THE INTERNATIONAL ALLOCATION OF ECONOMIC ACTIVITY

Proceedings of a Nobel Symposium held at Stockholm

Edited by

Bertil Ohlin
Per-Ove Hesselborn
Per Magnus Wijkman

First published 1977 by
THE MACMILLAN PRESS LTD
London and Basingstoke
Associated companies in Delhi
Dublin Hong Kong Johannesburg Lagos Melbourne
New York Singapore and Tokyo

Text set in 10/11 pt IBM Press Roman, printed by photolithography,
and bound in Great Britain at The Pitman Press, Bath

British Library Cataloguing in Publication Data

The international allocation of economic activity
1. Industries, Location of – Congresses   2. Commerce
– Congresses
I. Ohlin, Bertil   II. Hesselborn, Per-Ove
III. Wijkman, Per Magnus
338.6'042   HD58
ISBN 0-333-21423-4

Contents

List of Participants

Åke E. Andersson, Department of Economics, University of Gothenburg, Sweden

Bela Balassa, Department of Political Economy, Johns Hopkins University, and The World Bank, U.S.A.

Ragnar Bentzel, Department of Economics, University of Uppsala, Sweden

Jagdish N. Bhagwati, Department of Economics, Massachusetts Institute of Technology, U.S.A.

Dieter Biehl, Technische Universität, Berlin, West Germany

William H. Branson, Woodrow Wilson School, Princeton University, U.S.A.

Harold Brookfield, Department of Geography, University of Melbourne, Australia

Sune Carlson, Department of Business Administration, University of Uppsala, Sweden

Hollis B. Chenery, The World Bank, U.S.A.

Michael Chisholm, Department of Geography, University of Cambridge, England

W. Max Corden, Department of Economics, the Australian National University, Australia

Erik Dahmén, Stockholm School of Economics, Sweden

John H. Dunning, Department of Economics, University of Reading, England

Ronald E. Findlay, Department of Economics, Columbia University, U.S.A.

Gottfried Haberler, American Enterprises Institute, U.S.A.

Gary C. Hufbauer, Office of International Tax Affairs, Department of the Treasury, U.S.A.

Torsten Hägerstrand, Department of Social and Economic Geography, University of Lund, Sweden

Walter Isard, Department of Regional Science, University of Pennsylvania, U.S.A.

Harry G. Johnson, Department of Economics, University of Chicago, U.S.A., and the Graduate Institute of International Studies, Switzerland

Ronald W. Jones, Department of Economics, University of Rochester, U.S.A.

Charles P. Kindleberger, Department of Economics, Massachusetts Institute of Technology, U.S.A.

Lawrence R. Klein, Department of Economics, University of Pennsylvania, U.S.A.

Melvyn B. Krauss, Department of Economics, New York University, U.S.A.

Wassily Leontief, Department of Economics, New York University, U.S.A.

Assar Lindbeck, Institute for International Economic Studies, University of Stockholm, Sweden

Staffan Burenstam Linder, Stockholm School of Economics, Sweden

Erik Lundberg, Stockholm School of Economics, Sweden

Nils Lundgren, Institute for International Economic Studies, University of Stockholm, Sweden

Akin L. Mabogunje, Department of Geography, University of Ibadan, Nigeria

Fritz Machlup, Department of Economics, New York University, U.S.A.

Michael Michaely, Department of Economics, The Hebrew University of Jerusalem, Israel

Hla Myint, London School of Economics and Political Science, England

Bertil Ohlin, Stockholm School of Economics, Sweden

Göran Ohlin, Department of Economics, University of Uppsala, Sweden

Kjeld Philip, Department of Economics, University of Copenhagen, Denmark

Allan R. Pred, Department of Geography and Institute of Urban and Regional Development, University of California at Berkeley, U.S.A.

Harry W. Richardson, School of Urban and Regional Planning, University of Southern California, U.S.A.

Tibor Scitovsky, Department of Economics, Stanford University, U.S.A.

Robert M. Solow, Department of Economics, Massachusetts Institute of Technology, U.S.A.

Bo Södersten, Department of Economics, University of Gothenburg, Sweden

Gunnar Törnqvist, Department of Social and Economic Geography, University of Lund, Sweden

Organising Committees and Sponsors

COMMITTEE FOR NOBEL SYMPOSIA 1976

S. Ramel, Chairman, Executive Director of the Nobel Foundation
L. Hulthén, Professor, Chairman of the Nobel Committee for Physics
A. Fredga, Professor, Member of the Nobel Committee for Chemistry
B. Gustafsson, Professor, Secretary of the Nobel Committee for Physiology
or Medicine
L. Gyllensten, Professor, Member of the Swedish Academy (Literature)
T. Greve, Director of the Norwegian Nobel Institute (Peace)
E. Lundberg, Professor, Chairman of the Prize Committee for Economic
Sciences
N-E. Svensson, PhD, Executive Director, the Bank of Sweden Tercenten-
ary Foundation

ORGANISING COMMITTEE OF NOBEL SYMPOSIUM 35: THE
INTERNATIONAL ALLOCATION OF ECONOMIC ACTIVITY

B. Ohlin (Chairman), Professor Emeritus, Stockholm School of Economics
R. Bentzel, Professor, University of Uppsala
S. Carlson, Professor, University of Uppsala
T. Hägerstrand, Professor, University of Lund
A. Lindbeck, Professor, University of Stockholm
E. Lundberg, Professor Emeritus, Stockholm School of Economics

SPONSORS

The symposium was financed by the Nobel Foundation through
grants from the Bank of Sweden Tercentenary Foundation and by grants
from the Marianne and Marcus Wallenberg Foundation, and the Svenska
Handelsbanken Foundation for Social Science Research.

Foreword

This volume gives an account of the proceedings of a Nobel Symposium on The International Allocation of Economic Activity held in Stockholm, 8–11 June, 1976. A special aim of the symposium was to bring about an exchange of ideas between economists and economic geographers interested in trade and movements of the factors of production. It provides a somewhat different approach to international and regional trade than that which is commonly used with more emphasis on the location of production and less on trade itself.

International monetary relations and business cycles were excluded from the programme, having been the subject of a great deal of scientific analysis in the postwar period. Aspects of monopoly and imperfect competition were not given a special place on the programme due to the limited time available for discussion. For this reason, it was found necessary also to omit the Link project, which combines econometric systems for different national economies.

Attention was concentrated on *positive* theory – including analyses of the effects of several much used policy measures. The programme left out normative theory concerned with the choice of the best possible policy. As it was, the range of subjects for discussion was wide enough.

An analysis of essential aspects of international economic development with the aid of positive theories of causal connections between different elements – including some measures which have often been used in practice – can serve as a basis for a normative theory involving optimisation of policies with definite goals. The positive price and distribution theory of economic textbooks is generally accepted as indispensable even though it only indirectly helps an analysis of optimum policy problems. The same must hold for the *international* aspects of price theory. It goes without saying that economists are particularly interested in fields where important policy problems have appeared and are likely to appear, for example the international differences in social conditions and their economic effects. The programme for the symposium has been influenced by this consideration.

As indicated above, the programme, papers and discussions place **greater** emphasis on decisions about the *location* of economic activity and less on the different aspects of international trade than has been common in the scientific literature on international economic relations. Of course, decisions regarding location depend partly on the conditions for trade. But they also depend on the supply of factors of production in the different countries – which is affected by international factor movements and the transfer of knowledge – as well as on non-factor costs, risks and many social rules and other elements which affect the technology used in industries producing and transporting different commodities. A main idea behind the symposium was that a more comprehensive explanation of the size and changes of production in different regions is required than the usual factor proportion model can offer, although it has proved very useful in the theoretical analysis in the postwar years – particularly after the impetus given by Paul Samuelson's two brilliant papers in 1948–49.

As the adaptation of production, factor supply and demand takes time, it is obviously desirable that a theory in static equilibrium terms – expressed in prices or opportunity costs – should be supplemented with an analysis of a time-using development and process of growth.

So much for the symposium and its proceedings. Let me add a few words of thanks on behalf of the Organising Committee. We are grateful to the participants – many from afar – who accepted our invitation and made the symposium highly stimulating. We are also indebted to the Nobel Foundation and its Symposium Committee which – with the aid of grants from the Bank of Sweden Tercentary Foundation – made the symposium possible. We are equally grateful to the Marianne and Marcus Wallenberg Foundation and the Svenska Handelsbanken Foundation for Social Science Research which through additional grants enabled us to cover a larger field at the symposium than would otherwise have been possible.

The Institute for International Economic Studies rendered valuable assistance in the preparation and running of the symposium. Per-Ove Hesselborn and Per Magnus Wijkman, research fellows at the Institute, carried the main load of administering the symposium, assisted in editing this volume, and skilfully summarised the symposium's discussions. Vicki Olvång has throughout cheerfully provided secretarial assistance.

Stockholm   BERTIL OHLIN
September 1976

I know that all the participants of the Symposium shared my feelings of grief upon learning of the death of Professor Harry G. Johnson, one of the pioneers in the scientific analysis of international economic relations. We all deeply regret that our science has lost not only a colleague from whom we expected many more important contributions, but also a man with a charming personality, who spread warmth and vivacity at our meetings.

July 1977   B. H.

1 Survey of Circumstances affecting the Location of Production and International Trade as Analysed in the Theoretical Literature

Gottfried Haberler

I. INTRODUCTION

Suppose Ricardo had been asked why Portugal had a comparative advantage in wine; he surely would have answered, in effect though not in these words, because Portugal was well supplied with factors of production needed for wine growing, that is to say suitable land and plenty of sunshine. If the questioner had continued and asked whether there were not still other factors to be considered such as capital, Ricardo would have answered: Yes, certainly; in poor countries where labour is cheap capital will be invested in labour-intensive industries and in rich countries capital will be invested in industries that use comparatively little labour.

How do I know Ricardo's answers? Now, the answer to the first question is so obvious that there hardly can be any doubt. The answer to the second question I know because Ricardo said so in so many words in the *Principles* (not buried in the many volumes of letters): '. . . the capital of poorer nations will be naturally employed in those pursuits, wherein a great quantity of labour is supported . . . In rich countries, on the contrary, where food is dear, capital will naturally flow, when trade is free, into those occupations wherein the least quantity of labour is required. . .'.[1]

I say this not in order to make the point that Ricardo said everything, but merely to stress the continuity of the theoretical development from Ricardo via Mill and Marshall to Heckscher, Ohlin and Samuelson. There is an unmistakable family likeness between the modern theories, based on Ohlin's pathfinding work, and the early classical theories, just as there is between a modern jumbo jet and the Wright brothers' contraption. But I fully agree with Ohlin that Viner failed in his attempt to uphold the classical labour theory of value in the form of a real cost theory for the purpose of 'providing guidance on questions of national policy',[2] let alone as an explanation of the international division of labour. Strictly speaking the labour theory of value was already breached by the doctrine of comparative cost and the breach was widened when the assumption of geographical or occupational immobility of labour was applied to the national economy in the theory of non-competing groups. John Stuart Mill's theory of international values constitutes, in effect, an abandonment of the labour theory of value although Mill, as well as Alfred Marshall later, did not present their theories as a revolutionary new start but as elaboration and improvement of the Ricardian doctrine.

I still believe that the most fruitful way to get as much as possible out of Ricardo's theory is to reinterpret the theory of comparative advantage in terms of opportunity cost. Ohlin is surely right when he insists that this approach effectively abandons the labour theory of value, but helps 'little' unless it is 'connected with a mutual interdependence [theory of the] price ✦ system'.[3] To establish this connection was, of course, the intention of the opportunity cost interpretation right from the beginning. In the form of the 'transformation or production possibility curve' the opportunity cost approach has become one of the basic tools of the modern theory, although the word 'opportunity cost' has gradually faded away.[4] This type of analysis has been found very useful especially in the analysis of the welfare (normative) aspects, both of international trade and domestic economic problems. In fact the artificial dichotomy between international and domestic trade and value theories has disappeared.[5] The general price theory and the theory of international trade have gradually been merged and the merger has been explicitly and definitively accomplished in Ohlin's *Interregional and International Trade.* The fusion process has enriched both fields and on many occasions the theory of international trade has been the source and initiator of new modes of analysis.

There has been a widespread tendency in the modern theoretical literature on international trade to exaggerate the contrast between the old classical (Ricardian) theory and what is now referred to as the Heckscher-Ohlin theory; and both theories are often interpreted rather narrowly which to my mind is unfair to both. This tendency we find both in the purely theoretical literature and among the 'empiricists' who try to test statistically (or otherwise) the hypotheses attributed to the two schools.

On the empirical side let me mention the attempts by G. D. A. Mac-Dougall, Robert Stern and others at testing the Ricardian theory by comparing labour efficiency in some U.K. and U.S. manufacturing industries. These exercises surely have their proper uses, but as a test for the validity of the Ricardian theory of comparative advantage I find them either superfluous (if Ricardo's labour theory of value is taken literally), or inconclusive (if Ricardo's theory is interpreted more generously so as to admit factors other than labour and land.[6] Suppose the 'tests' work extremely well — even better than in fact they, surprisingly, seem to have worked — would anybody be prepared to give up modern economics and go back to the labour theory of value? Or the other way around, if the results of the 'tests' were negative, if they seemed to contradict the Ricardian theory — would anybody be prepared to give up the theory of comparative advantage?

II. TWO-FACTOR MODELS: LABOUR AND CAPITAL

In the theoretical as well as in the empirical literature the Heckscher-Ohlin theory is often interpreted as a model that explains international division of labour solely or predominantly in terms of different endowment of different countries with *two* factors of production — labour and capital. The two-factor model lends itself to easy graphic manipulation. An elaborate, elegant analytical—geometrical theory has been developed which is displayed with great flourish and ingenuity in modern textbooks. This extension was largely the work of Samuelson and Meade. With a few additional simplifying assumptions — two commodities and two countries, constant returns to scale and identical factors and identical production functions in both countries — a highly abstract but suggestive model of world trade can be constructed. All this constitutes a permanent and most valuable addition to our analytical apparatus and an invaluable pedagogical device. But we should not forget that the extreme simplifications 'disregard', in H. G. Johnson's words, 'some of the more penetrating insights' of the original work by Heckscher and Ohlin.[7] The two-factor assumption especially deviates sharply from the original Heckscher-Ohlin theory. These theories assumed many factors right from the beginning although in illustrative examples sometimes a truncated two-factor version of the general theory was used by the two authors.

The theoretical attraction of the two-factor model is that it permits the application of the Edgeworth-Bowley box diagram which has amply proved its great analytical and pedagogical worth. But it should be kept in mind that some of the best known generalisations derived from the production box diagram break down in a more-than-two-factor world — namely the Stolper-Samuelson and Rybczynski theorems, so beloved by modern textbook writers.

Also the famous theorem of factor price equalisation through free commodity trade has to be severely qualified, if there are many factors. This is in addition to several other more fundamental simplifying assumptions that have to be made, such as that factors are qualitatively the same and production functions identical in both trading countries, that production functions are homogeneous to the first degree and that there are no 'factor intensity reversals'. Keeping all this in mind makes it clear that what the theory really proves is *not* that factor prices will be equalised, but on the contrary that in practice there *cannot* be a factor price equalisation.[8]

Apart from its intrinsic value and obvious ingenuity, Leontief's famous demonstration that American export industries are largely labour-intensive and import-competing industries capital-intensive had its strong impact because of the widespread misinterpreation of the Heckscher-Ohlin theory as a two-factor model. Since it was taken for granted that the United States is, compared with the rest of the world, capital-rich and labour-poor, Leontief's results came as a shock; they were widely regarded as a blow to re-

ceived neoclassical theory. This conclusion is incorrect, but it had the
fortunate consequence that it helped to steer empirical economists away
from the two-factor models, that it forced them to distinguish different
types of labour and capital, and to pay attention to dynamic, institutional
and policy complications. This development marks a return not merely to
the intentions but to actual observations and hints in Heckscher's article
and especially in Ohlin's book.[9] Many of the modern explanations which
we shall discuss presently are more or less explicitly and clearly foreshadowed in Ohlin's book.

III. 'NATURAL RESOURCE TRADE'

The most obvious factors that explain a good deal of international trade
are 'natural resources' — land of different quality (including climatic conditions), mineral deposits, etc. No sophisticated theory is required to explain why Kuwait exports oil, Bolivia tin, Brazil coffee and Portugal wine.
Because of the deceptive obviousness of many of these cases economists
have spent comparatively little time on 'natural resource trade'.[10] Economic geographers have more to say on that very important subject.
   While it is easy to explain why Kuwait has a 'comparative advantage' in
oil, Bolivia in tin, etc., the existence of natural resources presents the economist with certain theoretical complications which should not be slurred
over. Natural resources are much less homogenous and less versatile and
mobile (domestically) than capital or labour. For example oil in different
countries differs in chemical composition (sulphur content), geographical
location (proximity to the sea), distance from the surface, etc. The same is
true of other mineral deposits. In other words natural resource factors in
different countries differ enormously not only in quantity but also in
quality. Hence production functions can no longer be assumed to be the
same in all countries or to be homogeneous to the first degree (display constant returns to scale) in terms of capital and labour. As a consequence, to
speak of international factor price equalisation becomes meaningless when
reference is made to *all* factors, and equalisation is quite uncertain if not
practically impossible when applied to factors of comparable quality (such
as capital and labour). Similarly, excluded are sweeping generalisations
about the effects of trade on internal income distribution, such as the
Stolper-Samuelson theorem.
   If production functions in terms of capital and labour (or more generally
in terms of internationally comparable factors) are different in different
countries because the natural resource endowment (including climate,
atmosphere) is different, the production of the same (or similar) products
may be capital-intensive in one country and labour-intensive in the other.
For example the production of rice in the United States is capital-intensive
while in the tropics it is labour-intensive. The same is true of rubber (dis-

regarding the quality difference between the natural and synthetic variety).[11] In the same vein several writers have suggested that the Leontief paradox can be wholly or partly explained by assuming that American capital is a better substitute for foreign natural resources than American labour.[12]

IV. DETERMINANTS OF TRADE OF MANUFACTURED GOODS

The pattern of international trade in manufactured goods is much more complex and more difficult to explain than trade in raw materials and crude foodstuffs, because the latter is largely and conspicuously dominated by the availability of 'natural resources' (including climate) and transportation costs. In recent years an enormous literature has sprung up which deals primarily with trade in manufactured goods. A bewildering array of often interrelated and overlapping explanations, refurbished old theories as well as more or less novel ones, have been presented.[13] The various strands of thought which have emerged will be discussed in greater detail and depth in the following session of this symposium. I must confine myself to giving an overview and to mentioning some forerunners of the new theories – indicating some connections between the new and the old literature. References to the older literature are almost completely missing in many recent contributions. I repeat, most of the new ideas are mentioned or foreshadowed more or less explicitly in Ohlin's *Interregional and International Trade*, but since this book is so well-known I shall refrain from making specific references.[14]

Some of the explanations stressed in the recent literature are in fact elaborations or applications of Ohlin's factor proportion theory. Thus, labour and capital are not homogeneous masses, but can and have to be subdivided in various ways.[15] This is, in effect, done in the theories that stress the 'R and D' (research and development) factor, human skills and human capital, as 'an important source of the United States' [and other industrial countries'] comparative advantage position'. (Baldwin, p. 142).[16]

There are different ways to look at these problems. One is to regard them as a 'relatively abundant supply of engineers and scientists' (Baldwin). This approach continues the tradition of F. W. Taussig who explained the pre-eminence of the German chemical industry before 1914 by the abundant supply of highly trained chemists which in turn was due to cheap and easily accessible technical education.[17]

Another way of looking at essentially the same circumstances, foreshadowed by Taussig's reference to technical education, is to stress the private or social costs of providing human skills – 'investment in human being', 'human capital'. Peter Kenen,[18] Harry Johnson and others have suggested that the Leontief paradox would largely disappear if labour skills were taken out of the labour supply and put into the capital coefficient where they belong.

Others have emphasised the dynamic aspects of the problem. R and D, investment in human skills, the creation of 'human capital' are, of course, essentially dynamic phenomena. R and D products are not just there for the taking but have to be continuously created, in western countries typically by private enterpreneurs.

I can do no better than to quote from the Caves-Jones treatise where the new approach is well summarised:[19]

> A new product is developed or a new production process embodied in a novel kind of capital equipment. The innovating firm tests its discovery on the market — presumably first . . . on its home market.[20] If the innovation proves profitable, the firm looks for wider markets abroad . . . The innovation . . . is likely to bestir imitators at home or abroad . . . Some countries may regularly prove to be sources of innovation. Their export lists would always contain new products that have not yet been successfully imitated elsewhere. We would have to explain their trade, then, not solely by their factor endowments . . . but rather in part as 'technological gap' exports. Do some countries enjoy special talents as innovators? For the United States, the answer may be yes . . . The United States, as the country with the highest labour cost, seems to offer the strongest incentive to labour-saving innovations. In the nineteenth century, economic historians have argued, the scarcity and dearness of labour made the United States a fruitful source of mechanical inventions. Coupled with an abundance of labour skills (invention itself requires a high proportion of skilled labour) and congenial cultural traits, American inventive dominance has continued. Thus a significant proportion of U.S. exports probably consists of 'technological gap' trade . . . The United States is of course far from being the only source of innovations. The role is also filled by countries with abundant skilled scientific labour, such as Great Britain, or . . . Germany (and Japan). The empirical evidence, however, is particularly clear for the United States. Industries making the strongest research effort (measured, for instance, by research and development expenditures as a percentage of sales) account for 72 per cent of the country's exports of manufactured goods.

The process of innovation has been further analysed and 'stylised' in the theory of the 'product cycle'.[21] Typically, the innovation process runs in several distinguishable stages. Again I quote from Caves and Jones

> Someone has invented and marketed the radio . . . At the start its market success is uncertain. The new product does not automatically appeal to many customers. Its manufacture is small-scale. Production techniques are likely to be novel and to require large inputs of skilled labour. 'Mass production' is unsuitable because of both the small market and technological uncertainties. The good must be produced near its market, because the producer needs a quick feedback of information in

order to improve its performance, reliability, and general appeal. Hence the innovator's home market will be the first served.

When the product is established at home . . . the location of production may start to shift . . . Standardisation and general consumer acceptance allow for mass production. This demands lesser labour skills . . . As the product grows standardised and its market becomes more competitive, the pull of cost advantages on the location of production grows stronger . . . Imitative competition is likely to arise (and to undermine the monopoly position of the original inventors of the product) . ... Costs start to tell. Unless the country where the innovation first becomes established has an ultimate comparative advantage, production will spread or shift to other countries . . . Once again, this model helps to explain changes in production and trade in new product lines, such as electronics. The United States had been a principal innovator, but production has also spread (with a lag) to other countries . . . Furthermore, for goods whose manufacture is spreading abroad we observe a shift from processes heavily dependent on skilled labour to automatic assembly processes using relatively more capital and unskilled labour.

'The product cycle, as an explanation of changes in production and trade, involves shifts in patterns of consumption as well as in the technology of production. As a consumer good matures, it passes from being a luxury to being a necessity. But 'necessity' is a relative term . . . As production standardises, a good will become cheaper relative to other goods.' (Caves and Jones *op cit.*, p. 221).

By now any reader who is moderately versed in the recent history of economics will realise: All this is pure Schumpeter. Indeed it is essentially an elaboration, variation, verification and application to international trade of Schumpeter's classical theory of capitalist development.[22]

Another related factor which surely often is very important in shaping the pattern of manufactured goods trade is increasing returns to scale. It is one of the oldest themes in economic theory that international trade enables the participating countries to reap the advantages of large-scale production. The scale factor was analysed in depth by Ohlin and has received much attention in the recent literature along with skills, R and D and innovation.

Let me mention a few recent cases. American dominance in the market for aircraft, especially the large, long-distance jets, is surely due to the large domestic market. Heavy military demand has greatly added to the size of the market and was decisively involved in the early development of the industry. It has been demonstrated that American industries in many cases have a great advantage over Canadian industries, because the large domestic market makes long production runs possible.[23] Needless to add that protectionist policies and the ubiquitous transport costs interact with the scale factors in intricate fashion. These factors will receive further attention in other contributions to this symposium.

American industries have the same advantage over European industries.

It was, indeed, one of the major economic objectives of the European economic unification to overcome this handicap. Perhaps the most important
reason why this goal has been reached only to a limited extent is the enormous growth of the public sector. Without political unification it is practically impossible to coordinate sufficiently nationalised industries and
public procurement policies to come near the degree of exploitation of the
advantages of large-scale production that would be possible in a competitive
economy.[24]

The ever present danger that new barriers of trade may be introduced
or old ones increased is a great handicap for small countries; it often makes
it too risky to take advantage of large-scale production by setting up
factories specially for exports. Jacques Drèze has tried to show that product differentiation between national markets (not only of consumer
goods but also of capital goods) is often prevalent even in the absence of
tariffs, and operates like tariffs to handicap small countries with small
national markets. Belgium, he says however, has partly overcome this disadvantage by exporting undifferentiated intermediate products – steel,
glass, non-ferrous metals, wool products.[25] Irving Kravis and Robert E.
Lipsey have discovered '. . . a number of cases in which the size of the U.S.
market enables U.S. producers to reach a large volume production for
relatively specialised product variants for which markets are thin in any
one of the smaller, competing economies. In the antifriction bearing industry, for example, the United States imports commonly used bearings which
can be produced in large volume both here and abroad, but the United
States has nevertheless enjoyed a net export position in bearings owing to
exports of specialised kinds capable of meeting precision needs, resisting
heat or rust, or bearing great weight'.[26]

These examples which could be multiplied *ad libitum* demonstrate the
enormous complexity of manufactured goods trade among modern industrial countries. At first blush the facts, for example ball bearings being
exported and imported at the same time, are often baffling and may give
the impression of wastefulness and inefficiency. But the actors in the
market, private producers and dealers, know what they are doing. While
for the researching economist it requires a major effort to find out what is
going on and the true answer may often elude him, the market if left alone
solves even the most intricate problems with dispatch and efficiency. This
is a matter of utmost importance for the development of theories and their
testing as well as for trade policies. It is safe to say, nevertheless, that this
fact is often not sufficiently realised in either area.

The various theories stressing labour skills, R and D innovation, technological gaps, product cycles, product differentiation, and scale economies
have been subjected to numerous empirical tests – historical case and
country studies and sophisticated statistical analyses. Most instructive and
illuminating I find are case studies of particular industries – plastics,
nylon, electronics, petrochemicals, consumer durables, etc.[27] Electronic

watches is one of the most recent innovations which has started in the
United States. In this case the product life cycle seems to have run its
course very rapidly, judging from the fact that U.S. producers have already
asked for high import duties on electronic watches to protect them from
foreign competition.

Comprehensive statistical testing, using American and world trade
statistics (trade matrices) have been attempted by Baldwin, Gruber and
Vernon, and Hufbauer.[28] These are very ambitious studies and it would
lead much too far to discuss them in detail. The authors claim that on the
whole the results support their theoretical expectations. But most of the
data are not very good (especially for other countries than the United
States) and the vital classifications of types of product, factors (for
example different skills) and processes are admittedly often rather arbitrary
and haphazard. Thus it is very doubtful whether it is possible statistically
to separate the effects of the skill, scale, R and D investment and innovation factors.[29] What the massive statistical operations have added to our
knowledge is therefore not clear. Fortunately it is probably not very important to know the precise comparative contribution of skill, scale, R and
D, product differentiation and product cycles.

V. WHERE DO WE STAND?

Our brief sketch of post-Ohlinian theory has presented an array of overlapping models and theories which stress a variety of circumstances, factor
proportions and others, that determine the 'international allocation of
economic activity'. But I could consider only a part of the problem. For
example, I did not address specifically the trade problem of the less
developed countries (on which there exists a vast literature). These problems will occupy other sessions of this symposium. Let me make bold,
however, and assert that the existing body of theories applies equally to
LDCs as to countries on a higher level of development. It goes without
saying, however, that the long run impact of trade on the factor supply,
especially on the human factor (human capital) and the transmission of
factors — including the transfer of technological and managerial knowledge
— from country to country requires special attention when dealing with
LDSs.

The importance of the development problem in the minds of present-
day economists is underscored by a remark of a participant at a recent
conference on trade problems. He was moved to say that 'trade theory is
foredoomed to become an extension of growth and development theory',
admitting, however that 'the latter is still struggling toward its successful
synthesis'.[30] This statement echoes, although in inverted form, Alfred
Marshall's famous though somewhat baffling dictum that the 'the causes
which determine the economic progress of nations belong to the study of

international trade'.[31] No doubt, international trade and international division of labour have played an enormously important role in modern development including the first and second industrial revolution. 'It is simply not possible to imagine what sort of economic development would have taken place over the last hundred (or two hundred) years without international trade' (Ohlin *op. cit.*, 2nd ed. p. 413).

Nor are these omissions all. Government policies, both foreign trade measures (import restrictions and export subsidies) and domestic policies such as taxes, subsidies and others, can have lasting effects on the patterns of trade. Finally I may mention monetary and business cycle phenomena. Although they have been excluded (in wise self-limitation) from the present conference, monetary and cyclical disturbances may well have permanent effects on the structure of the economy and the pattern of trade as Ohlin has pointed out. It would not be difficult to cite concrete cases of lasting effects of short-run disturbances. For example severe depressions often leave significant changes in the economic structure and comparative cost situations in their wake, largely but not wholly, via their profound impact on economic policy.

The picture which emerges is that of a mosaic of interrelated, overlapping and occasionally conflicting theories and models, each applicable to certain situations. This is a far cry from the imposing unified structure of the theory of international trade which has been developed by neoclassical writers — with appealing transparency in graphic form for two-commodity, two-factor and two-country models and generalised by Paul Samuelson and others in mathematical terms to many countries, commodities and factors.

It could be argued that there is no use for vast general equilibrium systems covering the whole economic universe, either in disaggregated form à la Walras or in highly aggregated form as in the post-Keynesian literature. Let me quote from the celebrated *Theory of Games and Economic Behaviour* by John von Neumann and Oskar Morgenstern

> Let us be aware that there exists at present no universal system of economic theory . . . Even in sciences which are far more advanced than economics, like physics, there is no universal system available at present . . . It happens occasionally that a particular physical theory appears to provide the basis for a universal system, but in all instances up to the present time this appearance has not lasted more than a decade at best. The everyday work of the research physicist is certainly not involved with such high aims . . . The physicist works on individual problems, some of great practical importance, others of less. Unification of fields which were formerly divided and far apart may alternate with this type of work. However, such fortunate occurrences are rare and happen only after each field has been thoroughly explored.[32]

The Neumann-Morgenstern injunction against applying what they call a 'super-standard' (*loc. cit.*), in other words postulating a universal system, is surely well taken not only with respect to sweeping economic or social laws which chart the course of economic and social evolution, à la Hegel and Marx, Spengler and Toynbee, what Karl Popper[33] calls 'oracular philosophy', but also to many contemporaneous overambitious econometric models which try to describe the working of the economy as a whole and project the course of the economy of single countries or of a large part of the world with or without its cyclical ups and downs in considerable detail for longish periods in the future.

I submit, however, that the static (or comparative static) neoclassical general equilibrium theory (in the broad sense including Heckscher and Ohlin) — even the truncated two-country, two-commodity model — is an extremely useful tool of analysis. Of course the general theory does not tell us, and should not be expected to tell us, which country is going to export what, or how the international terms of trade will move, just as nobody will say that 'the ordinary single-market theory' of demand and supply 'is useless because it is not dynamic'[34] and does not tell us what the price of sugar will be and who will produce how much.

It is true, general equilibrium theory is largely competitive theory (just as a theory using demand and supply curves for a particular commodity is). Monopolistic islands in a competitive economy can be easily accommodated in the general equilibrium system. But if monopolistic markets cover large areas of the economy, it becomes difficult to incorporate them in the general equilibrium system. This is especially true of oligopolies and bilateral monopolies. But the competitive theory has two very important functions, a positive and a normative one. The positive function (in Robert Solow's words) is to give 'an idealised description of how resources are allocated and incomes distributed in a competitive capitalist economy'. However, if you try to answer not that descriptive [positive] question but the normative . . . one of how scarce resources should be allocated by a society anxious to avoid waste', in other words a society whose aim is to maximise real national income, 'you rediscover the same theory in the guise of shadow prices or efficiency prices'.[35] The competitive equilibrium is, in a sense, an optimum. I need not here discuss in detail in what sense it is an optimum. Let me simply say in the sense of a 'Pareto optimum', which is also the sense in which Ohlin speaks of 'the gain from interregional trade'.[36]

Viner stressed the normative or 'welfare analysis orientation', as he called it, of the classical doctrine.[37] The classical theory of international trade', he said, 'was formulated primarily with a view to its providing guidance on questions of national policy, and although it included considerable descriptive (positive) analysis of economic process, the selection of phenomena to be scrutinised . . . was almost always made with reference to current issues of public interest'.[38]

Thus the classical and neoclassical theory was and is often used to defend and propagate the policy of free trade. But it can and it has in fact been increasingly used for the opposite purpose. For example, the competitive theory can be effectively used to demonstrate the optimum tariff argument; in other words the terms-of-trade argument for import restrictions. Ohlin is surely right when he urges not 'to mix viewpoints which are tinged with normative considerations with the objective [positive] analysis'.[39] But how easy it is to slip from the objective analysis into 'normative' welfare consideration, Ohlin himself demonstrated, unwittingly I suppose, by arguing already early in his book, in the midst of the 'objective' analysis, in typical classical fashion, that interregional trade increases real national income in terms of commodities.[40] The precise meaning of such statements and the conditions under which it is true that free interregional and international trade increase and maximise real national income have been clarified in modern welfare economies. The essentials can be very effectively demonstrated diagramatically in a two-commodity model. Roughly speaking the conditions are free competition and absence of external economies and diseconomies.[41] We know that these conditions are never fully realised. Whether they are as a rule sufficiently realised to justify the free trade prescription I shall not discuss here. The purpose of this discussion is to argue that the competitive general equilibrium theory is useful or even indispensable as an ideal type which enables us better to visualise, evaluate and measure aberrations from the ideal conditions which abound in the real world.

Perhaps I have already strayed too far into welfare economics. The agenda of this conference expressly exclude the discussion of policy questions. I trust, however, that this injunction does not entirely bar the mentioning of problems of welfare economics. This would be a pity for the reason that the theories of positive and welfare economics are so closely interrelated.

APPENDIX A

ALFRED MARSHALL ON TECHNOLOGY TRADE, INTERNATIONAL TRANSMISSION OF TECHNOLOGY AND THE PRODUCT LIFE CYCLE[41]

Alfred Marshall devoted great attention to the role of technology and its transmission in an international setting in his *Industry and Trade*.[43] He describes in detail the various methods by which technology is transmitted from one country to another, and its impact on comparative advantage. He points out the debt that British technology owes to the French in many instances, and how the British adoption of French techniques had, on occasion, reduced the volume of trade and eventually reversed the pattern comparative advantage

... the Revocation of the Edict of Nantes in 1685 was a chief incident in a sustained policy of Continental autocrats, which rid them of sturdy subjects. More than half a million of the ablest of them came to England, bringing with them that knowledge of technique, which was most needed by her just at that time. In particular the Huguenots taught her to make many light glass and metal wares, in which French genius excelled: and in a very short time such wares . . . were being sent to France and sold at a good profit.

Laying particular emphasis on the British ability to standardise the inventions and new products of others, he continues

Another side of the same faculties is shown in such manufactures as those of the bicycle, motor car, submarine, and aeroplane: where French inventors have led, and a few French operative mechanics displayed a skill, a judgment and a resource which are nowhere surpassed. As these new delicate industries have reached the stage of massive production, the faculty of disciplined steadfast work becomes more important: the motor car, the submarine and the aeroplane tend to find their chief homes in other countries, as the bicycle did long ago.[44]

Another example: The German, American, and British faculty for organisation, coupled with the impossibility of French fashion designers to prevent imitation of their goods, results in the following product cycle largely foreshadowing the work of modern theorists.

This same tendency is shown even more conspicuously in those industries in which the leadership of France has been long established . . . Thus new Parisian goods (dresses, etc.) are sold at very high prices to the richest customers in all countries. In the next stage copies of them, made chiefly by local hand labour, are sold at rather high prices to the richest customers in all countries. In the next stage copies of them . . . are sold at rather high prices to the moderately rich. The last stage is the adoption of the new fashion for general use: and, for that purpose, people in commercial countries, endowed with a high faculty for organisation, study the imported French model, catch the keynotes of its ideas; they translate these ideas as far as possible into mechanical language and produce passable imitations for the middle and working classes.

To meet such competition France is driven to make a little use of massive methods herself, even in industries to which they are not wholly appropriate. But the tendency of the age is to require the producer to show his goods to the purchaser. The purchaser does not, as a rule, now go to the producer unless he is in quest of goods of a very special kind: therefore, when the French goods have reached the stage of semi-mechanical imitation, the untiring push and bold energy of the travellers for German and other firms have had an advantage over their French rivals. Meanwhile, however, Paris may have made one or more new models, which can be sold at scarcity prices to those who are tired of the last model, partly because it has become somewhat vulgarised.[45]

Nor does Marshall neglect the 'public' nature of many inventions, nor the distinction between invention and innovation, nor the problem of rapid, free imitation of them abroad.

> Whether he [the inventor] communicates his results to a learned society, and leaves others to earn money by them, or applies them in practice himself (with or without the protection of a patent), they become in effect the property of the world almost at once. Even if he uses them in a 'secret process', enough information about them often leaks out to set others soon on a track near to his own.[46]

In discussing the comparative advantage of Germany '. . . in industries, in which academic training and laboratory work can be turned to good account . . .' Marshall gives the following account of German efforts to import technology by various methods

> In the early stages of modern manufacture scientific training was of relatively small importance. The Germans accordingly, recognising their own weakness in practical instinct and organising faculty, took the part of pupils, whose purpose it was to outrun their teachers. They began by the direct copying of English machinery and methods: (despite the British prohibition on the exportation of machines in effect at that time) and they next set themselves to get employment in English firms; and to offer steady, intelligent services in return for a low pay in money, and a silent instruction in the inner workings of the business . . . And all the while Germany has been quick to grasp the practical significance of any master discovery that is made in other countries and to turn it to account.[47]

Numerous other passages could be cited. The above should suffice to indicate the depth to which Marshall explored the role of technology, the methods of its transmission, the effects upon comparative advantage, and how

> . . . broad ideas and knowledge, which when once acquired pass speedily into common ownership; and become part of the collective wealth, in the first instance of the countries to which the industries specially affected belong, and ultimately to the whole world.[48]

It should be mentioned that Marshall draws heavily on earlier English literature. He quotes, for example, Daniel Defoe's *A Plan of the English Commerce 1728*[49] as follows

> Defoe had said, "It is a kind of proverb attending the character of Englishmen that they are better to improve than to invent, better to advance upon the designs and plans which other people had laid down,

than to form schemes and designs of their own . . . The wool indeed was English, but the wit was all Flemish". But he went on to show in detail how we outdid our teachers; how "we have turned the scale of trade, and send our goods to be sold in those very countries, from which we derived the knowledge and art of making them".[50]

What Defoe — and Marshall — said about the English, contemporary writers have been saying about the Japanese.

APPENDIX B

SOME CONSEQUENCES OF THE EXPANSION OF THE PUBLIC SECTOR FOR THE INTERNATIONAL LOCATION OF PRODUCTION

While the rapid technological progress in the area of transportation and communication, and the resulting reduction of the costs of transportation and communications have operated to expand international trade and international division of labour, the enormous growth of the public sector and the increasing involvement of the state in all branches of economic life have worked in the opposite direction. This is especially conspicuous in the vast area of public utilities — railways, postal services, telephone, telegraph, airlines and the governmental administration itself. But it is also true of other nationalised industries, although to a lesser extent, because these industries are usually under the discipline of competition of private firms at home and abroad.

A cursory comparison between the situation with respect to public utilities in the United States and in the European Economic Community is instructive. While in the United States public utilities, whether government operated (such as the postal service) or in private hands (such as railways, telephone, telegraph, airlines, etc.), operate freely over the whole expanse of the country and tend to select the optimum size and optimum location unobstructed by political boundaries, in Europe there exist as many such enterprises as there are sovereign states. Since the advantages of large-scale production are especially pronounced in the public utility area, the multiplicity of national enterprises involves a heavy burden of economic overhead cost and operating expenses. In other words, if Europe wanted to take full advantage of economic integration and approach the level of economic integration that has been achieved in the United States, it would be necessary to consolidate and merge many of the national railways, airlines, postal, telephone and telegraph (PTT) services. It is very doubtful whether this could be done without far-reaching political integration. If railway, telephone, telegraph and airlines were in private hands, as is the case in the United States, rational economic integration would be comparatively simple.

This does not, of course, mean that the railway, postal, telephone services inside the smaller European countries, as well as between them, are inferior to those in the United States. There exist great national differ-

ences in the quality and efficiency of these services between the different
European countries and the United States. In some of the European countries these services are just as good as, or even better than, in the United
States. But the point is that they could be still better, cheaper and more
efficient if there were no political boundaries or if the public utilities were
in private hands. In the absence of political boundaries public enterprises
would presumably buy their capital equipment, instruments, materials, etc.,
from the cheapest sources. As it is, government-operated public utilities
such as railways, telephone, and telegraph etc. produce much of their
capital equipment (locomotives, freight cars, coaches, etc.,) themselves or
buy them from national private firms. This is the rule even in the small
countries of the European community. As the E.E.C. report on *Public
Purchasing in the Common Market*, which was quoted in the text, says
public procurement has remained 'unaffected by the Customs union'.

Suppose now that most of the public utilities, like the railways, telephone and telegraph, were in private hands as is the case in the United
States. Then these national private concerns would merge and operate
across political boundaries and their procurement policies would surely, in
a customs union (i.e., under free trade and in the absence of governmental
protectionist measures) ignore the political boundaries. As Jacob Viner
said 'private enterprise, as such, is normally non-patriotic, while government is automatically patriotic'.[51]

It will be observed that these advantages of private enterprise over public enterprise are independent of the question whether private enterprise *as
such* (that is to say given the spatial extension of the operation) is more
efficient than public enterprise. I myself have no doubt that the evidence
is overwhelming that private enterprise is practically always much more
efficient than public enterprise, although it is true that the comparative inefficiency of public enterprise differs enormously from country to country.
This inefficiency is especially pronounced in less developed countries.

Trade problems of the centrally planned countries of the East — both
intra-East and East-West trade — have been excluded from consideration
in this symposium. But it is clear that the rapid growth of the public sector
in all Western countries make those problems increasingly relevant for the
understanding of intra-Western trade.

NOTES

[1] Quoted from Ricardo's *Principles* by Jacob Viner in *Studies in the
Theory of International Trade* p. 504. Viner quotes other, similar passages
from Ricardo, Malthus, McCulloch and other classical writers.

[2] See Ohlin, 'Reflections on Contemporary International Trade Theories',
Appendix II to second revised edition of *Interregional and International
Trade* (Cambridge, Massachusetts, 1967) p. 307.

[3] *Interregional and International Trade*, 2nd ed. p. 8.

[4] In connection with intertemporal (rather than interspatial) exchange
the transformation curve was already used by Irving Fisher in his book *The
Rate of Interest* (New York, 1907).

[5] A. Marshall's famous 1879 papers were still entitled 'The Pure Theory of Foreign Trade' and 'The Pure Theory of (Domestic) Values'. See London School of Economics *Reprint of Scarce Tracts* No. 1 (London, 1930).

[6] R. Caves' and R. Jones' view to the contrary notwithstanding. See their *World Trade and Payments. An Introduction* (Boston, 1973) p. 187.

[7] Harry G. Johnson, 'The State of Theory in Relation to Empirical Analysis' in *The Technology Factor in International Trade*, conference volume edited by R. Vernon. National Bureau of Economic Research (New York, 1970), p. 11.

[8] This has not prevented some writers, for example,Myrdal, from criticising classical theory for teaching that free trade will equalise living standards internationally. Neither the writers in the old classical tradition, nor Heckschernor Ohlin have taught that standards of living will be equalised. And contrary to a superficial impression the modern mathematical literature on the subject proves that factor price equalisation through free trade, although not 'inconceivable' is in reality 'absolutely impossible' (to use words which A. Marshall used in another connection).

Moreover, complete equalisation of factor prices does not imply equalisation of living standards, if the latter is defined as national income per head or per unit of labour. Suppose country A is better supplied with natural resources than country B, then its national income per head (per unit of the factor labour) will be higher even if wages and other factor prices are the same in A and B.

[9] It should also be observed that Leontief himself did not regard his findings in contradiction to the neoclassical tradition. (I use the world 'neoclassical' in a comprehensive sense, including Heckscher-Ohlin as well as as those who, like Marshall and Viner, emphasise the roots of modern theory in the writings of the old classical economists.) Leontief did not fully spell out the theoretical model underlying his empirical work, but it was clearly not a two-factor model; for in the verbal discussion of his results he assumed, in addition to capital and labour, the existence of other cooperating factors of production such as enterpreneurship and management in order to clear up the seeming clash between his findings and accepted principles.

[10] See, however M. A. Diab, *The United States Capital Position and the Structure of its Foreign Trade* (Amsterdam, 1956) and Jaroslav Vanek, *The Natural Resource Content of U.S. Foreign Trade 1950–1955* (Cambridge, Mass., 1963).

[11] Differences in the production function should be distinguished from 'factor intensity reversals' which may occur even with identical, homogeneous production functions merely as a consequence of dissimilar endowment with qualitatively identical factors. There may exist borderline cases where it is difficult to decide whether to speak of factor intensity reversal, dissimilar production functions, factors of different quality or product differentiation. Fortunately it would probably not make much difference for most purposes.

[12] See my *Survey of International Trade Theory* 2nd ed. (Princeton, 1961), pp. 22–23, J. Vanek, *op. cit.*, and Robert E. Baldwin, 'Determinants of the Commodity Structure of U.S. Trade' *American Economic Review*

Vol. 61 (March, 1971), p. 142. It should be kept in mind that Leontief's statistics relate to the United States only. He does not say that *foreign* production of American imports is labour or capital or natural resource-intensive. What he does say is that *American* industries competing with imports are capital-intensive compared with *American* export industries. But some of them are also relatively natural resource-intensive compared with American export industries.

[13] An attempt at classification of theories, at their statistical testing, and a comprehensive bibliography can be found in the excellent article by G. C. Hufbauer under the mouthfilling title 'The Impact of National Characteristics and Technology on the Commodity Composition of Trade in Manufactured Goods', in *The Technology Factor in International Trade: A Conference of the Universities*, National Bureau Committee for Economic Research, edited by Raymond Vernon, (New York, 1970), pp. 145–232. Robert M. Stern, 'Testing Trade Theories' in *International Trade and Finance Frontiers for Research*, edited by Peter B. Kenen (Cambridge, 1975), pp. 3–50, presents a comprehensive account of recent theorising with an extensive bibliography.

[14] Harry Johnson in his Wicksell Lectures *Comparative Cost and Commercial Policy Theory for a Developing World* (Stockholm, 1968) has put the new theories which stress the technology factor in a broader framework. He mentions that the Heckscher–Ohlin model can be 'easily adapted' to take care of differences in technology. For an early discussion of this new trend see also the excellent article by M. V. Posner, 'International Trade and Technical Change' in Oxford Economic Papers Vol. 13 (October, 1961), pp. 323–341.

[15] It should be recalled that A. Marshall (especially in his *Industry and Trade* (1927) and F. W. Taussig (in numerous writings) have explicitly and systematically dealt with different types of labour.

[16] See especially Baldwin and Hufbauer, *op. cit.*, Donald B. Keesing, 'Labour Skills and Comparative Advantage, *American Economic Review* Vol. 56 (May, 1966). W. H. Gruber, D. Mehta and R. Vernon, 'The R and D Factors in International Trade and International Investment of U.S. Industries', *Journal of Political Economy* (February, 1967) and Gruber-Vernon, 'The Technology Factor in a World Trade Matrix' in *The Technology Factor in International Trade* (cited above).

[17] See F. W. Taussig, *International Trade* (New York, 1928). Taussig had given a similar, though less complete analysis as early as 1906 in 'Wages and Prices in Relation to International Trade', *Quarterly Journal of Economics* Vol. 20. For further references on Taussig see Viner, *op. cit.*, p. 495. Irving Kravis in his well-known article '"Availability" and Other Influences on the Commodity Composition of Trade', *Journal of Political Economy* (April, 1956) mentions Taussig and other earlier sources.

[18] P. E. Kenen, 'Nature, Capital and Trade', *Journal of Political Economy* Vol. 73 (1965), pp. 437–460. Leontief had already pointed out that American export industries are more skill-intensive than American industries competing with imports (see W. W. Leontief, 'Factor Proportions and the Structure of American Trade: Further Theoretical and Empirical Analysis', *Review of Economics and Statistics* Vol. 38 (1956), pp. 386–407.

[19] Caves-Jones *op. cit.*, pp. 218–222.

[20] The importance of the home market as a base for international trade was stressed by Staffan Burenstam-Linder in his well-known stimulating book *An Essay on Trade and Transformation* (New York, 1961). Furthermore he puts forward the thesis that trade in manufactured goods will be 'most intensive' between countries that are 'similar' in their basic pattern of demand which in turn is largely determined by the level of per capita income. Linder contrasts this explanation of trade in manufactured products with the factor proportion theory. He thinks that the latter applies to trade in primary products but not to that in manufactured goods. Linder's theory was statistically tested by Hufbauer (*loc. cit.*) and by Seev Hirsch and Baruch Lev ('Trade and Per Capita Income Differentials: A Test of the Burenstam-Linder Hypothesis' in *World Development* Vol. 1, No. 9 (September, 1973), pp. 11–19). The results of the former test were unfavourable, those of the latter favourable for Linder's thesis.

In my opinion both tests must be judged as inadequate. For it is extremely difficult to separate the influence of differential labour skills, R and D, scale factors, transport cost, tariffs (trade barriers), product differentiation and per capita income differentials. Investigation in much greater depth would be required. But the relevance and usefulness of such an exercise must be doubted. The contrast between Linder's theory and the factor proportion theory seems to me overdrawn. It may be true that new lines of production are usually started in the home market and that international trade then first spreads between countries on the same level of development (although exceptions to this rule surely exist). But as Caves and Jones say (see text below) 'unless the country where an innovation first becomes established has an ultimate comparative advantage, production will spread or shift to other countries'. This has been confirmed in many cases by the 'product cycle' analyses (see below, page 7), where it is shown how the production of new product spreads to other countries. Linder says that trade in primary products is governed by factor proportions. But there is little trade in which primary products are exchanged for primary products; most trade involving primary products is an exchange of primary for manufactured products. That large chunk of trade surely is primarily determined by factor proportion.

[21] See especially Louis T. Wells, 'International Trade: The Product Life Cycle Approach' in *The Product Life Cycle and International Trade* pp. 3–38, edited by L. T. Wells (Boston, 1972).

[22] Joseph A. Schumpeter, *The Theory of Economic Development*, Translated from the German by Redvers Opic (Cambridge, Mass., 1934, first German edition 1912). Schumpeter's theory is nowhere mentioned in the whole literature on technology trade and product cycles (nor in any of lengthy bibliographies of that subject), although these theories were largely developed in Schumpeter's own University — at the Harvard Business School where Schumpeter's work was continued in the 'enterpreneurial history' project. Schumpeter, it is true, did not put forward his theory of economic development in opposition or criticism of neoclassical economics. This may explain why he is not mentioned. Raymond Vernon, to whose initiative and drive we owe to a large extent the rapid development of this

very valuable line of research, mentions J. H. Williams, Donald MacDougall and others who expressed 'discontent' with the static classical trade theory and used (rather, misused) Schumpeterian thoughts to make a case for the existence of a permanent dollar shortage — an idea which, despite its obvious weakness, was very popular in the postwar period, until the dollar shortage gave way to a dollar glut. To get a hearing for one's thoughts it is evidently better to present them as a heresy rather than as what they really are — an extension of the existing body of theory. Michael Connolly, University of Florida has drawn my attention to the fact that A. Marshall has anticipated much of the product cycle thesis. For excerpts from Marshall's *Industry and Trade* see Appendix A to this paper, pp. 12–15.

These grumbles should, however, not dampen our gratitude for the new material and insights which we owe to the recent research on technology trade, innovation and product cycles.

[23] On the instructive comparison of U.S. and Canadian industries see D. J. Daly's paper 'Uses of International Price and Output Data' in *International Comparisons of Prices and Output*, edited by D. J. Daly, Studies in Income and Wealth Vol. 37 National Bureau of Economic Research (New York, 1972), pp. 120–121 and the literature quoted there.

[24] On the situation in the European Common Market see the report on *Public Purchasing in the Common Market* by M. Guy Charpentier and Sir Richard Clarke to the Commission of the European Communities (EC) Brussels, 1974. The authors' conclusion is that there exists practically no Common Market policy on public procurement and that a very large part of the European economy (bearing in mind the [large and growing] volume of the [public] purchases involved) is unaffected by the Customs Union' (see Conclusions of the Report, p. 93).

For some further reflections on the importance of the expansion of the public sector on the international division of labour see Appendix B, page pp. 15–16.

[25] Jacque Drèze, 'Quelques reflexions sereines sur l'adaptation de l'industrie Belge au Marché Commun', Comptes rendues des Travaux de la Société Royale d'Économie Politique de Belgique, No. 275 (1960). Quoted by Caves and Jones, *op. cit.*, p. 224.

[26] *The Technology Factor in International Trade, loc. cit.*, p. 289. In the two authors' massive and comprehensive study, *Price Competitiveness In World Trade* (NBER New York, 1971), can be found many examples of other 'non-price factors affecting the competitive position of the U.S.' such as technological leadership, large scale of domestic market, quality of product, speed of delivery (pp. 31–38).

[27] See especially G. C. Hufbauer, *Synthetic Materials and the Theory of International Trade* (London, 1966), Seev Hirsch, *Locations of Industry and International Competitiveness* (Oxford, 1967), and Louis T. Wells, editor, *The Product Life Cycle and International Trade* (Boston, 1972) containing eight industry and country studies by the editor and others.

[28] Baldwin (*op. cit.*), Hufbauer, 'The Commodity Composition of Trade in Manufactured Goods' (*loc. cit.*), W. H. Gruber and R. Vernon, 'The R and D Factors In A World Matrix' in *Technology Factors In International Trade*, NBER (1970).

[29] On the limitations of the data and difficulties of classification of industries, labour skills, etc., see especially the lengthy explanations in small print (footnotes) in Baldwin's article where the statistical procedures are discussed at some detail. See also the critical comments on Baldwin's article by Lawrence Weiser and Keith Jay and the author's reply in *American Economic Review*, Vol. 62 (June, 1972), pp. 459–472.

[30] Donald B. Keesing at Conference on *The Technology Factor in International Trade, op. cit.,* pp. 275–276.

[31] Quoted from Marshall's *Principles* by Ragnar Nurkse. *Equilibrium and Growth in the World Economy. Economic Essays by Ragnar Nurkse*, edited with an Introduction by G. Haberler (Cambridge, Mass., 1961).

[32] *The Theory of Games and Economic Behaviour*, 1st ed. (Princeton, N. J., 1944), p. 2.

[33] Karl R. Popper, *The Open Society and Its Enemies*, revised edition, (Princeton N.J., 1950), see especially Part II, 'The High Tide of Prophecy. The Rise of Oracular Philosophy'.

[34] Ohlin, *op. cit.*, 2nd ed., p. 319.

[35] Robert M. Solow, *Capital Theory and the Rate of Return*, Professor F. de Vries Lecture (Amsterdam, 1963), p. 15.

[36] *Op. cit.*, 1st ed., pp. 39–40, 2nd ed., pp. 27–28.

[37] J. Viner, *Studies*, pp. 437 and 501 fl.

[38] *Ibid.*, p. 437,

[39] *Op. cit.*, 1st ed., p. 590. This passage occurs in an appendix that has been omitted in the second edition.

It should perhaps be pointed out that strictly speaking it is misleading to call welfare economics a normative science (if there is such a thing). Welfare economics is economics and not a branch of ethics. The welfare economist does not say: 'The policy-maker *should* maximise national income'. What he says is: '*if* the policy-maker wishes to maximise income, he should pursue such and such a policy'. The welfare economist does not exclude that the policy-maker may have objectives other than, or supplementary to, maximisation of income. For example, he usually has supplementary objectives with respect to the distribution of income. Of course, the welfare economist selects his hypothetical value judgements in such a way as to reflect as faithfully as possible the policy objectives that the policy-maker more or less consciously entertains or reveals by his preferences. Whether the welfare economist is, in fact, faithful in his choice, is a problem in positive science which, in principal, should be subject to empirical confirmation or refutation.

[40] *Op. cit.*, 1st ed., p. 41, 2nd ed., pp. 27–28.

[41] It should be observed that free competition implies flexible prices (of commodities and of factors of production including wages), not free mobility between industries of factors of production (except if immobility of factors is the consequence of monopolistic anticompetitive forces such as labour union restrictions on new entrants into a particular industry or labour group). To say that the case for free trade maximising national income does not depend on the assumption of perfect mobility of factors does, however, not mean that increasing the domestic mobility of factors by better information, educational and training measures and the like is

unimportant. Thus Staffan Linder (*op. cit.*) argues that LDCs suffer from total inability of reallocating factors of production. I think he exaggerates tremendously the alleged inability and the conclusion that it makes trade for LDCs counterproductive is quite wrong (see H. G. Johnson's review of Linder's book in *Economica*, New Series, Vol. 31, No. 121, London (February, 1964). But he is certainly right that comparative immobility of factors is a very important handicap for LDCs.

[42] This appendix has been adapted from an unpublished PhD thesis by Michael Connolly.

[43] London, Macmillan, 1919.

[44] *Ibid.*, p. 118.

[45] *Ibid.*, pp. 118—119.

[46] *Ibid.*, p. 204.

[47] *Ibid.*, pp. 132—133.

[48] *Ibid.*, pp. 174—175.

[49] On Daniel Defoe (1660 or 1661—1731) see *Palgrave's Dictionary of Political Economy*. Edited by Henry Higgs, Vol. 1 (London, 1926).

[50] *Ibid.*, p. 40.

[51] Jacob Viner, 'International Relations between State-controlled National Economics', *American Economic Review*, Vol. 34, supplement (March, 1944) reprinted in *Readings in the Theory of International Trade* (Philadelphia, 1949), pp. 437—456. See also on this whole problem G. Haberler, 'Theoretical Reflections on the Trade of Socialist Countries' in *International Trade and Central Planning*, ed. by Alan A. Brown and Egon Neuberger (University of California Press, Berkeley and Los Angeles (California, 1968), pp. 29—46.

REFERENCES

Baldwin, R. E., 'Determinants of the Commodity Structure of U.S. Trade', *American Economic Review*, Vol. 62.

Caves, R. and R. Jones, *World Trade and Payments. An Introduction* (Boston, 1973).

Charpentier, M. G. and R. Clarke, *Public Purchasing in the Common Market* (E.C., Brussels, 1974).

Connolly, M., Alfred Marshall on Technology Trade, International Transmission of Technology and the Product Life Cycle (Unpublished Ph.D. thesis).

Daly, D. J., 'Uses of International Price and Output Data' in D. J. Daly (ed.) *International Comparisons of Prices and Outputs*, Studies in Income and Wealth, Vol. 37 (NBER, New York, 1972).

Defoe, D., *A Plan of the English Commerce* (1728).

Diab, M. A., *The United States Capital Position and the Structure of its Foreign Trade* (Amsterdam, 1956).

Drèze, J., 'Quelques reflexions sereines sur l'adaptation de l'industrie Belge au Marché Commun', *Comptes rendues des Travaux de la Société Royal d'Économie Politique de Belgique*, No. 275 (1960).

Fisher, I., *The Rate of Interest* (New York, 1907).

Gruber, W. H., Mehta, D. and Vernon, R., 'The R & D Factors in International Trade and International Investment of U.S. Industries', *Journal of Political Economy* (Feb. 1967).

Gruber, W. H. and Vernon, R., 'The Technology Factor in a World Trade Matrix' in R. Vernon (ed.) *The Technology Factor in International Trade* (NBER/Columbia Univ. Press, New York, 1970).

Haberler, G., 'Theoretical Reflections on the Trade of Socialist Countries', in A. A. Brown and E. Beuberger (eds.) *International Trade and Central Planning* (California Univ. Press, Berkeley and Los Angeles, 1968).

Haberler, G., *Survey of International Trade Theory* (2nd ed.) (Princeton, 1961).

Higgs, E. (ed.), *Palgrave's Dictionary of Political Economy*, Vol. 1 (London, 1926).

Hirsch, S., *Locations of Industry and International Competitiveness* (Oxford, 1967).

Hirsch, S. and Lev, B., 'Trade and Per Capita Income Differentials: A Test of the Burenstam-Linder Hypothesis' in *World Development*, Vol. 1, No. 9 (Sept. 1973).

Hufbauer, G. C., 'The Impact of National Characteristics and Technology on the Commodity Composition of Trade in Manufactured Goods' in R. Vernon (ed.), *The Technology Factor in International Trade* (New York, 1970).

Hufbauer, G. C., *Synthetic Materials and the Theory of International Trade* (London, 1966).

Johnson, H. G., *Comparative Cost and Commercial Policy Theory for a Developing World* (Wicksell Lectures, Stockholm, 1968).

Johnson, H. G., 'The State of Theory in Relation to Empirical Analysis' in R. Vernon (ed.) *The Technology Factor in International Trade* (New York, 1970).

Johnson, H. G., book review of S. B. Linder, *An Essay on Trade and Transformation, Economica*, New Series, Vol. 31, No. 121 (Feb. 1964).

Keesing, D. B., 'Comments on Hufbauer, Gruber and Vernon', in R. Vernon (ed.), *The Technology Factor in International Trade* (New York, 1970).

Keesing, D. B., 'Labor Skills and Comparative Advantage', *American Economic Review*, Vol. 56 (May, 1966).

Kenen, P. E., 'Nature, Capital and Trade', *Journal of Political Economy*, Vol. 73 (1965).

Kravis, I., '"Availability" and Other Influences on the Commodity Composition of Trade', *Journal of Political Economy* (April, 1956).

Kravis, I. and Lipsey, R. E., *Price Competitiveness in World Trade* (NBER, New York, 1971).

Leontief, W. W., 'Factor Proportions and the Structure of American Trade: Further Theoretical and Empirical Analysis', *Review of Economics and Statistics*, Vol. 38 (1956).

Linder, S. B., *An Essay on Trade and Transformation* (New York, 1961).

Marshall, A., *Industry and Trade* (Macmillan, London, 1919).

Marshall, A., 'The Pure Theory of Foreign Trade' and 'The Pure Theory of (Domestic) Values', 1879, in London School of Economics *Reprint of Scarce Tracts*, No. 1 (London, 1930).

Morgenstern, O. and von Neumann, J., *The Theory of Games and Economic Behavior* (1st ed.) (Princeton, N.J., 1944).

Nurkse, R., *Equilibrium and Growth in the World Economy. Economic Essays*, G. Haberler (ed.) (Cambridge, Mass., 1961).

Ohlin, B., 'Reflections on Contemporary International Trade Theories in *Interregional and International Trade* (2nd rev. ed.) (Cambridge, Mass., 1967).

Popper, K. R., *The Open Society and Its Enemies* (rev. ed.) (Princeton, N.J., 1950).

Posner, M. V., 'International Trade and Technical Change', *Oxford Economic Papers*, Vol. 13 (Oct. 1961).

Schumpeter, J. A., *The Theory of Economic Development* (Translated from first edition in German, 1912) (Cambridge, Mass., 1934).

Solow, R. M., *Capital Theory and the Rate of Return*, Professor F. de Vries Lecture (Amsterdam, 1963).

Stern, R. M., 'Testing Trade Theories' in P. B. Denen (ed.), *International Trade and Finance Frontiers for Research* (Cambridge, 1975).

Taussig, F. W., *International Trade* (New York, 1928).

Taussig, F. W., 'Wages and Prices in Relation to International Trade', *Quarterly Journal of Economics*, Vol. 20.

Vanek, J., *The Natural Resource Content of U.S. Foreign Trade 1950– 1955* (Cambridge, Mass., 1963).

Viner, J., 'International Relations between State-controlled National Economics', *American Economic Review*, Vol. 34 (March, 1944), reprinted in *Readings in the Theory of International Trade* (Philadelphia, 1949).

Viner, J., *Studies in the Theory of International Trade* (New York, 1937).

Weiser, L. and K. Jay, Review of R. Baldwin 'Determinants of the Commodity Structure of U.S. Trade', *American Economic Review*, Vol. 62 (June, 1972).

Wells, L. T., 'International Trade: The Product Life Cycle Approach in L. T. Wells (ed.), *The Product Life Cycle and International Trade* (Boston, 1972).

2 Some Aspects of the Relations between International Movements of Commodities, Factors of Production, and Technology

Bertil Ohlin

I am happy to have the privilege to speak after my old friend Gottfried Haberler, who in his paper once more demonstrates his exceptional ability in making difficult problems easily understandable and his reliable judgement in scientific surveys.

The four days of our symposium provide an occasion for illuminating not only a series of concrete problems but important methodological questions as well. What I have in mind is, for example, the advisability of letting the highly simplified models — two factors of production, two commodities, two countries — dominate large parts of the analysis as much as they have done during several decades.

Unrealistic basic assumptions can — and often will — raise doubts about the realism of the conclusions from such models. Should not their relevance for the 'real world' be subject to more scrutiny and discussion than we have had? How are we to know more about the realism of the conclusions from highly simplified models, if we do not — in some cases at least — compare them with results of an analysis of more realistic settings of the problems? Is perhaps the marginal utility of further exercises with variations of the very simple models in many cases rather low compared to that of a greater concentration on *relatively* neglected problems and more realistic assumptions? I am thinking of the international effects of, for example, economies of scale, different tax structures, social legislation and risk as well as international factor movements and factor supply reactions. These aspects can be illuminated a great deal by comparative static analysis and by less simplified assumptions. This is also true of the adaptation of the demand for commodities and possibly also of the influence of technological change.

The simple models are, of course, a useful introduction. Under fortunate circumstances they can be much more than that.[1] They have permitted a greater precision in the conclusions than otherwise possible. However, in many cases the problems and the solutions owe their existence to special assumptions, which have nothing to do with the real world and its problems.[2] As an example I refer to the limited applicability of the factor price equalisation theorem. In my opinion, the chief importance of this theorem lies in its demonstration of *tendencies* towards price equalisation. Obviously a complete equalisation is only conceivable under *very* unrealistic assumptions (see section II, page 28).

What I have now said does not prevent me from expressing my admiration for the great scientific ability, which a number of economists have demonstrated in the use of well-known simple models in the treatment of new and old problems. Gottfried Haberler's survey is illuminating, as indicated by Ronald Findlay's references. In recent years he has himself made skilful use of such models. I only hope for an equal concentration of effort on the use of models which emphasise things like the structure of tax systems, social rules and legislation as well as risks in different countries.

I. SOME LIMITATIONS OF THE ANALYSIS

The general approach employed in this survey is that of *a price theory* of international trade — chiefly in equilibrium terms — and of location of industry and trade in terms of an economic development. The interdependence of factor and commodity movements is also a part of the analysis — as the subject for this session indicates. To explain the motives behind the supply of commodities, one has to take into consideration all the circumstances which affect the quantities available and the costs of output in terms of money — that is, the ordinary business cost account — as well as demand and market conditions. Most of the supply facts refer to places, regions, countries or larger groups of territories. The same holds for accounts of demand conditions.

Under conditions of perfect competition and full employment of the factors of production, calculations in terms of opportunity costs and in prices come to the same thing. But an analysis in terms of prices can more easily be adapted to conditions of incomplete employment and to price policies, which include elements of imperfect competition. Furthermore, cost of production includes not only payments to factors but also taxes and other 'non-factor expenses' and their sums are expressed in money. Besides, the relations between factor movements and commodity movements are chiefly concerned with prices in monetary terms. On the other hand, the concept opportunity cost is well suited for an analysis of alternatives for production under full employment and for a study of gain from variations in trade and factor movements.[3] It can with advantage be used as a supplement — a very important supplement — to the more general price theory approach.

Among the problems I take up for brief analysis — after some remarks on the factor price equalisation theorem — some emphasis is placed on things which, in my opinion, received relatively scant attention in the scientific texts and debates before 1960. Fortunately, the decades since then have brought considerable improvements in several of these directions. Except for a few sentences I pass over for example, the effects on trade of border obstacles which have been the object of penetrating analysis for more than a century.

In a survey of this kind it is obviously out of the question to present in each section a number of precise models. Like several other authors of 'introductions', I have had to confine myself to somewhat scattered observations on certain problems, knowing well that I may be criticised for not preferring the use of precise models in more narrow fields. My justification is that my main task is to illuminate the general character of the relations between trade and factor movements and, thereby, the international division of labour. It goes without saying that any change in part of a mutual interdependence equilibrium price system may affect any other part. But close connections which can be specified are a particularly interesting subject of analysis. To this category one may count, for example, the relations between international trade, factor supply and factor movements, including the spread of technical knowhow. Changes in border obstacles, non-factor expenditure and financial and social conditions as well as changes in the volume and structure of demand will affect these relations.

The business cost account approach to price theory and the factor proportion reasoning lead directly into an analysis of such relations. At the first stage it is based on the assumption that *ceteris paribus* each country has an advantage in the production of commodities into which enter a relatively large quantity of factors that are relatively cheap in that country. It is the difference in *the relative scarcity* of the factors of production, and the fact that they are used in different proportions in the production of different commodities, which leads to an international division of labour and trade under the simple assumptions made. Commodities containing a large proportion of cheap factors are exported. No assumptions are made that the number of commodities is small or that all factors exist in all countries, where two or more are taken into account.

The influence of trade will be to increase demand in all countries for factors which are relatively cheap in that country. But, there are exceptions to this conclusion — particularly under conditions of substitution of different factors for one another in cases of radical technological inequalities.

The influence of (1) trade on factor prices and (2) the influence of factor movements on trade makes it obvious that *international commodity and factor movements can act as substitutes for one another.* Reduced exchange of commodities will under many circumstances lead to factor price discrepancies which will increase factor movements. Reduction of factor movements will in many cases increase trade. I naturally deal also with some cases where the relation between commodity and factor movements is not one of substitution but one of supplementation. The importance of domestic factor supply reactions for factor price variations is stressed although — owing to lack of space — not much analysed. Emphasis is laid on the effects of other cost elements like taxes, social circumstances, etc., on trade and factor movements and their relations. Of course, a theory of factor movements is not necessarily subordinate to a theory of commodity movements.

II. SOME ASPECTS OF THE FACTOR PRICE EQUALISATION THEOREM[4]

For reasons indicated above, a transition from a situation with various trade obstacles to a situation where commodities but not factors of production move freely without any cost will under certain conditions call forth a tendency to international factor price equalisation. The reasoning is well known from numerous books and need not be repeated here.

The mutual interdependence equilibrium price system with one market and many goods and factors (for example of the Walras-Cassel type) in each country can be expanded to cover several markets. Among other things it can be used to illuminate the probably incomplete equalisation of international factor prices through trade in the absence of transport costs, which Heckscher discussed as a separate question. In the real world there are not only many factors of production and many commodities but also different tastes and demand conditions in different countries and seldom perfect competition on all markets for goods and factors.

It is no doubt interesting to ascertain the conditions under which — in the well-known simplified case of 2 x 2 x 2 — a complete factor price equalisation through trade takes place in the absence of factor movements. A still more important task is to gain knowledge about the influence on trade and factor prices of changes in transport costs, market imperfections, taxes, risks etc. — that is, circumstances that are left out of account in the simplified case. It is true, of course, that the conclusions about the conditions of complete factor price equalisation in the simple case tells us that the non-fulfilment of these conditions can be regarded as belonging to the causes of *incomplete* factor price equalisation. But this hardly gives us much more than an enumeration of *some* types of relevant circumstances. It so happens that the relevance of some of them is self-evident — at least market imperfections and different production functions in different countries. There remain all the other circumstances, which the simple case leaves out. The influence of their variations on factor prices and trade — its character and size — is a problem which can be studied with the aid of different factor proportion models and other models. The analysis of complete factor price equalisation is a useful preparation but the main part of the problem remains.

When a large number of countries is taken into account, it is possible that an expansion of trade may increase the demand for a factor F in a certain country, even though it is high up on the scale of relative factor scarcity. This factor may be needed for the increased output of a commodity which for other reasons — such as, a low price of another much-needed factor — is produced relatively cheaply in that country. Increased trade will then raise the demand for F and its relative price. However, the larger the number of commodities, the smaller the percentage of such cases will probably be.[5]

The relation of the price of factor X to that of factor Y in country A may be high in comparison with the relation in country B but low in comparison with countries C and D. Evidently, in the case of more than three countries it is very difficult to characterise the influence on trade of the relative scarcity of different factors in different countries in any other way than through systems of equations and matrices. A comparison of the factor prices in terms of money in the different countries, in situations with different volumes of trade, may *ceteris paribus* illuminate the relation between factor scarcity and trade expansion due to different causes. It is necessary to specify the cause of the trade expansion when analysing its effects!

The foreign exchange rate is affected by demand conditions. A large expansion of trade could change the relative scarcities of factors in the two countries and bring about such an equilibrium exchange rate for their two currencies, that the factor F passes from relative cheapness in A compared to in B to being relatively expensive in A. There is nothing peculiar in this case of 'relative factor intensity reversal'. The use of simple two-factor models has — it seems to me — created a paradox which in some cases is due to unrealistic assumptions rather than to the nature of the real problem.

There are, however, some *more special cases of factor intensity reversal* through trade. The new trade may imply *new methods of production or consumption* in the importing country. The growth of trade between China and the United States may have led to the importation and use of motor cars for part of the transportation in China as a substitute for 'rickshaws' and other vehicles requiring much labour. The relative scarcity of unskilled labour in some Chinese districts may have been reduced, although such labour was the relatively cheap factor. Similar substitution effects may appear in industrial production (see section VII on technological differences).

The obvious influence of demand and the difficulty in explaining what one means when saying that the factor F is relatively less scarce in country A than B when many countries and many factors are taken into account is one reason why since the early 1920s I have felt that the factor proportion model as a basis for trade theory cannot stand on its own legs, as it were. It is not sufficient to supplement it by a consideration of reciprocal demand à la John Stuart Mill. It is better to make the use of this model a part of a theory of mutual interdependence of different national price systems, when explaining international trade in general. This, furthermore, brings the advantage that international differences in the qualities of certain factors can be taken into account in the system of equations of the price systems. It has to be granted, however, that in most cases the explanatory value of such a system is limited, if one does not demonstrate *how* different the production functions are as a result of the qualitative differences of the factor in the various countries.

III. ON THE MEASUREMENT OF 'CAPITAL INTENSITY' AND SOME OTHER COST ASPECTS

Three different methods of measuring 'the capital intensity of the production of a commodity' are sometimes used in factor proportion analysis.

(1) The quantity of capital *per individual working place* used in the activity under consideration.

(2) The quantity of capital *per worker*. If production in a certain country is going on in two shifts — 80 hours per week instead of 40 — the number of workers in a factory of a certain size is doubled. The quantity of capital per worker is cut in half (although the increased wear and tear and investment in stocks of commodities must be considered).

(3) *The percentage share of 'the total unit production costs'* which consists of capital costs, in other words, the interest and depreciation costs. Other costs are chiefly labour costs. The comparison can be made with the cost situation 'abroad' in the production of the *same* commodity. It might seem natural to use this last method in measuring the capital intensity in the two countries but this would be a mistake. The use of a relatively large quantity of capital — in the meaning of (2) above — in the production of a certain commodity in country A which has a low interest level is quite compatible with a relatively low capital cost in A — compared to in B — if it is measured as a percentage of total unit cost. Obviously, the most relevant concept as far as *fixed capital* is concerned is the quantity of capital per worker in the second sense.

The circumstances touched upon above may help to explain why countries with relatively high wage levels and low interest levels may nevertheless export goods which 'contain' relatively large quantities of labour. The production may benefit from a high value of capital instruments per working place but a small quantity of capital per worker. Furthermore, traditions and slight differences in labour quality can enable them to keep the machines going faster than elsewhere. This is a very incomplete comment on Leontief's famous 'paradox' concerning the factor proportions in the trade of the United States. Economies of scale may also play a great role as well as may the advantages of technological pioneering activity and other technological discrepancies.[6]

The cost of using capital instruments includes not only interest payments but also the cost of depreciation. 'Time-depreciation' will be independent of the current output. But 'use-depreciation' will be roughly parallel to output. Thus, *marginal* costs in an existing establishment which lengthens the work period per month will as a capital cost include only use-depreciation — to the extent it exceeds time-depreciation. (This may be important particularly during imperfect competition and dumping.)

In the usual factor proportion reasoning the quantities of factors used refer to *the total process of production* of each commodity. It is, however, much more realistic to think about costs at different stages of production. In other words, total costs refer to the costs incurred by manufacture at *each stage of production.* Under equilibrium conditions the total unit cost is equal to 'the value added by manufacture' at a certain stage.

The factor proportions should evidently refer to each stage of manufacturing (production) which can be kept separate from other stages that are to some extent handled by other firms or productive units. This is necessary if the analysis is to explain trade where different stages of production are situated in different countries.

What I have said above about capital intensity can *mutatis mutandis* be applied to other factors, except the depreciation aspects. Initial expenditure for 'new workers' — costs of training, for example — may, however be divided between annual accounts through 'depreciation'. The difficulties for cost calculation arising from incompletely variable costs and fixed costs and from 'joint supply' of different commodities are on the whole the same as those in the one-market analysis.

IV. ECONOMIES OF SCALE AND SIZE OF THE MARKET

The most obvious modification of the simple factor proportion model implies a consideration of the economies of scale in economic activity — not only in production but also in transportation, research, etc. They have to do with the lack of divisibility of some productive units and the advantages of specialisation. Every textbook on economic principles explains the existence of both internal and external advantages of size and of agglomeration. In some cases size is measured in value terms, in other cases in the number of products.

As such economies mean that the cost per unit moves downward when output of a product or groups of products is increased up to a point — in the firm, in the concern, in the city, in the region or in the country —

they will tend to stimulate division of labour and trade, internal as well as between nations.

The larger the market is in a country, the more remunerative it may be to specialise in industries where economies of scale are important — if there are international border costs or large transport costs. This is part of the explanation why during some decades before and after the First World War, motor cars were chiefly produced in the United States.

At least for a time the relative scarcity of factors which are much used in industries profiting from a large scale will be increased through trade. In many cases the domestic supply of such factors will rise as time passes. Besides, technological innovations may be more easily 'produced' in large enterprises.

The consequence is that in countries with a very early development of manufacturing industry and high income levels, the economies of scale may be large and serve as an important cause of trade irrespective of any difference in relative factor prices.[7] *New factor price differences may be created.* The economies of scale can also tend to strengthen the equalising effect on relative factor prices which trade may exercise. The volume of output in an industry, which is dependent on factors of production that are relatively cheap in a certain country, may be subject to extra growth owing to the economies of scale. They play a greater role in that country than in some others. In such cases the increase in demand for the relatively cheap factors in the former country will be strengthened by the economies of scale. They make exports grow even more than would otherwise be the case.

Some of the economic advantages of specialisation can be obtained *in small firms* which concentrate on inexpensive parts or goods and produce a large number of them. In Belgium and Holland the Benelux free trade was expected to drive many firms out of business and force the workers to settle elsewhere. A number of these firms chose to specialise more than before and, thereby, reduced their costs so much that they could survive. Economies of scale contributed to this cost reduction.

The fact that many less developed countries are 'economically' small and enjoy relatively insignificant advantages of large scale, tends to keep back their industrial development. It also tends to limit the influx of foreign capital and high quality labour when they are needed for other purposes than the utilisation of raw material resources.

Can one say that international trade will create a tendency for *equalisation of costs* of producing the goods that are subject to trade even if factor price differences are not reduced? The answer will depend chiefly on the relative strength of the effects of trade on factor prices, on the one hand, and the reduction of costs owing to economies of scale, on the other hand. Consider an exchange between two countries of shoes against textiles and assume economies of scale to be considerable — then the difference between costs in the two countries will grow. In each country costs fall in the export industry but not in the import-competing industry, which may maintain a certain home production of some qualities. The increased demand for the factors in the exporting industry may raise their prices. But the effect on costs may be more than offset by the economies of scale.

Evidently, it must not be taken for granted that a reduction in the price differences for factors in different countries through trade will as a rule reduce the differences in the costs of production for all types of goods in which there is international trade. The elasticity of factor supply and several other circumstances have to be considered.

V. BRIEF REMARKS ON THE REACTION OF DEMAND FOR COMMODITIES AND OF SUPPLY OF FACTORS

Obviously, the effect of trade expansion on the real national income — generally in a positive direction — will affect the demand for commodities, both import goods, export goods and non-trade goods. Besides, the change in the distribution of income will also exercise an influence on demand. For these reasons — and others which are mentioned below — the primary effects of trade variations indirectly affect relative factor prices — probably differently in different countries — as well as the later currents of trade.

Furthermore, the international movements of labour, capital and technology[8] will change the relative factor prices, output, national income, distribution of income and — indirectly — the demand for commodities and trade (see section VI).

It is probable that the changes in many factor prices — which when measured in real terms will chiefly move upwards when the GNP is increased through trade expansion — will affect *the domestic supply* of some of them, quite apart from the obvious effect of the influx or outflux from and to other countries. In some cases, the reaction of supply to higher pay may be negative, for example a shortening of the working day or increased irregular absence from work.

If the interest level is raised in a country, it is possible — but far from certain — that the volume of saving will grow in that country. To judge from experience in industrialised countries it is almost certain that a rise in the G.N.P. will in the long run increase savings unless a changed distribution of income brings about an offsetting affect.

Furthermore, industrial development will increase the skill of some labour — in other words increase the domestic supply of certain labour qualities. The more one studies economic development during one or more decades, the more obvious it becomes that effects of commodity and factor movements on one another are interwoven with many other aspects of development, which are due for example, to the use of growing economic resources for improvements in education, technical training, research, communication, etc. (see section XII below, page 46).

With regard to the influence of some kinds of policy on factor supply, I refer to some later sessions.[9]

VI. SOME TYPES OF FACTOR MOVEMENTS AND THEIR ECONOMIC EFFECTS, PARTICULARLY ON TRADE, OTHER FACTOR MOVEMENTS AND FACTOR SUPPLY[10]

(1) SOME SPECIAL RELATIONS

A theory of international movements of factors of production can be built only in close contact with the theory of international commodity movements. The relations between the movements of different factors are important in both cases. In a simple two-factor—two-countries model with commodities as mobile as in the real world and with factors incompletely mobile — four possibilities occur: (i) F_1 moves from country A to country B (ii) F_2 moves from B to A (iii) both factors move but in opposite or (iv) the same directions. Obviously, the degree of mobility of the factors and the size of the factor price differences under the influence of trade is essential. A part of the trade is made superfluous — or brought into being — through the factor movements during a certain period of time. The outcome will depend also on the size of the 'remaining' production cost differences for the different commodities relative to the trade obstacles to be overcome, and partly on the 'new' demand conditions. In many of the cases below *the reactions of the terms of trade* must be considered, as they may influence the demand and factor price reactions.[11]

In this survey I can hardly do more than present a list of some characteristic connections, referring for the sake of brevity chiefly to a country which *receives* factors from other countries

(a) Increased factor movements will in many cases tend to reduce international cost differences and to curtail trade. New obstacles to factor movements will tend to bring about trade expansion.

In other cases, increased mobility of factors will lead to an expansion of the national income particularly in LDCs and, thereby, to a growth of trade. Yet the international differences in factor prices and commodity prices may be reduced. The growth of the volume of trade may nevertheless imply a reduction of trade, measured as a percentage of the national income in the factor-receiving country. On the other hand, internal and external economies of scale may increase trade more than the national income in such countries.

(b) It is impossible to understand the influence which the transfer of European labour and capital to LDCs exercised on trade, factor prices and G.N.P. in Europe in the last hundred years without considering the kind of production which was created in LDCs and to what extent it led to exports to Europe. In some cases the increased output and exportation consisted of raw materials which made it possible to extend the manufacturing industry in Europe and pay higher wages. In other cases the result was an exportation of textile goods from LDCs to Europe. In due time this led to a relative pressure on wages in the European textile industries. A consideration of different types and skills of labour is necessary in order to make a more precise account possible. In one way or another, the interaction between growing trade, factor movements and economies of scale affected the development and contraction of European industry and international price differences. It should not be too difficult to construct some models which will illuminate various alternatives inside such a general development — referring to different periods of time. Import of capital by LDCs led to an influx of skilled labour.

(c) It goes without saying that the long-run effects will be affected by the influence on domestic factor supply of changes in factor prices which are due to the international factor movements and to trade. Furthermore, industrial development and national income growth will indirectly affect the volume of savings and probably the training of skilled labour.

(d) There are many cases where two or three different factors move together in an organised manner. For example, multinational corporations may send risk-bearing capital plus leading managerial and technical labour from one country to establish a new factory in another country. Capital subsidies in the receiving countries may stimulate supplementary factor movements of this sort to these countries. One combination of factor movements may be an alternative to another, perhaps in the opposite directions.

(e) Increased 'border obstacles' to commodity imports may lead to an influx of capital and highly skilled labour, perhaps other labour qualities as well. The establishment of branch factories in protectionist countries has been a common phenomenon in the postwar period (see also sections XII(2) and (3) below, pages 47–50).

(f) In other cases a reduction of imports of commodities due to protection leads not only to an influx of foreign capital and knowhow but also to a reduction of emigration of labour from LDCs. Thus, immigration of one factor may be an alternative to emigration of another. Which alternative will be realised will depend on all those things which affect the different factor movements and trade may be one of them. (Cf. point (d) above.)

(g) A gradual expansion of the productive capacity follows from the influx of highly trained labour and capital, whereby the demand for ordinary labour is enlarged. There will be a tendency for ordinary wages to rise. More capital is needed to serve as a kind of 'wage fund', as the increased wages are paid out at an earlier date than that at which the sale of the product takes place. Thus, only the rest of the imported capital will 'materialise' in new investment goods and increased capacity of production!

This is a unique aspect – let me call it 'the Wicksell capital effect' – which has no correspondence in the case of an influx of labour.

(h) Besides, there will in some capital-importing countries be a tendency towards an increase of the relative price of factors which are used in relatively large quantities *in home market industries* – putting out non-trade commodities. This is due to the well-known adjustment mechanism in the case of capital movements (note (i)).

(i) A special relation between factor movements and trade is the influence of international capital movements on the balance of trade. The importation of capital takes the form of increased imports and/or a relative decline of exports of commodities, be it raw materials, finished producers' goods, articles for consumption, semi-manufacturer or services. Hence, a certain adaptation of the productive process takes place.

(j) The international migration of labour is not due simply to price differences, that is, differences in *nominal* wage levels. Inequalities in *real* wages are due also to differences in the costs of living, the climatic conditions, the availability of land at low prices and many other circumstances. All of them can more or less affect international labour movements.

(k) It is quite possible that the quality of labour will rise already after a few years as a result of a rise in the living standard in a capital-importing LDC. The supply of several different labour qualities must be considered.

(l) The mere fact that a worker from southern Europe emigrated to the United States in the 1920s probably increased his efficiency: he was at once caught by the 'quicker rhythm' in American factories.

(m) This effect is similar to the more general and usually slower effect of 'learning by doing' which implies a transition of an individual from unskilled to semi-skilled or skilled labour. In many cases this factor quality improvement comes during the years immediately after the immigration to an industrialised country, which offers opportunities of employment, such as in manufacturing industries.

(n) International capital movements are naturally influenced by several types of *risk*. Hence, a prospect for higher returns is in many cases a necessary condition for investment in foreign countries. In other cases, a mixture of risks from investments both abroad and at home may be more attractive to a capital owner than the placing of all his capital in the home country. Capital exports will have a tendency to raise the interest level at home, while they will tend to reduce or keep down the interest level in the capital-importing country. But, it is far from certain that the latter effect will come about, if the money is used to 'buy factories' or important machines abroad and if a new enterprise is in that way quickly created. The same holds for the case when foreign branch factories are established with foreign capital and highly qualified labour.

(p) Export credits may be used to stimulate sales from the lending to the borrowing country. This is an obvious and organised connection between capital and commodity movements. It is one of the many cases where factor movements stimulate trade and do not serve as a substitute for trade.

(q) The effects of factor movements on production and trade naturally depend also on economies of scale, social regulations and costs, etc. (see later sections).

(r) The demand reactions, such as when population is increased through immigration, will influence trade and indirectly capital movements.

(s) Special aspects of factor movements are due to the power of attraction of national resources and their location. (See Chisholm's and Richardson's contributions (Chapter 3) and the later discussion.)

(t) The effects on countries other than those directly involved cannot be ignored. They may be significant and exercise a secondary influence on the economy of the factor-exporting and importing countries.

(u) Temporary 'guest workers' may affect labour supply and industrial development, for example in the case of Switzerland.

(2) DO FACTOR MOVEMENTS INVALIDATE TRADE THEORY?

Professor Maurice Byé has emphasised the fact that the theory of international trade since the days of the classical economists has rested on the assumption that the factors of production are not mobile between nations or that their movements are so insignificant that a realistic trade theory need only refer to the existing domestic supply of productive resources. A growing factor mobility, for example inside Europe, will in his opinion make such a theory more and more unrealistic and make the conclusions about the advantages of trade and factor movements between nations in some essential respects erroneous.[12] My own opinion may be briefly indicated.

The short-run effects of factor movements on trade can be regarded as minor modifications of the trade that is going on if there are small variations in *domestic* factor supply. The relevant viewpoints in section VI can be utilised. Capital movements and the establishment of branch factories as well as the movement of highly specialised labour and the prospects for future movements deserve special interest.

The long-run effects of factor movements on development of industry in different countries and on trade between them can, however, be very considerable. Countries with large immigration and borrowing abroad can in a decade expand their trade in a way which is much affected by the changing total supply of productive resources, whether due to domestic variations or international movements. The insufficiency of static trade theory and the need for adding a theory of development to explain international economic relations is obvious. Thereby, the complications for trade theory connected with factor movements can be taken care of (see also section XII below).

One reason why simple formal static models of *factor* movements are less practical than simple *trade* models is that the degree of commodity mobility can be fairly well indicated through measures of the obstacles to trade, that are due to transport costs, tariffs, special sales costs, etc. all expressed in money costs per unit. But, the incomplete mobility of labour cannot be measured by the costs of transportation and resettlement of workers in another country. Besides, trade may conceivably follow an unchanged pattern year after year in constant volume. Factor movements alter the total supply of productive resources and thereby production and trade through a time-using process.

VII. ABOUT THE INFLUENCE OF TECHNOLOGICAL DIFFERENCES ON INTERNATIONAL ECONOMIC RELATIONS

(1) CAUSES OF INTERNATIONAL TECHNOLOGICAL DIFFERENCES

It may be natural to group the causes of inequalities in technical methods in five categories

(a) Different factor combinations due to the differences in relative factor prices.

(b) The absence in some countries of certain factors — present in others — like managerial and technical labour of high quality. A very common example is the absence of certain types of natural resources, for example, high-quality copper mines, which makes it natural in some countries to use low-grade mines and a different technique for the production of raw copper.

(c) The third type is due to the fact that certain technical knowledge may be available in some countries but not in others. Specialist knowledge about production methods may also be kept secret in one or several companies — or be monopolised through patent rights — and not be available for others.

(d) The fourth type — already discussed above — is dependent on social legislation or traditions about the hours of work, the availability of night work and extra hours of work, the number of labour shifts and the rate of additional pay for such 'extra work'. These matters may play an important role. Production which requires a great deal of capital will — other things being equal — tend to be located in countries where the workers accept working longer hours, for example, in several shifts. The expensive real capital will be better utilised in such countries.

(e) A fifth cause is, of course, the utilisation of the economies of scale and specialisation which is affected by the size of the market. In a world which still has many border obstacles to trade, it is easier to build up factories using a modern technique in LDCs like Brazil and

India which have very large domestic markets, than it is to do so in a LDC with only a small domestic demand. Unless these small countries have a special aptitude for the production, appropriate natural resources, for example.

It follows from what I have said in previous sections that differences in transport conditions, like the supply and quality of roads, railroads, harbours and other kinds of internal and external transport conditions can influence the technique of transportation and the volume of production and, thereby, the technique used in production. This is an example of causation of the second and fifth sort — with some special aspects. All this will influence the technical methods and factor prices in different countries. Hence, costs of production in monetary terms will be affected. So will international trade, and, in some cases, factor movements.

In my old analysis of international economic relations (1933), I chose to disregard the causes of differences in technology, which is referred to as the third type above. This was, of course, a conscious but serious omission. Other differences in technology were considered to some extent, although largely without the use of formal models.

(2) NEW ANALYSIS OF TECHNOLOGICAL DIFFERENCES AND TRADE

Considerable progress in the analysis of technological differences and their influence on industry and international trade has been made, chiefly after 1955. Inequalities in technical knowledge and different production functions have often been regarded as a separate condition of production, which has not been tied up with the quality of some special 'subfactor' of labour. This method has brought valuable results in the hands of skilful economists.[13] A pioneer in this field was Harry Johnson in the 1950s with an analysis he later followed up — most recently through his excellent contribution to this symposium. Like many of the other prominent contributors, he took part in the conference on 'The Technology Factor in International Trade' (proceedings edited by R. Vernon, 1970). The high quality of the analysis and the statistical testing attempts, in my opinion, make this volume extremely useful for students in a very important field. If for my purposes I refer to the two papers by Hufbauer and Jones, it does not mean that I fail to appreciate the high quality of the other essays in this volume or of earlier contributions by Balogh, Bruno, Cairncross, Chenery, Chipman, Findlay, Grubert, Hicks, Johnson, Myint, Nörregaard-Rasmussen, Perroux and Vernon about the international transfer of technology.

In one respect the new analysis has some affinity to a return to the approach used by the classical theory of international trade. Some writers talk about the international inequalities in the efficiency of production due to different levels of technique without going into an explanation of how the inequality has come about and why it is able to remain during long periods in a world of continuous change.

Some of the writers mentioned above have demonstrated the applicability of the factor proportion model in a study of the role played by technological differences which influence trade as well as movements of the factors of production. Another step in the direction of realism in the use of this model is possible if one counts with different qualities of labour and takes into account the causes of technological differences I mentioned above.

Let me specify *four* types of labour ('subfactors'): ordinary unskilled labour (OL), skilled labour (SL), managerial and technical labour of lower rank (MTLL), and higher managerial and technical labour (MTLH). Several of the less-developed countries, which belong to the upper half of the LDC group with regard to living standard and industrial development, have a seriously insufficient supply of the MTLL. It has proven easier, for example for some Arab countries as well as India and Pakistan, to train, import and maintain a rapidly growing supply of labour with high technical knowledge (MTLH). The industrialised countries — ICs — naturally have a relatively more abundant supply of all three skilled groups and relatively less of ordinary unskilled labour than the above-mentioned LDC. This difference in labour supply — as well as differences in the supply of risk-bearing capital — is reflected in their industrial development and trade, to judge from my impressions during brief visits and from discussions with experienced people.

It is, however, important to realise that an equilibrium position does not necessarily mean that certain scantily supplied labour qualities, like MTLL, are more highly paid in terms of money in LDC than in IC. The quality of the same 'subfactor' of labour may in some respects be lower in LDC than in IC. The willingness to keep a high rhythm of work and the reliability with regard to a regular presence in the factory and good care of the machines may be far from equal everywhere. Statistical illumination of speed and durability of standard machinery in different countries should be possible.

(3) TECHNICAL TIES BETWEEN NEW COMMODITY MOVEMENTS AND NEW TECHNIQUE

In some cases trade may be inseparably tied to a change of the technology in importing countries, as indicated in Section II above. Export of textile machinery from Europe to a non-industrialised country using home-spinning and weaving will reduce the relative scarcity of the cheapest labour quality in the latter country, which will start exporting textile goods to Europe. The increased output of textile machinery and reduced output of textile goods in Europe will increase the scarcity of capital and skilled labour. In both countries trade will reduce the relative scarcity of the unskilled labour. Through its direct influence on the technique used in industry, export of producers' goods can evidently exert influence on relative factor scarcity in a different way from what usually happens in other cases. As pointed out by Jones, the explanation is that in such cases trade and the new technology will have similar effects as a labour-saving invention in the LDC (see the Vernon volume referred to in (2) above).

The lowered tariff levels or the elimination of import duties on machines in many countries in the last two decades has made trade in such products easier. A part of it has probably had the above-mentioned effect, being in fact combined with changes in technology.

The surprising possibility of 'immiserising growth' — that a country can get poorer as a result of an improvement in the technical methods — has been demonstrated by Bhagwati and others. It may happen if the demand abroad has a low price elasticity. The increased exports can then lead to more unfavourable terms of trade and to a consequent loss which exceeds the gain from a cheaper supply at home. The lower real income for certain labour factors may lead to the emigration to other countries and districts.

To sum up: Technological conditions will to some extent lead to other commodity and factor movements than those which would have tended to equalise factor prices internationally. Differences in factor qualities make the meaning of the expression 'international factor price equalisation' vague. The marginal utility of increased formal precision in the use of simple models becomes lower than expected.

VIII. NON-FACTOR EXPENDITURE AND EXTRA FACTOR REQUIRE-MENT: THE TAX STRUCTURE

Apart from certain border obstacles — like tariffs — there are many other types of 'extra' expenditures in industry and trade. They can be called 'domestic non-factor expenditures' and consist chiefly of internal taxes and social payments. In other cases social conditions, for example, social customs and legislation and pollution aspects, may create a need for factors which would not otherwise exist. This 'extra factor requirement' will raise costs of production and transportation.

These elements make commodity and factor prices differ from what they would otherwise be! Social legislation and labour market agreements may affect not only the demand for but also the supply of factors, such as through a reduction of the number of normal working hours. The conditions in all the above-mentioned respects in the different countries are relevant. If the ordinary business cost account approach is used, these cost elements are taken into consideration. But the indirect effects on factor prices and on the rest of the price system are usually a very complicated matter. It goes without saying that factor movements and trade are influenced also.

Taxes that do not appear as cost elements, taxes on net income, for example, may affect location of industry and factor movements more indirectly. Assume that the public purse takes an increased part of profits or wages and salaries. Thereby, capital movements and labour migration may be influenced. In general countries with 'favourable' tax treatment of both national and foreign capital may attract capital, which would otherwise go to 'third countries' or 'stay at home'. Ordinary income taxation may affect migration of labour in a similar manner. Such taxes can also influence the choice made by *rentiers* when they decide where to live. Thereby, demand for consumption goods is affected, and, possibly, also the willingness to invest in the different countries. The economic development in the country where a capital-owning person lives is easier for him to follow and understand.

Company taxes that are proportional to wage and salary payments tend to bring about lower nominal earnings for labour and need not affect the cost account and competitive ability of the firms in the long run. In some cases it is fairly obvious that taxes weigh more heavily on certain industries than on others. Consequently, they tend to keep back investment in the former. The effect may be a slower development of their export capacity or reduction of their capacity to compete with imports.

Internal *indirect* taxes on certain commodities can, of course, exercise the opposite influence, if they are not levied on exports. Such taxes reduce the domestic use of these commodities and may tend to keep down the demand for — and the relative prices of — the factors, which are required in relatively large quantities for their production.

In some cases an indirect tax on 'value added by manufacture' — a common construction nowadays — is combined with a tax on imports and a subsidy for exports. Thereby, the effects on international trade and factor prices can be eliminated. It will depend on the use of the tax proceeds by the state, whether real earnings are regarded by the people as lower than they would otherwise be. If they are so regarded, an outflow of labour may be stimulated or an influx counteracted.

In the absence of a tax on imports and a subsidy for exports 'the value added tax' will tend to depress factor prices given the exchange rate. After adaptation to an equilibrium exchange rate, the effects on trade and factor movements will be slight if any. The use of the tax proceeds can, of course, play a role.

Indirect taxes on the home production of certain commodities and not on others tend to reduce their production and exports.

The effects of taxation on international economic relations depend naturally on the tax systems in all the trading countries. To a large extent it is *the international difference in the structure of the tax systems* and in the level of taxation that influence output and trade.

Unequal rules of tax-free depreciation in different countries raise special and important problems. The different opportunities to make tax-free savings by corporations may *stimulate industrial development* in some countries, chiefly because it will increase the supply of risk-bearing capital and, thereby, stimulate risky investments. Borrowing is usually not regarded by businessmen as an equally attractive alternative. Anyway the total supply of capital is increased.

'Low tax industries' like agriculture are 'artificially' stimulated compared to 'high tax industries', which are in many countries subject to a varying degree of double taxation. Here again the international differences in the tax structure deserve special consideration — with regard to effects on trade as well as factor movements.

There are few more complicated scientific economic problems — which are also of great practical importance — than the effects of internal tax systems on international economic relations. It is fortunate that in the last decades Hufbauer, Krauss and several other economists, building on foundations laid by Musgrave, have taken up this part of economic theory in valuable pieces of analysis. The brief examples of problems I have made serve chiefly as a basis for the argument that increased attention to them and some other tax and subsidy questions is highly justified.

I want to stress that the use made of the tax receipts can affect the direction of demand, allocation of resources and international trade. In his paper, Haberler rightly emphasises that the growing public purchases of goods and services are a major factor influencing international trade. They affect both the direction of demand and the choice of producers.

IX. SOCIAL CONDITIONS OF PRODUCTION

The social milieu which society provides for economic activity varies greatly from one country to another. It is important to distinguish between the social conditions, which affect the quantity and quality of the *available factors* of production — and thereby, production costs — and those, which affect costs through the addition of *non-factor* costs, like taxes and social payments. Thirdly, there are those which exercise a direct influence on the *demand for and combination of factors*, independently of relative factor prices (such as for pollution reduction).

In the first type of case I am thinking about legislation, which forbids a normal working week of more than 40 hours, limits overtime and puts obstacles in the way of night work for female labour. These and many others may be grouped under the heading *institutions.* Most of these non-factor costs and extra costs will probably weaken the tendency of trade to diminish the international factor price differences and reduce the competitive power and exports of certain industries — compared to other industries in the same country.

Let me return to the effect of the public demand and quote from a report which has attracted only little attention in scientific circles.[14] The state may use a part of its income

> to promote industrialisation of their underdeveloped regions by providing basic facilities in such fields as power, communications and urban land development and by creating or maintaining appropriate arrangements for the education and training of workers, the efficient organisation of the employment market, adequate public administration, banking and credit institutions and a system of taxation, at both national and local levels, that will encourage domestic saving and investment and will not constitute an unnecessary deterrent to foreign investment.

On the other hand, industries which would otherwise be able to compete on the world market may suffer from less favourable social rules and traditions than those existing elsewhere and may be unable to survive. The pattern of production, trade and factor movements will then be affected. But, it is quite probable that productivity rises for other reasons. The quality of labour may be improved as a result of more spare time, greater security, more stable employment. Higher social payments by firms may help to finance training and research.

X. RISK

The importance of risk and expectations and valuations of risk in economic life is obvious and nowadays dealt with extensively in economic theory, particularly in the analysis of entrepreneurial behaviour.[15] Its influence on investments abroad — for production and sales organisation — on other international capital movements (like portfolio purchases), on migration, on the choice of training, etc., is beyond doubt. The political instability in some countries, the unreliability of the legal system, the risk of expropriation of capital as well as of additional restrictions on the transfer of profits and on the right to import necessary raw materials and 'spare parts', can make an otherwise promising investment and settlement in such countries unattractive. So can a low degree of honesty in business dealings.

The need for risk-bearing capital will be different than in the case of investment in the home country and some other countries. Hence, both trade and factor movements and their relations are affected by such and other risk elements. The *gross* rate of profit required will be higher. The volume of investment abroad by people living in 'the stable countries' will be kept down. On the other hand, outflow of capital and some scarce labour qualities from LDCs may grow in order to spread and reduce risks. In general, international trade is probably kept on a lower level. So are movements of capital and high quality labour to the 'insecure' countries. There will be a tendency to develop particularly industries which require only little capital per worker, unless special natural resources which are particularly attractive exist in these countries.

Typical risk-bearing capital may flow from country A to country B, whereas capital seeking safe return may go from B to A. Uncertain investments may be attractive, if the chance of high profits is judged to be relatively great. Countries with a rapid growth of industry often fulfil this condition. Expectations about the future naturally influence both investments abroad and trade and the combination of them.

Lack of space makes it impossible for me to go more fully into risk aspects, which are touched upon in my earlier writings. I must refer to modern textbooks on international economics, like the one by Caves and Jones. In the collections of scientific papers about international economics before 1970, not much was said about risk in its relation to the location of industry and international trade, except in connection with the foreign exchange markets and capital movements.

XI. A BRIEF COMMENT ON SOME MONOPOLISTIC ASPECTS

I am sorry that I must pass over the very important monopolistic aspects of trade and factor relations, for example, international commodity price controls or agreements to regulate the supply of raw materials. Trade union monopolies which raise wages in some industries compared to the levels in other industries illustrate the importance of a theory which takes account of several 'types of labour'.[16]

The extreme case of monopoly is, of course, the dependence of industry and trade in some countries on a communistic centrally directed economic system. However, as everyone knows, even in countries where the market system dominates, the character and development of monopolistic institutions can exercise a very considerable influence on production and trade, whereas these economic variations in their turn affect the development of institutions. It is impossible to explain the global allocation of resources and economic activity without taking these and other institutional variables into account. This is one important reason why theoretical models alone cannot be expected to provide a satisfactory account and explanation of the development of international economic relations, in particular factor movements and trade. More about institutions in the next section.

XII. HISTORICAL DEVELOPMENT AND LOCATION THEORY APPROACHES

(1) INTRODUCTORY OBSERVATIONS ON DEVELOPMENT

Current international trade is, of course, affected by foreign exchange variations, inflationary movements, business cycles and other, in a wide sense, 'monetary circumstances' and the existing contracts and contacts between firms. It is, however, chiefly dependent on the present location of industry and population in different regions and countries. Therefore, to explain the current pattern of trade requires primarily an investigation of *economic development during preceding decades and centuries in different parts of the world with special reference to the local spread of the new economic activity as well as the spread of the disappearing activity*. The local distribution of population and of consumers' demand is included in this chain of causation. Among the circumstances which affect this development, many are exogenous like wars and political changes in the economic systems. Such exogenous circumstances and their effects must, I think, be analysed separately. It is chiefly institutional changes which are tied up with the variations in consumption standards, investment, factor supply, production, trade and 'learning by doing', that is, with the ordinary economic process, which can be treated as endogenous in theoretical models. See Myint and others in following sessions of this symposium.

For economic analysis in a more narrow sense it is the economic actions by individuals, firms and public bodies which have to be studied as causal elements — inside a framework of partly or wholly exogenous variations including technical progress, changes in fertility, education, government purchases and changes in tariffs, taxation, economic and social policy and monopolistic tendencies. But general comments on the economic causes of the exogenous variations can serve as realistic modifications and should not be excluded for reason of orthodoxy in pure theory. Why dig a ditch between ordinary theory and institutional analysis?

It is self-evident that the conditions for and development of international trade and factor movements belong to the circumstances which influence the general economic development of which trade and factor movements are parts. But, in a way, the decisions year after year to start new economic activity and expand or contract existing activity in different countries — and decisions by consumers to vary their purchases — can be regarded as central causes of the development of international trade, if we remember the influence of trade possibilities particularly on these production problems.

Individuals and businessmen make mistakes, for example, in their investments. But, in the long run they will be largely corrected through the effect of competition. This is much less the case with the actions of states. Hence, the decisions of politicians will partly, perhaps largely, be exogenous elements. However, organisations like GATT and OECD make recommendations to standardise political behaviour with some success.

Real capital becomes obsolete through technical progress and changes in relative factor prices, tariffs, transport conditions, etc. In every period of time inefficient forms of capital play a role and influence costs, but as a rule their owners have to accept a low remuneration. A continuous adaptation of the technical form of productive instruments is part of ordinary renewal and new investment.

(2) SOME LOCATION ELEMENTS

Investment and trade decisions always refer to an activity situated somewhere. Hence, they can be regarded as decisions to locate production somewhere and to sell and buy the products on certain markets. A theory of location of economic activity can, therefore, be regarded as a foundation for a theory of that part of economic development which, together with exogenous elements, will govern the international spread of economic activity in a somewhat later period. It will thereby throw light on international trade as well as on international factor movements — to the extent they are influenced by economic circumstances.

The optimum location of a new industrial establishment inside a country is dependent on a number of domestic circumstances and the prospects for their future changes — apart from the influence of conditions in other countries. Let me mention some important domestic elements

(a) the total supply and prices of the mobile factors,

(b) the quantities, local spread and prices of natural resources and of other immobile or incompletely mobile factors,

(c) the transport conditions — roads, railways, canals, harbours, surface of the earth, etc.,

(d) the relative transportability of raw materials, semi-manufactured goods, machines and finished goods,

(e) external economies from certain forms of agglomeration,

(f) internal economies of scale,

(g) the local spread of productive units, which are already in existence and either deliver goods which are used by the new factory or buy goods produced by the latter,

(h) the local spread of markets, which among other things depends on the spread of population and other demand conditions, including public purchases, foreign buyers, import duties etc.

(i) the institutions and the costs of living in different parts of the country,

(j) the relative height of local taxes and

(k) interregional differences in wage rates and labour qualities.[17]

Lack of space prevents me from adding more than a few examples of the importance of the location approach for an understanding of the international allocation of resources, international trade and factor movements.

Transport costs and transport facilities influence the location of the process of production, which can be divided into several stages. In most cases there will be 'break' expenditure if the process is divided between different establishments. Furthermore, the transportation of raw materials, semi-manufactured goods, machines and finished consumers' goods between the productive establishments leads to costs. The relative height of the transportation costs for the different types of products leads to different stages of production, of which some are concentrated in the neighbourhood of the markets, others are situated near sources of raw material or in districts, where the sums of the transportation costs for several needed materials are sufficiently low.

A great part of this kind of analysis is applicable whether the region comprises parts of a country, a whole country, parts of several countries, a number of countries or the whole world. The national borders add some relevant circumstances. Although the concrete facts underlying the abstract reasoning differ in the international and the domestic regional case, it would be strange to build up entirely separate and different theoretical constructions.

I believe that the kind of descriptive location analysis done by specialists in economic geography in the last 50 years is worthy of much more attention from economists than it has received. But many geographers have been rather slow in benefiting from the location and trade analysis of economists. Fortunately, contacts between them seem to be improving.

(3) THE ILLUMINATING CASE OF CHANGES IN THE LOCATION OF INDUSTRY IN ITALY

Increased freedom of movement for commodities and capital as well as technical knowhow will not always lead to a more rapid economic development of industry in all parts of the territory concerned whether they are parts of the same country or *belong to different nations.* To make my argument a little more concrete let me present a brief examplification through a quotation from the I.L.O. report mentioned above. It deals with the Italian experience in the last century (page 15).

In actual practice the elimination of tariffs between the southern

and northern areas led to the virtual disappearance of the southern
industries, while those of the north (which initially were only weakly
protected) enjoyed most of the advantages of the new national market.
Between 1883 and 1888 the northern industries were given a new
impetus by the introduction of highly protectionist policies but since
no special measures were taken to foster industrial development in the
south that area remained stagnant and indeed suffered as a result of the
deterioration of the terms of trade between agricultural and industrial
products following the introduction of duties on industrial goods.

Indeed, during the post-war inflationary periods considerable amounts
of capital flowed from the south to the north, where conditions for investment were regarded as favourable. Generous depreciation rules between
the two wars permitted northern industries to write off their capital investments rapidly whereby their competitive position was strengthened. The
external economies due to local concentration probably had some influence
on this expansion.

In the Italian case and many others the unfavourable results in some
regions of greater economic freedom was intimately connected with
insufficient institutional arrangements. I refer to public administration,
credit institutions, local tax policies and other things, which could
encourage the accumulation and the investment of capital. There was also
an insufficient supply of communications and local supply of power. The
fact that local taxes were often high in less developed areas discouraged
investment.

This was obviously the case also in the so-called 'devastated areas' in
Great Britain, where unemployment remained large between the two world
wars, while other parts of the country attracted new productive establishments. The effect was, of course, that labour to some extent moved from
the former to the latter districts. But traditions in certain areas — where a
few industries like coal mining had long dominated — made many
unemployed workers remain in such regions rather than migrate to others
which had expanding industries.

The possibility that more freedom of factor movements and trade may
keep back industrialisation in some regions — whether the region is a
country or a large part of one — has led to some debate about the European
Economic Community. There is a risk that, unless special measures are
taken, it will lead to a concentration of economic activity in the central
parts of the union — the major manufacturing districts — and discourage
development in Greece and Southern Italy as well as in parts of Spain,
Portugal and Africa. New institutions, larger education subsidies,
favourable tax systems, preferential tariffs are measures which can be
adopted to avoid such a concentration.

The brief account above is not only an exemplification of the relations
between commodity and factor movements. It also throws some light on
the connection between interregional and international commodity and

factor movements, on the one hand, and *the existence of suitable institutions*, on the other hand. The latter are often referred to as 'the social infrastructure'.

(4) SOME FURTHER REASONS FOR A LOCATION THEORY APPROACH TO A STUDY OF THE INTERNATIONAL ECONOMIC RELATIONS

The outcome of the tendencies which I have briefly commented upon may be to bring about a concentration of industry to certain parts of a LDC. In some cases large capital investment per worker employed is made in some districts even if there is a great relative scarcity of capital in the country as a whole. Thus it is not always possible to explain the relation between the trade and the factor supply *if each country is regarded as a unit*. For example Mexico demonstrates a concentration of industries to relatively small parts of the country, where most of the capital is invested, whereas slow development and poverty is characteristic of some other parts. Thus, in spite of a relatively scanty supply of capital, Mexico may export some commodities that are produced with the aid of much expensive machinery and other forms of capital. Similar conditions exist to some extent in most industrial countries and almost all LDC's. This seems to me to be one of several reasons why it is natural in an analysis of international trade and factor movements to supplement the introductory reasoning about factor proportions, technology, etc., with approaches of the location theory type and those used in regional economies.

Another advantage of the location theory approach is that the international trade in semi-manufactured goods and productive instruments will thereby be illuminated. Attention cannot be concentrated as much on finished commodities as has been the case in conventional trade theory. As a matter of fact a natural way of explaining trade in non-finished goods is through parts of a location analysis, as I have tried to indicate in my earlier writings. That factors and productive units can be attracted by natural resources, by advanced knowledge in technology and by favourable institutional conditions in certain countries has been mentioned above. In such a theory there will be much emphasis on production, factor movements and other changes in factor supply.

The approach of location theory leads attention more directly to the actions of leaders of business firms and to the spread of information than the conventional theory of international trade has done. One extra advantage is that the former approach brings the analysis directly to the problems and effects of *multinational corporations*.

(5) SOME THEORETICAL AND METHODOLOGICAL CONCLUSIONS

I hope my brief and highly selective reasoning in this paper demonstrates a need for more emphasis on the *economic development* and *location of productions*, and more analysis of *tax structures, social institutions and risks* in the study of international economic relations. This means *more attention to other non-factor costs than tariffs* and to some special costs. I repeat that I am happy that particularly in the last fifteen years scientists, several of whom are present here today, have made important contributions to this kind of research — thereby making the analysis much more realistic than it was before the Second World War.

In particular, progress has been made in the analysis of *development aspects* of international economic relations through the merger of trade and factor movement theory with the theory of growth — both in modern textbooks and elsewhere.[18] I refer particularly to the contributions during the symposium which deal with important growth aspects, such as those by Chenery, Solow and others.

Closely related to development are also some special and highly interesting theories of international trade, which deal in detail with some special trade problems of LDCs, with 'stages of production' of a certain group of commodities (for example, Caves-Jones), 'product cycles' (Vernon), and 'preference similarity' (Linder) — all described in Haberler's introductory survey. I should like to emphasise that these special theories can be regarded as important supplements to — not substitutes for — the older more general theoretical constructions, classical and 'modern'. If the latter are extended in the direction of an account of growth and development, the 'special' theories will find their natural place as important parts. A greater realism will be obtained in the analysis. Some steps will also be taken towards a treatment of institutional changes as endogenous variables in the economic process.

It goes without saying that an understanding of the economic development of different nations — such as, the numerous cases of growing differences in living standards after the Second World War — can be gained only through a study and analysis of many other aspects than international trade and factor movements. The less the quality of factors and the relevant institutional setting varies differently in the countries under investigation, the better a factor proportion model — with several amplifications which I have referred to — can help to explain the role of trade and international factor movements, including the spread of technical knowledge, which comes about partly through importation of modern machinery and through multinational enterprise. However, trade and factor movements as a rule lead to higher incomes and larger savings in countries at different stages of development and, thereby, increase the possibilities of a rise in productive investment, improved infrastructure, better education and more research. A consequence is economic growth.

All this means that between commodity and factor movements there are many indirect connections which are due to their role in a general economic growth and development of the different nations. The special connections dealt with in trade and factor movement theory — and in the greater part of this paper — are chiefly selected cases of relatively direct and clear causal relations.

The chief causes why so little equalisation of factor prices in ICs and LDCs has come about *in spite of expanding trade and considerable international factor movements* and why, on the contrary, a growing discrepancy in wage levels has been created between some of them, seems to lie in the fields of population growth, administration and production. No theory of trade and factor movements could be expected to give more than a minor part of the explanation of such a manysided dynamic process. What is needed for better insight is, of course, a continuation of the efforts to combine this theory with the analysis of growth and development — including institutional variations. Trade has been 'an engine of growth' — a much quoted expression from D. H. Robertson. So have international factor movements. But several other powerful engines have also been at work. Some of the latter have been more effective in many industrialised nations than in most LDCs.

NOTES

[1] See for example the use of three factors and three commodities in the following comments by William Branson.

[2] Professor R. W. Jones has reminded me of the sceptical attitude to the use of the 2 x 2 x 2 model, which is represented by I. Pearce, M. Kemp, and F. Hahn. Jones does not share their view.

[3] The pathbreaking and decisive use of the opportunity cost concept in international trade theory was, of course, Haberler's work: *Die Theorie des Internationalen Handels und der Zollpolitik* (1933), although members of the Pareto school had presented the opportunity cost idea in their writings, chiefly in the one-market theory.

[4] About the early development of this part of theory, I refer to some Swedish contributions. E. F. Heckscher, 'The Effect of Foreign Trade on the Distribution of Income', *Ekonomisk Tidskrift* (1919); B. Ohlin, (a) *Handelns Teori* (1924), (b) 'Die Beziehung zwischen internationalem Handel und internationalen Bewegungen von Kapital und Arbeit', *Zeitschrift für Nationalökonomie*, (Wien, 1930), and (c) *Interregional and International Trade* (1933 and several later reprints, abbreviated ed. in 1967 and reprint). See also G. Cassel, *Theoretische Sozialökonomie* (3rd ed., 1927) in which a section on international trade was added. Cassel generously referred to my theory of 1924, but gave too little credit to Heckscher's pioneer paper. There is no indication that Cassel's textbook, well-known on the European continent, and the paper by G. Mackenroth, 'Zollpolitik und Produktions mittelsversorgung, *Weltwirtschaftliches Archiv*, Vol. 29 (1929, pp. 77—105), or my own paper of 1930 influenced other writers before 1933 — apart from Mackenroth, who studied in Sweden, and a small textbook by Barret Whale (1932) who lectured in London.

Two brilliant and very important papers by Paul Samuelson — in the *Economic Journal* of 1948 and 1949 — developed a more precise analysis chiefly of factor price equalisation in a highly simplified case, with some qualifications. See also his penetrating paper in the *Swedish Journal of Economics* (1971) which brought a further addition and precision. The impressive literature on this subject — chiefly after Samuelson's first papers and papers by Tinbergen (1949), Metzler (1949), Meade (1950) and Lerner (published 1952, but circulated at a London seminar in 1933) — cannot be referred to here. A penetrating survey and a list of important papers are to be found in Caves, *Trade and Economic Structure* (1960).

To avoid too many references in this introduction to passages in my own earlier writings, I will, I hope, be excused if I make a general reference to the above-mentioned volume (ed. of 1933 and 1967). The topics I have in mind are particularly reactions of factor supply and factor prices, economies of scale, taxes, social payments, social milieu, risk, location theory approach including internal transport conditions, institutional changes and development aspects. In the 1967 edition some sections were left out; an appendix was added containing a lecture given at Kiel in 1960. Further extension of similar ideas has been attempted in my contributions to 'Festschrifts' in honour of Haberler (1965), Iversen (1969), Harrod (1970) and in a paper in the *Swedish Journal of Economics* (1970).

[5] This reasoning is quite different from one which attaches weight to the question whether the number of commodities is at least one greater than the number of factors. As the borderlines between what is the same or a different commodity — or the same and a different factor — are rather arbitrary, the precise counting of the relative number is also arbitrary and, consequently, uninteresting.

[6] See Klein's observations in the following discussion and the analysis in later sessions.

[7] See Hicks' well-known 'inaugural lecture' and observations on American exports.

[8] Observations by Machlup, Hägerstrand and others during the symposium rightly emphasise the separate role of the spread of technical and economic *information* as distinct from the change in technical labour qualities.

[9] I will perhaps be excused for referring not only to Heckscher's famous paper but also to the treatment in my Harvard volume, for example in Chapter VII on factor supply reactions. About the effect on trade of factor movements, including the tendency of trade to increase the international differences in factor supply, when the domestic supply has a positive reaction to the price increase for the relatively abundant factors which trade brings about in some cases, see chapters IX, XI, XIII; § 6, and XVII (XVI in the 1967 edition). See particularly pp. 167–182, 224–236, 261 and pp. 339–371 (first ed.).

[10] I ask the reader to remember that monetary disturbances, business cycles and balance-of-payment disequilibria fall outside the framework of the symposium. About the effects of taxation, social conditions and risk on factor movements and the consequent effects on trade, see sections

VIII to X below. The mechanism of international capital movements is an old and special story, being much interwoven with balance of payments variations. These aspects are left out in the present survey.

[11] The fact that commodity and factor movements may to a large extent serve as substitutes for one another was — apart from the early analysis by Heckscher and myself — taken up by Iversen (1936), Ellsworth (1938), by Samuelson in a more precise form (in the period 1948—53), by Meade (1955), Mundell (1957) and Caves (1960) as well as by many other writers in the 1960s. Less attention was given to 'covariations' of international commodity and factor movements. About the relation of changes in factor and commodity prices and movements to changes in the terms of trade, see e.g. the book by Caves and the paper by Gorden in the reference list.

[12] See for example his personal statement in the ILO report on 'Social Aspects of European Economic Cooperation' (1956). His policy valuations will not be discussed in this paper. Some observations on his theoretical observations are presented by me in the ILO report. See also the famous paper by J. H. Williams.

[13] See, for example, S. Laursen, 'Production Functions and the Theory of International Trade', *American Economic Review* (1952). A realistic and illuminating account of the international spread of new technology is to be found in *The Diffusion of New Industrial Processes*, edited by Nabseth and Ray (1974).

[14] *Social Aspects of European Economic Co-operation*, ILO (1956), p. 19. On the relation of factor movements to trade, see pp. 21—25 and 66—68, 73—77, 96—110. On social changes and costs, see pp. 32—41, 70—73, 90, 140. On monopolistic practices, see p. 26 ff. On taxes, pp. 153—159. The reader is, as usual, also referred to the discussion during later sessions — in this case by Philip, Hufbauer, Krauss, Biehl and others.

[15] The pioneer works were in my opinion Knight: *Risk, Uncertainty and Profit* (1921), and Myrdal: *Prisbildningsproblemet och föränderligheten* (*Price Formation and the Change Factor*) (1927).

[16] On the theory of 'the second best' for protectionist countries with monopolistic labour practices, see the extensive survey by Magee: 'Factor market distortions, production and trade. A survey', *Oxford Economic Papers* (1973). See also Meade: *Trade and Welfare* (1955) and textbooks by Caves and Jones as well as by Ellsworth and Leith.

[17] See books and papers by Hawtrey, Hoover, Isard, Lösch, Perroux, Samuelson, Vining and many others. Basic contributions were made by von Thünen, Weber and Palander, for example about the influence of relative transportation costs for materials and finished products. The German 'Standortstheorie' in the 1920s also made contributions, which helped me in location theory analysis (1933). See the papers in this book by Chisholm, Richardson, Isard, and Hägerstrand, and the following discussions. Hägerstrand emphasises innovation and the spread of information ('building blocks of ideas'). The pricing of transport services, e.g. in shipping during varying general business conditions, can affect the currents of trade. See the paper by C. M. Wright (1955).

[18] About international aspects of development see well-known works by Balassa, Bardham, Beckerman, Bhagwati, Burenstam-Linder, Caves and Jones, Chenery, Cooper, Corden, Domar, Ellsworth and Leith, Findlay, Harrod, Hirschman, Johnson, Kemp, Kindleberger, Levin, Lewis, Maizel, Meier, Myrdal (in 1956), Nurkse, Oniki-Uzawa, Pearson, Prebish, Richardson, Scitovsky, Södersten. See also collections of papers edited by Bhagwati, by Okun and Richardson, by Little and by Kenen. In the latter Kindleberger expressed very well an attitude to the relation of trade theory to development analysis which comes close to my own. Very suggestive introductions to a more dynamic trade analysis — building on parts of established trade theory — are two early and brief works: Nurkse, *Patterns of Trade and Development* (1959), and Haberler, *International Trade and Economic Development* (1959). In his 'Comments' Findlay emphasises the further development through the dynamic model of Oniki-Uzawa (1965). A valuable illumination of growth and trade is to be found in Svennilson, *'Growth and Stagnation in the European Economy'*. (U.N. Report, 1954.)

REFERENCES

Bhagwati, J., 'The Pure Theory of International Trade', *The Economic Journal* (1964).

Cassel, G., *Theoretische Sozialokonomie* (third edition, 1927).

Caves, R. E., *Trade and Economic Structure* (1960).

Corden, W. M., 'The Economic Limits to Population Increase', *The Economic Record* (1955).

Ellsworth, P. T., *International Economics* (1938).

Haberler, G., *Die Theorie des Internationalen Handels und der Zollpolitik* (1933).

Haberler, G., *International Trade and Economic Development*, Cairo, 1959.

Heckscher, E. F., 'The Effect of Foreign Trade on the Distribution of Income', *Ekonomisk Tidskrift* (1919).

Hicks, J., 'An Inaugural Lecture', *Oxford Economic Papers*, NS 5, pp. 117—35 (1953).

Iversen, C., *Some Aspects of the Theory of International Capital Movements* (1935).

Knight, F., *Risk, Uncertainty and Profit* (1921).

Krauss, M., *'The Economics of the "Guest Worker" Problem: A Neo-Heckscher—Ohlin Approach'*, *The Scandinavian Journal of Economics* (1976) pp. 470—478.

Laursen, S., 'Production Functions and the Theory of International Trade', *American Economic Review* (1952).

Linder, S. B., *An Essay on Trade and Transformation* (Almqvist and Wiksell, Stockholm and John Wiley & Sons, New York, 1961).

Mackenroth, G., 'Zollpolitik und Produktionsmittelsversorgung', *Weltwirtschaftliches Archiv*, Vol. 29 (1929), pp. 77—105.

Magee, S. P., 'Factor Market Distortions, Production and Trade: A Survey', *Oxford Economic Papers*, Vol. 25 (March, 1973), pp. 1—43.

Meade, J. E., *Trade and Welfare*, London, 1955.

Mundell, R. A., 'International Trade and Factor Mobility', *American Economic Review* (1957) pp. 321–335.

Myrdal, G., *Prisbildningsproblemet och föranderligheten* (Price Formation and the Change Factor) (1927).

Nabseth, L. and Ray, G. F., eds. *The Diffusion of New Industrial Processes: An International Study* (Cambridge University Press, 1974).

Nurkse, R., *Patterns of Trade and Development*, Stockholm, 1959.

Ohlin, B., 'Die Beziehung zwischen internationalem Handel und internationalen Bewegungen von Kapital und Arbeit', *Zeitschrift für Nationalökonomie*, Wien, 1930.

Ohlin, B., *Handelns Teori*, Stockholm, 1924.

Ohlin, B., *Interregional and International Trade* (Cambridge, Mass., 1933 and 1967), (Harvard Economic Studies, Vol. 39).

Samuelson, P., 'International Trade and the Equalisation of Factor Prices', The *Economic Journal*, Vol. 58 (June, 1948), pp. 163–184.

Samuelson, P., 'International Factor–Price Equalisation Once Again', The *Economic Journal*, Vol. 59 (June, 1949), pp. 181–197.

Samuelson, P., 'Ohlin Was Right', *Swedish Journal of Economics*, Vol. 73, (1971), pp. 365–384.

Social Aspects of European Economic Co-operation, report, International Labour Office, 1956, Geneva. (Contains also statements by M. Byé and by B. Ohlin and an appendix by B. Ohlin on 'Taxation and Foreign Trade'.

Svennilson, I., *Growth and Stagnation in the European Economy* (U.N. report, 1954).

Vernon, R. (ed.), *The Technology Factor in International Trade* (NBER/Columbia U.P., New York, 1970).

Williams, J. H., 'The Theory of International Trade Reconsidered', *The Economic Journal* (1929).

Wright, C. M., 'Convertibility and Triangular Trade as Safeguards against Economic Depression', *The Economic Journal* (Sept., 1955).

For further references see also endnotes 4, 17 and 18, pp. 52–53 and 54–55.

Comment
Ronald E. Findlay

Professor Haberler's paper is organised as a commentary on the 'factor proportions' approach to comparative advantage and its relation to various alternatives. Professor Ohlin, together with Eli Heckscher, was of course the pioneer of this approach in his 1924 doctoral dissertation and more fully in his great treatise of 1933. His paper today moves further on that same majestic trajectory. It reminds us once more that though he did make factor proportions the core of his general equilibrium analysis his vision of the 'international allocation of economic activity' is much broader and richer in scope than this alone would imply, embracing as it does indivisibilities and the economies of large-scale production, location and transport costs, and the movement of capital and labour across national boundaries. The common practice of hyphenating their names together as a prefix to words like 'model', 'theory' and 'approach' tends to make Heckscher and Ohlin indistinguishable, like those two other famous Scandinavians Rosencrantz and Guildenstern. In fact I once had a student in Rangoon who wrote in an examination that 'The factor proportions theory of comparative advantage was put forward by a very famous Swedish economist named Heckscher Ohlin'.

My comments will take the form of a bird's-eye view of the development of trade theory, with the work of Ohlin as the focal point. In particular I hope to show how the concept of 'specific factors' provides a link between the work of the two great trade theorists that we have heard today.

I. A RICARDIAN FACTOR PROPORTIONS MODEL

Let us begin, as Professor Haberler does, with David Ricardo. The Ricardian trade model that most people are familiar with is his celebrated numerical example in the seventh chapter of the *Principles* about the exchange of cloth and wine between England and Portugal, with labour as the only scarce input, and extended by later writers to many countries and commodities. In the Ricardian model of the closed economy, however, the centrepiece is diminishing returns from population growth on scarce land, leading to a rise in rents and a fall in the rate of profit until the stationary state is reached. What has happened to all this in his theory of international trade?

The explicit link is provided in his earlier *Essay on the Influence of a Low Price of Corn on the Profits of Stock*, in which the case for the repeal of the Corn Laws is discussed in terms of an implicit dynamic model that integrates growth and trade through the determination of the distributive shares. As Professor Hla Myint reminded us long ago Ricardo and his contemporaries were not solely or even primarily concerned with the efficient allocation of given resources but with the forces governing the changes in productive resources over time. I believe that the basic continuity in the analytical framework of pure trade theory from Ricardo to Ohlin is best demonstrated by an explicit formulation of the model sketched in the *Essay on Profits* rather than by scattered quotations, illuminating though these often are. An attempt to do this, drawing on the work of Pasinetti (1960), is contained in Findlay (1974).

In this model the size of the labour force at any moment is determined by the wage-fund, which is a stock of corn, and the 'natural wage rate', given in terms of corn. There are two outputs produced, corn and manufactures, and there is a uniform time-lag between the input of labour and the appearance of final output in each sector. Wages are paid at the start of each production period. Output of manufactures is simply proportional to the input of labour in that sector but the production of corn requires land as well, which is in fixed supply. These assumptions imply a transformation curve that is concave to the origin since the transfer of labour from manufactures to corn will produce diminishing increments of the latter commodity for every unit by which the output of the former commodity is reduced. At any given price-ratio of the two goods competition will ensure that the rate of profit is equalised between the sectors, which determines the supply of each commodity. Demand is determined by income distribution, with rent spent entirely on manufactures and wages and profits on corn. The wage-fund grows so long as the rate of profit is positive but continued accumulation raises the rent of land and reduces the profit rate asymptotically towards zero.

If two such economies trade with each other it can be shown that the one with the higher ratio of land to labour (or to 'capital' since the two are proportional in this model) will export corn and import manufactures. Trade will raise the rate of profit and lower rent in the manufacturing country while the opposite will happen in the agricultural country. With identical technology and the same natural wage-rate in both countries commodity price equalisation will imply equalisation of rent per hectare and the rate of profit as well. Trade raises the growth rate in the manufacturing country and lowers it in the corn-exporting country. Eventually of course, the common profit rate and hence growth rate of both countries tends to zero. This model shows the dynamic basis of Ricardo's arguments in favour of repealing the Corn Laws, since this would reduce rent and raise the profit rate in England and hence postpone the arrival of the stationary state.

It is remarkable how starting with Ricardian assumptions we end up with results that one usually associates with the modern factor proportions approach. The necessary ingredients all seemed to be there but perhaps the lack of sufficient analytical apparatus, particularly with respect to the determination of the terms of trade which was not available before Mill and Marshall, prevented sharper conclusions from being obtained. What is more surprising is how the faithful Ricardians of modern times, such as Taussig and Viner, were so content to remain essentially within the confines of the one-factor model. A clear statement of the factor proportions approach did not appear until Heckscher's pathbreaking article of 1919, which apparently had no direct antecedents except for the stimulus of some critical remarks by Wicksell on an earlier work. A possible link between Ricardo and Heckscher might have been Davidson, reputedly a deep student of Ricardian doctrine. This is pure speculation on my part but it might be worth pursuing by someone to whom Davidson's work is accessible.

II. HECKSCHER AND THE LERNER-SAMUELSON MODEL

Heckscher's article is astonishing not only for its originality but for the deep intuitive understanding that it displays of the relations between factor supplies, production and trade. The peerless economic historian could also clearly have been a theorist of the first rank. It is very difficult, however, to follow the steps by which he reached his startling conclusions, such as the complete equalisation of factor prices by commodity trade, since he usually does not specify a model explicitly. The several numerical examples are not very helpful either. The essential logic underlying Heckscher's conclusions, however, emerges clearly from the 'two by two by two' model that Lerner and Samuelson independently developed. This model clearly shows that commodity price equalisation through trade must lead to full equalisation of the prices of the completely immobile factors each country is endowed with, if technology is identical, both countries produce both goods and 'factor intensity reversals' are ruled out. Heckscher was clearly aware of the necessity of assuming identical technology and incomplete specialisation but does not indicate any concern about the factor intensity reversals. Perhaps he was thinking in terms of fixed coefficients of production, in which case reversals obviously cannot occur. He also does not appear to restrict the relative number of factors and goods in any way, though it was later shown by Samuelson (1953) that the number of factors cannot exceed the number of goods if factor price equalisation is to occur.

This Lerner-Samuelson model was also used by Robinson (1956), Jones (1956), Lancaster (1957) and Johnson (1957) to rigorously deduce the conditions under which a country with a relatively abundant endowment of a factor would export the commodity in which this factor is used relatively more intensively. The main logical point emerging from these papers is that identical technology and tastes are alone not sufficient to ensure this result. It must also be assumed either that factor-intensity reversals are technically impossible or that the factor endowments of the countries are such that no factor-intensity reversal occurs at any feasible factor price-ratio in either country. Identical tastes alone are insufficient to rule out 'perverse' cases since income-elasticities different from unity may result in, say, the land-abundant country importing the land-intensive good if the income-elasticity of demand for this good was sufficiently high to offset its relative cheapness form the supply side. Consequently the preference map has to be 'homothetic' to make income-elasticities of demand unity.

Minhas (1963) made an international comparison of production functions which indicated that factor-intensity reversals in fact occurred and put this forward as a possible explanation of the celebrated paradox of Leontief (1956) but his results were severely criticised by Leontief (1964).

III. SPECIFIC FACTORS

In the Lerner-Samuelson model both factors are regarded as freely transferable internally between both sectors. An alternative simple model is to have a specific input in each sector, such as wheat-land and cotton-land, and another factor such as labour which is freely transferable between both sectors. A production model of this type was introduced in Haberler (1936, chapter 12). After many years of neglect this powerful and flexible approach is now becoming rather popular. It is dubbed the Viner-Ricardo model in Samuelson (1971), who uses it to demonstrate the proposition that 'Ohlin was right', which is the title of his paper.

What Samuelson is alluding to is the fact that Ohlin had maintained that complete factor price equalisation was 'almost unthinkable and certainly highly improbable' while Heckscher had flatly asserted complete equalisation, though of course only under stringent assumptions. While nobody would expect complete equalisation to hold empirically it is an interesting question in the pure logic of economic theory if complete commodity price equalisation must lead to complete factor price equalisation or not. As we know there are models in which this result necessarily follows, though it requires even stronger assumptions than Heckscher apparently realised. What Samuelson now does is to use the 'specific factor' model to show that complete commodity price equalisation does *not* imply complete factor price equalisation, except for a knife-edge case, but that it does imply a tendency towards equalisation, which is the weaker version of the theorem to which Ohlin had always adhered.

Both Haberler (1961, p. 21) and Hicks (1959, p. 266) in discussing the relation between trade and factor prices have drawn attention to the role of specific factors in qualifying some of the strong results of the Lerner-Samuelson model. I suppose that both of them, and perhaps Ohlin as well, would therefore prefer Samuelson (1971) to Samuelson (1948). The specific factors model has the great merit of linking trade theory with economic geography through the role it provides for various natural resources such as mineral deposits, which are the truly immobile factors of production to which the others have to come.

At the formal level the 'specific factors' model can be treated as a 'short-run' version of the Lerner-Samuelson model when one factor is temporarily immobile, so that there is a discrepancy in the return it obtains in different sectors, which must, however, be equalised in the long run. The transformation curve of the Lerner-Samuelson model can then be looked upon as the long-run envelope of an infinite number of Haberler transformation curves, each one of which corresponds to a certain allocation of the immobile factor between the sectors. Mayer (1974) and Mussa (1974) proceed along these lines. It is also interesting to observe that the Ricardo-Pasinetti model discussed earlier leads to the 'specific factors' model if say coalmines are added to labour as an input to manufactures while it leads to the Lerner-Samuelson model if land is used in both sectors and is freely transferable between them.

IV. INTERNATIONAL FACTOR MOBILITY

The modern analysis of international factor mobility essentially begins also with Heckscher's amazingly seminal 1919 paper. Noting that under full factor price equalisation through commodity trade alone there would be no incentive to factor mobility or need for it, he goes on to explain that it is the existence of wide disparities in factor endowment ratios resulting in incomplete specialisation that makes for differences in factor prices and hence provides an incentive and a need for factors to move. His discussion of nineteenth-century emigration from Europe to America fits in beautifully with this model.

Heckscher also discusses the effect of protection inducing an increased supply of a factor from abroad. He states correctly that protection could only temporarily raise the reward of the factor used intensively in the protected sector, since with perfect international mobility there will be a sufficient inflow of this factor from abroad to drive the price down again to its former level. He did not see, however, the implication noted by Mundell (1957), that this leads to the elimination of commodity trade.

The Heckscher analysis and its modern refinements in terms of the Lerner-Samuelson model, as we have seen, leads to the view that international factor mobility is not necessary for the efficiency of world production if the conditions for complete factor price equalisation through commodity trade alone are satisfied. A very different picture emerges from the Ohlin approach, as illustrated by the 'specific factor' model. Here factor price equalisation through trade is only partial, so that except in the knife-edge case alluded to earlier, there is still a vital role for factor mobility to play in increasing the global efficiency of production. Samuelson draws attention to the fact that with n goods and n specific factors international mobility of labour alone will equalize *all* factor prices. The reason is that with constant returns to scale production functions with only two inputs (labour plus a specific factor) for each good, equalising the marginal product of labour equalises each of the specific factor marginal products as well, but this is of course only a very special case.

V . VARIABLE FACTOR SUPPLIES

In the recent literature on the Heckscher-Ohlin-Samuelson model factor supplies are taken as exogenously determined, in other words they are regarded as being perfectly inelastic with respect to price. Both Heckscher and Ohlin, however, were well aware that factor prices will exercise a strong influence on factor supplies and consequently that factor endowments could be the 'effect' as well as the 'cause' of trade. Ohlin's mathematical appendix assumed that factor supplies were fixed and this assumption has been retained in most subsequent mathematical and geometric models, with only a few exceptions such as Kemp and Jones (1962) and Martin (1976).

The opening-up of trade can be expected to lead, on Heckscher-Ohlin reasoning, to a rise in the price of the abundant factor and a fall in the price of the scarce factor. With positive supply elasticities of both factors this would cause a widening of the difference in factor proportions that lay at the basis of the initial trade; and hence would tend to promote still more trade, though we would expect the system to converge towards a solution in which factor prices, factor supplies and trade flows are all in equilibrium. The likelihood of complete specialisation by either or both trading partners, however, will increase and hence reduce the possibility of complete factor price equalisation. 'Backward bending' supply curves could produce all sorts of perverse cases.

The welfare interpretation of the case with positive factor supply elasticities raises some interesting issues since the divergence produced in capital—labour ratios might at first glance be taken to support the widespread contention of Balogh, Myrdal, Prebisch and others that free trade tends to widen the income gap between advanced and less developed countries. We will not pursue the subject further, however, both for reasons of space as well as obedience to the injunction to this conference to avoid welfare and policy issues.

VI. ECONOMIC GROWTH AND LONG-RUN COMPARATIVE ADVANTAGE

Under the influence of Hicks' Inaugural Lecture on the long-run dollar problem several papers appeared in the late 1950s and early 1960s that used the Lerner-Samuelson model to examine the effects of changes in factor endowment and technology on the pattern and terms of trade. The famous Rybczynski (1955) theorem, the 'immiserising growth' proposition of Bhagwati (1958), and the analysis of the effects of neutral and biased shifts in production functions by Findlay and Grubert (1959) were all part of this literature, which was largely initiated by Johnson (1955) and concluded by his comprehensive synthesis in Johnson (1959).

These studies in the comparative statics of growth and trade were followed by a full-fledged dynamic model presented in Oniki-Uzawa (1965), which was an application of the two-sector neoclassical growth model, itself inspired by the static Lerner-Samuelson model, to a consideration of trade between two countries. In this framework the capital-labour ratios of the countries become endogenous variables, whose ultimate values depend upon the technology, the savings functions in each of the countries and the common rate of growth of population. Many other exercises along these lines have since appeared so that, in a formal sense at least, Professor Haberler's (1961) observation that 'there exist only rudiments of truly dynamic analysis in the field of non-monetary trade theory' is now no longer true.

Once the capital-labour ratio becomes a state variable in a dynamic model it is useful to distinguish between instantaneous or short-run comparative advantage, determined by the current capital-labour ratio, and ultimate or long-run comparative advantage, determined by the propensity to save and the rate of population growth. A country could clearly switch or reverse its comparative advantage as a result of endogenous changes in its capital-labour ratio. So long as capital is perfectly malleable, however, there is no conflict between short-run and long-run comparative advantage since it always pays to specialise in the direction indicated by the current capital-labour ratio even though this is changing over time. This raises the question of 'specificity' once again. If new capital goods are 'putty' but become 'clay' once they are installed in a particular sector it becomes possible for there to be a conflict between present and future gains if endogenous changes in factor proportions or the terms of trade require the capital stock in some sector to contract in future. The nature of expectations about the future held by entrepreneurs becomes of crucial importance in this connection and what Arrow calls the 'myopic decision rule' of investing where the *current* return is highest can be shown to lead to misallocation of resources. These issues are analysed further in Findlay (1973, part 3) while Bardhan (1970) examines several other related aspects of trade and growth in a dynamic context.

VII. CAPITAL AND TRADE

The relation between capital theory and trade theory is a large and difficult subject but its importance requires some attention. As argued in the first section of these comments it is possible to specify a Ricardian model in which circulating capital in the form of a wage fund of corn is an input along with land and labour. In that model I assumed that there was a uniform lag between input and output in the two sectors of the economy so that the rate of interest did not affect relative prices. Once we permit different time-intensities of production the difficulties rapidly mount as recent work by Metcalfe and Steedman (1973) and Samuelson (1975) demonstrates. 'Reswitching' and other paradoxes and perversities discovered by modern capital theory disrupt the tidy world of the orthodox trade models.

As Ohlin has stated repeatedly his approach to trade theory has always been in terms of an application of the Walras-Cassel general equilibrium system. That system has always been regarded as seriously deficient in its treatment of capital. Ohlin and other Swedish economists under the influence of Wicksell have taken the view that capital is not a factor of production on the same footing as primary inputs like labour and natural resources. The integration of the Walras-Cassel system with Wicksellian capital theory was a task undertaken by Erik Lindahl and explicitly left aside by Ohlin (1933, p. 553) in the formal statement of his system in the mathematical appendix although there are very many interesting passages and asides in the main text of his treatise and in the present paper, such as for example the role of the Wicksell effect in the analysis of international capital movements.

The current standard trade models either interpret the two factors usually considered as labour and land, or assume that capital is perfectly malleable. In an interesting paper Kenen (1965) thinks of 'capital' as being something that 'improves' the quality of labour and land, which appears to be in the spirit of the 'stored-up services' of the Austrians and Wicksell, but the way in which this is accomplished is not brought out very clearly. Upgrading the quality of labour is of course something that has received considerable attention recently in terms of the 'human capital' approach, and it has been used by Kenen and others to 'explain' the Leontief paradox. It is most interesting that Ohlin's 1933 work shows full awareness of the relationship between wage differentials and the cost of education and training in determining the supply of skilled labour.

VIII. DIFFERENCES IN PRODUCTION FUNCTIONS AND THE TRANSFER OF TECHNOLOGY

Ohlin's treatise took it as axiomatic that the same information about the technological means by which inputs are transformed into outputs is available to all countries, in other words, that production functions are identical. It is possible to argue that any difference observed in output when n known inputs are held constant is due to either (i) differences in the quantity of some other unspecified input or (ii) differences in the quality of the n known inputs. The approach (i) leads to the view that it is 'organisation' or 'climate' that is the 'missing factor', inclusion of which would make the production functions identical; approach (ii) would make the production functions identical if the various non-homogeneous inputs are reduced to some common 'efficiency units'. Both approaches however lead to metaphysical contortions so it is best, as Haberler (1961, p. 19) pointed out, to abandon the assumption of a necessary identity, a position which Ohlin accepts in his present paper.

Differences in production functions between countries would obviously lead to trade even if factor proportions and tastes are identical. We can return to a Ricardian interpretation (in the narrow sense) of comparative advantage determined by relative 'technical' efficiency, but in a wider framework than labour being the only scarce input. In terms of the 2 x 2 x 2 model we only need to regard the analysis of once-over change in time of the production functions, as for example in Findlay-Grubert (1959), as applying to differences between countries. An elegant example of such an approach is Jones (1970).

While these models consider new techniques for making existing products considerable attention in recent years has been given to the introduction of new products into international trade, with contributions by Posner (1961), Hufbauer (1965) and Vernon (1966) as well as many others. Johnson (1968) gives a suggestive synthesis of all this work. The idea of this 'product cycle' approach is that firms in high income countries where there is a market ready to be tapped for new products have the advantage of being close to the consumer and are able to design and manufacture these products to suit special tastes and requirements. Once the product has become standardised production will once again be determined by cost considerations, which may transfer it overseas, perhaps in the branch plants of the innovating country's firms.

The tendency in much of the literature has been to consider factor proportions and the product cycle as mutually exclusive and competing hypotheses about the determinants of trade. However, it should not be forgotten that factor proportions operate on the *demand* side as well as on the cost or supply side. Many new products such as computers are developed to economise on high labour costs and such products as vacuum cleaners and washing machines reflect the high opportunity cost of the housewife's time in a capital-abundant economy.

Development of new products and processes creates an international market for trade in technological knowledge. There is a considerable literature on patents, royalties and so on of a descriptive nature. Rodriguez (1975) however is the only contribution so far that incorporates trade in technology within the standard general equilibrium model.

The 'advanced' part of the world economy has experienced continuous technological progress ever since the Industrial Revolution. A major problem in economic development concerns the determinants of the rate of diffusion of this technological progress from the 'centre' to the 'periphery' of the world economy. One idea, developed by Richard Nelson (1968), is that the rate of technological progress in the backward region is an increasing function of the gap or distance between its current level of technological efficiency and that of the advanced region. Another suggestive idea is the analogy between diffusion and 'contagion' as in the spread of an epidemic. In this connection it is natural to think of the 'carriers' as being multinational firms which leads to the hypothesis that the backward region's technical progress will be faster, the more open it is to foreign investment. I have made an attempt to combine the 'gap' and 'contagion' hypothesis in a simple dynamic model in Findlay (1976). Other models of endogenous technical change in open economies are Chipman (1970) and Teubal (1975).

IX. OHLIN'S VISION

In his great history of economic doctrine Schumpeter emphasised the role of what he called 'vision' in the development of the subject. I think it is true to say that Ohlin's vision of the forces determining the pattern and evolution of world trade, migration and capital movements is the most concrete and penetrating that is available in the entire history of the discipline. In addition to the factor proportions approach, with which my comments have been mainly concerned, the brilliant third chapter of his treatise offers an entirely different and also extremely powerful explanation of trade in terms of indivisibilities and the economies of large-scale production. In a particularly elegant and illuminating formulation he points out how commodity trade can substitute not only for the immobility but also for the indivisibility of the factors of production. It is only very recently, in an as yet unpublished paper, that a formal model along these lines has been developed, in Lancaster (1975). I leave Ohlin's ideas on location to the many experts at this conference.

If I may quote Haberler (1961, p. 17) on Ohlin 'His imagination, intuition and vision outrun his capacity for systematic, precise theoretical presentation — which is true of every empirical scholar worth his salt'. I

would only add that his vision is so rich and manysided that it has outrun
not only his own capacity for systematic presentation but that of an entire
generation of specialists in the field of international economics as well. I
think of the works of Bertil Ohlin as a deep, rich mine, on which all of us
can draw. In the case of this particular natural resource the possibility of
exhaustion is so remote that even the Club of Rome need have no fear.

REFERENCES

Bardhan, P. K., *Economic Growth, Development and Foreign Trade*
(Wiley, 1970).
Bhagwati, J. N., 'Immiserizing Growth: A Geometrical Note', *Review of
Economic Studies* (June, 1958).
Chipman, J. S., 'Induced Technical Change and Patterns of International
Trade' in R. Vernon (ed.) *The Technology Factor in International
Trade* (NBER, 1970).
Findlay, R., *International Trade and Development Theory* (Columbia
University Press, 1973).
Findlay, R., 'Relative Prices, Growth and Trade in a Simple Ricardian
System', *Economica* (Feb., 1974).
Findlay, R., 'Relative Backwardness, Direct Foreign Investment and the
Transfer of Technology: A Simple Dynamic Model', unpublished
manuscript (Stockholm, 1976).
Findlay, R. and Grubert, H., 'Factor Intensities, Technological Progress
and the Terms of Trade', *Oxford Economic Papers* (Feb., 1959).
Haberler, G., *The Theory of International Trade* (Hedge, 1936).
Haberler, G., *A Survey of International Trade Theory* (Princeton, 1961).
Heckscher, E., 'The Effect of Foreign Trade on the Distribution of
Income' (1919), English translation in Ellis and Metzler (eds.) *Readings
in the Theory of International Trade* (Blakiston, 1949).
Hicks, J. R., *Essays in World Economics* (Oxford, 1959).
Hufbauer, G., *Synthetic Materials and the Theory of International Trade*
(Duckworth, 1965).
Johnson, H. G., 'Economic Expansion and International Trade', *Manchester
School* (May, 1955).
Johnson, H. G., 'Factor Endowments, International Trade and Factor
Prices', *Manchester School* (Sept. 1957).
Johnson, H. G., 'Economic Development and International Trade',
Nationaløkonomisk Tidsskrift (1959).
Johnson, H. G., *Comparative Cost and Commercial Policy Theory for a
Developing World Economy* (Almqvist and Wiksell, 1968).
Jones, R. W., 'Factor Proportions and the Heckscher-Ohlin Theorem',
Review of Economic Studies (Oct., 1956).
Jones, R. W., 'The Role of Technology in the Theory of International
Trade' in Vernon (ed.) *op. cit.* (1970).
Kemp, M. and Jones, R. W., 'Variable Labor Supply and the Theory of
International Trade', *Journal of Political Economy* (Feb., 1962).

Kenen, P. B., 'Nature, Capital and Trade', *Journal of Political Economy* (Oct., 1965).

Lancaster, K., 'The Heckscher-Ohlin Trade Model: A Geometric Treatment', *Economica* (Feb., 1957).

Lancaster, K., 'A Theory of Trade between Similar Industrial Economies', unpublished manuscript (Columbia University, 1975).

Leontief, W. W., 'Domestic Production and Foreign Trade: The American Capital Position Re-examined', *Proceedings of the American Philosophical Society* (1953).

Leontief, W. W., 'International Factor Cost and Factor Use', *American Economic Review* (June, 1964).

Lerner, A. P., 'Factor Prices and International Trade', *Economica* (Feb., 1952).

Martin, J. P., 'Variable Factor Supplies and the Heckscher-Ohlin-Samuelson Model', unpublished manuscript (Nuffield College, 1976).

Mayer, W., 'Short-Run and Long-Run Equilibrium for a Small Open Economy', *Journal of Political Economy* (Oct., 1974).

Metcalfe, J. S. and Steedman, I., 'Heterogeneous Capital and the Heckscher-Ohlin-Samuelson Theory of Trade' in M. Parkin (ed.) *Essays in Modern Economics* (Longman, 1972).

Minhas, B. S., *An International Comparison of Factor Costs and Factor Use* (Amsterdam: North-Holland, 1963).

Mundell, R. A., 'International Trade and Factor Mobility', *American Economic Review* (June, 1957).

Mussa, M., 'Tarriffs and the Distribution of Income: the Importance of Factor Specificity, Substitutability and Intensity in the Short and Long Run', *Journal of Political Economy* (Dec., 1974).

Nelson, R. R., 'A Diffusion Model of International Productivity Differences', *American Economic Review* (Dec., 1968).

Ohlin, B., *Interregional and International Trade* (Harvard University Press, 1933. Revised edition 1967).

Oniki, H. and Uzawa, H., 'Patterns of Trade and Investment in a Dynamic Model of International Trade', *Review of Economic Studies* (Jan., 1965).

Pasinetti, L. L., 'A Mathematical Reformulation of the Ricardian System', *Review of Economic Studies* (Feb., 1960).

Posner, M. V., 'International Trade and Technical Change', *Oxford Economic Papers* (Oct., 1961).

Ricardo, D., *An Essay on the Influence of a Low Price of Corn on the Profits of Stock* (John Murray, London, 1815).

Robinson, R., 'Factor Proportions and Comparative Advantage', *Quarterly Journal of Economics* (May, 1956).

Rodriguez, C. A., 'Trade in Technology and the National Advantage', *Journal of Political Economy* (Feb., 1975).

Rybczynski, T. N., 'Factor Endowment and Relative Commodity Prices', *Economica* (Nov., 1955).

Samuelson, P. A., 'International Trade and the Equalization of Factor Prices', *Economic Journal* (June, 1948).

Samuelson, P. A., 'International Factor Price Equalization Once Again', *Economic Journal* (June, 1949).

Samuelson, P. A., 'Prices of Factors and Goods in General Equilibrium', *Review of Economic Studies* (Oct., 1953).

Samuelson, P. A., 'Ohlin Was Right', *Swedish Journal of Economics* (Dec., 1971).

Samuelson, P. A., 'Trade Pattern Reversals in Time Phased Ricardian Systems and Intertemporal Efficiency', *Journal of International Economics* (Nov., 1975).

Teubal, M., 'A Neo-Technology Theory of Comparative Advantage', *Quarterly Journal of Economics* (Aug., 1975).

Vernon, R., 'International Investment and International Trade in the Product Cycle', *Quarterly Journal of Economics* (May, 1966).

Comment
Harold Brookfield

DISSENT FROM THE PERIPHERY*

For a human geographer, straight out of 18 months in the field in the
South Pacific, to be asked to comment on papers by Gottfried Haberler
and Bertil Ohlin is a somewhat awesome experience. I comment mainly
on Haberler's contribution in what follows, since Ohlin's remarks are
themselves to some degree a commentary on the symposium as a whole. I
expected to comment on a paper concerning the historical evolution of
the international allocation of economic activity since about 1800, but I
find that Haberler has instead provided us with an elegant survey of theory,
classical and modern, which is — as Ohlin remarks — masterly in its
simplicity. However, it concerns a world largely innocent of tariffs, bilateral trade agreements, multinational corporations, O.P.E.C.,
U.N.C.T.A.D., C.O.M.E.C.O.N., the E.E.C., and so on. Ohlin does introduce these complications, and very effectively, but he leaves open to some
degree the central argument posed by Haberler who concludes, at page 12,
that: 'Competitive general equilibrium theory is useful or even indispensable as an ideal type which enables us better to visualise, evaluate and
measure aberrations from the ideal conditions which abound in the real
world'.

I found Haberler's survey illuminating and provoking. I intend to be
provoked, and from the point of view of a resident in a small LDC where I
first read his paper, and first drafted this commentary. For the past 18
months I have been deeply involved in studying the effects of the international and interregional allocation of economic activity among people
allocated to become and remain primary producers, for both international
and national markets. This experience was while I was working for the
United Nations, and though by the time of my final preparation of this
discussion comment I have returned to academic life, it is none the less
necessary to add that nothing I say here in any way commits the United
Nations, and represents solely my own views.

My own central argument will return to the quotation from Haberler's
paper with which I began. First, however, I find in his paper four rather
telling points concerning the state of reality. These are, if I interpret him
correctly

*For empirical data introduced in this paper I rest not only on my own
work but also on that of T. Bayliss-Smith in Fiji, and S. B. Iton in
St Vincent.

(1) The effect of distinguishing qualities within and among the factors labour and capital (and also land) is to reinforce the conclusion that there can be no factor-price equalisation, and that production functions must therefore always remain infinitely variable.

(2) The existing body of international trade theory — or any theoretical system that has validity — is applicable equally to less developed countries as to developed countries, meaning I think countries with respectively lower and higher levels of per capita productivity.

(3) International trade theory is part and parcel of the whole theory of growth and development, and the converse of this statement.

(4) If we incorporate welfare considerations into our analysis, we are entitled to ask if international and interregional trade increases the whole sum of real national income in terms of commodities; if this is true, then trade, and specialisation of production, are themselves indispensable elements in growth and development.

I agree with all these statements, but it does not follow from this measure of agreement that I also concur with the tenor of argument that follows from them in Haberler's paper. I am led in somewhat different directions, and argue accordingly.

The question of factor-price movements is important not only in international trade, but also to the whole theory of regional development which, especially since the 'centre-periphery' model was incorporated by John Friedman (1966) has unmistakable links with the 'centre-periphery' view of international trade argued since a generation past by Latin American economists. While the theory of regional development calls also on industrial location theory, a very significant part of the total argument concerns the exchanges between regions, and incorporates the element of factor mobility whose absence is a crippling weakness in all efforts to relate the classic theory of international trade to reality.

It is not only location theory that is at issue here, but also the wider — though weaker — theory of regional development. The great value of this theoretical system, one which it perhaps derives from Perroux (1955), is that it offers a means of ridding us of the obsession with countries as compartments between which commodities flow but not factors of production, and which are supposed to be equal entities as trading partners. Two centuries ago, Adam Smith recognised that trade between Great Britain and her West Indian colonies should be regarded as domestic trade, so closely were the economies of the latter linked with that of the former. One century ago, Marx regarded the undeveloped portion of the world as simply a space to be occupied, or being occupied, by the expansion of Western capitalism. Fifty years ago, a young Peruvian journalist J. C. Mariategui (translated 1971), recognised that the whole economic development of Latin America in the nineteenth century was an integral part of the industrial development of Great Britain, and later of Europe and North America. Most recently, Selwyn (1975) has ably shown how no international trade theory can account for the present economic condition of the lesser countries of southern Africa; this can only be interpreted in terms of a centre-periphery system focused on the southern Transvaal.

There is a point of some importance here. On page 4, Haberler remarks that 'No sophisticated theory is required to explain why Kuwait exports oil, Bolivia tin, Brazil coffee and Portugal wine'; these he regards as simply 'natural resource trade'. But is this really so? Kuwait exports crude oil rather than refined oil (or did) for reasons which a theory of industrial location on an international scale, compounded with a theory of the politics of international commerce, are required to explain. Bolivia exports tin, because it has tin; true. But a more relevant question to ask is why Bolivia lacks a metallurgical industry. Britain once exported tin, but almost two centuries ago the whole production was absorbed in the local industrial market which then cried out for more. Brazil exports coffee because among a range of crops which could be grown under its historically selected system of plantation production, coffee emerged as both adapted to resource endowment and more importantly to market opportunities in the period during which the industry became established. Portugal exports wine rather than manufactures for an even deeper set of reasons going back into the Middle Ages. Suppose, for example, that Portugal had succeeded in the sixteenth century as Britain did in the eighteenth in drawing together the profits of colonial empire and the benefits of an aggressive maritime trade policy to finance and find markets for the first industrial revolution in one country: would we then have found a Portuguese Ricardo explaining by means of comparative advantage why England exports wool — for which it is well-endowed in natural resources and climatic need — while Portugal exports, say, industrial alcohol? And would even Ricardo have explained the export of grain from wet Ireland to drier Britain by reference to Irish endowment in the factors needed for grain production? Or would he have taken some account also of the deindustrialisation of Ireland, landlordism, and the diversion of trading opportunities to England that flowed from the mercantilist policies of the previous century? We cannot take 'capital' and even 'labour' as given; each has its antecedents, and the concentration of capital in particular is subject to forces which no $2 \times 2 \times 2$ model can help us understand.

I thus lead on to the second and third points which I isolated from Haberler's paper: that theory applies equally to LDCs and DCs, and that international trade theory is part and parcel of the theory of growth and development. I have previously published argument that all development is interdependent (Brookfield, 1975). I disagree with the views of Frank and some other writers of Marxist persuasion that there is need for a

'discrete' theory of underdevelopment. There is no such need. The set of
forces that created one-crop or one-mineral economies supplying
industrial markets elsewhere in the world are also the set of forces that
created the industrial economies. They are therefore the same forces that
destroyed the former self-sufficiency of European agriculture and, by
creating locational advantage in selected areas of the developed countries
have *ipso facto* marginalised others, and hence created the so-called
'regional problem' of the EEC, as Ohlin demonstrates in the Italian case.
The 'internal colonialism' of some Latin American writers is also the
exploitation from the centre complained of by Scots, Bretons and Sicilians.
Factor immobility is not only a problem of the LDCs; it is also the problem
of Clydeside and the coal towns of central Pennsylvania. These are large
statements, but scarcely new; what I am now saying is that the problems
of polarisation and marginalisation relate to a set of forces which operate
within boundaries, across them, and across the world. The problem of
allocation of production is also the problem of location of production,
and perhaps more properly put as such. The utility of international trade
theory in this context (and I emphasise 'in this context') lies in the
elements which it can contribute to a general theory of the location of
economic activity. And this latter, to be useful, needs to be a dynamic and
not a static equilibrium theory, for any equilibrium in the interregional
and international web of activity location can only be unstable, so that
any new force creates disequilibration far beyond its own impact.
Schumpeter argued thus, though not at all in a locational context, and I
am very much at one with Haberler in calling for a fuller recognition of
his signal contribution.

But what of the sum of benefits, and *its* allocation? That there are
benefits from specialisation is incontrovertible. Individual farm units
specialise the production of different parts of a single holding. There is
specialisation within any small integrated region, however little it trades
with the rest of the world, and the underlying principles of this allocation
were worked out more than 150 years ago, by Ricardo and von Thünen.
There is some real utility in extending these ancient models to a view of
the allocation of activity on a world scale: I tried to show this, in
examining the trade pattern of the 'outermost supplier in an "isolated
state" world', in a book I wrote on the Melanesian islands in the South
Pacific some seven years ago.

But my point here concerns welfare as much as it concerns specialisation. There is aggregate benefit from specialisation, but how is it shared?
Did Portugal gain as much from its wine as England from its manufactures?
Perhaps the real question to be asked is this: does the activity allocated to
each place by the international system achieve the optimal potential of
that place within a constraint that the potential of the whole system is also
maximised? If not, and the answer is surely 'no' for a great majority of
places, then wherein does the major source of weakness lie? Does it lie in

an overemphasis on production for international rather than interregional trade or would the most efficient system (taking the objective function as above) be achieved by an even greater degree of international specialisation?

The mind (at least this mind) boggles at the scale of computation required in such an exercise, but the question is of great importance at every scale from that of the whole world down to the smallest regional unit. Thus great emphasis is being placed in many countries on the creation of new 'growth centres' which are always centres of manufacturing industry, which is thus — at least in the minds of planners — becoming more and more dispersed. One supposed effect of such policies is the stimulation of intraregional trade, but a more obvious immediate effect is stimulation of interregional trade in semi-manufactures and consumer goods. This is on a within-nation scale. On an international scale, the industrialisation of whole countries may similarly be treated as the creation of new 'growth centres', and it seems clear that a great expansion of international trade in raw materials, semi-manufactures, manufactures and consumer goods is to be anticipated, now as in the past. But we also observe casualties; the depressed manufacturing areas based on industries that have lost their semi-monopoly in world trade are only the most obvious illustration.

And what of the primary producer? When E.C.L.A. economists first proposed that the terms of trade had moved steadily against the primary producer in the late 1940s there was widespread dissent. The events of the last six years have given room for new doubt, and they have also exhibited the relative long-term weakness of the primary producers. We now live in a world in which successive U.N.C.T.A.D. conferences demonstrate the conflict over pricing and protection more and more sharply.

The welfare question grows insistent. Is it in fact true, as most representatives of Third World countries and the depressed regions of the 'developed' countries argue, that the benefits of specialisation accrue overwhelmingly to the importers of raw materials and the exporters of consumer goods and final manufacture? And that their specialisation is to their disadvantage given the present and historical terms of trade? If so, then the fact that the total product of trade is, under some sort of competitive equilibrium, an optimum, will give little satisfaction. In the 1970s, when many LDCs suffer the combined effect of inflation on their imports and depression on their exports, these are quite crucial questions demanding a new examination.

Haberler excludes this question from his own terms of reference, although he hints at its importance. I regard it as fundamental, whether we look at it in historical perspective, or purely in contemporary terms. I therefore propose to introduce some empirical discussion drawn from my own recent experience and concerning two islands, one in the Pacific and the other, smaller but much more populous, in the Caribbean.

(1) TAVEUNI (FIJI) AND ST VINCENT

These young, mountainous, volcanic islands of high soil fertility are useful to us in this context because they demonstrate how specialisation is, in fact, allocated. Both were brought into the international trading system as plantation economies — divided into units of land worked by an imported unskilled labour force resident on the estate, and substituting rigid management for skilled labour. In both cases, though at different times, the initial staple was sugar cane, but a wide range of other export crops was tried, including coffee, tea, cocoa and coconuts, and in St Vincent, arrowroot. Choice was limited structurally by the plantation system, and more fundamentally by the capacities of remote metropolitan markets for semi-processed products culled from a range of sources to supply final consumer-goods industries in the metropolitan countries.

In each case the higher-value export staples successively failed and gave way to staples of lower value per unit area of land. In St Vincent, little remains of the plantation system proper, and the international export staples are now bananas and arrowroot, grown on peasant farms. Both industries are demanding of labour, and in 1972 we calculated that if the cost of a farmer's own labour were valued at the going agricultural wage, bananas were being produced and sold to Great Britain at a loss. The arrowroot industry was unable to get labour at this wage, and was seeking methods of mechanisation.

Taveuni fell back early on its base crop, the coconut, and copra became and has remained the base crop for plantation and peasant sectors alike. In the 1930s and again in the 1970s, the received price has closely approximated the cost of production even after economies, and periods of boom have been relatively brief.

The effects are of some interest for this symposium. On the basis of a calculation of energy equivalents of cash incomes obtained from copra and certain competing activities, my project found that under boom conditions in 1973–74 the productivity in terms of MJ/hour was a little better for copra than for subsistence production or the sale of a local stimulant. In the inflation/depression year of 1975–76, on the other hand, the comparison gave copra only 60 per cent of the reward from subsistence production and 30 per cent that of growing the stimulant. Moreover, the per hectare productivity of copra production was far lower than that of competing activities, and the large land demand of this low-yielding crop led to very low densities of population supported per hectare of producing land. Yet this crop occupies 21 per cent of the good arable land of the country, and it is small wonder that the current development plan proposes 'diversification'. This is a consequence of 'international allocation of economic activity' brought about by a set of time-specific forces in an earlier generation, and relatively inflexible both because of the long life

of the coconut palm and the whole set of institutional arrangements that
have grown up around the copra industry.

Both islands also produce for regional markets, for urbanised Barbados
and Trinidad in the case of St Vincent, and for the urban market of the
Fijian capital in the case of Taveuni. St Vincent sells mainly root crops to
Barbados and Trinidad, the trade being in the hands of some 50 middlemen called 'speculators' who ship their cargoes on the dwindling fleet of
inter-island schooners. Root crop production in Taveuni is marketed
through a National Marketing Authority, but in both cases the cash
reward is low. Indeed, in energy terms, the Fijian farmer could buy only
25 000 MJ of store-bought foods with the return from a tonne of taro
at present prices, or 37 000 MJ if the whole sum were spent on rice and
flour in equal proportion. If on the other hand he and his family consumed
the taro themselves they would gain over 50 000 MJ from a tonne. It is
not surprising that many farmers are coming to regard this crop, too, as a
waste of time and energy; in a literal sense this is exactly what it is
(*U.N.E.S.C.O./U.N.F.P.A. Project*, in press). Only the local stimulant
offers a satisfactory return.

Several points of some interest can be drawn from this brief comparison.
In the first place it must be emphasised that these are highly fertile islands,
suffering no severe constraints other than steep slope. They are capable of
very high productivity, but this is depressed by production for international and interregional trade. Both in agronomic and in economic terms,
the productivity of the export economy is low. This is not universally
true; sugar cane is among the most efficient of all energy converters; tree
crops grown on land that will not consistently bear more intensive
production may be the best use of such land, as for example in much of
Malaysia. But very commonly, a characteristic of the internationally
traded production of much of the developing world is a persistent
emphasis on activities that rank low on the scales of returns to labour,
land, and to improvements. But these are the activities for which the
market has provided a consistently reasonable if poor return over the
longest time, whereas more intensive and temporarily more rewarding
activities have proved more risky because more is at stake in times of
depression.

Second, we might call attention to the manner in which price
reduction is absorbed in these conditions. It has to be passed on to the
producers, meaning the labour force under plantation economy, or
peasant living standards where peasant production has become the mode.
Small wonder that a large subsistence sector is 'obstinately' retained by
peasant producers, who decline to follow any theoretical stages of
'progress' toward complete commercialisation of their farming.

The international specialisation of economic activity has reshaped the
world, and while creating on the one hand a great deal of wealth, mainly
concentrated in a limited number of countries, it has also created very

large populations which depend entirely or partially on the production of primary products which enter international trade. Such specialisation of production has also stimulated the growth of interregional and intra-regional trade through which benefits are more widely distributed, but nonetheless often remain concentrated at the commanding centres of the trading and producing economy. Most of the 'speculators' of St Vincent make a pretty poor income, though they do better than the farmers. The companies which have formed to control larger sectors of the trading economy, and which have diversified their interests in order to obtain internal factor mobility, do far better. I have always been impressed by the fact that during the depression of the 1930s, when Pacific planters were going to the wall in considerable numbers, many estates ceased production, and many peasants returned to a largely subsistence economy, the trading companies continued to pay dividends to their shareholders. Even today, the larger trading companies will readily pull out of this or that area of activity that has become unprofitable to them. Most often other smaller entrepreneurs will enter the space created, but only to be taken over or squeezed out if the companies decide to re-enter under improved economic conditions. The behaviour of 'national marketing authorities' is not notably different from that of commercial companies in this regard.

(2) DISCUSSION

Galbraith's (1967) analysis of the manner in which power gravitates to the scarce factor in a system is relevant in this context, for the international specialisation of activity is best thought of as a highly complex set of systems within which the most integrated elements are the set of vertical structures which extend from control of trade itself into production, manufacture and distribution. They emerged very early in international trade, and indeed the great trading houses of the seventeenth and eighteenth centuries were the first truly multinational corporations, wielding a relative power greater than that of any of their modern successors. They grew in an era when capital for trading ventures and shipping was the most scarce element; they declined as power shifted to the centres of manufacture, but they have re-emerged in a post-industrial era (so-called) in which managerial and technical control over the complex processes of production, trade and distribution has become critical. The weakest element in the system is composed of those producers who are separated by the whole intermediate structure from their market. Even in the already classic case of oil, their attempts to unite to secure bargaining power have been only partially successful, since the intermediate structures have succeeded in retaining and enlarging their own profit margins instead of simply absorbing the increase in the price of crude oil; hence, they have caused consumers to unite to exert political pressure on the producers, with some real effect.

It will be apparent that I find 'departures from the ideal type' encountered in the real world too wide to accept Haberler's contention that general competitive theory is useful as a basis for analysis of reality. I prefer Ohlin's wider-ranging search for new approaches in which the empirical relevance of assumptions is a major criterion. But I would also go further, and suggest that the historical analysis of process may yet have a great deal of instruction to offer, however little this may appeal to positivists among economists or in my own profession. After all, the contributions of Innis in export-base theory and of Heckscher in international-trade theory are widely acknowledged, yet both were historians. The leading structuralists, such as Furtado, are both economists and historians.

It may be helpful to conclude by recalling a phrophecy which has not yet come true. Writing of the history of economic theory, Heimann (1945, p. 10) remarked that

> economic theory is the doctrine of the system of free enterprise, and initially of nothing else. It is a historical discipline, in the specific sense of the word, emerging at a certain moment and bound to be reabsorbed into a more comprehensive and complex structure of social science as the system of free enterprise itself is transformed and absorbed into a more centralised structure of economic society, with central and local controls in complicated proportion.

If this is true of the whole, it is true also of theory concerning allocation of economic activity, and is true of geographical theory as well as of economic. To say this is in no way to belittle the enormous contribution made by theoretical constructs built on clearly stated but restrictive premises; we have learned a great deal from them. It is, however, to say that in this matter as also in others, we perhaps need now to look backward, and understand how international allocation of economic activity has come about and also look around to examine its consequences, if we are more effectively to go forward.

REFERENCES

Brookfield, H., *Interdependent Development*. London: Methuen, (1975).
Friedmann, J., *Regional Development Policy: A Case Study of Venezuela.* (Cambridge, Mass., M.I.T. Press, 1966.)
Galbraith, J. K., *The New Industrial State* (Boston, Mass. 1967).
Heimann, E., *History of Economic Doctrines: An Introduction to Economic Theory* (New York; O.U.P., 1945).
Mariategui, J. C., Trs. 1971, *Seven Interpretative Essays on Peruvian Reality* (Trs. by M. Urquidi from *Siete ensayos de interpretacion de la realidad Peruana*, Lima, 1928).

Perroux, F., 'Note sur la notion de pôle de croissance', *Economie Appliquée* 8, pp. 307–20 (1955).

Selwyn, P., *Industries in the Southern African Periphery* (London, Croom Helm, 1975).

U.N.E.S.C.O. (in press), *The Eastern Islands of Fiji: Ecology, Population and Development: Report No. 1 of the U.N.E.S.C.O./U.N.F.P.A. Population and Environment Project in the Eastern Islands of Fiji* (Canberra, for U.N.E.S.C.O.).

Comment
William Branson

I. INTRODUCTION

It is an *honour*, and a thoroughly unearned pleasure, for me to be asked to comment on papers on trade theory by Gottfried Haberler and Bertil Ohlin. So it is with considerable diffidence that I offer my comments here. The papers by Professor Haberler and Ohlin are surveys of a literature that is at least decades, even centuries, old. A discussant can hardly touch on a majority of the points made in these surveys; rather he has to find a point of departure related to his particular *comparative advantage* with the hope that he can contribute to the discussion. As I read the two surveys, I decided that my contribution might lie in a discussion of recent empirical work on three-factor 'explanations' of the composition of trade in manufactured goods, and in a partial defence of the factor-proportions hypothesis concerning the source of comparative advantage. Here I put the word *explanations* in quotation marks, and mention a *partial defence* of the factor-proportions hypothesis because almost all of the recent empirical work has been on the factor content of trade; hardly any has been reported on relative factor endowments.

During the last ten to fifteen years the factor-proportions hypothesis seems to have been losing ground as a positive model of trade in 'non-natural resource' goods in the views of both the educated public and the economics profession. Evidence of this is the appearance of the 'neo-technology' models of trade, discussed at length in the book edited by Raymond Vernon (1970), and referred to by both Haberler and Ohlin. Running opposite to this current has been a recent series of studies that, taken together, tend to reconfirm partially the importance of factor proportions as a major explanatory factor for variations in the commodity composition of trade. I will discuss these studies and some work I have been doing along these lines.

Recent studies have focused on a three-factor model, with human capital as the third factor, along with physical capital and raw labour inputs. Haberler's survey gives relatively short shift to this model as a *positive* model of trade. While in his last five pages he extols the factor-proportions model as a *normative* one, in his section IV on determinants of trade in manufactured goods, just two out of twelve pages discuss the three-factor model. The rest focus on versions of the neotechnology approach, and Haberler does not provide an evaluation of recent empirical studies along the three-factor lines.

Ohlin is more encouraging on the question of the three-factor model's positive value. On page 40 of his paper he argues for disaggregation of labour into skill classes in a factor-proportions model, and in his section XI on international differences in real incomes, much of the discussion runs in terms of changes in the quality of labour that differ across countries. So the Ohlin factor-proportions models of 1933 and 1976 can be interpreted as including human capital, suggesting that Ohlin is more inclined to view that model as useful positively than is Haberler. But in his introduction to this session, Ohlin's positive view of the empirical studies was carefully hedged: 'But it is self-evident that a very simple model — like the factor proportion model — cannot alone explain the structure of international trade, its variations and relation to productive-factor movements'. This qualification is fair enough, I suppose.

The two excellent surveys by Haberler and Ohlin are brief in their discussion of the recent three-factor, human-capital approach, and are ambivalent in their evaluations of it. Thus a more extensive survey and discussion of recent results seems warranted. I will turn briefly to this now. Once I get beyond Leontief and Baldwin most of the references here are additional to the Haberler and Ohlin surveys.[1]

II. MINI-SURVEY OF THE LITERATURE ON THREE-FACTOR MODELS

In 1953 Wassily Leontief published his demonstration that U.S. exports in 1947 embodied a lower ratio of capital to labour inputs than did U.S. imports, contradicting the factor-endowment hypothesis combined with the widely held presumption that the U.S. was better endowed with capital relative to labour than was the rest of the world. These results were subsequently confirmed by Leontief (1956) using the 1951 trade pattern, by Gary Hufbauer (1970) using the 1958 input—output (I—O) table and 1963 trade data, and by Robert Baldwin (1971) using the 1958 I—0 table and 1962 trade data. Similar calculations have been done for Canada by Donald Wahl (1961), for West Germany by Karl Roskamp (1963), for India by Ranganath Bharawaj (1962), and for Japan by Masahiro Tatemoto and Shinichi Ichimura (1959), to cite a few examples of the internationalisation of Leontief's work. Hufbauer and Baldwin also found that the paradoxical result even holds for the U.S., although not as strongly, when only trade in goods that are not agricultural or natural-resource intensive is considered.[2] Recently Harkness and Kyle (1975) showed that Baldwin's results are reversed when capital and labour inputs of varying skill classes are used to explain not variations in the volume of net exports, but the probability that an industry is a net exporter, using logit analysis.

Leontief suggested that his findings were due to higher labour productivity in the U.S. than in its trading partners. In support of this conjecture in his 1956 paper he showed (table 2, page 399) that production of U.S. exports employed relatively more skilled labour than did production of import-competing goods. At about the same time, Irving Kravis (1956) published a paper showing that leading U.S. export industries paid, on average, higher wages than leading import-competing industries. Both Leontief's conjecture and Kravis' findings point to the importance of a third factor of production in explaining U.S. trade patterns. If the high productivity of U.S. workers were due to a relatively large endowment of capital (physical capital, that is), then U.S. net exports should, by the factor-proportions theory, be capital-intensive. But if there were a third factor involved, namely human capital, then a relatively high endowment of human capital relative to physical capital could explain both Leontief's and Kravis' results within a three-factor model. This was noted by Gary Becker (1964, page 60).

These original empirical findings were strengthened by Donald Keesing (1966, 1968), who showed the correlation of net exports across commodities with the percentage of skilled labour in total employment in the industries producing the commodities.[3] Helen Waehrer (1968) also showed the correlation of net exports with skilled labour input and with average wages. Waehrer also pointed out that if relative employment of skilled labour explains both wage differentials and net export differentials across industries, the correlation of net exports and skill ratios should exceed that of net exports and average wages. In simple regression equations using 1960 census data, she found support for this hypothesis.[4]

The human capital explanation of the pattern of U.S. trade has been used to rescue the two-factor hypothesis. Peter Kenen (1965) aggregated physical and human capital and found (using a 9·0 per cent discount rate to compute human capital) that U.S. net exports were capital-intensive after all.[5] Roskamp and Gordon McMeekin (1968) performed a similar calculation for West Germany with the same result. Bhagwati and Bharawaj (1967) did the calculations for India, and found that under reasonable assumptions, Indian net exports were capital-intensive too! Hal Lary (1968) studied value-added per worker in trade across countries, taking value-added as a return on total capital input, and also found U.S. net exports to be capital-intensive. This rehabilitation of the two-factor model has been accepted fairly widely. For example it is favourably cited in the survey article by Bhagwati (1964), and it is the basis for William Travis' (1972) paper examining the role of tariffs in explaining U.S. trade patterns in a two-factor, many-commodity world. In his paper here, Haberler notes that 'Peter Kenen, Harry Johnson, and others have suggested that the Leontief paradox would largely disappear if labour skills were taken out of labour supply and put into the capital coefficient where they belong (page 5)'. It is not clear when he is saying 'where they

belong' whether Haberler is stating his view or paraphrasing Kenen,
Johnson, and others.

This aggregation is questionable on several grounds. First, it eliminates
the possibility of detection of positive correlation of net exports with
human capital inputs and negative correlation with physical capital inputs,
if such exists in the data. Second, it seems unlikely that the two types of
capital are close substitutes in production, which is a condition for such
aggregation in production models. Finally, economists who investigate
the role of human capital in production directly more frequently combine
it with the labour input as an 'effective labour' adjustment.[6]

The closest approaches to a study of the independent influences of
physical capital, human capital, and labour inputs on net exports are
Baldwin (1971) and Harkness and Kyle (1975), reanalysing Baldwin's
data. They both look at the capital-labour ratio and ratios of various
skilled labour to total labour inputs, and obtain differing results. Neither
compares skill measures of human capital with the discounted wage
measure as a variable explaining trade patterns.

The literature on factor inputs into U.S. trade leaves open five questions,
which provide the focal point of the paper by Branson and Monoyios
(1975). The questions, and the short answers are as follows.

(a) What is the correlation between U.S. net exports (*NX*) and inputs of
physical capital (*K*), human capital (*H*), and labour (*L*) in their
production? Answer: Human capital is significantly positive, labour
significantly negative, and physical capital negative but only
marginally significant in regressions explaining net exports across
commodities.

(b) Are these results altered by 'scaling' the data to industry size? This
question was raised by comments on an earlier paper by Branson
and Junz (1971, pp. 344–45), by Stern (1973), and by Harkness
and Kyle (1975). Answer: No.

(c) Does conversion of the dependent variable from quantity or value
of net exports to a binary variable describing whether the commodity was a net export or import, and using maximum-
likelihood logit or probit analysis yield a positive coefficient for
capital-intensity in production? This is the result of Harkness and
Kyle using Baldwin's data. Answer: No.

(d) Are skill or discounted-wage measures of human capital more
significant in explaining variations in net exports? Answer: Unclear.

(e) Should physical and human capital be aggregated in collapsing the
three-factor model to two factors: capital and labour? Answer: No.

These answers come from a study of cross-section 1963 data for manufactured goods originally constructed by Gary Hufbauer (1970, pp. 212–
23) and extended by myself and N. Monoyios to 1967 to check the results.

Whether these results would hold on other data samples remains to be seen.

III. THE DATA

Hufbauer (1970, pp. 212–23) has compiled data on capital per employee and wages per employee in the industries producing 102 three-digit SITC traded manufactured goods (SITC Groups 5–8) in 1963. Both are measured in 1963 dollars. Privately, he provided the underlying data on total employment in 1963 for these industries. Multiplying employment by capital per man yields estimates of physical capital, K_i, in millions of 1963 dollars.

The human capital variable, H_i, was calculated by discounting the excess of the average wage in each industry, $\bar{w}_i$, over the median wage w earned in 1963 by a male with eight years of education in the U.S. (taken to represent unimproved labour) and multiplying by employment, L_i, in the industry.[7] Thus,

$$H_i \equiv \frac{(\bar{w}_i - w) \cdot L_i}{0 \cdot 10} \qquad (1)$$

defines aggregate human capital employed in each industry i.[8] H_i was then converted to millions of dollars, comparable to K_i. Of the 102 three-digit categories, Hufbauer could not compute either capital or labour inputs for eight of them, and four more were eliminated in the process of conversion from the four-digit SIC to the three-digit SITC classifications, so we have 90 usable observations.

To measure size of industry data were used on the value of annual shipments, S_i, from the Census and Survey of Manufactures. Trade data on U.S. exports X_i, imports M_i, and net exports, $NX_i = X_i - N_i$, across three-digit SITC commodity groups 5–8 were obtained from OECD, *Trade by Commodities, Series C*, relevant issues. These are also in millions of dollars. Given the production characteristics for 1963, a choice had to be made between 1963 and 1964 trade data, since presumably part of each is produced and shipped in 1963. In fact, the results are not at all sensitive to this choice, so only the 1963 data are used in sections 3–5.

Hufbauer also presents data giving the fraction of the labour force in the skill categories professional, technical, and scientific, for the 28 two-digit SITC groups that cover the 102 three-digit groups. The three-digit data on trade, physical capital, human capital, and labour were aggregated to the two-digit level. Then the labour force in each two-digit group was split into skilled labour LS_i, and unskilled labour LU_i, in order to test Waehrer's hypothesis that the variables K_i, LS_i, and LU_i, could explain variations in net exports better than could K_i, H_i, and L_i.

The basic data on physical capital, human capital, and labour inputs and net exports were also developed for 1967 to check the 1963 results. All data are reproduced, and described in detail, in the mimeographed Appendix A to Branson and Monoyios (1975) available from the author.[9]

VI. RESULTS AT THE THREE-DIGIT SITC LEVEL FOR 1963

The basic regression equation to be estimated is of the form

$$NX_i = \alpha_0 + \alpha_1 K_i + \alpha_2 H_i + \alpha_3 L_i + u_i. \tag{2}$$

We expect $\alpha_2 > 0$ and $\alpha_3 <$, but have no *a priori* expectation concerning the sign of the coefficient of K in view of the ambiguous results in the literature. If H and K are perfect substitutes and can be aggregated we would expect $\alpha_1 \approx \alpha_2 > 0$. On the other hand Leontief's paradox might manifest itself through a negative α_1.

The simple correlation matrix of the variables for the 90 three-digit SITC groups in 1963 appears in table 1. The units are millions of 1963 dollars except for labour which is in thousands of man-years. In row and column 3 note that no single variable is very strongly correlated with NX. Of the three factor inputs H has the largest correlation coefficient with NX at 0·57.

Among the three input variables the correlations are quite high, especially that of 0·83 between H and L. This is to be expected from the way H was constructed in equation (1). Simple observation cannot tell us what level of collinearity is too high for the independent variables in a regression equation. However if such a problem exists it manifests itself in a regression which might have a significant explanatory power as a whole but with all of the individual variable coefficients insignificant. As we shall see, the analysis suggests that the degree of multicollinearity among K, H, L and S is not severe.

From Table 1, r^2 between NX and H is 0·32 ($= 0·57^2$). This means that H alone explains 32 per cent of the variation in NX.

In Table 2 the results of the basic regression equations are shown. The first column identifies the dependent variable NX, X or M. The next three columns show the estimated coefficients of K, H, L, and the constant terms of the regressions in that order. The numbers in parentheses under the coefficients are the t-ratios. Those marked with one asterisk identify coefficients that are significantly different from zero at the 5 per cent confidence level, while those with two asterisks are significant at both the 5 per cent and 1 per cent levels. In the sixth column the multiple correlation coefficient R^2 for the regression is given, and in the last column, the identifying number for the equation.

TABLE 1: CORRELATION MATR X FOR 90 THREE-DIGIT OBSERVATIONS
FOR 1963, MEANS AND STANDARD DEVIATIONS

Column Row	Exports (X) 1	Imports (M) 2	Net Exports (NX) 3	Physical capital (K) 4	Human capital (H) 5	Labour (L) 6	Shipments (S) 7
1	1·00						
2	0·40	1·00					
3	0·90	−0·05	1·00				
4	0·59	0·58	0·36	1·00			
5	0·70	0·39	0·57	0·79	1·00		
6	0·47	0·43	0·31	0·62	0·83	1·00	
7	0·69	0·60	0·46	0·77	0·79	0·74	1·00

	Mean	Standard deviation
X	158·69	264·39
M	81·31	116·89
NX	77·38	242·76
K	1190·16	1449·06
H	5012·76	7276·83
L	146·28	211·94
S	3292·64	4829·66

NOTES

[1] The following discussion draws on W. H. Branson and N. Monoyios (1975).

[2] Baldwin found that the capital-labour ratio in the import-competing industries was 1·27 times that in the export industries when all industries were included. This ratio fell to 1·04 when natural-resource intensive industries were excluded (see Baldwin (1971), p. 134).

[3] More recently, A. E. Fareed (1972) reanalysed Leontief's original 1947 data, adding an estimate of human capital based on the cost of education of the labour force of 146 industries in the 1950 census. He found that U.S. exports embodied more human capital per man than did U.S. import-competing industries.

[4] See Waehrer (1968, p. 31).

[5] Kenen's aggregations of human and physical capital came in a brief empirical excursion at the end of a theoretical paper that developed a model of human and physical capital accumulation with two endowed factors, labour and land. He repeated his analysis in an excellent survey article covering research up to 1968 (see Kenen, 1970). Whether one can aggregate human and physical capital meaningfully in a production model is not an important question from the point of view of Kenen's path-breaking theoretical piece in 1965. However, his aggregation has been taken as showing that the U.S. is capital-intensive after all by many subsequent writers.

[6] See Zvi Griliches (1970), especially pp. 80–87, and the comment by John Conlisk (1970) for examples of the more common approach. Griliches presents a tentative test of the hypothesis that human capital and physical capital are, in fact, *complements* in production. His results are not clear, but they certainly do not suggest that the two factors are perfect substitutes (see Griliches 1970, pp. 106–109).

[7] This is the standard technique for computing H values in the human capital-production function literature. See Griliches (1970, p. 85) for an example.

[8] The median wage for males with eight years of education in 1963 is $2,397, taken from *Current Population Report*, Series P-60, N. 42 (June 12, 1964), p. 39.

[9] Write W. H. Branson, Economics Department, Princeton University, Princeton, N.J. 08540.

[10] See Branson and Monoyios (1975) for details.

REFERENCES

Baldwin, R. E., 'Determinants of the commodity structure of U.S. trade', *American Economic Review,* LXI (March, 1971), pp. 126–46.
Becker, G. S., *Human Capital* (New York: Columbia University Press, 1964).
Bhagwati, J. N., 'The pure theory of international trade: A survey', *Economic Journal* 74, (March, 1964), pp. 1–84.

Bhagwaj, R., 'Factor proportion and the structure of Indo–U.S. trade', *Indian Economic Journal* 10 (Oct., 1962), pp. 105–16.

Bharawaj, R. and Bhagwati, J., 'Human capital and the pattern of foreign trade: the Indian case', *Indian Economic Review 2*, (Oct., 1967), pp. 117–42.

Branson, W. H., 'Review of Morrall (1972)', *Journal of International Economics 3* (Aug., 1973), pp. 300–2.

Branson, W. H. and Junz, H. B., 'Trends in U.S. trade and comparative advantage', *Brookings Papers on Economic Activity 2* (1971) pp. 285–346.

Branson, W. H. and Monoyios, N., 'Factor inputs in U.S. trade', *Journal of International Economics* (forthcoming, 1977).

Conlisk, J., Comment on Griliches, in W. L. Hansen (ed.), *Education, Income, and Human Capital* (New York; Columbia University Press, 1970) pp. 115–24.

Fareed, A. E., 'Formal schooling and the human capital-intensity of American foreign trade: A cost approach', *Economic Journal* 82 (June, 1972) pp. 629–40.

Griliches, Z., 'Notes on the role of education in production functions and growth accounting', in Hansen (ed.), *Education, Income, and Human Capital* (1970) pp. 71–115.

Harkness, I. and Kyle, J. F., 'Factors influencing United States comparative advantage', *Journal of International Economics* 5 (May, 1975) pp. 153–165.

Hufbauer, G. C., 'The impact of national characteristics and technology on the commodity composition of trade in manufactured goods', in R. Vernon, ed., *The Technology Factor in World Trade,* (New York: Columbia University Press, 1970) pp. 145–232.

Keesing, D. B., 'Labor skills and comparative advantage', *American Economic Review* (May, 1966), pp. 249–58.

Keesing, D. B., 'Labor skills and the structure of trade in manufactures', in P. B. Kenen and R. Lawrence (eds.), *The Open Economy* (New York: Columbia University Press, 1968) pp. 3–18.

Kenen, P. B., 'Nature, capital, and trade', *Journal of Political Economy,* LXXIII (Oct., 1965), pp. 437–60.

Kenen, P. B., 'Skills, human capital and comparative advantage', in Hansen (ed.), *Education, Income, and Human Capital,* pp. 195–230.

Kravis, I. B., 'Wages and foreign trade', *The Review of Economics and Statistics*, XXXVIII (Feb., 1956) pp. 14–30.

Krueger, A. O., 'Factor endowments and per capita income differences among countries', *Economic Journal* 78 (Sept., 1968), pp. 641–60.

Lary, H. B., *Imports of Manufactures from Less-Developed Countries* (New York: Columbia University Press, 1968).

Leontief, W., 1953, 'Domestic production and foreign trade; the American capital position re-examined', in R. E. Caves and H. G. Johnson (eds.), *Readings in International Economics* (London: George Allen and Unwin, Ltd., 1968), pp. 503–27.

Leontief, W., 'Factor proportions and the structure of American trade: Further theoretical and empirical analysis', *The Review of Economics and Statistics,* XXXVIII (Nov., 1956), pp. 386–407.

Morrall, J. F., *Human Capital, Techmology, and the Role of the United States in International Trade* (Gainesville: University of Florida Press, 1972).

Roskamp, K. W., 'Factor proportions and foreign trade: the case of West Germany', *Weltwiotschoftliches Archiv* (1963), pp. 319–26.

Roskamp, K. and McMeekin, G., 'Factor proportions, human capital, and foreign trade: The case of West Germany reconsidered', *Quarterly Journal of Economics* 82 (Feb., 1968) pp. 152–60.

Stern, R. M., *Testing Trade Theories: Research Seminar in International Economic Discussion Paper no. 48* (University of Michigan, Ann Arbor, Michigan, 1973).

Tatemoto, M. and Ichimura, S., 'Factor proportions and foreign trade: the case of Japan', *Review of Economics and Statistics* 41 (Nov., 1959), 442–46.

Travis, W.P., 'Production, trade, and protection when there are many commodities and two factors', *American Economic Review,* LXII (March, 1972), pp. 87–106.

Vernon, R. (ed.), *The Technology Factor in International Trade* (New York: Columbia University Press, 1970).

Waehrer, H., 'Wage rates, labor skills, and United States foreign trade', in Kenen and Lawrence, *The Open Economy* (1968), pp. 19–39.

Wahl, D. F., 'Capital and labour requirements for Canada's foreign trade', *Canadian Journal of Economics* 27 (August, 1961), pp. 349–58.

Summary of the Discussion

The discussion first dealt with the validity of the factor price equalisation theorem and the relation between commodity and factor movements. It also considered the assumption of identical production functions in different countries and the possibility of factor intensity reversals. Suggestions were made to extend the factor proportions model to incorporate growth in factor supplies, indivisibilities, discontinuous space and historical irreversibility. The discussion ended with some reflections on the purpose and the methodology of standard trade theory, in particular on the value of 'simple' models based on 'unrealistic' assumptions. This session was chaired by *Charles P. Kindleberger*.

Gottfried Haberler opened the discussion with a comment on Bertil Ohlin's paper and the alleged tendency towards factor price equalisation. He noted that under certain well-known assumptions complete factor price equalisation logically follows. However, he felt that talk of a mere tendency toward factor price equalisation, when stringent conditions for complete equalisation are not fulfilled, was ambiguous. Problems arise as soon as there are many factors, immobile factors or internationally incomparable factors. When there are many factors, conceptual problems arise in classifying them and in measuring returns to identical categories in different countries. When factors are specific in the sense that they cannot move to other sectors or occupations, factor price equalisation may not occur. Nor can one speak of factor price equalisation for a factor that is specific to a particular country. Furthermore, if the existence of several categories of labour skills is recognised, the single category 'labour' is very ambiguous and Haberler could attach no meaning to the statement that there is a tendency to equalise the 'wages of labour'. He did not find it useful to derive statements about the effect of trade on the domestic distribution of income between factors, a point to which he returned in his concluding remarks.[1]

Bertil Ohlin replied that if there were no common factors at all in the different countries, one could not, of course, talk about equalisation. The Walras-Cassel price system would nevertheless establish a mutual interdependence price system that would illuminate trade relations.[2] However, he found it very simple to talk about a tendency towards factor price equalisation when there were factors of identical quality in the countries and hence, factor price differences could be measured. One could then use the index technique developed by Haberler and others many years ago. One could surely take price differentials for each factor in all those countries where these factors are to be found, and construct an index number of the size of the factor price differences. From variations in this index one could see whether or not factor price differentials had diminished with increased trade. If one asks for more than an index number of that kind, most of the measures that we use in economics would not be permitted. If there are some differences in the quality of broadly similar factors, he added, the comparison becomes somewhat vague and margins of error arise. Such differences may exist between different regions in the same country.

Finally Ohlin spoke of the dismal consequences for the usefulness of trade theory if Haberler were right that in reality there are no qualities similar enough to admit being treated as factors common to different countries. In that case, the greater part of the theory we discuss — and not only the factor proportion theorem and the factor price equalisation theorem — would lose its meaning. If we are to obtain a useful trade theory, we need to find at least some comparable factors of production in different countries, and we must be willing to accept certain margins of error in defining them, he concluded.

Bela Balassa asked whether Haberler's suggestion that the tendency towards factor price equalisation would not follow when certain assumptions were not fulfilled meant that we could go towards greater inequality. This could happen, he suggested, if factor intensity reversals occurred or if the production functions differed in a particular way. This proposition was testable, and he thought such an outcome might occur for trade between developed and developing countries. However, factor returns within the Common Market did not move in the opposite direction in different countries even though the familiar conditions of the theory were not fulfilled.

The discussion then turned to interpretations of actual factor price differences and the role of factor movements. *Lawrence Klein* observed that several decades of unprecedented rise in the volume of trade had not been accompanied by factor price equalisation. Instead, massive movements of labour, in particular from the Mediterranean and Balkan areas to Western Europe, had occurred. On the other hand, one could find a tendency towards factor price equalisation — albeit over a long period — for countries between which there had been no such migration such as the U.S.A., Germany and Japan. Trade flows between these countries had expanded very rapidly during the sixties and the seventies. Klein urged trade theoreticians to provide guidance on the length of the time period necessary for trade to equalise factor prices and also to explain why factor movements sometimes take the place of commodity movements.

Replying to Klein, *Assar Lindbeck* pointed out that a two-factor model could explain why factor movements could substitute for commodity movements and which factor — capital or labour — would move. Part of the explanation of the guest worker phenomenon in Europe may simply lie in government regulations in combination with different factor endowments in the regions of Europe. Governments, he said, have prevented capital from going to Southern Europe for fear of balance of payments problems, so instead labour has gone to Northern Europe and this has contributed to equalising factor returns in Europe. Similarly, the equalisation observed by Klein between the U.S.A., Germany and Japan, may be partly due to capital movements after the Second World War when labour movements between them were restricted.

Melvyn Krauss noted that the Heckscher-Ohlin model could incorporate factor movements. He claimed that the guest worker phenomenon in particular could be handled in a similar manner as Mundell had analysed capital movements in a seminal article.[3] Like capital exports guest worker migration would be treated as if the factor owner were stationary and the factor service mobile. This is because typically the guest worker produces income in one country and consumes it in another. Krauss had developed the implications of this in his Comment and in an article. He drew attention to the existence of a similar 'guest manager' phenomenon, which he had observed while on vacation in Italy. Whereas guest workers generally produce in the north and consume in the south, he suggested that guest managers in seasonal occupations like the hotel industry did the opposite. Factor movements, he furthermore noted, were important where factor price differentials were due to a large non-tradable sector. He concluded that more phenomena could be analysed by the Heckscher–Ohlin model than is generally recognised.

Lindbeck added that if Italian guest workers in Germany were instead considered as Italian residents, being abroad only temporarily, factor price equalisation would be even more pronounced.

Gary Hufbauer noted that the slow movement toward factor price equalisation observed by Klein was connected with the slow rate of trade specialisation between European countries. He suggested two explanations for this. First, governments have undercut their free trade policies with more or less invisible types of subsidies. Second, it takes considerable time for firms to adjust their production methods to increased competition from abroad.

Krauss held that the question of full or partial equalisation of factor prices was really not the important issue. The model can give either result according to the assumptions employed. Instead he felt that the important point to be derived from the theorem of factor price equalisation was that it laid the basis for conceptualising commodity trade and factor movements as related substitutes and not as independent variables. Policy makers had not fully understood the implications of this substitutability when formulating tax and tariff policies, he argued – a point developed in his Comment.

Ronald Findlay recalled that the controversy over partial or complete equalisation and the question whether commodity trade and factor movements were substitutes were but two different ways of formulating the same theoretical relationship. Therefore, one could not say that one was more important than the other.

Another issue central to standard trade theory was whether it was conceptually possible to define production functions so that it was meaningful to speak of their potential identity in all countries.

Fritz Machlup objected to Haberler's view, as expressed by Findlay in his Comment (page 65), that it was necessary to abandon the traditional assumption of potentially identical production functions in different countries. He felt that we should be able to judge whether differences in the patterns of production between different countries are to be attributed either to differences in technology — that is, in knowledge of certain physical relationships — or rather to other things, such as differences in the availability or quality of productive factors. Conceiving of technology as a cookbook containing recipes, he insisted that the recipe for ham and eggs was the same whether you had ham and eggs or not. He believed that production functions were the same for countries with access to the same cookbook. It was important to know if a country's failure to produce tasty ham and eggs was due to ignorance of the recipe or to non-availability of ham (or of eggs). One could, he claimed, say that English entrepreneurs knew the production function for wine, but England lacked the sunshine, the precipitation, the appropriate soil quality, etc., to produce wine competitively. So Machlup was prepared to accept some supposedly 'metaphysical contortions' in order to be able conceptually to distinguish between knowledge of hypothetical production possibilities on the one hand and availability of quantities and qualities of factors on the other.

Nils Lundgren, defending Ohlin's original statement that the laws of nature were given and were everywhere the same, also found that the assumption of potentially identical production functions made theory much more effective. He found it more convenient to attribute observed intercountry differences in the relation between inputs and outputs to differences in the quality of factors rather than to differences in production functions.

Findlay, replying to Machlup and Lundgren, maintained that it was not feasible to make production functions conceptually identical. One could in principle extend the list of inputs in order to take account of neglected factors, such as sunshine, moisture, etc. Similarly one could in principle differentiate between factor qualities. But he felt that the metaphysical contortions involved would not provide operationally helpful results. Therefore, he took it to be the standard view that it was tautological to say that the production function is identical all over the world.

Klein added that empirical approximations of production functions must abstract from some inputs and that these should therefore vary locally even when cookbooks were the same. He emphasised that contradictions to the scarce factor paradox of Leontief could be found if the assumption of technologies was chosen carefully. He thought that the main deficiency with regard to Leontief's original investigation was in not

considering the technology in both countries. A recent study of bilateral
trade between Taiwan and the U.S.[5] produced 'Leontief results' when the
input—output system of Taiwan was used, but contradictions to these
results occurred both when one used the U.S. input-output system and
when the two countries' systems were used simultaneously.

William Branson observed that even if production functions were
identical, in practice, the occurrence of factor intensity reversals caused
problems which tended to be swept under the carpet by trade theorists
because they were so destructive to the predictions of the directions and
effects of trade. Minhas' result,[6] which he felt was more impressive than
subsequent attempts to refute it, indicated that factor intensity reversal
could be an empirically important phenomenon.

Harry Johnson noted that even though reversals occurred in a number
of industries, as Minhas had claimed to have shown, they might not be
sufficient to cause reversals in the aggregate factor requirements of trade.

Åke Andersson drew attention to a central aspect of Ohlin's paper not
referred to by the commentators, namely the importance of transportation
and communications facilities for the structure of international trade.
By focusing on a region's transportation and communication capacity,
one might appreciate the importance of accessibility — a standard concept
used in location theory. He felt that important spatial dimensions and
different qualitative characteristics of the transportation problem are
often neglected by trade theorists and urged that trade theory take these
important aspects into account by adopting a so-called multiple network
approach. Such an approach might be able to explain the total volume
and the country composition of trade; it might illuminate an empirical
regularity he had noted, namely that the industrial economies dominated
world trade, that their trade consisted largely of intra-industry trade, and
that this resulted in large gross flows but small net flows of trade between
countries. By treating countries as points rather than as areas and by
neglecting two-way trade, trade theory, he claimed, had traditionally
focused on net trade rather than on gross flows and on the commodity
composition rather than on the country composition of trade.

Lundgren elaborated on Harold Brookfield's complaint that the factor
proportion theory gave little guidance in explaining the growth of nations.
He felt that it was not good enough to start with capital as given. If we
treat a country's endowment of capital as something which explains its
exports and imports, we bypass what we want to explain. Why, he asked,
do some countries have abundant supplies of capital? He suspected that
rents from natural resources and cultural factors such as religion might
have something to do with this.

Bo Södersten felt that it was important to investigate the consequences
for economic development of having a comparative advantage in a
particular sector. Different sectors have different linkage effects and
income-use patterns. It might be more conducive for development to have

a comparative advantage in, for example, a sector yielding high returns to skilled labour rather than to natural resources if rents could be squandered more easily than wages. He noted that historically Sweden's comparative advantage had continuously been transformed since it occurred in its industrial sector. Södersten also suggested that trade theory would benefit from incorporating specific factors and elements of Ricardian theory as put forward by Findlay. In this way trade theory might reflect more of the richness of Ohlin's own work.

Findlay found Brookfield's and Lundgren's objections ill-founded. Capital accumulation can easily be handled within the framework of a factor proportions model — and in fact had been! The work by Oniki and Uzawa[7] and a half a dozen of the participants at the symposium had incorporated capital accumulation, population growth and changes in technology in the factor proportions approach to comparative advantage. One should not keep on repeating Haberler's statement of 15 years ago that pure trade theory was not dynamic. That was correct then but not now.

This led to a discussion of the purpose of trade theory, the role of assumptions and the relative usefulness of simple and complicated models. *Brookfield,* acting as *advocatus diaboli,* claimed that neither the factor proportions theory nor other trade theories could explain why Brazil at a particular point of time should have specialised in coffee rather than in some other crop. He remained convinced that in this as in many other cases the assumptions of the two-by-two model were so unrealistic as to invalidate it.

Machlup warned against making snide remarks about unrealistic assumptions. Economics was concerned with making negative as well as positive predictions. Indeed, economists were superior specialists in predicting that certain things could not happen and in explaining why not. Therefore, he said, unrealistic, improbable, or counterfactual assumptions should enjoy a highly respected status in their theories.

Brookfield's dissatisfaction led *Robert Solow* to reflect on what one could legitimately ask theory to do. Questions directed at trade theory should be neither too detailed nor too general. There is presumably an optimal scale for most maps, he said, and one-to-one is not the right scale for any map. Similarly, we must find questions with the right degree of detail to pose to theory. It may admittedly have been too easy for trade theory to explain why Brazil specialised in agriculture rather than in manufacture in Brookfield's example. But it may have been too difficult a question to ask why Brazilian farmers cultivated coffee rather than some other crop. Similarly Solow felt that one should not ask the Heckscher-Ohlin theory to try to explain why when an automobile is assembled in one place the fuel tank may have been made in another country and the engine block in a third, or why when shaving that morning he should have found a Belgian mirror in a seventeenth century Swedish castle. This

detailed pattern of international trade presumably occurs because of
accidents of history. So once an industry appears, it stays because it is
difficult and not terribly important to dislodge — precisely because the
industry does not depend on any important comparative advantage. This
suggested that there might be something important to say about the
adult industry problem. Such industries may be due to irreversibilities in
time which are the opposite of the possibility of establishing infant
industries. He suspected that these irreversibilities were neglected by
theorists simply because they were difficult to deal with. Time symmetry
is a much more simple proposition, in equilibrium theory especially, but
it is possible to deal with irreversibilities and they ought to be dealt with.
Solow suspected that they were important for the 'fine structure' of
international trade but did not think we should expect theory to explain
this structure. Nevertheless, as Machlup had suggested, it could rule out
some possibilities.

Michael Michaely pursued a similar line of thought. He suggested that
trade theorists could probably devise a model that would satisfy
Brookfield and explain in an exhaustive and precise way why Brazil
started by exporting coffee rather than some other crop. Such a model
would, however, explain little else and he felt that most trade theorists
would not regard it as a useful theory. Every theory suggested could
certainly explain something and thus one could run tests, as Hufbauer
had done, to find some justification for any theory. Michaely therefore
saw the following problem: If trade theorists were to search for a universal,
exhaustive theory to replace the Heckscher-Ohlin model and to explain
all patterns of trade, they might wander in the desert for 40 years and
wind up without their disciples behind them. They were therefore left
with a basket of different theories. Since they would not wish to take
every conceivable theory and put it in the basket, the question arose: how
should one judge whether a particular theory belonged in the trade
theorist's basket of theories or not? He regretted that he had no answer
to this important question.

Balassa agreed that we should not expect one theory to explain everything. Different explanations may apply to different trade relations.
However, he had been very much impressed by the applicability of the
Heckscher-Ohlin theory to the trade of developing countries. Countries
at different stages of development exported different types of goods. For
instance, Japan started by exporting labour-intensive goods, moved via
skilled labour-intensive exports to capital-intensive exports. One should
distinguish between relevant development stages.

Simple models were defended by *Ronald Jones,* who felt that the real
contribution of the post-Samuelson development based on Haberler,
Heckscher and Ohlin, was that simple general equilibrium models were
used in a systematic way to obtain comparative static results. This was the
primary place in economics where general equilibrium had been put to use

to answer such questions as how a change in tariffs would affect factor prices and the volume of production. He also wondered whether the simple two-by-two model was as simple as many people claimed. He remembered struggling through it as a student and was continually surprised that his own students did not master it as quickly as one would expect for a simple model. He reminded its critics that even if one ignored the demand side and took prices as given in the open economy, the two-by-two model would still be a system of eight equations. This was not to suggest that the model was the end, but rather that it was a very good begining and could easily be expanded to *n* commodities and to *n* factors and solved with the use of a little matrix algebra. This would give clues as how to incorporate things like transport costs which varied for different goods and countries, non-traded goods, specific factors, etc. His teaching experience indicated that a model with specific factors, such as Findlay had suggested in his Comment, was an intermediate model helping to bridge those of Ricardo and Heckscher-Ohlin. It was an easier model because one did not have to look at all things at once. One can explain what happens if one adds more labour to a sector where another factor is 'trapped' and one can follow the analysis in terms of marginal products in a way students find easier to understand. In the Ricardo type model, in which non-trade aspects are included in the way Findlay suggested, one can use the language and the insights of the Heckscher-Ohlin theory.

Harry Johnson added that the purpose of models, and of teachers in general, is to instruct students in the simplest elements of a problem. Once they have that basic understanding of interconnections, the next stage is to look at the real world and try to see the simple interconnections operating. Economists tend to be divided into those who like to build simple models and those who like to see how complicated the world is. He did not consider it to be a confrontation when one person looked at the world and saw all kinds of strange things going on where another only saw capital and labour. Viewing models as instruments of teaching and of understanding, he saw the two-sector model as the simplest which still captures a lot of real problems. One thing that a two-good model did not capture was complementarity, which comes up in some of the things that Jones referred to. When one has fixed factors, one gets complementarity coming out of the relations between that factor and the other two in the model. The real problem in making the models more realistic is to find plausible and widely observable instances of complementarity which contradict the results one obtains with the simple models. Otherwise, one can always add more details, but the question is whether one adds anything more about the possibility of substitutability or whether one changes the economic essence of the problem. Most practical people are skilled, he suggested, because they can see such substitutabilities operating in all sorts of directions other than those suggested by the simple model, but it is not a basic conflict of interpretation of a theory. One has to have a simple theory to see and understand the connections, the way one needs observations of reality to see that reality is rather complicated and that one can only organise it according to general principles.

Findlay joined Jones and Johnson in defence of simple models. He made an analogy with macroeconomics. Keynes' vision, he said, was a very penetrating one, to which Ohlin's vision was analogous in international trade. Macroeconomics does not do full justice to Keynes, as Axel Leijonhufvud had pointed out. Obviously the IS-LM diagram and the 45 degree line did not capture all the subtleties of Keynes' thought, but macroeconomics would be enormously backward had we not had these simple tools. He thought there was a close analogy with the kind of simple models used in trade theory. The reason why we have Keynesian economics and not Hayekian or Hawtreyian economics is that Keynes was capable of being 'vulgarised', whereas Hayek is on such a lofty level that the only Hayekian in the world is Hayek. That may save him from vulgarisation, but it does not spread any message.

In his closing remarks *Haberler* warned against making too much of the factor proportion theory. For example, foreign trade theory explains why Portugal exported wine and Britain cloth; it does not also attempt to answer the further question why Britain rather than Portugal experienced industrial development. Similarly, when today we ask why Kuwait exports oil and Bolivia tin, and both import machinery from Europe and the U.S.A., we take the current situation of the economy as given. We leave it to economic historians, or maybe to philosophers, to explain why industrialisation started in Europe and the U.S.A. and not in Kuwait and Bolivia. These are very important questions, he said, and one can find very useful answers in Marshall's *Industry and Trade,* which quotes Hegel's philosophy of history extensively. So trade theories take the present situation as given and do not ask why things have developed in the course of history so that we find the situation as it is now.

In reply to Ohlin, Haberler concluded that he still found the suggested tendency towards factor price equalisation an ambiguous proposition, when the conditions for perfect equalisation were not given. If factors are qualitatively not the same in different countries, the question loses its meaning altogether. But even if each factor is qualitatively the same in both countries, he could not attach a precise meaning to the equalisation of factor prices if there were many factors. He did not agree with Ohlin that trade theory would lose much if such generalisations could not be made, since trade theory could still say a lot about how, under what conditions and in what sense, trade increases economic welfare.

Haberler also stressed that even if factor prices were perfectly equalised that did not mean that standards of living were equalised, since a country better supplied with natural resources or capital would have higher income per capita. He agreed that inequalities in income distribution were important, but suggested that people were more interested in the interpersonal than in the functional distribution of income. Except for some special situations, one could not derive general statements from the factor endowments of countries to the effect that trade makes poor people poorer and the rich richer or the other way round. If we want to redistribute income, the proper measures are taxes and government expenditures rather than interference with trade. An exception may be when a sudden opening up of trade causes poverty in certain areas in the short run.

Ohlin closed the discussion. He felt that the greatest challenge to the factor proportions model was to incorporate differences in technology. He saw at least two ways of dealing with differences in technology between countries. They could be viewed as due to a difference in 'cook-books' containing knowledge which was distinct from factor quality. This was the approach suggested by Machlup and by Jones in the Vernon volume.[8] Or they could be viewed as due to different composition of the labour force with respect to the four labour qualities mentioned in his contribution, partly due to investment in human capital (for further suggestions see his paper, section VII).

Ohlin did not agree with Andersson that traditional trade theory explains net trade rather than trade. Also he felt that the volume of trade, as well as its commodity composition, had been illuminated for instance by considering country size. However, he agreed that much remained to be done. He supported Klein's request for more dynamic considerations in trade theory. He felt that economic and social geographers had made important contributions to the analysis of development in different countries, which might be useful for economists. Even if their conclusions may be of a less precise nature than those from mathematically formulated economic models, he thought it important to pursue both approaches. He warned against the danger of developing models without checking them against reality, since they then threaten to live lives of their own.

Simple models were useful as long as they were realistic in the sense that they explained important phenomena in the real world. However, he feared that many simple models had lost touch with reality. Many important elements had been left out, such as taxation, location aspects and economies of scale, He thought that Hayek, whom Findlay had referred to, drew the wrong conclusion because his model, unlike Keynes', did not conform to the reality he was trying to explain. This illustrated, he thought, the necessity of choosing realistic assumptions. He felt that it must be very difficult to make very simple assumptions that are relevant in all the cases where the conclusions are applied. A question then arises concerning the relative importance of contributing to the pure logic of economic models and of explaining certain aspects of reality. He hoped that economists would allocate more of their intellectual resources to such neglected issues as the international aspects of taxation, social regulation, risk, internal transport costs, and development.

The tasks ahead were truly enormous. He recalled the advice once given by Jacob Viner: when you feel something is important don't ask others to do it, do it yourself! Choosing not to follow this advice, he urged other economists to tackle these important issues.

NOTES

[1] Haberler also discussed the effect of the growth of the public sector on the pattern of trade. He treats this topic now in Appendix B to his paper (pp. 15–16).

[2] See *Interregional and International Trade*, 2nd rev. ed. Appendix 1, *Simple Mathematical Illustrations of Pricing in Trading Regions* (Cambridge, Mass., 1967), p. 297.

[3] R. Mundell, 'International Trade and Factor Mobility', *American Economic Review*, 47, (June, 1957).

[4] M. Krauss, 'The Economics of the "Guest Worker" Problem: A New Heckscher-Ohlin Analysis', *Scandinavian Journal of Economics* (No. 3, 1976).

[5] J. T. H. Tsad, *Theoretic, Econometric, and Input-Output Analysis of Taiwan's Foreign Trade* (University of Pennsylvania, 1976).

[6] B. S. Minhas, 'The Homohypallagic Production Function, Factor-Intensity Reversals and the Heckscher–Ohlin Theorem', *Journal of Political Economy,* Vol. 70 (1962), pp. 138–56.

[7] H. Oniki and H. Uzawa, 'Patterns of Trade and Investment in a Dynamic Model of International Trade', *Review of Economic Studies* (Jan., 1965).

[8] R. Vernon (ed.), *The Technology Factor in International Trade,* (NBER/Columbia University Press, New York, 1970).

3 Regional Growth Theory, Location Theory, Non-renewable Natural Resources and the Mobile Factors of Production

Michael Chisholm

I. INTRODUCTION

Periodically, thinking men become worried about the pressure of demand on limited natural resources. Malthus was primarily concerned about food supplies for the world's population, an anxiety that during the nineteenth century receded only to return in the twentieth — as witness the many publications of the Food and Agriculture Organisation. During the 1960s and the present decade, a new spectre has emerged — the prospect that the world's supply of non-renewable minerals and fuels may be exhausted within the foreseeable future. Pessimists argue that the stock of these resources is finite and that exponential growth in consumption can lead to only one outcome, the complete depletion of the resources. Optimists opine that the supply of minerals and fuels yet to be discovered is vast, that technological improvements will permit leaner deposits to be worked, deposits in remote locations and/or at great depths (both on land and at sea) to be exploited, and that in any case the price mechanism will ensure substitution of materials, economy of use and recycling.

The present paper is not the appropriate place to enter the lists of this debate. For the present purpose, it is sufficient to note that the nineteenth-century assumption that minerals and fuels are abundant and relatively cheap is no longer generally accepted. We may also assume that global consumption of most non-renewable resources will continue to rise over the foreseeable future. The pertinent question in the present context, therefore, is whether we can say anything useful about the *distributional* consequences that follow from the prospective continued increase in consumption in an era of threatened, if not actual, scarcity. As a general point, the literature about the 'impending' shortages takes a world view and ignores the likely impact on the various nations/regions; perhaps the major exception is the anxiety felt in the United States as her self-sufficiency is steadily eroded (Cameron, 1972; Park, 1975). Yet in fact the spatial implications are important and may be a major factor in the pattern of economic development in the future.

The strategy to be adopted in the present paper is as follows. After a brief review of the concepts of 'land' and 'mobile' factors of production, discussion will focus on existing theories of regional development and industrial location that incorporate considerations of the natural resource endowment. Thereafter, an attempt will be made to indicate some of the major changes in circumstances that have occurred and to relate these to the theories that have been examined. This will lay the foundation for a schematic interpretation of the historical experience of the past two centuries or so and the identification of the ways in which future development patterns may differ. It would appear that in the future possession of non-renewable minerals and fuels will be an increasing asset for development, but that the form this development takes will differ from that which has occurred in the past.

II. LAND, LABOUR AND CAPITAL

In economic analysis, it is traditional to treat land as a geographically immobile resource, whereas labour and capital are conceived as mobile. This elementary distinction should be qualified in at least two ways. Land must be disaggregated, at the very least into (a) the soil—climate—vegetation complex, relevant for agriculture and forestry, and (b) non-renewable minerals and fuels. Furthermore, the notion that land resources are immobile is questionable. Clearly, the place of first exploitation is determined by the range of options offered by nature. However, this first stage — mining a mineral or cultivating a crop — may be only a minor part of the whole chain of processing and manufacture, all of which may be done either at the location of the first stage or elsewhere. Once won from the ground, natural (or land) resources are potentially mobile.

Thus, as an initial proposition, some natural resources are processed and consumed more or less *in situ*, whereas others require only a limited operation to win them from the earth and are then transported elsewhere for both processing and final use. The limited areas of subsistence agriculture still remaining in the world are examples of the former situation; extraction of iron ore in north-west Australia for shipment to Japan, Europe and elsewhere exemplifies the second situation. At this very general level, the questions relevant for this Symposium are the following: how are the various natural resources distributed along the continuum indicated above, how has this distribution changed over time and how in the future is it likely to alter, and what reasons may be adduced for observed and expected changes?

Now these are very big questions and it is impossible in one short paper to do them full justice. For the purpose of this paper, attention will be directed to only one part of the natural resource complex, the non-renewable minerals and fuels; the climatic and agricultural components of 'land' will receive only passing mention. Furthermore, for the purpose of this paper attention will be directed to those minerals which are relatively localised, such as most metalliferous ores; excluded from consideration will be materials such as sand, gravel and limestone which are very generally available in most regions of the world.

III. THEORIES OF REGIONAL ECONOMIC GROWTH

Reviewing the evolution of ideas about economic development, Hirschman (1965, p. 1) observed:

> The intensive study of the problem of economic development has had one discouraging result: it has produced an ever-lengthening list of factors and conditions, of obstacles and prerequisites. The direction of the enquiry has proceeded from thoroughly objective, tangible, and quantitative phenomena to more and more subjective, intangible, and unmeasurable ones. For a long time, certainly until 1914 and perhaps until 1929, natural resources held the center of the stage when the chances of a country's development were considered. Later on capital, a man-made and quantifiable entity, came to be considered the principal agent of development.

In subsequent paragraphs, Hirschman continued his review of the ever-widening range of factors to be taken into account, including questions that properly belong to the domain of the psychologist.

Whether natural resources, centre of the stage until 1914 or later, are 'thoroughly objective, tangible, and quantitative phenomena' is a matter that many would dispute. What is not in doubt is the fact that in recent decades students of economic growth and development in general, and of regional development in particular, have paid surprisingly little attention to the geography of natural resources. In this respect, Richardson's 1973 work on regional growth theory is typical, including as it does only six brief allusions to natural resources (compare also Kuznets, 1966 and 1971).

The lack of interest in natural resources displayed by economists concerned with economic development has not been compensated for by the work of geographers. As Keeble (1967) noted, comparatively few geographers have devoted their attention to the processes of economic growth and development. Furthermore, the relationship of natural environment to patterns of development has not been a major theme in geographical writings in recent decades, perhaps as a reaction to the excessive claims of the environmental determinists. Amongst geographers, Ginsburg (1957 and 1960) stands out as having an interest both in development and in natural resources.

Perhaps the main reasons for the apparent lack of interest in natural resources in general, and the non-renewable ones in particular, are:

(a) The difficulty of measuring the natural endowment of a region/ nation in a manner commensurate with other development and trade variables. Whereas population, G.N.P., industrial output, etc. are amenable to measurement, there is no comparable measure of 'natural resource endowment'.

(b) The fact that the natural resources of a region/nation are not absolute, given quantities. Climatic, topographical, biological and mineral resources, but especially mineral resources, are subject to constant re-evaluation. In particular, new discoveries of minerals and the exhaustion of old deposits is constantly changing the endowment of regions/nations.

For the purpose of economic model-building, the supply of natural resources is generally assumed to be an exogenous variable about which little can usefully be said. Consequently, in most of the formal literature on regional economic development natural resources are ignored. The limited amount of work by geographers has not been adequate to fill the gap.

IV. EXPORT BASE THEORY

To incorporate elements of the natural environment into formal development models constrains the researcher to use very primitive constructs. The most notable of these, and virtually the only 'theory' explicitly to take account of natural resources, is the 'export base theory'. The idea of the export base has a long antecedence (for example, Innis, 1930), though North (1955) was one of the first writers to incorporate it into a formal, albeit descriptive, model of economic development (see also Perloff *et al.*, 1960; Perloff and Dodds, 1963). In North's formulation, the impulse for development in a region (intranational development) arises from external demand for one or more locally produced goods. These may be agricultural in origin, forestry products or minerals, though North himself clearly was thinking of agricultural products in particular. He envisaged a cumulative process in which the extra local income arising from the export industry would generate a demand for goods and services that could be locally produced; the processing of the export staples would become more thorough (greater value added); infrastructure improvements would create opportunities for further development; and external scale economies would be realised, adding another twist to the upward development spiral.

Students of economic development have noted a commonly recurring sequence of manufacturing activities, summed up in the words of Maizels (1963, pp. 55–56) as follows:

At these earlier stages of industrialisation, manufacturing is generally confined to the processing of primary products (such as grain milling, spinning yarn or smelting metals) and, at a later stage in development, to the simple transformation of materials (such as clothing, footwear, furniture or paper). A more mature phase of industrialisation can be said to commence with the production of capital equipment based on machine technology.

This picture is based on the common evolution of manufacturing in the main industrial countries. . . . [It should not] be interpreted as implying any necessary sequence in the pattern of industrial growth.

Notwithstanding Maizels' final word of caution with respect to the future, the picture he presents is representative of the experience of many countries. Implicit is the idea that initial development is sparked off by the export of 'raw' primary products, including minerals, followed by further processing of these materials in the country of origin, thereby enhancing the value added retained in the developing country, improving the quality and/or extent of the infrastructure and widening the skills of the indigenous population.

The picture of development painted in the previous paragraphs is consistent with theories of trade and comparative advantage, even though empirical tests designed to establish whether trade actually does conform to comparative advantage have been rather inconclusive. Suffice to note that there are two schools of thought concerning the origin of comparative advantage. The tradition which can be traced to Ricardo and Mill emphasises relative labour costs. In contrast, Heckscher and Ohlin stress relative factor endowments, particularly of labour and natural resources. The reality probably is that both contribute (Moroney, 1975), though no doubt in varying degree.

Thus, at a very primitive level it is apparent that the distribution of natural resources is one factor, and an important one, governing the spatial distribution of economic activity.

V. WEBER ON INDUSTRIAL LOCATION

Alfred Weber was one of the pioneers of industrial location theory and his ideas figure prominently in the literature. The problem that he formulated can be stated in the following terms. Given that a firm's product has been decided and the scale of output determined, and given also that the production-function is known, what will be the optimum location for the firm when the sources of materials inputs and locations of markets are known? To solve this problem, Weber made some simplifying assumptions, notably that transport costs are directly proportional to tonne/kilometres and that transport facilities are freely available between any pair of points on a uniform plane. More recent and realistic versions of the problem are couched in terms of a specified transport network with known transport costs on each link in the system; linear programming techniques then provide a suitable framework in which to solve the problem.

Of particular relevance at present is Weber's distinction between materials and market locations. If, in the manufacturing process, the bulk of materials is large relative to the bulk of the final product, then transport costs would be minimised by a location as near as possible to the sources of the materials. A clear example is the location of pig-iron manufacture in the eighteenth and nineteenth centuries, when as much as 8 to 10 tonnes of coal was requisite to produce one tonne of pig-iron. At this period, most pig-iron manufacture was located on the coalfields (excepting the manufacture of high-quality charcoal iron and steel). Other products involve either an increase in bulk (for example, bread), are perishable or are fragile and are therefore expensive to transport (for example, optical instruments); in such cases, the best location may be as near to the major markets as is feasible.

The relative importance of materials and market locations will clearly vary from one industry to another. The Weberian formulation of industrial location clearly provides a *partial* explanation of comparative advantage that is consistent with the economic development sequence discussed in the previous section. However, with the passage of time the relative importance of the location factors will change for each industry. Technological developments have generally made for much greater efficiency in the use of both materials and fuels needed to achieve a given end product. In addition, the manufacture of some metals (notably steel) has been adapted to the use of scrap, either in whole or in part. Both tendencies imply that the best locations will be near the major markets rather than the original sources of the primary ores and fuels. This tendency has been reinforced over the past 150 to 200 years by dramatic improvements to transport facilities: transport costs relative to other costs have fallen, implying that locations which minimise transport costs are less relevant than hitherto; consequently, location decisions will be taken in the light of other considerations. Yet other changes have worked in the same direction, such as the rise of multinational companies and the problems of minimising the incidence of tax.

This train of reasoning leads to the conclusion that, other things being equal, mineral and fuel resources that have been won from the ground are increasingly mobile in their raw, or semiprocessed, state. Furthermore, there is plenty of empirical evidence to show that in recent decades this is exactly what has been happening. For example, in 1950 world exports of iron ore accounted for rather less than 20 per cent of all production; by 1967, the proportion had jumped to just under 36 per cent (Manners, 1971, pp. 348–9).

Clearly, the development sequence outlined in the previous section, however relevant it may have been in the nineteenth century, must be re-examined for its validity in the twentieth and twenty-first centuries. In particular, it would appear that exploitation of mineral and fuel deposits by countries that are currently underdeveloped will be of particular importance as creating a source of capital available for investment in other sectors of the economy (Ginsburg, 1957); the relative importance of this role is probably rising.

VI. THE SUPPLY OF MINERALS AND FUELS

Reviewing the development of the international economy during the nineteenth century, Ashworth (1975, p. 54) noted that:

> For many years the task of keeping up adequate mineral supplies was among the more straightforward of those imposed by industrialization. The main need was to extract more of familiar minerals in familiar places. As late as 1880 the three chief industrial countries, Britain, the U.S.A., and Germany, with much smaller contributions from France and Belgium, accounted for all but a tiny fraction of the world's coal output, and major changes in the countries supplying other minerals were rare, though not unknown . . .
> In the late nineteenth century the situation was changed by the approaching shortage of some of the familiar minerals in what had been the main producing districts and by the demand for new minerals that were not to be found in familiar places . . .. The mid-nineteenth century had seen the inauguration of geological surveying on an extensive scale and this helped to make mineral prospecting a less chancy business. In the next fifty years the improvement of survey techniques . . . and their application to many large areas previously of little commercial significance showed the existence of enormous and varied mineral resources . . .

The relationship of consumption rates to known reserves is not a matter for which reliable long-run historical data are available. Indeed, there is considerable argument about the relationship even for the present and recent past. Nevertheless, there is no reasonable doubt that for very many minerals, and also petroleum, current consumption would exhaust the presently known reserves in a matter of decades. If the presently known reserves would be exhausted within decades, it seems highly likely that each deposit which is being worked will itself have a useful life which is also measured in decades. In practice, we must take account of the fact that many of the new discoveries which are constantly being made are extensions of already proved deposits. Nevertheless, it seems likely that as global consumption rises, the useful life of a resource of any given size will decline. Only if discoveries consist of ever-larger deposits will this tendency be offset. During the past 100 or 150 years, the size of individual deposits has indeed risen as progressively leaner resources are pressed into service (Peach and Constantin, 1972), and this may well have served to offset higher rates of extraction and so maintain the useful life of individual deposits. Whether the tempo of technological development will permit the continuation of the trend to leaner ores to continue at the same pace, and consequently maintain the useful life of new enterprises in the future, is a matter for debate; my own judgement is that it will not.

A distinct, though related, development is also working to shorten the life of any one resource deposit. As the more accessible reserves in the inhabited portions of the globe are discovered, exploited and exhausted, the search for new deposits is pushed into inhospitable, even uninhabitable, regions, such as the Sahara, Antarctica and the oceans. The costs of exploration, but more especially of making extraction possible, must rise in relation to total costs. If sunk costs account for a rising portion of total costs, the rate of extraction from those resources which are developed must be raised, especially in the initial years until the sunk costs are recouped. Alternatively, the search for minerals leads to greater depths of extraction — the deepest gas well is about 7000 m — or to the use of lower grade deposits. The former clearly implies increased initial capital costs; the latter does also, usually in the form of installations to handle and concentrate massive quantities of material. As an example, in the early 1920s it was profitable to mine copper ores with about 1·5 per cent of copper; by 1970, the lower limit was 0·5 per cent, implying a threefold increase in the volume of material to be handled for a given output of useful metal (Park, 1975, p. 36).

Much the most important consideration, however, is the location of workable deposits. We have already noted Ashworth's view that as industrialisation proceeded, first in Britain and then in Europe and America, it was the 'familiar' places that were first ransacked for minerals and fuels. The same idea was expressed by Perloff and Dodds (1963) as a partial explanation of development within the United States. They identified the decade 1840–1850 as the start of an era in which the insatiable demands of the eastern seaboard and mid-west led to the opening up of mineral ventures in previously sparsely populated regions. (Following the export base model, demand for minerals acted as a stimulant for economic growth.) With the unfolding of the twentieth century, it is manifest that a rising proportion of world mineral and fuel production is obtained from regions that are inherently inhospitable. The deserts of the Middle East, Australia and the Sahara are the scenes of intense extractive activity. The northern wastes of Siberia, Canada and Alaska are also being combed for their riches. And now the search has turned to the major seas and oceans; the exploitation of oil and gas in the North Sea is the most ambitious project of its kind to date. Yet none of these areas is inviting for long-term settlement on a significant scale.

The conclusion to which all this leads is really self-evident. The hunt for minerals and fuels is taking mankind into parts of the globe where he will not wish to remain once the resource in question has been exhausted. Although this same phenomenon has occurred previously in history, the relative importance of supplies from inhospitable regions is undoubtedly greater than ever before, and is apparently growing. In all such cases, the traditional mode of analysis, framed in terms of Weber's least-cost transport location or the export-base model of regional development, either ceases to be relevant or has at best only a tenuous relationship with reality. Once the resource has been won from the earth, it will be transported elsewhere for further processing. We may thus visualise the inhabited areas surrounded by uninhabitable wastes that witness a transient interruption to their tranquillity.

This somewhat simple picture must be modified to take account of developments within the inhabited regions. As marginal resources become either deeper or leaner, already known but hitherto uneconomic resources will be tapped and yet others discovered. However, the more favourable the region for long-term habitation, the greater the constraints on mineral and fuel workings imposed by the need to safeguard other activities. An excellent example is provided by England's new Selby coalfield, south of York. Approximately 600 million tonnes of workable reserves have been proved, but on present plans only 40 per cent will be extracted; the balance of 60 per cent must be left in the ground to prevent subsidence, in Selby itself (with its famous Selby Abbey) and elsewhere (see *The Times*, 2 April, 1976). The general point is that mining operations in the more habitable parts of the globe will necessarily compete with other existing or potential uses; the more dense the population, the harder will it be to reconcile the conflicts of interest. Reconciliation will inevitably mean higher costs for the mining operation, thus artificially (but perhaps rightly) raising the price of these marginal deposits. Thus may attention first be focussed on deposits in the somewhat less favourable regions and in the inhospitable wastes.

If we take account simultaneously of the tendency for mineral supplies to be obtained from relatively inhospitable regions and of the probable shortening of the useful life of each deposit, it seems clear that the impact of non-renewable resources on economic development does not now and will not in future conform to the pattern that was described briefly earlier in this paper, a pattern relevant for the nineteenth century and earlier. The natural resources, once obtained from the ground, will be moved to the centres of population; in this sense, and in the context of long-term development, it will be the 'land' resources that are mobile.

VII. CONCLUSION

Mikesell and others (1971) compiled a fascinating set of case-studies of the effects on development of petroleum and mineral exploitation. In all cases, the exploitation was by capital foreign to the host country, the countries in question being relatively poor and underdeveloped. In an essay reviewing the findings of the case-studies, Mikesell (1971, p. 25) comments:

> Our preliminary conclusion is that, by and large, these industries have
> little direct impact on the course of development in the host countries
> since they engage only a small portion of the domestic labor and
> capital and of land having alternative uses. Their indirect impact on
> both the rate and pattern of social and economic change may be enor-
> mous, but this depends upon governmental policies in allocating revenue
> and in providing inducements to broadly based development, on the
> one hand, and upon the ability of society generally to utilise the returns
> from the subsoil for maximum social and economic progress, on the
> other.

If we set aside the social problems inherent in the development process,
minerals and fuels are seen as contributing to economic development
principally as a source of public revenue which will permit of investment
in other sectors of the economy. Mikesell might have added that this will
frequently imply investment at locations which may be far removed geographically from the place or places whence the minerals and fuels are obtained. Thus it is not surprising that in recent years considerable interest
has developed in the difficult problem of how best to tax resource-based
enterprises with the twin objectives of ensuring that the project can be
profitable and simultaneously that the host nation obtains the maximum
revenue advantage (Behrman, 1971; Garnaut and Ross, 1975; Pearce, 1975).
The problems are of course compounded for some resources by the problems of monopoly pricing.

Thus it seems that the export-base model of development may have
been of particular relevance up to and including the early twentieth
century. Especially during the nineteenth century, the search for minerals
and fuels was conducted largely, though not entirely, in regions which are
intrinsically habitable even though they may have been previously uninhabited. As exploitation has pressed onward into inhospitable regions,
the non-renewable products of the soil are exported from the region of
origin, as must be the profits. In this sense, therefore, the 'land' resource is
mobile, being brought to the existing centres of population whose locations
will remain relatively unchanging.

Two consequences follow from this general conclusion. Where the
extraction is designed for home consumption, the major problems facing
the country will be the nature and extent of restoration of the landscape
to be undertaken after mining operations have ceased and the reconciliation of conflicts with other forms of land use (recreation, water supplies,
etc.). Much more difficult problems are faced by those nations which
possess valuable mineral or fuel resources in demand on the world markets,
and are at an early stage of development. Libya and Morocco and the oil
states of the Persian Gulf are cases in question. For long-term prosperity,
it is essential for these countries to convert the profits from mineral and fuel

extraction into other forms of productive resource, whether agricultural, industrial or commercial. The poorer the natural endowment (other than minerals), the greater the need to jump to sophisticated high-technology activities but the harder this transition may be on account of the poverty of the people, high level of illiteracy and strength of custom. The paradox is that in such cases it is this indigenous labour which is the least mobile of the three factors of production, both geographically and occupationally.

REFERENCES

Ashworth, W., *A Short History of the International Economy since 1850* (Longman, 1975).
Behrman, J. N., 'Taxation of extractive industries in Latin America and the impact on foreign investors', in Mikesell, R. F. *et al.* (1971), pp. 56—80.
Cameron, E. N. (ed.), *The Mineral Position of the United States, 1975—2000* (University of Wisconsin Press, 1972).
Garnaut, R. and Ross, A. C., 'Uncertainty, risk aversion and the taxing of natural resource projects', *Economic Journal*, 85 (1975), pp. 272—87.
Ginsburg, N. S., 'Natural resources and economic development', *Annals of the Association of American Geographers*, 47 (1957), pp. 197—212.
Ginsburg, N. S. (ed.), *Essays on Geography and Economic Development*, Research Paper 62, Department of Geography, University of Chicago (1960).
Hirschman, A. O., *The Strategy of Economic Development* (Yale University Press, 1965). First published 1958.
Innis, H. A., *The Fur Trade in Canada. An Introduction to Canadian Economic History* (Yale University Press, 1930).
Keeble, D. E., 'Models of economic development', in R. J. Chorley and P. Haggett (eds.), *Models in Geography* (Methuen, 1967), pp. 243—302.
Kuznets, S., *Modern Economic Growth. Rate, Structure and Spread* (Yale University Press, 1966).
Kuznets, S., *Economic Growth of Nations. Total Output and Production Structure* (Harvard University Press, 1971).
Maizels, A., *Industrial Growth and World Trade* (Cambridge University Press, 1963).
Manners, G., *The Changing World Market for Iron Ore 1950—1980. An Economic Geography* (Johns Hopkins, 1971).
Mikesell, R. F. *et al., Foreign Investment in the Petroleum and Mineral Industries* (Johns Hopkins, 1971).
Moroney, J. R., 'Natural resource endowments and comparative labor costs: a hybrid model of comparative advantage', *Journal of Regional Science*, 15 (1975), pp. 139—150.
North, D. C., 'Location theory and regional economic growth, *Journal of Political Economy*, 63 (1955), pp. 243—258.
Park, C. F. and Freeman, M. C., *Earthbound. Minerals, Energy and Man's Future* (Freeman, Cooper and Co., 1975).

Peach, W. N. and Constantin, J. A., *Zimmermann's World Resources and Industries* (Harper and Row, 1972).

Pearce, D. W. (ed.), *The Economics of Natural Resource Depletion* (Macmillan, 1975).

Perloff, H. S. *et al., Regions, Resources and Economic Growth* (Johns Hopkins, 1960).

Perloff, H. S. and Dodds, V. W., *How a Region Grows. Area Development in the U.S. Economy* (Committee for Economic Development, 1963).

Richardson, H. W. (1973), *Regional Growth Theory* (Macmillan, 1973).

Comment

Harry W. Richardson

NATURAL RESOURCES, FACTOR MOBILITY AND REGIONAL ECONOMICS

Professor Chisholm's analysis is easily summarised. After a brief discussion of the role of natural resources in the export base model and in Weberian location theory, he stresses that mineral resources — the main type of non-renewable resource to which his paper is restricted — are likely to become exhausted within decades. The implications of this belief are that resource developments will increasingly take place at inhospitable locations. One consequence is higher capital costs. Another is the failure for such locations to generate long-term settlement, so that the natural resources then become the mobile factor and are transported to existing, and stable, population centres. Outside inhospitable areas, and especially at high-density locations, the major problem is the conflict between natural resource exploitation and environmental protection. Where extraction is for the world market an additional problem is how to convert resource revenues into local economic development.

With the exceptions mentioned below, there is little to disagree with in this diagnosis. I would like to use the space available to explore further some of the issues raised by Professor Chisholm and to introduce a few others. First, I should mention the points of disagreement. The economists' neglect of natural resources has recently been remedied, especially from the point of view of theoretical analysis. The revival and extension of Hotelling's economic theory of depletable natural resources (Hotelling, 1931; Gordon, 1967; Solow, 1974; Schulze, 1974; Pearce and Rose, 1975) with the critical equilibrium condition that the rate of increase of resource royalties over time must be equal to the interest rate, shows that formal theorising is feasible and productive. Indeed, some of the assumptions, such as the existence of perfect futures markets, suggest a little too much rather than no abstraction and rigour. A more substantial criticism is that theorists have not attempted, let alone succeeded in, the integration of the concept of exhaustibility (which demands analysis over time) with the retreat to increasingly inaccessible sources (which implies locational ana-lysis). A time-space model of natural resource development is an impor-tant research priority. But spatial economists have not been conspicuously successful in designing theoretical models that simultaneously deal with time and space, even in relatively thoroughly researched areas such as regional growth theory or urban structure. Natural resource economics is, apart from the historical landmarks (for example, Gray, 1914, as well as

Hotelling), a new subfield and can hardly be accused of tardiness in this task.

Despite some *caveats*, Professor Chisholm appears to accept the case for imminent mineral resource depletion. And this assumption underlines much of his analysis. The depletion issue is a technical one, and it is inappropriate here to spend much time on it. The important point is that the definition of reserves in terms of what could be mined at today's prices and current technology grossly underestimates availability. To quote two respected mineral economists, 'vast quantities do exist of mineral resources that could be mined and . . . either as their price goes up or as their cost goes down (which is to say, as technology of extraction improves), the volume of mineable increases significantly — not by a factor of 5 or 10 but by a factor of 100 or 1000' (Brooks and Andrews, 1973, p. 7). Moreover, on the demand side, there is fairly strong evidence that the intensity of use of minerals tends to decline at high levels of development. The demand growth paths of some developing countries might offset this tendency to some extent. Even so, trend projections of the past probably overestimate future demand. There is little reason to dispute that in this area high prices are an effective adjustment mechanism, especially as a stimulus to supply but also in dampening demand.

Professor Chisholm is right in his stress on the indirect mobility of natural resources, but there is at least one far from trivial exception that merits a few words. It was excluded from his analysis since it is a non-exhaustible resource. I am referring, of course, to climate. As a major amenity resource, climate has had a major influence on the mobility of both labour and capital within and between countries. In the United States, migration to the so-called 'Sunbelt' has been an important phenomenon in recent decades, and several analysts (see Greenwood, 1970; Alonso, 1971) have found that climate has a statistically significant influence on migration flows. Climate has also affected international migration in a similar though less consequential way, since affluent retirees have figured prominently among the migrants. The most marked economic impact has been the influence of climate as a determinant of international capital flows associated with the opening up, in the form of infrastructure investments, of major new tourist areas around the world.[1]

I. INTERNATIONAL AND INTERREGIONAL ECONOMICS

It is unnecessary here to discuss the implications of natural resources for international trade theory and analysis. These have been examined in Professor Haberler's paper (pp. 4–5) and were treated more extensively in the monograph by Vanek (1963). A key finding of Vanek's analysis was that complementarity between capital and natural resources could alter the ranking of relative factor requirements of a country's exports and imports (pp. 32–4). This might explain the capital intensity of United States competitive import industries relative to export industries (the Leontief paradox) if these industries were also relatively natural resource-intensive.

Historically, the development of regional economics owes a substantial debt to international trade theory. Presumably, one of the main ideas behind this session is that it might be possible to reverse this flow of knowledge so that insights gained from regional economics could be applied to analysis of the international allocation of economic activity. There are very few examples of such a reverse flow; the use of gravity models in the analysis of international trade flows (see Isard and Peck, 1954; Linnemann, 1966) is one, but it is difficult to think of others. Unfortunately, from the point of view of our present perspective, location theorists have had little to say about natural resource impacts. However, there may be some virtue in analysing the problem within an interregional system, on the grounds that this provides a more manageable focus than the international economy, by treating the interregional system as if it were equivalent to a system of nations under free trade (this is the approach adopted by Moroney and Walker, 1966). More particularly, the interrelationships between Alaska and the mainland states in the United States offer a neat analogue to a 'one country and the rest of the world' model, partly because of the dominance of natural resource development in the Alaskan economy, but especially because of the spatial separation between the two regions. Testing hypotheses on the locational pulls of natural resources using the Alaska-mainland testbed might be very fruitful.

II. NATURAL RESOURCES AS AGGLOMERATION ECONOMIES

The most recent analysis of the influence of natural resources on trade theory (mentioned by Professor Chisholm) is by Moroney (1975). In attempting to explain industrial specialisation in the southern United States, he argues that the original emphasis of Heckscher and Ohlin on labour and natural resource endowments is more appropriate than the modern interpretation in terms of labour and reproducible capital. Also, the classical stress on labour-cost differentials is relevant. Earlier (Moroney and Walker, 1966), Moroney had been puzzled by the specialisation of the South in capital-intensive industries. His recent finding is that specialisation is explained by low relative wages and by high natural resource endowments per unit of output. The paradox of high capital intensity is explained by the fact that capital is closely complementary to natural resources.

This argument may be generalised and extended a little. A characteristic of the South is the presence of abundant sources of relatively cheap labour. This is not common in frontier regions (defined as areas where natural resource exploitation is the dominant type of development). In this case it may be argued that both labour and capital are complementary to natural resources. In fact, natural resources become equivalent to agglomeration economies as a determinant of the direction of factor flows. Capital and labour both flow into frontier regions, partly because of the complementarity hypothesis, partly because of economies of scale in natural resource development (such as mining). Thus, returns to both capital and labour may increase simultaneously.

Although not a direct contradiction of the factor price equalisation theorem since the assumptions of the standard model have been changed, this argument is nevertheless troublesome for the received theory of factor mobility. Fortunately, it remains a theoretical wrinkle more than a major revision because its practical significance is probably — except in rare cases — relatively slight. There are several reasons to support this conclusion. Frontier regions and natural resource areas remain a relatively small part of the total universe, regardless of whether we are thinking in terms of Alaska in the United States or O.P.E.C. oilfields in the world economy. The labour requirements for natural resource development are usually low, and the amenities of frontier regions are frequently very poor, so the higher wages earned (whether in the form of increasing returns or 'compensation payments' to offset the disamenities) do not distort the national (or world) wage structure. Where frontier regions specialise in exhaustible resources, the duration of intense development may be quite limited. Spatial polarisation of factor flows due to scale economies will cease at a farily early stage of development, because of the effects of increasing resource inaccessibility on returns to capital. Natural resource development does not lead to permanent and continuous growth unless urban agglomeration economies take over, typically via the route of industrial development and processing, from the stimulus of natural resource extraction. The low labour requirements make such a transition improbable. Finally, in subsequent stages of development the profits from natural resource extraction are more than likely to be reinvested outside the frontier region. Whether this is explained within the framework of a 'dependency' model or as a search by natural resource producers (such as the O.P.E.C. nations) for higher returns both at home and abroad, the result is the same — a reversal in the capital flow. The probability of this flow is primarily due to the frequency with which natural resource zones fail to develop beyond enclaves since they rarely generate broad areal economic expansion.

III. ENVIRONMENTAL CONSIDERATIONS AND INTERNATIONAL DEVELOPMENT

Natural resource activities and the processing and manufacturing industries with which they are associated tend to be high polluters. There is often a hard choice to be made between pursuit of growth and environmental preservation. Since the benefits of growth may be widely diffused whereas the environmental costs tend to be spatially concentrated, the distributional consequences of the tradeoff are serious. These issues are treated more seriously in the developed countries, since the relative weights in the tradeoff shift from growth to environmental quality at higher levels of income. Krutilla (1967) argued that extractive activities have two major problems: the use of land for resource extraction precludes its use for other value-creating purposes, especially leisure and recreation (in the case of rapidly disappearing wilderness areas, the 'option demand' (Weisbrod, 1964) of the next generation may be quite important); and they are irreversible. These considerations are probably less critical in developing countries if only because policy-makers are less able to afford the shorter-term costs of sacrificed growth to their populations. Producers and governments in developed countries may be very willing to provide capital, or even subsidies, to promote natural resource extraction and processing in developing countries since they not only gain the resource as importer but also avoid the environmental costs (Clawson, 1972).

At first sight, there might appear to be a reasonable basis for international co-operation between the capital and technology of the developed countries and the resources of the developing countries. Unfortunately, this strategy has been attacked in many quarters as 'exporting pollution' and as the latest dirty trick of the multinationals. But the economic benefits for both sides may be compelling. In many cases the natural resources in the developing countries are more abundant, more accessible and hence more productive. Concern with environmental quality is a function of income, and it is arguable that some redistribution of polluting industries to developing countries is consistent with maximisation of world social welfare. Since population densities in *frontier regions* in developing countries are often lower than in resource regions in the developed countries, the numbers directly affected by environmental disturbance in the former may be lower. Finally, Krutilla's argument notwithstanding, some environmental costs are reversible, for instance, air pollution as opposed to physical despoliation or ecological destruction.

This argument is not a defence of the distributional effects of any particular set of institutional arrangements. If most of the economic rents from natural resource extraction accrue to the foreign producer rather than to the host country, or if within the country (as is very probable) one group gains the income from mining royalties while others suffer the environmental impact, some revision of these arrangements might be desirable. In more general terms, however, as the recent history of O.P.E.C. obviously demonstrates, the redistributional consequences of natural resource ownership may be drastic. The main reason is that, although the long-term substitution possibilities for natural resources may be substantial (Barnett and Morse, 1963), in the shorter run the elasticity of substitution between capital and natural resources is much lower than, say, between capital and labour. For resources where ownership is heavily concentrated or well-organised, the opportunities for monopoly pricing may be considerable. This strengthens the case for a flexible international capital market as a corrective 'recycling' mechanism.

IV. REGIONAL PLANNING

There are two other major research (and practical planning) problems that arise from consideration of natural resources. I suspect that they are more ciritical at the regional than at the international level, and hence I will discuss them only briefly. The first is how to evaluate the locational impacts of natural resource exploitation in densely populated, high-income regions (this is, of course, one aspect of the growth-environmental tradeoff). Most of the impact evaluation methodologies available measure net impacts only, whereas what is needed are gross impact, spatially disaggregated and relocational models. As an illustration, consider the effects of the development of offshore oil and gas resources off the California coast. Onshore terminals and facilities may generate all kinds of locational readjustments and *intra*regional factor mobility that are not picked up in current models. Prominent among these will be the 'environmental repulsion' effects of environmental deterioration on high income coastal residents and the offsetting 'job attraction' pull of the facilities for workers, either in the facilities themselves or in other industries that might be created in (or relocated to) their vicinity. It is possible that these flows might cancel out in a net impact model but the changing socioeconomic mix might have severe consequences on, say, community tax bases and public service requirements. Also, in the case of metropolitan regions the indirect locational repercussions of these initial changes might reverberate through the whole region.

The second research problem has a much wider significance than the environmental sensibilities of high-income societies. As implied in Professor Chisholm's analysis, the distinguishing characteristics of future natural resource developments may be inaccessibility and exhaustibility. These two features create daunting obstacles for planners. The problem is how to develop resource regions, *but for a limited period of time*. Rapid initial development is usually followed by outflows of labour and capital, and eventually by abandonment, as resource exhaustion approaches. The unpalatable choice is between boom towns that turn into ghost towns or temporary 'camps'. One strategy is a conservation policy approach since this will spread out development over time, simultaneously reducing the scale of settlement required and prolonging its life. The major planning issue is associated with the fact that urban infrastructure as fixed capital is immobile. The theory of the *mobile* growth centre has yet to be developed, while the alternative of perishable infrastructure (towns that fall apart after ten, twenty or thirty years) remains an untested but plausible technological possibility. If technology is capable of developing urban infrastructure to an acceptable amenity level that is either mobile or disposable, this perennial problem of natural resource settlements might be solved.

V. CONCLUSION

Natural resources exert a considerable influence on the mobility of factors of production both within and between countries, but not in ways that might be suggested by traditional international trade theory. Also, natural resources raise some interesting questions about growth-environmental tradeoffs and about the world income distribution. On the other hand, I doubt whether natural resource developments have major impacts on the location of production, unless location is defined very broadly in terms of the distribution of industries among countries. Only the *extraction* of natural resources is locationally tied, and processing and complementary industries can take place at a wide variety of locations. In some circumstances natural resources are conceptually similar to agglomeration economies exerting a gravitational pull on both labour and capital; the theoretical flow mechanism is much the same in both cases. However, the transient nature of natural resource locations implies that they will not have a major permanent impact on the spatial distribution of economic activity unless urban and industrial agglomeration economies are created. The probability of this conversion depends upon the scale of natural resource exploitation, its potential complementarity with other activities, and the attractiveness of the area for immigrants. Since, as Professor Chisholm points out, the cities and industries may be developed at sites distant from the natural resource zone (even outside the country), the attractiveness condition becomes critical. If most new frontier regions are inhospitable to permanent human habitation, the locational repercussions of natural resource expansion will be quite weak.

To illustrate these arguments with a familiar case, consider petroleum extraction in O.P.E.C. countries. Do the events since 1973 suggest that this particular resource is becoming more important? No, the simpler explanation is that a sudden realignment of relative prices, to which the world has now adjusted, corrected for a chronically low price of energy resources. Of course, the increased flow of petroleum revenues relaxed the capital constraint on development enabling the oil-producing countries to import capital and technology. Although this induces some shift in the international distribution of economic activity, its effects should not be exaggerated. Capital is not the only bottleneck: shortages of administrative and technical manpower, capacity constraints in the production of physical materials difficult to transport (such as building materials) and other limits on domestic absorptive capacity now become important. Even if there is a relative shift in international allocation (due to growth rate differentials), it would be surprising to find marked intranational locational changes within the natural resource economies. These countries are typically centralist in outlook and planning practice, reluctant to decentralise economic activity, administrative capacity or political power. Natural resource extraction and related industries remain capital-intensive and the resources tend to be located in the less habitable and more isolated areas. Clearly, there will be flows of capital from the centre to the periphery, but in the absence of either locational *diktat* or commitment to decentralisation the national settlement pattern will not change radically in response to natural resource development (though it might change for other reasons). Without such a change in the permanent settlement pattern natural resource extraction will not exert a locational pull much beyond its own narrow limits.

NOTE

[1] The role of a warm climate as a stimulus to economic development contrasts with the traditional argument that over secular time a colder climate has become increasingly associated with high rates of economic development. An early wide-sweeping study by Gilfillan (1920) on 'the coldward course of progress' argued that the average temperature of dominant cultures and economic systems has fallen progressively from ancient to modern times. Perhaps the critical contrast is between temperate (whether warm or cool) and extreme climates. Unfortunately many of the major unexploited resource deposits are found in the latter.

REFERENCES

Alonso, W., 'The System of Intermetropolitan Population Flows' (Berkeley: Institute of Urban and Regional Development, University of California (1971, WP 155).

Barnett, H. G. and Morse, C. W., *Scarcity and Growth: The Economics of Natural Resource Availability* (Baltimore: Johns Hopkins Press, 1963).

Brooks, D. B. and Andrews, P. W., 'World Population and Minerals Resources: Counterintuitive or Not?' (Stockholm: U.N. Symposium on Population, Resources and Environment, 1973).

Clawson, M., 'Economic Development and Environmental Impact: International Aspects', pp. 163—83, in École Pratique des Hautes Études, VIe Section, *Political Economy of Environment: Problems of Method* (Paris: Mouton, 1972).

Gilfillan, S. C., 'The Coldward Course of Progress', *Political Science Quarterly*, 35 (1920), pp. 393—410.

Gordon, R. L., 'A Reinterpretation of the Pure Theory of Exhaustion', *Journal of Political Economy*, 75 (1967), pp. 274—86.

Gray, L. C., 'Rent under the Assumption of Exhaustibility', *Quarterly Journal of Economics*, 28 (1914), pp. 66—89.

Greenwood, M. J., 'Lagged Response in the Decision to Migrate', *Journal of Regional Science*, 10 (1970), pp. 375—84.

Hotelling, H., 'The Economics of Exhaustible Resources', *Journal of Political Economy*, 39 (1931), pp. 137—75.

Isard, W. and Peck, M., 'Location Theory and International and Interregional Trade', *Quarterly Journal of Economics*, 68 (1954), pp. 97—114.

Krutilla, J. V., 'Conservation Reconsidered', *American Economic Review*, 57 (1967), pp. 777—86.

Linnemann, H., *An Econometric Study of International Trade Flows* (Amsterdam: North Holland, 1966).

Moroney, J. R., 'Natural Resource Endowments and Comparative Advantage', *Journal of Regional Science*, 15 (1975), pp. 139—50.

Moroney, J. R. and Walker, J. M., 'A Regional Test of the Heckscher-Ohlin Hypothesis', *Journal of Political Economy*, 74 (1966), pp. 573—86.

Pearce, D. W. and J. Rose (eds.), *The Economics of Natural Resource Depletion* (London: Macmillan, 1975).

Schulze, W. D., 'The Optimal Use of Non-renewable Resources: The Theory of Extraction', *Journal of Environmental Economics and Management*, 1 (1974), pp. 53—73.

Solow, R. M., 'The Economies of Resources and the Resources of Economics', *American Economic Review*, Papers 64 (1974), pp. 1—14.

Vanek, J., *The Natural Resource Content of United States Foreign Trade, 1870—1955* (Cambridge, Mass: MIT Press, 1963).

Weisbrod, B., 'Collective-Consumption Services of Individual-Consumption Goods', *Quarterly Journal of Economics*, 78 (1964), pp. 471—77.

Summary of the Discussion

A major part of the discussion concerned the relevance of export base models for analysing economic development based on natural resources and whether these resources had decreased in importance as was argued in the paper. The role of migration policy for the applicability of the export base theory and the importance of agglomerations for development were also touched upon. The rate at which regions would deplete local non-renewable natural resource deposits in the future was compared with previous experience and the consequences of local depletion as well as the probability of global depletion were discussed. This session was chaired by *Harold Brookfield*.

Max Corden registered his surprise at finding the main point in a paper on geography to be that geography was unimportant. It was a plausible point he said that resources were currently being exploited in increasingly less hospitable places and that the location of natural resources did not affect the location of industry. He concluded from this that the usual international trade considerations would decide where industry will be located.

Harry Richardson and *Michael Chisholm* felt rather that geography as a discipline was in a state of flux and in particular that human geography was becoming more important than physical geography.

Harold Brookfield suggested that some renewable natural resources could still serve as an export base sparking regional development. In tropical regions, such as Malaysia, rubber and oil palm served as an export base. On this a large regional structure was being established and intraregional and interregional trade were expected to be stimulated and substantial urban growth to follow. He felt that this was a very relevant feature of land development policy in a number of developing countries and asked why Chisholm should claim that the relevance of the export base model declined after the early twentieth century.

Bela Balassa noted that the export base theory applied in certain circumstances but not in others. He objected to Chisholm's claim that labour in the oil countries was the least mobile factor of production, both geographically and occupationally, and recalled that both skilled and unskilled labour was very mobile into the Arab oil countries. In fact, in some of these countries the guest workers were up to three times as many as the locals. Since the reaction of other oil countries was to restrict immigration, they clearly preferred to adapt their production structure to existing factor endowments according to the Heckscher-Ohlin model rather than to adapt their factor endowments to their natural resource base according to the export base model. From his own experience he mentioned the cases of Kuwait and Venezuela. The former wanted to establish very capital intensive industries in order to reduce its reliance on foreign labour. In Venezuela, where there is relatively little skilled or technical labour, he had advised the government to adjust its trade patterns to its factor endowments according to the Heckscher-Ohlin model. Balassa also emphasised that the effects on development of natural resource extraction depended on the structure of backward linkages in the production of the export staple as well as on how domestic income was used.

Assar Lindbeck emphasised the importance for development of the type of natural resource and the type of ownership. Development in Sweden he noted, had been based on forest exploitation. Trees grew mostly everywhere in Sweden whereas mines were generally highly localised. Therefore, the labour incomes generated by production were spread over the country. Furthermore, ownership of the forests was decentralised to the peasants, so that rental incomes also were widely dispersed over the country. Exploitation of a mine owned by a government of a multinational firm would generally result in a rather different development pattern.

Charles Kindleberger observed that a favourable transport location was itself a natural resource which could serve as an export base and attract an agglomeration of economic activities. As a recent economic historian he had been particularly interested in the case of the Netherlands which in the eighteenth century had grown rich on carrying trade with virtually no production of goods. The major cities specialised in buying goods where they were cheap and selling them where they were dear, often packing or repacking the goods before re-exporting them. This created a very open economy, with few of the goods coming from domestic production or going to domestic consumption. Typically we think of trade as being an engine of growth, he said, and as leading to production of goods. International trade theory, starting with Ricardo, may have ignored carrying trade as a source of wealth. Noting that this type of growth historically leads to banking rather than to production, and that banking leads to aristocratic ways of life, which lead nowhere, he concluded that wealth may be sterile even with agglomeration.

Harry Johnson took issue with the author's statement that natural resources were difficult to fit into models of economic development. There existed, he recalled, a large literature concerning both development based on resource extraction and conservation of resources starting with Harold Innis' work and containing contributions by many other Canadian economists. This literature was relevant to Chisholm's topic. He further noted that in a long perspective economic development did not depend on the permanence of existing agglomerations. He thought that it was a methodological construct to think of development as though it concerned settled populations proceeding to support themselves through the centuries by exploiting particular natural resources. We have, he recalled, a long history of populations and capital moving from resource base to resource base.

This mobility he said is a far more appropriate guideline than agglomerations for the study of resource based development.

Chisholm closed the discussion. He replied to Brookfield by stressing that he had confined the topic of his paper to non-renewable resources. It would have been too enormous a task to consider also renewable resources whose availability was influenced by a wide range of topographical, climatical and vegetational conditions. Thus, conclusions concerning the importance of renewable resources for development could be quite different from those for non-renewable resources.

An issue which had been the object of lively discussion, was whether the non-renewable natural resources of the world would be exhausted in the foreseeable future. In his paper Chisholm had pointed to evidence that the location of extraction of any one mineral was likely to be changing fairly rapidly due to the high rate of usage, given the size of the known deposits. He was sceptical of the horror stories about the imminent depletion of the non-renewable resources of the world he said in reply to Lindbeck and others who had charged him with spreading such stories himself [in a table illustrating his introduction but not included in this volume]. He clarified that he was speaking of the exhaustion of local and of global deposits of a particular non-renewable resource. The rate of depletion of these resources had been expanding very rapidly and as new discoveries continued to be made the locations of exploitation had been changing dramatically. Population and income growth made exploitation of marginal deposits profitable. These were increasingly located in inhospitable regions. The combination of high wages necessary to attract labour to the deposit and of falling transport costs to ship out the unprocessed raw material increased the incentives to process the raw material in locations away from its deposits. Thus, he concluded, the kind of trigger mechanism for development that natural resources constituted in the nineteenth century and earlier may be of greater use to explain past history than to predict future development.

4 The Location of Economic Activity since the Early Nineteenth Century: A City-systems Perspective*

Allan R. Pred

The institutional, technological and overall contextual framework within which the location of economic activity occurs in economically advanced countries has changed greatly since the early nineteenth century. The most prominent changes are more or less common knowledge. The focus of economic activity has shifted from the countryside to the city. The sectoral centre of gravity has shifted from agriculture and other 'primary' activities, to 'secondary', or manufacturing activities, to the so-called 'tertiary' sector, that is, consumer, business and government services and retailing. The 'secondary' sector, as well as the 'tertiary' sector has increasingly employed people in administration, management, clerical work, research and other office-bound activities. That is, to a growing extent the job-providing economic units materialising at different locations in advanced economies have been principally involved with the processing and exchange of information rather than the processing and transportation of natural resources and inter- mediate- and final-demand goods. The typical decision-making entity responsible for the location of manufacturing and related activities has in- creased in size from the locally oriented workshop controlled by one or a few men, to the regionally oriented single-product factory, to the horizon- tally merged multiplant corporation enjoying a regional or national oligo- poly, to the more elaborately administered nationally oriented corporation with several vertically integrated products, to the nationally oriented multidivisional corporation with a variety of integrated and unintegrated manufacturing and non-manufacturing functions and a great number of locationally divorced units. Overland transportation costs fell sharply with the spread of railways. This, in combination with the scale economies and specialisation made possible by new production technology, enabled ever larger market areas to be served from a single location. Later, as techno- logical advances required production systems to become increasingly characterised by an intricate division of labour — and as the volume of goods crisscrossing between components factories, assembly plants, ware-

* This paper was prepared in conjunction with a research project funded by the U.S. National Science Foundation.

houses, wholesalers and retailers consequently increased dramatically —
trucking and other developments ironically reduced the relative importance
of transport costs in the locational calculus of most classes of industrial
activity. In recent years, however, the rapidly expanding demand for face-
to-face contacts within and between both business and government organisations has magnified the importance of locational variations in the time
and monetary costs of passenger travel for a growing number of administrative, office, and service activity units.

Despite these and many other relevant changes, it can be maintained
that the underlying feedback processes currently influencing the location
of economic activity in advanced economies are essentially similar to those
which influenced economic activity location in the early nineteenth century. In order for such an argument to be made, it is necessary that the
locational pattern of a country's non-agricultural economic activities for
any given period of time be seen from the perspective of city-system growth
and development. (A city-system, or system of cities, can be defined as a
national or regional set of urban or metropolitan units which are interdependent in such a way that any significant change in the economic activities, occupational structure, total income, or population of one member
unit will directly or indirectly bring about some modification in the economic activities, occupational structure, total income, or population of
one or more other set members.) Since contemporary international trade
to a very great degree consists, in effect, of the exchange of goods and
services between the metropolitan units of different advanced economies,
such a national-level city-system perspective may perhaps serve as a useful
backdrop for this symposium.

I. EXPLICIT AND IMPLICIT LOCATIONAL DECISIONS

The growth and development process of a system of cities may be viewed
largely as an accumulation of decisions directly and indirectly affecting the
location and size of job-providing activities in the private and public sectors.
These decisions fall into two broad categories: explicit locational decisions,
and implicit locational decisions. Explicit locational decisions occur whenever an entrepreneur, small firm, corporation or government body decides
to establish or physically expand a job-providing facility. Implicit locational
decisions occur whenever a business or government unit decides to purchase
goods or services, to award a contract or subcontract, or to make some
miscellaneous allocation of capital. These latter decisions are not usually
conceived by their perpetrators as being locational in nature. However,
such decisions are locational in so far as they must involve some places
rather than others.

Neither explicit nor implicit locational decisions are made in a vacuum.
Decision-makers can only choose from alternatives which they become

aware of either through information search or unintentional information acquisition. Hence, both decision types are not only influenced by traditionally recognised geographical variations in supply and demand factors (themselves related to previous locational decisions), but also by existing 'spatial biases' in the availability of specialised information. That is, because of the means by which private and public specialised information circulate through contact networks, the probability of a particular bundle of specialised information being known or acquired varies from place to place during any given period of time. Conversely, any decision-making individual or group possessing specialised information at a given location is more likely to have actively sought or accidentally obtained it from some contacts or places rather than others.

Explicit and implicit locational decisions are especially sensitive to spatial biases in the circulation and availability of specialised information since such decisions are usually made from a small range of alternatives, or after limited search. Numerous inquiries into the decision-making behaviour of individual entrepreneurs and organisations indicate that — regardless of decision type — only a very limited scanning of the environment normally occurs before what is judged to be a 'satisfactory alternative' is selected (for example, Cyert and March, 1963; Aguilar, 1967; and North, 1973). Limited search behaviour is often economically rational since the marginal cost of search is apt to quickly begin exceeding the marginal improvement in alternatives identified. (The early nineteenth-century entrepreneur was discouraged from extensive search because of the costly and extremely slow procedure of obtaining information from non-local sources. Today, high-level administrative decision-makers are usually dissuaded from undertaking extensive search in connection with any one decision, because there constantly is such a great number of new planning and coordinating decisions to be reached.) To the extent that decisions are based upon limited search they are likely to be based upon the most readily accessible specialised information. And, the most readily accessible specialised information is almost certain to be spatially biased, most probably in the sense that it is obtained from or near the decision-making unit's already existing economic-linkage partners and related contacts of both a direct intermediary character.

Each of the particular types of job-providing facilities and technological advances allocated in space in conjunction with explicit locational decisions may be regarded as an innovation. The somewhat more specific impact of spatially biased specialised information availability on explicit locational decisions can therefore be phrased in innovation diffusion terms. Information circulation is central to innovation diffusion processes for several reasons (cf. Hagerstrand, 1967). Obviously, specialised information circulation may influence the spatial dissemination of knowledge regarding either the existence of any given economic innovation, or the market justification necessary for an organisation to internally develop or perfect an innovation.

Furthermore, because of the technical, cost, or marketing uncertainties to be overcome, and the risk-taking frequently involved (Schon, 1967; Zaltman, Duncan and Holbek, 1973), adoption or rejection of a growth-inducing innovation usually requires that redundant and new information be searched for or otherwise acquired. At this point spatially biased information concerning the reactions and experience of previous adopters is frequently crucial, especially if the potential adopter is 'passive' and reluctant to act unless excess demand, falling profits, or increasing competition make it necessary. Finally, under modern circumstances, once a decision to adopt is reached, spatially biased specialised information — especially the market contacts and spatial structure of the adopting organisation — is likely to affect the selection of a location at which to implement (cf. Lasuen, 1971, 1973; Pred, 1973a, 1975a). However, this need not be so if the innovation is a technological one that can be appended to an already functioning facility.

Implicit locational decisions are either of a routine or non-routine character. Routine implicit locational decision-making normally rests on the direct feedback of information from ongoing business or organisational activities. Direct feedback may indicate, for example that stocks of a given item have declined to a level where additional purchases from an already identified source are necessary. Such routine decisions require no new search for alternatives since the search and spatially biased information employed previously in a succession of similar decision situations has, via experience feedback, resulted in a learning process and the identification of what is judged to be a satisfactory standard solution. In contrast, non-routine locational decisions have few or no precedents and demand the use of new search and spatially biased specialised information to identify and select alternatives. In particular, it would appear that those who make non-routine locational decisions frequently attempt to reduce uncertainty and avoid perceived risks by choosing alternatives that are similar to those opted for in the recent past either by themselves or by other firms or organisations of which they have become aware through their local and non-local network of contacts and economic linkages.

In addition to being influenced by existing spatial biases in the availability of specialised information, implicit and explicit locational decisions contribute to further spatial biases in the circulation of specialised information. This is owing to the fact that such decisions always create or expand goods, service, administrative or capital-flow linkages whose existence and maintenance is dependent upon information flows. In other words, for 150 years or more, in currently advanced economies the process of city-system growth and development — and thereby the location of non-agricultural economic activities — has been dominated by the constantly repeated interplay between: (a) existing local and interurban economic linkages; (b) spatial biases in the circulation of specialised information; and (c) implemented locational decisions, or new and expanded local and interurban linkages. This assertion can be expanded upon by juxtaposing a heuristic probabilistic model describing how early nineteenth-century city-system growth and development unwound in the United States — and with some modification in other countries — with a similar model describing how city-system change occurs during the 1970s in advanced economies. Since national and large regional city-systems in advanced economies have been characterised by a very long-term stability in the population rank of their leading urban units (for example, Lukermann, 1966; Robson, 1973), these models initially focus on the means by which large centres reinforce the growth of one another.

II. EARLY NINETEENTH-CENTURY CITY-SYSTEM GROWTH AND DEVELOPMENT

Imagine a comparatively large mercantile city (M_1), that is, a city whose principal functions lie within a complex of wholesaling–trading sectors.[1] Its relative size indicates the city has begun to outdistance most of its competitors within the national or regional city-system in which it is embodied. Much of the previous and on-going growth of the city's population is attributable to a series of locally self-perpetuated feedbacks which are here only diagrammatically represented as a submodel in figure 1. The feedbacks

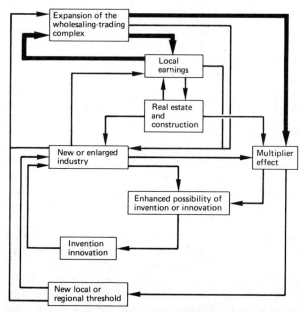

Figure 1 A submodel of locally generated urban size-growth for a single large United States mercantile city, 1790–1840. For an elaboration see Pred (1973b).

occurring in M_1 between (a) the local wholesaling–trading complex and its dependent manufacturing activities, and (b) local earnings and multiplier effects, are collapsed into a shorthand version in the lower lefthand portion of figure 2. The simplified local-growth submodel is also shown at the upper left of figure 2 as simultaneously operating for other comparatively large mercantile cities $(M_2, M_3, \ldots, M_n)$ belonging to the same national or regional system of cities.

While the functioning of the local-growth submodel is important, the continued accumulation of economic activities and population growth at M_1, or any other large mercantile city, to a great extent springs from its trading linkages and economic interaction with other leading centres. More precisely, each sizeable increment in the wholesaling-trading complex of M_1 not only enhances local employment opportunities, but also directly or indirectly causes increased economic interdependence, or interaction, with other large centres within the same city-system. This interdependence, by increasing the dimensions of wholesaling-trading activities in other large cities, triggers the local-growth submodel of those places and thereby brings them further economic expansion. Direct increases in interdependence occur when expansion of the M_1 wholesaling–trading complex is owing to a larger scale of shipments to M_2, M_3, or M_n of either local and hinterland specialities or of goods originating in another country or region. Expanded interdependence also occurs when the wholesaling–trading complex of M_1 enlarges the scale of its operations by increasing agricultural or industrial imports originating in or passing through the hands of wholesaling–trading middlemen in M_2, M_3, or M_n. Interdependence between M_1 and other high-ranking centres expands indirectly when population increases in M_1 (or M_2, M_3, or M_n) create a greater demand for the locally consumed agricultural and industrial goods normally received from or through one or more of those other major cities. (The population increases which precipitate the indirect increase of interdependence may stem from wholesaling–trading complex increments other than those associated with the direct expansion of large-city interdependence). Enlarged economic interaction between M_1 and other large centres is often preceded or accompanied by a widening of human spatial interaction between those places. This is so because of the frequent necessity for merchants or their agents to travel to the purchase-source or sales-destination city in order to bargain and consummate business transactions.

Each increase in commodity spatial interaction between M_1 and other leading mercantile cities contributes to spatial biases in the circulation of specialised information. (Business travel is not the sole source of these spatial biases. The expansion of interdependence between M_1 and other highly ranked cities can add to spatially biased information flows by inducing improvements in the quality, speed and frequency of transport and postal linkages between those centres; by causing a larger volume of interurban business mail; and by engendering a greater interurban movement

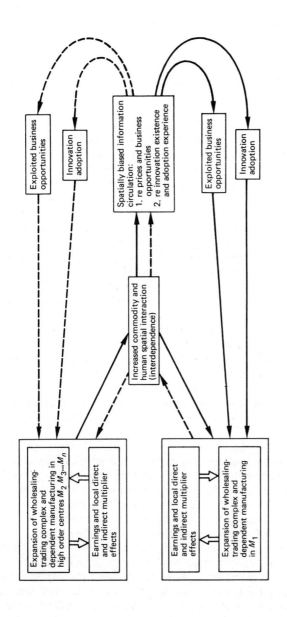

Figure 2 The feedback processes generating large-city rank stability (or the large-city accumulation of non-agricultural locational decisions) in the national and regional city-systems of the early nineteenth-century United States.

of commercially relevant newspapers via the mails and passenger and freight services).[2] Whatever their source, compounded spatial biases in the circulation of specialised information in turn lead to yet further large-city interaction and spatially biased information flows through one of two pairs of feedback loops (figure 2). The net impact of these two feedback sequences is a continued domination of the national or regional system of cities by the same large urban units; in other words, a continued concentration of non-agricultural locational decisions in already large cities.

One pair of feedback loops involves *spatially biased* information about market changes, prices and business opportunities in general. That is, information either originating in or entering the national (or regional) city-system at one large mercantile city has a greater probability of being early acquired and exploited by the entrepreneurs of another large mercantile city than by the businessmen of smaller cities within the system.[3] This is so because smaller cities have both fewer and less frequent contacts with M_1 and other large mercantile cities, and greater time lags from those places.[4] Should a major business opportunity (implicit locational decision) be exploited at one large mercantile city, for example, M_1, it will eventually be synonymous with an expansion of the local wholesaling–trading complex, employment opportunity additions, and population growth. For one of two reasons, this in turn leads both to increased interdependence with one or more other large mercantile cities and to reinforced spatial biases of specialised information circulation – (a) the previously unexploited opportunity directly involves another large mercantile city rather than a smaller city in the same national or regional city-system, and (b) the previously unexploited opportunity involves either a smaller city, or another national or regional city-system, but the consequent population growth in M_1 fosters a greater demand for locally consumed agricultural and manufactured goods normally acquired from or through one or more other large mercantile cities.

The second pair of feedback loops involves specialised information concerning either the existence of, or demand for, commercial, financial and industrial innovations, as well as information on the experience of those who have already adopted such innovations. Due to spatially biased information circulation, any innovation originating in or entering the city-system at one large mercantile city will have a significantly greater probability of being early (and multiply) adopted at other large mercantile cities than at smaller urban units within the system. That is, the adoption probability is lower at those smaller and medium-size places within the national or regional city-system which have either fewer and less frequent contacts with the initially accepting city, or greater time lags from that same city. (The chances of adoption in smaller cities will be especially low when the characteristics of a particular innovation are such that its successful application depends either on the fulfilment of large market, capital or labour-supply requirements, or on the local availability of external economies.) For one of two reasons the consequences of adoption at one large mercantile city (for example, M_1) are increased interdependence with other large mercantile cities and strengthened spatial biases in the circulation of specialised information — (a) single or multiple adoption of the innovation brings into being previously non-existent forms of interdependence between the national or regional city-system's largest units, and (b) innovation adoption in one large mercantile city brings local employment multiplier effects and population growth, which in turn breed a greater local demand for the agricultural and manufactured products generally imported from or via one or more other large mercantile cities.

Given the probabilistic quality of these feedback loops, any given business opportunity may be exploited — or any specific growth-inducing innovation may be adopted — in one, some or all of a city-system's leading centres. Hence, via the occurrence of business opportunity- and innovation-derived local employment multipliers of varying magnitude, the model allows for some adjustment in the population ratios of a city-system's largest units and perhaps even for some minor rank-shifting among them. More importantly, the probabilistic aspect of the feedback loops sometimes permit business opportunity exploitation or innovation adoption in lower-probability smaller and medium-size cities at the same time that exploitation is limited in other system units (including M_1 and other large mercantile cities). Thus, in accord with reality, small or medium-size cities can occasionally receive the telescoped economic stimulus necessary for relatively rapid progress through the urban size ranks.[5] Size-rank progress would be attributable to sizeable and temporally concentrated local employment multipliers, increased economic interaction with other cities, and a higher probability of business opportunity exploitation or innovation adoption at later dates.

The model diagrammed in figure 2 may be expanded upon, so as to include more explicitly all those interdependencies extending either between large mercantile cities and less populous hinterland and non-hinterland cities, or between urban pairs consisting of two medium- or small-sized cities. When this is done (figure 3), the entire process of early nineteenth-century city-system growth and development — or the entire locational accumulation of non-agricultural economic activities — can be synthesised in admittedly oversimplified terms.

III. CITY-SYSTEM GROWTH AND DEVELOPMENT IN ADVANCED ECONOMIES DURING THE 1970s

(1) THE INFLUENCE OF MULTILOCATIONAL ORGANISATIONS

The current process of city-system growth and development in advanced

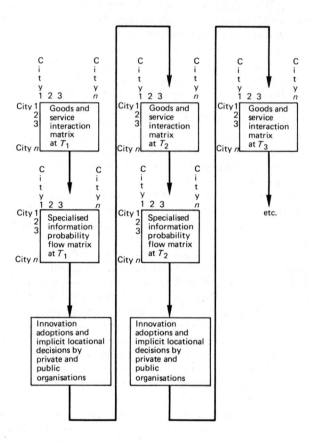

Figure 3 A simplified description of the growth and development process for an entire national or regional city-system. In the version of this model for the early nineteenth-century United States, the goods and service interaction matrix mostly involves the movement of agricultural commodities and simple manufactures, and locational decisions are reached by individual entrepreneurs rather than organisations. In the version of this model for advanced economies during the 1970s, the goods and service matrix mainly consists of: (1) goods that are involved in lengthy production or marketing systems associated with multilocational organisations; and (2) a wide range of services that are either provided by or to multilocational organisations, or move between spatially separated units of a single organisation (cf. footnote 6).

economies is largely associated with the explicit and implicit locational decision-making behaviour of multifunctional business and government organisations which simultaneously operate units at numerous locations. In terms of number of jobs provided, income generated and total revenues, the economy of every 'post-industrial' country is dominated by multi-locational corporations — whether or not of international scope — and government bodies.

The importance of the explicit and implicit locational decisions reached by multilocational organisations is reflected by the following simple observation. In each advanced economy, virtually all of the private-sector employment which is not directly under the control of multilocational corporations and firms is assignable to one of two categories: (a) single-establishment firms connected by backward or forward goods and service linkages to multilocational business and *government* organisations; and (2) single-establishment firms providing goods and services to members of the household sector, most of whom derive their income from private- and public-sector multilocational organisations.

Regardless of their multifunctional attributes, the multilocational organisations which dominate advanced economies are usually spatially structured along intentional or *de facto* hierarchical lines. At the national (or large-scale regional) level, the hierarchy normally consists of three or more tiers (such as national, regional, local). Each unit at a successively higher tier serves a successively larger area or number of places. A high degree of asymmetry usually becomes apparent when hierarchical spatial structures are compared with one another — especially in the private sector.

Varied evidence for the U.S.A., Canada, Great Britain, Sweden and elsewhere consistently indicates that asymmetrical spatial structures (along with lengthy production and marketing systems) contribute to a rather complex pattern of intraorganisational and interorganisational linkages between urban units (Pred, 1975b, 1976). More specifically, in the national and regional city-systems of contemporary advanced economies, the most significant aggregate economic interdependencies do not exist between large metropolitan complexes and their traditionally defined retail-trading, or central-place theory, hinterlands. Instead, the greatest volume of non-local economic transactions and specialised information contacts crisscrosses between nationally and regionally highly ranked metropolitan centres. Furthermore, the domestic intraorganisational and interorganisational linkages extending between a large metropolitan complex and smaller towns and cities outside its 'hinterland' are typically more important than the sum of those extending to all 'hinterland' places — regardless of population. Put otherwise, because of the asymmetrical spatial structure of multilocational organisations, whenever and wherever major new investment or activity expansion occurs some non-local multiplier effects are quite likely to appear at a nearby or *distant* large metropolitan complex.

(2) HEURISTIC MODEL

With the above skeletal observations on multilocational organisations in mind, the model presented for the early nineteenth century can be para-phrased in order to describe the present process of city-system growth in advanced economies.

Imagine a large metropolitan complex (M_1) situated within an advanced economy. Being in an advanced economy, all but a small portion of its on-going and recent population growth is in one way or another associated with the birth or expansion of job-providing activities belonging to multi-locational business and government organisations. Much of the growth pro-cess of the metropolitan complex is locally self-sustaining in a manner telegraphed by the lower left-hand portion of figure 4. The stripped-down local-growth submodel is also shown at the upper left of figure 4 as con-currently operating for other large metropolitan complexes of high national or regional rank $(M_2, M_3, \ldots M_n)$. In particular, each major increment or birth of organisational activity propagates *local* employment multiplier effects — both directly, through backward and forward linkages (locally implemented implicit locational decisions), and indirectly, as a result of employee income expenditures. Some of the activities benefiting from initial direct and indirect multiplier effects will call forth secondary local multiplier effects of their own. The combined impact of all these local multipliers most probably will sooner or later be an increase in population and the attainment or duplication of one or more local or regional thresh-olds. The surpassing of market thresholds eventually leads to the establish-ment or large-scale expansion of organisational units and another round of local-growth feedback. Additional rounds of local direct and indirect multi-plier effects are also likely to occur as a result of the investment of earnings from previous rounds in non-threshold activities, that is, organisational units which are not particularly sensitive to the scale of the local or regional market. Such a local ploughing back of earnings is apt to be stimulated by the increasingly complex *intra*urban network of organisational information exchange that accompanies urban-size growth (which, among other things, influences the perception of local opportunities); and the availability of 'localisation' and 'urbanisation' economies.

Although repeated iterations of the local-growth submodel are vital, the continued amassing of economic activities and population growth at M_1 and other large metropolitan complexes depends considerably on its organ-isational linkages and economic interaction with other leading centres. Each major increment or birth of organisational activity in M_1 not only increases the size of that complex, but also directly or indirectly engenders organisa-tional and economic interdependence, or interaction, with other large metropolitan complexes within the same regional or national city-system. This interdependence, by enhancing the magnitude of organisational activity in M_2, M_3, or M_n, contributes to the local-growth submodel of those metro-

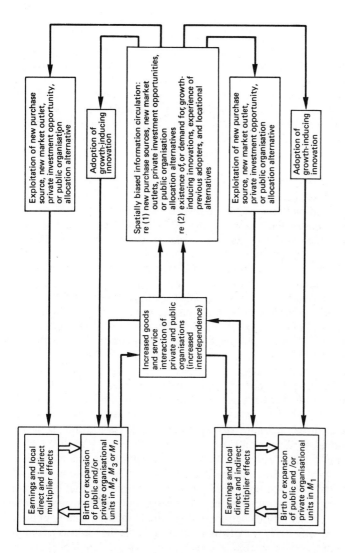

Figure 4 The feedback process of urban-size growth for large metropolitan complexes in advanced economies during the 1970s.

politan complexes and thereby yields them additional growth. Direct expansion of interdependence occurs when the initial major increase in organisational activity at M_1, through backward or forward goods and service linkages, causes interorganisational or intraorganisational *non-local* multipliers at M_2, M_3 or M_n.[6] Indirect growth of interdependence between M_1 and other large metropolitan complexes results when local direct and indirect multipliers at M_1 itself generate additional demands for goods and services from those complexes. Interdependence can also arise indirectly when the direct and indirect non-local multipliers propagated by M_1 at another major centre are reflexive, that is, they increase the demand for goods or services normally obtained at M_1. In the same manner, each major increment or birth of organisational activity in another large metropolitan complex, not only enhances the size of that complex, but is also capable of directly or indirectly producing organisational and economic interdependence with other major centres.

Each expansion of interdependence between any pair of large metropolitan complexes has a physical manifestation in the movement of goods and services (and monetary payments when interaction occurs on an *inter*-organisational basis). Each new or enlarged interurban goods and service linkage also has a parallel, or dual, flow of routine or non-routine specialised information. In addition, when subordinate organisational units are involved, increased goods and service interaction between two metropolitan complexes may, at least initially, be further accompanied by: (a) specialised information flows between those complexes and the head-office metropolitan complexes of the involved organisations; and (b) specialised information flows between the two headquarters centres. Whatever the case, each increment in goods and service interaction between M_1 and other large metropolitan complexes contributes to spatial biases in the availability of specialised information.[7] These spatial biases, in turn, through one of two pairs of feedback loops, generate additional interaction between major metropolitan complexes and, hence, additional spatial biases in the availability of specialised information (figure 4). As a consequence of these two feedback sequences, the same metropolitan complexes continue to dominate the national or regional city-system.

One pair of feedback loops is fuelled by *spatially biased* specialised information capable of affecting the implicit locational decision-making of multilocational organisations. More precisely, information that either comes into being or enters the city-system at one large metropolitan complex will have a higher probability of being early acquired, and non-locally exploited, in one or more other major metropolitan complexes than in less populous centres within the same system. This is largely owing to the fact that the aggregate non-routine organisational contacts of smaller cities with M_1 and other large metropolitan complexes are fewer and less frequent than those among M_1 and its size-group peers. Should an organisational unit in one large complex, for example, M_1, implement a major implicit locational decision, or exploit an opportunity, that involves another city, it quite likely will sooner or later result in local expansion of the organisation, new jobs, and some local population growth. For one of two reasons, this should be accompanied by both greater interdependence with one or more other highly ranked metropolitan complexes and strengthened spatial biases in the circulation of specialised information — (a) the major implicit locational decision directly involves another large metropolitan complex rather than an intermediately or lowly ranked urban unit in the same city-system; and (b) the major implicit locational decision involves either a smaller city, or another national or regional city-system, but the resulting local multipliers and population growth create an expanded organisational demand for goods and services customarily acquired from one or more other large metropolitan complexes.

The second pair of feedback loops is fed by specialised information regarding the existence of, or demand for, new product or service innovations, and other growth-inducing organisational innovations whose adoption often requires an explicit locational decision. This pair of feedback loops also involves specialised information concerning both the experience of previous adopters of particular innovations, and alternative locations to which a managerial unit of the adopting organisation may 'steer' diffusion. Once again, the spatial biases of innovation-relevant information circulation are such that any growth-inducing innovation perfected or introduced within the city-system at one major metropolitan complex has a probability of being adopted early and on a larger or multiple basis at other major complexes that is greater than the probability for smaller places within the system. Or, adoption probabilities are lower at those intermediately and lowly ranked cities which have fewer, less frequent and more costly[8] non-routine organisational contacts with the large metropolitan complex(es) where early acceptances have occurred. (However, if the innovation in question is a new manufactured item, and if standardised output becomes feasible, competition may sometimes force the adopting organisation to 'trickle down' production units to smaller cities where labour, tax or other cost savings are available.)[9] Through one of two mechanisms, organisational adoption at one large metropolitan complex (for example M_1) is inclined to bring increased interdependence with other large metropolitan complexes and the further entrenchment of spatial biases in the circulation of specialised information: (a) single or multiple organisational adoption of the innovation itself requires the establishment of new forms of interdependence between the city-system's largest metropolitan complexes;[10] (b) the local multiplier effects and population growth resulting from organisational adoption of an innovation in one large metropolitan complex create a greater demand within other local organisations for goods and services normally secured from other major centres.

Due to the probabilistic nature of the implicit and explicit locational decision feedback loops (Pred, 1973a), this model also permits: occasional rapid advances in population rank by small and medium-size cities; and some population-ratio modification and minor rank-shifting among the largest metropolitan complexes of a city-system.

Here too, the model under discussion may be amplified so as to more specifically take into account the entire complicated web of interdependencies which connects: (a) large metropolitan complexes with nearby and distant cities of small or medium size, and (b) pairs of intermediately and lowly ranked urban units with one another. When this step is taken, the entire process of current city-system growth and development in advanced economies can be summarised in terms that are once more admittedly oversimplified (figure 3).

IV. THE ROLE OF TRANSPORTATION NETWORK IMPROVEMENTS

Over forty years ago Bertil Ohlin (1933) once noted that the 'improvement of transport relations through a local concentration of economic activity where they are already good tends to concentrate population and production [or trade] still further'. The succession of transportation improvements that have occurred in advanced economies since the early nineteenth century have not transpired entirely haphazardly, that is only occasionally and randomly benefiting already existing major concentrations of economic activity. Instead, certain transportation network developments are describable in feedback process terms that provide further insight into the constantly repeated interplay between the geographical pattern of economic linkages existing at a given date as a result of implicit and explicit locational decisions, spatial biases in the circulation of specialised information, and new locational decisions, or new and expanded local and non-local linkages.

According to an empirically verified model formulated by Janelle (1969), increased economic interaction between large metropolitan centres calls forth transport improvements which, after an indefinite lag to allow for decision-making adjustments, encourages increased large-centre interaction to the detriment of smaller intervening cities.[11] More specifically, the non-local economic exchange of highly ranked centres where specialised private-sector or government job-providing activities are accumulating, 'leads to further demands for increased accessibility', or demands for more varied, more frequent, and faster transport services and routes (figure 5). (During the late nineteenth and early twentieth centuries, the pressure and capital for transport [railway] improvements often came from metropolitan based large-scale manufacturers interested in the preservation and extension of market areas. Under present conditions, transport-improvement demands may emerge due to the overextension of facilities, traffic congestion, organisational desires to more quickly obtain and distribute inputs and outputs, or a collective organisational desire to ease the non-local face-to-face exchange of specialised information). When these demands are satisfied

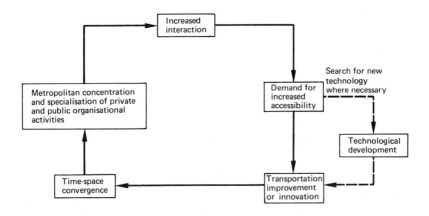

Figure 5 Feedback relationships connecting transportation improvements and economic interaction between the large metropolitan complexes of an advanced economy (modified from Janelle, 1969). The wording of the 'metropolitan concentration' cell, which refers to the multilocational organisations dominating present conditions, can be altered so as to refer to the decision-making units of earlier periods.

through transportation improvements or innovations, travel-time between places decreases and 'time-space convergence' occurs. The attributes of time-space convergence rates[12] are such that any particular transport improvement brings the greatest convergence, or accessibility gains, to the most distant centres served by the improvement; that is, normally to the large metropolitan places at either end of the route. Consequently, the highly ranked centres that initially generated demand now experience a further accumulation of job-providing activities and additional economic specialisation. (Concentration and specialisation in highly ranked centres is now primarily associated with the information-processing office and service activities of multilocational organisations, as opposed to manufacturing production 50 to 100 years ago, and wholesaling—trading activities in the early nineteenth century.) This is partly due to the internal scale economies and division of labour made possible by improved accessibility to other large centres and hinterland and non-hinterland smaller places; partly due to the possibility of spreading external agglomeration economies over wider areas or markets; and partly due to the expanded receipt of non-local specialised information. Finally, increased metropolitan concentration and specialisation is synonymous with increased non-local economic interaction, which thus paves the way for new transport-improvement demands and another cycle of the positive feedback process.

V. CONCLUDING REMARKS

Through juxtaposing two models of city-system growth and development, it has been contended that — despite great economic, technological and institutional changes — the underlying feedback processes influencing the location of non-agricultural economic activities in presently advanced economies have remained more or less the same since the early nineteenth century. Put differently, the existing locational distribution of non-agricultural economic activities in a given country or large region is but one of many possible outcomes resulting from a process of information feedbacks that is deeply rooted in the past.

Much research remains to be carried out in order to more precisely identify the means by which existing economic linkages and contact patterns influence the domestic implicit and explicit locational decision-making of multilocational organisations. Nevertheless, on the basis of what has been said, it may be speculated that a city-system information–circulation conceptualisation of implicit and explicit locational decisions has some utility for interpreting international activity allocation and trade among economically advanced countries. In other words, something may be gained by using such a framework as an interpretive supplement to the comparative advantage and other schema traditionally employed by economists. The urban networks of the United States and Canada are economically interwoven to such a degree that they may be regarded as a single system of cities. Because of the growing reliance of organisational units in different western European countries on one another for manufacturing inputs and specialised services, and because of the specific multinational characteristics of so many of the largest business organisations based in western Europe, it is also possible to regard the metropolitan areas of the post-industrial economies of western Europe as constituting a single system of cities. Given the increasing number of intraorganisational and interorganisational economic linkages being formed between variously sized metropolitan units in O.E.C.D. countries it may even be possible to speak of an emerging system of cities which spans all of the world's advanced capitalist economies.

If the possible usefulness of the proposed framework is admitted, then a number of questions become quite apparent. For example, to what extent does the international contact network and trading linkages of multinational corporations affect their input purchases and contract awards, or implicit locational decisions, within advanced economies? How does the spatial structure of multinational corporations affect the international movement of administrative and business services between advanced-economy metropolitan units? To what degree do international city-system interdependencies bias the diffusion of growth-inducing innovations from one advanced economy to another? Perhaps most importantly, in what ways are the feedback mechanisms within the international city-system related to the widening per capita income gap between 'post-industrial' and 'third-world' countries?[13]

NOTES

[1] This complex encompassed four major types of commercial activity: the coastal and interregional distribution of hinterland and local production; the hinterland and coastal redistribution of interregional and foreign imports; the foreign export of hinterland commodities; and the re-export of imported carrying-trade commodities. The relative importance of these four component functions varied over time and from city to city. Moreover, almost all mercantile-city manufacturing activities were either directly or indirectly linked to the wholesaling—trading functions of those places (Pred, 1966).

[2] There is extensive empirical evidence that between 1790 and 1840 there was a parallel development between large-city economic exchange and superior large-city access to specialised information. (Pred, 1973b.)

[3] These probabilities can be expressed in simple equations (Pred, 1973b).

[4] Prior to the diffusion of the electromagnetic telegraph, specialised information moved very slowly over distance. Thus, such information could be spatially biased by time lags as well as by contact network patterns.

[5] Data for a number of advanced economies consistently indicate that the variance in population growth rates, or size-rank stability, for urban units is inversely proportional to population class.

[6] Here, 'services' may also refer to those functions performed by a head office or other administrative, marketing or research unit for an elsewhere-located intraorganisational unit.

[7] For empirical evidence see Törnqvist (1970, 1973); and Goddard (1975).

[8] Non-routine contacts with large metropolitan complexes are apt to be more costly from intermediately and lowly ranked cities because of poorer travel connections and longer average transit times.

[9] Many of the largest metropolitan complexes of advanced economies have been losing their share of the more or less stable number of manufacturing production jobs (see, e.g., Berry, 1973). This trend, which is most pronounced among footloose, or transport insensitive, production units, is facilitated by the developments in telecommunications and computer technology which have weakened the need for proximity between organisational office units and the plants they control.

[10] The new interurban interdependencies may be *intra*organisational or *inter*organisational.

[11] The model presented in this section is a modified and abbreviated version of Janelle's schema. In addition to Janelle's own U.S. evidence, there is a wealth of historical and contemporary evidence on transport-route developments, suggesting the validity of his framework as well as the model summarised in figure 3.

[12] The average rate of 'time-space convergence' between any pair of urban places may be expressed as $TT_1 - TT_2 / Y_2 - Y_1$, where TT_1 and TT_2

are interurban travel times at two different dates, and Y_2-Y_1 is the time interval separating the two dates.

[13] The 'dual economy' phenomenon, and the widening economic gap between rich and poor nations, has resulted partly because the leading urban centres of poor countries have functioned primarily as outlying units of economically advanced national city-systems, rather than as the principal nodes of domestic city-systems. Or, underdeveloped countries lack truly integrated national city-systems. Until such systems emerge, the feedback processes described in this paper cannot operate; that is urban-economic growth cannot serve as the principal means by which new employment opportunities are spread throughout the national space.

REFERENCES

Aguilar, F., *Scanning the Business Environment* (New York: Macmillan, 1967).

Berry, B. J. L., *Growth Centers in the American Urban System*. 2 vols (Cambridge, Mass: Ballinger Publishing Co., 1973).

Cyert, R. M. and March, J. G., *A Behavioral Theory of the Firm* (Englewood Cliffs, N.J.: Prentice-Hall, Inc., 1963).

Goddard, J. B., *Office Location in Urban and Regional Development* (London: Oxford University Press, 1975).

Hägerstrand, T., *Innovation Diffusion as a Spatial Process* (with postscript and translation by A. R. Pred) (Chicago: University of Chicago Press, 1967).

Janelle, D. G., 'Spatial reorganization: a model and concept', *Annals of the Association of American Geographers*, 59 (1969), pp. 348–364.

Lasuén, J. R., 'Multi-regional economic development: an open-system approach', in T. Hägerstrand and A. R. Kuklinski (eds.), *Information Systems for Regional Development – A Seminar*, pp. 169–211. Lund Studies in Geography, Series B, 37 (1971).

Lasuén, J. R., 'Urbanization and development – the temporal interaction between geographical and sectoral clusters', *Urban Studies*, 10 (1973), pp. 163–188.

Lukermann, F., 'Empirical expressions of nodality and hierarchy in a circulation manifold', *East Lakes Geographer*, 2 (1966), pp. 17–44.

North, D. J., *The Process of Locational Change in Different Manufacturing Organizations*. Occasional Papers, No. *23*, Department of Geography, University College, London (1973).

Ohlin, B., *Interregional and International Trade* (Cambridge, Mass: Harvard University Press, 1933).

Pred, A. R., *The Spatial Dynamics of U.S. Urban-Industrial Growth, 1800– 1914: Interpretive and Theoretical Essays* (Cambridge, Mass: The M.I.T. Press, 1966).

Pred, A. R., 'The growth and development of systems of cities in advanced economies', in A. R. Pred and G. E. Törnqvist, *Systems of Cities and Information Flows: Two Essays*, pp. 1–82. Lund Studies in Geography, Series B, 38 (1973a).

Pred, A. R., *Urban Growth and the Circulation of Information: The United States System of Cities, 1790–1840* (Cambridge, Mass: Harvard University Press, 1973b).

Pred, A. R., 'Diffusion, organizational spatial structure, and city-system development', *Economic Geography*, 51 (1975a), pp. 252–268.

Pred, A. R., 'On the spatial structure of organizations and the complexity of metropolitan interdependence, *Papers of the Regional Science Association*, 35 (1975b), pp. 115–142.

Pred, A. R., 'The interurban transmission of growth in advanced economies: empirical findings versus regional planning assumptions', *Regional Studies*, 10 (1976), pp. 151–71.

Schon, D. A., *Technology and Change: The New Heraclitus* (New York: Dell Publishing Co., 1967).

Törnqvist, G. E., *Contact Systems and Regional Development*. Lund Studies in Geography, Series B, 35 (1970).

Törnqvist, G. E., 'Contact requirements and travel facilities: contact models of Sweden and regional development alternatives in the future', in A. R. Pred and G. E. Törnqvist, *Systems of Cities and Information Flows: Two Essays*, pp. 83–121. Lund Studies in Geography, Series B, 38 (1973).

Zaltman, G., Duncan, R. and Holbek, J., *Innovations and Organizations* (New York: John Wiley, 1973).

Comment
Gunnar Törnqvist

I. THE CITY-SYSTEM PERSPECTIVE AT NATIONAL LEVEL

The theme of this symposium is The International Allocation of Economic Activity. Questions concerning regional growth, location, agglomeration, natural resources, trade etc. will mainly be dealt with in an international or global perspective.

The lines of thought and basic approach presented in Allan Pred's paper may for many be new in this context. Allan Pred starts off from analyses of the structure and function of modern city-systems and the processes of change taking place through time in these systems. The relevant definition is: A city-system, or system of cities, can be defined as a national or regional set of urban or metropolitan units which are interdependent in such a way that any significant change in the economic activities, occupational structure, total income, or population of one member unit will directly or indirectly bring about some modification in the economic activities, occupational structure, total income, or population of one or more other set members.

Allan Pred's basic hypothesis is: For 150 years or more, in currently advanced economies, the process of city-system growth and development – and thereby the location of non-agricultural economic activities – has been dominated by the constantly repeated interplay between

(a) existing local and interurban economic linkages;
(b) spatial biases in the circulation of specialised information;
(c) accumulation of decisions directly and indirectly affecting the location and size of job-providing activities in the private and public sectors.

II. EMPIRICAL EVIDENCE

Allan Pred's model can be rooted in a number of empirical studies carried out in various countries in recent years. Findings can, for example, be drawn from studies done in the United States, Canada, Australia, Great Britain and perhaps above all in Sweden.[1] This research, which has been done by both economists and geographers, has been concerned with the following factors.

(1) CHANGES IN OCCUPATIONAL STRUCTURE

Experiments with the functional classification of employment which show marked shifts in employment from goods-handling to information-processing work functions.

(2) SPATIAL ORGANISATION OF ACTIVITY SPHERES

These are studies of the spatial organisation of, for example, corporations and production systems; and studies of an increasingly diversified regional division of labour and specialisation.

(3) INTERACTION AND LINKAGES

Studies of how workplaces and work functions, as well as entire urban regions, are linked together by goods transports, flows of payments, contacts via telecommunications and direct face-to-face contacts.

The main finding of these studies has been the great importance of information transmission and direct face-to-face contacts in the post-industrial society. Consequently, passenger transportation and time spent have become vital factors in studies of development potentials for different types of economic activities in various areas.

(4) TRANSPORTATION NETWORKS

Large-scale studies of how the structure of different kinds of transport networks affect transport and travel facilities in national and international city-systems.

III. APPLICATION

In recent years, the city-system approach has come to play a major role in regional planning and in the regional policies of various countries. In Sweden, for example, we often speak of a city-system policy instead of regional policy. One of the aims of this policy is given as the creation of a city-system that provides a fair distribution of facilities for different interest groups.[2]

IV. WHAT ABOUT THE INTERNATIONAL LEVEL AND THE GLOBAL PERSPECTIVE?

The theoretical model presented by Allan Pred in his paper is primarily intended to explain the growth and function of the city-system in the United States. The empirical studies on which it is based have mainly been concerned with individual nations and the national systems of cities. In addition, the examples are drawn from societies which can be described as post-industrial.

As Allan Pred suggests in conclusion, it is of interest to discuss how relevant these lines of thought are in an international and global perspective. I would like to have seen these concluding views discussed in more detail. The fact that the international aspect has been left in the background is my main criticism of Allan Pred's paper.

Can the city-system approach be used in studies of the problems facing the developing countries? Can studies of the interdependence in international city-systems give rise to new thinking in the field of international trade theory?

My own personal opinion is that there is every reason to catch hold of the basic ideas in Allan Pred's paper and consider these in an international perspective. We are in urgent need of comprehensive studies of spatial organisation, interdependence and contact patterns in international city-systems. Our knowledge in this field is very poor.

However, I should like to stress that I *do not* think that experience gained from studies of national city-systems is directly applicable at the international level. In many respects, international city-systems are probably more complex, more irregular and diversified than the comparatively well-structured national city-systems we are familiar with at present. The spatial biases, which Allan Pred has demonstrated as arising within a nation, are probably of a somewhat different nature at the international level. I am also convinced that these spatial biases play a much more prominent role in an international than in a national perspective. This is probably bound up with the fact that strong forces throughout the world have succeeded in their attempts to achieve greater regional equality at the national level. But on the other hand, efforts to promote equality at the international level have not been able to influence development to a comparable degree.

I shall try to explain what I mean by giving a few examples from studies now in progress.[3] These are far from complete and are on a limited scale, and it is too early to say whether findings will be generally valid.

V. NATIONAL BARRIERS

National frontiers often function as very effective barriers to, or filters for, all types of interaction. This is also true in fields where there are no tangible antagonisms between the nations which border on to one another – in Scandinavia, for instance. The studies which have been done of interaction between economic activities in border areas are telling examples. The volume of goods, personal contacts and telephone calls passing between closely located urban regions on each side of a national frontier is surprisingly small. Interaction is on much the same scale as if the regions were thousands of kilometres away from each other in the same country. These barriers to the exchange of information and the flow of goods may possibly be a consequence of one or several of the following conditions or factors (this is not a complete list, of course, but just a few examples):

(a) Commercial policy which includes tariffs and other restrictions on imports as well as taxes and subsidies on exports (see papers presented by Bela Balassa and Bertil Ohlin)
(b) Legislation and social conditions (see the paper by Bertil Ohlin)
(c) Language and cultural traditions
(d) Transport costs (in time and money)
(e) Institutional and organisational conditions within corporations and production systems
(f) Private information fields and information barriers.

Each of these types of conditions should be examined in an historical perspective.

Current studies show that the conditions listed under (e) and (f) are particularly important. It appears that national frontiers have an unexpectedly strong impact on the spatial organisation of activity spheres, on the direction and scale of flows of information and on the attitude of the individual to the world around him.

VI. SPATIAL PERSPECTIVES ON INDUSTRIAL ORGANISATION

As Allan Pred points out in his paper, large corporations and other organisations are often multilocational today. Moreover, a great deal of manufacturing is done in complex production systems, which consist of large assembly plants at the head of a very great number of subcontractors in several strata.

At the national level, the picture of these complex and spatially divided systems is fairly clear. Administration and information processing is concentrated on one or two of urban regions in the country concerned. Manufacturing and goods-handling – particularly the routine type – have a more scattered or dispersed locational pattern. Production at these manufacturing units is becoming more and more remote-controlled, that is to say, is controlled from a head office in one of the country's main control centres. In many countries, trends towards greater remote-control are just as obvious in the public sector. The development I describe here has meant that particularly the flows of information in modern societies are clearly focused, that is, business travel and telephone contacts are very much oriented towards these control centres. In many cases, goods transportation networks have a similar pattern, but the focusing is much less tangible.[4] Thus, if anything, the 'inner unity' of national economies has increased over time, as Bela Balassa writes in his paper (p. 232).

Studies now in progress show that national control centres are components in different supranational city-systems. In Europe there are at least two such supranational systems, one West European with about six or seven control centres, and one East European.[5]

Finally, a few examples in a more global perspective. Figure 1 shows the spatial organisation of a large corporate structure, a multinational corporation consisting of 135 firms spread throughout the world. The head office of the group is in London, and a great deal of management, administration and sales is run by units in the London area. Outside Great Britain, there are local head offices in each host country's largest city.

The extraction of raw materials and routine manufacturing is done in various parts of the world. The group employs about 17,000 workers in Kenya (see figure 2), about 28,000 in India and about 5000 in Argentina, just to mention a few examples.

It is interesting to note the information flows in this giant concern. They are probably very typical. There are very few contacts between local units with routine production and very little exchange of information. Contact flows are directed towards the local head office in each host country (see Nairobi, for example, in figure 2). There are no contacts or exchange of information between the local head offices themselves. Contact flows go via the head office in London. Flows of goods are also mainly directed towards Great Britain. Finished products are then distributed from Great Britain via local units to a West European market. It has not been possible to chart how the economic transactions are managed in this complex system.

In 1974, the eight corporations illustrated in figure 3 had close to 1400 registered subsidiaries and associated firms spread over 69 countries. Their strategic activities are within the agricultural sector of developing countries. Important products are thus vegetable oils, cocoa, coffee, tea, peanuts, animal feed and meat. Vertically integrated product-lines are common, and they regularly have substantial interests in functionally supplementing branches, such as packaging, printing, paper, chemicals, shipping, clearing/forwarding, insurance and engineering. These characteristics imply that the interaction flows generated by the corporations should be biased by intra-

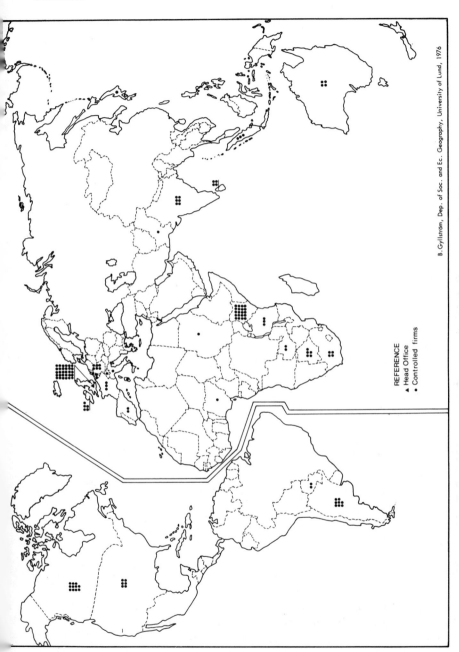

B. Gyllström, Dep. of Soc. and Ec. Geography, University of Lund, 1976

REFERENCE
▲ Head Office
• Controlled firms

Figure 1 Geographical distribution of subsidiary and associated firms controlled by a multinational, agrobased corporation (1974)

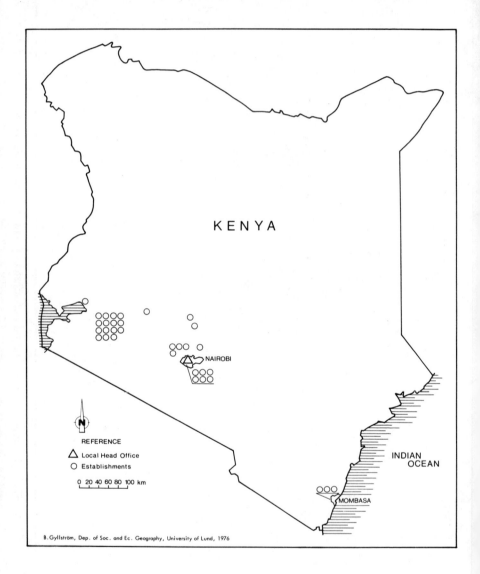

Figure 2 Geographical distribution of establishments controlled in Kenya by a multinational, agrobased corporation (1974)

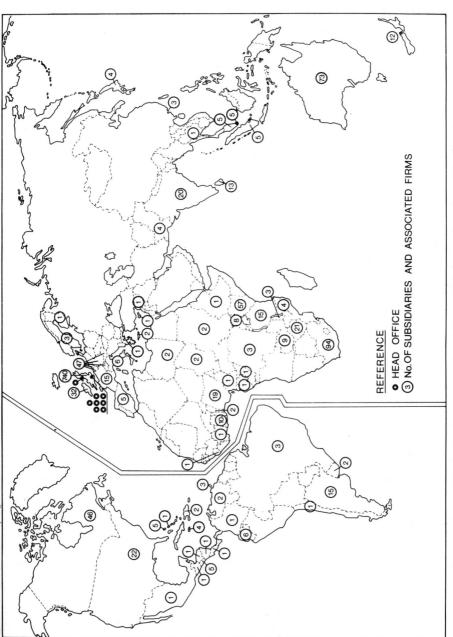

Figure 3 Subsidiaries and associated firms of eight agrobased, multinational corporations in 1974

organisational considerations. In more general terms, it supports the supposition that global networks of stratified information and material flows should follow from a parallel expansion of international trade and large corporate structures.[6]

At this point I therefore think it is very important to observe what John Dunning writes about 'internal transaction' in his paper. I also want to underline Akin Mobogunje's words that an important circumstance affecting the development and trade of developing countries is the overwhelming role of multinational corporations in mediating the pattern, scope and content of their international economic relations.

Many similar examples can be found in different parts of the world. Taken together these show that there are probably several overlapping global city-systems. The primate (nationally dominant) cities in Africa belong more to a West European city-system, the primate cities in South America to both a North American and a West European system, just to mention a few of these examples.[7]

VII. THE STRUCTURE OF THE TRANSPORTATION SYSTEM

It should be pointed out here that the transportation system plays an important role in regional development. As Allan Pred mentions in his paper, studies show that changes in the transport sector have tended to accentuate regional differences in various countries. In the case of Europe, at least, the differences at international level have also become more pronounced.

When it comes to routes, the frequency of services and trafficability, the largest nodes in national and international city-systems are best off. In the case of accessibility and range, the differences between large and small nodes tend to increase through time. This development is particularly pronounced in the case of passenger transportation on long distances (air travel and express train travel).

So we find that a small number of urban regions become particularly attractive to activities which are dependent on contacts. The concentration of these activities then results in the increased focusing and expansion of the transport system. This development is comparable to a causal cycle with interdependence and interaction between the location of economic activities and the gradual expansion of the transport system. The question of what is cause and effect in this process is much the same as the question of which came first, the chicken or the egg?

VIII. INFORMATION SPACE

I shall conclude my comments by discussing a question I think is very important —.this concerns the role of information in the process of regional development. I know that Allan Pred holds much the same views as I do on this subject, even if he did not go into any details on this point in his paper.

How do decision-makers in corporations and public authorities and so on interpret the world around them? How much all-round information have they about their surroundings?

There are plenty of studies of how individuals see their environment in a geographical perspective. These pictures are usually called 'mental maps' in Anglo-Saxon literature. Other concepts are 'environmental image' and 'cognitive space'. Studies have been done in differing environments in various parts of the world.[8] These studies reveal that people often have a very limited and usually distorted picture of their surroundings; distorted in the sense that it diverges from the actual, measurable conditions (cf. 'cognitive imperfections' in the paper presented by John Dunning). The bias and distortions become the more pronounced the greater the area under review. We are fairly well acquainted with our immediate surroundings, but even at a national level our knowledge becomes very limited. At the global level, the geographical picture we have of our environment is extremely confined and fanciful. Studies now being done show that this is also very true of accomplished decision-makers at all levels of society.

The mental maps are built up gradually by direct and indirect information. The first, which presupposes that we make our own observations, is the most important. Via mass media the individual gets information which at the national level is stamped by the fact that the mass media, like other information processing activities, are concentrated to large control centres. At the international level, the pictures individuals have of the world vary greatly according to the countries and the environments in which they have grown up.

The main factor which seems to influence the picture decision-makers have of the world around them is the sphere of information they are concerned with in their jobs. People with the same kind of jobs often have fairly similar pictures of their environment. In other words, the mental map is very much a product of the decision-maker's own contact network and his own pattern of movement when discharging his duties.

It is reasonable to assume that a decision-maker's mental maps affect the strategical decisions and the daily routine decisions made in a corporation, other organisations and political bodies. *The hypothesis thus is that information flows and contact networks, via decision-makers' mental maps, greatly influence various kinds of decisions, intentionally or unintentionally.* These decisions in turn often affect the transactions which can be measured in the form of flows of goods and flows of payments, for instance. If this hypothesis is correct, it means that the geographer's studies of information space are of interest to the theory of international trade and other theories affecting the international allocation of economic activity.

NOTES

[1] See references in Allan Pred's paper.

[2] Swedish Government Official Reports (Statens Offentliga Utredningar, SOU) not available in English.

[3] 'The Oresund Project', studies of the spatial organisation of activity spheres, interaction and linkages in areas around the border strait (the Sound) between Denmark and Sweden.

[4] See Törnqvist, G., Spatial Organization of Activity Spheres, in H. Swain, R. D. MacKinnon (eds.), *Issues in the Management of Urban Systems*, IIASA, Schloss Laxenburg, Austria, 1975.

[5] Studies on the European city-system (forthcoming).

[6] Gyllström, B., *Spatial Impacts of the Formal Organization of Production Systems in Underdeveloped Countries* (Ph.D. thesis, forthcoming) (Department of Social and Economic Geography, University of Lund).

[7] Gyllström, B., *On Organizations, Production Systems and Regional Planning in Underdeveloped Countries* (Department of Social and Economic Geography, Lund, 1976); and Pedersen, P. O., *Urban-regional Development in South America. The Process of Diffusion and Integration* (Monton, 1974).

[8] See presentation and references in Gould, P. and White, R., *Mental Maps* (Harmondsworth and Baltimore: Penguine Books, 1974); Gould, P., *People in Information Space* (Lund Studies in Geography, Ser B., No. 72, Lund, 1975).

5 Location Theory, Agglomeration and the Pattern of World Trade*

Walter Isard

I. INTRODUCTION

When Professor Ohlin invited me to present a paper to this conference, he asked me to discuss agglomeration economies, particularly as they are related to the advantages of being a firstcomer, or a latecomer. Hence you have a paper which emphasises a lot of good, old-fashioned location theory — aimed at exposing some of these advantages. I use concepts such as isodapanes and margin lines. But I imagine that a more fundamental reason for my being here is to be involved in a continuing discussion on the interrelations of trade and location theory — whether location theory is a special case of trade theory, whether trade theory is just a special case of a general location theory, or whether they are one and the same thing. My opinion is that 'realistic' trade theory and 'realistic' location theory are one and the same thing. They are as the two sides of the same coin. Flows of goods, factors (labour and capital) and ideas are between locations. To be able to fully explain these flows, we necessarily must come to know and simultaneously explain what exists at these locations. Or, to be able to fully explain what exists at a set of interacting locations, we must come to know and simultaneously explain the flows of goods, factors and ideas among these locations.

Let me develop some of my ideas more extensively. It seems to me there are certain basic primitives for us in examining the question of international allocation of economic activities. Among others they are

   (a) the distribution of productive factors — labour, capital, mineral and all other relevant resources among different nations;
   (b) physical and other distance, and transport cost as a function of distance;
   (c) that relative immobility of these factors and resources which goes beyond transport cost and which may reflect social, cultural,

*Research for this paper was supported by National Science Foundation grant P 251018.

ideological and other forces;

(d) production functions which may very among nations;

(e) scale economies in production, and externalities due to localisation, urbanisation and other types of agglomeration economies;

(f) behaving units with preference and payoff functions (producers, consumers, traders, nations, multinational enterprises);

(g) time as affecting technology, tastes and other exogenous and endogenous processes; and

(h) commercial policy as reflecting different political, social and other values and institutions among nations.

Now it is clear that both 'realistic' trade and location theories have and must consider all these and other factors. But then it is also clear that if we are to move in the direction of obtaining probing insights for effective trade *and* location policy, we must abstract from many of these factors in view of our limited intellectual capacity to conduct complex analysis. Accordingly there must, be and are, specialised theories, such as that 'pure' trade theory associated with the 2 x 2 models of two nations with given and different factor endowments. Such theory frequently simplifies by taking the transport cost between two nations as fixed, by abstracting from scale and other agglomeration economies, time, multinationals, and so forth. In contrast stands specialised location theory, such as that employed in this paper, which places major emphasis on transport costs as a variable and agglomeration economies while abstracting from exchange rate variation, the balance of payments constraint and other forces. Both these specialised theories are extremely useful for developing effective policy, as well as a number of other specialised theories. My point is that there are basically no inherent differences among different trade and location theorists. There are just differences among these theorists when they choose to work with different assumptions. Yet at the same time we should recognise that each theory could be still more realistic and effective if each could be extended (broadened) to include some of the strong analyses of these other theories, without sacrificing depth of analysis. We do need to remove at least some of the isolation among different groups of theorists which has characterised the last three decades. I trust that this will be one of the outcomes of this conference.

Against this background, I shall proceed with the specific task assigned to me. In section II which follows, I shall define agglomeration economies and then present in very elementary fashion some of the basics of agglomeration analysis, with emphasis on agglomeration at cheap factor (labour) locations. In section III I shall speak of a case study relating to agglomeration analysis in practice, namely the industrial complex development in Puerto Rico. In section IV I shall discuss the advantages of being a firstcomer or a latecomer, with emphasis on scale economies and technological development. In section V I shall briefly discuss cheap environmental locations and their implications for new agglomerations in the future and the future pattern of world trade. In section VI, I shall make some general projections and concluding remarks about the world pattern of economic activity and trade and relevant methodology.

II. DEFINITION AND WEBERIAN THEORY

Following Ohlin, Hoover has neatly classified agglomeration (deglomeration) economies as follows:

(a) *Large-scale economies within a firm*, consequent upon the enlargement of the firm's scale of production at one point.

(b) *Localisation economies* for all firms in a single industry at a single location, consequent upon the enlargement of the total output of that industry at that location.

(c) *Urbanisation economies* for all firms in all industries at a single location, consequent upon the enlargement of the total economic size (population, income, ouput, or wealth) of that location, for all industries taken together.

The reader may refer to the standard literature for a detailed discussion of agglomeration (deglomeration) forces.[1]

Agglomeration theory in essence begins with Weber (1909). To state his basic theory succinctly, suppose there are three units of production putting out a like product, located as in Figure 1 at P_1, P_2 and P_3. Each

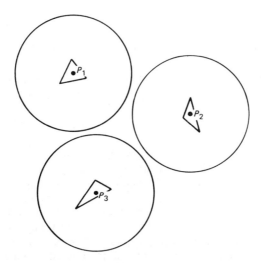

Figure 1 Non-intersecting critical isodapanes: no agglomeration

location is a point of minimum transport cost for its respective unit in assembling required raw materials and transporting the finished product to the unit's market. Around the location of each unit are drawn the unit's locational triangle and critical isodapane. In this situation, the critical isodapane for a unit of production is that locus of points for each of which transport costs in assembling the raw materials and shipping the finished product to the market exceed the corresponding transport costs associated with the optimal transport point for that unit by a constant amount. This amount is taken to be equal to the agglomeration economies (primarily localisation economies) that would be realised by that unit were it associated with other units in an effective agglomeration. In figure 1 the critical isodapanes do not intersect. Agglomeration is infeasible. In contrast stands the situation depicted by figure 2 where these same three

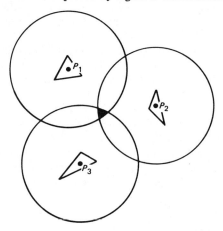

Figure 2 Intersecting critical isodapanes: agglomeration

units are closer to one another. Here their critical isodapanes do intersect. À la Weber, agglomeration will take place at a site within the common segment which is shaded.

At this point I do not wish to go into the discussion by Weber and subsequent theorists on the question of identifying that point within the shaded area (the agglomeration set), or even outside it, which is optimal or which will be realised as the point of agglomeration.[2] Rather I wish to go to a next question, namely, the question of the deviation of location to a cheap factor location, that is a location at which a factor is, because of certain immobilities or relatively large transport cost or both, significantly lower in cost than at a typical optimal transport (minimum transport cost) point. For example, let this be a cheap-labour location, L, as depicted in figure 3. We now ask to what extent will the units of production at P_1, P_2, P_3, be deviated to the cheap-labour location L.

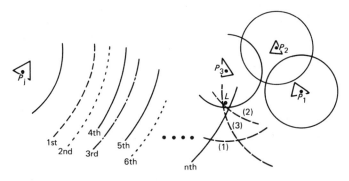

Figure 3 Critical isodapanes and agglomeration at a cheap-labour location

(a) To begin to answer this question we first construct around the location P_i of any unit i ($i = 1, 2, 3$) its critical isodapane with respect to the cheap-labour location L. See the right-hand side of figure 3, ignoring for the moment the centre and left-hand side. The critical isodapane in this situation is that locus of points for each of which the additional transport costs in assembling the raw materials and in shipping the finished products to the market when compared to P_i just equals the labour cost savings per unit of output if unit i were located at L. In the diagram presented only one unit of production, namely unit 3, will shift to L, which lies within unit 3's critical isodapane, but not within the critical isodapanes of units 1 and 2.

(b) Interject agglomeration economies. Suppose the agglomeration economies that can be realised if all three locate at the same location are $2.00 per unit of output. Then to take into account both cheap labour and agglomeration economies we need to construct for each unit an adjusted critical isodapane − a first adjusted critical isodapane − the dashed lines of the figure. Now we see that L lies within the first adjusted critical isodapanes of all three units of production. Hence each unit of production would find it profitable to deviate and agglomerate at L if all were to do so.

(c) Consider the possibility of replacement deposits − that is of the use by a unit of production of new raw material sources closer to L, or from which raw materials can be obtained more cheaply by a unit at L, than when that unit of production is located at its optimal transport point. To consider this factor and others to be noted, let us now focus our attention on unit of production j whose optimal transport point is P_j at the extreme left of figure 3. Around it we have constructed the critical isodapane re the cheap-labour location L − the solid line − and the first adjusted critical isodapane − the dashed line. Now we can construct a second adjusted critical isodapane to take into account the fact that it would use a source or raw material deposit closer to L than it currently uses if it were agglomerated at L with the other units.[3] We see that unit j is not yet motivated, in this relatively simple framework, to deviate to L.

(d) The presence of cheap labour at L in general will induce factor substitution, that is the substitution of cheap labour for other factors in production, leading to a still greater gain from agglomeration at L. We indicate this by the third adjusted critical isodapane re unit j.

(e) Production at the cheap-labour location L may entail certain dis-advantages. For example, unit j may find fuel costs higher there than at P_j; water costs too, may be higher, but taxes may be less. So we need to adjust the analysis for j to recognise all these other cost differentials (and factor substitutions and the like which they imply). Suppose on net these are disadvantages for j. Thus the fourth adjusted critical isodapane, which takes into account these factors as well as all those already mentioned, lies closer to j than the third does.

(f) As firms 1, 2 and 3 operate at point L and as other activities locate at L to serve the workers at L (in firms 1, 2 and 3, and in their own activities), additional market for each unit of production located at L (or that would be located at L) comes to exist, leading to additional profits through decreasing average delivery costs per unit product. This leads to a fifth adjusted critical isodapane.

(g) Additional economies may be associated with import substitution at L as the population there increases. As firms 1, 2, 3 and perhaps j and others locate at L, new enterprises find it profitable and also possible to produce at lower cost some of the commodities imported from elsewhere. If these commodities are also inputs into firms 1, 2, 3 and j, then additional savings are possible in time by location at L via 'backward linkage' — a factor akin to that of replacement deposits. Hence we obtain a sixth adjusted critical isodapanè, based on anticipated growth.

(h) With time, additional agglomeration economies may be anticipated, going well beyond localisation economies and encompassing the full range and diversity of urbanisation economies. For example, it may be reasonable to anticipate, because perhaps of the centrality position of location L, that a number of enterprises might locate there which would use the output of firms 1, 2, 3 and j in their production processes — thereby leading to still greater profits through decreasing still more average delivery costs per unit product. Such anticipated 'forward linkages', coupled with all kinds of local income and employment multiplier effects (in part anticipatable via input-output methodology — see Isard, 1975a, chapter 7) and the emergence of perhaps a wide range and diversity of service activities characteristic of urban-industrial agglomerations may lead the nth adjusted critical isodapane to be as indicated in figure 3. Under such circumstances, it would then be 'rational' for firm j to locate at L, thereby adding to the snowballing agglomeration process that might be set in motion there.

We have thus far presented, in an oversimplified step-by-step manner, one scenario which identifies various factors which contribute to agglomeration economies. More sophisticated statements are available elsewhere, which also include the basic factor of scale economies to be considered later. The important point to be made is that agglomeration does affect significantly the location of economic activity and hence the movement of goods between locations whether these locations are within several regions of a nation, or within the nations of a world region composed of many nations, or within the world itself. Their major significance has been attested to by the past — for example, in the development of basic steel and steel-fabricating activity at relatively few concentrated locations in the world which has strongly affected the pattern of world trade — and will be in the future — for example, as is apparent when we project major nuclear fuel development or nuclear complexes with which major agglomeration economies will be associated on account of required security measures and control of radiation hazards, to name just a few elements.

III. AGGLOMERATION ANALYSIS IN PRACTICE

It is one thing to talk of theory such as agglomeration theory or the related theories such as growth pole analysis. It is another thing to speak of agglomeration in practice. It is in connection with the latter that I want to say a few words about the story of the industrial complex development in Puerto Rico — to deepen our perspective.

In presenting the Puerto Rican study (Isard, Schooler and Vietorisz, 1959) it should be kept in mind that we can expect many similar developments among the third world nations — which in at least a few will be gigantic as it may well turn out to be in Puerto Rico. The implications for a changed pattern of world trade are then obvious. The second point to be kept in mind is that, unlike the simple theoretical structure in the previous section, I must introduce scale economies as well as localisation and urbanisation economies because I am in fact dealing with a situation of reality and cannot abstract from it. As I have already indicated, because of space limitation on this paper, I have postponed the discussion of scale economies until the next section.

As many third world countries are today, Puerto Rico in 1950 was a region of extreme poverty. At that time we were called in to conduct research by the Economic Development Administration (E.D.A.) of Puerto Rico. This Administration desired to avoid a one-industry region based on cheap labour, and the typical one-industry instability and vulnerability associated with fly-by-night firms. It sought basic economic development of a long-run competitive character that could spark a 'takeoff'.

It was clear after much thinking and examination of previous research that no isolated manufacturing activity by itself could be profitably located in Puerto Rico except in the cheap labour-oriented directions considered undesirable for further development. Hence, having in mind the various types of agglomeration economies noted in the literature (only some of which have been mentioned), we had to think of ways of putting together sets of operations into industrial complexes meaningful for Puerto Rico. We defined an *industrial complex as a set of activities occurring at a given location and belonging to a group (subsystem) of activities which, because of technical, production, marketing and other linkages, generates significant economies to each activity when spatially juxtaposed.* Given that Puerto Rico had no resources, it was extremely difficult to identify any meaningful industrial complex. We had to look around for resources that were close by — the nearest was Venezuelan oil at a distance of 965 km (600 miles) by water. We then considered oil-refining together with fertiliser production as a possible import substitution activity, since fertiliser could be produced through several stages from the gas streams of an oil refinery and since fertiliser imports into Puerto Rico dominated the import list. However, we had to add on synthetic fibres which though contrary to the objective of avoiding dependence on cheap labour industries provided in fact the only hope to obtain something definitely profitable from Puerto Rico. To oil-refining, synthetic fibres and fertiliser-production there was further added the diverse petrochemical operations required at intermediate stages.

Those of us who know the great variety of ways to go from oil through petrochemicals to final products recognise the tremendous number of complexes that could be established as technically feasible. Our problem was to isolate from the very large number of technically feasible complexes one or a few for Puerto Rico that could stand competition from the mainland and other world regions, and that could operate profitably. Given limited resources for research, we arrived at several useful criteria to guide us through the maze of possibilities

(a) We recognised that in operating any one plant, such as an oil refinery, there would most likely be scale economies. We knew that in most cases we could not achieve the full-scale economies in Puerto Rico because of small markets there and because of the large capital investments that would be involved. But we also knew that we would have to operate the plant at a level that would capture a large part of the available scale economies if we were to have any chance of finding an economically feasible complex. Thus, for each activity we set up a minimum plant size for being included in a complex. Of course, except for fertilisers, the output from a minimum-size plant in an activity would be above any conceivable demand level in Puerto Rico itself.

(b) We required that there be an end product which would use a very large amount of the cheap needlework labour of Puerto Rico. Because of the decided advantage it had in the costs of this resource, the more such labour could be used, the more likely we could find a profitable complex for Puerto Rico. We found that synthetic fibres required the greatest amounts of such labour, generally speaking. So we almost always included the production of synthetic fibre in any complex examined.

(c) We recognised that private mainland business (on which Puerto Rico would have to depend for substantial capital investment) would find an operation less risky if its outputs were products whose mainland markets were growing at a faster rather than a slower rate. Hence, we considered the production of only those synthetic fibres for which demand was growing rapidly in the United States in the 1950s and which was expected to continue into the 1960s.

(d) We required that, where technically possible, no byproducts should be wasted. Accordingly, we introduced the commodity LPG (liquified petroleum gas) as one to be produced (and sold on the local market) from the unused gas streams and liquid fractions of the refinery.

(e) In order to spark industrialisation, we almost always required that any complex considered be a 'full' complex, in the sense that it contained the full range of activities in going from the refinery to fertilisers on the one hand, and from the refinery to the synthetic fibre endproducts on the other. In this way, we hoped to achieve maximum stimulus for development of entrepreneurship, management, and a pool of labour, with a diversity of key skills. Of course, we had to recognise that a few items might need to be imported from the mainland, because scale economy and other considerations would make production in Puerto Rico exceedingly costly.

With all these and other criteria in mind we began testing and experimenting with diverse complexes. I shall not go through the details of the analysis on (a) how we derived total input requirements; (b) how we developed comparative costs between a Puerto Rican location and the most efficient mainland location pattern (the Gulf Coast with synthetic fibre operations in Tennessee); (c) how we calculated location cost differentials by commodity; (d) how we handled linear relations on the one hand, and non-linear on the other; (f) how we adjusted for different factor proportions and process mixes that would be used as well as for different mixes of product that would be produced; (g) how we developed the framework so that each decision-maker could put in his best estimates of relevant labour cost differentials, scale disadvantages and other items on which there might be great differences of opinion among businessmen and political leaders. We derived a set of tables such as table 1, and we concluded 'for at least a limited type of development, the advantages of a Puerto Rico location with regard to a relatively fully integrated industrial complex are clearcut. Exactly how extensive this development should be — under favourable circumstances it could be quite extensive — and what its

TABLE 1 OVERALL NET ADVANTAGE OR DISADVANTAGE OF A PUERTO RICO LOCATION, IN $/YR, BY TYPE PROGRAM* (ON THE BASIS OF'MODERATE' SCALE DISADVANTAGE)

Program	(1) Transport Cost Disadvantage (approximate)	(2) Advantage on Textile Labour	(3) Disadvantage on Chemical and Petroleum Labour	(4) Overall Net Advantage: Identical Complex Comparison	(5) Scale and/or Process Disadvantages: Fibre and Fertiliser Production	(6) Adjusted Net Overall Advantage or Disadvantage
Dacron A	− 263,000	+ 3,963,000	− 2,229,000	+ 1,471,000	− 1,160,000	+ 311,000
Dacron C	− 339,000	+ 3,962,000	− 2,226,000	+ 1,397,000	− 1,909,000	− 512,000
Orlon B	− 608,000	+ 3,986,000	− 2,329,000	+ 1,049,000	− 2,017,000	− 968,000
Orlon J	− 565,000	+ 3,960,000	− 2,217,000	+ 1,178,000	− 708,000	+ 470,000
Dynel A	− 760,000	+ 4,046,000	− 2,590,000	+ 696,000	− 2,916,000	− 2,220,000
Dynel F	− 437,000	+ 4,000,000	− 2,390,000	+ 1,173,000	− 1,445,000	− 272,000
Nylon A	− 457,000	+ 4,055,000	− 2,624,000	+ 974,000	− 2,543,000	− 1,569,000
Nylon G	− 772,000	+ 3,974,000	− 2,275,000	+ 927,000	− 335,000	+ 592,000

*All data rounded to the nearest $1,000.
Source: W. Isard, Methods of Regional Analysis (Cambridge: M.I.T. Press, 1960), p. 395.

specific form should take obviously depend on a host of subsidiary factors which fall outside the scope of this study' (see Isard, Schooler and Vietorisz (1959), page 215).

It has in fact turned out that by 1973, some 7000 jobs had come to exist in the petrochemical sector. Moreover, other new jobs had been created, though some of the strong linkages anticipated had not materialised. But much more important is the drastically new industrial psychology that has come about. Businessmen are confident about Puerto Rico's capability for engaging in industry on a competitive basis, and thus are vigorous in their pursuit of further opportunities. Thus, one can definitely state that the impact was positive, and that successful economic development was generated, primarily by the conjunction of agglomeration economies and cheap labour.[4]

IV. THE ADVANTAGES OF BEING A FIRSTCOMER OR A LATE-COMER

We have just completed a summary of a case study of an industrial complex development which has had major impact upon Puerto Rico. Without question there are going to be numerous other industrial complexes, or the equivalent, developed throughout the world; and many non-economic factors – political, social and cultural – which will govern subsidies provided, the setting of prices and quotas, etc. will greatly alter the economically efficient pattern based on narrow concepts of economists. Undoubtedly there will be major developments in all parts of the world especially in the underdeveloped regions so that the pattern of trade can be expected to change greatly. But before we go into this, let us consider agglomeration in a more dynamic framework and in particular to consider the advantage of being first and the advantage of being last.

The advantage of being first can be best illustrated by a figure first developed by Hoover for a very simple situation. Suppose there exists a producer located at A at the right-hand side in figure 4 with a typical U-shaped average cost curve as indicated in the left-hand side of figure 5. Suppose consumers are fairly uniformly distributed along the line AR and that each consumer comes to A to buy the goods produced by the firm there. Suppose, too, that the producer follows the practice of average cost pricing.[5] If the producer at A were to supply the needs of the consumer at A only, and if that consumer purchased only one unit, the producer's average cost would be AK, and that would be the price he would charge the consumer at A. However, other consumers not at A purchase from the producer. Suppose these consumers were to come from as far away as L, and suppose sales to them and output are such under average cost pricing that the average costs owing to economies of scale fall

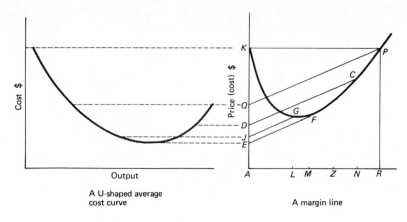

Cost $ | Output

A U-shaped average
cost curve

Price (cost) $ | A margin line

Figure 4

to AJ; then so would the factory price.[6] Adding transport costs (borne by
the consumer) to the average cost AJ yields for the stretch AL a delivered
price-line JG whose vertical height at any point is the delivered price to
the corresponding consumer along stretch AL; JG is also a transport
gradient line since it indicates how transport costs on a unit of product
rises as distances from A increases.[7]

In figure 4, sales under average cost pricing are taken to correspond to
that output at which average costs fall to the minimum AE when consumers
come from as far away as M. At this output, the derived delivered price-
(transport gradient) line is at its lowest level. For all other outputs, average
costs (factory price). Hence the delivered price-line are higher. For
example, if A's market is enlarged to AN, average costs turn out to be AD;
and the transport gradient line starts from point D and parallels EF at a
higher level. The delivered price to the consumer at N is AD plus transport
cost, or *in toto CN*.

If points K, G, F and C are connected with other points, each of which
by its vertical height represents for a given size market area the delivered
price to the consumer on the edge (boundary), the curve $KFGC$ is obtained;
Hoover has designated this a margin line. It indicates how delivered price
at the edge of the market varies with the geographical extent of the
market. It is evident that the margin line changes in form as the pricing
practice at the factory changes.

Note that the stretch from A to R might be said to correspond to the
producer's natural market area when competition is absent and under
average cost pricing. For all points within this stretch, the scale economies
(in producing for the consumers contained by the entire stretch) outweigh
the diseconomy of transport; and at point R scale economies just equal
the diseconomy of transport. If the market were extended beyond R, the

scale economies (which owing to rising marginal cost are less than KQ) would fail to match transport costs (which exceed KQ) in reaching locations beyond point R. If consumers beyond R wish to consume, they can either produce for themselves (assuming free entry), or purchase from another producer.[8]

(There are a whole host of issues which should be discussed concerning the possible relevant pricing practices for different situations and the dependence of the spatial pattern and size of consumer demand on the pricing system. These are particularly important in a world trade context, since pricing systems often reflect specific cultural practices. Space limitations, however, preclude such discussion.)

Alternatively, let us think of A as a place where there are many producers of a like product operating under conditions of pure competition who are located there because of externalities, say localisation economies. Again, let consumers be arrayed along the stretch AR. Assume that each producer when producing in a location by himself confronts a U-shaped average cost curve whose minimum point corresponds to an average cost as great or greater than AK. However, when producers are spatially juxtaposed, they gain from localisation economies, so that the minimum points of their like average cost curves fall from AK to AJ to AE (see figure 4) and then rise to AD and AQ as the stretch of consumers in their market, under average cost pricing, grows from A to AL to AM to AN and to AR, respectively, and once there develops historically at a location, say A, two or more producers of the same product serving a continuous market stretch starting from A and extending to the right to Z (where $AZ < AR$), it is unprofitable for any one producer at A to consider relocating elsewhere by himself to serve any of the demand generated by consumers in the stretch. When the market stretch become as large as AR, then one of the firms agglomerated at A may find a move to location R to be a non-losing relocation.

Or, imagine an industrial complex at A, where in general average cost pricing is pursued, and where consumers of its diverse products are arrayed from A to the right. *In general* the same kind of argument can be put forth. *In general* it would not be feasible for a producer or subset of producers *to begin to produce* elsewhere as long as the market stretch fell short of AR. *In general*, the agglomeration (scale, localisation and urbanisation) economies achievable at A would lead existing producers at A to choose to remain at A, and would lead all new producers to locate at A for any market stretch $AZ < AR$. When the market stretch reaches the size of AR, then production might begin at R for the market at R. In short, the existence of production at A precludes production elsewhere in any market stretch AZ for $AZ < AR$.

This type of analysis points up the advantage of being first. Note that the results under symmetry assumptions are independent of whether production first started at A or at R; and with certain extensions of the analysis, at any one intermediate point.

Now with the passage of time there are two important effects to consider. One is technological advance in producing the product or products under consideration. The other is the growth in demand density at all points along the line *AR*. (This latter could reflect technological progress say in agriculture or other economic pursuits providing income to consumers along the stretch *AR*.) Accordingly if we were to imagine that the effective demand of consumers was so increased by year *t'* that sales corresponding to the output at which average cost is minimum (for the firm, or set of small firms producing a like product, or industrial complex) were now obtainable, under average cost pricing, from consumers in the substretch *AM'* (see figure 5) rather than *AM*, then the margin line in effect would have shifted down and to the right from *KFTP* to *KF'UP'*.[9]

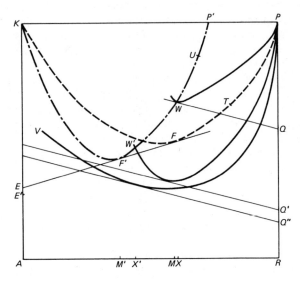

Figure 5 Margin lines for agglomerations at *A* and *R*

And with further technological progress and time, the margin line would continue to shift down and to the right.

With the shift of the margin line to the new positions, we can now see from figure 5 that it becomes feasible for a producer, or a few small producers of a like product, or for an industrial complex to begin operations at *R*. At the start, and for quite some time, operations cannot be expected to reach their optimal level. For example at time *t'* operations at *R* may have reached the level where average costs are as low as *RQ*. A margin line for that scale of output might be *PW*. Accordingly, location *X* defined by the intersection of the two margin lines *KF'WP'* and *PW* at

W is the location at which the delivered price from both *A* and *R* would be the same (with average cost pricing). It thus is, at time t', the boundary point between the market areas of the two producing sites *A* and *R*.

At a still later point of time t'' the production of the single firm, or the group of small producers, or the industrial complex may have reached a size closer to optimal and the minimum average cost may have fallen to the level RQ'. The new margin line relevant for production at *R* would be PW'. The boundary point dividing the two market areas would be X'. Conceivably, too, the single firm, or the group of small firms, or the industrial complex at *R* may have been so much more efficiently designed in terms of latest technology, or organised so much more efficiently in terms of avoiding congestion, controlling pollution, achieving internal coordination, and avoiding certain types of diseconomies (which had come to exist at *A* but could not have been foreseen) that the relevant minimum average cost point falls to as low as RQ'' and is reached when output is quite large. The margin line might then be PV; and should this turn out to be the case, production at *A* is eliminated from the competition.[10]

In the above manner, we see how the advantages of an early start forestalls development elsewhere, but where with time and increase in technology and the density of demand, new agglomerations can begin to develop elsewhere, utilising new technology in many cases (a latecomer advantage), ultimately to achieve greater size than the first agglomeration and to obtain a larger share of the market than the first or even to eliminate it. Historically, one may well argue that this was the situation with regard to iron and steel agglomerations, the great advantages of the early British iron and steel agglomerations having gradually been eroded, and in certain respects transformed into significant disadvantages so as to lead to the effective elimination of British iron and steel from world trade.

V. HIERARCHICAL WORLD ORGANISATION AND CONSTRAINTS ON AGGLOMERATION

Having discussed a number of issues from a more or less traditional standpoint, except for cheap environmental locations, in the previous section, let me now introduce another new type of variable into the analysis. It is by now obvious to all that as we continue in our era of major population growth, rapid expansion of industry and energy use, etc., that the problem of environmental management and of control of the ways we utilise the earth's resources becomes increasingly critical. Without doubt a new type of world organisation will emerge, or the current world organisational structure (the United Nations) will adapt in a major way, or both. Elsewhere, I have spelled out several of the basic forces that will be operating and will lead to a more effective hierarchical world organisation. (Isard, 1974b and 1975b.)

It is clear that the world organisation of the future will have at least limited taxing powers, at least some authority to control monetary, tariff and economic development policies, etc., and at least some important regulatory powers over the use of the world's resources (certainly ocean) and environment. What is not clear is *how much* authority and power it will have in these several and other areas.[11] To me, however, it is clear that relatively small differences in authority and decision-making power granted the node at the top of the hierarchical world organisation can lead to major differences in Gross World Product (G.W.P.) and in the world pattern of industrial agglomerations engaged in the output of that product. For example, suppose there emerges a strong world unit at the top, determining a relatively few but critical kinds of decisions and policies in a few basic areas, and utilising highly sophisticated techniques: location theory; multinational, multiregional input—output models; and LINK-type multinational, multiregion econometric models; among others. I can envisage how major curbs may be placed on the growth of G.W.P., as is narrowly and most inadequately defined by our current economic concepts, in order to achieve more rapid growth in world social welfare. I can also envisage that a strong hand will be used to prevent the emergence of excessive industrial agglomerations and concentrations at a number of points in this world such as at Nagoya and Puerto Rico, and the use of preclusion powers based on preclusion analysis in areas like Tokyo and Philadelphia. (Preclusion analysis essentially is industrial complex analysis *in reverse*. . . The objective of such analysis is to define sets of inter-related, interconnected activities which can be effectively removed at low cost (or great gain) from an existing regional structure, or precluded from normal development in that structure at low cost (or great gain) considering the environmental and like social costs involved — see Isard, 1974a.) Also I envisage how a strong distributional policy might emerge, to meet the pressing demands for development by third world countries, which would allocate new industrial agglomerations in a way not to be anticipated from the operation of a market economy.

On the other hand, the node at the top may turn out to be weak in authority, and have little control over the growth of Gross World Product, excessive industrial concentrations, and the increasing disparities in per capita income and welfare among world regions and their parts. The resulting size and patterns of industrial agglomerations and world trade would then of course be much different.

VI. CONCLUDING REMARKS

I have spelled out in some detail the nature of agglomeration as seen by a location theorist. In many ways this paper is a listing of factors well known to economists, geographers and other social scientists. However, what has not been done, except by location theorists, is the synthesis of these factors to depict and understand better past, current and future spatial distributions of economic activity, population and related magnitudes. In effecting his synthesis, the location theorist plays down a number of factors considered extremely important by trade theorists, such as exchange rates, balance of payments, and quotas. To a location theorist such important factors enter into the specific properties of a location with regard to its various markets and can often be treated as readjustments of its critical isodapanes, or in similar ways.

Also, I have spelled out at some detail one case study of an agglomeration simply because it is my view that one cannot obtain a full understanding of the contributions of agglomeration theory without going into detail on locational cost differentials as they take specific form in a case study.

Moreover, like a good location theorist, I sit back and use our existing stock of theory to make projections of the future world pattern of agglomerations and economic activities, and view this future world pattern as in large part determining the pattern of world trade. On the other hand, I recognise that my approach overemphasises supply conditions, and gives inadequate attention to demand conditions. This reflects in part the fact that location theory first places emphasis on supply and locational cost differentials and later brings in demand. In this sense, location theory tends to be more relevant for the long run than the short. In contrast, input-output analysis and econometric modelling seems to me to be more relevant for the short-run and less for the long, when basic structural supply conditions may have changed. Actually, good analysis must incorporate both approaches and use their associated models. For example, one can speculate on a step-by-step procedure in the joint use of these two approaches. As a first step one might use a LINK econometric model to specify demand conditions today and over the next few years. Then he might examine these estimates for their locational implications — for middle and long-run shifts in the world pattern of supply points, by intranational regions, nations, and world regions. Next he might redo the LINK model inserting new data on supply points and relationships, and obtain a second round of estimates and projections. In turn, he might redo the location analysis. And so forth. One might speculate that a procedure involving a few rounds of iterations of this sort might well come to constitute a basic component for world development and trade models. But perhaps not. Only time will tell.

NOTES

[1] See Ohlin (1933), Hoover (1937), Palander (1935), Isard (1956), Engländer (1926), Lösch (1954), Isard *et al.* (1959), among others.

[2] See the literature already cited and W. Isard *et al.* (1959) chapter 9.

[3] We assume that the agglomeration economies realisable at L would not be affected were j agglomerated there or not — an assumption to be dropped later.

[4] Here one must be very careful to make sure that the term 'economic development' is used only in the narrow sense of economics. For there were important non-economic outcomes, significant from the standpoint of measuring social welfare, which cannot be measured by dollar figures or number of jobs. These outcomes can be viewed, by and large, as negative.

[5] It is implicitly assumed that each producer charges the identical factory price to all consumers.

[6] If the factory price were set equal to marginal cost, the factory price would be lower, sales higher and average cost lower so long as the producer was operating in the falling part of his average cost curve; also the market area would extend beyond the consumer at L if the delivered price to the consumer at L based on average cost pricing was the maximum any consumer would be willing to pay (that is if in figure 5 LG were the maximum).

[7] Hoover (1973), pp. 8—11. Where irregularities in rate structure exist, these will be reflected in the transport gradient line. The transport gradient line of figure 4 is constructed to portray a rate structure proportional to weight and distance. If the rate structure is graduated and less than proportional to distance, the transport gradient from J would rise continuously but curve downward.

[8] It should also be borne in mind that consumers at and close to R along the stretch AR might find it advantageous to produce for themselves and gain scale economies when they would consume more than one unit.

[9] To keep figure 5 from becoming complicated, we assume that technological progress does not lower the minimum average cost AE obtainable from optimal agglomeration at A. Actually, such can be expected to occur, in which case a transport gradient line should proceed from say E', and the new margin line $KF'WU$ would be shifted to be tangent to the transport gradient line from E'.

[10] Of course, were there use of new technology at A so as to lower its minimum average cost significantly below AE, production at A would not be eliminated from the competition.

[11] The question of optimal hierarchical world organisation involves consideration of decision-making cost differentials from different assignments of functions among the nodes of any given hierarchy, and with respect to different hierarchical structures. See Isard (1969), chapter 3, and forthcoming manuscript with P. Kaniss.

REFERENCES

Engländer, O., 'Kritisches und Positives zu einer allgemeinen reinen Lehre vom Standort', *Zeitschrift fur Volkswirtschaft und Sozialpolitik*, Neue Folge, Vol. V (1926) Nos. 7—9.

Hoover, E. M., Jr. *Location Theory and the Shoe and Leather Industries* (Harvard University Press, Cambridge, Mass., 1937).

Isard, W., *Location and Space Economy* (M.I.T. Press, Cambridge, Mass., 1956).

Isard, W., Schooler, E. W. and Vietorisz, T., *Industrial Complex Analysis and Regional Development* (Cambridge: M.I.T. Press, Cambridge, Mass., 1959).

Isard, W., 'General Theory: Social, Political, Economic and Regional', (M.I.T. Press, Cambridge, Mass., 1969).

Isard, W., 'Activity-Industrial Complex Analysis for Environmental Management', *Papers,* Regional Science Association, p. 127, Volume 33 (1974a).

Isard, W., 'World Environmental Conflicts: Some Relevant Analytical Frameworks', *Papers*, Peace Science Society (International), p. 139, Volume 23 (1974b).

Isard, W., *Introduction to Regional Science* (Prentice-Hall, Englewood Cliffs, New Jersey, 1975a).

Isard, W., 'Notes on an Evolutionary Theoretic Approach to World Organisation', *Papers*, Peace Science Society (International), p. 113, Volume 24 (1975b).

Isard, W. and Kaniss, P., 'Structure, control and language hierarchies and world organization', *Journal of Peace Science*, forthcoming.

Lösch, A., *The Economics of Location* (Yale University Press, New Haven, 1954). (English translation.)

Ohlin, B., *Handelns teori* (Stockholm, 1924).

Ohlin, B., *Interregional and International Trade* (Harvard University Press, Cambridge, Mass. (1933, p. VII).

Palander, T., *Beitrage zur Standortstheorie* (Almqvist and Wiksells Boktryckeri – A. B., Uppsala, 1935).

Weber, A., *Über den Standort der Industrien*, Tubingen (1909). English translation with introduction and notes by Carl J. Friedrich, University of Chicago Press, Chicago, 1929.

Comment

Torsten Hägerstrand

Location theory as presented in Professor Isard's paper is concerned with where a producer is likely to succeed in capturing and holding a market. It also suggests some of the circumstances which might cause him to lose it as time goes to somebody in a different location. I propose to limit my comments to this latter aspect, using some of the results obtained by studies of innovation and diffusion, an area which is — just as economic location theory — much concerned with questions of location and circulation. My emphasis though, will be on the location and circulation of *information* rather than goods.

New and evolving patterns of demand call forth new or adjusted industrial products. New inventions as well as research and development efforts create the base for introduction and spread of new methods of production. In either case an almost inevitable effect is the birth and growth, decline and death of industries at various locations.

Although exogenous to location theory proper these phenomena are implicitly present in Professor Isard's discussion when he for example talks about density of demand and technological advance. I would like to use this opportunity to take a few steps back in the order of events and introduce some locational aspects of innovation and diffusion processes *per se*. I do so because I believe that the concomitant understanding of industrial location and the emergence and spread of innovations is an important twin problem to deal with when we are seeking new theoretical orientations where international division of labour and international trade are concerned. It brings in social processes against which economic processes should be seen.

Let me then first point out that the phenomenon of agglomeration is as essential in 'innovation theory' as it is in location theory. (Clearly, what we know about innovation and diffusion is based on empirical generalisations and not on deductive reasoning.) The term agglomeration is perhaps not used in the former context but the fact is nevertheless there. In industrial location theory agglomeration in all of its three different forms is assumed to give the firms that are involved certain economic advantages. What concerns original innovation (to be distinguished from borrowed) it is probably true to say that agglomeration is, if not a necessary so at least a very important, condition for an innovation to reach the stage of take-off. So, while firms are seeking to appear in agglomerations because of their calculable economic interests, agglomerations, once they have come into being, might — in ways which are impossible to anticipate in detail — start to act as centres of change in production technology and patterns of demand.

What happens is that when creative minds and tangible resources have been brought together they start to interact. Building blocks of ideas and of hardware pieces are there side by side waiting to be put together in new ways. A stage is set for action in case cultural and structural circumstances so permit. This is a socioenvironmental process which can hardly be predicted or planned but can perhaps to a certain degree be influenced by strategic policies. The characteristic thing is that in the process *big leaps are rare but many small steps are the rule.* And when big leaps occur it takes a very flexible environment for digesting the results in non-harmful ways.

It is well known that the mega-innovations of world history have been highly localised phenomena in areas where the interaction between the step-takers has been high. Closest to our concern is the rise of modern industry with Britain as the heartland. But other less dramatic innovations — or should we say secondary innovations — seem to behave in a like manner; they may consist of changes in lifestyles or simple shifts in consumption, or the birth of new industries or the introduction of new production processes. Odd inventions and ideas may appear almost anywhere. But the chance that they will combine to become workable and spreadable innovations is much higher inside than outside agglomerations, be these industrial or urban. A critical mass seems to be needed for a population to be able to stay at the forefront of technology and to feel at an early stage when changes in demand are approaching — or else to influence demand within limits.

Let us now consider the discussion of the advantages of being firstcomer and latecomer, respectively (pp. 169—73 and figure 5 in Professor Isard's paper). The model given tells us among other things that the firms agglomerated at A would experience such advantages because of their early start that they would be able to 'forestall development elsewhere ...'. Yet 'with time and increase in technology and the density of demand, new agglomerations can begin to develop elsewhere, utilising new technology in many cases (a latecomer advantage), ultimately to achieve greater size than the first agglomeration and to obtain a larger share of the market than the first or even to eliminate it'. Thus there are two factors that could break the monopoly of firms being at A: *technological advance and increased density of demand.*

Both processes could be interpreted as instances of innovation and diffusion. The first requires development and adoption of innovation in production. The second is the result of diffusion of demand for a product on the market.

How plausible now is Professor Isard's scenario from the point of view of what we know about innovation and diffusion? The answer to this question depends to a large degree on where we choose to locate A and R, respectively.

At this point we must first bring in the question of geographical scale into the picture. Professor Isard does not directly specify this, but since we are dealing here with international and even global matters I assume that I have the right to think that the $A-R$ distance could be quite large.

What I would like to do now is to place the cross-section $A-R$ in a few different areas and directions on the globe.

(1) Both A and R are placed at agglomerations inside the United States or inside Europe. If so, of course A and R are not only point-located agglomerations *per se*. They are also members of what one might call *agglomerations of agglomerations*. Some of the economic effects of agglomeration recognised by location theory are present to an even more powerful degree in these huge agglomerations of agglomerations than in the single point-located agglomeration. The same is still more true for the interaction factors behind innovation and diffusion. The European and American industrial and urbanised belts have been the breeding-ground and the normative centres for the global spread of technologies, lifestyles and consumption patterns. They have been that powerful because of their pooled and gradually growing resources of creativity, scientific knowledge, physical outfit and managerial skill (and political ruthlessness).

Now, this location of the cross-section $A-R$ means that A and R could be considered about equal in terms of circulation of ideas and access to technical building-blocks for new constructs. There are good preconditions present for new and more advanced technologies to become developed at R independently from specific firms located at A. The producers at A might well be thrown out of business by somebody at R (and they would soon find out something else to do).

The second kind of change — increased density of demand — frequently proceeds in a spatially ordered fashion as a wave out from the initial centre of adoption. This wave moves sometimes very fast, sometimes slowly. Whatever the case may be, the rise in demand tends to lag in areas away from A and thus help to postpone the moment when firms at R become competitive. But on the whole, inside the United States or inside Europe — with their intense internal circulation of people and ideas — the diffusional lag effect is so weak today that it can be disregarded in matters related to consumption of goods or adoption of technical knowhow. Thus R is not much hindered in its development for diffusional reasons.

Clearly, much of the technological advance of the West and the growth of variability in consumption has come about just as location theory suggests: *by competition between actors in innovative agglomerations inside agglomerations of agglomerations*. At least Europe had the suitable geographical structure with densely located competing centres long before industrialisation started.

(2) The situation becomes entirely different if A is still assumed to be located in one of the industrial belts of the Northern hemisphere but R somewhere in a less-developed region of the Southern hemisphere, perhaps a metropolis. Then we cannot expect that the millions of people present at

R would provide a breeding-ground for competitive innovation. They are not the kind of critical mass to generate high-level technology. And even if there existed a core of technologically sophisticated individuals among them and some other useful resources — which is actually the case in many places — they would not have the advantage of belonging to a well-integrated agglomeration of agglomerations within which competition takes place. They would, in fact, be alone in a technological desert. So, if a competitive enterprise should appear at all at *R*, its advanced technology must come from the North — but clearly not necessarily from *A*. But this technology would in all likelihood represent a big leap at *R* without much chance of being incorporated in an integrated system of step-by-step innovation there.

Where increased density of demand is concerned there are two strongly retarding factors at work in holding back *R*. One is the slow or non-existing rise in general purchasing power in areas around. The other is the gradient of diffusional spread which in this environment must be assumed to be very steep from *A* to *R*. Even low-cost items are hindered in their adoption because even they might require from people cultural quantum jumps and not just changes little by little.

What has just been said does not imply that there can be no development and change generated at *R* and spread out from it. But the dominating step-by-step principle of innovation makes this process qualitatively different. It moves on a level which is too far from developments at *A* for being able to offer competition.

Given the situation just described, the firstcomer at agglomeration *A* is most likely to retain his monopoly position. Advantages of being late with respect to *A* do hardly exist at *R*. The reasoning offered by location theory does not seem to be applicable during a foreseeable future because of the nature of the process of innovation and diffusion. Cheap labour as a competitive factor is a different matter. Economic development on that base, Professor Isard seems to indicate when speaking about what actually happened in Puerto Rico (p. 169), must be looked at very carefully from a social welfare point of view.

(3) Finally we assume that *A* and *R* are both located inside the developing world, say for example at agglomerations in Africa. This location of the cross-section would in several respects take us back to a situation like the first case in the sense that we would find (a) a high degree of development homogeneity along *A*–*R*; and (b) fundamental similarities in terms of knowhow capability between agglomeration *A* and its potential competitor *R*.

Provided that the production going on at *A* were of a kind where the developed industries of the North had nothing to say (for example, some superior equipment for harnessing solar energy) or if they were kept out of competition by institutional arrangements, then again a true dialogue between firstcomers and latecomers would be a real possibility.

The great difference compared with the first case would be that the cross-section would not (yet) be embedded in an agglomeration of agglomerations. It would run between relatively isolated agglomerations far apart. Intensity of interaction between pools of ideas would be bound to be low or at least very costly to uphold. Similarly, increase in the density of demand would still be slow both because of the slow growth of purchasing power in general over wide areas and because of the steep gradients of diffusion also internally in the region. But still a situation of competition would be present between agglomerations on an approximately equal footing. A gradual step-by-step development over a broad front under mutual competition, starting from the level now given, would be a clear possibility, just as Professor Isard's scenario suggests.

The conclusion of this short exercise in wedding location theory to innovation theory seems to be that trade in market areas shared between equals promotes development and change under preserved equality whereas trade in markets between unequals preserves inequality. Competition between equals also means that diffusion of new items and lifestyles is likely to give a more smooth and peaceful advance than a halting influence emanating from unequal centres of change. This is so because items under spread would be reasonably congenial with already existing values, habits and institutions.

Comment
Åke E. Andersson

I. INTRODUCTION

In his role as father of Regional Science, Walter Isard has vigorously advocated the necessity of an explicit consideration of time and space in theorising about social development. It is also one of his major achievements that he has deepened our understanding of the importance of a *simultaneous* introduction of time and space in economic models.

Consequently I was a little disappointed by the somewhat partial approach chosen in his paper. The presentation in his paper is a reflection of early regional science and has very little in common with his recent research on interdependencies in allocation in a framework of continuous time and space.

To put Isard's contribution in the correct scientific perspective, I would like to classify his regional economic analysis as well as international economics within the framework of some general regional science. My first instrument of classification stresses the representation of time and space.

TABLE 1

Space / Time	Implicit	Discrete	Continuous	
Implicit	Classical international economics	Walrasian theory of location and trade	One-dimensional urban economics	Two-dimensional European school of location
Discrete	N-region growth theory	Regional growth models		
Continuous	Dynamic international economics	Maximum principle models for networks	Time–space allocation theory	

The current work by Isard is solidly referred to cell (3, 4). In his presentation today he has preferred to reflect upon earlier work — belonging mainly to cells (1, 2) and (1, 4). Thus he reduces the importance of the development of current regional science analysis as one basis of a more general theory of allocation in space.

Let me now turn to one of the main themes of the symposium: to further an integration or unification of interregional and international economic analysis. Such an integration or unification cannot be achieved or evaluated, unless the characteristics of the now very different spatial theories of international economics and regional science are properly understood. Table 1 shows that neoclassical international economics and modern regional science have different specifications of time and space. But this is not at all a sufficient basis of comparison. I would thus like to introduce another table of basic assumptions.

It must be stressed that table 2 is intended to emphasise generalities rather than to pinpoint all exceptions to the rule that we can find in any of the two spatial disciplines. The table shows that the common ground is limited today. There could consequently be a great potential advantage in synthesising the two theories of spatial allocation — whether normative or descriptive.

The theoretical and empirical problems associated with a synthetic approach should, however, not be underestimated.

In his paper Isard exemplifies some of the problems of synthetic model building. Even in cases when elements of *well-known* problems are to be treated in a more synthetic way, there are plenty of examples of rapid increase in complexity.

Combining assumptions 3, 6, 7 and 8 in a comprehensive model of industrial complex analysis is a now classical example of such fruitful — but often extremely difficult — synthetic work pursued by Isard, Chenery, Westphal and Nijkamp, to name a few.[1]

The combination of two-dimensional space and neoclassical possibilities of substitution is another example, mentioned by Isard, that is still an insufficiently solved problem of regional economics.

The need for a synthetic approach in international and interregional economics is highly warranted. The search for a synthesis can be expected to be a much more complicated matter than is implied in the final section of Isard's paper.

II. TOWARD A SYNTHESIS OF REGIONAL SCIENCE AND INTERNATIONAL ECONOMICS

In spite of my own fear of complexity I would like to propose a scheme of synthetic analysis.

I will try to consider the problem under the simplification of a theory of allocation and trade in *discrete space* and *discrete time* on a network that is given and with explicit links. A further simplification is the

TABLE 2

		Dominant trade theory	Dominant regional science theory
1.	Price-induced substitution in production	Yes (neoclassical assumptions)	No (fixed coefficients)
2.	Price-induced substitution in consumption	Yes (neoclassical assumptions)	No (Keynesian assumptions)
3.	Factor mobility	No	Yes
4.	Differential land-use in different economic activities	No	Yes
5.	Transportation network explicit	No (important exceptions: Dutch and Finnish schools)	Yes
6.	Propensity to trade explicit function of distance	No (important exceptions: Dutch and Finnish schools)	Yes
7.	Direct inter-dependencies	No (important exception: international input-output analysis)	Yes (interregional input-output analysis)
8.	Increasing returns to scale allowed	Seldom	Common
9.	Political factors included	Yes	Yes
10.	Trade flows determination	Deterministic search for trade partners	Stochastic search for trade partners subject to profit constraints

assumption of general equilibrium as the principle of solution.

I will further assume price-induced substitution in production, complete factor mobility (as in Chisholm's state of recycling), direct interdependencies in production of commodities and labour, increasing returns to scale and the propensity to trade to be an explicit function of distance. Migration, commuting and similar labour moves are considered to be special aspects of trade.

The general aspects to be interconnected in this 'regional science, international trade and growth model' are

(a) Endogenous technological development and technical choice at the national level.
(b) International trade flows between sectors located in regions.
(c) International allocation of production over time.

The structure of the model is first presented as a flow diagram:

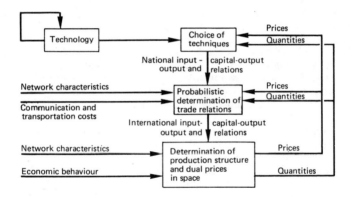

The next diagram presents the model's structure more precisely.

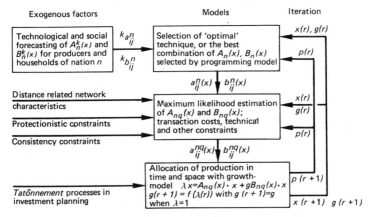

$A_n^k(x)$ = $k \cdot m$-dimensional rectangular matrix of input coefficients as functions of
the production vector for the m sectors and n nations (x)
$B_n^k(x)$ = corresponding matrix of capital-coefficient functions
$A_{nq}(x)$ = a square matrix of technically efficient and spatially consistent imput—output
and trade coefficients
λ = capacity slack (positive if less than 1); r = iteration
g = rate of growth (and interest); f = adaptive control function of stabilisation
policy

With suitable (and reasonable) assumptions about irreducibility, continuity, compactness, and net productivity we can use the general Brouwer fixed-point theorem to ensure the existence of equilibrium solutions to the whole system, even in the case of increasing returns to scale. Furthermore, we can use a theorem by Nikaido to ensure the existence of at least one positive rate of growth for the non-linear input-output international growth model.

The computational possibilities for this model (of interconnected models) have increased considerably in the last two years. Geometric programming can now be used to solve technical choice problems with continuously increasing returns to scale.

A remarkable estimation procedure by mathematical statisticians of the Royal Technological Institute in Stockholm has solved the problem of large-scale maximum likelihood estimation of trade patterns with numerous different constraints.[2] Finally, I myself and a physicist from Chalmers Technological Institute — Håkan Persson — have developed a method for efficient computation of the intrinsic growth rates and the production vector of non-linear input-output systems for international location, trade and growth analysis.

III. CONCLUDING REMARKS

The model presented above should be used as an example of one of many possible approaches to a synthesis between modern international trade theory and regional theory. As such it could be used as an example of a *general* equilibrium approach in contrast to the partial approaches advanced by Isard in his paper.

In the model presented above location of production and trade flows are simultaneously determined in a dynamic process. The model is also of such a construction that it can determine the creation of agglomerations in space as a consequence of the *conjunction* of economies of scale, interdependencies in production and advantages of accessibility to communication and transportation networks.

There are, however, also disadvantages with this approach: It cannot handle questions about economically advantageous subdivisions or fusions of nations or other economic regions. This is a consequence of the discrete subdivision of space in the model.

The characteristics of the communication and transportation systems as well as protectionist measures are also determined as exogenous factors.

Isard has, however, recently constructed continuous optimisation and equilibrium models of *endogenous* determination of trade, locations and communication systems. These models are also very helpful in the analysis of the development of functional regions as well as the diffusion of technology in continuous time and space. It is consequently somewhat frustrating that his paper to this conference does not give a reflection of his achievements in continuous time-space, social development and allocation theory, but halts at a partial analysis of a few aspects of applied location theory of the 1950s and 1960s.

NOTES

[1] Chenery, H. and Westphal, L., 'Economics of Scale and Investment over Time', in J. Margolis and H. Guitton (eds.), *Public Economics* (Macmillan, London, 1969). P. Nijkamp, *Planning of Industrial Complexes by Means of Geometric Programming*, RUP, Rotterdam, 1972).

[2] Snickars, F. and Weibull, J., 'A Minimum Information Principle: Theory and Practice', *Regional Science and Urban Economics*, 1977; 1—2. See also Marksjö, B. and Hårsman, B., 'Efficient information adding', in Å-E. Andersson and I. Holmberg (eds.), *Demographic, Economic and Social Interaction* (Ballinger Publishing Company, Cambridge, Mass., 1976).

Summary of the Discussion

A special purpose of the symposium had been to assemble economists and economic geographers to compare approaches to the analysis of the international allocation of economic activity. This session took advantage of the opportunity for the two disciplines to develop an 'informal communications network and to gain from trade', as Max Corden put it. The first issue discussed was whether location theory and trade theory tried to solve the same set of problems with different approaches or addressed different problems. Both views were advanced. The papers by Allan Pred and Walter Isard, as well as the Comments upon them, explored the cumulative nature of economic agglomerations and the consequent advantages of being a firstcomer. The discussants scrutinised the relevance of these concepts for the subject of the symposium. This session was chaired by *Lawrence R. Klein.*

Walter Isard asked whether trade theory and location theory were concerned with the same set of problems, and suggested that they were. *Ronald Jones* felt rather that the theories addressed different questions and employed different assumptions. Trade theory, he said, was concerned with situations where resources are immobile in the sense that they cannot move to some other area. Areas need not be defined in location theoretical terms, but can consist of groups of factors. Trade theory assumes that these 'trapped' resources are going to do something and the basic question it asks is what they are going to produce. Jones illustrated this by referring to the Ricardian model with one factor — labour. The question for any particular group of labourers, for example those in a country, was in what activities they had a comparative advantage. This could be seen as a problem of labour economics — of assigning jobs to people. While location theorists were often concerned with where in space production of something takes place, trade theorists were concerned with what given resources produce and only indirectly with where they do it. Trade theory has little to say about transport costs except for the assumption that they are very high, on the one hand, or negligible, on the other.

Trade theory furthermore was concerned with the consequences of exogenous changes for the group. How will changes in tastes, in world market prices, etc., influence the production pattern, volume of trade, real income, factor prices and distribution of income of the group? In addition there were questions having to do with the adjustment mechanism. Jones suggested that location theory would not be able to answer the questions posed by trade theory even if it abandoned the assumption of fixed coefficients in production, which Åke Andersson

claimed characterised it, while trade theory could answer the same
questions as before even if this assumption were incorporated.

Harry Johnson noted that in order to compare approaches a common
problem was required. He felt that trade theory was appropriate for
certain kinds of problems, while location theory may be important for
another range of problems. The two theories, he said, assumed different
resources to be 'trapped'. Location theory assumes distance to be trapped
factor and considers attempts to overcome distance by means of i.a.
agglomerations. Trade theory considers factors of production to be
trapped and is concerned with how far this can be overcome by trade.
Trade is a means to overcome factor immobility, whether natural or
manmade. We try, he exemplified, to solve the problems of developing
countries by transferring capital or technology to them, but are not
prepared to admit their unskilled people into our territories. The factor
price equalisation theorem tells us that if may be possible to solve the
problem of world welfare without allowing people to move freely from
place to place. It may also tell us that we might be able to solve the
problem by transferring technology without transferring either people
or capital, or by transferring capital without transferring technology.
From this viewpoint he felt the factor price equalisation theorem to be
an important one.

While Jones and Johnson had emphasised the differences in problems
which trade and location theorists dealt with, *Max Corden* compared the
assumptions of the two theories. What modifications, he asked, were
necessary to build a bridge between location theory and trade theory?
Firstly, trade theory tended to assume that the factor supply is given in
each country at a particular moment of time and did not stress the
mobility of factors in determining the pattern of trade. So, he suggested,
systematic allowance in trade theory for some mobility of factors, possibly
even for perfect mobility of some factors, would bring it closer to location
theory. Trade theorists could for example assume that capital is perfectly
mobile internationally and natural resources utterly immobile with
different skill-categories of labour somewhere in between. Secondly, while
trade theory did refer to economies of scale, the recent literature tended to
neglect them and their implications had not been sufficiently worked out,
in spite of their early extensive treatment in Ohlin's book. So, he said,
location theorists would perhaps be happier if trade theorists redefined
economies of scale and called them agglomeration economies and if they
continued the work started by Linder and others. In addition, Corden
suggested that trade theory could easily include external economies
internal to countries to allow for free information flows within countries.
Trade theory would then have information spreading processes familiar
to location theorists. Thirdly, while trade theory did take transport costs
into account, it was in a primitive way, simply stating that transport costs
reduced trade, without changing its nature. So Corden suggested that trade

theorists make more systematic allowance for transport costs, for instance by comparing transport costs for inputs with transport costs for final goods. He referred to the body of theory on effective protection which allowed for different tariffs on inputs and on final goods, and suggested extending it to cover transport costs. This might give effective rates of protection by transport costs conceptually similar to those by tariffs, and perhaps many results familiar to location theorists. Corden thought that trade theory, modified in this way, would have most of what location theory had and yet something more, namely relative costs. These modifications would establish a new body of theory bringing the two approaches together, rather than simply reconstruct location theory.

Åke Andersson stressed the need for trade theory to consider transfer costs more systematically. An important point made in location theory, he held, was that comparative advantage is endogenously created and that transport and communication policy plays an inportant role in its creation. Location theorists thus tended to view comparative advantage as the result of decisions to invest in communication networks and to invest human capital in specific nodes. He thought that in the past this had been a dividing line between trade and location theorists. To further a convergence of theories, he felt trade theory should emphasise more the functioning and construction of networks for transferring goods, services and ideas, while location theory should emphasise more the problems of substitution in production and the endogenous determination of technology.

Concluding this part of the discussion, *Bertil Ohlin* argued that the combination of location theories and trade theories was essential. Trade theory had historically not paid much attention to entrepreneurs or leaders of business firms. The factors of production were assumed to come together automatically in an enterprise. Location theory on the other hand had a leadership of firms which counted costs to determine where it was most profitable to locate production and sales. Transportation costs and planned transfers of productive factors were at the very centre of cost calculations and decisions in location theory, whereas in trade theory transportation costs had been regarded chiefly as obstacles to trade. To be more realistic, trade theory should be influenced by location theory in these respects. Furthermore, Ohlin noted, transport costs and reloading costs played a special role when several raw materials were used and fetched from different and perhaps distant natural resources. Trade theory models concentrated attention on transport costs for the finished goods but as a rule disregarded internal costs of transportation. However, the choice of location inside a country was also important. It determined whether country *A* or country *B* had a comparative advantage in the production of a certain commodity.

The discussion also dealt with agglomeration and network economies as treated in the papers by Allan Pred and Walter Isard and their alleged consequences for the international allocation of economic activity. *Charles Kindleberger* suggested that location theorists could be interpreted as claiming that information follows channels created by hierarchies of cities and other information networks. When it moves, labour is not perfectly mobile but follows information networks. The first immigrant sends for his cousin, then for his uncle, brothers and family. Therefore the Italians do not end up evenly dispersed in the New World on a von Thünen plain but in San Francisco, while the Hungarians end up in Bufflao, and the Poles in Baltimore. Capital also flows through organised networks and the same is true for trade. He noted that location theorists should recognise that historically these networks decay. Obsolescence overtakes Amsterdam whèn its merchant network finally loses its monopoly and other countries buy directly from Australia. This happens in financial networks too. He concluded that location theory may teach trade theorists that their extreme assumptions of either immobility or perfect mobility of capital does not provide enough nuances to allow for spatial hierarchies which historically change over time. A theory which included these networks would be a richer theory but also, he feared, what Robert Solow had called a futile exercise — a one-to-one mapping of eternity.

Dieter Biehl also emphasised that past agglomerations do not grow indefinitely. Referring to basic German contributions to regional theory[1] he mentioned the example of the Hanseatic City League which — under the leadership of the town of Lübeck — for more than four centuries dominated the Baltic and North Sea Trade as a 'multinational' system of cities, but finally lost its firstcomer position to Hamburg when large scale commercial transactions with the New World developed. Biehl also suggested that the notion of transportation costs should be extended to cover all communication costs. Those costs may be decisive even if they represent but a small share of total costs, since they influence locational decisions at the margin.

Gunnar Törnqvist also stressed the importance of including information costs which for certain activities could far exceed transportation costs. A medical firm for instance could spend 150 million Scr per year for information and only 200 000 Scr to transport its goods. This was explained by its high costs for conferences and direct personal contacts arranged to save expensive time.

Michael Chisholm emphasised the need to specify the time period for which Pred claimed his argument was valid. Like Biehl, he felt that a firstcomer could be overtaken by others in the longer run. If the argument about the firstcomer's supremacy were valid due to a continuation of agglomeration economies, then Great Britain would not be in its present difficulties. Chisholm thought that the evidence presented by Pred did not support the extension of his city-system approach from the national to the international scale.

Assar Lindbeck felt that omission of prices and costs in Hägerstrand's analysis gave too pessimistic prospects for latecomers to catch up. After all the United Kingdom was an example of a firstcomer which had been overtaken by many others. Sweden and Japan were latecomers at the turn of this century. Spain, Taiwan and South Korea were latecomers in the postwar period. They were all able to compete successfully. This could be explained once prices and wages were introduced into the analysis in addition to technological superiority.

Torsten Hägerstrand replied that he had neglected economic factors deliberately in order to concentrate on the innovative process in a society. Elaborating on the model developed in his Comment, he noted that already before industrialisation Europe had a well developed system of central places and of agglomerations. Its cultural climate stimulated production of technological ideas. The creation of ideas resulted from the interaction between minds rather than from economic mechanisms. So he questioned whether the transfer of American technology to technologically less sophisticated countries would help them develop the desired creative climate. The transfer of technology to Japan was probably an exception because of the special structure of the country. This was largely an empirical question and he thought that a study of industrialisation in Japan would help us understand how one might transfer technology to developing countries today.

Kjeld Philip felt that Hägerstrand's view of the innovative process could help to explain why factories in the developing countries used the same factor intensities as those in the developed countries. This technology was designed in developed countries to economise on a factor of production — labour — which was scarce there but cheap in developing countries. It was transferred more of less automatically to the LDCs who lacked a research and development activity of their own which he felt was necessary to establish and use techniques adapted to their factor endowments. Transfers of technology between less developed countries, Philip suggested, could help overcome this by stimulating an innovative process in these countries. Once they were able to develop locally a technology which employed their abundant factors, their development would proceed much faster.

Robert Solow was interested in the emphasis that Pred had put on biases in the flow of information and the possibility that locational decisions made centrally in a large enterprise may be subject to biases that come from the sort of information channels that Kindleberger had described. He asked Pred and Törnqvist if they thought that because of informational biases the headquarters of a large international enterprise making locational decisions was likely to choose high cost rather than low cost locations when the margin is very large. Was it perhaps more likely that the cost function arranged by place rather than by output was relatively flat so that if there was a really low cost place somewhere the enterprise would hear about it — biases or no biases? It was then likely to make only small mistakes. He thought the question was important because the location decision may mean little to the enterprise but be important for the place where the factory gets built.

Harry Johnson concluded that the question of firstcomers versus late-comers was a semantic trap. The real question was who is a comer and who is not. The early starter has the advantage that it knows the ropes before others, who have to make a lot of investments to catch up. But a latecomer can avoid the mistakes of the earlycomers provided it is a comer at all. The real question is under what circumstances there are opportunities for people to create something new and for countries to be comers.

In his final comment *Pred* started with a reply to Törnqvist. He had left the international aspect of city systems in the background since he assumed that his audience was largely unfamiliar with these models which had been developed mainly for the national level. Information networks and feedbacks certainly played a pivotal role on the national level and he thought they may be even more important on the international level. In reply to Chisholm who had questioned the international applicability of his observations, Pred said that since the United Kingdom began to recede before an international system of cities had begun to emerge, he did not think that this example contradicted his proposal to apply the city systems view internationally. In reply to Solow, he suggested that locational decisions of organisations would lead to small rather than large mistakes as a result of spatial biases. Given the number of decisions required and the imperfect knowledge they possess, most firms would be ruined by too extensive a search for marginally superior explicit of implicit locational solutions.

Referring to Biehl's emphasis on communication costs as opposed to transport costs, he observed that the former were of special importance for the costs of moving services — including information — within as well as between organisations. Pred expressed surprise that trade theorists in the post-industrial era concentrated on the movement of goods and neglected the movement of services.

Isard closed the discussion. On the issue of the continuity and rigidity of the current world pattern of agglomerations, he emphasised that an international city system had not yet crystallised. Basic changes were still possible. Environmental problems for instance would increase loca-tional cost differentials and make it possible for a number of major nodes to emerge in less developed countries. He welcomed Corden's suggestion to incorporate into trade theory economies of scale, agglomeration economies, factor mobility, transport costs and external economies of information, and felt that trade theory and location theory would then be very similar. He did not agree with Jones that the questions raised by the two theories were basically different. In particular, trapped resources did not constitute a basic dividing line. In fact, his study on Puerto Rico was concerned precisely with what kind of jobs to assign to the trapped cheap labour resources of the island. He concluded that in a realistic framework location and trade theory were really the same.

NOTE

[1] Cf. Walter Christaller, *Central places in Western Germany* (translated from: Die Zentralen Orte in Süddeutschland by Carlisle W. Baskin, Englewood Cliffs, N.J., 1966); August Lösch, *The Economics of Location* (translated from the 2nd Edition of the Räumliche Ordnung der Wirtschaft; eine Untersuchung über Standort, Wirtschaftsgebiete und Internationalen Handel) (New Haven and London, 1954); Bernhard Harms, *Volkswirtschaft und Weltwirtschaft, Versuch einer Begründung einer Weltwirtschaftslehre (National Economy and World Economy, a Suggested Justification for World Economics)* (Jena, 1912); Fritz Rörig, *Mittelalterliche Weltwirtschaft — Blüte and Ende einer Weltwirtschaftsperiode (Mediaeval World Economy — Flowering and Decay of a World Economic Period)* (Jena, 1933, Kieler Vorträge Nr. 40).

6 Conceptual and Causal Relationships in the Theory of Economic Integration in the Twentieth Century*

Fritz Machlup

My first proposition is that the theory of interregional and international trade and the theory of interregional and international economic integration are co-extensive or, to state it more boldly, are concerned with the same conceptual and causal relationships, though perhaps with some minor shifts in emphasis. I shall begin with a few comments on the term 'economic integration'.

I. ECONOMIC INTEGRATION

In his great book on *Merkantilismen* (1931), Eli Hecksher described the countless obstacles that had long existed to hamper interprovincial trade. Obstacles to trade among the French provinces before 1790 and among the German splinter states before 1834 had resulted in a *splittring* and *upplösning* of the national economies of France and Germany. Mendel Shapiro, the translator of Heckscher's book into English (1935), rendered these words as 'disintegration'.

In a Swedish article, published in the *Ekonomisk Tidskrift* (1939), Wilhelm Röpke spoke of the *förfall* of the world economy — which he translated later as disintegration — and attributed it to the economic nationalism and protectionism that fragmented the world after 1914.

---

*Prefatory note: I am indebted to scores of economists who have in countless articles and books presented their thoughts on the subject of this paper. The sources from which I have drawn most, perhaps excessively, are my own writings. I mention my Harms-Prize Lecture on 'Integrationshemmende Integrationspolitik' in *Bernhard-Harms Vorlesungen* 5/6 (Kiel: Institut für Weltwirtschaft, 1974); my Presidential Address at the Fourth World Congress of the International Economic Association, held in Budapest in 1974, on 'A History of Thought on Economic Integration', to be published in *Economic Integration: Worldwide, Regional, Sectoral* (London: Macmillan, 1976); and finally my book *A History of Thought on Economic Integration* (Macmillan, 1977).

Several German writers in the 1930s and early 1940s employed the terms integration and disintegration to describe the changing patterns and trends of world trade. In 1942, Folke Hilgerdt, the Swedish economist in charge of the trade statistics of the League of Nations, published the volume on *The Network of World Trade*, in which he presented statistical evidence pointing to the 'world-wide integration of the economy of different countries'. These men are among the first who discussed interprovincial, interregional, and international trade, and the geographic division of labour which it implies, in terms of economic integration.

The promotion of economic regionalism and bloc formation after 1945 gave a strong impulse to the development of the theory of geographic economic integration. It was conceived as a theory of the effect of preferential trade arrangements among nations and was studied chiefly as the theory of customs unions and free-trade areas (Viner, 1950, Meade, 1953, 1955). This led some writers to narrow the concept of economic integration to that of multinational trade (intrabloc trade) as distinct from interprovincial trade (intranational trade), on the one hand, and world trade, on the other (Balassa, 1961). While the political problems are surely different, for economic analysis it makes no difference whether the geographical areas in question are provinces, countries, blocs of countries, or the whole world. Economic integration of different areas always implies movements of goods, people, capital funds, moneys, and technological or organisational knowhow. It becomes apparent that the theory of economic integration has become coextensive with the theory of interregional and international trade.

In making this pronouncement, we should bear in mind that the fusion of the mentioned sets of causal propositions has taken place under two stimuli: a strong orientation to pragmatic policy considerations, and an accelerated development of theoretical analysis. The former is easy to understand, since virtually all international economic policy discussions after the Second World War were concerned with closer economic integration both through general liberalisation of payments and trade and through the formation of regional arrangements in the form of free-trade areas, trade blocs, customs unions, and currency areas. The faster rate of development of theoretical analysis in international economics goes farther back in time, as theorists replaced simpler two-country models with more complex multicountry models and replaced the assumption of international immobility of productive factors with assumptions allowing for international movements of capital and labour.

Of course, for didactic reasons, expositors of the theory of *customs union* still begin with excluding migration of labour and flows of capital across national frontiers, but they drop this restriction at some point in the analysis. The limitation to 'trade integration without factor movements' is therefore only provisional, and theorists introduce capital movements and labour migration as early as they can manage. The model of *economic*

union, which combines integration of factor markets with integration of
product markets, has become the centrepiece of integration theory.

II. DEFINITIONS OF ECONOMIC INTEGRATION

The literature has furnished us with a variety of definitions of economic
integration, but all agree that it may be understood either as a process or
as a state of affairs reached by that process. Whether that state of affairs
has to be the conceivable terminal point or any intermediate point in the
process is not always clear, but this ambiguity can be taken care of by distinguishing between complete and incomplete integration. More difficult is
the question as to what it is that is to be integrated: people, areas, economic
sectors, markets, production, goods, resources, policies, activities, or what?
Everyone of these possible subjects of integration may to some extent be
involved; this was clear to many writers when they attempted to use adjectives in order to modify or specify the noun, for example, when they spoke
of sectoral integration, trade integration, factor integration, market integration, policy integration, and so forth. Division of labour within a specified
geographical area is for many economists the sum and substance of trade
integration, though not many have made it clear whether there is a minimum of exchange of products that would justify speaking of integration.
And, in this context, one may complain that the relationships between
international movements of factors (labour and capital) and the volume
and composition of international trade are still insufficiently explored,
which seems incredible 43 years after Ohlin's pioneering work.

I submit that the idea of complete economic integration implies the
actual utilisation of all *potential* opportunities of efficient transfers of productive resources and efficient division of labour. This makes it clear that
the totality of economic activities within the area or areas in question is
what is to be integrated. However, whether unused opportunities for a
beneficial transfer of resources or a beneficial exchange of potentially produced goods exist, or whether all such opportunities have been fully taken
advantage of, can be ascertained only by benefit-and-cost analyses, in
which benefits as well as costs are hypothesised with the help of a highly
imaginative marginal calculus. Available data of observation are not sufficient to answer such questions; the calculations relevant for the evaluation of
actual and potential transfers of resources and actual and potential exchanges of products are so complex because they involve an indefinite
number of inputs and outputs indirectly related to one another by alternative employment, alternative location, and alternative production.

Complete economic integration presupposes that all enterprises and all
agencies in charge of planning and allocation have made their calculations
on the basis of opportunity cost. Every means of production, wherever
actually used, has to be valued according to the social utility that could

potentially be derived from alternative uses.[1] Such alternative uses may be anywhere in the (supposedly) integrated area and in any sector, industry, or branch, however remote. All means of production have to be in competition for all possible uses, and all branches of production have to be in competition for all possibly usable means of production. In this inter-relatedness and interdependence among all economic activities I see the essence of general economic integration. This is the principle, and it applies equally to a single country, a group of countries, or the whole world.

III. DEGREES OF ECONOMIC INTEGRATION

Several economists have suggested that we describe, estimate, or measure the degree of integration attained. Erich Schneider held that an understanding of the concept presupposed differentiation of degrees of integration between the two extremes, complete isolation and perfect integration (Schneider, 1957). Jean Weiller wrote an article on 'Les degrés de l'intégration', in which he hinted at the possibility of an 'optimal degree of integration' to be far short of an 'ideal maximum' (Weiller, 1958). I suspect, however, that Weiller's idea was quite different from Schneider's, and I have not been able to find any consistent body of thought on these conceptions, least of all among the quantitative analysts who have tried to measure integration and compare the progress made in different regions or blocs of nations.

The difficulty or impossibility of measuring economic integration, or even of suggesting methods of doing it, is embarrassing. There are philosophers' dicta to the effect that a concept ought to be subject to *operational definition* and that propositions employing the concept ought to be subject to *operational testing*. I am inclined to disregard these dicta as neopositivistic prejudice, and to reject the still more extreme position which denies that anything but empirical operations can give meaning to concepts and to propositions involving them. Thus I insist that the concept of a degree of economic integration has meaning even if we do not know how to measure it. However, if one asserts that a concrete historical situation represents a higher degree of integration than another such situation, one cannot reasonably refuse to tell on what evidence his assertion rests. For example, if somebody compares the progress made or degree attained in the economic integration among the C.M.E.A. countries and the E.E.C. countries (or among the states of the U.S.A., or between the U.S.A. and Canada) he has to present statistical evidence – and present also the theoretical basis on which one can agree that it really is evidence for what is being asserted. This holds also for comparisons of the progress of integration in a given area over stated periods of time.

The indices offering themselves for comparisons of this sort refer either to *conditions* or to *effects*. Among the conditions are those that are likely to affect *mobility*, and among the effects are actual *movements*. Both mobility (the elasticity of responses to stimuli) and actual movements refer to goods, people, capital funds, enterprise and management. Mobility of goods can be affected by tariffs and customs formalities (with their delays and chicaneries), quotas, licence requirements, payments restrictions, currency allocations, deposit requirements, and all sorts of controls, regulations, and their operations. One can furnish similar lists for conditions affecting travel, migration, trade credits, capital transfers, securities purchases, direct investments, and whatever else may contribute to economic integration.

The effects of mobility may be seen not only in actual movements of goods, people, and capital funds but also in relative prices; hence, comparisons of relative prices of goods, labour services, loanable funds, and securities in the supposedly integrated countries are valuable tests of the adequacy of mobility, on the one hand, and of the degree of integration achieved, on the other. For standardised products such tests are easier than for differentiated ones. The simplest tests are based on the rule that, in the absence of restrictions, prices for the same commodity will not differ from one place to another by more than the transport cost between these places and, if one of the places in question is the site where the good is produced, delivered prices should not differ by less than the transport cost. Tests for prices of the same securities on different stock exchanges are even simpler, whereas tests of interest rates for loanable funds are complicated by the fact that various risks — risks of default or future restrictions on payments, exchange risks, etc. — are involved and may be differently evaluated by different lenders for different borrowers. Tests for prices of the 'same' kind and quality of labour in different countries are very difficult, first because one can never be sure that the efficiency of the workers is really the same, secondly because differences in working conditions, fringe benefits, and non-pecuniary advantages and disadvantages of residing in different places and countries are hard to take into account, thirdly because variations in exchange rates may play havoc with the comparisons, and fourthly because adjustments of existing differences in earnings through migration are very slow, what with the risky investment in moving expenses and the psychological obstacles to moving to a foreign country.

One of the most widely used tests consists in comparisons of various *trade ratios*: what portion of total purchases in any part of a supposedly integrated (or intentionally to be integrated) region is of goods and services produced in that same part (province, state, country), what portion is of goods and services produced in other parts of the region, and what portion is of things produced in the rest of the world? Analogous tests are made for total sales of output: what portion is sold to residents of the same part of the region (province, state, country), what portion sold to other parts of the region, what portion to the rest of the world? Studies of this sort have been made with most surprising results. They show a remarkable provincialism in Europe, where in the larger countries the bulk of all purchases are of goods and services produced in the same country, and the bulk of all sales are to residents of the same country. Analogous estimates for the United States yield very much larger shares of purchases and sales, respectively, from suppliers and to buyers residing in other states of the union.

While these and other tests, despite all their weaknesses, may shed some light on the connotations of economic integration, they cannot be admitted as conclusive in an attempt to measure the degree of economic integration attained. The main reason for this scepsis lies in the fact that integration is essentially, as I have said before, a *relative* achievement, a ratio of actually realised to potentially realisable opportunities for effective division of labour. We may have learned how to measure actual trade, actual migration, actual capital movements, but we have not yet learned how to measure the unused potential.

IV. DEGREE OF INTEGRATION VERSUS EXTENSION OF AREA INTEGRATED

Additional difficulties of a conceptual nature arise from the fact that economic integration is relative not only to unknown potentials but also relative to the area under consideration. We must distinguish the *degree* of integration achieved within a *given territory* from the *extension of the territory* to be integrated.

If new territory is added to a region with the intent of having the resources and activities in the new territory integrated with those of the 'old' area, one must expect a reorganisation of some of the activities and a reallocation of its resources in both parts and, of course, more trade between the old and the new parts of the extended region. This calls for caution in appraisals of the degree of integration, especially if actual movements of goods and factors are measured and the results considered as aids in such appraisals. Any increased division of labour between the old and the new parts of the extended region should express itself in new trade flows which increase the share of intraregional trade in total world trade. Of course, the combined shares of domestic trade and of what was previously counted as intraregional trade within the old region may then be lower. This reduction should not lead to wrong conclusions concerning either the degree of integration in the old or in the extended region. As the network of trade widens and the relative share of trade among the closest neighbours is reduced in the process, it would surely be erroneous to infer from this that the extension of external trade and the smaller relative share of internal trade mean a lower degree of general economic integration of the original 'home area'.

Let us then affirm that *the notion 'degree of integration' calls for a specification of the area or combination of areas to which it is supposed to apply*. We should note that different degrees of integration may have been reached (a) within the old region; (b) between the old region and one newly joined with it; (c) between the old region and the rest of the world; and (d) between the extended region (the combined area) and the rest of the world. If other regional blocs exist, even more combinations would be interesting, especially, the degree of integration (e) between the extended region and the other regional blocs.

If we thus accept the idea that the degree of integration may be estimated (or at least a rough impression formed) separately for each area and for each combination of areas, we shall find it possible to speak of a relatively high degree of integration within area A, a lower degree within area $A + B$, a still lower one within $A + B + C$, and so on until we have the entire world. This is not inconsistent with expressed policy statements of several governments. They are, as a rule, determined to take advantage of all efficient opportunities for division of labour within their own country; they very much want to utilise many such opportunities within the regional group of which they are a member; they hold that considerable gains could be derived from trade with other regional blocs (for example, East-West trade) or, in general, with the rest of the world. It would be unnecessarily confining to estimate the degree of integration just for the economic activities within the regional bloc. The concept makes sense for any and all combinations of territories, even if we are still far from knowing how to measure it.

The worst difficulty arises from the fact that the emergence of new opportunities for efficient division of labour with any part of the world outside the area on which something is to be predicated will almost certainly change the original set of opportunities; the comparative advantages of various productive activities will be altered with each inclusion of productive resources available outside the original area. The inherent conceptual difficulties are as yet insufficiently explored. One might construct a few simple models with a small number of factors, goods, and countries, with given production functions and given preference systems, and then try to compare different combinations of 'integrated' areas. Such an exercise might yield some elucidation of what is implied in 'higher' and 'lower' degrees of integration when the extension of the area in question is varied in a variety of ways.

V. INTERNAL VERSUS EXTERNAL INTEGRATION

Pending the solution of the problem of how degrees of integration may be conceived, it seems rather daring to pronounce on the possible welfare effects obtainable by the two modes of utilising opportunities of efficient division of labour: more intensive exchange within the area in question or outward extension of the area. Yet, pronouncements on this question have been made and, we must admit, with a ring of plausibility. The question was formulated as a comparison between two possible policies: toward a *partial* approach to a *wider* union and, alternatively, toward a *more complete* approach to a *narrower* union. The answer suggested an application of the law of diminishing returns; if there has been a good deal of integration achieved within the given area, it would seem more promising to look for extending trade with the outside world (Meade, 1953). That is to say, larger net additions to the economic welfare of the inhabitants of the original area may be expected from extended than from intensified integration.

This view obviously took it for granted that the degree of internal integration in the original area was reasonably high. If one assumes, however, that serious obstacles have existed to economic integration within the area — say, that strong trade unions have effectively closed entry into some of the most productive activities, or that industries with entrenched positions of monopoly or oligopoly have restricted the production of important materials — the removal of these obstacles and, hence, the attainment of a higher degree of internal integration of the economy (national or regional) may well make a greater contribution to economic welfare than could be expected from an extension of division of labour with other countries. It happens that the conflict in judging the merits of the alternative policies may be more apparent than real, since the extension of external trade may at the same time reduce the power of the disintegrating elements within the economy (nation or region). For example, competition from imports may reduce the restrictions imposed by organised labour and monopolistic industry. In this case the outward-looking policy, securing a higher degree of economic integration with the outside world, would at the same time raise the degree of internal integration.

That this happy result of more extensive (international) integration aiding internal integration — a chance of killing two birds with one stone — cannot reasonably be generalised, may readily be seen if one assumes that the obstacle to internal integration is not a monopoly situation that can be overcome by foreign competition but, instead, a condition that will not yield to it. Take, for example, a case of government regulation restricting domestic transport through distorted freight charges that bear no relation to the cost of hauling goods by railway, highway, barge, or ship. This kind of disintegrating regulation will not be alleviated by an increase in foreign trade, and benefits derived from an increase in international division of labour may well be smaller than those obtainable from allowing a higher degree of domestic integration by replacing the bureaucratic follies of public regulation of transport with the anonymous forces of competition among truckers and rival haulers of goods.

The point made by these examples is, again, to warn against facile generalisations. It may be safe to pronounce a judgement to the effect that a nation (or region), starting from a high degree of internal economic integration and a low degree of international (interregional) economic integration, may expect a larger increase in its total product from extending its division of labour with the outside world than from trying to intensify its internal integration. To go beyond this judgement would not be safe; where internal economic integration has been hindered (or obstructed) by obstacles to the movement of factors and products, by institutional rigidities, and by administrative bungling, removal of these disintegrating roadblocks may deserve the highest priority on the nation's (or region's) agenda.

However, the comparison of the welfare effects obtainable from stepping up the degree of internal integration and those from an extension of external trade would make good sense only where the two policies were disjunctive alternatives, each excluding the other. Where this is not the case, where the nation or region does not have to choose between the two courses of action but can proceed with both, the benefits it can obtain need not be measured against each other. Economic integration can reach higher degrees internally, internationally and interregionally at the same time.

VI. INTERPRETING THE CHANGES IN TRADE RATIOS

In statistical descriptions of developments in international trade certain ratios of trade to other magnitudes have been assigned significant roles, particularly with regard to what is purported to indicate 'progress' in economic integration. The ratio of a country's trade with other *members* of its trading bloc, customs union, or free-trade area to its *total* international trade, and the changes in the ratio over the years, have been regarded as highly significant. Other widely advertised ratios have been those of intraregional, interregional, and world trade, to the gross national product of the country or group of countries concerned. Unfortunately, the theoretical support for the inferences drawn from the statistical observations was often lacking: and if the ratios, and any trends shown by their changes, were said to be significant, one can hardly help asking: 'significant for what?'

A simple example may explain why this rude question had to be asked. If, for any reason (say, because of the removal of obstacles or because of some 'positive' actions of government), a country's trade increases both with other bloc members and with non-member countries, it depends on which increase happens to be greater relative to the previous trade volumes, whether the ratio of intraregional trade to total trade will be higher or lower than it had been. A decrease in that ratio, in the face of an increase in the absolute volume (physical or value) of intraregional trade, would surely *not* indicate a decline in the degree of regional integration. Even if intrabloc trade remained unchanged and only the trade with non-member countries was increased, the fall in the ratio of intraregional trade to total trade need not be indicative of a decline in regional integration.

More relevant to the problem of integration are changes in the basic shares of a country's expenditure (absorption, intake).[2] These basic shares are for domestic production, imports from member countries, and imports from non-member countries (Truman, 1975). Other things remaining equal, the reduction or abolition of intrabloc tariffs and increase in regional integration can be expected to raise the relative share of imports from member countries at the expense of the shares of domestic production and of imports from non-member countries. A reduction in the share of expenditure on domestic products would indicate trade creation, and a reduction in the share of expenditure on imports from non-member countries would indicate trade diversion. Since other things may have changed, besides the preferential treatment of imports from bloc countries, actual expenditures would, for purposes of empirical estimation, have to be corrected for the effects of these other changes, so that the residual changes in the three basic shares could be attributed to the deliberate promotion of regional integration.

Such an approach, however, can at best give some clues regarding the progress of regional integration, but usually not even that, because the increase in the share of expenditures for imports from bloc countries may be due to disintegrating changes within the national economy and/or to disintegrating obstacles to imports from non-bloc countries. Of course, the econometrician may have 'caught' all these other changes and corrected the observed data for their presumed effects. (Many changes in the country's wage structure brought about by collective bargaining may have disintegrating effects in the national economy. They are difficult to catch and even more difficult to take into account in correcting the recorded expenditure data.) Equally difficult to deal with are the effects of changes in commercial policy vis-à-vis non-bloc countries; for example, reductions of duties on imports from these countries may have occurred together with the abolition of the duties on intrabloc trade. Simultaneous progress in regional and worldwide integration could, however, be ascertained only by hypothetically eliminating in turn the effects of the changes promoting first the one and then the other; otherwise the relative share of expenditures on imports from non-bloc countries might rise at the expense, not only of the domestic share, but also of that of imports from bloc countries, and wrongly indicate a decline in regional integration.

Some economic analysts, trying to assess the degree or progress of trade integration, have focused on trade/income ratios and their changes. Before one can see the relevance or irrelevance of these ratios, one must first understand the implications of the relative size of the countries for their trade ratios. If by 'size' one means a country's total (national or domestic) product, and by 'trade' the value of its exports plus its imports — and if one assumes, for the sake of simplicity, that countries are approximately equal in every respect that matters in this context (chiefly the stage of industrialisation, degree of economic integration, the peoples' tastes and wants, the wealth and incomes per head) — it follows that the trade/income ratio will vary inversely with the countries' size.[3]

This relationship between the trade/income ratio and the relative size of countries makes the ratio useless for comparisons of the degree of integration, national or worldwide, of different countries. On the other hand, changes in the trade/income ratio over the years may be significant as symptoms of progress of international economic integration. If the foreign trade of a given country, with its political frontiers unchanged, grows consistently at a faster annual rate than its national (or domestic) production, the resulting increase in the trade/income ratio may indicate that the country's economy is getting more closely interwoven with the world economy. A steady increase in the trade/income ratio for a group of countries will tell the same story for the group, as will the world trade/world income ratio for the entire world.

If foreign trade is divided into intraregional, interregional, and worldwide trade, one may use the changing ratios of each of these figures to the income of a country (or group of countries) as clues to the progress of the various kinds of trade integration over the years. But, to repeat for emphasis, while changes in the said ratios over time may be relevant for appraisals of trends in these respects, the ratios cannot be used for comparisons of the degree of integration attained by different countries at any particular moment of time.

One other statistical indicator may be briefly mentioned: the ratio of trade balances to the total value of trade. If a country's foreign trade is disaggregated to show its trade (exports plus imports) with all its trading partners, and its balance of trade is likewise disaggregated by country, the ratios of the balance to the total may indicate the degree of bilateral balancing. Complete bilateral balancing makes the ratio infinite, since all balances are zero. For a country using all its proceeds for its exports to one group of countries to pay for its imports from another group of countries, the ratio of the sum of its trade balances (surpluses *plus* deficits) to its total trade (exports *plus* imports) will be unity and will indicate completely triangular or multilateral trade patterns. What matters, however, is less the degree of bilateralism in any given year than the changes over the years. A consistent decline in the balance/volume ratio over time may indicate an increase in bilateral trade arrangement; a consistent increase in the ratio, increase in multilateralism. Multilateralism is associated with a higher degree of worldwide integration.

VII. METHODOLOGICAL DISTINCTIONS REGARDING THE EFFECTS OF INTEGRATION

Virtually all distinctions which economic theorists have made for their various techniques of reasoning have found a place in the literature dealing

with the effects of trade liberalisation, trade discrimination, and the formation of trading blocs. There are, of course, the usual dichotomies and
trichotomies of direct and indirect effects; primary, secondary, and tertiary
effects; short-run, medium-run, and long-run effects; static and dynamic
effects; effects inferred from partial-equilibrium analysis and those consistent with general equilibrium. All these distinctions have been applied to
the analysis of effects on product prices, factor prices, resource allocation,
production, employment, trade, gains from trade, movements of productive
factors, distribution of income and wealth, investment, economic development and growth, and all the rest.

In some instances the distinctions were more confusing than helpful,
and often they were rather arbitrary and idiosyncratic. It made good sense,
however, to designate the effects of establishing a customs union as primary
in so far as they bore on the changes in imports resulting directly from the
reduction or removal of import duties; as secondary in so far as they modified the prices and quantities of substitutes and complements of the products primarily affected; and as tertiary in so far as they were repercussions
of adjustment processes necessary to restore balance in international payments (Meade, 1955). It was quite evident that any limitation of the analysis to the primary effects involved partial equilibrium only and left the
processes associated with general equilibrium unexplored. On the other
hand, effects derived from partial-equilibrium analysis are, as a rule, more
fully determinate than those derived from general-equilibrium analysis,
which calls for an infinitely greater number of specifications of conditions
(and policy decisions) if the degrees of freedom are to be reduced sufficiently to make the problem manageable and the outcome more 'predictable'.

The least helpful distinction proposed in the analysis under consideration was that between static and dynamic effects. The use of this pair of
adjectives has had a long and spotty history, but in recent years economic
theorists had more or less agreed to associate the terms with the use of
dated and lagged variables in their models or systems of relationships. It
was then entirely in contravention to this usage if some economists decided
to speak of dynamic effects of the removal of tariffs, not in order to
characterise the type of analysis employed in explaining the effects, but in
order to separate realisation of economies of scale, increase in competition,
and diversion of investment, from all other induced changes of resource reallocation. Any and all of these changes can be explained by means of
static or of dynamic analysis, and there just is no sense in which a particular
change is a 'dynamic effect'. Of course, as in most terminological and
methodological discourses, no harm to the validity of the analysis of the
investigated problems follows necessarily from the inappropriate use of
language.

VIII. ECONOMIC WELFARE, SOCIAL WELFARE, PRIDE AND ENVY

There is wide agreement on the pronouncement that the analysis of economic integration constitutes only a bare skeleton of positive economics
and that virtually all its meaty substance is welfare economics. This has at
least two reasons: (a) The chief problem of economic integration is the
division of the gain in material output among different regions, different
countries, and different groups of people, and any statement about net
benefits from integration involves, therefore, an evaluation of gains enjoyed
and losses suffered by different persons. (b) It is not only the distribution
of material products that is involved, but also of satisfactions and dissatisfactions of a merely 'psychic' nature, including the pleasures and displeasures associated with non-tangible changes which may induce feelings
of pride and envy.

Considerations of the distributional aspects of changes in economic welfare and of the sentimental aspects of changes in social welfare are entirely
in the domain of evaluative (normative) economics. This does not relegate
matters into the dustbin of metaphysical speculation; for better or for
worse, the value judgements about the effects and side-effects of economic
integration are crucial in the policy decisions of governments acting for
their constituencies. Their actions may include such things as the gratification of national pride at the expense of efficient production for increased
material consumption (Johnson, 1965; Charles Cooper and Massell,
1965), or their actions may be motivated by envy and resentment and
imply the acceptance of sacrifices of potential gains just in order to avoid
that larger gains accrue to others. These are, therefore, very pragmatic
questions about national choices. Perhaps the magnitude of the costs and
sacrifices is not always known to the nations clamouring for such decisions
but, apart from this incomplete knowledge, one cannot contend that the
basic considerations are irrational — even if other people with more accurate
knowledge of the benefits and costs or with different preferences and
appreciation of social welfare might advocate very different policies.

IX. THE INCLUSION OF PUBLIC GOODS

Among the most frequently 'demanded' intangibles are the gratifications
of national pride in being able to produce something within the country
instead of importing it from abroad. While economists acknowledge that
such satisfactions are 'public goods' that are part of total welfare, they
question whether the choices in favour of the merely psychic incomes are
made in full awareness of the cost, that is, of the material goods sacrificed
by producing at home what could be had much more cheaply from abroad.

Similar doubts may be raised in connection with other public goods
which can be produced more efficiently for smaller communities than for

large ones (Richard Cooper, 1976). There is a real conflict — a contradiction, in Marxian jargon — between the optimal scale of production for most private, material goods and that for many collective, intangible goods. If it were established that private, material goods are most efficiently produced at a scale so large that only a very large integrated region, if not the whole world, can fully utilise the appropriate productive capacity, while the services that are rated as public, collective goods are most efficiently provided in the small and cosier, culturally coherent environment of a small community, a serious question of the 'optimum area of integration' would arise. Almost 50 years ago, John Maynard Keynes raised it and tentatively concluded that, since services were becoming more important than material goods, free trade was becoming less and less significant for total welfare. This argument, downgrading free trade, would by implication downgrade international division of labour and economic integration of extended areas. A counterargument suggests, however, that most nations can afford to devote increasing portions of their incomes to the types of services regarded as public goods only because private material goods, the necessities of life, have become so much less expensive thanks to international division of labour.

X. COMPROMISE BETWEEN FREE-TRADERS AND PROTECTIONISTS

A customs union or any regional trade bloc may be seen as a compromise between two groups of antagonists promoting seemingly irreconcilable principles of policy: free-traders and protectionists. Having made the compromise, the former are happy about the abolition of barriers in intrabloc trade, the latter about the continuation of barriers against extrabloc imports. Does it make sense to ask who has made the greater concession in reaching the compromise?

The question makes sense indeed, and the answer depends on the height of the trade barriers abolished and that of the barriers retained. But, as a matter of fact, a good many free-traders (with a 'more realistic' world outlook) had not been seriously concerned about the tariff walls retained around the region and about the trade discrimination which it implied, because (as eternal optimists) they counted on both a gradual lowering of the walls and a gradual pushing outward of the walls: more countries would join the union and a continuing growth of world trade would not only be admitted but actually desired and promoted.

This optimistic prognosis has often been made, sometimes founded on a strange faith in the basic rationality of human action, including political action, sometimes on nothing but wishful thinking. More recently, rigorous mathematical proofs have been furnished, using set-theoretical methods, demonstrating that an incentive to form and enlarge customs unions persists until the world is one big customs union, that is, until universal free-

trade prevails (Kemp and Wan, 1976). That this process is so slow is explained by game-theoretic problems (choosing partners, dividing spoils,
enforcing agreements), non-economic national objectives, inertia and ignorance. With good will and luck, these obstacles on the path of economic
rationality may eventually be overcome.

XI. POLITICAL INTEGRATION

The two groups of friends of trade blocs and customs unions, those aiming
at regional protection and those aiming at eventual worldwide trade integration, were greatly aided by a third group: those who cared far less about
economic integration as an objective, but saw it as a catalyst of political
integration. They were hoping that closer economic relations among the
members of a customs union would lead to closer political ties and eventually to political unification.

The literature is rich on contributions to the theme whether economic
integration could and would lead to political integration, or the other way
around. The pragmatic implications of this question were, at several junc-
tures in history, of utmost importance. The question was hotly debated in
the years of the formation of the German *Zollverein*, but the discussion
was resumed on many occasions. Economists of the historical school made
solemn pronouncements on the subject, usually to the effect that a
'historical law' made it most unlikely for any arrangement of economic
integration ever to succeed if it was not preceded or at least accompanied
by political integration; the one great exception, the German *Zollverein*,
was said to have been just the 'exception that proved the law'.

This controversy has lost some of its steam after the exceptions to the
alleged historical law became too notorious. No longer can it be denied
that regional trade arrangements and regional economic integration are
possible without prior political integration. What has remained open is,
first, the question whether these economic arrangements can be permanently viable if they are not followed by some degree of political integration, and, second, the question whether ever higher degrees of economic
integration will strengthen the forces that operate to bring closer political
integration and federation or unification of now sovereign countries into
being.

XII. SUMMARY AND A FEW AFTERTHOUGHTS

Complete economic integration, I have said, means that all potential opportunities of efficient transfer of productive resources and efficient division
of labour are actually utilised. This idea is difficult to sell, because potentials are often not subject to quantitative estimation, let alone measurement. I will summarise some of the major obstacles to quantification.

(a) Division of labour and transfer of resources are imperfect substitutes (that is, they would be perfect substitutes only under excessively strong, counterfactual assumptions) and we do not know just what sizes and kinds of flows of products and flows of factors would be equivalent in their effects.

(b) The 'efficiency' of a geographical transfer of labour is to a large part a matter of subjective evaluation by people with different personal feelings for the risks and psychic costs of migration, temporary or definitive.

(c) The 'potential' is not invariant; it changes with every variation in supply, technology, demand, tastes, etc., and such changes may increase or reduce the unused opportunities for 'efficient' movements of products and resources.

(d) If 'degree' of integration refers to the remaining distance from 'complete' integration, and if this ideal terminal point is subject to continuous change, the notion is not only statistically non-operational, it is not even conceivably operational.

(e) Even the notion of 'progress' in economic integration becomes difficult to defend, because, although we may have increased the distance from 'zero integration', new opportunities for efficient movements of factors and products may have arisen and may have increased our distance from complete integration; thus we may have moved forward and yet be farther away from the terminal point.

(f) All these conceptual difficulties are compounded if the geographical area, which is progressing towards greater internal integration, is extended to include territories previously 'outside'. (Assume that six countries, none of which has a completely integrated economy, form a union and begin to move towards an integrated economy; next that three additional countries join the union, and a process of integration between the six and the three is getting under way; finally, that the walls around the nine are lowered and division of labour with the rest of the world is initiated. We now are confronted with four different degrees of integration, each suffering from all the conceptual infirmities described in the previous five points.) The problem is so messy that one can well understand if some economists refuse to go on with it.

Some have even expressed their inclination to scrap the phrase economic integration altogether. I admit that there may be problems that disappear when confusing terms are replaced by less misleading ones, but I do not believe that the problems I have indicated are of this sort. They will not go away when we invent more felicitous words. The literature of the last twenty-five years is full of attempts to measure the progress of economic integration in the E.E.C., in the C.M.E.A., in various other regions, and in the world as a whole. Most of these attempts have been confined to trade shares and a variety of trade ratios, and the conceptual basis of the analyses was often anything but clear, the statistical data employed were usually quite poor, and the correspondence between the empirical data and the theoretical constructs was questionable. Thus, the results were not conclusive; but there can be no doubt that the analysts were dealing with what they conceived to be meaningful problems. Even if all these studies are vulnerable and can be criticised for having disregarded or covered up some fundamental conceptual defects, the idea of 'progress' in economic integration cannot be thrown out on the ground of its vagueness or complexity.

Perhaps it will help if we recall that there are a number of widely used terms that are closely akin to, and in some contexts full equivalents of, 'integrating' measures (or 'integrating' changes in conditions and constraints). Economists speak, for example, of institutional changes that are 'monopoly-reducing', 'mobility-increasing', 'distortion-reducing'. Every one of these expressions connotes the removal of an insulating, immobilising, distorting device or condition. The existence of 'non-competing groups', groups', 'market-failure' or 'market-imperfection' are other phrases favoured by many economists in the same context; the relaxation or removal of such 'imperfections' reduces the fragmentation of the (national, regional, world) economy and is thus a factor promoting the 'integration' of the economy in question. Nowhere, to my knowledge, have all market imperfections, all immobility-fostering or allocation-distorting constraints ever been removed at one stroke; but there have been periods in which imperfections of this sort were gradually reduced and I can see no good reason why these developments should not be denoted as progress in economic integration. The problem of measurement is not changed with the linguistic changes. It is not one bit easier to measure the progress made in 'reducing distortion' than it is to measure progress in 'economic integration'. As a matter of fact, the two, defined in a defensible manner, are the same.[4]

An unrelenting operationalist will regard all these problems, whatever terms are used to denote them, as pseudoproblems; if he is consistent, he will also have to reject Walrasian general-equilibrium theory, since it is incurably non-operational. It is not possible to substitute statistical data, obtained from empirical observation, for the terms in the Walrasian functions. Assume that, despite substantial changes in available resources, in technological opportunities, and in peoples' tastes, all productive resources and services are immobilised; assume next that this period of immobility is ended and a universal *tâtonnement* towards general equilibrium is started, with various paths, roads, and avenues towards complete equilibrium. Depending on the dynamics of 'equilibration', productive services will be reallocated, prices of products and factors will be revised, and products made in larger or smaller quantities; and all these changes may continue for a very long time, with fluctuations and oscillations due to different time-lags of adjustments behind price signals in different markets, different industries, different sectors. However, depending on a variety of conditions (including the completely unrealistic assumption that no further changes take place in resources, technology, and tastes, or the less unrealistic assumption that the speed of such changes is substantially below the speed of the adjustment tending towards an 'equilibrium solution'), I submit that it makes good sense to raise the question of how much progress towards equilibration has been made in a number of 'market days' or 'output-changing decisions', etc. Not that anything of this sort can be done in the world we live, but it can be done in the world which we 'model' in our minds.

The process of a general-equilibrium system approaching a solution in which no further adjustments (reallocations, price changes, output revisions) take place unless further changes in resources, technology, and tastes occur is equivalent or analogous to the process of economic integration. The only conceptual difference is that the Walrasian model in its simpler forms abstracts from space and distances, whereas the models for geographical economic integration have territories and areas among their essential properties. Economists willing to admit general-equilibrium models to their theoretical instrumentarium cannot reasonably resist the admission of models of economic integration – even if neither of them is equipped for operational tests, except where statistical proxies are recognised as remote relatives of the mental constructs employed in the models and theories in question.

NOTES

[1] Social utility takes account of external benefits and costs but does not disregard private evaluations. For example, if people give much weight to non-pecuniary advantages and disadvantages when they choose between migrating or staying where they are, these considerations are integral parts of social evaluations – though they are unknown and practically unknowable.

[2] The term 'absorption' for a nation's real expenditures was coined, as far as I know, by Kenneth E. Boulding, *Economic Analysis* (New York: Harper, 1941). It was later used, in setting forth the 'income-absorption approach', by Sidney S. Alexander, 'Effects of a Devaluation on a Trade Balance', *International Monetary Fund Staff Papers*, Vol. 2 (April, 1952), pp. 263–278. The term 'intake' was proposed by me as a more suitable member of the set: input, output, income, and intake (where all the nouns are formed by compounding a preposition with a verb). See my 'The Terms-of-Trade Effects of Devaluation upon Real Income and the Balance of Trade', *Kyklos*, Vol. 9 (1956), pp. 417–452.

[3] If this is not immediately obvious to the reader, let him imagine a world of only three countries of equal size (national income) and equal trade/income ratios; now let two of these countries merge into a double-sized one. Total national income of this large country will, of course, be twice that of each part; its total foreign trade, however, will not be doubled, because half of what was foreign trade is now counted as domestic trade between the two halves of the united country; the actual foreign trade of the two halves will therefore add up to an unchanged trade volume of the

enlarged country. With the national product doubled but foreign trade unchanged, the trade ratio of the double-size country will be one-half that of the small country.

This may be the place to explain why some relatively small but highly industrialised countries may have trade/income ratios close to unity or even above. If there is much trade — exports plus imports — in materials and semi-finished products, which enter trade statistics with their full value, foreign trade may exceed national income, which contains only the value added by domestic activities to the values of materials and semi-finished products. Cases in point are Belgium and the Netherlands, whose foreign trade (exports plus imports) in 1973 and 1974 exceeded their national incomes, was about equal to their gross national products and only slightly below their gross domestic products.

[4] Distortion can be defined either as a *condition* (constraint) or as an *effect* of the condition (constraint). Under the first definition, tariffs, monopoly positions, minimum wages, etc., *are* distortions; under the second definition, they *cause* distortions in relative prices, marginal products, etc. The same semantic differences exist regarding 'integration': abolition of tariffs may *be* or may *permit* or may *bring about* integration. I prefer the definition in terms of relative prices and resource allocation.

REFERENCES

Alexander, S. S., 'Effects of a Devaluation on a Trade Balance', *International Monetary Fund Staff Papers*, Vol. 2 (Apr., 1952), pp. 263—278.
Balassa, B., 'Towards a Theory of Economic Integration', *Kyklos*, Vol. 14 (1961), pp. 1—17.
Balassa, B., *The Theory of Economic Integration* (Homewood, Ill.: Irwin, 1961), pp. 1—3.
Boulding, K. E., *Economic Analysis* (New York: Harper, 1941).
Cooper, C. A. and Massell, B. F., 'Towards a General Theory of Customs Unions for Developing Countries', *Journal of Political Economy*, Vol. 73 (1965), pp. 461—476.
Cooper, R. N., 'Worldwide versus Regional Integration: Is There an Optimum Size of the Integrated Area?' in Fritz Machlup, (ed.), *Economic Integration: Worldwide, Regional, Sectoral*, Proceedings of the Fourth World Congress of the International Economic Association (London: Macmillan, 1976, pp. 41—53.
Heckscher, E. F., *Merkantilismen* (Stockholm: Norstedt and Söners, 1931). English edition, *Mercantilism*, authorised translation by Mendel Shapiro (London: Allen and Unwin, 1935).
Hilgerdt, F., *The Network of World Trade* (Geneva: Economic Intelligence Service, League of Nations, 1942).
Johnson, H. G., 'An Economic Theory of Protectionism, Tariff Bargaining, and the Formation of Customs Unions', *Journal of Political Economy*, Vol. 73 (1965), pp. 256—283.
Kemp, M. C. and Wan, H. Y., 'An Elementary Proposition Concerning the

Formation of Customs Unions', *Journal of International Economics*, Vol. 6 (Feb., 1976), pp. 95–97.

Machlup, F., 'The Terms-of-Trade Effects of Devaluation upon Real Income and the Balance of Trade', *Kyklos*, Vol. 9 (1956), pp. 417–452.

Meade, J. E., *Problems of Economic Union* (Chicago: University of Chicago Press, 1953).

Meade, J. E., *The Theory of Customs Unions* (Amsterdam: North Holland Publishing Co., 1955).

Ohlin, B., *Interregional and International Trade* (Cambridge, Mass.: Harvard University Press, 1933).

Röpke, W., 'Världshushallningens förfall och därmed sammanhängande grundfrågor', *Ekonomisk Tidskrift*, Vol. 41 (Jan., 1939), pp. 11–29.

Schneider, E., 'Lineamenti di una teoria economica del mercato commune', *Rivista Internazionale di Scienze Economiche e Commerciali*, Vol. 2 (Feb., 1957), pp. 107–118.

Truman, E. M., 'The Effects of European Economic Integration on the Production and Trade of Manufactured Products', in Bela Balassa, (ed.) *European Economic Integration* (Amsterdam: North Holland Publishing Company, 1975), pp. 3–40.

Weiller, J., 'Les degrés de l'intégration et les chances d'une 'zone de coopération' internationale', *Revue Economique*, Vol. 9 (Mar., 1958), pp. 233–254.

Comment
Assar Lindbeck

INTERNATIONAL ECONOMIC INTEGRATION

I have no serious quarrel with Fritz Machlup's various definitions and descriptions of the *general* concept of 'economic integration'. In fact, his distinctions are both thoughtful and clarifying. As I do not really feel qualified to elaborate upon these concepts, I can probably make more of a contribution by discussing various problems connected with one *specific* type of economic integration, namely integration across national borders, which I will call *internationalisation*. This type of integration is, of course, particularly interesting from the point of view of economic policy, as the targets, instruments and design of economic policy are still largely attached to national states.

To begin with, it is important to ask, as Machlup does: *integration of what*? I think it is useful to concentrate on the international economic integration of three things: markets, institutions and externalities. With a further breakdown of these concepts, the following more detailed classification is obtained:[1]

(1) Internationalisation of *markets* for (a) commodities and services, (b) money and credit, (c) labour and human capital, (d) technology and entrepreneurship.
(2) Internationalisation of *institutions*: (a) political, (b) interest groups, (c) market-oriented institutions.
(3) Internationalisation of *externalities*: (a) on the production side (e.g. environmental disturbances), (b) on the consumption side (e.g. taste equalisation).

It is quite clear that international economic integration, like other types of economic integration, has been caused both by market forces and by institutional developments, in particular by political decisions. What I would like to emphasise is the *interrelations* between market forces, institutional changes and political decisions in the process of international economic integration, even though it is often difficult to say which developments should be classified as 'autonomous' and 'induced', respectively. Political decisions and institutional changes have released and facilitated integrating market forces, and these market forces have in turn influenced institutional changes and political decisions, with considerable effects on the integration process — sometimes speeding it up, sometimes modifying or retarding it.

The discussion here about these issues will be organised around three questions: (a) What are the dominating features of the internationalisation process? (b) What are the effects on the national economies? (c) What are the reactions of politicians to these effects?

I. WHAT IS INTERNATIONALISATION?

(1) MARKETS

Commodities and services
It is, I think, useful to distinguish between three different aspects, or 'dimensions', of integration of markets:

(a) Larger *flows* ('movements') between countries of goods and factors.
(b) Higher sensitivity ('mobility') of these flows between countries.
(c) Larger *stocks* of assets and factors of foreign origin.

All these aspects will be considered here. However, what particular aspect of market integration over national borders that is of relevance in a specific case depends, of course, on the problem at hand. For instance, if we want to study how international events influence short-term fluctuations in *domestic output*, for example by the help of an export multiplier model, the share of *trade flows* (exports) to GDP may be a useful measure of the degree of internationalisation. As this ratio has been fairly constant during the postwar period — the O.E.C.D. average has increased from about 11 per cent in the early 1950s to about 13 per cent in the mid 1970s — and as the amplitude of the fluctuations in real world trade has been rather small (except possibly for the years 1973—75), it is difficult to avoid the conclusion that 'externally' generated macroeconomic disturbances of output for individual countries have been *less* pronounced in the post-Second World War period than earlier. However, there *might* have been a tendency during the last decade to a closer *synchronisation* of volume fluctuations among countries. This is of some policy interest, as the world economy would be more stable if the large economies — U.S., West Germany, Japan, etc. — could avoid a close synchronisation of their fluctuations in aggregate demand.

If we are instead interested in *price disturbances* from international markets, the *direct* impact on the national economy is presumably related more to the share of the flow of *tradeables* than to the share of trade. (The *total* 'static equilibrium' effects depend largely on how the exchange rate and the stock of financial assets, including money, will change as a result of increased international prices for tradeables.) As the share of tradeables has probably increased over time during the postwar period — due to larger international flows and tighter price links also for many goods and services which could earlier be regarded as non-tradeables — it is likely that international price changes have a *stronger* direct (short-term) impact than earlier on the national price levels in various countries. We would expect this to show up both as smaller price differentials between identical and similar products in different countries, and in a closer synchronisation among nations of price movements for tradeables (both adjusted for exchange rates). Scanty empirical studies seem to give some support for both of these hypotheses. (Genberg and O.E.C.D., 1970.)

The internationalisation process looks more dramatic if we shift the interest from the *macro* level to the *micro* level. Empirically speaking, whereas the share of total exports (or imports) to GDP (or domestic absorption), as mentioned above, has increased rather moderately, the export and import shares have increased drastically *within* practically all sectors. In many sectors, these shares have, in fact, increased by some 50 to 100 per cent during the last decade. Thus, individual firms are confronted with foreign competition to a much greater extent than earlier. The increasingly international character of the environment for individual firms is, of course, largely obscured if we look at aggregate figures over export (or import) of goods and services as a fraction of GDP (or domestic absorption).[2]

The fact that the flows of commodities and services across national borders are larger than before does not necessarily mean that also the *sensitivity* has increased — as measured by, for instance, the elasticities of the flows with respect to prices, income and various policy instruments — as this would require that the marginal ratios have increased more than the average ratios. Nevertheless, scanty empirical evidence suggests that this is in fact so, at least in the case of the elasticity of import with respect to national income (Lindbeck, 1973). This higher sensitivity corresponds to what Machlup calls consequences of the 'conditions' of integration, whereas the larger flows correspond to part of what Machlup denotes the 'effects' of integration. The 'sensitivity aspect' of international economic integration is, of course, of particular relevance if we want to study how various national target variables are (directly or indirectly) influenced by changes in various parameters and variables in the economic system such as relative prices, incomes and interest rates.

Money and credit
It is a rather generally accepted fact that international economic integration has been more spectacular for money and financial capital than for commodities and services (as measured in both cases by the size of the flows across national borders relative to domestic flows). It is also well known that both the size of the flows and their variability over time have increased much more for short-term financial capital than for long-term

financial capital. Moreover, the relative spread of interest rates between nations, as measured by the coefficient of variations, has fallen over the last 15 or 20 years. And the synchronisation of interest rate changes has also increased. For instance, the correlation coefficient of short-term interest rates among countries has increased considerably; in the early 1970s it has reached a level of about 0·8 to 0·95 for several developed countries.[3] What may be not quite clear is to what extent this synchronisation is an expression of more closely integrated credit markets, and to what extent it reflects a more synchronised timing of national monetary policies, possibly in response to a greater synchronisation of the business cycle or to a more coordinated policy.

It is also not clear whether the larger variability in recent years in short-term capital flows is an expression of higher sensitivity of the flows (greater elasticities) or of greater fluctuations in the explanatory variables. It is, in fact, easy to construct examples, according to whether it is the large changes in expected exchange rates in the early 1970s, rather than greater elasticities, that account for the high movements of short-term capital (Lindbeck, 1973).

Labour
The international integration of the labour market is a rather complicated matter, even to describe. However, a bird's-eye historic perspective of the movement of labour (and capital) may serve to illuminate the issue. During the nineteenth and early twentieth centuries, intercontinental ('global') movement of labour mainly took the form of movements of unskilled or semi-skilled labour from countries with little labour per unit of land and/or capital to countries with much labour. This type of international movement of labour can perhaps best be explained by relative factor proportions, and therewith connected factor prices — rather than by using the factor proportions to explain only trade patterns. During the period after the Second World War, when restrictive immigration laws stopped mass immigration of unskilled labour from one continent to another, capital was instead in fact stimulated to move in the opposite direction, particularly in the form of direct investment. Heavy import protection in many LDCs has accentuated these effects on capital movements, whereas increased political uncertainty for investors in the LDCs has had the opposite effects.

The situation is quite different *within* the continents, for instance within Europe. Unskilled or semi-skilled labour comes to the richer European countries from the less developed countries within Europe, particularly from the Mediterranean countries, as a large-scale movement of labour has been allowed without much restriction.

In a fundamental sense, the movement of labour has during the last decade been larger than the movement of long-term capital between these countries. For instance, the size of the Swedish capital stock abroad might roughly be measured by the return on Swedish equity capital abroad. The return to Sweden amounted in the early 1970s to about 100 million dollars per year in the form of interests and dividends; a similar amount of profits is probably reinvested in foreign countries. By contrast, the return in the form of wages and salaries of the 250,000 foreign employees in Sweden was about 1·2 billion dollars, that is, an amount of a rather different order of magnitude. In this sense, the stock (and flow) of labour of foreign origin are much larger than the stock (and flow) of Swedish capital abroad. Similar relative magnitudes would probably be found in a number of other Western European countries. In this specific sense, the factor of production labour has been more internationally mobile *within Europe* than the factor of production capital — in spite of the 'inherent' difficulties for the mobility of labour connected with intercountry differences of a social and cultural character.

Part of the explanation for these relative movements of labour and capital within Europe is probably that movements of labour do not create the same difficulties for the balance of payments, in the context of a system with fixed or quasi-flexible exchange rates, as does movement of capital. Permanent migrants become 'currency citizens' in the host country, which means that no serious balance-of-payments problems will arise for the country that exports labour and human capital. (The balance of payments is rather *improved* in the emigration country, as some remittances are sent back.) Permanent emigrants move their production and absorption *simultaneously*.

The effects are somewhat different in the case of *temporary* movements of labour, as in this case part of the labour income earned by the emigrants is spent in the emigration country, which then export labour *services*, the return from which can be used to import commodities (or other services). However, there is no reason to expect any *serious* balance-of-payments problems to be caused by this export of labour services either in the emigration country (where the capacity to export commodities is increased) or in the immigration country (where the capacity to import commodities is increased).

Financial capital movements, by contrast, may create severe adjustment and balance-of-payments problems both when the original capital flow takes place, and when the return is paid out to the capital-exporting country.

We have here an example how *government regulations*, in the form of tariffs, immigration rules, and regulations of capital movements, greatly influence the relative mobility of labour and capital, and hence also the international allocation of economic activity. More specifically, government interventions have stimulated *inter*continental movements of capital, and *intra*continental movements of labour, in particular among European countries. One result has been that intercontinental factor movements are dominated by movements of *knowledge*, in the form of physical investment and the movement of skilled labour ('brain drain'), whereas factor movements within Europe are dominated by more 'conventional' labour and (short-term) financial capital.

Technology and entrepreneurship

It is quite difficult both to define and to measure the internationalisation of technology and entrepreneurship, partly because of the difficulty to distinguish volumes from prices. However, it would seem that the *value* of exports of machines in the world economy has expanded more rapidly than exports in general. It would also seem that payments of royalties from patents have usually increased even more rapidly. For instance, whereas the value of world exports of goods expanded by some 9 per cent per year during the 1960s, trade in machines expanded by about 13 per cent, and receipts from royalties by some 15 per cent. Casual observations also suggest that exports of 'key-ready factories' have increased very much.

A likely effect of all this is that the production functions — and, due to factor mobility, factor proportions as well — will be more and more similar for a large group of countries, and that product qualities will differ less and less. Trade patterns will then probably depend less on differences in production functions (à la Ricardo), and on differences in factor proportions (à la Ohlin-Heckscher), than on 'historical accidents' (such as skilful entrepreneurs in individual firms) and returns to scale.

(2) INSTITUTIONS

So far I have discussed only internationalisation of markets. In the case of *institutions*, the internationalisation process is clearly most striking for market-oriented institutions, such as multinational firms — in manufacturing, raw material exploitation, credit market operations, insurance, consulting, travelling, etc. — rather than political institutions and interest group institutions such as labour unions.

Most likely the increased importance of international *market-oriented* institutions has in many cases increased the international movements and mobility of goods and factors, as the information and communication channels have been improved by these institutions. (The welfare implications are a more complicated matter which will not be discussed here.) The internationalisation of the *interest group* organisations, by contrast, is still a rather insignificant development, though they have probably to some extent improved international information channels, for instance concerning technology, demand conditions, labour market situations, etc. However, it is still an open question whether the internationalisation of market-oriented and interest-group organisations has meant any really fundamental ('qualitative') change in the operation of the global market system — in addition to the just-mentioned improvements in the efficiency of the channels of information and communication.

In the case of *political institutions*, the consequences, and the mutual interaction between the internationalisation of markets and institutions, is more obvious. A small but extremely important aspect is, of course, that international agreements between national governments – in the context of institutions like G.A.T.T., I.M.F., E.E.C., E.F.T.A., L.A.F.T.A., etc. – created a 'liberal' trade and currency system after the Second World War, whereby international markets could develop strongly and efficiently. Trade liberalisation and currency convertibility were perhaps the two most important institutional arrangements in this context. The hypothesis of the importance of political institutions and decisions for the development of international markets and the global allocation of economic activity is supported by the fact that an expansion of internationalisation trade has largely been prevented in the sector where trade liberalisation has been most resisted – that is, in European agriculture.

One reason why the liberalisation process has been politically feasible is probably that the expansion of trade to a large extent has been *intra*-sectorial rather than *inter*sectorial, which means that the process has been possible without much closing down of large parts of branches of industry. Domestic reallocations of resources have largely taken place within industries, and in fact often within individual firms by changes in the range of their product mix. This means that serious social problems, and therewith connected political setbacks, linked to the reallocations have to a considerable extent been avoided.

It is interesting to note that protectionism has been most difficult to remove in the fields where free international competition would have led to *inter*sectorial rather than *intra*sectorial reallocation of resources, such as in agriculture and labour-intensive products. A future integration of the manufacturing sectors of the LDCs into the international division of labour would probably require much more expansion of *inter*sector trade and therewith connected reallocation of resources between sectors in the developed countries.

(3) EXTERNALITIES

However, perhaps the most dramatic internationalisation during the post-war period has occurred for the *externalities* of the consumption and production process.

In the case of consumption, the improvement in international information about consumption in various countries means that consumption in a country (to an increased extent) enters the preference functions of households in other countries. The most obvious consequence is probably the 'demonstration effect' for households regarding levels and patterns of consumption in other countries, and therewith connected changes in the aspiration level of households. Increased sales promotion in other countries, in connection with increased exports, may have a similar effect.

However, there is at least a theoretical possibility that also new knowledge in the rich countries about the poverty in the poor countries will in the long run affect the consumption behaviour in the rich countries, by their acceptance of large transfers to the poor countries.

The internationalisation of the externalities on *the production side* — that is the entering of the volume of production in one country into the production or preference functions in other countries — is more obvious and concrete. In fact, it can probably be argued that the dominating production externalities in the world of today are international rather than national; in other words they are 'external' to nations as well as to individual firms. Obvious examples are, of course, waste disposal in the air and the sea, or more generally the disturbance of the worldwide ecological system, as well as the exploitation of the oceans, manifested by the 'fish wars' between countries and the competing (geographically overlapping) claims of nations concerning the exploitation of oil and minerals lying on or under the seabed.

II. EFFECTS ON THE NATIONAL ECONOMIES

There is not room here for an elaborate discussion of the effects on the national economies of various types of international economic integration of markets, institutions and externalities. However, already an *enumeration* of some likely effects indicates that a number of important target variables will more than earlier be influenced by forces outside the country itself:

(a) a greater synchronisation (in time) among nations of fluctuations in output and prices, particularly if exchange rates are not very flexible;

(b) a falling profit margin due to increased international competition (and hence flatter demand curves);

(c) a more rapid rate of change in comparative advantage among nations;

(d) a more rapid rate of structural change;

(e) tendencies to increased structural unemployment and possibly also increased wage differentials within countries;

(f) increased geographical dispersion of unemployment, and possibly also of income, within countries;

(g) an increased tendency to mergers because of the fall in the profit margins and the more rapid rate of structural change;

(h) a tendency to weaker investment incentives for private firms;

(j) stronger effects on the domestic economy of decisions by large organisations outside the jurisdiction domain of the individual country — by international organisations, multinational firms and perhaps also interest group organisations;

(k) greater environmental disturbances and demonstration effects from abroad on domestic citizens.

It would seem that available empirical data give support for most of these hypotheses (Lindbeck, 1973).

III. REACTIONS OF GOVERNMENTS

It is natural that governments have not looked passively upon these consequences for the domestic economy of growing integration and disturbances from abroad. Not only have important *target variables* tended to be 'pushed out of focus'; a number of *policy instruments* are no longer very useful for domestic policy purposes, either because of international agreements (such as in the case of tariffs) or because the internationalisation of markets has reduced the efficacy of some instruments (such as for interest rates). The policy difficulties have been further accentuated by the fact that the national targets have tended to become *more ambitious and detailed*, in particular for employment and income distribution, including the regional and branchwise distribution of employment and income.

As a result, governments have felt it necessary both to use earlier available instruments more aggressively and to develop new policy instruments. The most obvious examples are perhaps the use of (a) taxes and subsidies on investment, employment, and research and development; (b) public capital grants of equity capital and lending priorities; (c) selective import fees and export subsidies; (d) the tying of foreign aid; (e) protectionist government purchases; and (f) government use of product and environmental standards and regulations, sometimes in fact as protectionist devices. Basically, all this amounts to a replacement of the traditional tariffs with *both* various types of non-tariff barriers *and* 'modern' mercantilist methods — both of a temporary and a more permanent nature (Lindbeck, 1973 and 1975).

The building up of new non-tariff barriers amounts, of course, to some *retreat* in the process of international economic integration, *except* that temporary 'safety measures' sometimes may prevent the raising of more permanent barriers to trade. The mercantilist policies are more difficult to characterise and classify. If international economic integration is defined as large flows between countries — one of Machlup's definitions — the mercantilist policies can perhaps be said to result in *more* international economic integration. If, by contrast, we follow another of Machlup's definitions of economic integration — as 'the actual utilisation of all potential opportunities of efficient transfer of productive resources and efficient division of labour — the mercantilist policies may instead be characterised as *disintegration*, in the sense that trade may be 'artificially' stimulated in some sectors.

Thus, whereas political decisions immediately after the Second World

War helped to release internationally integrating market forces, these forces became so strong after a while that governments sometimes found it necessary to undertake new *dis*integrating and trade-modifying measures — when the governments found that they had, like the Sorcerer's Apprentice, released forces outside their own control. One way to avoid these new disintegrating forces may, of course, be to rely on *temporary* 'safety measures', internal income compensations and help to domestic reallocations rather than permanent non-tariff barriers and mercantilistic measures.

These considerations raise some awkward but rather fundamental questions of positive economics, welfare economics and policy advising.

(1) POSITIVE ECONOMICS

Firstly, as to positive economics, we have to ask whether it is reasonable to analyse the effects on the allocation of resources of changes in certain policy instruments without making assumptions also about the effects on the behaviour of the governments themselves. For instance, the effects on the domestic economy of tariff policies cannot really be realistically analysed without considering also the consequences for the actual use of non-tariff barriers and 'mercantilist' taxes and subsidies. In other words, is it reasonable to stop the analysis while treating other aspects of government behaviour as exogenous variables when the effects on the economy of a specific policy instrument are analysed?

(2) ANALYTICAL WELFARE ECONOMICS

Secondly, in the field of analytical welfare economics, it is not self-evident that the distortions of relative prices and the allocation of resources will always be smaller with these 'new' policy interventions, such as non-tariff barriers and various neomercantilist devices, than with traditional protectionism, the reduction of which has *induced* the implementation of the new policy interventions.[4] However, *temporary* 'safety measures', income compensation, and the facilitation of domestic reallocations may very well, in the long run, *help* achieve the desired effects of trade liberalisation.

(3) POLICY ADVISING

Thirdly, we are — as is well known — confronted with the issue of whether it is really possible at all to prevent governments, for instance by way of international agreements, from using distorting policy interventions. More specifically, we are as policy advisers faced with the issue whether economists really should recommend policy interventions with expected 'desirable' effects *ceteris paribus* for other government policies, even if the net effects may be 'non-desirable' on balance when we consider also the effects on other facets of policy. In other words, should economists recom-

mend policy actions which in the view of the economist himself will most
likely result in *other* policy changes, so that the *net effect* may be detrimental from the point of view of the original targets established?

All these questions point, of course, to the potential importance of
occasionally treating politicians as endogenous rather than exogenous variables — both in positive economics and in welfare economics, including the
art of policy advising.

NOTES

[1] As always, the classification is not entirely straightforward. For instance, there are some border cases and overlapping in the classification.

[2] The reason why these changes have not resulted in a corresponding
change in the export and import shares for the economy as a whole is, of
course, that the *composition* of production and demand *in current prices*
has shifted from high-trade to low-trade sectors (mainly from manufacturing
to services, in particular public services).

[3] Calculations by the author on the basis of figures in *International
Financial Statistics*; Monthly Report of the Deutsche Bundesbank, various
issues.

[4] An even stronger statement could perhaps be made. If the 'new'
policy interventions imply, as I think is the case, stronger and more
differentiated changes in relative prices between industries than did tariffs,
and if interventions also discriminate *between individual firms* within
industries, which certainly is the case, distortions in the allocation of
resources are likely to be *greater* than before the tariff reduction. Efficiency
losses will be accentuated because the new interventions give politicians
and public administrators power to make investment and production
decisions — tasks for which they normally have little competence. Thus,
the general assertion in the pure welfare theory of public interventions,
that production subsidies imply less distortions than tariffs (as the former
do not distort relative prices for consumers) does not necessarily hold —
and is most likely incorrect — when considering the behaviour patterns of
politicians and public administrators ('endogenous politicians and
bureaucrats').

REFERENCES

Genberg, H., 'The Concept and Measurement of the World Price Level and
Rate of Inflation', *Journal of Monetary Economics* (forthcoming).
Lindbeck, A., *The National State in an Internationalized World Economy*,
Institute for International Economic Studies, Seminar Paper No. 26,
Stockholm (1973).
Lindbeck, A., 'The Changing Role of the National State', *Kyklos*, Fasc. 1
(1975).
O.E.C.D., *Inflation: The Present Problem*, Paris (Dec., 1970).

Summary of the Discussion

The discussion first concerned the difficulties and pitfalls involved in attempts to measure economic integration by the degree of price equalisation. Factor price equality, suggested as one definition of integration, could be achieved, it was argued, in other ways than through market integration. Attention was also given to the problem of measuring integration when prices are used for other purposes than to clear markets. A second issue concerned the need to consider actual political units and their policy aims when discussing geographic integration. This session was chaired by *Jagdish N. Bhagwati.*

Charles Kindleberger noted that economists, nurtured on the law of one price, think of integration in terms of 'oneness' and suggested factor price equalisation as the basic definition of integration. However, he excluded the case where this occurred as the result of prices being equalised by chance or by evolution due, for example, to skewed demands being matched by skewed resources. Nor was he inclined to accept the case where the result was achieved by outside factors, such as when German and French wages or interest rates were equated through a third market. To serve as an indicator of integration, factor price equalisation should be achieved by movements of either factors or goods directly within the markets concerned and not by accident or through outside markets.

William Branson agreed with Kindleberger that observed covariances between similar variables in different countries may be an inadequate indicator of the degree of international market integration. The factor price equalisation theorem itself, he noted, illustrated that factor prices could be equalised without any integration of factor markets. Branson recalled that Assar Lindbeck in his Comment had induced from increasing covariances of interest rates that money and credit markets were increasingly integrated. However, the same phenomenon could have been obtained without increased capital market integration if the covariance of business cycles had been increased through foreign trade multipliers. Branson, therefore, stressed the need to guard against a high level of 'implicit theorising' when talking about economic integration.

To Jagdish Bhagwati's question whether it mattered if economic variables were equalised directly or indirectly, Branson replied that this knowledge could suggest to a government where it must erect a barrier in order to break the link. *Assar Lindbeck* noted that it might also affect the possibility for governments to pursue monetary policy. If increased covariance of interest rates is due to increased integration of capital markets, it reduces the autonomy of monetary policy. If instead the higher co-variance is due to more synchronised cycles, this implication for monetary policy does not follow.

Michael Michaely added that integration within a nation could be brought about by international factor movements. Thus, using Kindle-berger's criterion of factor price equality in an integrated area, Michaely observed that Italy or Finland might now be more integrated nationally due to the migration of labour, not from their less to their more developed regions, but rather to foreign countries.

Other difficulties in using market price differences as a measure of economic integration were noted. *Jagdish Bhagwati* pointed out that two definitions of integration mentioned in Machlup's paper — the 'free trade' definition meaning equalisation of interest rates, wages, etc., and the definition meaning equalisation of the social utility of a certain factor in alternative uses — could lead to contradictory indications of the degree of integration reached, and that therefore Machlup could not have both criteria but must choose one.

Åke Andersson emphasised the need for developing methods that would make it possible to measure an area's degree of integration when prices are not used for market clearing but for income distribution and similar purposes. He envisaged a situation where countries with identical price structures have production structures that do not conform to a proper international division of labour.

In reply to Kindleberger, *Melvyn Krauss* noted that integration in Europe was often defined in terms of 'sameness' in addition to 'oneness'. Economists, he noted, sometimes considered the striving for harmonisation foolish, but he interpreted it as an effort by politicians to establish uniform tastes in the community. For example, fixing exchange rates required countries to have similar rates of inflation and he suggested this would eventually make them view the same rate of inflation as optimal. Similarly, he felt that a uniform size of the public sector, while inefficient at first, might eventually be optimal when tastes become more 'European'.

Kindleberger felt that macrointegration may call for harmonisation or coordination of economic policies — fiscal as well as monetary — and that it was necessary to investigate further the extent to which sameness of tastes is necessary in order to have macrointegration.

Bo Södersten thought that it might be useful to consider actual policy aims when discussing integration. Capital movements would be viewed differently by various groups, and depend on the type of economic system prevailing in a country. For instance, differences in Swedish labour migration policy in the 1960s and the 1970s he believed could only be explained with reference to a 'social welfare function' that took income distribution effects into account.

Hollis Chenery recalled that the basic decision-making unit was still the nation state and not the international community, and that it made integration decisions in the light of its own interests. Developed nation states might not be interested in factor market integration with poor nations, but only in exploiting gains from trade through commodity market integration. Therefore, he felt that the appropriate integration criterion for developed countries was commodity rather than factor price equalisation. In theory, factor price equalisation usually followed once commodity prices were equal, but in practice this occurred only after a time span of perhaps several centuries when the union was between countries with very different resource endowments. Consequently he felt that integration discussions were an academic exercise useless for policy questions unless the policy-makers' interests were specified.

Fritz Machlup closed the discussion. He replied to Chenery that he was all in favour of academic exercises for economists. Since the concept of economic integration was basically the same whether integration was interprovincial, interregional or international, he believed that it was valuable to form apolitical concepts which could deal with various and particular problems.

Machlup elaborated on the problems encountered in measuring and defining integration. Replying to Bhagwati he said that, of course, social and private opportunity costs often differed and that this created problems. He preferred, in principle, to accept the actors' valuation. For instance, personal psychic aversion to migration ought not to be disregarded in any social valuation. Some people do not like to move from their area of residence and prefer low income there to higher non-psychic income elsewhere. However, he did not know of any mechanism by which a government official could measure such personal valuations.

Replying to Kindleberger, Machlup doubted that the factor price equalisation criterion was operational. We can, for example, never know if factors in different places are of the same quality. How do we know if labour in Malaya is of the same quality as labour in Pennsylvania? Therefore, he felt that this criterion was ruled out as a measure of integration as a state of affairs. It might, however, provide some insight into the process of integration assuming that existing differences in factor quality did not change over time.

Finally, Machlup noted that Gunnar Myrdal once defined economic integration in terms of income — rather than factor price — equality. But factor price equalisation was compatible with enormous income differences. For instance some people may choose to work 20 hours a week and others 100 hours a week; since Machlup himself belonged to the latter group, he strongly suspected that his factor return was very low compared with that of most of his colleagues.

7 Effects of Commercial Policy on International Trade, the Location of Production, and Factor Movements*

Bela Balassa

For purposes of this paper, commercial policy is defined to include tariffs and other restrictions on imports as well as taxes and subsidies on exports. Since a devaluation is equivalent to the simultaneous application of tariffs on imports and subsidies on exports at equal rates, it will be considered together with commercial policy measures.

In order to indicate the possible effects of commercial policy on international trade and the location of production, one first needs to examine the relationship between interregional and international trade. This will be done in section I, with attention given to efforts made to place the theory of international trade in the framework of location theory.

In turn, section II will consider the impact of commercial policy measures on imports and on industrial composition in particular countries. Also, empirical tests will be offered to explain intercountry differences in imports and in the degree of industrial specialisation in terms of *per capita* incomes, population, and the level of protection.

Section III will investigate differences in import shares and in the degree of industrial specialisation in interregional versus international relationships, with a view to analysing the effects of national frontiers on the location of production. For this purpose, use will be made of data for Northern Ireland and the Republic of Ireland as well as for nine U.S. regions and comparable industrial countries.

If commercial policies influenced the location of production, the question remains as to how the elimination of tariffs would affect locational patterns. This question will be examined in section IV in the context of the European Common Market, with further attention given to the impact of trade liberalisation in the United States.

Finally, section V will deal with the effects of trade barriers on factor movements. Consideration will be given to both capital and labour move-

---

*This paper has been prepared in the framework of a consultant arrangement with the World Bank. The author is indebted to Dominique de Crayencour for computational assistance.

ments, with reference made to available empirical evidence for the European Common Market, the United Kingdom, Australia, and Canada.

I. THE RELATIONSHIP BETWEEN INTERREGIONAL AND INTER-NATIONAL TRADE

The *locus classicus* on the relationship between interregional and international trade is Bertil Ohlin's *Interregional and International Trade* (1933). Ohlin considers international trade theory as a special case of the theory of interregional trade, 'where the regions are different countries' (p. 68). In turn, the theory of interregional trade is regarded as a form of location — in Ohlin's terminology, localisation — theory (chapter XII), thus linking international trade theory and location theory.

This linkage is made explicit in the statement that places the theory of international trade in the framework of location theory. 'When . . . the costs of transport *within* regions and countries are taken into account, there is need for a general localisation theory, which considers at the same time regions and districts of many different kinds, among which are the various countries . . . A theory of international trade must, therefore, be founded upon the general localisation theory; indeed, it consists of a localisation theory which gives special attention to the circumstances arising from the existence of a number of countries' (p. 243).

Taking Ricardo and his followers to task for having neglected transport costs in formulating the doctrine of international specialisation, Ohlin reiterates that 'the theory of international trade is nothing but *internationale Standortslehre* (international location theory)' (p. 589). And, he considers one of the principal objectives of his work is 'to demonstrate that the theory of international trade is only a part of a general localisation theory . . .' (p. vii).

According to Isard and Peck, 'the inspiration for Ohlin's statement can be traced to Alfred Weber's criticism of classical trade theory for ignoring the significant amount of industry which is transport-oriented . . .' (1954, p. 97). Weber's ideas (1911) were further developed by Lösch (1956), who suggested replacing the classical doctrine of international specialisation by location theory.

In Lösch's view, 'National economies have no inner unity as the theory of comparative costs postulates. Nor is the mobility of the factors of production obstructed by political frontiers as such. Contrary to widespread opinion, national currency differences have been shown to be harmless . . . In essence, the processes of national and international trade are the same' (p. 63). Instead of comparative cost theory, Lösch purports to explain international specialisation in locational terms, with reference to supply and market areas being located on two sides of the frontier. And while he admits that 'tariff boundaries alter the number and position of location centres, particularly near the frontier' (p. 53), tariffs play a subordinate role in his analysis and exchange rates do not enter at all.

Tariffs and exchange rates receive no mention in Isard's *Location and Space Economy* (1956), which represents a further extension of Lösch's work. At the same time, Isard regards international trade theory as a special case of the general theory of location and space economy: 'One proceeds from the latter to the former by assuming a given locational structure of economic activities, by erecting appropriate barriers to correspond to the boundaries of nations, and so forth' (p. 53).

It appears, then, that location theorists have come to increasingly emphasise the role of transport costs and other locational factors in determining international specialisation at the neglect of commercial policies. In so doing, they have departed from Ohlin's tradition, according to whom 'protective tariffs bar the different national markets from one another more completely than the other costs of transfer (such as transport costs) could do alone' (p. 296). Ohlin further noted that 'varying currency systems cause the mechanism of trade between countries to differ from that of other sorts of trade' (p. 244), 'that cumbersome customs formalities, government preference for domestic products, and a variety of other factors, too, create obstacles to international trade' (pp. 245–46).

The increased emphasis on transport costs and the reduced emphasis on commercial policy in recent contributions to location theory would lead one to expect that transport costs have become more – and commercial policy less – important in affecting international specialisation. In fact, the opposite has been the case; since Ricardo's time, transport costs have declined in importance while commercial policy has assumed an increasingly greater role.

To begin with, as a result of successive revolutions in transportation, transport costs have decreased more-or-less continuously, leading to a fall in their ratio to production costs. At the same time, the advances made in ocean shipping notwithstanding, compared to Ricardo's time the decline has been more pronounced in the cost of surface transportation, with railways and subsequently trucks taking the place of more primitive means of transport. Thus, if anything, the 'inner unity' of national economies has increased over time.

This is indicated by data on transportation costs for pig iron, reported in Appendix A. Taking account of freight, insurance, and the interest cost involved in shipping, we find that the ratio of the cost of land to sea transport per ton mile decreased from 80 to 130 in the second half of the eighteenth century to 8 in 1976. During the same period, the cost of ocean transportation between the U.S. Atlantic Coast and London, expressed as a percentage of the factory price of pig iron, decreased from 18 to 29 per cent to 11 per cent while that of land transportation, calculated for a distance of 160 km (100 miles), fell from 70 to 3 per cent.

The decline in transport costs has been reinforced by changes in the commodity composition of world trade that entailed a fall in the relative share of transport intensive commodities in world trade through the rise in the proportion of manufactured goods in total trade and the increase in the share of commodities with a higher value of weight ratio within manufacturing. The described changes have further been enhanced by innovations in communication, greatly reducing their cost as well as elapsed time.

In turn, commercial policies have come to assume a greater role. Despite reductions in tariffs undertaken during the postwar period, tariffs in the developed countries are higher today than they were at the time of Ricardo and John Stuart Mill, not to speak of the period of practically free trade in Western Europe during the second half of the nineteenth century (Bairoch, 1972). Furthermore, developed countries limit the importation of various commodities by formal and informal quotas that was not the case in the nineteenth century.

Apart from the actual use of quotas, international trade is affected by the risk of their imposition. This is of particular importance for developing countries who fear that new exports will be subjected to quantitative restrictions once they enter developed country markets in substantial quantities, as it has happened in regard to textiles (Balassa, 1965, p. 70). The flexibility of exchange rates also creates uncertainty in international trade that did not exist under the gold standard.

The effects of uncertainty due to the risk of the imposition of quotas and changes in exchange rates deserve emphasis since they have been neglected in most contributions to international trade theory. With producers being by-and-large risk-averters, uncertainty as regards changes in relative prices resulting from such actions will provide inducement to expand domestic sales at the expense of foreign sales. In particular, risk considerations will influence decisions and new investment, thereby affecting the industrial structure.

These effects may be especially pronounced in developing countries which have not yet embarked on the exportation of various manufactured goods. The development of export industries in developing countries is also discouraged by the high level of protection in these countries, which greatly exceeds levels of protection present-day developed nations had at any stage of their existence (Little, Scitovsky and Scott, 1970, Chapter 5). In addition to tariffs, protection in developing countries takes the form of quantitative restrictions, foreign exchange licensing, and import prohibitions, all of which tend to differentiate international from domestic transactions.

Various other forms of government interventions, too, tend to favour domestic production over imports in developed as well as in developing countries. They include, among other things, public procurement rules, production subsidies, regional policy measures, and health and sanitary regulations. These measures have assumed increasing importance in recent years and they further distinguish the processes of international trade from those of interregional trade.

We may conclude that, paradoxically, locational theory would have had greater relevance for international specialisation in Ricardo's time than today. In turn, the emphasis on the distinction between international and domestic trade prevalent in the writings of Ricardo and John Stuart Mill is more appropriate under present-day conditions than it was in their lifetime.

II. THE IMPACT OF COMMERCIAL POLICY MEASURES ON IMPORTS AND ON INDUSTRIAL COMPOSITION

The conclusions, according to which the greater role of commercial policy and the reduced importance of transport costs tend to increase the cleavage between international and interregional trade, should not be interpreted to mean that transport costs would have no bearing on international specialisation. In fact, following earlier efforts by the German Statistical Office (1928), applications of gravitational models by Savage and Deutsch (1960), Pöyhönen (1963), Pulliainen (1963), and Linneman (1966) have shown the role of transportation costs, more exactly distance, in affecting trade flows.

These gravitational models did not incorporate the level of protection on the grounds that its 'average or normal trade-reducing effect is incorporated in (the) definition of potential foreign trade . . .' (Linneman, p. 31). However, in explaining bilateral trade flows in 1959, Linneman successfully used variables expressing preferential trade ties among the countries of the British Commonwealth, the constituent parts of the French Community, as well as between Belgium and Portugal and their colonies. Subsequently, introducing dummy variables to represent the creation of the E.E.C. and E.F.T.A. in gravitational models estimated for the years between 1951 to 1967, Aitken (1973) showed the effects of European integration on trade flows.

The use of dummy variables to denote preferential ties cannot be interpreted in terms of elasticities. In turn, estimates of price elasticities of import demand, reviewed most recently by Stern, Francis and Schumacher (1975), have often been used to calculate the expected effects of tariff reductions on imports (Officer and Hurtebise, 1969). But these estimates will not appropriately indicate the responsiveness of imports to tariffs as they relate imports to variations in prices, irrespective of whether these are autonomous or result from tariff changes, although there is reason to believe that users react differently to autonomous price changes than to changes in tariffs. This is largely because they tend to consider the former to be temporary and the latter to be permanent.

Given the cost of adjustment, reactions to temporary changes may be small while users will respond to changes they consider permanent (Balassa, 1966, p. 187). Also, with effective tariffs exceeding nominal tariffs on most commodities and production responding to effective rather than to nominal rates, a change in nominal tariffs on a particular product will have a greater impact on imports than a price change of equal magnitude that resulted from higher input costs. As Kreinin notes (1967), this result will apply also under all-round tariff reductions as long as larger reductions apply to the product than to its inputs.

Correspondingly, in order to indicate the effects of commercial policy on international trade, the impact of tariff changes on imports needs to be directly investigated. In making estimates in a time-series context, Johnston and Henderson (1969) found that the import surcharge imposed at a rate of 15 per cent in October 1964, reduced to 10 per cent in April 1965, and abolished the following year, had no lasting effect on U.K. imports. This result may be largely explained by the fact that the import surcharge was imposed on a temporary basis; the same comment applies to estimates of the effects of a temporary surcharge on Canadian imports (Officer and Hurtebise, 1969). At any rate, time-series estimates of the elasticities of import demand with respect to price and tariff changes are subject to a downward bias for reasons which are all too well known to mention here.

These objections do not apply to estimates of the effects of permanent tariff reductions that may involve comparing trends before and after tariff reductions, analysing cross-section data, or making use of control groups. The application of the first of these methods gave tariff-elasticity estimates of −4·5 for the United Kingdom in the early 1930s (Scott, 1962, pp. 168−69) and −9 for Germany in the mid-1960s (Wemelsfelder, 1960). In turn, Krause (1962) obtained tariff elasticities (−4·5) much exceeding price elasticities (−1·5) in a sample of 91 commodities for the United States in the 1947−54 period when substantial tariff reductions took place.

Also for the United States, Kreinin (1961) derived a tariff elasticity of −6 for commodities on which tariffs were reduced, using a control group of duty free imports. The control group method was further applied by Finger in estimating the effects of tariff concessions in the Dillon Round (1974) and in the Kennedy Round (1976). Confining ourselves to the results pertaining to the Kennedy Round when tariff reductions were substantially larger, Finger's estimates of tariff elasticities were −9·5 and −14·8 for U.S. imports, −5·4 and −3·9 for E.E.C. imports and −8·0 and −11·9 for Japanese imports from developed and from developing countries, respectively (1976, p. 89).

The cited results point to the fact that tariffs affect imports to a considerable extent, thereby favouring import-competing industries at the expense of export industries. The location of production is further influenced by the structure of tariffs. As Ohlin noted, 'in the case of high import duties, raw materials free of duty or slightly taxed are sent instead of manufactured goods with heavy duty charges' (1933, p. 211).

This question is of particular importance for developing countries as the escalation of tariffs from raw materials and unprocessed goods to finished products imported by the developed nations discriminates against their exports of processed goods. In 1964, on the average, nominal tariffs in the developed countries were 4·5 per cent on products in the first stage of transformation, 7·9 per cent in the second stage, 16·2 per cent in the third stage, and 22·2 per cent in the fourth stage, with the corresponding effective tariffs being 4·6, 22·6, 28·7, and 38·4 per cent.

Tariff discrimination against the imports of processed commodities from the developing countries tends to offset the cost advantages these countries possess on account of decreases in transportation costs as a proportion of export value from lower to higher stages of transformation. This may in large part explain the fact that the structure of imports into the developed nations is inversely correlated with the height of nominal and effective tariffs.

In 1964, the relative shares of developing country exports from the first through the fourth stage of transformation were 71·2, 23·8, 2·9, and 2·1 per cent, respectively. Among the importing countries, the share of processed commodities (stages two to four) was the highest (45·5 per cent) in Sweden, where tariffs escalate the least, while it was only the smallest (9·5 per cent) in Japan, where tariff escalation is the most pronounced (Balassa, 1968a, p. 589).

Tariffs have been reduced in the framework of the Kennedy Round without, however, appreciably affecting the degree of escalation. While average tariff rates in the developed countries have declined somewhat more on commodities in the second (29 per cent) and in the third (30 per cent) stage of transformation than on those in the first stage (26 per cent), products in the fourth stage (24 per cent) have experienced the smallest decline (Balassa, 1968b, p. 207). At the same time, the bias against the processed exports of the developing countries is aggravated by the imposition of quantitative restrictions on the imports of several of these commodities.

The data of table 1 show that the developing countries have continued to export a relatively small proportion of their raw materials and foodstuffs in processed form in 1970, following the virtual completion of the Kennedy Round tariff reductions. Comparisons with the composition of exports from the developed countries are particularly noteworthy as a substantial part of trade among the developed countries takes place under tariff-free conditions in the framework of the E.E.C. and E.F.T.A.

In discriminating against the exports of processed goods from the developing countries, tariff protection in the developed nations thus affects the location of production, with developing countries having a smaller share of processing activities than they would have had in the absence of tariff escalation. In turn, protection in the developing countries tends to increase the use of their domestic resources in protected industries as compared to a free trade situation. In this connection, the effects of the structure of protection on industrial composition in the developing countries is of particular interest.

TABLE 1 EXPORTS OF SELECTED COMMODITIES IN PROCESSED AND UNPROCESSED FORM, 1970

	SITC No.	Shares of		Proportions for	
		Developed	Developing	Developed	Developing
1. MEAT					
Fresh and frozen meat	011	80·4	19·6	82·2	76·8
Meat preparations	013	74·6	25·4	17·8	32·2
2. FISH					
Fresh and frozen fish	031	73·5	26·5	70·7	84·6
Fish preparations	032	86·3	13·7	29·3	15·4
3. FRUIT					
Fresh fruit	051	57·5	42·5	69·8	83·3
Preserved fruit	053	74·5	25·5	30·2	16·7
4. VEGETABLES					
Fresh vegetables	054	70·7	29·3	68·9	84·6
Preserved vegetables	055	85·8	14·2	31·1	15·4
5. COCOA					
Cocoa beans	072·1	0·9	99·1	1·9	88·1
Cocoa powder	072·2	79·8	20·2	33·6	11·3
Chocolate	073	97·9	2·1	64·5	0·6
6. LEATHER					
Hides and skins	211	70·8	29·2	47·3	51·0
Leather	611	70·5	29·5	42·4	46·4
Leather manufactures	612	91·2	8·8	10·3	2·6
7. GROUND NUTS					
Groundnuts	222·1	19·6	80·4	63·0	58·7
Groundnut oil	421·4	17·0	83·0	37·0	41·3

TABLE 1 (CONTD.)

	SITC No.	Shares of		Proportions for	
		Developed	Developing	Developed	Developing
8. COPRA					
Copra	221·2	0·0	100·0	0·4	50·2
Coconut oil	422·3	10·9	89·1	99·6	49·8
9. PALM KERNEL					
Palm kernel	221·3	0·1	99·9	0·4	64·6
Palm kernel oil	422·4	26·9	73·1	99·6	35·4
10. RUBBER					
Natural rubber	231	29·0	71·0	67·2	99·4
Rubber products	621	97·2	2·8	32·8	0·6
11. WOOD					
Wood in the rough	242	45·3	54·7	27·2	71·8
Wood, shaped	243	84·9	15·1	72·8	28·2
12. PULP AND PAPER					
Pulpwood	251	98·1	1·9	32·7	36·6
Paper and paperboard	641	99·0	1·0	57·2	35·6
Articles of paper	642	95·6	4·4	10·1	27·8
13. TOBACCO					
Tobacco unmanufactured	121	69·8	30·2	56·4	79·4
Tobacco manufactured	122	87·3	12·7	43·6	20·6
14. COTTON					
Cotton	263	23·5	76·5	34·1	77·3
Cotton fabrics, woven	652	67·0	33·0	65·9	22·7

	Code				
15. JUTE					
Jute	264	4·0	96·0	14·6	37·9
Jute fabrics, woven	6534	13·0	87·0	85·4	62·1
16. WHEAT					
Wheat unmilled	041	95·0	5·0	88·6	83·7
Wheat, meal or flour	046	72·6	7·4	11·4	16·3
17. IRON					
Iron ore	281	53·9	46·1	20·2	79·1
Pig-iron	671	87·0	13·0	11·7	8·0
Iron steel, primary forms	672	96·8	3·2	22·2	3·4
Iron steel, shapes	673	95·7	4·3	45·9	9·5
18. COPPER					
Copper ores	28311	30·4	69·6	7·0	8·4
Copper unrefined	68211	14·0	86·0	4·7	15·3
Copper refined	68212	37·9	62·1	88·3	76·3
19. PETROLEUM					
Crude petroleum	331	5·3	94·7	17·5	78·3
Petroleum products	332	48·9	51·1	82·5	21·7
20. ALUMINUM					
Bauxite	2833	8·2	91·8	2·8	85·0
Aluminum unwrought	6841	94·6	5·4	97·2	15·0
21. ZINC					
Zinc ores, concentrates	2835	75·8	24·2	44·9	51·7
Zinc alloys, unwrought	6861	80·5	19·5	55·1	48·3

Source: United Nations (1974) *Yearbook of International Trade Statistics, Volume II* New York, and FAO (1974) *Trade Yearbook,* Rome

The International Allocation of Economic Activity

In an empirical investigation of Pakistani industries, Guisinger (1970) showed that protection was positively correlated with the expansion of production although it was not associated with import shares. In turn, Westphal and Kim (1976) found a positive correlation between subsidies to exports and export expansion in a cross-section study of Korean industries; however, the relationship between protection rates and the growth contribution of import substitution was not statistically significant, and protection rates and import shares were positively correlated. According to Westphal and Kim, the latter results may be interpreted as suggesting that import substitution progressed the least in the most inefficient industries, which needed high protection to survive. At any rate, the use of the null hypothesis in these investigations (that is, assuming import shares of all industries to be the identical in the absence of protection) will hardly be appropriate for examining the effects of protection on import structure and industrial composition.

A different benchmark was used by Leamer (1974) who assumed that, in the absence of protection, trade in particular commodity categories among pairs of thirteen developed countries would be explained by their gross national product, population, and distance. Having further introduced tariff variables in the models for 28 commodity categories, Leamer obtained tariff elasticities above −5 in absolute value in ten cases, elasticities of between −2 and −5 in seven cases, and between −1 and −2 in five cases; tariff elasticities were less than −1 or positive in six cases. While the *t*-values exceed one in only eleven cases, we may accept Leamer's conclusion: 'The fact that most of the estimates of the tariff elasticities are negative and comparable in magnitude gives us a feeling of greater confidence than seems justified by the standard errors on individual coefficients' (1974, p. 8). This conclusion is strengthened if we consider that tariff elasticities with a positive sign have *t*-values clustering around 0·3.

In influencing the volume as well as the composition of imports, tariffs affect the industrial structure of individual countries and the location of production in the world economy. Confining our attention to the country's own tariffs, we would expect that tariffs will reduce the actual extent of trade — imports as well as exports — below its potential level under free trade and will also increase the degree of industrial diversification by limiting possibilities for international specialisation.

These propositions have been tested by the present author in a sample of 21 industrial and industrialising countries. In explaining intercountry differences in imports, a protection variable representing average tariffs on manufactured goods[1] has been added to the per capita income and population variables that have been conventionally used for this purpose (Chenery, 1960). The same independent variables have been utilised to explain intercountry differences in industrial specialisation, as measured by the Theil coefficient of inequality which has desirable theoretical properties (Theil, 1967, pp. 91−93). The higher the coefficient of industrial specialisation the more specialised (the less diversified) is a country's industrial structure.[2]

The results of the regression analysis excluding and including the tariff variable are shown in equations (1) and (2).[3] It appears that the elasticity of imports with respect to per capita income and population are somewhat lower than those obtained by Chenery (0·98 for per capita income and 0·72 for population). The differences may be explained by the fact that Chenery's sample contained a larger proportion of developing countries.

$$\log M = \underset{(1·17)}{0·45} + \underset{(7·05)}{0·81} \log \frac{Y}{P} + \underset{(7·93)}{0·58} \log P \qquad R^2 = 0·86 \qquad (1)$$

$$\log M = \underset{(2·63)}{1·03} + \underset{(7·66)}{0·76} \log \frac{Y}{P} + \underset{(9·67)}{0·63} \log P - \underset{(2·75)}{0·45} \log T$$

$$R^2 = 0·90 \qquad (2)$$

Adding the protection variable increases the explanatory power of the regression and raises the absolute value as well as the statistical significance of the constant term of the regression equation. Its introduction further reduces the coefficient of the per capita income variable and increases that of the population variable while raising the level of statistical significance of both of the variables.

The protection variable itself has the expected negative sign and it is significantly different from zero at the 1 per cent level. The relevance of the protection variable for intercountry differences in imports can further be indicated by calculating from the regression equation hypothetical values of imports at different levels of protection.

For a country with a per capita income of $2241 and population of 35·6 million, corresponding to mean values in the 21 country sample, estimated import values are $35·7 billion for a zero tariff on manufactured goods, $12·6 billion for a tariff level of 10 per cent, $9·3 billion for a tariff level of 20 per cent, and $7·7 billion for a tariff level of 30 per cent. For the same tariff levels, the ratios of estimated imports to the gross national product are 36·8 per cent, 13·0 per cent, 9·6 per cent, and 7·9 per cent, respectively. These figures compare to average imports of $10·3 billion and an average import share of 10·6 per cent in the sample.

In turn, one would expect that the degree of industrial specialisation decreases — the degree of industrial diversification increases — with per capita incomes, population size, and tariff levels. Per capita incomes may be considered to express the degree of technological sophistication which leads to a more diversified industrial structure. Population size will have the same effect as economies of scale can be appropriated in the framework of a larger market. Finally, by discriminating against export industries and providing protection to import-competing industries, tariffs on manufactured goods tend to reduce the degree of specialisation within the manufacturing sector according to comparative advantage.

These *a priori* expectations are borne out by the regression results that are shown in equations (3) and (4).[4] The explanatory power of the regression increases by nearly one-third when we add the protection variable. At the same time, the protection variable, as well as the per capita income and population variables, are significantly different from zero at approximately the 2·5 per cent level

$$C = 71 \cdot 73 - 7 \cdot 46 \, \log \frac{Y}{P} - 7 \cdot 32 \, \log P \quad R^2 = 0 \cdot 35 \qquad (3)$$
$$(4 \cdot 92) \quad (1 \cdot 72) \qquad (2 \cdot 65)$$

$$C = 87 \cdot 40 - 8 \cdot 72 \, \log \frac{Y}{P} - 5 \cdot 79 \, \log P - 12 \cdot 30 \, \log T \qquad (4)$$
$$(5 \cdot 39) \quad (2 \cdot 11) \qquad (2 \cdot 12) \qquad (1 \cdot 91)$$
$$R^2 = 0 \cdot 46$$

The negative correlation between levels of protection and the degree of industrial specialisation can be represented by using equation (4) to calculate the coefficient of industrial specialisation for the hypothetical country with average per capita incomes and population in the sample of 21 countries. The estimated coefficients are 0·491 for nil tariffs, 0·368 for tariff levels of 10 per cent, 0·331 for tariff levels of 20 per cent, and 0·310 for tariff levels of 30 per cent.

III. TRADE SHARES AND INDUSTRIAL DIVERSIFICATION

In the preceding section, we examined the effects of tariffs on international trade and on the location of production taking countries as units. These estimates do not indicate, however, the full impact of commercial policies on international specialisation as they relate imports to the level of tariffs at a given point of time, or to changes in tariffs over a short time-interval. In so doing, one neglects the historical experience of the country's economy responding to changes in tariffs over time; disregards the effects of quantitative restrictions on imports; and leaves out of account the risk element due to the possibility of the imposition of trade barriers and changes in exchange rates.

In order to gauge the effects of all these factors, we need to reintroduce the distinction made between the processes of international and interregional trade. Interregional trade is characterised by the absence of tariffs and other policy instruments affecting trade flows as well as by fixed exchange rates in the form of a common currency. Accordingly, comparisons of trade shares and the extent of industrial diversification between countries and regions with similar characteristics may shed light on the effects of national policies in general, and commercial policy in particular, have on trade and industrial specialisation.

Such comparisons have been made for Northern Ireland and the Republic of Ireland by McAleese (1976). These two areas offer a good standard of comparison, since they are at similar levels of economic development; their manufacturing sectors are of about equal size; they share a common language and culture; their currencies have been at parity since 1922; and both have enjoyed free access to the British market during the postwar period. However, they differ in the availability and use of commercial policy instruments: while Northern Ireland admits British goods duty free, until the mid-1960s the manufacturing sector of the Republic of Ireland was heavily protected, with nominal and effective rates of protection, respectively, averaging 25·5 and 85·0 per cent (McAleese, 1971, p. 23).

Using data for Northern Ireland pertaining to 1963 and for the Republic of Ireland in the year 1964, McAleese found substantial differences in trade ratios and in the extent of diversification in their manufacturing sector. Thus, average import-consumption ratios were 45·7 per cent and 16·5 per cent, and average export-production ratios 59·7 per cent and 21·2 per cent, for Northern Ireland and the Republic of Ireland, respectively. In turn, in a 29-industry breakdown, the Florence coefficient of industrial specialization[5] for value added was estimated at 45·6 per cent and 23·2 per cent in the two cases, indicating the specialised character of the regional economy of Northern Ireland as against the diversified industrial structure of the Republic of Ireland. Northern Ireland is also characterised by a high degree of intraindustry specialisation as 20 out of its 29 manufacturing industries had both export-production and import-consumption ratios exceeding 30 per cent, while there was not even a single such case in the Republic of Ireland.

It may be added that the liberalisation of trade during the second half of the 1960s, entailing reductions of import tariffs by roughly one-half, has led to an increased opening of the economy of the Republic of Ireland. Between 1964 and 1971, average import-consumption ratios rose from 16·5 per cent to 19·6 per cent while export-production ratios increased from 21·1 per cent to 28·3 per cent. During the same period, the coefficient of specialisation increased from 23·2 to 25·0 per cent. Nevertheless, these ratios remain considerably lower than in Northern Ireland.

Information on interregional trade is not available for the United States. However, net trade balances for individual regions can be derived from data on production and consumption. This has been done for four regions (North-east, North, Central, South and West) in a six-industry breakdown (metals, machinery, transport equipment, chemicals, textiles and clothing, and other manufactured goods) by Hufbauer and Chilas (1974). These authors have calculated specialisation indices by relating the sum of the absolute values of net trade in the individual commodity categories to value added in manufacturing. The specialisation indices average 0·65 as against 0·16 for the European Common Market whose larger member countries are comparable in size to the four U.S. regions. Hufbauer and

Chilas also found that interindustry specialisation is much greater in the United States than in the Common Market (1974, p. 8).

These results on the extent of interregional specialisation are consistent with the observation that industries tend to be more concentrated within the United States than within Western Europe. Thus, while U.S. textile, clothing, shoe, automobile, electronics, and aircraft industries are regionally concentrated, textile, clothing and shoe industries can be found in even the smallest European countries and half-a-dozen European countries have their national automobile, electronics, and aircraft industries.

More detailed comparisons of industrial structure have been made in the 27-industry breakdown used in the regression analysis. Nine U.S. regions have been selected for this purpose: New England, Middle Atlantic, East North Central, West North Central, South Atlantic, East South Central, West South Central, Mountain, and Pacific. These regions vary in terms of population from 8.3 million for the Mountain region to 40.3 million in East North Central and in terms of per capita gross product from $3558 in East South Central to $5425 in the Middle Atlantic region.[6]

Defining economic size in terms of gross national product (or regional product), the U.S. regions are comparable to the major European countries, Canada, and Japan, although the comparisons are influenced by the apparent overvaluation of the U.S. dollar in 1970. Table 3 (pp. 246—47) shows data on population, per capita gross product, and total gross product for the nine U.S. regions as well as for the 21-country sample. Average tariffs on manufactured goods, the value of imports, and coefficients of industrial specialisation derived utilising the Theil measure of inequality are also shown in the table.

The results conform to the pattern observed in Northern Ireland and the Republic of Ireland. U.S. regions generally have the highest coefficients of industrial specialisation, indicating that they are less diversified industrially than European countries, Canada and Japan. An exception is one of the smallest European countries in the sample, Sweden, which has a higher localisation coefficient than some of the U.S. regions. In turn, for reasons noted below, the East South Central Region has the lowest coefficient of specialisation.

Comparisons have been made for four groups of geographical areas selected on the basis of their economic size. In the first group, average specialisation coefficients for the Middle Atlantic (gross product of $202 million) and the East North Central ($200 million) regions are about one-third higher than those for Japan ($199 million) and Germany ($194 million). The same relationship holds between the Pacific ($135 million) and the South Atlantic ($133 million) regions on the one hand, and France ($157 million) and the United Kingdom ($127 million), on the other.

Differences between regional and national specialisation coefficients are even greater in the next group, composed of Italy ($94 million), Canada ($78 million), West South Central ($78 million), West North Central ($73 million), and New England ($61 million). They range from 36 per cent to 120 per cent.

Finally, in the fourth group, the coefficient of industrial specialisation for the Mountain region ($36 million) exceeds that for Sweden ($32 million), the Netherlands ($32 million), and Belgium ($26 million) by 17 to 84 per cent. In turn, as noted earlier, the East South Central region has the smallest coefficient of industrial specialisation in the group. This may be explained by the fact that the region, consisting of Kentucky, Tennessee, Alabama, and Mississippi, is more agriculturally oriented than any other U.S. region and it has primarily assembly and other 'finishing touch' industries ranging across the manufacturing sector, its largest industry being printing and publishing.

East South Central is also the only region whose coefficient of industrial specialisation is smaller than that for the United States taken as a whole. In turn, the average specialisation coefficient for the nine regions (0·470), calculated by weighting with value added in manufacturing, is one-third higher than for the U.S. (0·356), and there are five regions whose coefficients of industrial specialisation are at least two-fifths higher than the U.S. coefficient.

We have further calculated hypothetical values of specialisation coefficients for the eight U.S. regions from equation (4). Calculations have been made assuming zero tariffs for the regions as well as a tariff of 11·5 per cent, corresponding to the U.S. tariff. These represent possible extreme values since the trade of each region with other United States regions is not subject to duties while U.S. tariffs apply to its trade with foreign countries. The results are presented in Table 2.

TABLE 2 COEFFICIENT OF INDUSTRIAL SPECIALISATION

	Actual	*Hypothetical*	
		Zero tariff	*11·5 per cent tariff*
New England	0·496	0·394	0·263
Middle Atlantic	0·387	0·320	0·189
East North Central	0·577	0·319	0·188
West North Central	0·569	0·380	0·249
South Atlantic	0·357	0·341	0·210
East South Central	0·225	0·404	0·273
West South Central	0·443	0·373	0·242
Mountain	0·554	0·424	0·293
Pacific	0·519	0·343	0·212

Except for the aberrant East South Central region, the hypothetical coefficients of specialisation are always lower than the actual coefficients. If

TABLE 3 REPRESENTATIVE DATA FOR 19 INDUSTRIAL AND INDUSTRIALISING COUNTRIES AND 9 U.S. REGIONS

	Population million	per capita product $U.S.	Gross product $U.S. billion	Tariffs per cent	Imports $U.S. billion	Coefficient of localisation
Countries						
United States	204·8	4670	975·2	11·5	40·0	0·356
Canada	21·4	3700	79·2	16·0	13·8	0·326
Belgium	9·7	2720	26·3	11·0	11·4	0·301
Denmark	4·9	3190	15·7	7·8	4·4	0·400
France	50·8	3100	157·4	11·0	19·1	0·325
German Federal Republic	61·6	2390	180·4	11·0	30·0	0·315
Italy	53·7	1760	94·5	11·0	14·9	0·260
Netherlands	13·0	2430	31·6	11·0	13·4	0·364
Norway	3·9	2860	11·1	7·8	3·7	0·374
Sweden	8·0	4040	32·5	6·6	7·0	0·474
United Kingdom	55·7	2270	126·5	15·2	21·7	0·346
Japan	103·4	1920	198·5	16·1	18·9	0·393
Australia	12·6	2820	35·4	16·2	4·5	0·344
New Zealand	2·8	2700	7·6	13·4	1·2	0·480
Brazil	92·8	420	39·0	48·0	2·8	0·308
Ireland	2·9	1630	4·8	17·9	1·6	0·509
Israel	2·9	1960	5·7	32·5	2·1	0·308
Korea	13·9	250	3·5	10·7	1·2	0·381
Malaysia	10·9	380	4·2	13·0	1·4	0·445
Singapore	2·1	920	1·9	2·9	2·5	0·536
Taiwan	14·7	386	5·7	15·6	1·5	0·582
U.S. Regions						
New England	11·8	5195	61·3	na	na	0·496
Middle Atlantic	37·2	5425	201·8	na	na	0·387

East North Central	40·3	4953	199·6	na	na	0·577
West North Central	16·3	4487	73·1	na	na	0·569
South Atlantic	30·7	4323	132·7	na	na	0·357
East South Atlantic	12·8	3558	45·5	na	na	0·225
West South Central	19·3	4048	78·1	na	na	0·443
Mountain	8·3	4306	35·7	na	na	0·554
Pacific	26·5	5260	139·4	na	na	0·519

Source: Population, per capita product, and gross product (1970): Countries – IBRD (1972) *World Bank Atlas*, Washington, D.C. U.S. Regions – U.S. Bureau of Census (1972) *Statistical Abstract of the United States*, Washington, D.C.
Tariffs (average tariffs on manufactured goods, various years): To be provided on request.
Imports (1970): IMF–IBRD (1974) *Direction of Trade*, Washington, D.C.
Coefficient of Localisation (Theil measure of inequality, various years): Countries – United Nations (1973), *The Growth of World Industry, Vol. I, General Industrial Statistics*, New York; U.S. Regions – U.S. Bureau of Census (1971) *Census of Manufacturers, Vol. II. Industry Statistics*, Washington, D.C.

comparison is made with the zero tariff alternative, differences equal
approximately the standard error of the estimate (0·086) in three cases,
one-and-a-half times of the standard error in one case, and two standard
errors in three cases. Should we instead make comparisons with the 11·5
per cent tariff alternative, the differences between actual and hypothetical
values range between 1·7 and 3·7 standard errors of the estimate.

The results support the hypothesis that tariffs do not fully reflect the
obstacles to international trade. At the same time it should be emphasised
that the results for U.S. regions underestimate the degree of industrial
specialisation. This is because the definition of regions is an administrative
rather than an economic one; it cuts across economic regions by dividing
several metropolitan areas between different administrative regions and by
combining natural economic units into one region.

IV. HOW THE ELIMINATION OF TARIFFS AFFECTS LOCATIONAL PATTERNS IN AN E.E.C. CONTEXT

The comparisons of trade shares and industrial structure in the intercountry
versus interregional context reported here indicate the importance of commercial policy in determining trade patterns and industrial specialisation.
The estimates further provide support to the proposition that one tends to
understate the effects of commercial policy by limiting attention to tariffs
alone.

The question remains, however, if the relationship between commercial
policy, on the one hand, and international trade and the location of production, on the other is fully reversible. Should this be the case, the elimination of tariffs would lead to the restructuring of production so as to
establish a situation that would have existed if tariff barriers had never
been imposed. In this connection, the experience of the European Common
Market since its establishment offers particular interest.

In the Common Market, tariffs and other protective measures were
abolished over the 1958—67 period and a common commercial policy was
established on the E.E.C. level. It would be too early for the full effect of
these measures on industrial location to have taken place during the short
period that has elapsed since. Nevertheless, it is possible to discern the
direction of changes that have occurred.

The traditional theory of international trade would lead us to expect
that the elimination of tariffs gave rise to interindustry specialisation
through the reallocation of resources from import-competing to export
industries, with consequent changes in the location of production. As the
author first noted in 1963, this had not in fact happened following the
Common Market's establishment; instead of interindustry specialisation,
the expansion of intra-E.E.C. trade was characterised by intraindustry
specialisation, in other words increases in the mutual trade of the member

countries within particular commodity categories (Balassa, 1963, p. 179).

Subsequent statistical testing carried out in a 91-commodity group breakdown has confirmed these conclusions (Balassa, 1966a and 1974). The tests involved estimating rank correlation coefficients between the export composition of particular pairs of countries and calculating 'representative ratios' of trade balances. The latter has been defined as the unweighted average of the ratios of the absolute differences between exports and imports to the sum of exports and imports in each commodity category.[7] Should interindustry specialisation predominate, we would expect this ratio to approach unity since the country would export *or* import a particular commodity (commodity group). Conversely, in the event of intraindustry specialisation, the ratio would approach zero as exports and imports would tend toward equality within each category.

Rank correlation coefficients of export composition in the individual member countries rose to a considerable extent following the Common Market's establishment, pointing to increasing similarity of the export structure of the participating countries. Thus, unweighted averages of the rank correlation coefficients calculated for all pairs of countries rose from 0·53 in 1958 to 0·67 in 1963 and, again, to 0·76 in 1970 (Balassa, 1974, p. 120).

In turn, while the 'representative ratios' for the individual E.E.C. countries were in the 0·39 to 0·58 range in 1958, they were between 0·32 and 0·52 in 1963 and between 0·27 and 0·41 in 1970. From 1958 to 1970, the average decrease in the ratio for all the E.E.C. countries was 30 per cent, the largest decline taking place in Germany (38 per cent) and the smallest in Belgium (26 per cent). The elimination of tariffs, then, has led to increasing intraindustry rather than interindustry specialisation.

These results can be explained if we consider the importance of product differentiation in trade among developed countries. Only a few manufactured goods (such as steel ingots, aluminium, and paper) traded among these countries are standardised products while the large majority are differentiated products that can be protected *and* exported. In the presence of national product differentiation, then, the elimination of tariffs would tend to lead to the exchange of consumer goods and to increased specialisation in narrower ranges of machinery and intermediate products.

The increased exchange of consumer goods is compatible with unchanged production in the consumer goods industries of each of the participating countries while changes in product composition can be accomplished in the framework of existing machinery and intermediate products industries. Correspondingly, the elimination of tariffs in trade among the developed countries does not necessitate radical changes in their industrial structure.

These findings are confirmed by the experience of the United States. Following multilateral reductions in tariffs, the 'representative ratio' for the United States, calculated for the same 91-industry commodity breakdown, fell from 0·59 in 1958 to 0·45 in 1970. Nevertheless, the 24 per cent decline in the U.S. ratio was less than for any of the Common Market countries, indicating that the elimination of tariffs has a greater effect on intraindustry specialisation than partial reductions in tariffs.

One may conclude that, once manufacturing industries have been established, the elimination of protective measures on trade among developed countries does not appear to reverse the effects these measures had on industrial composition and the location of industry. This conclusion points to the importance of the learning-by-doing process that takes place during the period of acclimatisation of an industry. It also indicates the role played by product differentiation in trade among the developed countries.

It cannot be assumed, however, that these conclusions would apply to trade between developed and developing countries, where differences in factor endowments and production costs are greater and exports of standardised products are more important. Correspondingly, the elimination of barriers to the mutual trade of these countries may lead to substantial shifts in resources. But, the effects of tariff changes on the location of production between the two groups of countries awaits further study.

V. THE EFFECTS OF TRADE BARRIERS ON INTERNATIONAL FACTOR MOVEMENTS

Thus far, we have considered the effects of commercial policy on international trade and on the location of production without giving attention to international factor movements. However, as Ohlin first pointed out, international factor mobility is a substitute for commodity trade to the extent that intercountry differences in factor endowments are reduced as a result (1933, chapter IX). Ohlin further suggested that obstacles to commodity trade tend to encourage the international movement of the factors of production. Thus, 'the tariff policy of recent decades, by placing obstacles in the way of international trade, has in many cases induced firms which were exporting a given commodity to establish production in the protected country' (1933, p. 334).

The effects of commercial policy on international factor movements were formulated in a rigorous fashion by Mundell (1957). In the framework of a two-country—two-commodity—two-factor model he showed that, if the assumptions of factor-price equalisation are fulfilled, under perfect factor mobility a small tariff will remove the conditions for commodity trade. In turn, Schmitz and Helmberger (1970) noted that trade and factor movements may be complementary if the model is amended to introduce intercountry differences in natural resource availabilities, in which case increased factor movements may lead to more rather than to less trade.

There is a considerable amount of scattered evidence on tariff protection giving rise to the inflow of capital in the United Kingdom (Dunning, 1958), Australia (Brash, 1966) and Canada (Dales, 1966). Also, in a statistical study, Horst (1972) found that tariff discrimination was positively related to the ratio of sales by the subsidiaries of U.S. companies located in Canada and in the United Kingdom to total U.S. sales (U.S. exports plus sales by U.S. subsidiaries) in these countries.

However, while the effects of E.E.C. tariff discrimination on U.S. investment have been subject to much research in recent years, the results are far from clearcut. A statistical investigation carried out by the present author did not show a positive correlation between the rate of tariff discrimination and the expansion of U.S. investment in the Common Market, irrespective of the statistical formulation employed (1964, p. 9). Results by Scaperlanda (1967) and by Scaperlanda and Mauer (1969) have confirmed this conclusion. Thus, using the ratio of U.S. exports to intra-area exports in the E.E.C. as the tariff discrimination variable, Scaperlanda and Mauer did not find evidence that increased tariff discrimination against American goods would have affected U.S. investments in the Common Market.

In turn, Schmitz and Bieri (1972) defined the tariff discrimination variable in terms of the share of the E.E.C. in total U.S. exports and found that changes in this share were positively correlated with changes in the share of the Common Market in U.S. foreign direct investment. These results have been taken as evidence for the effects of tariff discrimination on American investment in the E.E.C.

The conclusion reached by Schmitz and Bieri is open to objections on several grounds. To begin with, changes in the E.E.C. share in U.S. exports cannot be used as evidence of the existence of tariff discrimination, since the results are affected by changes in international competitiveness and growth in non-E.E.C. markets. In fact, the present author has found that the United States experienced external trade creation rather than trade diversion in its manufactured exports to the Common Market (1974, p. 128).

For similar reasons, the E.E.C.'s share in U.S. foreign direct investments will not appropriately represent the effects of tariff discrimination on U.S. direct investment. And, even if we find that U.S. direct investment in the Common Market rose more rapidly than exports, this is compatible with the thesis put forward by the present author that increases in the market area open to producers consequent upon the fusion of national markets has been the principal factor in the rise of U.S. direct investments in the E.E.C. (1964, p. 8).

In interpreting these results, it should be noted that in Mundell's model, the tariff will lead to the inflow of a particular factor of production if its relative remuneration increases as a result. Thus, depending on the effects of protection on factor prices, the inflow of capital or that of labour may result.

Labour mobility is of considerable importance in the European Common Market, where the protection of labour-intensive industries appears to have led to immigration at the expense of the importation of labour-intensive products. A systematic treatment of this question, however, awaits further study. More generally, there is need for research on the interrelationship of trade and factor movements under protection.

VI. CONCLUSION

This paper has examined the effects of commercial policy on international trade, the location of production, and factor movements. In the discussion, emphasis has been given to the increased importance of commercial policy in its impact on the processes of international as against interregional trade.

Given the inadequacy of import demand elasticity estimates to gauge the effects of tariffs on imports, direct estimates of tariff elasticities have been utilised for this purpose. Calculations have further been made to explain the effects of tariffs on imports and on industrial specialisation in an intercountry context. But these estimates too, are subject to limitations as they neglect the historical experience of the country's economy responding to changes in protection over time, disregard the effects of quantitative restrictions on imports, and leave out of account the risks due to the possibility of the imposition of trade barriers and changes in exchange rates.

In order to indicate the effects of all the relevant factors, comparisons of international and interregional trade have been made. Data for two areas with otherwise similar characteristics — Northern Ireland and the Republic of Ireland — show export-production and import-consumption ratios and specialisation coefficients to be substantially higher in the former, which admitted British goods duty free, than in the latter, whose economy was heavily protected. U.S. regions, too, engage in more trade and are more specialised — less diversified — industrially than comparable European countries, Canada, and Japan.

These results point to the importance of commercial policy in determining the pattern of international trade and the location of production. At the same time, the experience of the European Common Market fails to show the reversibility of the effects of commercial policy on the industrial structure. Rather than leading to the reallocation of resources among industries, the elimination of trade barriers on intra-E.E.C. trade has given rise to intraindustry specialisation through the exchange of consumer goods and different varieties of machinery and intermediate products. This conclusion may find explanation in the process of learning-by-doing through acclimatisation of industry and in the prevalence of product differentiation in trade among the developed countries.

Tariffs and other commercial policy instruments affect not only trade but also international factor movements. There is evidence that tariffs have led to the inflow of capital in the protected industries of some countries and the inflow of labour in others. However, further research on the effects of commercial policy on factor movements and on the interrelationship of trade and factor movements would be desirable.

APPENDIX A
A NOTE ON TRANSPORT COSTS*

The vicissitudes of transportation during the colonial period in North America are well indicated in the 'Diary of a Journey of a Moravian from Bethlehem, Pennsylvania to Bethabara in Wachovia, North Carolina 1753'.[8] According to the author, the 88-km (55-mile) wagon trip between Bethlehem and the present Womelsdorf took two to three days under normal conditions. However, the going was much slower following rains, with weather conditions affecting not only the speed at which wagons could move but also how much they could carry. Even as late as 1798, the heavy stage wagons that travelled through Philadelphia only attained speeds of five to six miles per hour 'over good roads . . . when pulled by four horses'.[9]

In 1760, the cost of transporting pig-iron from Colebrookdale Furnace in Berks County, Pennsylvania to Philadelphia was estimated at £1·2 pound sterling over a 64-km (40-mile) distance, corresponding to a per ton/mile figure of £0·03 or 0·6 shillings.[10] This compares to the price of pig-iron at the furnace of about £4·5. On a two-day journey the interest cost was negligible while the cost of insurance may have amounted to 3 per cent of the value of the shipment,[11] that is, £0·135 for the 64-km (40-mile) distance or 0·07 shillings per ton/mile, raising the per ton/mile cost to 0·67 shillings.

In turn, in 1751 the cost of shipping pig-iron from Baltimore to London was £0·5 per ton or 0·003 shillings per ton/mile for the 5140-km (3200-mile) distance. The journey took three months on the average while the cost of insurance was 6 per cent of the value of the shipment.[12] Calculating with an interest rate of 5 per cent[13] on a price of £4·5 for a ton of pig-iron, the interest cost of the shipment was 1·1 shillings per ton and the cost of insurance 5·4 shillings per ton, thus increasing the cost per ton/mile to 0·005 shillings.

The cost of ocean shipping cited here was on the low side, however. Pig-iron was shipped from Baltimore to London on vessels carrying tobacco, 'the pigs and bars being stowed among the tobacco hogsheads in the hold . . . This method of shipment limited the size of the consignments but also made freight inexpensive, since the rate for iron was based on cargo space rather than weight'.[14] For shipments of pig-iron through the port of New

*I am indebted to Paul Paskoff for information on prices, freight, and insurance rates of pig-iron in Colonial North America. Much of this information is contained in his Ph.D. dissertation, 'Colonial Merchant-Manufacturers and Iron: A Study in Capital Transformation 1725—1775' (Baltimore, The Johns Hopkins University, 1976).

York, Hasenclever shows marketing charges of £3·02 per ton in 1764 for pig-iron produced in the New Jersey iron works and sold in London.[15] This amount includes also the costs of inland transportation to New York and the cost of repeated loading and unloading; adjusting for these cost items, the cost of sea transport (including insurance) may have been around £1·3.[16]

In turn, in mid-1976, freight on pig-iron shipments between Troy and New York (246 km — 154 miles) was $7·39 per ton, insurance 20 cents per $100, and the interest charge negligible, resulting in a total cost of 5·04 cents per ton/mile. At the same time, freight to London was $20·5 per ton, insurance 15—30 cents per $100, and the real interest rate 2 per cent calculated for a 15-day period, resulting in a total cost of 0·65 cents per ton/mile. By comparison, the ex-factory price of pig-iron was $187·67 per ton.

These data are summarised in table 4. The results indicate a decline in the ratio of land to sea transport per ton/mile from 80 to 130 in the second half of the eighteenth century to 8 in 1976. Parallel with these changes, the cost of ocean transportation as a percentage of the price of the good declined from 18 to 29 per cent to 11 per cent while that of land transportation, calculated for a distance of 160 km (100 miles), fell from 70 to 3 per cent.

TABLE 4 TRANSPORT COSTS FOR PIG-IRON

	Second half of eighteenth century		Mid-1976	
	British shillings	Per cent of price	U.S. dollars	Per cent of price
Land (160 km — 100 miles)	62·7	70	5·50	3
Sea (5140 km — 3200 miles)	16·5—26	18—29	23·65	11
Factory price of Pig-iron	90		187·67	

NOTES

[1] In the case of industrialising countries, the averages also reflect the tariff-equivalent of quotas.

[2] The Theil-measure equals $y_i \log y_i N_i$, where y_i refers to the ith industry's share in total manufacturing output and N denotes the number of industries. It has been calculated in a 27 industry breakdown, corresponding to the three-digit International Standard Industrial Classification for the 21 countries included in the sample.

[3] In the equations M denotes imports, C the coefficient of localisation, Y the gross domestic product, P population, and T average tariffs on manu-

factured goods; *t*-values are shown in parenthesis. The underlying data are reported in table 3.

[4] Since this paper was prepared, it has been pointed out to the author that in an unpublished study Seev Hirsch (1976) correlated export, import, and output concentration with per capita incomes and population, without, however, adding a protection variable.

[5] For the purpose at hand, McAleese redefined the coefficient of localisation introduced by P. Sargent Florence to indicate the extent of industrial specialisation as

$$\frac{1}{2} \sum_i \left| y_i - \frac{100}{N} \right|$$

This coefficient is interpreted in the same way as the Theil measure and the same notation is employed.

[6] Population and income data relate to 1970 and have been taken from the *Statistical Abstract of the United States*; per capita gross product data have been derived by multiplying personal income figures for the individual regions by the ratios of G.N.P. to personal income in the United States.

[7] Denoting intra-E.E.C. exports in commodity category i by X_i, and imports by M_i the formula for the representative ratio is

$$\frac{1}{N} \sum_i \frac{|X_i - M_i|}{X + M}$$

[8] Cited in Mereness, N. D. (ed.), *Travels in the American Colonies* (New York, Macmillan, 1916), p. 328.

[9] Dunbar, Seymour, *A History of Travel in America* (Indianapolis, Bobbs-Merrill Co., 1915), Vol. I, p. 181.

[10] Bining, Arthur C., *Pennsylvania Iron Manufacture in the 18th Century*, Harrisburg, Pennsylvania Historical Commission, 1938, p. 31 — all data referred to here and hereafter have been expressed in terms of British pounds.

[11] In the absence of information on the cost of insurance on land transport, it has been assumed that this was one-half of insurance on sea transport.

[12] Johnson, Keith, 'The Baltimore Company seeks English market — a study of the Anglo-American iron trade, 1731—1755', *William and Mary Quarterly* (January, 1959), pp. 37—60. It should be added that the 6 per cent rate applied in peace time; in times of conflicts, the rate was 10, 12, 14, and even 20 per cent.

[13] Clapham, J. M., *The Bank of England*, Vol. I (Cambridge University Press, 1958), p. 298. No adjustment has been made for inflation as prices did not show any marked trend during this period.

[14] Johnson, *op. cit.*, p. 44.

[15] Hasenclever, Peter, *The Remarkable Case of Peter Hasenclever Merchant* (New York, 1773), N.Y. Public Library, Special Collection, pp. 76, 79—82.

[16] The cost of transportation to the port was assumed to be the same as between Colebrookdale Furnaces and Philadelphia (£1·2) while the cost of lighterage and wharfage in Baltimore was estimated at 3·5 shillings by Johnson (*op. cit.*). The latter amount has been tripled to account for the repeated loadings and unloadings.

REFERENCES

Aitken, N. D., 'The Effect of the EEC and EFTA on European Trade: A Temporal Cross-Section Analysis', *American Economic Review* (1973), 63 (4), pp. 881–92.

Bairoch, P., 'Free Trade and European Economic Development in the 19th Century', *European Economic Review* (1972), Vol. 3 (3), pp. 211–45.

Balassa, Bela, 'European Integration: Problems and Issues', *American Economic Review* (1963), 53 (2), pp. 175–84.

Balassa, B., *Economic Development and Integration* (1965), Mexico, Centro de Estudios Monetarios Latinamericanos.

Balassa, B., 'Tariff Reductions and Trade in Manufactures among the Industrial Countries', *American Economic Review* (1966a), 56 (3), pp. 466–73.

Balassa, B., 'American Direct Investments in the Common Market', *Banca Nazionale del Lavoro Quarterly Review* (1966b), No. 77, pp. 1–26.

Balassa, B., *Trade Liberalisation among Industrial Countries: Objectives and Alternatives* (New York, McGraw Hill, 1967).

Balassa, B., 'Tariff Protection in Industrial Nations and Its Effects on the Exports of Processed Goods from Developing Countries', *Canadian Journal of Economics* (1968a), 1 (3), pp. 583–94.

Balassa, B., 'The Structure of Protection in Industrial Countries and Its Effects on the Exports of Processed Goods from Developing Countries' in *The Kennedy Round and Estimated Effects on Trade Barriers*, New York, United Nations (1968b), pp. 197–217.

Balassa, B., 'Trade Creation and Trade Diversion in the European Common Market: An Appraisal of the Evidence', *Manchester School* (1974), 44 (2), pp. 93–133.

Brash, D. T., *American Investment in Australian Industry* (Cambridge, Mass., Harvard University Press, 1966).

Chenery, H. B., 'Patterns of Industrial Growth', *American Economic Review* (1960), 50 (4), pp. 624–54.

Dales, J. H., *The Protective Tariff in Canada's Economic Development* (Toronto University Press, 1966).

Dunning, J. H., *American Investment in British Manufacturing Industry* (London, Allen and Unwin, 1958).

Finger, J. M., 'GATT Tariff Concessions and the Exports of Developing Countries – United States Concessions at the Dillon Round', *Economic Journal* (1974), 84 (335), pp. 566–75.

Finger, J. M., 'Effects of the Kennedy Round Tariff Concessions on the Exports of Developing Countries', *Economic Journal* (1976), 86 (341), pp. 87–95.

Florence, Sargant P., *Investment, Location, and Size of Plant* (Cambridge University Press, 1948).

Guisinger, S. E., *Effective Protection, Resource Allocation, and the Characteristics of Protected Industries; A Case Study of Pakistan' 1963–64*, Cambridge, Mass., Ph.D. Dissertation prepared for Harvard University, 1970.

Hirsch, S., 'Rich Man, Poor Man, and Every Man's Goods. The Industrial Organization of International Protection and Trade', mimeo (1976).

Horst, T., 'The Industrial Composition of U.S. Export and Subsidy Sales in the Canadian Market', *American Economic Review* (1972), 62 (1), pp. 37–45.

Hufbauer, G. C. and Chilas, J. G., 'Specialization by Industrial Countries: Extent and Consequences, in *The International Division of Labour: Problems and Perspectives* (Herbert Giersch, ed.) (Tubingen, J. C. B. Mohr, 1974), pp. 3–62.

Isard, W. and Peak, M. J., 'Location Theory and International and Interregional Trade Theory', *Quarterly Journal of Economics* (1954), 68 (1), pp. 97–114.

Isard, W., *Location and Space Economy* (New York, M.I.T. Press & Wiley, 1956).

Johnston, J. and Henderson, M., 'Assessing the Effects of the Import Surcharge', *Manchester School* (1967), 35 (2), pp. 89–110.

Krause, L. B., 'United States Imports, 1947–1958', *Econometrica* (1962), 30 (2), pp. 221–38.

Kreinin, M. E., 'Effect of Tariff Changes on the Prices and Volume of Imports', *American Economic Review* (1961), 51 (3), pp. 310–24.

Kreinin, M. E., ' "Price" vs. "Tariff" Elasticities in International Trade – A Suggested Reconciliation', *American Economic Review* (1967), 57 (4), pp. 891–94.

Leamer, E. E., 'Nominal Tariff Averages with Estimated Weights', *Southern Economic Journal* (1974), 4 (1), pp. 34–46.

Linnemann, H., *An Econometric Study of International Trade Flows* (Amsterdam: North Holland, 1966).

Little, I., Scitovsky, T. and Scott, M., *Industry and Trade in Some Developing Countries* (London, Oxford University Press, 1970).

Lösch, August, 'A New Theory of International Trade', *International Economic Papers*, No. 6 (London, Macmillan Co. (1956), pp. 50–65. – originally published in German in *Weltwirtschaffliches Archiv* (1939).

McAleese, D., 'Effective Tariffs and the Structure of Industrial Protection in Ireland'. *The Economic & Social Research Institute* (1971), Paper No. 62.

McAleese, D., 'Do Tariffs Matter? Industrial Specialization and Trade in a Small Economy', *Oxford Economic Papers* (1977), forthcoming.

Mundell, R. A., 'International Trade and Factor Mobility', *American Economic Review* (1957), 47 (3), pp. 321–35.

Officer, L. H. and Hurtubise, J. R., 'Price Effects of the Kennedy Round on Canadian Trade', *Review of Economics and Statistics* (1969), 51 (3), pp. 320–33.

Ohlin, B., *Interregional and International Trade* (Cambridge, Mass., Harvard University Press, 1933).

Pöyhönen, P., 'A Tentative Model for the Volume of Trade between Countries', *Weltwirtschaffliches Archiv* (1963), 90 (1), pp. 93—98.

Pulliainen, K., 'A World Trade Study: an Econometric Model of the Pattern of the Commodity Flows in International Trade in 1948—1960, *Ekonomiska Sanfundits Tidskrift* (1963), 17 (2), pp. 78—91.

Savage, I. R. and Deutsch, K. W., 'A Statistical Model of the Gross Analysis of Transactions Flows', *Econometrica* (1960), Vol. 28 (3), pp. 551—72.

Scaperlanda, A. E., 'The EEC and U.S. Foreign Investment', *Economic Journal* (1967), 77 (305), pp. 22—26.

Scaperlanda, A. E. and Mauer, L. V., 'The Determinants of U.S. Direct Investment in the EEC', *American Economic Review* (1969), 59 (4), pp. 558—68.

Schmitz, A. and Helmberger, P., 'Factor Mobility and International Trade: The Case of Complementarity', *American Economic Review* (1970), 60 (4), pp. 761—67.

Schmitz, A. and Bieri, J., 'EEC Tariffs and U.S. Direct Investment, *European Economic Review* (1972), 3, pp. 259—70.

Scott, M., *A Study of United Kingdom Imports* (Cambridge University Press, 1962).

Statistischer Reichsamt, 'Der Güterverketer der Weltshiffahrt', *Vierteljahrshefte nur Statistik des Deutschen Reichs* (1) (Berlin, 1928).

Stern, R. M., Francis, J. H. and Schumacher, B., 'Price Elasticities in International Trade: A Compilation and Annotated Bibliography', *Seminar Discussion Paper No. 62* (Ann Arbor, Department of Economics, University of Michigan, 1975).

Theil, H., *Economics and Information Theory* (Amsterdam: North Holland, 1967).

Weber, A., 'Die Standortlehre und die Handelspolitik', *Archiv für Sozialwissenschaft und Sozialpolitik* (1911), 32 (2), pp. 674—77.

Comment .
Tibor Scitovsky

Professor Balassa's paper well demonstrates the great strides economic reasoning has made over the past half-century and the much greater caution and closer reliance on empirical evidence with which modern economists approach the old economic problems. In the good old days, we made sweeping assumptions about the mobility of products and the immobility of factors, and had implicit faith in the strength, the reversibility, and the monotonic nature of the relationship between tariffs, trade, international specialisation, and economic welfare. We have since learned, and are still learning, that none of those assumptions and relations is quite as simple as it once seemed, and that none can be taken on trust, without empirical evidence.

Balassa proceeds by small steps, carefully testing every link in the causal chain against the evidence; and the evidence he marshalls is surprisingly voluminous. If he comes up with few answers in the end and raises more questions than he resolves, he can hardly be blamed. I shall try to point out some of the gaps and unanswered questions; but let me first raise a philosophical question that comes to mind when looking at Balassa's findings.

Perhaps the most important and certainly the most interesting of his findings is the secular reduction of the natural barriers to trade and specialisation. The main element, according to Balassa, is the falling cost of transportation in relation to other costs. The figures he quotes show a reduction in the relative cost of ocean transport by about one-half over a period of two centuries; in the relative cost of land transport over the same period by as much as twenty-four twenty-fifths (96 per cent). A second element is what I take to be the declining importance of transport-intensive commodities in the consumer's budget as his real income rises; and a third element might well be the erosion of national and regional differences in customs, tastes and fashion brought about by cheaper transportation and the great technological advances in communication.

Balassa stresses the implications only of the great disparity between the reductions in the cost of land and sea transport; and especially (1) the increasing importance of commercial policy, (2) 'the increased cleavage between international and interregional trade', and (3) 'the greater inner unity of national economies'. I fully agree about the first; as to the second and third, they are true only to the limited extent that a higher percentage of domestic than of international trade is carried by land. One must beware of identifying land transport with domestic and sea transport with international trade. Balassa might have added, as a fourth fateful consequence, the greatly increased international mobility of capital funds due to better, faster and cheaper communications.

To my mind, however, the most important implication of reduced transport costs is the great actual and potential increase in interregional *and* international trade and specialisation, whatever the manmade impediments to trade.

The diminution in the natural barriers to trade has long been known and deplored in the developing countries, where complaints are often voiced about the import-intensity of growth and of the affluent consumer's tastes. Another and more general manifestation of the erosion of natural obstacles to trade, as well as of the increasing economies of scale, is the great rise in world trade in relation to world production throughout the postwar period — despite our many tariffs, restrictions, controls, and despite the political and economic risks besetting international trade, which seem much greater than those of earlier times.

All that confirms Balassa's conclusion; but it also raises an important and interesting question. While there were great natural barriers to trade and specialisation, the blessings of the division of labour seemed so much greater than its possible drawbacks that we unhesitatingly favoured every policy, every institutional change capable of lifting manmade obstacles to trade, and so bringing us closer to free trade — that Pareto-optimal situation which, we fervently believed, would maximise world welfare. Only on a temporary basis or on narrow nationalistic grounds did we envisage exceptions to that rule.

But now, when the natural barriers to trade have been so greatly lowered, and when trade free of man-made restrictions would lead to so much more specialization than before, do we and should we still favour the unrestricted flow of goods, funds and workers?

After all, specialisation has costs as well as benefits. It increases total production; but it also renders the income of each geographical area and the profit of each specialist firm more vulnerable to shifts in demand and changes in circumstances. In other words, increased specialisation across geographical space and national boundaries increases uncertainty — both the uncertainty of the individual's employment opportunities and the uncertainty of the business firm's investment opportunities. Presumably, there is an optimum degree of specialisation, where its marginal benefits equal its marginal costs. When the natural obstacles to trade were high, we took it for granted that actual specialisation always fell short of optimum specialisation. Hence the belief, once undisputed, that trade restriction is bad, free trade is good, and the freer the better. The question I am now raising is whether that is a universal law or whether it was just a nineteenth-century rule of thumb, valid in its own day but in need of qualification or revision in today's different world? I have no ready answer to that question. My guess would be that completely free international economic relations in today's world might well generate too much uncertainty; but I would be reluctant to conclude from that that trade restriction is necessarily the best remedy. There are several alternative remedies. It has been argued that uncertainty is a collective 'bad', in the sense that one person's or firm's defence against uncertainty inflicts on others the external diseconomy of increased uncertainty. If that argument is valid, then efficiency calls for collective defence against uncertainty, organised or underwritten by the State. Trade restriction is one form of that, Government-guaranteed export credits are another; and there may be many more.

Let me now proceed to some of the more concrete and better documented points either answered or raised in the paper. The best documented is the influence of tariffs on the volume of imports; but all the tariff elasticities cited measure the influence only of the *lowering* of tariffs. As to the imposition of tariffs, we are merely told that temporary surcharges had no permanent effects. One would also like to know whose and what kind of responses are measured by tariff elasticities: producers' or consumers' responses, capacity or merely output responses? Documentation to throw light on those issues would be more interesting but is much more scanty.

An interesting finding on which Balassa reports is the preponderance of intraindustry (as against interindustry) specialisation between members of the E.E.C. The reason for that seems obvious: it is the natural and easiest way to specialise for countries whose economies have been well-diversified by longstanding past policies of protection. It might also be the best form of specialisation, since it reaps the economies of scale at relatively low cost in terms of uncertainty. If that is so, the question arises whether other economic groups could achieve that desirable outcome more simply and directly than via Europe's circuitous route.

So much for the consequences of tariff reduction. More problematic are the consequences of the imposition of tariffs. The usual purpose of protection is to create, at the cost of some sacrifice of comparative advantages and economies of scale, a more balanced economy, in the sense of greater harmony between the structure of protection and the structure of absorption. That purpose is achieved, or supposed to be achieved, through protection creating monopoly profits and the monopoly profits motivating the establishment or expansion of manufacturing capacities which will contribute to a more diversified and more balanced productive structure.

Leaving aside the question of the desirability of the aim, its achievement depends on the effectiveness of the profit motive and the correctness of the structure of profits created by protection. On this latter subject, Balassa says nothing here; but we owe to him many of the best and most ambitious empirical studies of the structure of effective protection in both developed and developing countries; and estimates of effective protection are probably as close as we can come to the estimation of profit protection.

As to the first subject, most of us have great faith in the effectiveness of the profit motive under competitive conditions; and that faith is probably justified. But how about the effectiveness of monopoly profits created by protection? Are they equally effective in motivating the creation of capacity and the expansion of output?

In the developed countries they probably are: Balassa's table 1 contains impressive evidence of that. But the question is more open in the LDCs, part of whose lesser development may well consist in the lesser development of their businessmen's desire to maximise profits. An affirmative answer to that side of the question is contained in Balassa's discussion of the comparison of the Republic of Ireland with Northern Ireland. Irish businessmen do seem to be motivated to action by the lure of profit and never to have heard of Sir John Hicks' dictum that 'the best of all monopoly profits is a quiet life'. But can one generalise from the experience of the Irish? Are they not supposed to be the last upholders of puritanism and its values?

It is better therefore to ask the question in its most direct form. Have the monopoly profits created by the import-substitution policies of the non-European LDCs been effective in motivating the building up of capacity and the expansion of output? Balassa cites two studies (Pakistan and Korea), which give mutually contradictory answers. Tentative attempts at my university (Stanford) to correlate the growth of output of different industries with their effective rates of protection in a few LDCs show little or no correlation. Also relevant in this context is Balassa's table 3 which shows a coefficient of localisation that on average is significantly lower for the 19 countries of the sample than for the 9 U.S. regions. In other words, tariff protection seems to make for much lesser specialisation (greater diversity) of industry than one finds in regions unprotected from each other's competition. When one looks closer, however, one realises that the average of the coefficients of localisation differs much more between the developed and the less-developed countries of the sample than it does between the less-developed countries and the U.S. regions. It is true that the developed countries have practised trade restriction for very much longer; on the other hand, the LDCs have pushed their restrictive policies to much greater heights. The average height of the LDCs' tariff in Balassa's sample is twice that of the DCs; in addition, the LDCs also make much more use of import controls and quantitative restrictions. I would conclude therefore that in the LDCs of today, the effectiveness of tariffs and other instruments of protection in diversifying the economy is far from proven. Tariffs undoubtedly create monopoly profits; but we do not really know how effective these are in creating viable industries. We know that the structure of effective protection is often ill suited to encourage a well-diversified economy; and the economies of the LDCs in Balassa's sample are not well diversified. It must be noted, however, that Theil's index of inequality is a very crude index of what we are trying to measure. After all, industries of equal size do not add up to a balanced economy.

Comment
Melvyn B. Krauss

Both Professor Balassa's excellent paper and the subject matter with which it is concerned stimulate several comments.

The first relates to the proper definition of commercial policy. For the purposes of Professor Balassa's paper, 'commercial policy is defined to include tariffs and other restrictions on imports as well as taxes and subsidies on exports'. Balassa continues, 'since a devaluation is equivalent to the simultaneous application of tariffs on imports and subsidies on exports at equal rates, it will be considered together with commercial policy. measures'.

I find this definition, at the same time, too narrow and too broad for meaningful discussion. It is too broad because, despite a well-placed hedge on Professor Balassa's part, currency devaluation does not belong in the same category of policy measures as tariffs and export subsidies. It is too narrow, because it leaves out a host of policy measures that currently form the central focus of commercial policy discussions.

In light of the recent resurrection of David Hume by those stressing the monetary approach to balance of payments theory, I find it hard to accept currency exchange rate variation (either currency appreciation or currency depreciation) as anything but *monetary policy*. Traditionally, commercial policy has been concerned with measures affecting relative price. Balassa's argument that because currency devaluation is logically equivalent to the combined application of general tariffs on imports and general export subsidies — neglecting to mention, by the way, the important proviso that this is true only from the perspective of the balance of *trade* — it is similar to *either* a tariff *or* an export subsidy misses an important point of general equilibrium trade theory — that while the tariff alone distorts, and the export subsidy alone distorts, the combined application of the two at equal *ad valorem* rates does not distort. This, of course, is the essence of Abba Lerner's Symmetry Theorem. The combined application of import taxes and export subsidies of equal *ad valorem* rate from an initial free trade position is logically equivalent to switching from an export tax to an import tax — there will be a monetary effect from the switch but no real effect.

What I would like to hear discussed by commercial policy specialists, but which is only fleetingly referred to in Balassa's paper, is what the trade negotiators at the Tokyo Round presently are concerned with — policy measures that do not discriminate between the domestic and foreign sectors of the economy but nonetheless have a significant impact on international trade. Production subsidies are an example, border tax adjustments another, safety standards yet another. Currently such measures go under the somewhat misleading banner of 'non-tariff trade barriers'. They all affect trade, both trade volume and trade patterns, and are extremely important. Yet if one limits debate solely to measures that discriminate between domestic and foreign sectors, they are left undiscussed. It is worth noting at this juncture that if even more evidence is needed to demonstrate the unparalleled perspicacity of Bertil Ohlin, it could be this quote from *Interregional and International Trade* (p. 309, second edition):

> Besides the costs for the use of certain quantities of the factors of production — quantities needed for production and transportation — the costs of production also include *taxes and social welfare fees,* many of which bear an important relation to international trade and yet are not included in general systems. It has long been a mystery to me why existing accounts of international trade pay so little attention to these problems. So many books and articles discuss the impact of a certain type of taxation, *viz.,* tariffs levied at the border when goods are imported, yet they devote no space to the question of how *other kinds of taxation* can affect trade.

There can be no doubt that the international trade effects of taxation, other than trade taxes, have been an underexplored area of scientific investigation. This is and continues to be unfortunate, since there are many aspects of public finance which cannot be properly understood unless the openness of the economy is explicitly brought into account. Consider a question as basic as the form in which a domestic goods tax is applied — either as a production tax or a consumption tax. If a domestic tax is to be applied as a consumption tax, it must be supported by destination principle border tax adjustments — that is, compensatory import taxes combined with export tax rebates at the same *ad valorem* rate as domestically produced and domestically consumed goods. Otherwise the tax will appear as a production tax. The principle of border tax adjustment, in other words, determines the form that the domestic tax takes. The present G.A.T.T. rule that restricts destination principal border tax adjustments to so-called 'indirect taxes' greatly constrains the sovereignty of nations to apply their internal goods taxes as they, the nations, see fit. A case in point is the corporation income tax and the employer's social security tax which must be applied as production taxes under this G.A.T.T. rule, even though there probably are nations that would apply these 'direct' taxes as consumption taxes if the G.A.T.T. rule were changed.

Analogous to Ohlin's point as to how taxation can affect international trade, is that of how taxation can affect international factor mobility. As Balassa reminds us, in his classic 1957 paper Mundell demonstrated that even a small tariff could eliminate *all* 'goods for goods' trade if, in a 'two by two by two' general equilibrium model, under factor-price equalisation assumptions, one of the factors of production is mobile. The only effect of the tariff in this case is to change the pattern of international exchange from 'goods for goods' to 'factor services for goods'.

This same conclusion holds, with one important exception, if instead of a tariff, a production tax is imposed under conditions of capital mobility. Like the tariff, the production tax terminates 'goods for goods' trade and substitutes an equivalent (in terms of the domestic aggregate consumption point) 'goods for capital services' exchange pattern. The difference, however, is that while the *location of domestic production* is indeterminate with the tariff, it is fully determinate with the production tax – output of the taxed good must fall to zero. Hence, even a small production tax, or a small tax on one factor only in one sector only – the corporation income tax, for example – will shut down the taxed industry and dry up the tax base *completely* if there is international factor mobility.

Of course, the real world differs from the frictionless world of the 2 x 2 x 2 general equilibrium model. But the meaning for real world economic policy is clear enough. Governments in their taxing powers can have dramatic effects on the location of production when the factors of production are mobile. Hence, fiscal sovereignty may require stringent controls over the free movement of capital and labour both to preserve the tax base and prevent dramatic shifts in the location of production.

Professor Balassa rightly calls for a systematic treatment of labour mobility. But he fails to point out the two separate and distinct classes of labour mobility: 'short-run' and 'long-run'. The former is illustrated by Bertil Ohlin's 1933 case (pointed out to me by Ronald Findlay) of workers in southern Belgium who daily crossed the border into France to work in French factories and return home in the evenings. These workers produced income in a foreign country and consumed it at home. Today, this pattern of producing income in a foreign country and domestically consuming it is much more widespread than in the 1930s. Besides cases that involve a single border crossing, as did Ohlin's, there currently exists in western Europe a class of workers, euphemistically known as 'guest workers', who have had to cross many borders to get to work, travelling as they do from Europe's south to Europe's north. Guest workers typically work for short periods in the host countries, consuming very little there before going home. They represent a case of 'short-run' labour mobility in contrast to permanent migration.

Yet another current example of 'short-run' labour mobility, this time from north to south, concerns skilled labour. While guest workers represent a situation where a southern resource transports itself to work with other resources in the north, 'guest managers' represent the reverse, where a northern resource transports itself to work with other resources in the south. A case in point is the tourist industry. Tourism is a non-traded good, because its main factor input is geographically fixed in supply. That is, while one can import an Italian chef to cook spaghetti in Sweden, for example, one cannot import the Amalfi or Ligurian coasts from Italy (though some misguided soul did import London Bridge to the U.S.A.). It is a fact that the tourist industry in the south is often run by 'guest managers' from the north, who stay south for the tourist season and then return home to consume the fruits of their labours.

Economists have paid little attention to the phenomenon of 'short-run' labour mobility, in contrast to permanent migration, brain drain problems among other things. (A notable exception is Jagdish Bhagwati who at this symposium has stressed that the 'welfare implications of . . . to-and-fro migration . . . are quite serious' and 'drastically' different from the brain drain problem; also see Krauss (1976).) Yet this important and interesting problem is readily analysable by a somewhat modified version of the standard Heckscher-Ohlin-Samuelson general equilibrium model. This is because the definition of 'short-run' labour mobility, as a situation in which income is produced in the foreign country and consumed at home, permits this phenomenon to be treated *as if* the factor *owner* does not move, while the factor *service* does — the approach used by Mundell in his paper on commodity trade and capital mobility. Mundell's conclusion, that under factor price equalisation assumptions, capital mobility can substitute perfectly for commodity trade in terms of aggregate consumption and potential welfare, is relevant for the analysis of guest workers as well.

Indeed the analysis of guest workers could be a straightforward adaptation of Mundell where labour services instead of capital services are exported, because domestic protection increases the output of importables which are capital-intensive (or protection in foreign countries of importables which are labour-intensive — the idea put forward by Bela Balassa). A more interesting idea, and probably more relevant for 'short-run' labour mobility, is that guest workers compensate for certain non-traded elements in the international economy. It is reasonable to assume that for guest workers alternative employment possibilities at home would be in the non-traded goods sector — as waiters, barbers, government clerks, bus drivers, etc. Assume then that the two sectors of the Heckscher-Ohlin-Samuelson model refer to a capital-intensive traded good T and a labour-intensive non-traded good H. Also assume that the two economies are identical except for relative factor endowment; the home country (illustrated by figure 1) being labour-abundant and the foreign country capital-abundant. Let H be plotted on the horizontal and T on the vertical in figure 1. The slope of MN would represent free-trade commodity prices (assumed to be given for a small country), and CBP the trade triangle in labour-abundant economy were good H tradeable (which it is not). Hence, CBP is the 'hypothetical' trade triangle with the labour-abundant country exporting the labour-intensive good. The same result, in terms of domestic consumption and potential welfare, that would occur under free trade (were it possible), in fact, can take place by the home country exporting labour services along the Rybczynski line RR via guest workers. By comparison with hypothetical free trade, national income and consumption remain the same, at OM (or ON) and point C respectively. But unlike Mundell's case where both goods are tradeable, the location of production is fully determinate in this model. There is a unique production point at P' where the demand for and supply of the non-traded good is equal. Given production at P' and consumption at C, labour remittances equal CP' in terms of the tradeable good.

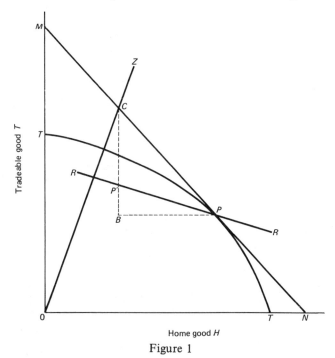

Figure 1

I have a good deal of sympathy for Professor Balassa's point that as the natural barriers to trade have come down (the decline in importance of transport costs), the artificial or policy-induced barriers have been more important. Balassa makes a convincing case. But I do not think it is correct to identify flexibility of exchange rates as one of the referred-to artificial barriers. Balassa writes (p. 233) 'The flexibility of exchange rates also creates uncertainty in international trade that did not exist under the gold standard'. (I take as a standard of comparison the gold-exchange standard which seems to be more relevant from a policy point of view than the gold standard.)

I don't want to belabour the difference between flexible exchange rates and widly fluctuating exchange rates — only to mention that wildly fluctuating rates reflect wildly fluctuating domestic macroeconomic policies, which would be a problem under any exchange rate régime. The point, as we all know from Milton Friedman, is that the lack of everyday adjustment under fixed rates creates a need for once-and-for-all discrete adjustment. This, in turn, not only creates uncertainty as to when and the form such adjustment will take, but often leads to illiberal solutions such as import quotas, travel restrictions and capital controls. Balassa notes 'the effects of uncertainty due to the risk of the imposition of quotas . . .' (p. 233), but either fails to recognise or fails to agree that flexible exchange rates have significantly reduced the risk that quotas will be imposed for reasons of the balance of payments.

Of course, critics could point to the recent case of Italy when, to bolster the collapsing Lira, the Italian government imposed the very controls that flexible exchange rates were supposed to preclude the need for. Hence, flexible exchange rates might be said to have led to illiberal restrictions. This, however, would be a misinterpretation in my view. While it is true that neither fixed nor flexible exchange rates could turn the at-that-time unstable situation in Italy into a stable one, at least under flexible rates the need for illiberal solutions such as import controls in the face of instability does not exist. What the recent action of the Italian government really proved is that the Italians were not willing to have a true flexible rate system (hence, this situation cannot be used as an argument against floating rates).

My final point relates to Professor Balassa's interesting finding that the experience in the European Common Market 'fails to show the reversibility of the effects of commercial policy on the industrial structure . . .' (p. 252). Perhaps here too the definition of commercial policy plays a role. A narrow definition of commercial policy leaves out the effects that 'non-tariff barriers' have had on the location of production and trade in the Common Market. Perhaps what was obtained with tariff reduction was lost through non-tariff barriers. Because governments were not willing to tolerate the implications of tariff reduction, they could neutralise such effects by means other than those constrained by E.E.C. obligations. The need to quantify the trade effects of non-tariff trade barriers clearly is a most pressing one.[1]

NOTE

[1] The work of the Office of Foreign Economic Research, U.S. Labour Department, to obtain such quantification should be noted.

REFERENCES

Krauss, M. B., 'The Economics of the "Guest Worker" Problem: A Neo-Heckscher-Ohlin Approach', *Scandinavian Journal of Economics* (formerly, *Swedish Journal of Economics*) (1976), No. 3.

Krauss, M. B. and Baumol, W. J., 'Guest Workers and Social Programs Financed by Host Governments', unpublished manuscript (1976).

Mundell, R. A., 'International Trade and Factor Mobility', *American Economic Review* (1957) 47 (3), pp. 321–35.

Ohlin, B., *Interregional and International Trade* (Cambridge, Massachusetts, Harvard University Press, 1933).

Reply to Comments

Bela Balassa

I am grateful to Professor Scitovsky for a careful reading of my paper and for the thoughtful comments he has chosen to make. I trust that these comments will stimulate further work on the subject. Some of these comments, however, call for discussion.

To begin with, Scitovsky expresses doubts concerning the validity of my statement as to the greater 'inner unity' of national economies today as compared to the time when the classical economists developed the theory of international specialisation. He warns that 'one must beware of identifying land transport with domestic and sea transport with international trade'. Yet, with rare exceptions, domestic transport proceeds on land while the sea route is used even in much of intra-European trade not to speak of trade with, and among, non-European countries. Also, Scitovsky neglects the fact that, compared to Ricardo's time, increased protection in the form of tariff and non-tariff barriers have increased the 'inner unity' of national economies.

In turn, Scitovsky claims that the erosion of natural obstacles to trade is manifested in 'the great rise in world trade in relation to world production throughout the postwar period – despite our many tariffs, restrictions, controls, and despite the political and economic risks besetting international trade, which seem much greater than those of earlier times'. Yet, barriers to trade among the industrial countries, where much of the expansion has taken place, have been reduced rather than increased during the postwar period. Quantitative restrictions on foreign exchange and on imports from the other industrial countries were dismantled during the early part of this period; tariffs have subsequently been reduced in the framework of successive multilateral negotiations; and, finally, barriers to trade within large groups of European countries have been abolished in the process of regional economic integration.

The results observed during the postwar period thus lend support to my thesis as to the importance of commercial policy in determining international specialisation. This thesis receives further support from evidence for earlier periods. The data show that during preceding decades, when barriers to trade multiplied, the share of imports in national income substantially declined. This was documented first by Werner Sombart (1913) and later by Deutsch and Eckstein (1961) who carry their comparisons up to the immediate postwar years.

The effects of increased trade barriers on trade are also shown by Hollis Chenery's results for Japan reported at the symposium. According to these results, export expansion was a major source of economic growth in the period 1914–35 when tariffs in Japan were low or non-existent. In turn, exports made a negative, and import substitution a positive, contribution to national income following the imposition of trade barriers during the Sino-Japanese War and the Second World War and the period immediately following.

Scitovsky next raises the question if we should 'still favour the un-restricted flow of goods, funds and workers' in the presence of 'the un-certainty of the individual's employment opportunities and the uncertainty of the business firm's investment opportunities'. To begin with the latter point, in my paper I have noted that, with producers being by-and-large risk-averters, uncertainty as regards changes in relative prices (resulting from the risk of imposition of quotas and changes in exchange rates) will provide inducement to expand domestic sales at the expense of foreign sales'. If private producers act in this fashion, the question is whether the social risk is greater than the private risk, thus necessitating the use of corrective measures in the form of trade restrictions.

I submit that the opposite is the case. The social risk will be lower be-cause of diversification in the portfolio of nations as against that of in-dividual firms. This conclusion is strengthened if account is taken of the 'bankruptcy effect', that is firms attach greater disutility to negative profits than nations do. Thus, in contrasting social risk with private risk for the firm, one may call for subsidising rather than taxing foreign trade.

Different considerations apply to employment. Nonetheless, for various reasons, I would not recommend the imposition of trade barriers for the sake of reducing uncertainty as regards employment opportunities. Firstly, trade appears to react little to temporary changes in exchange rates while persistent changes in exchange rates are generally associated with inter-country differences in the rate of inflation (Niehans, 1965). Secondly, assistance to the unemployed may be preferable to putting the burden of adjustment on the foreigner. Last but not least, second-best considerations call for exercising extreme caution in raising trade barriers in order to reduce uncertainty in employment, thus lending support to Scitovsky's conclusion that trade restriction is not necessarily the best remedy.

Scitovsky has recently done important work that brings into question traditional postulates on utility maximisation by the consumer (1976). By analogy, he raises the question of whether the monopoly profits created through protection will motivate 'the establishment or expansion of manu-facturing capacities which will contribute to a more diversified and balanced productive structure'. In this connection, he makes reference to Sir John Hicks' dictum that 'the best of all monopoly profits is a quiet life'.

Distinction needs to be made, however, between the inducement protec-tion provides for the establishment of an industry *and* for improvements in the firm's operations once it has been established. While there is evidence in developing countries on 'the effectiveness of tariffs and other instru-ments of protection in diversifying the economy', first from food production to simple consumer goods, and subsequently through the backward integration of the production process, Hicks' dictum applies to established firms inasmuch as high protection provides little inducement for improvements in production methods and technological change. This is well-documented in the Little-Scitovsky-Scott studies (1970) as well as in my own work (1971).

The impact of tariff protection on industrial diversification is also shown by the results of my regression analysis, which adjusts for the effects of variables such as per capita incomes and population. Nor can one compare average coefficients of industrial specialisation for the developed and developing country groups in the sample and the U.S. regions, without taking account of differences in terms of population and per capita incomes. Thus, while the (unweighted) averages of the coefficients differ little between the seven developing countries of the sample (0·438) and the nine U.S. regions (0·459), this is explained by offsetting influences of high protection and low per capita incomes on industrial specialisation in the developing countries.

In fact, hypothetical coefficients of industrial specialisation calculated from equation (4) under the assumption of nil protection average 0·558 for the developing country group. And, if we consider that the tariff data shown for the developing countries also include the effects of non-tariff barriers, there can be little doubt that protection has increased the degree of industrial diversification in the national economies of these countries.

Mr. Krauss makes some useful points on the effects of production taxes and on the phenomenon of guest workers, which well complement my own analysis. However, his comments on my paper appear to reflect a misinterpretation of my argument and lack of factual information.

To begin with the definition of commercial policy, Krauss' discussion of the monetary approach to the balance of payments and of Abba Lerner's well-known symmetry theorem is beside the point. It simply shows that Krauss missed the distinction made between the definition of commercial policy and the need to consider a devaluation together with commercial policy measures. In this connection, it should be recalled that balance-of-payments equilibrium can be obtained by different combinations of exchange rates, tariffs, and subsidies. The imposition of tariffs will in general permit balance-of-payments equilibrium to be reached at a lower exchange rate than under free trade; however, as Professor Johnson has shown (1966) under certain circumstances the exchange rate will be higher if tariffs are imposed.

Krauss' claim, according to which 'Balassa . . . either fails to recognise or fails to agree that flexible exchange rates have significantly reduced the risk that quotas will be imposed for reasons of the balance of payments' again reflects a misreading of my arguments. This is because I contrasted present international monetary arrangements with the gold standard as it existed during the nineteenth century and with common currency within a national economy, rather than comparing floating exchange rates with the adjustable peg. Under the gold standard, the mechanisms of international and interregional adjustment were essentially the same as countries did not follow independent monetary and fiscal policies, so that there was no exchange rate risk that exists under floating exchange rates *and* the adjustable peg under present-day conditions.

I come next to Krauss' statement: 'What I would like to hear discussed by commercial policy specialists, but which is only fleetingly referred to in Balassa's paper, is what the trade negotiators at the Tokyo Round are concerned with — policy measures that do not discriminate between the domestic and foreign sectors of the economy but nonetheless have a significant impact on international trade'. In this connection, Krauss refers to production subsidies, border tax adjustments, and safety standards.

Krauss is misinformed about the ongoing multilateral trade negotiations that used to be called the Tokyo Round. The main subjects being negotiated in Geneva are tariffs, quantitative restrictions, export subsidies, restrictions on agricultural trade, and the American Selling Price issue, all of which discriminate between the domestic and the foreign sectors of the economy. The border tax issue has been settled by the recent ruling of the U.S. Treasury which accepted border tax adjustments. Production subsidies are subject to discussion only to the extent that they provide implicit export subsidies as witnessed by the Canadian Michelin tyre and the Greek tomato case (Balassa and Sharpston, 1976). Safety standards too are considered as disguised measures of protection since they affect differently domestic and foreign goods. In this connection, one may refer to U.S. automobile standards or to the use of health regulations to exclude meat from Kenya in the E.E.C.

As far as my own discussion of the question is concerned, I may refer the reader to the statement on p. 233:

> Various other forms of government interventions, too, tend to favour domestic production over imports in developed as well as in developing countries. They include, among other things, public procurement rules, production subsidies, regional policy measures, and health and sanitary regulations. These measures have assumed increasing importance in recent years and they further distinguish the processes of international trade from those of interregional trade.

It would appear then that one can hardly blame me for using an overly narrow definition of commercial policy since non-tariff barriers were explicitly considered in my paper. Nor can one pretend that 'perhaps what was obtained with tariff reduction (in the Common Market) was lost through non-tariff barriers'. Thus, as shown in my recent book on *European Economic Integration* (1975) notwithstanding the use of various non-tariff measures, it cannot be assumed that governments would have 'neutralised such effects by means other than those constrained by E.E.C. obligations'.

Coming to the points put forward by Krauss in regard to factor movements, the production taxes applied by European countries are subject to border tax adjustments under the destination principle and hence do not affect international trade and the location of production. It is difficult to pretend, therefore, that 'fiscal sovereignty may require stringent controls over the free movement of capital and labour both to preserve the tax base and prevent dramatic shifts in the location of production'.

Finally, Krauss suggests that the inflow of labour to service industries producing non-traded goods is of greater importance than the inflow of labour to protected labour-intensive manufacturing. But the difference between the two cases is more apparent than real once we introduce a more realistic three-sector model. While foreign labour may be employed in the service industries, it releases domestic nationals for the protected manufacturing industries. If we assume that consumption patterns are given, the results will be the same, irrespective of whether foreign labour is employed in services or in protected manufacturing.

REFERENCES

Balassa, B. *et al.*, *The Structure of Protection in Developing Countries* (Baltimore, Md., The Johns Hopkins University Press, 1971).
Balassa, B. *et al.*, *European Economic Integration* (Amsterdam: North Holland, 1975).
Balassa, B. and Sharpston, M., 'Export Subsidies by Developing Countries: Issues of Policy', *Journal of World Trade Law* (forthcoming), 1977.
Deutsch, K. W. and Eckstein, A., 'National Industrialization and the Declining Share of the International Economic Sector, 1890−1959', *World Politics* (1961), 13 (1), pp. 267−98.
Johnson, H. G., 'A Model of Protection and the Exchange Rate', *Review of Economic Studies* (1966), 33 (2), pp. 159−67.
Little, I., Scitovsky, T. and Scott, M., *Industry and Trade in Some Developing Countries* (London, Oxford University Press, 1970).
Niehaus, J., 'Some Doubts about the Efficacy of Monetary Policy under Flexible Exchange Rate', *Journal of International Economics* (1975), 5 (3), pp. 275−82.
Scitovsky, T., *The Joyless Economy* (Oxford, Oxford University Press, 1976).
Sombart, W., *Die Deutsche Volkswirtschaft im neunzehnten Jahrhundert* (Berlin, Bond, Verlag, 1913).

Summary of the Discussion

Some discussants took issue with Balassa's statement that 'since Ricardo's time, transport costs have declined in importance while commercial policy has assumed an increasingly greater role' and that therefore 'locational theory would have had greater relevance for international specialisation in Ricardo's time than today' (p. 232 and p. 234). The importance of transportation costs was disputed and the need to consider other kinds of transfer costs was pointed out. In an attempt to reconcile different statements it was argued that transportation costs may be low and still important for location. The discussion also suggested alternative interpretations of Balassa's findings on the effects of trade liberalisation. This session was chaired by *Jagdish N. Bhagwati*.

Nils Lundgren noted that transport costs may well have declined more than Balassa's statistical evidence showed. Indices for services generally take quality changes and new products into account to a lesser extent than do price indices for goods. Quality improvements, he noted, consist of faster, safer and more punctual transport as well as of such changes in the goods that facilitate their transportation, for instance through freezing.

Wassily Leontief supported Balassa's observation about transportation costs and tariffs. He referred to his own study containing an analysis of the magnitude of tariffs as a percentage of delivered price of goods.[1] He thought it was unwise to explain international location mainly by reference to transportation costs since tariffs and other trade barriers were likely to be more important.

Bertil Ohlin did not dispute the relevance of Balassa's facts. But he wanted to expand the reasoning about transport costs to cover costs of overcoming economic distance, lack of contact, etc. Business leaders, he said, make very detailed investigations about the costs of getting necessary raw materials and want to know where they can best place a new factory in order to minimise transportation costs, overcome language barriers, and find favourable labour conditions. In their calculations the relation between the costs of transportation of raw materials, of semi-manufactured goods, and of manufactured goods and the distance to markets, plays a great role. Hence, international and national movements of factors of production are dependent on transport costs and on the other contact costs. For example the attractive power of natural resources on industry depends very much on whether raw materials are easy or difficult to transport relative to manufactured goods. If they are easy to transport while the manufactured goods are difficult to transport, there will be a tendency to locate production near the market. Moreover, once productive factors, including labour, are concentrated in certain districts, then you get a consumer market there which attracts other industries. This is also a consequence of transport and contact costs. So, in the long run countries with good internal and external transport conditions and a strategic location of natural resources attract factors of production, because of the costs of transportation.

While Balassa's observations about the great importance of tariff costs and the decline in the relative importance of transport costs were no doubt correct, Ohlin felt that one should not be content to compare with nineteenth-century conditions and to determine if things are moving in this or in that direction. A more important question is: do transport costs under present conditions considerably affect the location of production and thereby trade? The answer is in the affirmative. If this is left out, he said, we might wrongly conclude that the reasoning in location theory is of very little interest to international trade analysis.

Lawrence Klein noted that transport costs could be quite important even though rates are a small and declining share of price. He recalled that the oil crisis caused severe problems in spite of oil's small share of costs in general, since it was a necessary input in many processes and part of a complex interindustry structure. Transport services had these same attributes. Therefore their share of total costs would be misleading as an indicator of how important they might be to do without. He added by way of illustration that transport costs were the key obstacle to commercial exploitation of domestic sources of energy in the event of an oil embargo. Consider the enormous problems of the North Slope oil pipeline!

Assar Lindbeck remarked that given other costs, firms choose between alternative locations in order to minimise transport costs. These costs therefore may become low precisely because they have been highly important for location — high transport cost locations are avoided if other costs are equal. As *Lundgren* put it, firms' actual transport costs could be viewed as an endogenous variable which had been minimised.

Jagdish Bhagwati observed that even if transport costs for *any* alternative location were a small proportion of total product price, they could still affect location if they varied geographically more than other costs of production. It is geographical variability in transport costs relative to other costs of production rather than their level which determines whether they are important for location decisions.

Some participants objected to Balassa's generalisation and emphasised that the importance of transport costs varied considerably between commodities. *Allan Pred* suggested that Balassa was constructing a 'straw man' if he claimed that location theorists had increased their emphasis on transport costs. One could hardly emphasise transport costs more than classical theory did. He suggested that Balassa lacked familiarity with the great variety of rather complex problems that location theorists and economic geographers had recently dealt with in a manner not confined to transport costs.

Åke Andersson noted that the effects of transportation costs showed large sectorial differences. He referred to a study by Karen Polenske[2] which had treated interregional trade for different commodities in the U.S., using distance as an explanatory factor. For crude commodities transportation costs were insignificant while for services − a highly refined product − transportation costs significantly affected trade. In some cases 'distance elasticities' were between 2 and 3. He concluded that for the latter type of goods transportation costs may be more important, internationally, than commercial policies as a barrier to trade.

Gunnar Törnqvist added that the difference in opinion on the importance of transport costs might be due to comparing goods belonging to different stages of production. Information or communication costs stressed in his and in Pred's contributions, were most important at the final stage of production where today most manufacturing activity takes place. Classical location theory, he recalled, treated transport costs for activities in the first stages of production, such as mining.

Michael Chisholm also emphasised that the costs of transmitting information were increasing relative to the costs of transporting goods. He therefore thought that the approach used by Pred in his paper was relevant to the analysis of the effects of distance on international trade in goods.

The discussion turned to Balassa's methods of testing the effects of commercial policy on trade and economic structure and his results.

Both *Harry Johnson* and *Lundgren* suggested different interpretations of Balassa's findings regarding the effects of trade liberalisation. Johnson warned against generalising the results from European integration, since it was not a random experiment. Europe was able to establish the Common Market precisely because major industries in the major countries foresaw that they would not be wiped out but instead obtain opportunities to specialise, while retaining a similar structure and unchanged profitability. That this could occur was due to the phenomenon of intraindustry trade studied by Grubel and Lloyd.[3] We seldom have experiments which allow us to determine whether trade liberalisation wipes out big industries or not. If it does, liberalisation will not take place for political reasons. This is reflected in the literature in the idea that only countries at the same stage of development can afford to enter custom unions.

Lundgren suggested that in addition to the effects of liberalisation on location of economic activity we should consider its effects on welfare. It is possible that reductions in manmade barriers to trade may have great effects on trade flows and the location of production (high elasticities of domestic production in terms of price changes) but small effects on welfare in terms of the traditional welfare triangles.

Chisholm claimed that the observed differences in industrial and trade ratios between Northern Ireland and the Republic could not be explained solely by different commercial policies. He noted that these differences had existed for 100 to 150 years and consequently before the independence

of Eire in 1921. He was also surprised by the level of specialisation for the
U.S. (see table 2, p. 245). Because of its size and abundant natural
resources one would expect a low index of specialisation. In fact Balassa
listed the U.S. with a higher level than many smaller countries. This surprising result he felt should be further scrutinised.

Johnson commented on observations in the two Comments to the paper.
He supported Krauss' contention that exchange rate changes should not be
considered a commercial policy instrument. He noted that in fact Balassa's
statistical techniques did not correct tariff changes for exchange rate
changes and therefore his methodology for testing the effect of commercial
policy was inconsistent with his definition of it. He objected that he knew
of no evidence to support Tibor Scitovsky's assertion that more trade implies more risk, and referred to an IEA conference which showed surprisingly that more open economies did not seem to suffer worse cycles.[4] He
suggested that the reason was simply that the more insulated a country is,
the more stupid its government can be — and usually is! Openness acts both
as an exposure to external disturbances and as a discipline on government
to counter these disturbances.

Balassa closed the discussion. On the issue of whether transport costs
mattered, he referred to his paper which had clearly stated that his empirical observation should not be interpreted to mean that transport costs had
no bearing on international specialisation. He felt that he had provided incontrovertible evidence that transport costs had fallen as part of total production costs and become less important relative to the costs imposed by
commercial policy. He noted also that costs for transmitting information
internationally had declined tremendously, which however was perfectly
consistent with the emphasis, by the geographers present, on the increasing
importance of transmitting information between buyer and seller.[5]

NOTES

[1] 'Explanatory Power of the Comparative Cost Theory of International
Trade and Its Limits', *Economic Structure and Development. Essays in
Honor of Jan Tinbergen*, H. C. Bos (ed.) (Amsterdam: North-Holland Pub-
lishing Company, 1973).

[2] K. R. Polenske, *A Case Study of Transportation Models Used in Multiregional Analysis*, Ph.D. dissertation, Department of Economics, Harvard
University (1966).

[3] H. G. Grubel and P. J. Lloyd, *Intra-industry Trade — The Theory and
Measurement of International Trade in Differentiated Products* (London,
1975).

[4] L. Tarshis, 'The Size of the Economy and its Relation to Stability and
Steady Progress', in E. A. G. Robinson (ed.), *Economic Consequences of
the Size of Nations* (Macmillan, London, 1960).

[5] Several other questions raised in the discussion are dealt with in
Balassa's Reply to Comments (see pp. 270 ff.).

8 On Location of Production, Factor Movements, etc., as Affected by the Social and Fiscal Policies of Individual Countries and Economic Communities

Kjeld Philip

I. INTRODUCTION

The matters to be discussed here have a common trait: their impact on location is often thought to be great, though in most cases actual location is probably only slightly affected. Most factors affecting location are not easily influenced by political decisions. However, the social and fiscal policies of a country are shaped entirely through its political machinery. But such policies are almost exclusively aimed at something different than location.

In analyses of social and fiscal policies it will often be of advantage to consider the measures adopted in either sphere as being independent of each other, and thus as having expansive and contractive influences respectively on the economic activity. If however I should follow this procedure it would bring me into the field usually discussed under the heading 'fiscal policy' and it would bring the whole discussion onto the periphery of 'monetary policy'. The fact that countries take different monetary and fiscal measures may give them different levels of employment and different rates of inflation. This may exert an influence on migration of factors of production and on the rate of growth, etc., in the different countries. All this can certainly be of importance for the topics studied at the symposium, but it is obvious that it goes beyond the borders fixed for this paper. For the purpose of the present paper it is therefore assumed that each measure requiring expenditure will be balanced by another creating revenue, to such an extent that the effects caused on the level of employment, etc., will by and large cancel each other out. In the present analysis, it is not so very important what is understood by 'cancelling out'. The important thing is not that the two amounts are equal if they are measured in money but that the contractive and expansive influences on the level of employment, etc., are of equal strength.

Contrary to a great many other factors affecting location, the measures referred to are confined to geographically well-defined areas, such as those of local governments, towns, counties, countries, or associations of countries such as the European Economic Community (E.E.C.), the Latin American Free Trade Association (L.A.F.T.A.), or the East African Community (E.A.C.). Often, it will be seen that one part of a set of measures is applied within one geographical unit while its counterpart is found within one or more other units. Where this is the case, location will almost of necessity be affected.

Where, in area A, a change is made in the social and financial situations causing A to be a more attractive area for certain economic activities, the result may be accelerated growth of enterprises already domiciled in A and the moving-in of enterprises from outside. It seems practical to distinguish between four types of reactions

(a) Accelerated growth of enterprises existing in A.
(b) Moving-in from outside of already existing enterprises.
(c) Individuals in A about to set up in business or to seek employment will opt for the activity affected by the change.
(d) Individuals outside A will move into A to work or to set up in the business affected.

Among the various groups, the time-lag for reactions to materialise will vary greatly. People already living in A (that is groups (a) and (c)) may well be expected to react sooner than others. On the other hand, since more people live outside than inside A, the impact of the change may be much stronger in cases (b) and (d) than in (a) and (c). In the following, I shall deal primarily with group (b).

It seems practical to distinguish between two main ways in which social and financial measures affect location: direct and indirect.

Direct influence is where the very measure adopted motivates a decision-maker to a change in location. An example of this is where a man moves his business for reasons of lower company taxation, or moves house for reasons of lower income tax or better social benefits, such as higher old-age pension.

Indirect influence is where public measures affect changes in other economic factors, which in turn will motivate a person or an enterprise to seek a change in location. In the case of indirect influence it will be seen that it is other circumstances than the social and fiscal ones that motivate people for a new location, but these other circumstances are themselves created by something social or fiscal.

One and the same set of public measures may of course create an environment that is attractive to some people but not to others. A specific geographical area may be directly unattractive to one group of people and indirectly attractive, or vice versa. The country whose guests we are, Sweden, has pursued a direct fiscal policy that must be felt by many people to be unattractive. However, thanks among other things to this very fiscal policy, combined with her social and educational policies, Sweden has created such an economic environment that as a result she has developed into a country that seems attractive to many businesses.

Traditionally, public finance and social policy deal in the main with the direct influences. It seems reasonable, however, to ask whether, for the purpose of the questions studied at this symposium, the indirect influences are not often of greater importance. I shall therefore deal first with a few observations on various indirect influences.

II. THE INDIRECT INFLUENCES

The success of a business depends to a very high degree on the interplay between the business and the entire economic environment surrounding it. It is of the greatest importance to the progress of a business that it has easy access to a well-developed and well-functioning infrastructure (railways, roads, ports, telecommunications, etc.); that locally it can find qualified manual and non-manual employees; that in its neighbourhood there are people who can do repairs and maintenance work, or who can offer assistance or give advice, such as consulting engineers, legal advisers, accountants, and advisers on sanitary and health matters. Also important is the existence locally of a reliable legal system. When, in spite of their low-priced production factors and their various measures on trade policy, etc., many developing countries find it so hard to attract manufacturing industries, one reason is their lack or low quality of these externalities. All these advisory and service functions need to be carried out by highly educated people. Where a society is provided with all these externalities and with a well-functioning infrastructure, it is to a great extent the result of public expenditure in the transportation sector as well as in the educational sector, etc.

The modern welfare society as we know it best, that is, in the north-western half of Europe and in parts of North America, is very much the product of the social policy, the educational policy, and the public transport policy that these countries have pursued. The enterprises that are located here benefit from great advantages not available to enterprises outside the welfare areas, and which have strengthened their competitive position. If a business, situated in a developing country or in another country not favoured in the manner referred to, wants to secure for itself that kind of expertise, etc., the cost of so doing will easily be considerable. In comparison, businesses situated in the welfare society enjoy two sets of advantages: (i) the cost of such service and assistance is much lower, and (ii) part of the cost is borne by public authorities. To a great extent, the enterprises contribute to public spending through payment of taxes that are not included in their operating costs and that are not included in their price-fixing process (personal income tax and company taxation).

In this connection, it would be reasonable to comment on investment in education. For a great many years, such investment was mainly provided on a private basis — in particular with respect to the support of students and trainees. This is still the case in many countries, developing as well as industrial countries. Not only was the basis a private one, but the investments themselves were not financed through the channels of ordinary capital markets.

The mechanism which serves to ensure for investments in material goods that the same internal rate of interest will apply to all investments did not function within this field. For this type of investment, the capital market was limited to the near relatives. Thus, there was nothing to ensure that investment in education would be sufficient for all investments to lead to a level where the same marginal internal rate of interest was achieved everywhere or that it would be the same as for investments in material goods. The result was such a scarcity of educated people that generally investment in education carried interest at a rate considerably higher than that obtained on investments in material means of production.

In recent years, education has been heavily subsidised in the welfare states, and we are approaching a situation where such investments are borne entirely by public authorities. This has caused a rapid rate of expansion of investment in education. A common capital market has been created for these investments, but it has not as yet been entirely assimilated into the ordinary capital market, one reason being that many of these investments carry no interest at all. We cannot disregard the possibility that now 'too many people' are being educated, so that investment in material means of production will pay off better. However, for the time being, there is no doubt that the policy pursued has actually 'paid off'. As a result, enterprises are operating in an environment characterised by a great many external economies, all of which are the consequence of a society having a very great number of educated people at its disposal.

As to the social policy, developments have been on the same lines, only much weaker. The traditional social policy has not been very productive: pensions for disabled and old people, benefits for the sick and unemployed, and poor relief for the social losers in society. The last generation has, however, experienced an enormous development within the social field, for the purpose of improving productivity. Rehabilitation is the most obvious example, but also more child and youth welfare has been directed towards creating a more productive performance. A not unimportant part of the health sector aims at prophylaxis.

Modern social policy is to a considerable extent a result of and has further made possible the disintegration of the traditional pattern of sexual roles handed down to us from the past. The existence of crèches, kindergartens, organised neighbourhood child-care, etc., has enabled the exodus of women from the home, where much time was lost on technically inferior work, at a low rate of productivity. The result has been a substantial increase in available labour. It is clear that these measures have meant an increase in the supply of labour as well as of productivity.

In the picture of public investments aiming at stimulation of production should be included also the considerable public spending on infrastructure, such as railways, postal services, telecommunications, aviation, roads, ports, airports, and shipping services. Public authorities provide the funds for these investments and then make the various services available to the general public and private enterprise on terms that often do not ensure an ordinary rate of return. In other words, private enterprise enjoys this infra-structure at 'cut prices'. The rationale of this policy may be disputed, but clearly it is of advantage to producers, Such a policy, when actively pursued, helps make a country attractive to enterprises.

In the early decades of this century it was a characteristic feature of almost all public expenditure that it did not influence very much the quality and quantity of production factors or the infrastructure of a country. Public money was spent on 'unproductive' items such as the military, royalty, provision for the old, though also on productive factors such as schools, the police, and the legal system. What has been added during the last half-century in welfare states has, apart from military expenditure, almost exclusively been expenditure resulting in increased efficiency and productivity of production factors, which, as previously said, has created a novel composition of labour, according to education. However, many parts of the world have still not developed further than the stage at which the western world found itself before the onset of the welfare policy. Enterprises that set up in developing countries may have lower internal costs of production, such as lower wages, cheaper land, sometimes even lower rates of interest; but more highly educated employees, service factors outside the business, communication and transportation are much more expensive, of poorer quality, and less stable. Clearly, these factors are not the 'cause' of low development in the developing countries, but they are concurrent and influential factors.

The much steeper rise in consumption of public goods relative to con-sumption of privately produced goods is often explained by reference to the income elasticity of public goods, which is supposed to be greater than that of private goods. But this is probably only part of the explanation. The efforts made to create a more equal distribution of income must also be considered. At the turn of the century, the present welfare states saw the emergence of a relatively large group of wage-earners, who soon combined in a strong movement demanding a bigger share of the national product. Efforts were made to force up wages — hardly a measure that would increase their share of the cake. Also political means were tried, and thanks to the introduction of universal suffrage the lower classes now had a chance of achieving something through political channels. For instance, would gratuitous education and health services as well as a hefty increase in social benefits make possible an improvement in the living standard of the badly situated, without the improvement being included in costs or causing a rise in prices? While the impecunious received no greater part of privately produced goods than their income would allow, they did receive about equal shares of public goods. Progressive taxation meant that their payments towards these goods, in the form of limited private consumption, were relatively modest.

This policy has, however, had effects that can hardly have carried much weight with the decision-makers. The number of educated people increased rapidly; the number of women who could leave their household chores and join the labour market swelled; the general state of health improved, as did the average life expectancy.

The result of this particular form of distributive policy was thus not just something to do with income distribution but also the creation of an economic environment that, at least until today, has created a violent economic expansion.

Social and fiscal policies, which were initially aimed at ensuring distribution by political means, have thus led to a significant economic growth.

What has here been said on the productivity-stimulating forces of modern spending policies, comprises at one and the same time something self-increasing and also certain factors that may halt developments. In an area of rapid economic growth, existing scales of taxation create large public revenue, and thereby the possibility of further public spending. But certain public fields of investment have no built-in brakes to safeguard against 'too big' investments. While normally private investments are made only when profit is expected at least to equal that of other possible investments, there is, as already said, a risk that public investment in education — and in the health sector, etc. — provided the principle of gratuitousness is upheld, may be decided upon even though a greater return would have been obtained from investment in material production factors or in other forms of education. Obviously, similar possibilities are inherent in the social field, where 'productive' social measures can be imagined to be promoted to an extent where they are no longer productive. As in the educational sector, strong political forces primarily interested in the aspects of distribution may pull in that direction.

One thing in particular will be of decisive importance for the international distribution of industries, and that is differences in educational levels. It is usually said that the industrialised countries 'ought to' specialise in capital-intensive industries, while the developing countries 'ought to' specialise in the labour-intensive industries. The relevancy of this dichotomy may be disputed. Actually, capital is easily transferred, and to modern industries the rate of interest in a great part of the developing world is no higher than that for instance in Western Europe, which of course does not mean that other restraining factors cannot be found to exist. The real difference between industrialised and developing countries is to be found in the education of labour. Industries requiring a great number of educated people, much research, access to research institutes, etc., will decide on location in industrialised countries, while industries that may operate with relatively many unskilled employees and only a few highly educated officers, will seek a location in the developing countries. Thus, educational policy must be seen as an important location-deciding factor. In comparison, social policy will play only second fiddle.

Normally, within the boundaries of a country, the level of public benefits will be uniformly available. What has been dealt with above has therefore primarily been problems between various countries. However, within one country situations of a related nature can be found, affecting activities in the various parts of the country.

The revenue and expenditure of a government will normally affect local activities in a non-neutral way. This will be the case even though efforts are made to achieve a balance for the country as a whole between the revenue-created contraction and the expenditure-created expansion. Taxes are normally levied under uniform rules all over the country, but the bases for taxation may differ widely between regions. Certain public expenditures will find their outlets in a few geographically limited areas.

Social spending belongs among the items of public expenditure that have less centralising effects. Much social spending will be spread all over the country, such as child allowances and old-age pensions. Social institutions, such as homes for the aged, rest homes, children's homes, are found every-where in all regions. Nevertheless, even in the case of social spending certain centralising influences can be found, first because particular national institutions are often located where density of population is great, secondly because certain forms of social need are mostly found in large cities, and thirdly because the social coverage — perhaps unwittingly — is more complete in the most highly advanced parts of the country.

It is easy to see why local governments are so keen on housing central government institutions and why they compete for them just like states compete for international institutions. The funds that flow into a selected area will, through a local multiplier effect, intensify activities in many other fields within the favoured area. Sometimes, this effect has been deliberately utilised to further location policies, as when the central government in its regional development plans locate public institutions, educational or social, in an underdeveloped part of the country. The problem has clearly emerged through the discussions in recent years on the location of new universities.

Previously, it was widely held that a high rate of public activity would in itself have an equalising effect on regions with different bases of taxation. It was contended that regions with a poor basis of taxation would contribute relatively little per capita, and receive comparatively much through social benefits paid out of public funds. But the violent expansion of the educational sector, so characteristic of the present-day welfare

state, and the novel ideas in social policy-making benefits available to
'everybody', even offering generally 'compensation for lapse of income',
have reduced this equalising effect to the point where it may be said to be
non-existent.

However, the contention that public spending within a geographically
limited area has a locally expansive effect must be assumed to be at most
a half-truth. Where the influx of new residents into an area is great, the
cost of transportation will be high, as will the rentals for housing; agricultural produce will be expensive; and much time will be lost in
commuting to work. The cost of all this should be shifted onto the
employers — public and private — in the form of demands for higher
wages. But in modern society some of these mechanisms work only
imperfectly. The high cost of transportation is borne partly by public
transport authorities run at a loss, partly by central government through
deduction of travel costs from taxable income. The cost of housing is
spread over wide circles through public policy on housing. Collective
bargaining tends to make wages uniform all over the country. So, there
is a risk that centralisation of activities in a few areas will lead to costs
beyond what is economically warrantable.

Were decisions on location to be made by a single body responsible for
spending — public as well as such that, traditionally, in the western world
is private — and which would take into account all costs and benefits,
then the location of public institutions would presumably be different,
and to some degree more decentralised.

III. THE DIRECT INFLUENCES

The characteristic thing about indirect influences was that they affect
location via the economic environment in part created by them. The
characteristic thing about the direct influences is that they are among the
motives that lead a person or enterprise to a particular location. A few
examples are: moving out of an area to avoid taxation; removal of an
enterprise to a municipality known for its lower taxation; moving into a
district for the sake of better educational or social facilities; or the choice
of a business less burdened with taxes.

However, the social and fiscal motives behind a person's decisions are
normally just a few among several others. To form an opinion on the
influencial force of changes in social and fiscal data, we shall have to
examine also the forces of the many other factors that influence location.

For the purpose of a study of the influences of social and fiscal
measures, it may be practical to distinguish between three situations

(a) influence on the motives of the individual decision-maker;

(b) influence on the motives of the group of which the decision-maker is a member;
(c) relocation of units necessitated by the relocation of another existing unit (residence, place of work, school, etc.).

In the following pages I shall comment on each of these three.

(1) INFLUENCE ON THE MOTIVES OF THE INDIVIDUAL DECISION-MAKER

In the commodity market we are able to limit purchases of each article so as to ensure for ourselves the optimal satisfaction for that part of our income which is spent on purchase of goods. Each individual decides for himself what combination of goods he wants. Whereas, the decision to 'purchase' public services is imposed upon the individual. Payment of taxes is compulsory. Many public services will be rendered him whether he wants them or not, and he certainly gets them in a proportion different from that on which he himself would have decided had they been ordinary articles. Several services, of course, may be accepted or rejected; but rejection does not mean that others are available instead. To the individual, the choice is in principle limited to 'take it or leave it'.

It is generally held that satisfaction of individual requirements in respect of public goods is adjusted through the political machinery in that the individual consumer elects his political representatives, and that these will seek to find the balance that will provide maximum cover of requirements. This theory implies a uniform structure of consumer requirements which is non-existent. In a modern society there will be many people who will prefer a different 'mix' of public and private goods and of the various public goods.

As long as a citizen resides in the same place, he will, in practice, have no choice as to what public goods are offered him. But he may move to another municipality or another country. Thanks to these possibilities, he has a number choices. But in each case he will have to accept the public offers as a 'package'. Obviously, he cannot within one period pluck from each country the plum of his choice, for instance the Spanish tax policy and the Swedish health and welfare.

To the individual, the choice may be a difficult one. It is not easy to imagine in advance what public services one will need. A measure of adaptation lies in the possibility of moving around according to the requirements of age. An example is, the man who spends his first years as a pensioner in Spain but returns to Sweden when frailty and ailments set in.

However, what is said above is not a rule without exceptions. In many countries, farmers are actually treated differentially (subsidies, lower taxation). By choosing to be a farmer, you may secure for yourself a situation slightly different from that of other occupations. Other examples may be given, but they are mostly to be considered as flaws in the system and not of much interest.

The fact that changes in public measures and activities almost always emerge as a complex of which one part is attractive, another detractive, is one reason why the influence of sets of social and financial measures is often only slight. Often, a set of measures will affect an individual in both positive and negative ways.

The fact that often we are affected at the same time in a positive and a negative way, that often we are unable to tell what the implications of a certain measure will be for our own situation, will in many cases mean that we react by staying where we are.

(2) INFLUENCE ON THE MOTIVES OF THE DECISION-MAKER'S GROUP

In our reasoning we often assume that the individual is the decision-making unit. But in many cases the decision-making unit consists of a whole complex of persons, who will be unequally affected by a new measure, and who may subsequently go their separate ways.

Let me illustrate by giving an example: The economic unit may be a family comprising persons of differing ages and having different occupational interests. We may find a senior generation, where for reasons of taxation he wants to live in the Canary Islands, she wants to be close to the hospitals and rest homes of the Swedish health system. There is a middle generation, where he would like to move his business to Portugal, while she can find employment as a Swedish social adviser only in a Swedish environment. And then there is often a junior generation, anxious to take advantage of Swedish educational facilities — except for the one extraordinary person who says good-bye to welfare and economic growth and goes to Nepal in search of happiness. The mother of the black sheep hopes for relief from the Swedish authorities when the child returns home. Opinions on moving the business to Portugal may also be divided. There may be employees who opt for Swedish welfare and security, and who refuse to follow should the business be moved. Management and share-holders need not have identical interests. The introduction of a new set of social and fiscal measures may well cause much tension in such economic units, tensions that will then either almost cancel each other out — or in some cases cause a unit to disintegrate.

Where the economic unit is preserved, such tensions may easily result in no change at all, locationwise. So, the very complexity of economic units tends to dampen the influences of any measure introduced.

(3) RELOCATION OF THE UNIT

Also tending to dampen the influences of a new measure is the fact that relocation in the case of an existing enterprise is often less advantageous in secondary respects, relative to the advantages experienced by enterprises already established in the new location. A change in taxation could, conceivably, mean that a business ought to have been set up somewhere else if, at the time of its establishment, the owner had known what would happen. However, the new tax is something that was not expected. Adaptation to the new situation will mean the loss of employees, suppliers, customers, and other established contacts. Therefore, a new taxation situation is primarily of importance to those who have just decided to set up in business. The process started by new social and fiscal measures will therefore only very slowly have any perceptible influence on location structures of the economy as a whole.

Often, a person is not bound to one but typically to four places or points of reference: his residence, his own place of work, his wife's place of work, and his children's kindergarten, school, or place of work. A business will frequently, as such, be bound only to one place. But in an actual situation, many considerations different from those which will maximise business earnings will play their part. If the decision-makers are a group of the business staff, each group member's considerations of his other three points of reference will affect the common decision.

The reaction of the individual to a new social and financial situation depends fairly much on how many of his reference points he will have to move. To a wage earner it may not matter to any great degree where he lives if only he will not have to move his other references. He may even be prepared to change his job to avoid breaking his other ties. His willingness to move varies inversely with the number of ties he will have to break.

For these reasons, mobility is great within a certain radius. In spite of public transport and the general ownership of motorcars experienced over the last few decades, this area though it has been widened is still rather limited. In many countries, local districts have in recent years been combined, often in such manner that districts forming an economic entity have merged into one municipality. Each citizen will feel that, within the area of his effective mobility, the social and financial rules are the same.

From the liberal period we have inherited the political doctrine that rules of taxation and central government spending policy as far as possible shall have a neutral effect on economic activity, as also on its location. A brief suvey of present-day policies in most countries will reveal that, as a general principle, neutrality has been maintained but that, in certain cases, this principle is deviated from for the sake of policies of regional development. Attention to neutrality will easily conflict with considerations of local self-government.

Let me give two typical cases in point.

Within the borders of a country, the various local districts will often have differing bases of taxation. As already said, municipalities in the poorer parts of the country will tend to have a lower service level than that of the richer districts. Often, the poorer parts will nevertheless have a higher level of taxation. In these circumstances certain interests will aim at another pattern of location than the one that would be aimed at if the rules were the same all over the country. A desire to maintain neutrality may then lead to rules on granting of aid to municipalities, in particular to municipalities having a weak basis of taxation.

Also, it may happen that a local government decides to maintain a relatively high service level and therefore a higher level of taxation than that of other municipalities with a corresponding basis of taxation. A high service level will be typical of municipalities dominated by wage earners' interests, perhaps in particular where salaried staff are the most influential group. Such local government policy will be attractive to some people and detractive to others.

Local self-government is almost irreconcilable with a strict adherence to the principle of neutrality. In most countries, these problems are not very important, and nowadays of less importance than previously. One major reason is that local rates generally are low, compared with taxes payable to central government, something which again is explained by the policy found in many countries: that of making available large grants-in-aid to municipalities, for the sake of neutrality.

Analogous problems are now emerging in the economic communities. Where free mobility and free right of establishment are allowed among a number of countries, as is the case in the E.E.C., inequalities between the rules and levels of taxation may create unintended relocation of activities from one country to another. Considering that the E.E.C. has not as yet any right of taxation of its own, and that equalisation between member states therefore must remain very limited, it must be realised that great differences may be found between the states, differences that may cause relatively large, unintended transfers of enterprises and labour from one country to another. In the United States, similar problems are found among the various States, the severity of which however is mitigated by the relatively low State taxation compared with that levied by the Federal administration, but problems are aggravated by the fact that national differences between States are much less pronounced than in Europe.

Neutrality may be protected, not only by grants-in-aid to municipalities or, as in the United States by grants to the member States, but also by selection of types of taxation. In the nineteenth century this method found wide application. In public finance, distinctions for this purpose were made between the effects of differences between property taxes, income taxes, and consumption taxes.

The theory is the familiar one of incidence according to which taxation of land is shifted onto the price of land. It is no doubt correct, when it is said that these taxes only slightly affect local activity. And therefore it is no coincidence that such taxes have primarily been levied for the financing of local activities. In Europe they have typically been the local municipal rates, as also in the United Kingdom, where rates are the typical form of local taxation.

The next group among the important forms of taxation is the income tax. Different levels of income tax may motivate people to move. But experience seems to indicate that certain differences in levels of taxation can be maintained without causing migration of large numbers of people. As already said, there are so many other factors apart from the level of taxation that affect the situation.

Most detrimental to neutrality is probably differences in duties on goods, including different levels of value added tax. Where there is free exchange of goods between areas and no restriction on transportation, it seems that only very slight differences are tolerated before the duty-inspired trade between areas will gain momentum. Apart from such articles as petrol, to which special conditions apply, the differentiation of excise duties etc., within the same trading area has been abandoned almost everywhere. Differentiation of excise duties may also mean preferential treatment of production. When, as is the case in Denmark, the duty on Danish schnapps is lower than that imposed on other types of alcohol, it acts as protection of the schnapps producers and discrimination of production of cognac, whisky, etc. The reason for this policy is, of course, that Denmark has a production of schnapps but almost none of other types of hard liquor. Therefore, this policy has naturally been included in the agenda of the E.E.C., as something that it is thought should be altered.

The circumstances referred to above have been reflected in the traditional application of these taxes and duties to the financing of local and central government expenditures respectively. But the traditional distribution of fiscal income between the various levels of government proves to be meeting with growing difficulties.

In the light of arguments quite different from those discussed here, a development has set in that will reduce the significance of land taxes and cause income taxes to give way slightly to duties on production, turnover taxes, etc.

In this field a new set of problems has proved to be emerging. While economic problems within the individual states are largely solved by means of grants-in-aid to municipalities and by central governments levying much more than do the local governments, so that differences between municipalities are fairly small, the situation is quite different in the E.E.C.

As we know, the E.E.C. follows the principle of free mobility of goods and labour. But the levels of income taxes, excise duties, etc., are greatly different. There is no doubt that this affects location. How then, one may wonder, is it possible to create an approximation to neutral circumstances without extending the common activities of the E.E.C. much further than they are now? The existing widely different levels of service prevent a harmonising of taxes, and such harmonising would in itself not solve the problems unless accompanied by a harmonization of services as well. And is actual harmonisation feasible as long as wages and income levels are widely different, as in fact they are? Ought not the service level to be an entirely different and higher one in a high-income country like the Federal Republic of Germany, than in low-income countries such as Italy and Ireland?

If consistent and all-out harmonisation cannot be implemented, it may still be worthwhile to push for it in a limited field, such as business taxation, which probably is able to affect the location of certain groups of enterprises. It seems particularly sensible if attempts are made at adopting rules to prevent any region from trying to attract business by offering special advantages.

The determining factor in respect of how taxation of businesses will affect their location is the basis of taxation (how taxable earnings are defined, including rules on provisions for depreciation, assessment of stock-in-trade, treatment of increases in value, rules on transfer of losses, and special rules on taxation of allocation to reserves and of profits). In most countries, the location aspect of the problems has been solved by making business taxation uniform for the whole country. A likely consequence of this method is that other taxation will have to be varied more markedly between one local government and the next, and it may create problems if the proceeds will have to be distributed according to some formula or other between the local regions in which the businesses operate.

While along these lines it has been possible to solve the problems within individual countries, a comparable solution is not as easily arrived at within a Community. Here we have a combination of countries that have entered the community with different business taxation systems, some of them interested in upholding taxes that are attractive to businesses. But in the opinion of many people, taxes will have to be uniform to be accepted as neutral. Any attempt by the E.E.C. today to introduce absolutely uniform company taxation would probably be beyond the politically feasible and also beyond what would be reasonable, considering the unequal service levels. But the existence within the same economic area of a number of different systems of company taxation is an inducement to a great many transactions whose true purpose is to avoid taxation, and of which some do actually affect location. Therefore, much can be said in favour of making uniform certain aspects of company taxation. It would be desirable if there were uniform rules on where tax was to be paid; when liability would commence; on how earnings should be stated; and on the relationship between parent and subsidiary companies. Uniform rules on statement of earnings must include uniform rules on provisions for depreciation, on stocktaking, on appraisal of increased values, etc.

Company taxation must be considered in conjunction with personal taxation. Profits distributed as dividend will in many countries be taxed also as the dividend-receivers' income.

Differences may also be found in the degrees to which company taxation is levied on provisions for depreciation and payments of dividend. This may lead to location of companies paying dividend in some countries, and to location of those preferring increase of reserves in others. A policy strongly favouring retention of earnings may have a preservative effect on an existing business structure and may further accumulation of funds, while a policy favouring payment of dividend will to some extent increase consumption but will in particular cause new investments to keep flowing towards the area where profits may be most substantial.

Special problems are found in the multinational companies. Through their internal transfer operations, they may decide to a great extent in what place their profits will ultimately be registered. The possibility of transfer for purposes of taxation is greatly increased if areas have different fiscal years and if they define taxable earnings differently, including differences in rules on depreciation.

Even though it may not be possible to arrive at a uniform level of taxation, much should be attainable through harmonisation of the said underlying rules. The critical wind that has blown in recent years against the multinational companies could possibly be abated if it were possible internationally to agree on a code of good behaviour and a harmonising of rules (not levels) of taxation of these companies.

Within the E.E.C. pressure is at the moment being applied on member states to reach a common definition of earnings liable to value added tax. The main reason for this pressure seems to be the planned contribution to the E.E.C., payable by the member states, which will be based on V.A.T. rated income. Various rules on what turnover is V.A.T.-rated and the differentiation of V.A.T. rates practised in most countries may have certain consequences for policies of location. Therefore, it is no wonder that this is a field where the Common Market favours harmonisation. Implementation of uniform rules on V.A.T.-rated turnover should be feasible, but efforts to arrive at the same level of V.A.T. in all member states will hardly be successful as long as the E.E.C. has not developed beyond its present stage. Introduction of a uniform level may be countered even more strongly than in the cases of company taxation by considerations of the different service levels offered by the various states, and consequently of their differing fiscal requirements. Uniform V.A.T. would simply mean that other forms of taxation, especially taxation of income, would have to be varied correspondingly more.

Changes in V.A.T. have proved to be an effective tool in business-cycle policy. Until the day when the E.E.C. is itself capable of more effectively stimulating economic activity, it would be most unfortunate if the states were deprived of this suitably effective tool.

In general, the fiscal legislation within an area is initially intended to have a neutral effect on location. Only at a later stage are exceptions introduced to satisfy demands for regional development.

Political efforts in respect of location fall naturally into two groups: regional development and regional competition. Regional development is where a government within its area decides on measures to further economic development in parts of this area. Regional competition is where a government introduces measures to attract activities to the whole of its area, often from the areas of other governments.

Regional development is not a policy reserved for individual states. It may be applied within a union, as for example where the E.E.C. creates special benefits for its less developed regions, such as southern Italy, southern France, Ireland, the north of England and Greenland. Something related to regional development is found where industrial countries arrange for preferential customs treatment of goods from developing countries or where they grant aid to developing countries. By far the greater part of these measures is outside the scope of this article. Social and fiscal policies play some role in these connections but in most countries they are of only secondary importance. In regional competition, however, fiscal policy does play a part.

Within the borders of a country, national legislation normally prevents taxes from being applied for that purpose. But internationally, more than a few examples may be given of fiscal policy being used for the purpose of regional competition.

As late as in the 1950s, fairly keen competition prevailed among countries trying to attract industries by means of special favours. With the high rate of growth in the 1960s and with full employment in almost all industrialised countries, interest in regional competition dwindled. In the E.E.C. it still means something that Ireland continues to extend certain favours to foreign investors. In the developing countries, where we find massive unemployment and political desires for industrialisation, many different devices are used to attract manufacturing industry. Normally, favours are reserved for foreign investors. They may take the form of negative protection of the country's own investors. However, this policy is probably most often pursued where local industries of the kind contemplated are non-existent or found only at the stages of handicraft or cottage industry.

In the competition for new industries, taxation privileges play an important role. There are countries that grant tax holidays, for instance in the form of tax exemption for the first five or more years, or they grant duty-free importation on machinery, tariff protection for goods produced, and even undertake not to levy export duty on goods produced.

To some extent, countries hungering for more industries compete among themselves to attract such industry. Often, privileges are negotiated in each particular case. There are industrial firms which, before deciding on where to settle, approach a number of prospective host countries to find out which of them will offer the best terms. During negotiations, one country is played off against another. This procedure is of particular importance in the least-developed countries. It might be a good thing if these countries could agree on a code of good conduct. One way to avoid this form of competition would be to pass restrictive rules thereon within the established communities.

The most active participants in regional competition seem to be the least developed countries. To the extent that their policy succeeds, it will lead to a certain industrialisation of areas that would not otherwise by themselves have become industrialised. In the light of the considerations behind most development aid, this may be deemed only just. However, if the aim is to ensure location according to where production will be cheapest, then the procedure is a failure.

Such activities are unfortunate in that the countries will fail to obtain proceeds from some taxation and will therefore have to increase taxation of other persons and enterprises, and may even have to reduce their general level of services.

But such regional competition seems actually to have its limitations. In countries where growth has really gained momentum, competition is abandoned, presumably because it is no longer as strongly needed and because it begins to be costly. Even in the poorer developing countries, the importance of such policy is not very great. This is explained by the fact that precisely the countries that most eagerly offer tax holidays, etc., have at the same time pursued a controlling policy. It all seems to remind one of a mousetrap. First, you tempt by means of fiscal privileges. Next, when businesses have settled in the region, you apply quite a different set of rules: price restrictions, transfer controls, limitation of dividends, compulsory reinvestment liabilities. The unpleasant aspects of the mousetrap, though perhaps unknown in detail, make the temptation less alluring; the awareness of some future unpleasantness when first you are allowed in, makes you stay out. Until now, the actual influence of such tempting (with or without mousetraps) has been slight. In some cases, it has had some influence on selection of host country, but hardly much on the question of whether to invest or not.

The problems for potential investors in developing countries are more likely to be found in aspects other than those that can be solved by fiscal policies.

Comment

Gary C. Hufbauer*

TAXATION AND PUBLIC EXPENDITURES IN AN OPEN ECONOMY

In an seminal but neglected paper, Bertil Ohlin stressed that taxation and public expenditure can significantly alter the composition and direction of trade.[1] Ohlin analysed company taxation, sales taxation, and other levies in the context of factor immobility. Professor Philip has now broadened the discussion by examining the impact of taxation and public expenditure when labour and capital are free to move from country to country.

Using Professor Philip's paper as a point of departure, I would like to summarise certain key issues raised by taxation and public expenditure in an economy which is open both to the flow of international trade and to the movement of resources.[2] I must caution that, by contrast with Professor Philip's perceptive observations which are amply illustrated by real world examples, my own remarks draw on the ethereal world of neo-classical analysis. Among other things, I assume a world of small countries and frictionless flows of commodities and factor services (but I assume there is some stickiness in the movement of factor owners).[3] These are extreme assumptions, though less extreme today than 30 years ago.

One set of issues concerns the impact of taxation on the structure of domestic production and consumption of goods. In an open economy, the structural impact of taxation is potentially amplified because foreign production and domestic production are ready substitutes. The structural impact of taxation leads naturally to the question of border tax policy on commodity trade.

A related set of issues concerns the impact of taxation on the inflow or outflow of factor services from the rest of the world. This leads to the question of border tax policy on the exchange of factor services. Interesting parallels can be drawn between border tax policy on commodities and on factor services.

A third set of issues concerns the combined impact of taxation and public expenditure on the migration of factor owners. Although factor owners are generally loyal to their native land, an unfavourable fiscal environment can prompt them to seek more congenial surroundings.

---

*The views expressed in this paper should not be construed as the views of the U.S. Treasury Department, where the author is Deputy Director, Office of International Tax Affairs. He is grateful to M. B. Krauss for helpful comments and insights.

I. STRUCTURE OF PRODUCTION AND CONSUMPTION

If taxes were uniformly imposed on all goods and services, or on all categories of income, there would be almost no tax-induced distortion in relative prices.[4] Changes in the structure of economic activity would reflect only the difference between private and public consumption preferences, not distortions between the structure of world prices and the structure of domestic prices.

Modern taxation is not, unfortunately, characterised by uniform tax rates but rather by rates which are differentiated between types of goods and categories of income. Governments deliberately use the tax system to change the workings of the market. Some types of income are favoured, some disfavoured; some types of goods are lightly taxed, others are heavily taxed; some regions are preferred, others are penalised. These practices have can the greatest importance for international commerce.

Differentiated taxation produces price effects which work their way in a complex and unpredictable fashion through product and factor markets. Once a government has embarked on a course of differentiated taxation, and accepted the ensuing distortions,[5] the question is *not* how to restore the *status quo ante*, but how to channel the international consequences using border tax policy.[6] Restoration of the *status quo ante* is an almost impossible task, rather like putting Humpty-Dumpty back together again. But the Government can employ border tax adjustments to determine whether domestic taxes, in the context of an open economy, affect the 'uses of income' flow or the 'sources of income' flow. Two classes of border tax adjustments play a role in this determination — those relating to trade in commodities, and those relating to the exchange of factor services.

II. BORDER TAX ADJUSTMENTS ON COMMODITY TRADE

The two polar border principles for adjusting for commodity taxes are the *destination* principle and the *origin* principle. These two principles can be combined into a *dual* principle. For purposes of discussing commodity border tax adjustments, I shall assume that there is no exchange of factor services. Trade in goods must then be balanced.

Under the destination principle, something happens at the border: domestic taxes are imposed on imports and remitted on exports. By contrast, under the origin principle, nothing happens at the border: domestic taxes are not imposed on imports and there is no remission or exemption of taxes on exports. Under the dual principle, which is rarely if ever used, a partial adjustment happens at the border: taxes are imposed on imports, but not remitted on exports.[7]

The destination principle ensures that differentiated domestic taxes affect the uses of income flow, and thus the structure of consumption.[8] Domestic prices paid by consumers are raised by the amount of the tax, but since producers are free to export at prevailing world prices, their net receipts remain unchanged.[9]

Conversely, the origin principle ensures that domestic taxes affect the sources of income flow, and thereby the structure of production. Domestic prices paid by consumers remain unchanged, since these prices are determined by world markets. The impact of taxes is entirely felt by producers.

The dual principle affects both the uses of income flow and the sources of income flow. Under this principle, domestic taxation discriminates against *both* the consumption and production of heavily taxed goods. Because of this implication, the dual principle is rarely used as a border tax policy.

The choice between destination, origin, and dual principles can have dramatic consequences for the domestic economic structure, and for the composition of international trade. Border tax policy not only determines whether taxes impinge on consumption or production, but it importantly affects the economic fate of particular industries and regions of the country. For example:

(a) A shift from the origin to the destination principle will reduce consumption and increase production of heavily-taxed goods. Correspondingly, imports of these goods will fall, and exports rise.

(b) A shift from the origin to the destination principle will increase consumption and decrease production of lightly taxed goods. Correspondingly, imports of these goods will expand and exports contract.

(c) A shift from the origin to the dual principle will reduce consumption of heavily taxed goods and increase consumption of lightly taxed goods. Imports of the former will fall (or exports rise); imports of the latter will rise (or exports fall).

III. BORDER TAX ADJUSTMENTS ON FACTOR SERVICE EXCHANGE

Parallel to destination and origin principle border tax adjustments for commodities, similar principles apply to taxes on factor income. The two polar principles a country can use to channel the impact of its tax system on the movement of factor services are the *residence* principle and the *source* principle. These two principles can be combined into a system of *worldwide* taxation. For purposes of discussing income border tax adjustments, I shall assume that there is no trade in commodities. The exchange of factor services must then be balanced.

Under the residence principle, income is taxed only in the country where the factor owner resides; under the source principle, income is taxed only in the country where the income is earned. Under the world-wide system, income is taxed both in the country where the factor owner resides and in the country where the income is earned.[10]

Assuming the national allegiance of factor owners, the residence principle ensures that taxes on income cannot be avoided by the mere exportation of factor services. This is true because income is taxed in the country, and only in the country, where the factor owner resides.

By analogy, assuming the geographical specificity of factor services, the source principle ensures that taxes on income cannot be avoided by the emigration of factor owners. This is true because income is taxed in the country, and only in the country, where the factor service is employed.

The converse of these propositions should also be stated. Residence principle taxes can be avoided by the emigration of factor owners (even though factor services stay behind), while source principle taxes can be avoided by the emigration of factor services (even though factor owners stay put).

A Draconian answer to these possibilities is the worldwide system which taxes income both in the country where the factor owner resides and in the country where the factor service is employed. Under a world-wide system, income taxes cannot be avoided except by the simultaneous emigration of factor owners accompanied by their factor services.[11]

In a world with trade in factor services, but not commodities, the residence principle ensures that income taxes are reflected in lower factor earnings.[12] Domestic pretax factor returns are limited by competition from imported factor services, and local factor owners cannot escape the burden of domestic taxation by exporting their factor services.[13]

Conversely, the source principle ensures that income taxes are passed on in the form of higher pretax factor returns and ultimately higher commodity prices. The imposition of an income tax will impel factor owners (both domestic and foreign) to export their services until upward commodity price adjustments in the local market restore the aftertax return to factors. Thus, income taxes affect only the price of goods sold domestically, not the return to factor owners.

A system of worldwide taxation will both increase the relative price of goods made with heavily taxed factors, and ensure that domestic owners of heavily taxed factors experience a decline in their aftertax returns.

IV. PARALLELS IN BORDER TAX POLICY

In a sense, the destination and residence principles are counterparts: commodities are taxed where they are sold and income is taxed where it is used. The origin and source principles are also counterparts: commodities are taxed where they are made and income is taxed where it is earned. The dual and worldwide principles are likewise counterparts: commodities and income are taxed on the widest possible juridical basis.[14]

The parallel between commodity and income border adjustment principles extends, in contempory practice, to the question of which government collects the revenue.[15] Under the destination and residence principles, the exporting country exempts goods and factor service income from its tax while the importing country collects its tax.[16] Under the origin and source principles, the situation is just reversed. The exporting country collects, whereas the importing country exempts.

In a world which permits the free exchange of both commodities and factors, the combination of destination and residence principle adjustments achieves an assignment of taxes in keeping with common understanding. Consider a simple tax system with only sales taxes and personal income taxes. The destination principle ensures that sales taxes alter the structure of prices facing domestic consumers, but not the rewards of productive factors. The residence principle ensures that income taxes alter the returns to factor owners, but not the pretax factor service prices and hence not commodity prices.

By contrast, a combination of origin and source principle adjustments would tend to assign taxes exactly opposite to common understanding. The origin principle would tend to ensure that a sales tax affects the rewards of productive factors, but not the structure of prices paid by consumers (since the structure of commodity prices is determined by world markets). The source principle would tend to ensure that an income tax affects the local market price of commodities, but not the aftertax returns to factors (since aftertax factor prices are determined on world markets). However, in an open economy, with frictionless flows of both commodities and factor services, either the origin or the source principle would literally drain the country of factor services. A sales tax would impel domestic factor owners to export their factor services while an income tax would cause industries to shut down. In the process, the domestic tax base would disappear. Space does not permit a deeper exploration of these consequences, but it seems safe to predict that such topics will increasingly attract the attention of international fiscal experts.

V. THE MIGRATION OF FACTOR OWNERS

The conception of taxation as a price for public services seemed utterly natural to Grotius and Locke, but fell into disrepute with Mill and his contemporaries. The idea was rediscovered in the late nineteenth century by Italian economists, such as Pantaleoni and de Viti de Marco, and by Swedish economists such as Wicksell and Lindahl.[17] Twenty years ago, Tiebout added a new dimension when he pointed out that taxpayers can vote with their feet as well as their ballots to reach the most suitable combination of services and taxes.[18] As if to illustrate Tiebout's argument, Philip notes the double-edged example of the Swedish pensioner who retires to the warm sunshine and mild climate of Spain, but returns home when the ailments of age become severe and the attractions of public medical care become great.

If factor owners are prepared to change their national residence and take their factor services with them, then normal border tax adjustments will have little effect. The only border 'solution' to the phenomenon of footloose factor owners would involve capital controls and emigration restrictions. Rather than pursue such repressive remedies, democratic nations should instead seek to ensure a reasonable balance between taxes imposed and public benefits rendered to each significant segment of the community.

VI. INTERNATIONAL RULES AND FISCAL SOVEREIGNTY

The present era of high taxation has opened alluring but dangerous avenues for the fiscal control of international commerce. The preferential Danish schnapps tax mentioned by Professor Philip is a small but apt example of these temptations. While the age of tariff protection may be slowly setting,[19] the age of fiscal protection appears to be rapidly dawning. This prospect has rightly alarmed many economists.

One response to this troublesome prospect is the G.A.T.T. rule on commodity border tax adjustments. Under Article XVI, destination principle adjustments can only be applied to indirect taxes (sales, excise, value added), and not to direct taxes (property taxes, personal and corporate income taxes). While the goal of G.A.T.T. rules is laudable, the dividing line between the application of destination and origin principle adjustments is questionable.

Another response to the prospect of fiscal protection involves bilateral tax treaties limiting the scope of each country's income tax jurisdication. In the typical treaty, each country binds itself to apply its income taxes either under a modified residence principle or under the source principle.

A third type of response, still very much on the drawing boards, is the call for fiscal harmonisation. Despite its popularity in academic circles, fiscal harmonisation has two important drawbacks. Carried to an extreme, fiscal harmonisation would negate fiscal sovereignty.[20] National governments would be deprived of the power to alter the internal structure of prices as a means of achieving economic goals. And factor owners would be denied a meaningful choice of fiscal environments. Harmonisation would thus stifle the wholesome competition between governments in matching taxes collected with services rendered.

The challenge ahead is to fashion international rules which restrain the most egregious cases of fiscal protection, yet permit each country a measure of fiscal sovereignty to shape its own economic destiny.

NOTES

[1] Bertil Ohlin, 'Taxation and Foreign Trade', Appendix II in International Labour Office, *Social Aspects of European Economic Cooperation*, report by a Group of Experts, Geneva (Switzerland, 1956).

[2] My remarks draw extensively on a paper by M. B. Krauss and G. C. Hufbauer, 'Border Tax Adjustments on Commodities and Income', unpublished manuscript (July, 1976).

[3] Note that the mobility of factor services does not necessarily imply the mobility of factor owners. Factor owners can stay at home and export their factor services. Conversely, factor owners can emigrate and leave their factor services behind.

[4] However, even if uniform taxes were imposed on all goods and services, or on all categories of income, but leisure remained untaxed, the incentives to work and save would be distorted.

[5] When the domestic economy is severely distorted, free trade and free movement can sometimes diminish welfare by comparison with no trade and no movement of factors. For the present discussion, I assume that tax distortions are not so severe as to produce that unhappy result.

[6] The theory of border tax adjustments has been explored in a respectable, if minor, literature that can be traced to Ricardo. See P. Sraffa, editor, *Works and Correspondence of David Ricardo*, Cambridge University Press, vol. IV, pp. 216–219. More recent treatments include: Dieter Biehl, *Ausfuhrland-Prinzip Einfuhrland-Prinzip und Germeinsamer-Markt-Prinzip*, Carl Heymanns Verlag KG (Koln, 1969); Harry Johnson and Mel Krauss, 'Border Taxes, Border Tax Adjustments, Comparative Advantage, and the Balance of Payments', *Canadian Journal of Economics* (November, 1970); James E. Meade, 'A Note of Border Tax Adjustments', *Journal of Political Economy* (September/October, 1974).

[7] A reverse dual principle, conceptually bizarre because it would extend an open invitation to fiscal evasion, would exempt both imports and exports from domestic taxation.

[8] 'Consumption' is here broadly defined to include purchases of investment goods as well as consumption goods.

[9] This statement and the corresponding analysis of the origin principle depend, of course, on the extreme assumption of frictionless commodity trade.

[10] The issue of which government applies its tax *rates* should be distinguished from the question of which government ultimately collects the tax *revenue*. Factor owners are relatively indifferent to the division of revenue, but they will export and import factor services in response to tax rate differentials. The various border tax principles are fundamentally addressed to applicable rate structures, and they are theoretically compatible with alternative revenue sharing arrangements. But in practice, the government imposing its rates usually retains the revenue.

[11] U.S. factor owners must also renounce their citizenship if they wish to avoid U.S. taxes, since, under the United States version of a worldwide tax system, all citizens are subject to tax no matter where they reside.

However, foreign tax credits and liberal statutory exclusions substantially reduce U.S. taxation of citizens residing abroad.

[12] This statement, and the corresponding analysis of the source principle, depend, of course, on the extreme assumption of frictionless factor exchange.

[13] Note that the imposition of a differentially higher tax on the income of a single sector (for example, a surtax on steel profits) will drive the sector into the hands of foreign factor owners, if the tax is applied under the residence principle.

[14] In practice, dual taxation rarely occurs, while worldwide taxation is usually mitigated by foreign tax credits and statutory exclusions for income earned abroad by domestic residents and by reduced tax rate on income earned at home by foreigners.

[15] As noted earlier, the ultimate division of revenue between governments need not necessarily be decided by the choice of border adjustment principles.

[16] 'Exporting' and 'importing' of factor service income here mean payments to foreign countries and receipts from foreign countries respectively; the terms have an opposite usage in balance of payments terminology.

[17] English translations of the classic essays may be found in R. A. Musgrave and A. T. Peacock, editors, *Classics in the Theory of Public Finance* (Macmillan, 1958).

[18] C. M. Tiebout, 'A Pure Theory of Local Expenditures', *Journal of Political Economy* (October, 1956).

[19] Ever so slowly, according to Bela Balassa. See his contribution to this volume.

[20] The parallel with the loss of national monetary sovereignty under a regime of fixed exchange rates is obvious.

Comment
Dieter Biehl

I.

Professor Philip's paper is difficult to summarise. It deals with a large number of different aspects of social and fiscal policy influences on location which are analysed from varying points of view. This demonstrates the multifacet character of the topic to be discussed, but makes it at the same time difficult to isolate the set of criteria applied by Professor Philip in order to arrive at his conclusions.

II.

It seems as if his main conclusion (or is it perhaps the starting assumption?) is already contained in his first sentence, *viz.* that the impact of social and fiscal policies on location 'is often thought to be great, though in most cases actual location is probably only slightly affected'. This might be true as far as the impact of a *national* (community) budget in influencing the *international* location of a national (community) economy as a whole is concerned, especially if one assumes, as Professor Phillip does, that 'expansive' and 'contractive' effects cancel each other out. But social and fiscal policy measures may nevertheless have important repercussions on the *interregional* allocation of activities inside a national (community) economy. Since the regional case is not overlooked by Professor Philip, one wonders whether his general statement at the beginning of his paper gives the appropriate weight to it. Whether tax burdens and expenditure benefits are evenly distributed interregionally or not has important implications for the development, for example, of agglomerated regions compared with the less agglomerated ones and can, via this relationship, also influence the international location of economic activities. What frequently is labelled a 'market failure' when regional concentrations of economic activities exist, is in the last resort a 'politics failure' caused especially by concentration of public expenditures in already highly agglomerated regions and by other public 'deregulations' favouring these regions.

III.

Professor Philip is also not quite clear as to the opportunity cost or incidence concept underlying his analysis. It is possible to argue that the costs, for example, for public infrastructure investment are (partly) borne by public authorities. But this is a shortsighted view of incidence which especially in the case of a long-term analysis like locational analysis does not look very promising. Such expenditures have to be financed either by taxes or by borrowing and, therefore, reduce the resource use of the private sector. A similar partial approach is applied when the taxes are analysed in such a way as if total tax payments constituted a net burden on firms or individuals; here no mention is made of the corresponding expenditure benefits. Statements like the one that tax inequalities between E.C.-member states cause relatively large, unintended transfers of enterprises and labour from one country to another do not take into account that it is only the net result of tax burden minus expenditure benefits which is relevant.

But perhaps the main issue is not so much a methodological one, but an implicit preference for a centralist government structure as opposed to a federal one. A statement like the following: 'Local self-government is almost irreconcilable with a strict adherence to the principle of neutrality' and similar ones seem to reflect such a preference, which is based on the implicit desirability of a uniformly defined 'neutrality' for the total national territory. The alternative federalist position starts from the idea that a large number of public services do not only actually have servicing areas which are smaller than the national territory, but should even be used consciously in order to create more possibilities for regional populations to express differences in evaluating public sector benefits. In this respect, not so much a theory of central government, but a 'theory of clubs' or of 'Fiscal Federalism' à la Buchanan/Musgrave would be appropriate.

IV.

Among his 'indirect' influences, Professor Philip also lists infrastructure equipment. He stresses that these indirect influences are more important than the direct ones. At the end of his paper, he introduces another related distinction between 'regional development' and 'regional competition' (p. 294). His two approaches and the related arguments can be brought together and can be based on a more rigorous reasoning starting from an extended relative resource endowment approach à la Heckscher-Ohlin for regional development.

Assume that all resources can be classified according to their specific degree of mobility, divisibility, specialisation and substitutability. The thesis then is that only those resources which are highly immobile (that is, having fixed locations), highly indivisible (representing a large economic 'capacity'), not very specialised (that is, are 'polyvalent' in the sense that they can be used without additional resource costs in a large number of different lines of production), and substitutable only to a limited degree, determine the locational potential of a region. A region which is better equipped with those resources has a higher potential output per head or development potential and can have a higher actual income per head. These resources therefore 'limit' the realisable actual income per head and can on that count be considered as possible 'bottleneck factors'. Examples of these categories range from topography, climate, mineral resources, 'natural' population in the sense of not yet skilled labour (skills should be considered as mobile human capital), infrastructure equipment of all kinds (I prefer to include here also Professor Philip's educational and health facilities), up to agglomeration and sectoral structure (cf. for more details and a general presentation of this approach Dieter Biehl *et al.* (1975)). In addition, economic distance of a set of possible bottleneck factors from other regions as locations of other factor sets (the 'site potential') is important.

The potential output represented by a given regional set of bottleneck factors can be transformed into actual output, if the bottleneck factor capacity is fully (optimally) utilised by combining it with the adequate quantities and qualities of the mobile, divisible, specialised and substitutable resources. Whether a regional development potential is really optimally used depends on relative prices.

From the point of view of this approach, social and fiscal policy measures can have two kinds of influence: they can change the endowment with some of the bottleneck factors, and they can influence relative prices for the bottleneck factors on the one hand and the mobile factors on the other. Examples of the first type of influences are then all public investments, ranging from the normal infrastructure to office location decisions. Here all the examples Professor Philip discussed in his paper and others besides can be brought in. Most of the other social and fiscal measures, and most of other public policies too, presumably have greater impact on relative prices: pollution standards, land zoning, minimum wage policies, social security contribution systems, central government grants to lower-level governments, fiscal equalisation schemes between different levels and also between governments of the same level (*Finanzausgleich*).

Since most of these bottleneck factors are not tradeable or only to a limited degree, an important problem for fully utilising a given regional locational potential is that public decision makers, and also trade union leaders and entrepreneurs, attempt and succeed in devising regulations which favour full capacity use. A closer look at a number of existing regulations reveals that these are in fact more like deregulations, restricting relative prices and interregional and international competition. I shall mention only three types of them which I think are important and which are neglected in Professor Philip's paper.

(1) MINIMUM WAGE REGULATIONS

In a number of countries, minimum wage regulations exist for the relatively immobile categories of labour (unskilled women, young people looking for their first job, etc.), Sometimes, these regulations are combined with higher social security contributions.[1] Minimum wages are normally fixed in relation to national averages. This means that these wages are too high compared with the potential productivity level per job in regions for example with poor infrastructure, low degree of agglomeration and peripheral site, whereas they are too low for the economically stronger regions, especially the agglomerations. Although these measures have been introduced with the aim of helping 'the poorest of the poor', they in reality only increase the unemployment risk for these groups. Furthermore, they clearly disadvantage the poorer regions as potential competitors of the central agglomerations; they impose a 'tax' on immobile labour thus preventing these regions from making use of one of its comparative advantages: a relatively abundant supply of unskilled or less skilled labour.[2]

(2) FIXED PRICES FOR LAND AND RENT CONTROLS

These measures are normally only applied in highly agglomerated regions in order to prevent land prices and rents from rising to their true scarcity level. This decreases the price for one bottleneck factor in these regions, increases real income out of a given nominal wage and can even increase profits if the categories of labour concerned do not succeed in having the saved rent component paid to them. This may be particularly so in those regions which experience a strong immigration so that labour supply is increased compared with demand. Such policies, therefore, again benefit the agglomerations to the disadvantage of the other regions and distort interregional competition.

(3) FINANCING OF INFRASTRUCTURE EQUIPMENT IN URBAN AGGLOMERATIONS

Effecting this through central government grants is another example of distortion of relative prices. If the central government subsidies, for example, public passenger transportation systems or pollution abatement installations in these regions, it maintains a situation where private costs are kept below social costs. It is estimated that in Germany in the last few years about 1 billion DM has been spent in order to favour backward regions, whereas at the same time about 5 billion DM have been paid out

of federal funds for transportation schemes in urban agglomerations. The
negative effect from the point of view of regional development is still
larger, because a part of that 5 billion DM has been taken out of the funds
for the national highway system. Since normally highway projects in
peripheral regions have no great priority, presumably a large part of this
money would have been used in these regions in order to improve transportation infrastructure.

V.

Some evidence for some of the relationships discussed may be briefly
mentioned:

(a) That distance (site) and degree of agglomeration play an important
role for the development of a system of regions can be seen from the
enclosed graph. It shows for the 61 regions of the old 6 E.E.C.-member
countries how income per capita declines with increasing distance from
the Cologne/Düsseldorf area. The coefficient of determination, which is
0·71 for this regression, increases up to 0·81 when population density for
these regions is inserted as a second explanatory variable.

(b) A study of the relative infrastructure equipment of German labour
market regions (a 178 breakdown) shows the following differences in
relation to population and/or area: If the German average is set equal to
100, the mini—max ratio for the worst-equipped region compared with
the best-equipped one is 56:346 for all the seven categories taken together
(roads, railways, energy, education, health, dwellings, infrastructure). The
highest mini—max ratio has been found for a hospital beds index with
2:656; the lowest is for roads with 60:202.

VI.

On p. 290 ff., Professor Philip also discusses some of the problems of tax
harmonisation in the E.E.C. This discussion suffers from the lack of a
clear theoretical background. As long as the E.C.-member countries have
national currencies — and especially if these currencies are linked through
flexible exchange rates — differences in the net taxation/expenditure levels
will create no distortions as far as the weighted average of the net effects
are concerned. The traditional analysis applies only to specific taxes which
should then be 'neutralised' with the aid of the so-called 'destination
principle', that is, with restitution of these differentials for exports and
taxation of imports. But it can be shown that the alleged neutrality of the
country of destination principle only holds in a partial analysis (cf. Biehl
(1969)). As soon as the analysis is enlarged in order to allow not only for

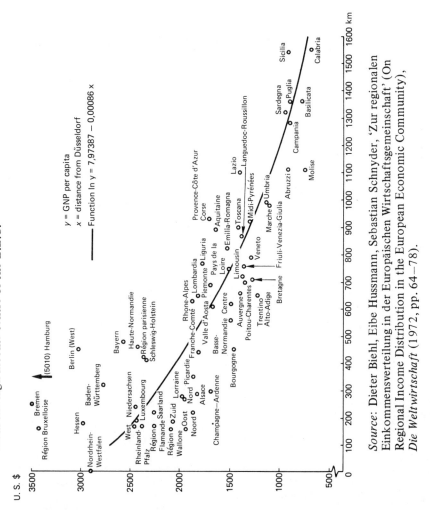

Figure 1 Relation in 1968 between regions' G.N.P. per capita and distance from the high-income centre of the E.E.C.

Source: Dieter Biehl, Eibe Hussmann, Sebastian Schnyder, 'Zur regionalen Einkommensverteilung in der Europäischen Wirtschaftsgemeinschaft' (On Regional Income Distribution in the European Economic Community), *Die Weltwirtschaft* (1972, pp. 64–78).

trade in goods, but also in factor services, and the possibility is taken into account that economic agents may choose their place of (legal) residence, their place of consumption, and their place where capital and labour is put to work, then this international tax principle will cause incentives and disincentives. Although the other possible taxation principles will create distortions, too (origin principle, residence principle, source principle), the number of distorted types of transactions is higher under the destination principle. Distortions are minimised if a combination of these simple principles is applied which corresponds to the requirements of a common market. But I nevertheless agree with Professor Philip that certain tax rules and definitions should be harmonised in order to avoid *specific* distortions in the Common Market.

As far as the financing of the E.C.-budget is concerned, the existing procedure that each country delivers 1 per cent of its value added tax revenue, calculated according to uniform criteria, implies a regressive taxation. In order to avoid this, the corporation tax could be given to the E.C. This would then also bring about a unifrom corporation tax system for all E.C. countries.

NOTES

[1] This is the case if social security contribution rates are applied only up to a certain wage, so that low-wage earners necessitate higher social security charges than high-wage receivers.

[2] The same, naturally, is true as far as the attempts are concerned to force underdeveloped regions to apply the severe pollution standards which are adequate — perhaps even still too low — for the already over-congested regions. Here, the immobile natural resources of the poorer regions are taxed by the richer agglomerations.

REFERENCES

Biehl, D., *Ausfuhrland-Prinzip, Einfuhrland-Prinzip und Gemeinsamer-Markt-Prinzip* (*Country of Export Principle, Country of Import Principle, and Common Market Principle*), (Köln, 1969).

Biehl, D., *et al.* 'Bestimmungsgründe des regionalen Entwicklungspotentials' (Determinants of Regional Development Potential), *Kieler Studie* 133 (Tübingen, 1975).

Biehl, D., Hussmann, E. and Schnyder, S., 'Zur regionalen Einkommensverteilung in der Europäischen Wirtschaftsgemeinschaft' (On Regional Income Distribution in the European Economic Community), *Die Weltwirtschaft*, (1972) 1.

Summary of the Discussion

Several discussants took issue with Kjeld Philip's general statement that differences in social and fiscal policies affected actual location only slightly. The quantitative importance of interregional and international migration and their effects were discussed. The need for international trade theory to consider social and fiscal policy instruments together with commercial policy instruments was stressed. This session was chaired by *Göran Ohlin*.

Robert Solow noted that the tremendous internal migration in the U.S. was largely motivated by differences between states in social services — a characteristic of large federal areas. He suggested that these differences were more important between Alabama and New York, for example, than between countries in Western Europe. Movements of blacks from the South to New York were motivated by a desire to escape discrimination but also occurred in response to different benefit levels.

Solow also pointed to the large number of illegal immigrants in the U.S. In the nature of the case, their number was difficult to determine but he estimated it to be 3 to 5 per cent of the population. Since they tend to concentrate in certain areas and since a larger ratio of their population is active than the U.S. average, there are places where the ratio of illegal immigrants in the labour force is quite large. Solow compared them with guest workers in Europe and stressed the important difference that they coexist with substantial domestic unemployment particularly among those groups which compete for similar jobs.

He also observed that New York City lost central offices of large corporations to New Jersey where there is no state income tax. Other large cities had similar experiences. This indicated that the need for face-to-face contacts by business people emphasised in other discussions at the symposium was perhaps exaggerated. Places like New York City, Solow thought, performed a genuine social function for business that required Mr. A to see Mr. B — and occasionall Miss C — but suggested that this sort of face-to-face interaction may be more of a consumer's good than a producer's good

Solow lastly commented on Philip's remark that property taxation had no effect on location since it was completely shifted. He noted that the level of property taxation varied substantially between cities and states in the U.S. Since this was mainly a tax on buildings it resulted in considerable distortion of industrial location.

Sune Carlson added that illegal immigrants existed also in Europe. He estimated their number to be between a half and 1 million in France. Since social benefits in France were 72 per cent of firms' labour costs and since firms did not pay these for illegal immigrants he thought that many firms particularly in Southern France were dependent on this kind of labour.

Dieter Biehl expected that the extension of the Common Market to include certain Mediterranean countries would lead to larger labour movements between countries similar to the American experience mentioned by Solow. In Turkey alone, 1 million people were registered for work in Germany. He also mentioned that his own investigations had shown that the fastest growing regions in the U.S. had the highest unemployment rates. This paradoxical result was perhaps due to the migration incentives provided by social benefits which were highest in the fastest growing regions.

Hollis Chenery observed that Philip's paper showed the difficulties involved in assigning particular policy instruments to particular objectives. It is difficult to say that a certain set of instruments particularly affects trade while other sets of instruments affect other things — and not trade. There is therefore a need to reconsider what is useful to discuss under the heading of international trade. The characteristic of policy instruments in general is that they affect the quality of factors, the location of factors and production, consumers' tastes, etc., as well as trade.

Bertil Ohlin emphasised the need for more research on the effects of social and fiscal policy on trade, factor movements and location. The choice and construction of such policies cannot be built on an analysis of effects in an isolated community. It must consider the effects of international relations. We need, he noted, a wide grasp of real world examples such as given in Philip's paper as a preparation for a more thorough analysis of important cases. And we also need to investigate further, he added, the general relationships between trade and factor movements on the one hand and government expenditures and receipts on the other. Ohlin illustrated this by way of a concrete example. An error of thinking in 1939 by the Swedish Minister of Finance, Mr. Wigforss, he said, was one of the most effective elements in fostering Sweden's industrial expansion and exports during the last 30 years. Wigforss thought that highly generous depreciation rules reduce the tax revenue only temporarily. Corporations declare high profits later on when the assets are 'written off' and then their tax payments will grow. It is only a question of 'tax credit'. Wigforss overlooked that in growing enterprises this credit may rise during several decades. Large supplies of tax-free profits in Sweden increased the risk-bearing investments there. Thus his generous depreciation rules led to a higher rate of investment in industrial enterprise than otherwise probable. The effect on Swedish exports and on imports of machinery was obvious.

Kjeld Philip closed the discussion. He felt that the commenters' contributions had been complementary to his own and he appreciated Gary Hufbauer's attempt to formalise the relationships between taxation, public expenditure and factor movements in a general equilibrium framework. It was important however, he felt, to extend the analysis to many variables and to account for differences between as well as within areas. Noting the clear connection between taxation, public expenditure and migration he was surprised that actual international migration was low in spite of large international differences in income, taxes and social benefits. The larger movements of labour between areas in the U.S., he said, could be explained by a common language, culture and legal system. In Europe, even in Scandinavia, language differences constituted serious obstacles to migration. He also suggested that the limited investment in countries with cheap labour and land was due to differences in the quality of infrastructure between countries. When establishing a plant in say Africa, a firm may have to train and educate its employees, provide them with hospitals and their children with schools, and perhaps even construct its own transportation system. It was therefore important not to forget that the supply of public goods as well as the level of taxation was a factor influencing the international location of production, he concluded.

9 Technology, Technical Progress and the International Allocation of Economic Activity

Harry G. Johnson

Economics offers two alternative approaches to the question of the influence of technology on the allocation of economic activity, which may be termed the microeconomic and the macroeconomic, though with some violation of the meanings commonly accorded to these terms.

What I term the microeconomic approach may be said to have originated with J. R. Hicks's *Inaugural Lecture* of 1953,[1] which was concerned with the possibility that technological progress in the United States might, through having a bias towards occurring in American import-substituting industries, create chronic balance-of-payments problems for the rest of the world (especially for Britain). It may be remarked, incidentally, that since that time international monetary theorists have become much more aware of the difficulties of making the analytical transition from 'real' disturbances to 'monetary' balance-of-payments effects.[2] For the present purpose, however, the relevant point is that Hicks's rather simple Ricardian constant-cost model stimulated a wave of intensive research on the effects of introducing technical change of various kinds into the (by then) standard Heckscher-Ohlin-Samuelson model of comparative advantage and international trade.[3]

That work, however, left largely unanalysed both the possibility that differences in real (absolute) factor prices resulting from technological differences would promote the diffusion of technology among countries, with consequent changes in comparative advantage and trade patterns, and the possibility that the same influences would promote the international migration of factors of production, with effects on the distribution of factors of production and of economic activity among countries (political units) and/or among geographical regions (climatic units). The first possibility, technological diffusion, has since been pursued along lines pioneered by Posner and especially by Vernon.[4] The second line has been pursued primarily in connection with work on the multinational corporation[5] and secondarily on so-called 'brain drain',[6] though the multinational corporation also involves as an integral part of its activities the diffusion or 'transplantation' of technology.[7]

The 'microeconomic' approach carries with it certain biases in the formulation of questions for scientific economic study, biases often not recognised by the economic scientists themselves. The central and crucial biasing factor is the acceptance of, and frequent identification of the social scientific observer with, the nation-state as the fundamental unit of human social organisation, and the unit with whose welfare the economist should be concerned – in contrast to the older economic-theoretical tradition, which stressed the individual and his welfare (though implicitly the patriarchal family was the point of reference). Along with this orientation goes a basically mythological structure of beliefs in the dispassionateness of the national state's government, and its superiority over the individual as arbitrator of the social welfare, beliefs fortified by conviction of the empirical reality and quantitative significance of phenomena variously termed 'divergences between marginal private and social costs or benefits', 'cases of market failure', and most recently 'distortions'.

What I term the 'macroeconomic' approach is concerned, by contrast, not with the nature of rational – competitive *or* monopolistic – responses to given technological-change stimuli, and the specification of optimising policies designed from the point of view of the national state as an optimising welfare-experiencing unit, but with the process of technical change itself, as a process of maximising response to opportunities for profitable technical change on the one hand, and the costs of producing technical progress on the other, a process whose operation may be stimulated or inhibited by governmental policies (and more broadly by social influences) but whose long-run trends condition, rather than are conditioned by, governmental and social institutions.[8] This approach, or so I take it, is the more appropriate one for the general problem with which this conference is concerned, namely 'the international allocation of economic activity'. It must, however, be recognised that 'the nation' is an artificial unit of organisation, and that to treat the problem with proper generality one must bear in mind a point emphasised by Edgeworth, Ohlin and other great trade theorists, that the same basic theory applies whether the problem is called 'international' or 'interregional' trade (or for that matter, following Bastable, trade among non-competing groups).

The 'macroeconomic' approach also suggests a much longer time-perspective than is customary in international trade theory, which has mostly concentrated on relatively short-run, 'contemporary' questions of trade among nations and the effects of their commercial policies, even though the basic principles of comparative advantage are explicitly presented as universal and timeless truths. And it requires somewhat more attention to human needs and wants, and the biological characteristics of human beings as an animal species, than is considered necessary for the usual purposes of trade theory.

To set the subject very briefly in long historical perspective, consider a rudimentary model of post-nomad, agriculturally-based-and-dominated economic activity, in which population tends in a broad sense to breed to some level of subsistence. The distribution of activity and population around the surface of the world would be dominated by the distribution of agricultural land, *subject* (and this is important) to the fact that the human species can exist most comfortably within a range of distances away from (and not too close to) the equator, and only with great difficulty if at all outside that range — the range itself being determined partly by the biological characteristics of the vegetation on which man fed, directly or indirectly through consumption of other animals. Population densities would vary with soil fertility; and 'civilisation' would be associated with the production of an agricultural surplus — or excess of agricultural-sector output over agricultural-sector consumption of food. Note that a potential agricultural surplus could be absorbed by population expansion in agriculture, so that the emergence of civilisation would require some means of preventing a general process of breeding to the level of subsistence — which in economic terms could be supplied by a system of property rights that captured agricultural rents for a sub-sector of the population, and of inheritance rights or rules that promoted limitation of the numbers of land-rent recipients.

Modifying the model to allow for the effects of climatic differences on comparative productivity in different types of agricultural production would introduce interregional trade — Ricardo's famous example of English cloth for Portuguese wine naturally springs to mind — and with it probably variations in population densities related to the relative labour and land intensities of agricultural production. Introducing the need for technologies of working up raw agricultural products into forms appropriate to human consumption needs would introduce further types of international exchange — especially cloth, pots for cooking and storage, and jewellery; also weapons. Weapons are a type of tradeable that economists, rooted in the ways of thought of the nineteenth century, find it uncomfortable to bring into their formal models; but war is a natural alternative to production when agricultural surplus is hard to generate, and other societies' surpluses invite plunder. The range and extent of trade over distance would itself be conditioned by the technology of transport — initially a byproduct of the process of hunting the waters for food in the form of fish.

Rather than attempt a series of models of world production allocation and trade in successive stages of world economic evolution under the influence of very slowly evolving technologies of production and consumption,[9] I shall skip ahead to the modern period in which improvements in agricultural and resource extraction technologies have made the agricultural surplus so large relative to the population employed in agriculture that the agricultural surplus has ceased to be a dominating or even important influence on the location of economic activity. (This generalisation contains an implicit assumption that population no longer breeds to the level of subsistence, and hence excludes the problem of the less-developed part of the world, where agriculture still dominates and population growth and rising standards of living are in sharp competition with one another. This range of problems is assumed to be dealt with elsewhere in the programme, though it will necessarily enter into the subsequent argument.) The reason why agricultural land, and resources in general, cease to exercise a dominating influence on economic activity is in large part the consequence of the alternative of interregional and international trade, as compared with local production: locational advantage for these particular types of production does not carry with it locational advantage (in the form of a multiplier relationship) for general economic activity except to the extent that the combination of numbers employed and earnings per head (a function of technological superiority) generates locational advantages in the form of proximity to the consumers and consumption markets.

If one assumed that population was anchored to national territories, and grew at a rate determined 'exogenously' or by sociological and other forces not amenable to economic analysis, *and also* that capital stocks per head were determined by national savings propensities, the international distribution of aggregate economic activity would be determined by population, capital, and technological level. Further precision in generalisation would have either to resort to complicated taxonomy, or make more specific assumptions about the interactions between savings propensities and capital accumulation on the one hand and technological level on the other. The theory of factor-price equalisation suggests that real income per head will vary fairly directly with capital stock per head, and later theorising suggests that, when human capital as well as material capital is allowed for, real income per head will vary more than proportionately with material capital per head. Differences in technology level, extreme cases of bias of technical progress aside, will tend to accentuate the non-proportionality in the relation of income per head to physical capital per head; and if one assumes what has not been satisfactorily either proved or disproved, that technical progress tends to be biased in the labour-saving capital-using direction, incomes per head will tend to vary more than proportionately with technological level.

These general remarks relate to the distribution of economic activity, rather than to international trade as such. Technology, and differences in technological level among countries, will generate international trade at both the partial equilibrium or extreme microequilibrium level (the level of Vernon's 'product-cycle' theory) of particular products in which a particular country or group of countries has established technological leadership (possibly reinforced by 'economies of scale'), and at the microeconomic level of comparative advantage based on superior technological level, superior 'endowment' (or past accumulation) of capital, or a combination of them. The fact that what is involved in the explanation of the trade in question is a combination of capital (both material and human) and technology is responsible for an analytical complexity that has frequently bedevilled policy discussions. The confusion in question involves identifying comparative disadvantage with a so-called 'technological gap', defined in narrow terms of absence of a particular piece or application of technological knowledge, when the apparent comparative disadvantage in question may be due *either* to the possession of relative endowments of factors, and corresponding factor prices, that make the application of more advanced technology uneconomic, *or* to a *generally* low level of technological resources and competence that makes comparative advantage depend on the gifts of nature, in the form either of abundant localised natural resources or of abundant low-skilled but low-cost labour. Further confusion arises from the fact that knowledge is costly to produce, but once produced is optimally to be treated as a public good rather than privately appropriated. This fact in turn inclines political and intellectual leaders in the less-developed countries, and their sympathisers in the developed countries, towards the assumptions that deriving an income stream from the private possession and use of technological knowledge created by sacrifice of one's own resources is somehow immoral, that the knowledge should instead be made available to others free of charge, and further that the failure of the private enterprise system to produce at its own cost knowledge that it is unprofitable either for itself or for governments in less-developed countries to produce, but that those governments might use if someone else bore the costs, constitutes a decisive criticism of the competitive process.[10]

The argument thus far has followed the main line of classical trade theory, or the microeconomic approach, as defined earlier. That is, it has assumed for each 'nation' a given population, capital stock, and technology, either directly or in the 'dynamised' form of exogenous population growth, equilibrium capital per head determined by an exogenous saving ratio, and technological opportunities improving by discrete exogenous shifting. Those assumptions have one great analytical advantage, in making national income and national expenditure identical, through the equilibrium requirement that the trade balance must balance at zero, so that 'the international distribution of economic activity' includes simultaneously the distribution of production and of consumption. It is, however, not realistic to assume each 'nation's' income and output to be determined by its own stock of factors and own technology applied within its own national territory, with international economic relations confined to trade in currently produced goods and services only. Instead, one would expect — and find in the actual international economy — movements of capital and labour in response to absolute differences in factor marginal products, and the international diffusion of technology and erosion of international differences of technological level. International non-current-product mobility of these various kinds would in turn give rise to unilateral flows of income, adding to or subtracting from current national output.[11] The nature of these flows would vary with the type of mobility considered, and in particular might be either 'permanent' or transitory; or, to put the point another way, in terms of the theoretic difference between comparative static models and equilibrium growth models, a 'permanent' international income transfer or unilateral flow might be generated by a once-over change in a comparative statics model, or instead occur only through the continual re-creation of the reasons for a transitory flow through the mechanics of equilibrium growth.

To be more specific, a once-over movement of capital through foreign investment would give rise to a permanent flow of interest and dividend payments from the country invested in to the country whose citizens made the investment. With labour migration of a permanent kind, on the other hand, one would expect the associated return flow of emigrants' remittances to dwindle to negligibility, as the parents and other immediate relatives of the original migrants either died off, or perhaps were assisted themselves to migrate, by their migrating forebears – in the case of parents, as non-producing consumer dependents. In the case of technological transfer (which might, of course, be mediated through the export of goods embodying superior knowledge rather than through transfer of technological knowledge itself), one would expect patent, royalty, and licence fees and other payments less obviously received for the sale of technological know-ledge gradually to disappear as legal and secrecy protection was eroded by the passage of time and the competitive imitation of the knowledge.

The international movement of labour raises some special analytical problems under present citizenship and immigration practices, that require notice, though their importance may not be great enough to require serious modification of the common assumption that capital and technology (and possibly skilled labour, managerial and technical, applied to the movement of the other two productive elements on a short-term or 'circulating' basis) are internationally mobile while labour in general is internationally immobile. One problem, relating to labour as a factor of production, is the now-common discrimination of national immigration laws in favour of skilled professional and technical labour, embodying a relatively high quantity of 'human capital', and against ordinary unskilled labour, except in cases in which it brings with it considerable financial capital. Another, in the same context, is the practice of licensing temporary immigration of unskilled and semi-skilled foreign labour, to perform tasks for which native labour is scarce or relatively expensive to obtain.[12] Both influences tend to accentuate the dispersion of incomes per head among countries, or perhaps of per capita consumption and standards of living of the native-born population, though a full treatment involving due attention to the economics of income taxation and social security legislation and careful attention to the limitations of consumption per head of residents as a welfare index is beyond the present purpose. A third aspect which requires some attention, though to the best of the writer's knowledge relatively less work has been done on it than on the so-called 'guest labour' problem of temporary immigration of foreign workers, or on the closely related economics of the foreign tourist industry, is the apparently growing practice of using private retirement funds or national public pension entitlements to finance retirement in other countries than the country of national citizenship and working life. This last aspect is related to a more general consideration, the influence of both production and consumption technology on the preferred climatic living location of human beings. Merely as two examples of this, one may mention the long-run influence of air-conditioning in making hot but otherwise attractive parts of the world comfortable for human living, and the influence of both modern medical technique and air transport in making retirement to cheap and attractive but distant and generally primitive environments feasible (quite apart from the increased feasibility associated with higher retirement income).

All of these, and other, aspects of labour migration join with the mobility of capital in partially divorcing the international distribution of total population and its consumption from the same distribution in terms of the international distribution of labour force and productive capital equipment and of current production of goods and services. One might, indeed, envisage a sort of post-national-state, more technologically advanced, or even ultimate technologically stationary state, in which production absorbed relatively little of total social time or total living population, and consumption and leisure, mostly done by the non-working population, was distributed over the world's surface in a way determined by peoples' preferences for scenic and climatic locational advantages for pleasant existence. Alternatively, perhaps less unrealistically, one might envisage the production, consumption, and childbearing and childrearing activities of a substantial portion of those of working age to be influenced by national barriers to the mobility of competitive productive people, but with a large proportion of consumption activity being 'internationalised' and 'consumption-preference-determined' through holiday and temporary-foreign-working residence in preferred foreign countries for those of working age and through retirement migration of those passing beyond the working age.

A conceptualisation more focused on the time-perspective and con-temporary stage of economic history or world economic development implicit in the formulation of the question posed for this paper and this session of the Conference would assume a world economy composed of countries with widely divergent levels of past accumulation of human and physical capital per head of population; widely different levels of technological or (more generally) productive efficiency, including the organisation of final and intermediate markets, distribution systems, and management and co-ordination; and widely different propensities to accumulate material, human, and informational and technological capital, as contrasted with the use of increase of potential productive efficiency in the expansion of population numbers. The international distribution of economic activity (disregarding for simplicity the differences between consumption and production activity generated by factors discussed earlier) would correspond to the distribution of population as modified by these factors, and the evolution of the distribution over time would be the outcome of the balance struck between the establishment of new positions of superiority achieved by further accumulation of human and material capital and the acquisition of improved technological knowledge, on the one hand, and the erosion of existing positions of superiority through the diffusion of technological knowledge and of propensities to accumulate human and material capital – a sort of generalised diffusion of superior technology – on the other.

At the 'advanced' end of the spectrum of countries ranked according to level of technological development, crucial determinants in this balancing process would be, first, the 'objective' factor of the availability and cost of acquiring and applying new technological knowledge and the uncertainty of the 'pay-off' from scientific pure and applied research and development. A second factor would be social attitudes and institutions favouring or impeding the pursuit of technology-improving activities, including the material and social rewards available to these seriously committed to, and the presumably smaller group successful at, such activities. A third factor would be social attitudes concerning the relative importance of improving material consumption, and of using increased productive efficiency either to reduce the proportion of time devoted to work as distinct from non-work activities, or to provide incomes and consumption to the non-productive population at the expense of the economically active population – alternatively expressed, the relative emphasis on 'quality of life' as opposed to quantity of consumption, or an redistribution of income as opposed to production of income, emphasis which could be roughly related objectively to the relative size of the government sector and the progressivity of the tax system, and the inter-income-group and inter-age-group redistributive effects of the government's expenditures and transfer payments. Perhaps the strongest force likely to promote a more equal (more accurately, more proportional to population) distribution of economic activity among nations – as well as changes in the identity and geographical location of the nations currently occupying positions of technological leadership in world economic activity – is the strong trend in the European and European-orientated advanced countries – especially the English-speaking ones – towards the general belief that growth has received too much emphasis by comparison with 'quality of life', and the not necessarily correlative tendency towards expansion of the non-productive role of the government and the 'public sector'.

At the other end of the spectrum, that of the less-developed countries, the key factor is obviously population behaviour, or the relative importance attached to improvement of average consumption as opposed to supporting an expanding population at a constant (sometimes even falling) standard of living. There is a possible analytical pitfall to be avoided here, however, both alternatives still raise the aggregate of economic activity in the expanding nation, though with different effects on the detailed composition of economic activity, so that for the choice to affect the distribution of aggregate activity it must involve a difference — presumably on the side of population limitation — in the propensities to accumulate material and human capital and raise the level of technical knowledge. Aside from this fundamental factor of population behaviour — fundamental at least once considerations of equality between nations or between citizens of different nations are introduced — social and organisational factors similar to those discussed in connection with the advanced nations apply. In particular, despite the rhetoric of 'development' reiterated by their political leaders, the social philosophies and the conceptions of the role and importance of government in the less-developed countries may either encourage or impede the process of 'catching up' with the more-developed countries through technological emulation, imitation, and application, and through the personal accumulation of material and human capital. In particular, just as one can observe among the current group of advanced countries significant differences in the relative emphasis placed on 'growth' versus 'equality', so one can observe among the less-developed countries significant differences in the relative emphasis placed on 'modernisation' and on the preservation of traditional social values, including preservation of the dominating positions and power of traditional social elites.

In conclusion, this very short and very general paper has attempted to sketch an approach to the question posed for this session which is not confined to the comparative static and microeconomic equilibrium framework suggested by the question as originally formulated. As already mentioned, the nation-state is itself a transient mode of human socio-political organisation, a mode whose basic character has itself evolved rapidly from what it was in the (roughly half a century past) interwar period during which the broad outlines of contemporary international trade theory were laid out by Bertil Ohlin and his contemporaries and successors. More important, technological levels, and differences in them, and changes in the differences, can no longer be taken as exogenous and exogenously changeable, from the viewpoint of international trade theory, in the same way as differences in comparative labour costs were taken in the Ricardian theory of comparative cost, and subsequently differences in national endowments of factors in the Heckscher-Ohlin-Samuelson model of international trade.[13]

Technology is a form of capital, and its availability alterable by investment. Consequently, satisfactory analysis of it must treat it in terms of the costs and returns of this kind of investment, and more broadly in terms of social and national-cultural encouragement or discouragement of this form of investment and of investment in general.

NOTES

[1] J. R. Hicks, 'An Inaugural Lecture', *Oxford Economic Papers*, N.S. Vol. 5 (1953): No. 2, pp. 117–35.

[2] Jacob Frenkel and Harry G. Johnson (eds.), *The Monetary Approach to the Balance of Payments* (London: Allen and Unwin, and Toronto: University of Toronto Press, 1976).

[3] For a bibliography of this work, see Harry G. Johnson, *Money, Trade and Economic Growth* (London: Allen and Unwin, 1962), pp. 99–103.

[4] Raymond Vernon, 'International Investment and International Trade in the Product Cycle', *Quarterly Journal of Economics*, 80 (1966): 2, pp. 190–207; (ed.), *The Technology Factor in International Trade* (National Bureau of Economic Research, New York and London: Columbia University Press, 1970).

[5] See for example C. P. Kindleberger (ed.), *The International Corporation* (Cambridge, Mass. and London: The M.I.T. Press, 1970).

[6] See for example Harry G. Johnson, 'Some Economic Aspects of Brain Drain', *Pakistan Development Review*, Vol. 7. No. 3 (Autumn, 1967), pp. 379–411, and abridged in Walter Adams (ed.), *The Brain Drain* (New York: Macmillan, 1968), pp. 69–91.

[7] For an attempt to put this work into perspective for a new approach to trade theory, see Harry G. Johnson, *Comparative Cost and Commercial Policy Theory for a Developing World Economy* (The Wicksell Lectures, 1968, Stockholm: Almqvist and Wiksell, 1968). For a non-technical survey of various economic aspects of technology, see Harry G. Johnson, *Technology and Economic Interdependence* (London: Macmillan, 1975).

[8] An important earlier contribution to this approach, in the field of economic development, is T. W. Schultz, *Transforming Traditional Agriculture* (New Haven, London: Yale University Press, 1964).

[9] While medieval history is marked by a very slow but noticeable improvement in the technology of agricultural production, the crucial stage ignored here is the 'agricultural revolution' that created the food surplus that made the 'industrial revolution' possible.

[10] See Harry G. Johnson, 'The Efficiency and Welfare Implications of the International Corporation', in C. P. Kindleberger, *op. cit.*, chapter 2, pp. 35–56; reprinted in I. A. MacDougall and R. H. Snape (eds), *Studies in International Economics: Monash Conference Papers* (Amsterdam: North Holland, 1970), as chapter 6, pp. 83–103. See also Harry G. Johnson, 'A New View of the Infant Industry Argument', chapter 7, pp. 105–20 in MacDougall and Snape, *op. cit.*

[11] For an early comparative statics approach on these lines, see Harry G. Johnson, 'Economic Expansion and International Trade', *The Manchester School*, Vol. 23 (May, 1955), pp. 95–112. Work on dynamic equilibrium-growth models of international trade began with the classic article by H. Oniki and H. Uzawa, 'Patterns of Trade and investment in a

Dynamic Model of International Trade', *Review of Economic Studies*, 32 (1965): 1, pp. 15—38. An early effort along 'Harrodian' lines was Harry G. Johnson, 'Equilibrium Growth in an International Economy', *Canadian Journal of Economics and Political Science*, Vol. 19 (November, 1953), pp. 478—500; reprinted in Harry G. Johnson, *International Trade and Economic Growth* (London: Allen and Unwin, 1958). See also Harry G. Johnson, 'A Formal Analysis of some Brinley Thomas Problems concerning the International Migration of Capital and Labour', *Osaka Economic Economic Papers*, 25 (1975): 1, pp. 24—36.

[12] This is the so-called 'guest labour problem', which has recently been the subject of theoretical investigation by Melvyn B. Krauss and others. Bela Belassa has pointed out in discussion that 'brain drain' is characteristic of English-speaking countries and 'guest labour' of Continental European countries, the difference presumably being accounted for by differences in the basic concept of 'citizenship'.

[13] For further discussion of this point, see Harry G. Johnson, 'Technological Change and Comparative Advantage: an Advanced Country's Viewpoint', *Journal of World Trade Law*, Vol. 9, No. 1 (January/February, 1975), pp. 1—14.

Comment
Sune Carlson

In the opening statement to our symposium, Bertil Ohlin asked us to broaden our interests beyond the customary 2 x 2 x 2 models. I think he got his wish. At the end of yesterday's session Kjeld Philip brought us far away into the domains of public finance. Today Harry Johnson widens the horizon towards archaeology and futurology.

In his 'macroeconomic' approach to the problem of international allocation of economic activity, Harry Johnson starts with an analysis of a post-nomad society in which the distribution of this activity around the globe is determined mainly by the availability of agricultural land. There are also restrictions caused by climatic conditions. As an act of politeness to the host country of this symposium, he also includes the areas where the human species can survive only with great difficulty, and in addition to agriculture he includes warfare as an economic activity. During the period he speaks about — which must be the time of the Vikings — Swedish imports meant loot from successful plundering in the East and West, an activity which for nearly a thousand years was to enrich our castles and museums with art treasures.

Since, like Harold Brookfield, I believe that an understanding of the present phase of a dynamic process — and technological change is certainly a dynamic process — presupposes an understanding of the past, I am rather fond of this part of Harry Johnson's paper. It is imaginative, stimulating and beautifully written. If it had been delivered not yesterday but a hundred years ago, it could have been set to music by Richard Wagner.

After a second part relating to our present time, which I shall return to soon, Johnson proceeds with an analysis of 'a sort of post-national state' with highly advanced technology giving people plenty of leisure time, which they can spend in the most pleasant parts of the earth. As an empiricist I am not particularly attracted by this kind of speculation. If I should live to see anything like the development Johnson talks about, I should probably be several hundred years old and so senile that I wouldn't notice if he had been right or not.

But let me return to the part of Harry Johnson's paper which deals with the present allocation of economic activity. One of the factors that determines this allocation, he says, is the differences in technological levels between various regions of the globe. These differences also give rise to international trade, what Haberler calls 'technology gap trade'. Thus, trade in technology-intensive products is one way by which technology is transferred and one of the means by which the differences between the technology levels become equalised. There is also a trade in technological knowledge *per se*, independent of the commodity trade, which gives rise to special income streams *i* Johnson treats technology as a kind of capital, the value of which is determined by the discounted income that it generates. The difficulty is, of course, to separate this kind of capital from human capital in general.

I am in agreement with all this. However, I want to extend the analysis to the microlevel, which might seem pedestrian, but which gives me a chance to take up the problem of technological uncertainty — a subject which has not been adequately considered in our deliberations.

In order to show what the problem of technological change looks like from the viewpoint of the individual firm, let me start with a production function of the type

$$O = f(\tau, A^{\alpha}, B^{\beta}, C^{\gamma}, \dots).$$

O is the output, which in the highly industrialised society consists both of hardware and software. $A, B, C, \dots$ are inputs of intermediate products, machines, staff, etc. The factor τ represents the product knowledge required in order to produce and market the hardware—software combination in question, and the exponents $\alpha, \beta, \gamma, \dots$ indicate the process knowledge needed for the appropriate use of the various inputs. In order to save time I shall limit my analysis to the uncertainty aspects of a change of the process technology, for example the substitution of the factor A and the process knowledge α by A' and α'.

The introduction of a new process technology is associated with a series of uncertainties. Firstly, the firm has no previous experience of how the factor A' behaves in the actual production process. Every input factor has a certain 'use-uncertainty', and the less standardised the factor is, the higher this use-uncertainty may be expected to be. Secondly, the firm does not know whether the required process knowledge α' really is available inside its own organisation. Process knowledge is generally more difficult to identify than product knowledge. While the latter is often embodied in drawings, laboratory minutes, etc., process knowledge is mostly accumulated in the heads of people. Since it often is transferred by word of mouth, it is hard to keep track of. Thirdly, the firm is uncertain as regards the technical aid it can get from the supplier of A'. Most hardware producers also furnish software of one kind or another. But to appraise a supplier's qualifications in this respect is even more difficult than to form an opinion about his future hardware deliveries. Sometimes technical services can also be bought independently, but since the requirements of process knowledge in most cases are hard to determine, and since its proprietorship is often uncertain, trade in process knowledge *per se* is rather rare.

Because of these uncertainties in connection with technological change, the selection of suppliers will be made more on the basis of personal trust than on objective technical criteria. The firm wants to feel confident in the supplier's will and ability to deliver the hardware and software needed. This generally means that an old supplier will be preferred to a new one, and a supplier from a region or a country with which the firm already has business connections will be preferred to suppliers from other regions or countries. As was mentioned in the discussions of Allan Pred's and Walter Isard's paper, the search area for new technology is generally very limited.

In their experimental study of the buying behaviour of purchasers in large and internationally oriented Swedish firms in the mechanical engineering industry, Håkansson and Wootz[1] have shown that the cultural distance between the buyer and seller influences both the selection of bidders and the actual choice of suppliers among the bidders. In the case of high-use-uncertainty goods the purchasers were particularly sensitive to distance, and often a supplier at a shorter distance was chosen even when his price was higher.

Thus, the presence of technological uncertainty affects the international allocation of economic activity by giving an extra advantage to already established industrial regions. Since it is easier and less risky to transmit technical knowledge inside an organisation than between organisations, it also favours the expansion of multinational firms. But it affects the software production much more than the hardware production.

My comments have been limited to process technology and the choice of input factors, such as machinery and intermediate products. But since this kind of goods represents a continuously increasing share of world trade, the circumstances which determine the location of their production become more and more important. Often their markets are highly oligopolistic, which means that the trade flows to a large extent are influenced by the behaviour of the individual firms. The purpose of this intervention has been to throw some light on these behaviour patterns. Assar Lindbeck made a plea yesterday that we should include the actions of the politicians in our analysis. Maybe the actions of the businessmen are just as important.

NOTE

[1] Håkansson, H. and Wootz, B., 'Supplier Selection in an International Environment — An Experimental Study', *Journal of Marketing Research*, Vol. XII (February, 1975).

Comment

Ronald W. Jones

Harry Johnson has provided a broad perspective from which to view the historical process whereby positions of comparative advantage are attained by the joint efforts of capital accumulation, checks on population growth, and investment in technological progress. In commenting upon his remarks I wish to focus more narrowly on two aspects of the interraction between technology and factor proportions.

First, consider how advances in technology are transmitted from one country to another. Many stories can be told. A new process developed in the advanced country may be disseminated by a multinational firm to its producing unit in the less-developed country. The transfer price charged may be closely dependent upon opportunities to minimise the joint tax burden reflected by different national tax structures. Alternatively, the new process may be described in sets of plans that can be sold directly to foreign firms. Patent agreements may ensure a stream of returns for the new technology. I step over these details in sketching the following possible pattern which may conform to some actual transfers of technology.

(a) I assume a continuous process whereby innovations are launched as a consequence of investment in the advanced country, characterised by a relative abundance of capital and high wages. A discrete view is provided in figure 1. The commodity in question is produced by combining labour and capital by the techniques shown generally by unit-isoquant (1), and shown particularly for the advanced country by point A, at which an iso-cost line representing A's wage/rental ratio is tangent to unit-isoquant (1). The result of innovative investment is a new set of techniques described by unit-isoquant (2). These techniques are not assumed to dominate the old for all factor prices — but they do represent an improvement at the advanced country's factor prices. It switches from point A on isoquant (1) to point B on isoquant (2).

(b) A less-advanced country has a lower wage rate and is using techniques shown by isoquant (1), but at a lower capital/labour ratio, shown by point C. At this relatively low wage rate the new techniques developed by the advanced country and shown by isoquant (2) have no cost-saving appeal.

(c) As time passes it is assumed that real wages are rising in both countries. In the advanced country innovative activity has continued, leading to the new isoquant (3). Although these new techniques would have been ignored by the advanced country at its old wage/rental ratio (shown by the slope of (2) at B), they are adopted by combining capital and labour in the proportions shown by point D on isoquant (3) once the

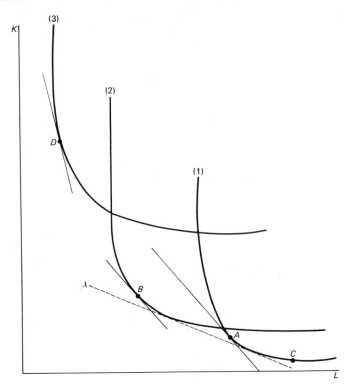

Figure 1

wage rate rises in the advanced country to the position shown by the slope of (3) at D.

  (d) Meanwhile, the wage rate has risen in the less-advanced country so that its factor-cost line is steeper than line λ. Once this happens, the technology represented by isoquant (2) becomes attractive to the less advanced country.

  (e) The process sketched above leaves out a potentially important ingredient — there is learning-by-doing, represented in the advanced country by a set of skilled labourers who were involved initially in developing the techniques shown by isoquant (2). These labourers as well possess skills acquired by on-the-job training which have resulted in isoquant (2) being drawn as close to the origin as it is. The point is that the skilled labour directly involved in the advanced country's experience in producing the commodity using techniques shown by (2) (especially near B) embody the knowledge that is exhibited by isoquant (2).

  (f) The techniques represented by isoquant (3) have been developed and learned by a younger set of skilled labour inputs in the advanced country. That is, each generation of skilled labour in the advanced country has made an investment in a particular set of techniques. A younger generation is associated with (3), an older one with (2).

(g) As wages in the less-developed country rise beyond the level shown by the λ-line in figure 1, this country demands the technology represented by isoquant (2), thus creating a demand for the advanced country's workers who were employed in using technology (2).

(h) The continuous improvement of technology in the advanced country, embodied in skills acquired by successive generations which are each linked to its own technology, and coupled with the possibility of international mobility of skilled labour, creates a setting in which the less-advanced country is continuingly demanding 'second-hand' technology from the advanced country.

(i) The impact of such labour mobility on the distribution of income may seem to run counter to the 'factor-price-equalisation' theme. In particular, older workers in the advanced country may find the local market for their obsolescing knowledge and skills collapsing as a newer generation is involved in learning skills associated with technique (3). But workers in the less-advanced country whose skills are linked to technique (1) could find their returns threatened by international mobility of the older generation of advanced country's workers skilled in (2)-technology as the general wage rate level in the less-advanced country rises beyond the λ-line. International labour mobility, as a vehicle for the transmission of technology, could prop up the returns to older skilled workers in the advanced country at the expense of the most skilled workers in the less advanced country.

(j) The younger generation of workers involved in the development and implementation of technique (3) in the advanced country have no international market at this point in the development process. The existence of a perpetual wage differential between countries coupled with the assumption of technology embodied in labour skills maintains a demand in less advanced countries for second-hand, cheaper technology plus labour now more suited to the lower-wage country's needs. With the passage of time the workers involved in isoquant (3)-technology will find their returns supported by the possibility of foreign markets for their skills.

This sketch of one possible sequence associated with the transmission mechanisms would need to be supplemented in many ways — for example, the considerations that lead to innovative investment in the advanced country, the underlying rationale for the continual advance in wage rates in both countries, etc. However, it does represent one possibility that captures the following basic elements: (i) new technology may be attractive to one country with high wages but not to another with lower wages; (ii) technology may be embodied in workers who have learned their skills by developing, using, and maintaining that technology; (iii) the trans-

mission of technology may hinge directly on the international mobility
of skilled labour, and (iv) such mobility may serve to prop up the returns
to older workers in the advanced country, whose skills are no longer
locally demanded, and keep suppressed the returns to younger workers
abroad who are skilled in even less advanced technologies.

This discussion has focused on the transfer of technology without
regarding the pattern of trade. To conclude these comments let me pick
up Johnson's theme that both technological differences and factor
endowment differences are involved in explaining trade patterns.[1]

Consider the case of a small country, whose technology need not
correspond to that of other countries. Suppose world prices are given —
beyond the control of this small country. The assumed lack of identical
technology with the rest of the world is reflected in figure 2's representation of a set of unit *value* isoquants for this small country. At world
prices the combinations of capital and labour (assumed to be the only
two factors) required to produce one dollar's worth of each of the five
commodities are shown by each unit-value isoquant. The doubling of any

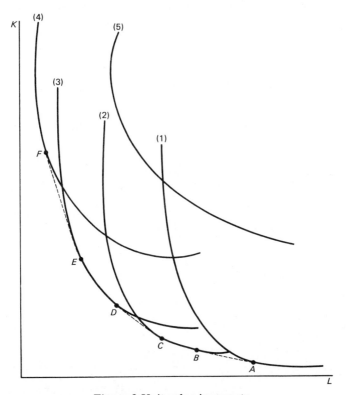

Figure 2 Unit-value isoquants

commodity price would contract its unit-value isoquant half-way to the origin.

A comparison of this country's technology with that in the rest of the world (as captured by world prices) reveals that commodity (5)'s production could not be supported locally. The unit value isoquant for commodity (5) lies everywhere above the convex hull of commodities (1)–(4). For commodity (5) there is a decided technological gap, quite independent of the small country's endowment proportions.

The pattern of production in this small country depends on its capital/labour endowment ratio. If this should intersect unit-value isoquant (3) between E and D, the country would specialise completely in commodity (3), and its wage/rental ratio would be shown by the slope of the commodity (3)-isoquant. Alternatively, if the factor endowment ray should intersect segment FE, the country would be incompletely specialised in producing both commodities (3) and (4). Thus, the pattern of production, and the associated distribution of income, depends on the economy's capital/labour ratio. This is made more explicit in figure 3. The dotted curves reflect only the home country's technology. The solid broken

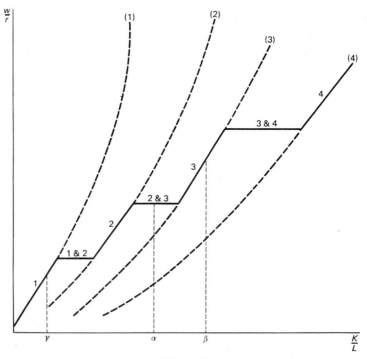

Figure 3

curve identifies the production pattern that is chosen by this small country facing given world prices. This pattern depends upon its factor proportions, as does its factor prices.

This model incorporates the basic Heckscher-Ohlin structure with two productive factors. But by not limiting the analysis to two commodities, and by not assuming identical technologies with the rest of the world, a richer set of conclusions emerges than in the 2 x 2 x 2 model. Specifically:

(a) Some commodities are never produced. The country is technologically inferior in producing commodity (5).

(b) The country may be completely specialised even though its factor endowment proportions are not 'extreme'. If β represents the country's capital/labour endowment proportions it produces only commodity (3). If its capital/labour ratio were higher, it could *also* produce commodity (4). Alternatively, a lower capital/labour endowment ratio (for example at α) could lead to production of commodity (2) as well as (3).

(c) A higher capital/labour ratio leads generally to a higher wage/rental ratio. But this relationship is interrupted at those endowment proportions at which the country is incompletely specialised. This is the factor-price-equalisation zone.

The role of factor endowments in affecting production and trade patterns if technology is assumed comparable can be analysed *not* by having the whole world share the same technology and climatic conditions, but by introducing *another* small country, identical to this one in technology, but differing in factor endowments. Let the original home country's endowment proportion in figure 3 be denoted by α. Then the other small country might:

(a) Have its factor prices equalised by trade (at world prices) if its endowment is near that of the home country.

(b) Have its factor prices different despite the equivalence of its technology if its endowment is sufficiently different. If the foreign capital/labour ratio is shown by γ, this lower capital/labour ratio is matched by a lower wage/rental ratio and a completely different pattern of production.

(c) Produce some commodity in common with the home country — for example commodity (3) if its endowment ratio is shown by β — and yet have different factor prices. Let me stress this point, since the factor-price-equalisation theorem in my opinion serves as a strong stumbling block in the way of accepting Heckscher-Ohlin theory. If the home country has endowment ratio α, and the other country with similar technical knowledge has ratio β, then the foreign country actually adopts different techniques in producing commodity (3), *because* its wage/rental ratio is higher, *because* its capital/labour ratio is higher. Differences in factor endowment proportions can as easily explain why actual techniques adopted by various countries differ — even if they read the same technological blueprints — as they can explain why they might be the same. Heckscher-Ohlin theory explains both why factor prices can be equalised by trade if endowments are fairly similar and why factor prices may not be equalised because endowments are sufficiently *dis*similar even though technological knowledge may be comparable. The two-commodity limitation typical of most textbook presentations (although not of Ohlin's pioneering work) tends to hide this point.

(d) Note how a model with many commodities helps to emphasise how trade offers a nation the possibility of producing many *fewer* commodities than it consumes. Furthermore, a typical country imports commodities that are both *more* capital-intensive and *less* capital-intensive than the commodities it exports. If the home country's capital/labour endowment ratio is α in figure *3*, it may export (2), or (3), or both. But if its consumption pattern is broadly based it will import (1), (4), and (5) (whose factor proportions are similar to (2) and (3)).

For my concluding remark I return to figure 2. The unit-value isoquants drawn there assume given world prices and given technology. Leave world prices alone, but pick up Johnson's point of having technical improvement involve at least some investment expenditure. The home country is producing commodity (3) with a capital/labour ratio shown between E and D. In which other commodities might to wish to invest resources in an attempt to improve technology? There is an answer — based on Heckscher-Ohlin factor-proportions theory. The commodities that are closest in capital/labour ratios to the one(s) produced are the most likely candidates for investment. The Heckscher-Ohlin emphasis on factor proportions not only helps explain what nations actually produce, but also what other commodities are the best candidates for being produced if investment in technology is forthcoming.

NOTES

[1] The following analysis is based on chapter 7 of the revised edition of Caves, R. E. and Jones, R. W., *World Trade and Payments* (Little, Brown, 1977).

Summary of the Discussion

The discussion suggested several directions in which to develop a theory of long-run technical progress as sketched by Harry Johnson in the paper. Historical as well as contemporary examples were given to illustrate the importance of technical breakthroughs for the global location of economic activity. Attention was given to the effects of warfare and of the military sector in developing new technology, and to nations as social groups initiating major technical innovations. Governmental attempts to close technological 'gaps' and the practice of applying Western technologies in LDCs were emphasised. The discussion also treated the interaction between technological change, geographic factor movements and migration policies. Finally, it was argued that the effects on trade patterns of economies of scale should be analysed. This session was chaired by *Michael Michaely*.

Jagdish Bhagwati noted the historical sweep of Johnson's paper. It stretched from a distant past in which nomads moved by foot or by camel to a future in which, like today's economists, they 'jet-setted' between different places, producing in one place — or even in two, like Johnson — consuming in another and possibly retiring in a third! This was essentially a 'nomad model' of the world economy.

Bhagwati suggested that this 'high-level' treatment of the links between technology and society might be illustrated by some historical breakthroughs in technology and he presented the invention of the stirrup as an example of a new technology causing systemic change in society.[1]

Bhagwati suggested that the paper might also refer to how contemporary technological change could radically alter international relations. For instance, the emergence of new technologies to exploit the resources of the oceans and of the seabed beyond existing national jurisdictions had provided fresh impetus to the less developed countries' demands for the new international economic order: by holding up agreement on the Law of the Sea, they could influence the entire set of negotiations concerning the evolution of new international rules of the game on many fronts. This was an excellent example of how technological change could have 'big' institutional effects.

Bhagwati turned finally to the question of the diffusion of new technology between countries. The growth of new technology created concepts such as 'technology gap' which he noted suggested to governments that it was desirable to 'catch up'. Many restrictions on trade and multinationals could be traced to this attempt. The resulting 'hewers-of-wood, drawers-of-water' attitude towards technological change was common for governments in many 'medium-level' countries such as France, as well as in many less developed countries. He therefore felt that the dissemination and use of technology followed such considerations rather than the ingenious sequences that neoclassical trade theorists such as Jones could construct. The role of political factors in creation and utilisation of technology was, of course, most evident for the Soviet Union where modern econometric research had shown that technical change in heavy industry has been faster than in light industry.

Observing that the Soviet emphasis on heavy industry was basically military in origin, *Harry Johnson* suggested that the role of warfare was more basic than the role of government in inducing technological change. Economic history testifies to the contribution of war in developing new techniques, for instance, methods involving mass production and interchangeable parts. Therefore he feared it would be a great mistake to neglect the influence of war on economic growth.

Sune Carlson suggested that war was just as important for the development of human capital as for the development of technology. The military had been extremely effective in training the labour force. In some countries, for instance Brazil, the army universities supplied the only really good technical education.

Charles Kindleberger noted that Johnson in his paper had questioned the relevance of the nation state as the basic unit of social organisation and for economic analysis. Kindleberger recalled Graham's words that trade is conducted between firms and individuals and not between nations. However, he felt that nations were important to the extent that policies were formulated on the national level. Moreover, beyond questions of national policies, societies behave in unified ways, sometimes getting bursts of energy, sometimes slowing down. The major inventions of the industrial revolution all occurred within a period of ten years. Such a burst of activity cannot be explained on technological, economic, or political grounds, but must be the result of social interactions between groups of people. He asked how we can explain that the centre of innovating civilisation moves from sixteenth-century Venice to seventeenth- and eighteenth-century Holland and nineteenth-century Britain. Modelling techniques are of little help in explaining that part of the social sciences that Braudel calls civilisation.[2]

Bela Balassa questioned the relevance of the 'common assumption' accepted by Johnson (p. 319) that capital and technology but not labour were internationally mobile. He believed that while capital may have been more mobile than labour for the Anglo-Saxon countries where capital exports had been very important, this was not generally true for countries in continental Europe. He suggested a similar bias in the general statement that skilled labour tended to move internationally more than unskilled. This might be true for India due to an antidevelopment bias in its policy and for Anglo-Saxon countries but not for continental Europe. Balassa noted that foreign unskilled labourers were more common in continental

Europe than in Anglo-Saxon countries. The term 'guest worker' was misleading as it suggested a temporary phenomenon. While individual workers
may be temporary visitors on the host country's labour market, the stock
of foreign workers could be a permanent phenomenon and of considerable
magnitude even in a recession. Noting that a country could choose between
immigration and imports of labour-intensive commodities, he believed
that it was important to study why there is more immigration and less
imports in Europe than in the U.S.A. Incentives matter and both natural
and state-made factors may explain the difference.

While it was common to assume that between nation states, capital
was more mobile than labour, *Harry Richardson* emphasised that within
countries and especially within less developed countries, labour was more
mobile than capital. He suggested one outcome of this asymmetry.
Capital from developing countries is either directly invested in resource
regions in less developed countries where it has little impact on employment, or, through the financial hierarchy, in the large primate cities there.
Domestic labour flows towards these cities but the foreign technology fails
to employ the labour force. He considered this concentration of foreign
capital and domestic labour in large cities in less developed countries to be
unsatisfactory. Johnson had suggested some form of population control as
a possible solution. Richardson recommended as complementary strategies
the design of labour-intensive technologies to absorb the urban unemployed
and the formulation of policies to dispense population.

Tibor Scitovsky commented on another asymmetry: the tendency of
economists, scientists and engineers alike to approach their various
problems much more often from the developed than from the developing
countries' point of view. That was understandable in professionals from
the developed countries; but he discerned the same bias even in the LDCs
own professionals. He attributed that partly to these having been too
strongly imbued with the built-in biases of the Western education they
received or their own educational institutions copied, and partly to the
LDCs' often distorted price structure, which, besides promoting
industrialisation, also gives the illusion of factor proportions typical of
an already industrialised society.

Hollis Chenery felt that an important problem of technology was
neglected in this discussion of technological change. It was clear, he said,
that because of economies of scale, large countries specialised differently
in trade than smaller ones, even when the latter become richer. He
suggested that because of its large economy, India may follow the
Brazilian path and export steel, motor cars and other products of heavy
industry at much lower levels of income and capital than smaller countries.
A poor small country looking at the technological cookbook available
from the advanced countries has to rule out three quarters of the recipes
because they require production on a scale much larger than the domestic
market allows. The influence of economies of scale on trade patterns

should be more systematically studied in trade theory, he felt.

Johnson closed the discussion. Bhagwati had referred to the 'hewers-of-wood and drawers-of-water' attitude to technology. Johnson suggested that this phrase, often used by Canadians, called attention to the 'ceremonial' or political element in scientific research and development. Governments' interest in scientific research was often due to a desire to have their own nationals participate 'at the highest level in international discussions'. He suggested that the present group might be an example of that. Many countries did not consider themselves to be in the modern world until they could send an economist to an international conference!

Kindleberger had emphasised cultural periods and Johnson referred to studies on the history of the potato, relating breakthroughs in cultivation to breakthroughs in diet. Although increases in the average size of individuals affect development, he feared that a self-defeating aspect might be involved: bigger people eat more, but the number of intelligences around is still the same!

Answering Balassa, Johnson suggested an explanation of the different attitudes to immigration in the Anglo-Saxon world on the one hand and in continental Europe on the other. The Anglo-Saxon principle was that once you let someone in, he is in to stay, while the Europeans consider it all right to let a man in for a limited period of time and then throw him out again. As permanent residents and retirees, immigrants must be provided with medical care and other social services, which makes them less profitable to the host country. The practice of various African countries of sending guest workers from villages to the mines is similar. It has the interesting result of reinforcing the home country's control over individuals' retirement opportunities.

Johnson agreed with Richardson that population dispersal policies alone did not make much sense. In his experience governments caused agglomerations which they themselves deemed undesirable. They worried about regional problems and tried to disperse population while setting up systems that necessitated the presence of firms in the capital to obtain government licences necessary for production. Efforts by policy makers to decentralise were to some extent offset by the centralising effects of the policy makers themselves in the capital. One hundred years of effort to disperse population in England had not prevented the growth of London. As an undergraduate at Cambridge, Johnson had read many reports on the need to disperse population, and Lawrence Klein, he remembered, had once prepared for the U.S. government a similar report on population dispersal in the event of an atomic war. Moreover, the development of technology which permitted the dispersion of population was itself expensive.

In reply to Chenery, Johnson emphasised that economies of scale were only a matter of location of activity and did not necessarily affect consumption levels differentially. Unless a monopoly captures the benefits,

others will participate in them. Thus everybody may benefit from
travelling by Concorde except the British and French taxpayer!

NOTES

¹ He referred to Lynn White, *Medieval Technology and Social Change*
(Oxford, 1962), which contained an interesting essay on how attempts to
raise a cavalry following this invention led to the growth of feudalism.
² See Fernand Braudel, *The Mediterranean and the Mediterranean
World in the Age of Philip II*, New York, Harper (translated from the revised
French edition of 1966), Vol. II (1975).

10 Changes in Labour Quality and their Implications for the Analysis of Questions in International Trade*

Jagdish N. Bhagwati

I have been asked to review the 'effects of changes in the quality of factors of production, with special reference to changes in labour quality, for example through learning by doing'. Such a review, however, poses special difficulties, as the only substantial analytical and empirical literature in the area of labour quality and its interaction with the questions of international economics relates to the numerous contributions on the effect of skills, R and D, knowhow and related aspects of labour and technical change on the pattern of trade. However, this area has not only been extensively reviewed by me earlier;[1] it is also precisely the subject matter of Gottfried Haberler's paper at this Conference and will doubtless be the focal point of his discussants' remarks.[2]

I have therefore deliberately decided to take a much wider approach to my subject and rather to develop a systematic classification of the effects of labour quality change on trade, distinguishing between the 'demand' and the 'supply' aspects in the main. Using this primary classification, I proceed then to sketch in a number of possible interactions between labour quality change and international trade, emphasising the scope for future theoretical model-building of interest while also drawing together the existing theoretical and empirical work, however meagre, on these possible interactions.

I make no apologies for allocating much of my limited space to indicating potential theoretical models and questions: the focus of the Conference would seem to me to be not merely to review existing work, but also to indicate the general directions in which the analysis of trade theorists can and indeed needs to be extended. I should also state that I have deliberately not confined my analysis exclusively to positive questions. For, as will be evident below, labour quality change inevitably raises welfare questions that should be noted in any sophisticated analysis

*I have profited from the comments of Ragnar Bentzel, Ronald Jones and Robert Solow. Thanks are due to Robert Dohner for research assistance and for partial financial support to the National Science Foundation, Grant No. SOC74-13210.

of the questions at hand; at the same time, by influencing policy, such welfare questions and answers thereto affect, in turn, the positive analysis to which I must principally address myself.

I. 'DEMAND' ASPECTS OF LABOUR QUALITY CHANGE

At the outset, I should note that the subject of my assignment would be too narrow if it were to be construed as referring exclusively to the effects of labour quality change purely from the side of supply. For, what distinguishes labour from other factors, and this despite Chicago's exclusivist preference for the concept of human capital, is precisely the fact that changes in labour quality, with or without investment expenditures, are not symmetric with changes in the quality of capital as, for example, analysed through vintage capital goods models. Thus, labour is not merely a factor of production; it is also the object of economic satisfaction, the recipient of utility. Hence, changes in the quality of labour immediately imply two things: (a) they can, and generally will, affect equilibrium patterns of production and trade, not merely through their effects on the supply side of our general-equilibrium models, but also through possible changes in the demand patterns as the perceptions and tastes of labour, *qua* consumer, change simultaneously; (b) moreover, the qualitative changes of labour, *qua* consumer, raise difficult questions for welfare analysis. As Marshall (1962, p. 79) said long ago, in relation to the law of diminishing marginal utility

> There is, however, an implicit condition in this law which should be made clear. It is that we do not suppose time to be allowed for any alteration in the character or tastes of the man himself. It is, therefore, no exception to the law that the more good music a man hears, the stronger is his taste for it likely to become; that avarice and ambition are often insatiable; or that the virtue of cleanliness and the vice of drunkenness alike grow on what they feed upon. For in such cases our observations range over some period of time; and the man is not the same at the beginning as at the end of it.

Clearly, similar difficulties afflict welfare analysis when tastes change with labour-quality change so that 'man is not the same at the beginning as at the end' of the process of change. While some limited progress towards analysing the welfare implications of changing tastes has been made, as in Weizsacker's (1971) interesting paper on the endogenous change of tastes, this is still virgin territory; and fortunately, the lack of systematic trade-theoretic analysis of this problem in welfare economics may be only noted but not regretted (except intellectually) since the conference specifically precludes extended discussion of welfare questions.

Turning rather to the former question then regarding the 'positive' effects of labour quality change, as operating through consequent demand changes, we can see that these changes may be regarded as exogenous or as endogenous to the policy changes that international trade theory often analyses. Thus, for example, the classic statement by John Stuart Mill (1848) considers the effects of labour quality change as brought about by the opening of trade

> . . . a people may be in a quiescent, indolent, uncultivated state, with all their tastes either fully satisfied or entirely undeveloped, and they may fail to put forth the whole of their productive energies for want of any sufficient object of desire. The opening of a foreign trade, by making them acquainted with new objects, or tempting them by the easier acquisition of things which they had not previously thought attainable, sometimes works a sort of industrial revolution in a country whose resources were previously undeveloped for want of energy and ambition in the people: inducing those who were satisfied with scanty comforts and little work, to work harder for the gratification of their new tastes, and even to save, and accumulate capital, for the still more complete satisfaction of those tastes.

It is easy for a theorist to think of possible models of trade and growth where the consequences of such an endogenous shift in the average propensity to save can be analysed; and even a cursory acquaintance with such literature would show that the long-term effects on equilibrium solutions to output, production and trade patterns, etc., will critically depend on the model being utilised.[3] Perhaps the neatest model which analyses long-term comparative advantage, and the effect thereon of shifts in the propensity to save, is that of Findlay (1973). In this model, the Oniki-Uzawa (1965) two-sector model is modified to allow for a non-traded good which is the capital good, and the small-country assumption is extended to two tradeables in the usual manner. It is, of course, clear that a model with this structure will have its domestic (relative) price of the capital good determined once the prices of the tradeables are specified, and that the resource allocation will reflect the demand structure in the model (since the supply of the non-traded good must be satisfied from domestic production alone). In the context of this model, Findlay manages to extend the Heckscher-Ohlin theory to a long-term concept of comparative advantage, showing that when the system behaves in a stable manner such that the rate of capital accumulation converges to the pre-specified rate of growth of the labour force, the associated capital-labour 'endowment' ratio comparison between two countries [with identical production functions and demand patterns (including of course the savings ratios)] will determine the pattern of trade in the two tradeables exactly as predicted by the Heckscher-Ohlin theory: in other words, that the capital-abundant country (in the physical endowment sense) will export the capital-intensive good and import the labour-intensive good. Findlay also shows that the effect of a rise in the savings ratio, in the short run, may well be to reverse the Heckscher-Ohlin pattern of trade because the effect of the increased production of the capital good may well be to require a corresponding shift in the relative production of the two tradeables such that the given *overall* capital—labour endowment ratio remains unchanged (as required in the short run); but that, in the long run, the rise in savings ratio will have restored, through capital accumulation, the Heckscher-Ohlin pattern of trade. Needless to say, the long run may not be realised before the quality of the labour force changes again, disturbing the system away again from the Heckscher-Ohlin pattern of trade.

Note that the Mill argument, at its most essential level, raises welfare questions of the kind that we raised but set aside earlier. It also leads naturally to more familiar welfare analytics: for example one could readily examine the welfare impact of an induced rise in the savings propensity in the framework of a standard intertemporal-utility model. Moreover, it is worth noting the essentially 'benign' view that Mill seems to hold of the impact of trade *via* the resulting increase in the savings propensity of an 'improved' population, and is even more manifest in his other, classic remark

> It is hardly possible to overrate the value in the present low state of human improvement, of placing human beings in contact with persons dissimilar to themselves, and with modes of thought and action unlike those with which they are familiar . . . Such communication has always been and is peculiarly in the present age, one of the primary sources of progress.

It is necessary, therefore, to contrast Mill's 'benign impact' view with that of recent analysts from the developing countries who take a 'malign impact' view of trade with the developed countries. Thus, in the classic description of the process as disintegration of the national economy through integration into the world economy, Oswaldo Sunkel (1972) has focused rather on the *deleterious* effects of international contacts with 'unequal partners': among these would be the Hirschman-type (1969) inhibiting effect of multinational corporations on the emergence of domestic entrepreneurship (an effect that is certainly describable as the effective prevention of change in the quality of the population in a direction required for rapid, self-sustaining growth) as also the induced rise in salary levels for professional classes as these become more integrated into the highly professional markets abroad (an 'international emulation' effect analysed recently in Bhagwati and Hamada (1974), Rodriguez (1975), and McCulloch and Yellen (1976) in the literature on brain drain and taxation thereof).

Next, we may note that the comparative-static effects of shifts in tastes, whether exogenous or endogenous to some policy change, are readily incorporated into the standard trade-theoretic analysis in the class-room.[4] This is because, basically, the analysis involved is identical to the analysis of the transfer problem: in the latter, as in the former, one is essentially examining the impact, at constant terms of trade, of a demand disturbance on the excess demand for each good to derive the criterion for the terms of trade change. Thus, in the usual analysis of the $2 \times 2 \times 2$ model, it is trivially obvious to a trade theorist that: given stability, the terms of trade will worsen or improve according as the country with the taste change shifts its consumption pattern at the margin towards increased consumption of the importable or the exportable good. And it is equally obvious then that the analysis can be extended similarly to models involving non-traded goods, intermediates, etc., much as transfer-problem theory has recently been extended to such models: the parallels are too obvious, and the relevance of such analysis too limited to our present concerns, to do this here.[5]

Finally, recalling Bertil Ohlin's (1933, p. 85) remark that 'trade changes the *quality* of people, teaches them to consume new things and to use old things in new ways', it may well be that models of taste change that extend merely to shifts in propensity to save and in the spending pattern for existing goods are not enough; and that analytical models involving new goods are probably more pertinent to the question at hand. The role of new goods in international trade, of course, has been elevated to importance by several quasi-theoretical writings, starting from Linder's (1961) well-known shift of attention from the pattern to the volume of trade in manufactures, the subsequent highlighting of the importance of intra-industry trade by Grubel and Lloyd (1975), and Kravis' (1956) emphasis on the role of 'availability' in determining the U.S. trade pattern and the subsequent reworking of this notion as a critical ingredient of the so-called 'product cycle' model of foreign investment, and related empirical research. Unfortunately, a general-equilibrium, Lancaster-type analysis of a model with emerging, new goods is yet awaited:[6] and until that is done, a rigorous analysis of Mill's problem in such a framework cannot be undertaken.

II. 'SUPPLY' ASPECTS OF LABOUR QUALITY CHANGE

Shifting focus now to the 'supply' side of the problem of quality change in labour, I would like to distinguish among the following areas of analysis: (1) the effects of 'learning by doing' on the pattern of specialization in international trade; (2) the effects of skills formation, not related to learning externalities, on the trade pattern; and (3) the effects of trade on domestic allocation of resources when account is taken of adjustment costs resulting from redeployment of trained labour to other activities requiring different skills from those possessed, and the reverse impact of such adjustment costs on the pattern of feasible tariff reductions.

(1) LEARNING BY DOING

Treating the problem of 'learning by doing' as one involving externalities in the Arrow sense (1962), one sees immediately that the effect is to point to a market failure, where intervention to subsidise the industry that enjoys differentially greater learning by doing would be called for. Moreover, following the principles of first-best policy intervention worked out in Bhagwati and Ramaswami (1963) and Johnson (1965), the optimal intervention would be a subsidy to factor employment if the externality was associated with factor input (such as investment in Arrow's formulation) or to output if it was a function of production (as would appear to be the case from the highly speculative evidence for the airframe industry that is usually cited in support of the learning-by-doing hypothesis).

Thus, for example, in the analysis of learning by doing to trade theory, in its optimal policy intervention version, Bardhan (1970) constructs a model where the current output is a function, not merely of current inputs, but also of cumulated output in a Hicks-neutral way; and he concludes, as one would expect, that an optimum production subsidy is called for; and his dynamic analysis of the problem is addressed to defining the time-path of the optimal production subsidy so required.[7]

A similar, and inevitable focus on optimal policy intervention in the presence of learning-by-doing externality is to be found in the work of Kemp (1974). Kemp works with a two-period model and essentially imagines that the second-period outputs are a function of the first-period outputs, so that if producers are not able to forecast perfectly, there will be a case for policy intervention (with production tax-cum-subsidy à la Bhagwati-Ramaswami-Johnson) to maximise social utility over the two periods together. In spirit, this problem and its solution are analogous to Findlay's (1973, chapter 8) elegant analysis of optimal policy intervention when capital is putty in period 1 but congealed into clay for period 2.

While therefore the trade-theoretic analyses of learning by doing have naturally focused on the welfare effects of this form of externality, the 'positive' implications can obviously be worked out within identical models; and, for that matter, as with the question of the effect of increased propensity to save (discussed in section I), there are innumerable growth models into which the phenomenon of changing production functions as learning proceeds through doing can be incorporated in the usual manner. Rather than address myself to analysing such effects within an arbitrarily chosen growth model, I think it is more profitable to note that, as far as the pattern of international specialisation and trade is concerned, learning by doing is likely to reduce current comparative advantage by having the latecomers learn from doing.[8] At the same time, while production gains would occur from inevitable learning as produced output and hence experience cumulates over time, this 'primary gain' would tend to be accompanied by secondary gain as well: presumably, the latecomer, learning industry produces the country's importable and hence augmentation of production through learning by doing there would appear to be biased, even ultra-biased, in favour of the importable and hence, *ceteris paribus* and given stability, to improve the latecoming learner's terms of trade.[9] Moreover, if one considers that infant industry protection is typically granted for alleged learning-by-doing reasons to new manufacturing industries, the international allocation of resources is surely affected so as to make the distribution of manufacturing to the latecoming, 'underindustrialised' nations progressively more rapid and substantial than would otherwise have been the case.

A few remarks on the learning process at a much more general, macro-economic level may be in order. The great debate in the postwar world, on import-substituting *versus* export promoting or inward-looking *versus* outward-looking trade strategy, has centred on the foreign trade policies of the less developed countries (LDCs) and doubtless concerns the international allocation of economic activity. While this is not the occasion to enter into the optimality aspects of these rival trade strategies,[10] it is clear that the learning process has affected the degree of trade restrictionism in the LDCs in the following manner:

(a) many LDCs that, through the 1950s, had highly restrictive trade régimes, had 'learnt by undoing' and shifted to less restrictive, outward-looking trade régimes;

(b) among those that were to make the transition most rapidly were countries such as Taiwan and South Korea, suggesting that the influence of the Japanese example[11] (through both geographical affinity plus 'learning by indoctrination' (?) as a result of earlier occupations) may have played a major role in determining the attitudes of the leaders and policy-makers — doubtless an important part of the 'quality-of-labour' phenomenon if one correctly includes here the quality of the élite groups; and

(c) a few of the countries that have stuck excessively to overly restrictionist trade-and-payments régimes, as in India, have in turn élite groups who were tutored in socialist doctrines which teach one to prefer the iron fist to the invisible hand.[12]

Finally, I should like to draw attention to yet another 'learning' phenomenon which has considerable importance for both the positive and normative aspects of trade-theoretic questions. I have in mind the fact that the acquisition of skills and learning occurs as 'migrants', both unskilled and skilled (the latter constituting the so-called brain drain), move from countries of 'immigration' back to countries of 'emigration'. In short, the customary theoretical analyses of the effects of migrating labour have been undertaken on the assumption that migration is permanent whereas what one has now is 'to-and-fro' migration or, at minimum, the phenomenon of the 'return of the native'.

Now, the welfare-analytic implications of such 'to-and-fro' migration are quite serious. Thus, take the question: how is the group over which we consider the welfare impact of the 'to-and-fro' migration from the LDC of emigration to be defined? Now, if migration were permanent, so that the immigrant could be taken to have left the LDC and arrived in the DC on a forever basis, then it would make some sense to consider the question as to what has happened to 'LDC welfare' as identical to the question as to what has happened to the 'welfare of those left behind in the LDC'. However, with to-and-fro migration, it may be more sensible to regard the welfare of the 'migrants' *plus* the non-mobile nationals as constituting the relevant LDC population.[13] Once this is done, it is easy to see that the welfare-analytic formulation of the relevant questions in regard to the implications of the brain drain can change drastically. Thus, in the context of a theoretical analysis of the so-called Bhagwati brain drain tax proposal which recommends that a surtax, for developmental spending in LDCs, be imposed on incomes of the skilled LDC emigrants by DCs on the incomes earned by them in DC's of immigration,[4] Bhagwati and Hamada (1976) have used an Atkinson-type model of optimal linear income tax to show that the failure to extend the domestic income tax to earnings abroad (that is the incomes of the 'emigrants') creates a sub-optimal situation and that a fully optimal, equity-cum-efficiency solution requires that the linear income tax be extended to such incomes.

Again, getting away from the welfare to the positive aspects of this 'to-and-fro' migration, one can readily see numerous possibilities for theoretical investigation. Thus, in regard to the short run, one could argue that the effect of losing skilled manpower would be to reduce comparative advantage in the output (presumably manufactures as against agriculture, in the broad alternatives defined in popular debate) of the activity using the skilled labour intensively.[15] However, if the same labour will return, augmented by acquired skills, this will restore and even reinforce the earlier comparative advantage in producing the skill-intensive outputs.[16] There are obvious empirical examples and studies to support the construction and exploration of such models, as evidenced for example by the case of Chinese atomic energy work by Chinese scientists returning from employment at M.I.T., Caltech, etc., to their homeland and in recent studies of skill acquisition by Turkish and Yugoslav workers in Europe.

Furthermore, in determining the impact of to-and-fro migration on the pattern of trade and specialisation, one should not ignore the consumption effect that was discussed earlier. Returning migrants can be a force for changing consumption patterns, not merely through their own direct con-

sumption reflecting acquired tastes during residence abroad; they can also
act as catalysts for dissemination of such taste change in their countries of
origin and occasional return.[17]

Finally, in concluding this line of thought, I might add that the 'to-and-
fro' migration model suggests that it may be useful theoretically to
analyse the effects of modern migration in terms of the life-cycle earnings
model.

In conclusion, note yet another aspect of the brain drain and its impact
on factor endowments and the pattern of specialisation in production and
trade. Suppose that the brain drain manages to draw away not merely the
better-educated — as is implicit in the discriminatory immigration
restrictions of DCs that favour skilled, as against unskilled, immigration —
but *also* the more talented among this subgroup. At the non-normative
level, of course, this would imply, *ceteris paribus*, that the degree of
innovation, serendipity, etc., would decline, thus reinforcing again the
LDCs' comparative disadvantage in modern manufactures of the newer
vintage. Again, if one were to examine the welfare impact of such
'selective' emigration of the talented labour force, there might be no
special cause for worry. However, it is possible to argue that the LDCs
do not have perfect markets in rewarding such talented labour, and that
the highly talented workers get the same rewards as the less gifted because
the market either cannot discriminate between them or cannot reward
them differentially owing to market pricing restrictions (such as hiring
and salary policies). If then the foreign market *can* do this, by both
recognising and rewarding the more gifted differentially, then it is easy to
show of course that the brain drain would, *ceteris paribus*, be causing
harm to the non-migrant population.[18]

(2) SKILLS AND THE PATTERN OF TRADE

Shifting next to the related but more mundane issue of the effects of skills
on the pattern of trade, considerable amount of evidence has been turned
up in support of this line of reasoning. For reasons outlined at the beginning
of this paper, I will largely bypass this literature and merely not that

(a) The impetus for this inquiry came largely from the interaction of
Leontief's (1954) conjecture that U.S. labour was more efficient than
foreign labour with the doctrine of human capital, with its consequent
implication that the U.S. had comparative abundance in human *plus*
traditional capital.

(b) This has naturally led in turn to the more sophisticated view that
human and other capital are not perfect substitutes as implied by the
empirical procedure of adding together the estimated amounts thereof
(Joan Robinson duly disregarded), so that the effect on production

advantage will depend on the usual Hicksian complementarity and substitution relationships among more than two factors.

(c) Finally, since one is not really dealing with costless technical change, and there is usually no 'free lunch' in getting new technology, one also needs to examine the tradeoffs between utilising existing skills to produce new technology, to produce new skilled labour, and to produce current output. Again, obvious implications exist for both welfare and positive trade-theoretic analyses.

I have predicated my analysis above on the assumption that skills affect trade. However, trade can affect skills, R and D, etc. Two obvious possibilities need to be mentioned. First, the impact of MNCs on host populations may come in the shape of accelerated acquisition of skills: the frequent LDC policy of imposing 'indigenous quotas' on MNC hiring policies is to be traced to this presupposition (though paradoxically it may lead to adverse effects such as those noted at the outset of section I). Second, and more interesting, the imposition of a restrictive trade régime may stimulate R and D activity in import-substituting industries. Thus, research on R and D in modern Indian industries such as pharmaceuticals and chemicals has shown that the inability to count on continuing imports of raw materials and on renewal of patents has stimulated the growth of R and D cells whose job it is to analyse the possibilities of adapting processes to the use of locally available raw materials, for example.[19] In a world where profitability is made critically conditional on inventing such new technology, one gets essentially the Weizsäcker-Kennedy type phenomena of induced technical innovation.[20]

(3) SKILLS, LABOUR ADJUSTMENT PROBLEMS AND TARIFF CHANGE

Finally, let me turn to an interesting and important new area of analysis that has recently developed, both empirically and at a theoretical level, in regard to the labour adjustment costs of tariff change and their effect, in turn, on the process of tariff reductions (and hence, of course, on the international allocation of economic resources).

Empirically, the most interesting work in this area has been that of John Cheh who, in his dissertation at MIT and then in a valuable paper in the *Journal of International Economics* (1974) has taken the opportunity provided by the Kennedy Round tariff cuts, and exemptions to the 50 per cent across-the-board tariff cuts, to examine if the degree of exemptions from the tariff cut of 50 per cent is related to characteristics of the industries, such as the presence of old and unskilled workers.[21]

Cheh uses therefore 'proxies' of labour adjustment costs: for example old workers imply that displacement will be more costly, as the returns from retraining for newer jobs would be less and the losses from losing employment using the existing training would be more; similarly, unskilled workers may have more difficulty finding new jobs: the contraction of their current employment may not be offset by more jobs in the expanding export industries, for example, if the latter are more skill-intensive (as seems to be the case for the United States); and so on. For his dependent variables, Cheh uses both nominal and effective tariffs, and he also uses explicit and implicit tariffs, the latter implying the inclusion of nontariff barriers.[22] Cheh argues that he would expect changes in nominal tariff rates, rather than in effective tariff rates, to correlate with the labour adjustment proxies: and, this is what happens also to be the case.[23] Similarly, Cheh's results are better also when the non-tariff barriers are additionally taken into account.[24]

Cheh's work has recently been reproduced by James Reidel (1976) for tariff concessions in the Kennedy Round in West Germany, with rather better results also for protective changes that *include* the changes in non-tariff barriers. Furthermore, using *direct* adjustment cost estimates, by working with estimated time of displacement and next-best employment possibilities, Bale (1976), in a subsequent contribution, has shown that, for a subset of the industries in Cheh, for which Bale could make such estimates, there is a nice correlation between the degree of exemptions granted and the estimated displacement costs.[25]

If, therefore, this line of empirical investigation is accurate, then it follows that the effect of skills, and lack thereof, and the relative costs and returns on acquisition of new skills at different ages in the life-cycle, will affect the possibility of effecting tariff changes and hence the eventual outcome on the international division of labour.

Turning finally to the theoretical analysis of such adjustment costs, there are again two basic lines of thought in trade-theoretic literature on this question: (a) the 'positive' approach consists in constructing models that distinguish between the 'short-run' and the 'long-run' impact of tariff change, with the short run being characterised by some form of factor rigidity that the long run escapes; and (b) the welfare approach extends the theory of optimal policy intervention to cases where adjustment costs are present.

In reviewing both these types of contributions, it is necessary to distinguish among the following ways in which the adjustment problems may be modelled. Principally, one could assume that factors are immobile, so that the production gain from reallocation of resources in response to freer trade, for example, is lost. Or one could assume that factor prices are inflexible, while factors are mobile, in which case one could have unemployment of the factor whose reward is inflexible and hence corresponding loss of output and income. One can, of course, have combinations of these two polar types of factor rigidity; and one could have factor immobility in only a subset of factors or factor price inflexibility in a subset of sectors. Trade theorists, in fact, have worked on all these

types of factor market imperfections. For example the early Haberler
(1950) analysis of the gains from trade dealt with total factor immobility
(which, in two dimensions, reduced the production possibility set to a
rectangle). He, and then Johnson (1965), Bhagwati (1968) and more
definitively Brecher (1974a; 1974b) have dealt with the factor price
inflexibility case where the shadow wage falls below the actual, minimum
or sticky wage. The case of sector-specific price inflexibility has been
considered by Harris and Todaro (1970), Bhagwati and Srinivasan (1974;
1976), and Corden and Findlay (1975). Finally, the case of sector-
specificity of factor immobility has been considered by Mayer (1974) and
Mussa (1974) who apply it explicitly to the question of short-run lack of
full adjustment, treating the case where capital is fixed but labour is
mobile in the short run.[26] While, however, the Mayer-Mussa analysis of
adjustment problems utilises the concept of immobility of one factor to
move in response to shifts in incentives, it is perfectly easy, and possibly
much more in correspondence with the facts of the real world, to utilise
the models involving some elements of factor price inflexibility as the
essential ingredient in the analysis of adjustment costs in the presence of
changed price incentives for resource allocation.

Finally, in regard to welfare analysis, it is clear that the presence of
adjustment costs, in any of the several forms discussed in the preceding
paragraph, raises the problem of optimal policy intervention. Thus, in the
context of reconsidering the national defence argument, where the earlier
work on non-economic objectives by Corden (1957), Johnson (1965), and
Bhagwati and Srinivasan (1969) has shown that the optimal method of
protecting domestic production is to subsidise domestic production rather
than to use a tariff, Mayer (1975) has recently argued that one can provide
an *economic* rationale for such intervention by assuming the presence of
exogenous uncertainty about import of the 'defence' commodity due to
embargoes (as in the case of the oil embargo), if there are adjustment costs.
While Mayer uses his (1974) model of short-run adjustment costs taking
the form of immobile capital to establish this proposition, a more general
analysis (of what amounts to the same problem), both in terms of the
nature of uncertainty and the nature of the adjustment costs entailed, has
been provided independently by Bhagwati and Srinivasan (1975) such
that Mayer's results become a special case of their analysis. The Bhagwati—
Srinivasan analysis is addressed to analysing the effects of *market disruption*, where it is assumed that a quota or a tariff may be invoked by the
importing country if the exports reach a certain critical level. Postulating
that the probability of invoking the quota at a specified level increases
with the excess of actual exports over this critical level, thus making the
uncertainty *endogenous* to the country's exports, they show that the
optimal policy intervention implied is a tariff that suitably corrects for
the marginal increase in the probability of invoking the quota. Then, by
introducing adjustment costs in a perfectly general way, such that the

feasible production vector in period 2 is a function also of the production vector in period 1, they show that the optimal policy intervention in this case also includes a production tax-cum-subsidy in period 1 to allow for this interaction effect.[27]

NOTES

[1] See my *Economic Journal* survey (1964) and the 1969 *Addendum* to it, reviewing the contributions that sought evidence in support of the hypothesis that skills affect the pattern of trade. See also section II (2) below for some brief remarks.

[2] In fact, William Branson's discussion of Haberler's paper happens to have been directly on this topic and can be usefully read in conjunction with my (1969) *Addendum*.

[3] For example, an increase in the propensity to save permanently raises the exponential rate of growth of output and investment in a Harrod-Domar model, but not in Solow's (1956) neoclassical amendment of the model.

[4] In addition, we may note also that the effects of shifts in *reciprocal* demand (which may, of course, reflect shifts in both demand and production) on the volume and terms of trade were already examined long ago by Marshall and Graham who arrived at apparently contradictory answers. The clarification of this Marshall-Graham 'controversy' was then provided by Bhagwati and Johnson (1960) and Kemp (1956).

[5] Cf. Chipman (1974) and Jones (1975) on the transfer problem with non-traded goods.

[6] An effort in the direction of such a general-equilibrium analysis, however, has been made in a recent, unpublished paper of Lancaster (1975).

[7] For details of the usual sort, for example, the focus on interior solutions, the transversality condition sufficient for optimality, the extension to learning in both countries in a two-nation international economy, etc., see Bardhan (1970, Chapter 7) in the original.

[8] In what follows, I am assuming that learning by doing applies only to manufacturing and that the latecomer country imports manufactures while exporting agricultural items.

[9] On the other hand, if we allow for 'learning by doing' of a behavioural type in regard to consumption of the importable, this could cause an *off-setting* bias in consumption and be a factor *increasing* the price of the importable over time.

[10] These questions have been reviewed, and the literature thereon synthesised, in Bhagwati (1975).

[11] The Japanese call the process of shift from domestic to export markets the 'flying geese pattern' phenomenon. Having never had the opportunity to observe flying geese, in either cross-sectional formation or in time-series motion, I can only assume that this description reflects what one observes and is not another disconcerting instance of Zen.

[12] Of course, there are different socialist doctrines. As Arthur Lewis is reputed to have told Thomas Balogh: 'Tommy, the difference between you

and me is that when you think of socialism, you think of yourself as behind the counter whereas when I think of socialism, I think of myself as being in front of the counter'. At the same time, it is necessary to recall that the invisible hand doctrine relates to Darwinian efficiency rather than to distributive justice; and in the year of the Adam Smith Bicentennial, one might well quip that Chicago took the theory from Smith and left the moral sentiments to the rest of us.

[13] In fact, even in the case of permanent, forever migrants, it is not entirely clear that they should be excluded altogether from the definition of 'LDC welfare'. Thus, as argued elsewhere: 'Skilled immigrants today enjoy low transport costs which permit frequent returns to the LDCs of origin and hence retention of LDC loyalties and affiliations. Their job opportunities also now tend to cut across different DCs, increasing their capacity to resist the assimilative pressures of the DC in which they reside — a passionate immigrant into the UK, who will not adapt to British phlegm, may be able to migrate to the back-slapping friendliness of the U.S.A. or to a convex combination of the two cultures in Canada. The identification with the DC of destination is not quite so inevitable in consequence. Furthermore, the melting pot now has itself melted in the U.S.A., the principal DC of immigration: ethnic diversity is encouraged and Dr. Kissinger finds his *realpolitik* hamstrung by ethnic groups who political and emotional affiliation to countries of emigration is considered a thoroughly acceptable part of the domestic, political process.

Thus, several factors have combined to make continuing link to LDCs of origin and failure to fuse into DCs of destination important aspects of modern, PTK migration from LDCs to DCs. This observation, plus the fact of extensive 'to-and-fro' migration, make it somewhat implausible to assert that, if one is interested in LDC-welfare, one must exclude the welfare of the migrants from the analysis.' Cf. Bhagwati and Rodriguez (1975), reprinted in Bhagwati (1976).

[14] See the detailed analysis of this proposal, its rationale and its legal, human-rights, constitutional and revenue implications, in Bhagwati and Partington (1976).

[15] In theoretical terms, one can think of the Rybczynski effect at constant prices, of course: the relative output of the activity using the migrating factor intensively would fall absolutely. Needless to say, one can qualify the argument if some capital also leaves with the skilled labour.

[16] Again, one can modify and adorn this basic argument in numerous ways, allowing for capital accumulation by the skilled labour abroad, for example. This is an area of analysis that requires explicitly dynamic formulation, however.

[17] At a broader level, they may even be a powerful source of 'systemic' change. For example, the Yugoslav workers' control system may well have been compromised in some degree by the reported permission to returning workers to invest their capital in small factories. The overall impact on political attitudes and forces may be slower but no less certain when the migration is of sizeable proportions, as in Yugoslavia, Turkey and Greece.

[18] The theoretical analysis involved is essentially another aspect of the Arrow-Spence screening theory; for an explicit theoretical analysis of the

problem of the brain drain that takes this imperfection into account, see Hamada and Bhagwati (1975), reprinted in Bhagwati (1976).

[19] Cf. the work of Desai (1975) and the discussion of this problem in Bhagwati and Srinivasan (1975a, Chapter 15).

[20] Needless to say, it may still pay firms to search for different types of techniques at the margin (cf. Samuelson (1965)).

[21] This is clearly much more interesting, and also more effective, than examining tariff *levels* and their relationship to industry characteristics. For, the tariff levels are largely a matter of historical accident and evolution whereas *changes* therein are more likely to reflect the effects of current adjustment and other such problems.

[22] Cheh was able to use estimates made by Baldwin (1970) of the changes in U.S. protective rates with the Kennedy Round, taking into account several (but not all) non-tariff barriers.

[23] For the arguments, which seem quite convincing, see Cheh (1974, pp. 326–28).

[24] To quote Cheh (1974, p. 335) 'By separating the independent variables that might be multi-collinear, the evidence reveals that percentage reductions in nominal tariff rates are significantly related to UL (unskilled labour), OL (old labour, over 45 years of age), and GS (growth rate of domestic shipments). The relationship becomes stronger when the percentage reductions in nominal rates include non-tariff measures as well as tariffs. When the dependent variable is percentage reductions in effective rates, however, the significance levels of the independent variables, even when run in separate regressions to avoid multicollinearity, remain very low. On the basis of reductions in effective rates, we might have concluded that United States exceptions at the Kennedy Round are not related to domestic labour adjustment costs, when in fact reductions in nominal rates tell us otherwise.'

[25] Whether old workers experience greater displacement costs due to specificity of their skills or due to institutional arrangements that interfere with mobility (such as loss of seniority, loss of pension rights, etc.) is a point of some interest here, of course. In the absence of detailed evidence on these underlying causes of displacement costs, I would be inclined to attach *some* weight, at least, to the argument that it is the loss of return on existing skills and the cost of acquisition of skills at later ages that makes the tariff change disruptive and necessary to resist. In terms of the topic assigned to me, it is really the enforced change in the quality of labour, that the tariff change imposes on the old workers in the import-competing industries, that causes the resistance to tariff cuts.

[26] Actually, it makes little empirical sense to assume that tariff-adjustment problems arise because of capital immobility while labour is fully mobile. As already argued above, it is the inability of *labour* to move or to accept cuts in real wages that seems to be the more realistic empirical situation.

[27] Thus, the Mayer analysis becomes a special case of the Bhagwati–Srinivasan analysis simply because, if the uncertainty is endogenous, the case for the tariff disappears; and the production in period 2 may be constrained by period 1's outputs in ways other than through the sector-

specific immobility of capital. Both Mayer and Bhagwati-Srinivasan use basically a two-period analysis; however, Bhagwati and Srinivasan also extend their results to steady state analysis.

REFERENCES

Arrow, K. J., 'The Economic Implications of Learning by Doing', *Review of Economic Studies*, June (1962).
Arrow, K. J., 'Higher Education as a Filter', *Journal of Public Economics*, Vol. 2(3) (1973).
Baldwin, R., *Nontariff Distortions of International Trade*, Brookings Institution (Washington DC, 1970).
Bale, M., 'Further Evidence on Cheh's Hypothesis Using Direct Estimates of Adjustment Costs', Mimeographed (1975).
Bardhan, P., *Economic Growth, Development, and Foreign Trade* (John Wiley and Sons, New York, 1970).
Bhagwati, J. and Johnson, H. G., 'Notes on Some Controversies in the Theory of International Trade', *Economic Journal* (March, 1960).
Bhagwati, J. and Ramaswami, V. K., 'Domestic Distortions and the Theory of Optimum Subsidy', *Journal of Political Economy* (1963).
Bhagwati, J., 'The Pure Theory of International Trade: A Survey', *Economic Journal* (1964).
Bhagwati, J., *The Theory and Practice of Commercial Policy*, Frank Graham Memorial Lecture (1967), International Finance Section (Princeton University, 1968).
Bhagwati, J., *Trade, Tariffs and Growth* (M.I.T. Press, Cambridge, 1969).
Bhagwati, J. and Srinivasan, T. N., 'Optimal Intervention to Achieve Non-Economic Objectives', *Review of Economic Studies* (1969).
Bhagwati, J. and Srinivasan, T. N., 'On Reanalyzing the Harris–Todaro Model: Policy Rankings in the Case of Sector-Specific Wages,' *American Economic Review* (1974).
Bhagwati, J. and Hamada, K. (1974), 'The Brain Drain, International Integration of Markets for Professionals and Unemployment: A Theoretical Analysis', *Journal of Development Economics*; reprinted in Bhagwati (1976).
Bhagwati, J., 'Protection, Industrialization, Export Performance and Economic Development', Paper prepared for U.N.C.T.A.D. IV Conference, Nairobi, May, 1976 (1975).
Bhagwati, J. and Rodriguez, C. (1975), 'Welfare-Theoretical Analyses of the Brain Drain', *Journal of Development Economics*, Vol. 2(3); reprinted in Bhagwati (1976).
Bhagwati, J. and Srinivasan, T. N., 'Optimal Trade Policy and Compensation Under Endogenous Uncertainty: The Phenomenon of Market Disruption', *M.I.T. Working Paper No. 164* (1975).
Bhagwati, J. and Srinivasan, T. N., *Foreign Trade Régimes and Economic Development: India*, National Bureau of Economic Research (Columbia University Press, 1975a).
Bhagwati, J. and Hamada, K., 'Optimal Policy Intervention in the Presence

of Brain Drain: Educational Subsidy and Tax on Emigrants' Income', *M.I.T. Working Paper No. 172* (1976).

Bhagwati, J. and Partington, M. (eds.), *Taxing the Brain Drain: A Proposal*, (Amsterdam: North Holland Co., 1976).

Bhagwati, J. (ed.), *The Brain Drain and Taxation: Theory and Empirical Analysis* (Amsterdam: North Holland Co., 1976).

Brecher, R., 'Minimum Wage Rates and the Pure Theory of International Trade', *Quarterly Journal of Economics* (Feb., 1974a).

Brecher, R., 'Optimal Commercial Policy for an Open Economy', *Journal of International Economics* (May, 1974b).

Cheh, J., 'United States Concessions in the Kennedy Round and Short-Run Labour Adjustment Costs', *Journal of International Economics* (1974).

Chipman, J., 'The Transfer Problem Once Again', in G. Horwich and P. A. Samuelson (eds.), *Trade, Stability and Macroeconomics* (New York: Academic Press, 1974).

Corden, W. M., 'Tariffs, Subsidies and the Terms of Trade', *Economica* 1957).

Corden, W. M. and Findlay, R., 'Urban Unemployment, Intersectoral Capital Mobility and Development Policy', *Economica* (1975).

Desai, A., 'Research and Development in India', *Margin* (Quarterly Journal of NCAER, New Delhi), Vol. 7(2) (1975).

Findlay, R., *International Trade and Development Theory* (New York: Columbia University Press, 1973).

Grubel, H. and Lloyd, P., *Intra-Industry Trade: The Theory and Measurement of International Trade in Differentiated Products* (New York) John Wiley and Sons, 1975).

Haberler, G., 'Some Problems in the Pure Theory of International Trade', *Economic Journal* (June, 1950).

Hamada, K. and Bhagwati, J. (1975), 'Domestic Distortions, Imperfect Information and the Brain Drain', *Journal of Development Economics*; reprinted in Bhagwati (1976).

Harris, J. R. and Todaro, M. P., 'Migration, Unemployment and Development; A Two-sector Analysis', *American Economic Review*, 60 (March, 1970).

Hirschman, A., *How to Divest in Latin America and Why*, Princeton International Finance Section (1969).

Johnson, H. G., 'Optimal Trade Intervention in the Presence of Domestic Distortions', in R. E. Caves, P. B. Kenen and H. G. Johnson (eds.), *Trade, Growth and the Balance of Payments* (Amsterdam: North Holland Publishing Co., 1965).

Jones, R. W., 'Presumption and the Transfer Problem', *Journal of International Economics* (1975).

Kemp, M. C., 'The Relation Between Changes in International Demand and the Terms of Trade', *Econometrica*, Vol. 24 (1956).

Kemp, M. C., *Three Topics in the Theory of International Trade*, Series in International Economics (Amsterdam: North Holland Co., 1976).

Kennedy, C., 'Induced Bias in Innovation and the Theory of Distribution', *Economic Journal* (1964).

Kravis, I., 'Availability and Other Influences on the Commodity Composition of Trade', *Journal of Political Economy* (April, 1956).

Lancaster, K. J., 'A Theory of Trade Between Identical Economies', *Mimeographed* (1975).

Leontief, W., 'Domestic Production and Foreign Trade: The American Capital Position Re-examined', *Economia Internazionale* (1954).

Linder, S., *An Essay on Trade and Transformation* (New York: John Wiley and Sons, 1961).

Marshall, A., *Principles of Economics*, 8th Edition (London: Macmillan, 1962).

Mayer, W., 'Short-run and Long-run Equilibrium for a Small, Open Economy', *Journal of Political Economy* (Sept./Oct., 1974).

Mayer, W., 'The National Defense Tariff Argument Reconsidered', *Mimeograhed* (1975).

McCulloch, R. and Yellen, J. (1975), 'Consequences of a Tax on the Brain Drain for Unemployment and Income Equality in the Less Developed Countries', *Journal of Development Economics*; reprinted in Bhagwati (1976).

Mill, J. S., *Principles of Political Economy* (London: Longmans Green and Co., 1848).

Mussa, M., 'Tariffs and the Distribution of Income: The Importance of Factor Specificity, and Intensity in the Short and Long Run', *Journal of Political Economy* (1974).

Ohlin, B., *Interregional and International Trade* (Cambridge: Harvard University Press, 1933).

Oniki, H. and Uzawa, H., 'Patterns of Trade and Investment in a Dynamic Model of International Trade', *Review of Economic Studies* (1965).

Reidel, J., 'Tariff Concessions in the Kennedy Round and the Structure of Protection in West Germany: An Econometric Assessment', *Mimeographed* (1976).

Rodriguez, C., 'Brain Drain and Economic Growth: A Dynamic Model', *Journal of Development Economics*; reprinted in Bhagwati (1976).

Samuelson, P. A., 'A Theory of Induced Innovation Along Kennedy–Weizsacker Lines,' *Review of Economics and Statistics* (1965).

Spence, A. M., *Market Signalling: Informational Transfer in Hiring and Related Screening Processes* (Cambridge: Harvard University Press, 1974).

Srinivasan, T. N. and Bhagwati, J., 'Alternative Policy Rankings in a Large, Open Economy with Sector-Specific, Minimum Wages', *Journal of Economic Theory* (1976).

Sunkel, O., 'Latin American Underdevelopment in the Year 2000', in J. Bhagwati (ed.), *Economics and World Order* (New York: Macmillan, 1972).

Weizsäcker, C. von, 'Notes on Endogenous Change of Tastes', *Journal of Economic Theory*, Vol. 3 (1971).

Comment

Ragnar Bentzel

Professor Bhagwati's paper can be regarded as consisting of three separate parts. The first of these deals with demand effects of labour quality changes, the second with supply effects, and the third with labour adjustment costs and tariff change. In my comments I shall stick to this partition and by turn give some views on these three parts.

I. DEMAND EFFECTS

Professor Bhagwati stresses the fact that changes in the quality of labour can affect the equilibrium patterns of production and trade through possible changes in demand patterns, as the perceptions and tastes of labour, *qua* consumer, change simultaneously. In his rather long discussion of these demand effects he refers to statements by J. S. Mill, Marshall and Ohlin. However, neither these statements nor Professor Bhagwati's own comments allow for very clear conclusions. It is obviously very difficult — also for such a prominent scholar as Professor Bhagwati — to draw non-trivial conclusions concerning the demand effects on trade. It is easy to say that such effects may arise, but it is far from easy to say something about the direction in which they affect trade. Moreover, without knowing something about this direction we cannot say anything but trivialities. Professor Bhagwati has solved this dilemma by supplementing his presentation with discussions of some problems which have nothing to do with labour quality changes.

As far as I can see, the supply (or production) effects of labour quality changes are far more interesting and important than the demand effects. This makes it a little difficult for me to understand why Professor Bhagwati pays so much attention to these latter effects. Do we really have to worry about them at all in the context of labour quality changes? I do not deny their existence but I have a strong feeling that they can be regarded as a second-order problem in the sense that they are rather unimportant in comparison with the supply effects. Maybe this is more so in the developed than in the less-developed countries. Anyhow, it is a pity that Professor Bhagwati has not said a word about how relevant the demand effects are.

II. SUPPLY EFFECTS

In his introductory remarks Professor Bhagwati states that his intention with his paper is 'to develop a systematic classification of the effects of labour quality change on trade, distinguishing between the 'demand' and the 'supply' aspects in the main'. The idea of developing such a classification seems to be all right. The question is, however, to what extent has Professor Bhagwati's intention been realised in the paper presented at this conference? Looking at the supply section I must admit that the systematic feature is not very easy to discern. I am more inclined to characterise this section as some scattered — though interesting — points of view rather than as a systematic classification. In my opinion such a classification should be designed in a different manner. It should, first of all, inclued a definition of the concept of labour quality change, and an explanation of how such a change affects production.

It seems rather natural to define a change in labour quality as a non-quantitative change in the labour force that results in a shift in the production function. Since it is rather unlikely that all types of such changes give identical effects on the existing production function, a systematic analysis requires a discussion of how quality changes occur. We need a list of different types of quality changes, and we have to try to find out how these different types affect the production function. Such a list should include a number of items, such as traditional education at different levels, learning by doing, R and D activities, transfer of knowledge by imitation and by migration, improved health, alterations in the age composition of the labour force, etc. It is, in fact, rather easy to enumerate a great number of such items, but it is very difficult to say how these different factors affect the production function. Will they cause labour augmenting, capital augmenting, labour saving or other types of shifts. This is an important question, since it has to be solved before the analysis can be integrated into general growth theory. And such an integration seems to be the main aim of the labour quality analysis.

Another strategic factor concerning the effects of labour quality changes is the localisation of these changes within the total labour force. Do they refer to all members of the labour force or are they concentrated on some subgroup of individuals? Probably the trade effects will depend upon whether the quality changes apply to all individuals or if they are limited to, for instance, people working in a certain branch of industry, or people with a certain level of education.

Before I leave the list of factors affecting labour quality, I want to make a plea for paying more attention than has been done so far to the impact of improvements in health. Compared to education, health improvements have been treated rather stepmotherly in human capital theory. Most growth economists seem to have accepted the view that the rise in the level of education has been a more important growth-promoting factor than the simultaneous improvement in health. But is this view really correct? That is not very easy to say. However, we can be sure we are right if we say that health improvement has been an extremely important factor in the economic development ever since the industrialisation process started. Perhaps this factor has lost some of its strength in the developed countries during the last two decades, but probably not in the less developed countries.

In the supply section of his paper Professor Bhagwati has laid much emphasis upon learning by doing. To me this is a little astonishing. Why should just learning by doing be placed in the limelight? I can't see that learning by doing is more interesting in this context than, for instance, health improvement and changes in the age composition of the labour force. And this one-sided concentration on learning by doing is clearly inconsistent with the intended systematic feature of the paper.

There are some other points in the learning-by-doing analysis that are a little puzzling. Professor Bhagwati argues as if learning-by-doing theory implies that latecomers learn more from doing than forerunners. I don't think this is correct. Professor Bhagwati seems to have combined, implicitly, the learning-by-doing theory with theories of technology dispersion. Further, it is not very easy to follow Professor Bhagwati when he states that 'presumably the latecomer, learning industry produces the country's importable . . . ' and that 'the international allocation of resources is surely affected so as to make the distribution of manufacturing to the latecoming underindustrialised nations *progressively* [my italics] more rapid and substantial than would otherwise have been the case.'

III. LABOUR ADJUSTMENT PROBLEMS AND TARIFF CHANGE

In the last section of his paper Professor Bhagwati deals with the relationship between labour adjustment costs and the process of tariff reductions. There he starts by referring to a recent investigation by John Cheh. This is characterised as 'the most interesting empirical work in this area'. I agree with this judgement about Cheh's work, but I think that there are some points in it which are open to discussion, so I shall devote a few minutes to giving some additional views on Cheh's results.

In his study Cheh considers the problem of the degree to which exemptions from the Kennedy Round tariff cuts within different groups of industries are related to the frequency of individuals having great adjustment problems when unemployed. He regarded old people and unskilled workers as representative for such individuals. In his econometric calculations he found that there are significant relationships between tax-cut exemptions and the frequencies of old and unskilled workers. This result is interpreted by Cheh as a positive outcome of a test of the hypothesis that interindustrial differences in U.S. tariff reductions reflect a government policy aiming at minimising labour-adjustment problems consequent on the tariff cuts.

Maybe we should be a little cautious with the interpretation of Cheh's findings. There are some weak points in the manner in which he draws his conclusions. The result of his econometric calculations can obviously be interpreted in alternative ways. Let me give some hints about this.

Firstly, the significance of Cheh's regression coefficients is not too impressive. In his large model, that is, the model which includes six exogenous factors, the regression coefficients of the two strategic factors — those representing the frequencies of old and unskilled workers — are not significantly different from zero at the 5 per cent level. Significant coefficients were found only in the small models, that is, the models including as exogenous variables only total employment and one more single factor. These facts make it natural to ask if the correlations in the small models are spurious in one way or another. Can it be so, for instance, that existing regional differences dominate the picture and that the government policy has been based on regional rather than labour adjustment considerations?

Secondly, Cheh takes it for granted that the adjustment problems are greater for unskilled workers than for other categories. But is it really so? There is, as far as I know, empirical evidence supporting the idea that old people have great adjustment problems, but what evidence do we have concerning the unskilled part of the labour force?

Thirdly, the outcome of the regression analysis is consistent not only with the policy target considered by Cheh, but also with the less-sophisticated target of reducing negative effects on the income levels on unskilled and old workers. This raises the question whether or not it is more likely that the government considerations pertain to income distribution rather than to labour adjustment problems. However, there are alternative interpretations applicable in this context, and I want to mention a recent study by a Swedish economist, Lars Lundberg (L. Lundberg, *Handelshinder och handelspolitik; studier av verkningar på svensk ekonomi*, IUI, Stockholm 1976.) He has shown that the Swedish tariffs before the Kennedy Round were correlated to the labour intensity of the different industry groups. Since high-labour intensity meant a comparative disadvantage in Sweden this tariff structure gave a protection to industries suffering from such disadvantages. Lundberg interprets this as an expression of a political desire to keep manufacturing industry reasonably diversified. Maybe a similar interpretation is valid in the American case too. As a parenthesis it can be mentioned that the correlation between tariffs and labour intensity in Sweden disappeared after the Kennedy Round tariff cuts. This is consistent with the above interpretation since these tariff cuts can be regarded as exogenous from a Swedish point of view.

The fact that there are many different ways of interpreting Mr. Cheh's econometric findings gives rise to the question whether or not it is possible to check these alternatives. There must be some documents from which it is possible to find out what arguments have been put forward in the negotiations between the government and the representatives of the various industries. Would it not be worthwhile to make a study of these arguments?

Summary of the Discussion

Part of the discussion concerned the quantitative importance of different kinds of labour quality changes. In particular, the effects of health, education and learning by doing were emphasised. A second issue was the alleged importance of demand side effects. A third issue concerned the interrelation between the structure of protection and sectoral differences in labour adjustment costs. Finally, the paper's 'asymmetrical' assumption that learning by doing could occur in the import-competing but not in the export sector was questioned. This session was chaired by *William H. Branson.*

Robert Solow thought that it would be worthwhile to study the improvement of health as an aspect of human capital as Ragnar Bentzel had suggested. Investigations in the U.S. indicated that education could account for an improvement of abour 1 per cent per annum in the quality of labour 'embodied' in a given number of bodies. Lengthening of the work life or reduction of absenteeism due to improved health could well account for an equivalent improvement. In less developed countries investment in education might contribute more, in value terms, than as equivalent investment in health which mainly increases the quantity rather than the quality of man hours of labour.

Åke Andersson thought that the paper's treatment of the consequences of labour-quality changes on consumption and demand was interesting, but felt that important empirical findings in the field of education had been neglected. He referred to a study by Michael[1] on the relation between education and consumption, and a study by Grossman[2] about the relation between education, income and the demand for health. He also mentioned his own study[3] concerning the demand for different consumer goods in relation to educational differences.[4]

The stock of education creates demand for human capital, which in its turn increases the stock of education, health, etc., thus increasing productivity. These results show the need to treat 'demand' effects together with the ordinary 'supply' effects and that the cumulative productivity changes from educational and information policy may be as important as the ordinary effects from learning by doing. The results are consistent for Sweden, the U.S. and Israel, in spite of differences in institutional and social conditions and, he claimed, ought to be integrated into future theoretical developments, both in development and trade theory.

Bertil Ohlin emphasised an aspect of learning by doing which he felt was important for development. Certain ways of industrial life might be difficult to acquire without personal experience. In LDCs people have to learn to go regularly to the job and work a given number of hours. Similarly, trade unions must learn to get along with each other and with owners to ensure that delivery contracts made by firms can be fulfilled. As examples of the importance of this, he mentioned that many Swedish industrialists preferred not to rely on imports from countries where the risk is great that labour disputes hinder regular deliveries. A similar uncertainty, he added, was beginning to be felt by Swedish firms when monthly wages replaced piece rates for blue-collar workers. This almost doubled absenteeism in their factories on Mondays and Fridays. Industrial leaders take this into account in their production plans, which makes the consequences less serious. The executive director of a Swedish automobile company recently suggested that employees should enter into formal contracts with the employer specifying the number of hours they were prepared to work per week.

Hollis Chenery felt that Bhagwati's juxtaposition of the supply and demand effects of changes in labour quality could usefully be applied to development policy problems, for instance to illuminate the view that trade is bad because favourable effects on the supply side may not be worth its effects on the demand side. Bhagwati's main point, he suggested, was to emphasise the need to consider how human beings will behave once they are changed by education. The general hypothesis behind such views is that increased education of the labour force biases demand towards high-quality employment and capital-intensive goods. He observed that increased demand for these jobs caused unemployment, with serious political and economic consequences, as had become apparent in, for instance, India and Sri Lanka as well as in an increasing number of African countries. The change in the demand for goods was biased towards imports and since trade restrictions were the easiest instrument, the usual reaction to some of the effects due to educating human beings in the development process tends to be: Develop by cutting off imports! Chenery felt that these policies might be partly due to governments being ignorant of alternative instruments and that the use of a more varied policy mix would enable governments to have the benefits due to changes in the supply side without the bad effects from the demand side. He feared that administrators were led to compare extreme policy alternatives: free trade or no trade.

Dieter Biehl referred to certain German studies[5] showing that some developing countries, which now successfully export labour-intensive products, started with import substitution. However, labour-intensive rather than capital-intensive products had been protected. The lines chosen had been infant industries in which the country had an ultimate comparative advantage.

Another study[6] also revealed that in a developed country like Germany, effective protection and the number of non-tariff barriers were larger the more labour intensive the commodity, so that profiting from learning by doing in a developing country is restricted by the protectionist policies of developed countries. These German studies support the conclusions in similar studies referred to by Bhagwati and Bentzel.

Observing that in most countries the public educational infrastructure was the main factor 'producing' changes in labour quality, Biehl suggested extending Bhagwati's analysis to include this. Isard had emphasised that the educational infrastructure was tied to given locations and consequently strongly influenced the location of economic activity. Biehl noted that even though the supply of education might be highly localised, migration could easily disperse educated people. However, this 'brain drain' could be regulated by taxing the movement of human capital, he noted, adding that this appeared reasonable when education was financed largely by public funds.

Bela Balassa elaborated upon differences among countries in the relation between the demand and the supply of 'skills'. He noted that India was characterised by an excess supply and other countries, such as Brazil and South Korea, by an excess demand. He felt that these differences should be explained by deliberate policies in the countries concerned rather than by the educational and cultural backgrounds of government officials. Bhagwati had observed that South Korea and Taiwan had perhaps adopted outward-looking policies due to cultural and geographical proximity to Japan and colonial status, while Indian development policy was formulated by Indian economists who at Cambridge had learnt to prefer the iron fist to the invisible hand. Balassa objected to this view. The former British colonies of Ghana, Kenya and Tanzania showed considerable diversity in their policies as did the former French colonies of the Ivory Coast and Senegal. Even South Korea and Taiwan pursued very different policies than Japan at the same level of development.

Ronald Jones and *Robert Solow* questioned Bhagwati's assumption that learning by doing only occurred in the import-competing industries. Through this assumption Bhagwati obtained a 'secondary benefit' from learning by doing in the form of an improvement in the terms of trade. Jones suggested that this asymmetrical assumption be moderated since doing could contribute to learning in the export sector as well. Was there any reason why learning should proceed systematically faster in the import-competing industries than in the export industries? Jones suggested that the former might be trying to catch up with or imitate foreign producers, while the export sector was 'tired' or had no foreign producers to imitate, or that the import-competing sector simply lends itself more easily to improvements than the export sector. However, he felt it was more reasonable to assume that people are doing and learning in other sectors as well.

Solow noted that Bhagwati's assumption that learning by doing reduces current comparative advantage implies that a late comer is better off in a world with learning by doing than in one without. Just the reverse might be true. Late comers may learn more quickly but they also have more to learn. All in all, Solow preferred to be a late comer in a world in which experience does not improve productivity than in one where it does.

Bhagwati closed the discussion. He felt that his contribution was in line with the general purpose of the symposium, that is to suggest ways for theoretical development, rather than to build specific models. He was convinced that the distinction between consumption and supply effects was important in analysing the interaction between labour quality change and the pattern of specialisation. He knew of no trade literature in which this distinction had been made and felt that it was a rather important thing to do.

NOTES

[1] Michael, R., 1972, *The Effect of Education on Efficiency in Consumption* (New York: NBER, 1972).

[2] Grossman, M., *The Demand for Health* (New York: NBER, 1972).

[3] Andersson, Å. E., 'Merit Goods and Micro-Economic Dependence', in Culyer, A. J., Halberstadt, V. (eds.), *Public Economics and Human Resources*, IIFP (Leiden, 1977).

[4] The largest *positive* 'education stock elasticities' were found for education, international travel, health and housing. The largest *negative* elasticities were found for alcohol, city and radio communications, tobacco and simple amusements, suggesting, he added, interesting cumulative human investment implications from education.

[5] Cf. for example Stecher, B., *Erfolgsbedingungen der Importsubstitution und der Exportdiversifizierung im Industrialisierungsprozess (Conditions for Success of Import Substitution and Export Diversification in the Process of Industrialization)*, Kieler Studie 136 (Tubingen, 1976).

[6] Cf. Donges, J. B., *et al., Protektion und Branchenstruktur der westdeutschen Wirtschaft (Protection and Industrial Structure of the West German Economy)*, Kieler Studie 123 (Tübingen, 1973).

11 The Place of Institutional Changes in International Trade Theory in the Setting of the Undeveloped Economies

Hla Myint

The topic assigned to this paper is 'The Possibility of an Analysis Treating Institutional Changes as Endogenous Variables together with the usual Economic Variables' in the study of the international allocation of economic activity.

I.

Taking the rough-and-ready notions which the economists have at the back of their minds when they speak of the 'institutional factors', it is possible to attach two distinct meanings to this term.

Firstly, the institutional factors may be interpreted as those factors influencing the *organisation* of economic activity in one sense or another. Thus, there are the 'international economic institutions', such as the I.M.F., the World Bank, G.A.T.T., U.N.C.T.A.D., etc. While some of them directly take part in international economic activity, most of them have the function of shaping the institutional framework of laws, regulations and conventions, which govern international economic relations. Next, we can think of the international network of transport and communications, finance and insurance, which provide the institutional channels through which economic activity flows from one country to another. Thirdly, coming down to the national level with which we are mainly concerned in this paper, we can think of the various institutional factors which shape the domestic economic organisation of a country participating in international economic activity.

These institutional factors operating on the domestic economic organisation of a country may be contrasted with the conventional assumptions of international trade theory.

(1) In the conventional theory, households are distinguished from the firms and the latter are assumed to be the Marshallian-type of small business enterprises depicted in the 'atomistic' model of competition. In contrast, it is possible to observe a variety of ways in which individual

economic units are organised in different institutional settings. At one end of the spectrum, there are the family-based economic units or the 'household-firms' which characterise peasant agriculture and the 'traditional sector' of the underdeveloped countries; these family-based economic units are still in a 'pre-atomistic' stage of development and have as yet not attained the degree of commercial specialisation and division of labour depicted in the 'atomistic' model. At the other end of the spectrum, there are the giant multinational corporations of the advanced industrial countries; these corporations, based on large-scale production and 'high technology', may be said to have 'exploded' beyond the 'atomistic' framework.

(2) The conventional model of perfect competition implies that the market institutions, both for the commodities and the factors of production, are fully developed and that the different markets and sectors of the economic system are sufficiently interrelated to be depicted by a general equilibrium model. Here again, it is possible to observe different degrees of development in the market institutions in different types of countries. In many underdeveloped countries, substantial proportions of their total output and resources still remain outside the market system. The development of the markets for the factors of production tends to lag behind the development of product markets and in particular the development of the domestic capital market is still at an embryonic stage. Moreover, the underdeveloped countries are characterised by a pronounced 'dualism' in the factor markets in their 'traditional' and 'modern' sectors. The small family-based economic units in the traditional sector have recourse to the 'informal' labour market for seasonal and casual labour and to the 'un-organised' market for loans from the moneylenders, shopkeepers or landlords; in contrast, the larger enterprises in the modern sector obtain their labour supply from the regular labour market and have access to the modern banking system and financial institutions. This relatively incomplete development of the market institutions and dualism represents significant divergences from the perfect competition model. But we may, however, note that these divergences arising from the *incomplete* development of the market institutions are conceptually different from the monopolistic elements and 'market imperfections' in the conventional sense. The monopolistic-type of market imperfections may be found both in the highly developed and integrated market systems of the advanced countries and in the underdeveloped countries. The incomplete development of market institutions and of the domestic economy is confined to the underdeveloped countries.

(3) In the conventional comparative costs theory, the role of government is considered mainly in relation to commercial policy, based on taxes and subsidies on particular products. We should not, however, overlook the more important general functions of the government's administrative and fiscal system in providing the appropriate social

overhead capital and public economic services which may have a vital role in enabling a country to take advantage of its potential comparative advantage. Thus, the conventional assumption that the resources are more mobile within a country than between countries implies the pre-existence of an administrative system capable of providing an adequate system of internal transport and communications. Similarly, the simplifying assumption that the production functions of a country are identical with those of the other countries implies the existence of a government which is capable of providing sufficient educational and research services to enable the country to adopt the best known technology in the rest of the world and to eliminate any 'technology gap' that may arise. Here again, it will be seen that the conventional theory implicitly assumes a well-developed administrative and fiscal system which does not obtain in most of the underdeveloped countries.

If we interpret the 'institutional factors' to mean those market and non-market institutions which shape the internal economic organisation of a country, the significance of these factors for international trade theory is now fairly apparent. The conventional procedure of deriving the static comparative advantage of a country from its 'given' resources, technology and tastes, is possible only with the implicit assumption that the domestic economic organisation or the institutional framework of the country is fully developed. Once we allow for the incomplete development of the domestic institutional framework, a country's capacity to realise its potential comparative advantage would depend not only on the usual economic data concerning its 'given' resources, technology and tastes, but also on the state of development of its market and non-market institutions.

We may now turn briefly to the second possible interpretation of the 'institutional factors', that is, to denote the politico-institutional influences on the economic decision-making process. It is a contemporary fact of life, both in the developed and the underdeveloped countries, that governments are not prepared to allow international economic forces to work freely on the domestic economic system. Instead, there seems to be an 'institution-alised' pattern of government action to protect and insulate certain parts of the domestic economy in response to the sectoral political pressures exerted through the voting system. Thus, for instance, the tendency of the industrially advanced countries to give special protection to agriculture or to the technologically stagnant labour-intensive industries cannot be satisfactorily analysed without taking into account the 'institutional factors' in the second sense. Given the increasing politicisation of economic decision-making, particularly in relation to international economic activity, the importance of these politico-institutional factors looms larger than ever.

However, this paper is concerned not with the alternative interpretations of the 'institutional factors' as such but with the question whether 'institutional changes' on either interpretation can be treated as endogenous variables in the analysis of international economic activity. Here it does seem that the institutional changes in the first sense are more susceptible to analysis as endogenous variables than the institutional changes in the second sense, at least in the setting of the underdeveloped countries. If we interpret the institutional factors as those affecting the domestic economic organisation of a country, then endogenous institutional changes may be regarded as the changes in the domestic economic organisation brought about by the process of international trade, these changes in their turn affecting the future pattern of the comparative costs of the country. Since both market and non-market economic institutions are less completely developed in the underdeveloped countries than in the advanced countries, there would be a larger scope for international economic forces to introduce institutional changes in the former type of countries. If, for the sake of isolating the institutional changes, we assume the initial set of economic data, that is, the endowment of resources, the best known technology and tastes and preferences remain unchanged during the process of change, then we may be able to use the static theory of comparative costs to chart the broad direction of these institutional changes.

On the other hand, given that very few underdeveloped countries possess a well-established democratic system of government, it is not feasible to treat institutional changes in the second sense as endogenous variables in the setting of these countries. This is, of course, not to deny the heavy politicisation of economic decision-making in the underdeveloped countries. As is well known, whatever their factor endowments, these countries tend to encourage and protect manufacturing rather than agriculture; and to encourage the 'sophisticated' type of manufacture based on capital-intensive methods with large-scale production and high technology rather than the simpler type of manufacture based on labour-intensive methods with smaller-scale production and low technology. As we shall see, this preference for sophisticated industry imposes severe political constraints on the potential development of domestic economic organization. But these political constraints may be more appropriately regarded as exogenously given constraints than as endogenous variables. In the absence of a properly functioning and effective voting system, the political preferences of the government may be changed in a discontinuous manner by a violent change of government or a 'change of heart' on the part of the government not necessarily related to the normal political pressures working in an institutionalised manner through a democratic voting system.

The plan of this paper is as follows. In section II, the institutional limitations operating on the domestic economic organisation of an underdeveloped country are represented in terms of its production feasibility curve and the differential gap between this curve and the conventional production possibility curve is used as a basis for the study of endogenous institutional changes. In section III, this method of analysis is applied to clarify the nature and effects of the political constraints operating on the underdeveloped countries. In the concluding section IV, we explore the possibility and the limits of treating institutional changes as endogenous variables in international trade theory in terms of the different kinds of shifts in the production feasibility frontier of the labour-intensive type of underdeveloped country.

II.

We shall begin by considering how the conventional theory of international trade may be modified and its assumptions reinterpreted to take account of the institutional characteristics in the domestic economic organisation of the underdeveloped countries. This raises three related issues which lead us straight on to the study of institutional changes as endogenous variables.

(1) In the conventional theory, the domestic economic organisation of a country which participates in international trade is represented by the perfect competition model. This implies that there are no institutional constraints which prevent the country from attaining a position on its production possibility curve, both before and after trade. Further, the position and the shape of the production possibility curve is supposed to be unambiguously determined once we are 'given' the factor endowments and the technology of the country. In analysing the consequences of the incomplete development of the domestic economic organisation in an underdeveloped country, we are concerned not only with its conventional production possibility curve but with its production feasibility curve, indicating the feasible quantities which a country can produce with the resources and technology actually available to the producers, given the institutional limitations which constrain their activities. The production feasibility curve may be expected to be below the production possibility curve. The study of the institutional changes of a country as endogenous variables in the analysis of its international trade may be approached in terms of the possibility of induced shifts in its production feasibility curve in the general direction of its potential comparative advantage indicated by its production possibility curve.

(2) In the standard trade theory model of a country producing two commodities with two factors of production, the main difference between the producers in the two sectors lies in their production functions. Otherwise they are assumed to be a more or less homogeneous collection of 'atomistic' competitive firms, having access to identical markets for products and factors of production. In contrast, the domestic economic organisation of the underdeveloped countries is characterised by 'dualism' or the co-existence of a 'traditional sector' consisting of a very large

number of small family-based economic units and a 'modern sector' consisting of a few larger-sized economic units organised on modern business lines. The traditional sector, dominated by peasant agriculture or craft industry, employs labour-intensive techniques, whereas the modern sector, consisting of modern manufacturing industry and mining and plantations, employs capital-intensive techniques. This technological difference holds more generally if we define 'capital' to include not only durable capital goods but also land and natural resources. The larger modern-style estates and farms in the underdeveloped countries use more machinery and land per unit of labour than the small peasant farmers. But technology, though important, is not the sole distinguishing feature between the small and the large economic units in the traditional and the modern sectors. Most notably, the small economic units in the traditional sector have access only to the retail markets for products and to the un-organised market for capital while the large economic units in the modern sector generally operate in wholesale markets and have access to modern banks and financial institutions. As we shall see, this has a significant influence on the characteristic shape of the production feasibility curve of an underdeveloped country.

(3) The 'pure' theory of international trade is still mainly based on an idealised concept of the domestic economy of the trading country which is capable of allocating its perfectly mobile resources in a 'frictionless' manner according to the assumption of perfect knowledge. For our purpose of studying the institutional limitations in the underdeveloped countries attention has to be focused on the 'frictions' and all the associated costs of overcoming them, such as transport costs, transactions and administrative costs and costs of search for economic and technological information. It will be argued that since the small economic units in the traditional sector and the large economic units in the modern sector have access to different types of factor and product markets and also to different levels of the administrative system of the government, the frictional costs or the transaction costs in a broad sense will be higher, per unit of economic activity, for the small economic units than for the large economic units. Assuming that one of the commodities is exclusively produced by the small economic units and the other by the large economic units, the differential incidence of the frictional costs will have a differential effect on the production feasibility curve of an underdeveloped country.

The simplest way of incorporating the transaction costs into the standard theory is to assume that the frictional elements are uniformly distributed throughout the domestic economic system. If we adopted this convenient assumption, then the effect of an incomplete development of the domestic economic organisation of an underdeveloped country would be merely to contract its production possibility curve in a uniform manner to indicate the reduced quantities of the two commodities that can be produced with the existing institutional limitations. Then the production feasibility curve would merely be a scaled-down replica of the production possibility curve and the two curves would be separated by a uniform gap. In this simple version, the *degree* of the underdevelopment of the domestic economic organisation would determine the width of the gap. But the institutional limitations as such would merely affect the absolute costs and not the comparative costs of the underdeveloped country.

Once we bring in the dualistic features of the domestic economic organisation of an underdeveloped country, this simple approach is no longer tenable. For now we should have to take account of the fact that economic units in the two sectors have a differential access to the markets for products and factors of production and to the public services provided by the government.

When we allow for the differential access to product markets, the assumption of a given international price ratio to the two sectors assumes a different significance. With a given f.o.b. price of the export commodity, the small producers in the traditional sector would receive a lower price than the large producers in the modern sector to cover the higher marketing and transactions costs. Conversely, with a given c.i.f. price of the import commodity, the small economic units in the traditional sector would have to pay a higher retail price than the big units of the modern sector who can purchase it wholesale. Thus the actual internal price ratios facing the economic units in the two sectors will diverge from the international price ratio — to the disadvantage of the small economic units in the traditional sector. Thus even if the production feasibility curve is assumed to be a scaled-down version of the production possibility curve, the institutional limitations will have a non-neutral effect on the international trade of the underdeveloped country.

To simplify analysis, we shall from now on ignore the differential effects in the product markets and assume a common international price ratio for the traditional and the modern sectors. Even then we shall see that the differential effects in the factor markets and access to public economic services can exert a powerful differential effect on the production feasibility curve of the underdeveloped country in at least three different ways.

(1) The cost of transmitting or retailing technical knowledge to the numerous widely dispersed small economic units in the traditional sector is very much greater than the cost of transmitting technical knowledge to the modern sector. On the other hand, international trade theory frequently assumes that the production functions are identical in different countries. This implies that, for any trading country, the 'given' technology means the most efficient technology available in the outside world, 'costlessly' embodied in the production possibility curve of the country. Once we allow for the higher cost of retailing technical knowledge to the traditional sector, it is apparent that with the 'given' state of technology in the out-

side world embodied in the country's production possibility curve, there would be a wider 'technology gap' for the small economic units in the traditional sector. In other words, the production feasibility curve which is constructed on the actual methods of production used inside the country will diverge from the production possibility curve as the country moves in the direction of increasing the output of the commodity produced by the traditional sector (see figure 1).

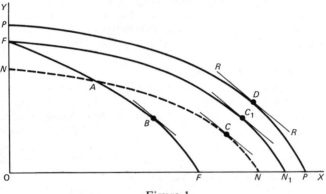

Figure 1

(2) Given the embryonic state of the capital market in the traditional sector, credit is either not available or available at generally much higher rates of interest than in the modern sector. The reason for this is not merely the overall scarcity of savings in the economy but also the incomplete development of the domestic capital market. The higher rates of interest reflect the genuinely higher transaction costs of organising a credit supply on a retail basis: the higher risks and the higher costs of obtaining information about creditworthiness and the higher costs of administering a large number of small loans. This means that even where the knowledge of more efficient techniques is transmitted to the small producers in the traditional sector, these techniques may not be feasible because they require a greater amount of capital investment or purchase of cash inputs. This will re-enforce the differential effect of the unequal 'technology gaps'.

(3) Even in the advanced countries with a well-developed fiscal and administrative system, the costs of providing public services to the widely dispersed rural communities is higher than the cost of providing the same level of services to the urban centres. Given the underdeveloped fiscal and administrative systems of the underdeveloped countries, these difficulties are accentuated. Even if they wished it (which is not always the case), few governments in these countries are able to provide the small economic units in the traditional sector with the same level of public economic

services, notably transport and communications, as that enjoyed by the large economic units in the modern sector. Thus the incomplete development of the non-market institutions re-enforce the incomplete development of the market institutions in creating a differential gap between the production possibility and feasibility curves.

We may now illustrate our argument diagrammatically. In figure 1, the production possibility curve *PP* for two commodities *X* and *Y* is drawn on the usual assumptions, including that the 'given' technology represents the best 'known' technology in the outside world, embodied costlessly in this curve, *X* is the labour-intensive commodity produced by the small economic units in the traditional sector and *Y* the capital-intensive commodity produced by the large economic units in the modern sector. The country is assumed to have abundant labour relatively to its endowment of capital (defined to include natural resources) and is therefore presumed to have a comparative advantage in producing *X* (abstracting from differences in tastes). The production feasibility curve *FF* represents the combinations of *X* and *Y* which the country can produce given its institutional limitations and *FF* is tilted downwards along the *X* axis to depict the differential institutional effects working on the traditional sector. The country was intiailly at point *A* on its feasibility curve and with the opportunity to trade at a given international price ratio *RR* tangential to *D* on *PP*, it moves from *A* to *B* where the international price ratio is tangential to the feasibility curve. It will be seen that for the labour-abundant type of economy depicted in figure 1, the differential institutional effects which we have described work against the direction of the country's potential comparative advantage indicated by its factor endowments. It should be emphasised that this differential effect against export production is not due to any deliberate government policy; it may be regarded purely as a spontaneous outcome of the existing institutional limitations reflecting a characteristic pattern of the incomplete state of domestic economic organisation in the underdeveloped country. Diagrammatically, the institutional effect against the production of the exportable commodity *X* may be illustrated by drawing a neutral production feasibility curve *NN* (a scaled-down replica of *PP*) to pass through the initial position of the country at *A*. The international price ratio is tangential to *NN* at *C*. The difference between the country's potential exports at *C* and its actual exports at *B* indicates the differential institutional effect with a more or less equal degree of underdevelopment of the domestic economic organisation.

We are now in a position to give a graphical interpretation of the topic of our paper. The institutional factors operating on the initial economic organisation of a labour-abundant underdeveloped country are represented by the production feasibility curve *FF*. The direct effect of international trade is to move the country from its initial position *A* along the *FF* curve to its immediately attainable position *B*. But it is possible to think of the indirect effects of trade which can operate on the economic organisation of the country in the longer run. These consist in the changes in the economic organisation, involving both market and non-market institutions, which take place in response to the opportunity to trade at a given international price ratio. Such 'endogenous' institutional changes may be represented by the shifts in the production feasibility curve *FF*. To obtain a fixed frame of reference to chart the direction of these institutional changes, we may assume that not only the international price ratio but also the initially 'given' factor endowments and technology embodied in the production possibility curve *PP* remain constant during the process of the institutional changes. The curve FN_1, a neutral replica of *PP* with the same intercept on the *Y* axis as *FF*, indicates the expanded production feasibility frontier the country can attain by counteracting the initial differential institutional effects operating on the traditional sector. It is important for our later analysis of the shifts in the production feasibility frontier in section IV.

III.

So far we have been concerned with the conceptual possibility of treating institutional changes as endogenous factors in international trade theory. This, however, presupposes that political constraints will not inhibit the endogenous changes in the domestic economic organisation and that the government is willing to pursue a free trade policy in combination with other policies which enable the domestic economic system to respond more effectively to the external economic opportunities. This is the assumption we shall be adopting in the next section. Before we do that, however, it is useful to apply the analysis of the preceding section to clarify the nature of the political constraints which prevail in the underdeveloped countries.

The underdeveloped countries' enthusiasm for domestic industrialisation and their distrust and hostility towards free trade seem to be rooted in their reaction against the so-called 'nineteenth century' or 'colonial' pattern of trade. This is identified with the export of primary products from the large foreign-owned mines and plantations which, it is maintained, created 'economic enclaves' cut off from the rest of the domestic economy and resulted in an overexpansion of the export production. Thus, it is argued that the newly independent countries should try to correct the 'export bias' and encourage the development of the domestic sector. This notion of the 'export bias' in the context of what may be described as the 'old-style' dualism can be readily illustrated by adapting our previous diagram.

In figure 2, the production feasibility curve *FF* is constructed on the same assumptions as before. But the production possibility curve is

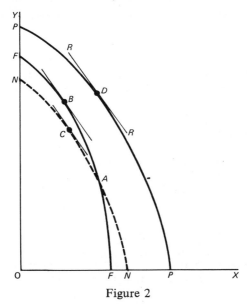

Figure 2

redrawn. Because of its relative abundance of capital (including its natural resources and the foreign capital which has flowed in to exploit these natural resources), the country is now depicted as having a comparative advantage in the production of *Y*, the capital-intensive commodity produced by the large economic units in the modern sector. Given the opportunity to trade at the international price ratio *RR*, the country moves from its initial position *A* on its production feasibility curve *FF* to *B* where the price ratio is tangential to *FF*. In this case, the differential institutional effect working in favour of the modern sector (against the traditional sector) is in the same direction as the country's comparative advantage derived from its factor endowments and this results in an 'export bias'. This can be seen by drawing a neutral production feasibility curve *NN* as a replica of *PP* to pass through *A*. The country is producing a greater amount of the exportable commodity *Y* at *B* than at *C* where the international price ratio is tangential to *NN*.

Now the case for correcting the 'export bias' is reasonable enough, given the appropriate assumptions. But frequently the argument appropriate for the capital-abundant country depicted in figure 2 is transposed to the case of the labour-abundant country depicted in figure 1 which is the more relevant model for a majority of the present-day under-developed countries. Further, in figure 2, the 'domestic sector' which is to be encouraged is the traditional sector employing labour-intensive methods to produce food or handicraft products for the domestic market. By a curious metamorphosis, the 'domestic sector' is now identified with the modern manufacturing industry employing capital-intensive technology. Thus, when the policies to correct the 'export bias' are transposed to the labour-abundant country depicted in figure 1, we have what may be described as the 'new' dualism. The traditional sector, the source of labour-intensive export production, is now doubly handicapped, both by the spontaneously operating differential institutional factors and by the government policies to encourage the modern sector at the expense of the traditional sector. Specifically, the government's policies of providing foreign exchange, capital funds and public economic services on excessively favourable terms to the large economic units in the modern sector can be pursued only by starving the small economic units in the traditional sector of these resources.

In the context of the underdeveloped countries, government interventions can also have adverse effects on the traditional sector without any deliberate policy intentions. In some cases, this arises from a mistaken analysis of the nature of the institutional limitations which operate on the traditional sector: from a failure to distinguish the *incomplete* development of the market institutions from the 'market imperfections' and monopolistic factors in the conventional sense. Thus, the higher rates of interest which prevail in the traditional sector are frequently attributed, not to the genuinely higher and unavoidable transaction costs of lending money on a retail basis, but to the 'monopolistic' power of the money-lenders – this, in spite of the fact that there is normally free entry into the moneylenders business. This mistaken diagnosis has led the government to 'correct' the market imperfections by introducing usury laws and licensing of moneylenders (which has the effect of limiting free entry); and by the diversion of capital funds from 'unproductive' money lending and trade to 'productive' manufacturing. The effect of such interventions has been to reduce or make more expensive the available source of credit to the traditional sector and repress the development of a more effective capital market in that sector.

In other cases, the adverse effect of government intervention arises simply from the underdevelopment and the ineffectiveness of the government's administrative apparatus when employed as a method of rationing scarce resources. As we have seen, the small economic units in the traditional sector, buying and selling on a retail basis, have to incur much higher transaction costs than the big economic units, buying and selling on a whole-sale basis. But it is not always appreciated that this retail-wholsale differential effect tends to operate in a more pronounced manner when an underdeveloped administrative mechanism is substituted for an underdeveloped market mechanism. The small economic units are even more handicapped in their dealings with the 'middlemen' of the administrative system and the red tape than the large economic units which have the necessary 'contacts' and influence. Thus, while a small man may have to pay a high price-differential to obtain a scarce commodtiy or resource under the market system, he may frequently get none at all when the rationing is done administratively.

The combined effect of government policies operating against the production of the labour-intensive export commodity from the traditional sector may be illustrated in figure 3 depicting a labour-abundant country

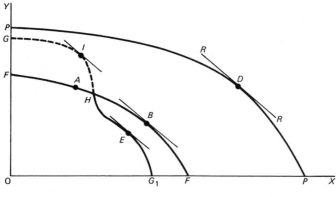

Figure 3

with a comparative advantage in producing the labour-intensive commodity X from the traditional sector. The production possibility curve PP and the production feasibility curve FF are the same as those in figure 1. We now introduce a new curve GG_1 to show the *ex post* effect of government domestic policies on the production feasibility frontier. More frequently than not, the only effect of government intervention is to impose an extra political constraint on the traditional sector in addition to the existing institutional constraints so that the country's production feasibility curve shrinks from FF to FHG_1. In practice, government intervention involves considerable restrictions on foreign trade but we shall hypothetically assume free trade at the given international price ratio RR in order to obtain a common basis of comparison. Thus, if the government pursued its domestic policies but permitted free trade, the country may be located at E on FHG_1 instead of B on FF. This means not only a lesser static gain from trade but also an inhibition of the possible endogenous institutional changes represented by a move from B on FF to C_1 on FN_1 in figure 1.

The dotted section of the GG_1 curve is added, with a stretch of 'increasing returns' between E and I, to allow for the possibility that government intervention may lead to a successful establishment of an 'infant industry'. In that rare event, the country will move under free trade conditions to the position I on the GIH section of the GG_1 curve. There are two things to note about the point I as we have drawn it. First, it is located within the production possibility curve PP; this is so because PP embodies the best known technology in the outside world in a 'cost-

less' manner whereas I represents the highest point on the production
feasibility curve attainable by a process of 'learning by doing', deducting
the cost of learning. Second, at the given international price ratio RR, I
is shown to be superior to B on the initial production feasibility curve
FF. But note that it is not necessarily superior to a point like C on the
neutral production feasibility curve NN shown in figure 1. It is probably
inferior to the point C_1 on FN_1 and clearly inferior to the long-run
equilibrium point D on PP. In a way, we may say that the opportunity
cost of fostering an infant industry, even if it were successful, consists in
the diversion of the path of institutional changes away from the direction
of potential comparative advantage indicated by the move from B to C_1
and thence to D.

IV.

We may now consider the various possible shifts in the production
feasibility frontier of the labour-intensive underdeveloped country and
their relation to the problem of incorporating institutional changes as
endogenous variables in the analysis of international trade.

In order to do this, we shall start from the initial situation depicted
in figure 3. Here, the country's traditional sector, which has a comparative
advantage in the labour-intensive commodity X, say a peasant agricultural
export, is constrained both by government policies and by an underdeveloped domestic economic organisation. Leaving aside the infant
industry case, the country's initial production feasibility frontier is FHG_1
in figure 3. In practice, the political constraints operate not only through
domestic policies which favour the modern sector at the expense of the
traditional sector but also through considerable restrictions on foreign
trade. But in order to obtain a common basis of comparison, we shall
hypothetically assume free trade. Thus, with a given and fixed international price ratio RR, the country's initial position may be located at
E on FHG_1. This indicates where the country would be if the government
pursued its constraining domestic policies but permitted free trade.

Starting from this position, we may distinguish three kinds of shift in
the production feasibility frontier. (a) There is the possible shift from
FHG_1 to FF moving the country from E to B in figure 3. (b) There is the
possible shift from FF to the neutral curve FN_1 in figure 1 moving the
country from B to C_1. (c) There is the possible uniform outward shift
from FN_1 towards PP moving the country from C_1 towards D in figure 1.

The first kind of shift in the production feasibility frontier, such as
from FHG_1 to FF, requires the removal of the political constraints
imposed by government policies. Now, as we have said at the outset, it is
not plausible to treat political factors as endogenous variables in the
setting of the underdeveloped countries. This can be illustrated by trying

to apply the Heckscher-Ohlin theorem in a routine manner to the determination of commercial policy in a labour-abundant country, assuming of course the existence of an effective voting system. The argument would run as follows: in such a country, free trade by increasing the output of the labour-intensive export commodity tends to raise wage incomes relatively to other incomes; but wage earners are likely to form the majority of voters; therefore, political pressures working through the voting system would tend to remove the political constraints on free trade and the expansion of exports! This convenient syllogism is clearly not applicable ot the underdeveloped countries. Here, the removal of the political constraints will have to be regarded as an exogenous change in data. Fortunately, we are not compelled to rule out-of-court the possibility of such an exogenous change in political constraints occurring at least in some underdeveloped countries. In spite of the general distrust of free trade and the lure of domestic industrialisation, some of the underdeveloped countries have become increasingly disillusioned by the failure of the import substitution policies. After this 'change of heart', they may be disposed to reverse their previous policies or switch them in the direction of export expansion. We may also appeal to some actual historical cases of exogenous changes in government policies; in particular, Japan during the Meiji era and Taiwan in the 1950s, started out as textbook examples of the labour-abundant underdeveloped country which succeeded in expanding labour-intensive exports, both agricultural and manufactured, after what may be regarded as an exogenous change in political constraints.

Let us now suppose that the political constraints operating on our underdeveloped country have been removed exogenously and that the government desists from its domestic policies of encouraging the modern sector at the expense of the traditional sector. In figure 3, this represents a shift of the production feasibility frontier from FHG_1 to FF. This may be contrasted with the conventional account of the change in the situation. In conventional analysis, the removal of the political constraints would be identified with the correction of the distortion in the allocation between the modern and the traditional sector, permitting the country to move directly to its full production possibility frontier represented by PP. The difference is that the conventional analysis implicitly assumes the pre-existence of a fully developed domestic economic organisation. On this basis, the adverse effects of the political constraints are identified merely with the static welfare losses arising from a divergence in the marginal rates of substitution between capital and labour in the two sectors and as is well known these usually do not amount to more than a small percentage of the *G.N.P.* On the other hand, we start from the fact that the domestic economic organisation, particularly in the traditional sector, is incompletely developed. Here the full effects of the political constraints cannot be appreciated until we take into account their longer-run consequences: for example, in repressing the future development of the domestic economic organisation and preventing the country from attaining its potential comparative advantage depicted by the subsequent shifts in its production feasibility frontier from FF to FN_1 and thence to PP in figure 1.

The conventional analysis assumes that there is a determinate production function for the traditional sector producing the labour-intensive commodity X on the same footing as the production function for the modern sector producing capital-intensive commodity Y. On the other hand, we explicitly start from an underdeveloped traditional sector, handicapped particularly by an embryonic capital market. The root of the trouble here is not only that interest rates are higher in the traditional sector than they need be, but also that there is a wide dispersion in the rates of return on investment among the small economic units making up that sector. Some of these rely on their own savings while others can borrow only from an 'unorganized' and 'fragmented' capital market in which the going rates vary widely for different borrowers. The effect of inappropriate government policies in this situation is not only to reduce the supply of capital funds for the traditional sector but also to discourage the future development of a more unified domestic capital market which combines the modern and the traditional capital markets into an effective network of wholesale-retail borrowing and lending. In this context, the problem is not merely that of equalising the marginal rates of substitution between capital and labour in the two sectors. The more important problem seems to be how to articulate the production function for the traditional sector by equalising the marginal rates of substitution between capital and labour at a microeconomic level for the different small economic units *within* the traditional sector. This calls for the development of a more effective capital market which reduces the lack of information about creditworthiness and the lack of coincidence between those who possess acceptable collaterals for raising the loans and those who possess investment opportunities to make a productive use of the loan.

The importance of promoting or not repressing the development of the capital market in the traditional sector is increased when it is remembered that it suffers from a wider technology gap than the modern sector and that there may be important financial constraints preventing the small economic units from adopting the more productive technology even if technical information were available to them. From the point of view of the conventional trade theory, it may appear paradoxical that the underdevelopment of the capital market should have such an important effect on the potential output of the sector producing the labour-intensive product. The reason for this may be traced to the conventional practice of treating labour and capital as substitutes and not as complements. That is to say, under conditions of 'atomistic' competition, it is implicitly assumed that each producer can procure the minimum amount of the complementary fixed factor required to reach an efficient scale of production with the given techniques and that there are no indivisibilities. Now, when the small economic units in the traditional sector are confronted with a new cash-intensive technology (say, improved seeds requiring a greater input of fertiliser and irrigation), they frequently face 'indivisibilities' in the absence of a capital market. The cash outlays they require to adopt the new technology may appear quite 'small' by conventional reckoning but may represent 'lumpy' sums in relation to their low cash incomes.[1] In these circumstances, the development of a capital market by overcoming these 'indivisibilities in the small' and filling in the gaps in the production function of the traditional sector may be capable of adding numerous small increments in output. The sum of these small additions to output is likely to be larger in the aggregate than the more spectacular gains from the economies of scale in a few large-investment projects in the infant industry of the modern sector. This is why the point I in figure 3 is likely to be inferior to the point C_1 in figure 1.

Let us now assume that the political constraints are removed. In a moment we shall see that this involves not only the reversal of the government's domestic policies but also the removal of restrictions on foreign trade and investment. Our underdeveloped country now moves from FHG_1 to FF in figure 3. But the traditional sector producing the export commodity X is still subject to the differential institutional effect of an underdeveloped economic organisation. The next shift in the production feasibility frontier requires a correction of this institutional bias by the development of a more effective economic organisation in the traditional sector. This may be represented in figure 1 by a shift in the production feasibility frontier from FF to FN_1. This depicts a net expansion in the production feasibility frontier with the output of X increasing without a contraction in the output of Y. It can be brought about only by a more effective adaptation of the domestic economic organisation to the opportunity of international trade at the given international price ratio and may be regarded as a genuine *endogenous* change of the domestic economic organisation. We may mention three main factors which can contribute to this process.

The first of these arises from the fact that the country's export has expanded because of the removal of the political constraints. In the setting of an underdeveloped country in which the government is heavily dependent on taxes on foreign trade, this initial increase in export is capable of generating important indirect effects. It can initiate the process whereby government revenues from the increased exports can be used to provide better economic services to the traditional sector to stimulate a further expansion of export production. Our previous analysis suggests that the differential institutional factors operating against the traditional sector may be counteracted in a significant manner: (a) by the improvement in the network of transport and communications which provides the physical basis for the development of the economic organisation in the traditional sector; and (b) by the improvement in education, research and the extension services transmitting the economic and technical information to the small economic units in the traditional sector which serves to narrow the 'technology gap' in that sector.[2]

Where government policy permits, the second factor which can contribute to the endogenous changes in the domestic economic organisation arises from the activities of the foreign entrepreneurs and merchants who form the institutional link between the small producers in the traditional sector and the world market. The conventional theory abstracts from the activities of these merchants and entrepreneurs by assuming that countries enter into international trade in an institutional vacuum, under conditions of perfect knolwedge about the possible sources of imports and markets for exports and on the basis of fullyfledged production possibility curves. But once we take into account the institutional channels through which international trade must flow from one country to another, it becomes evident

(a) that merchants and entrepreneurs operating in an underdeveloped country would have to invest a considerable amount of resources in their initial *search* for the sources of supplies and market outlets and in establishing and maintaining their channels of communications and commercial connections;

(b) that they would incur these overhead costs if they expect to recoup themselves by a subsequent expansion in the volume of trade;

(c) that the difference between the actual volume of export at the production feasibility frontier FF and the potential volume of export at the production feasibility frontier FN_1 in figure 1 provides them with this type of profit opportunity; and

(d) that, therefore, they would have the incentive to introduce new methods of production and organisation and frequently also to provide trade credit to stimulate the expansion of export production from the traditional sector.[3]

Up to the Second World War, the activities of foreign entrepreneurs and merchants were a potent source of endogenous change in the domestic economic organisation in the traditional sector in many Asian and African countries. Since then these activities have been severely curtailed by the political reactions against 'foreign economic domination': by the tendency to substitute state marketing boards in the place of private export–import firms; and by the popular belief that all forms of commerical and middlemen activities are 'unproductive' and the only 'productive' contribution which foreign enterprise can make is by investment in the manufacturing industry. Thus, in the current setting, the impact of the foreign entrepreneurs in the domestic economic organisation of the underdeveloped countries seems to be mainly shifted to the modern sector.

The third factor which can contribute to the endogenous shift in the production feasibility frontier arises from the response of the small

producers in the traditional sector themselves. As is well known, international trade, by introducing new commodities and new wants, provides
a powerful incentive for the small producers in the traditional sector to
make a fuller use of the 'surplus' resources which tend to exist in that
sector owing to the incomplete development of the exchange economy,
and imperfect knowledge of the location and availability of the unsued
resources. A part of the gap between the production possibility frontier
which assumes 'full employment' of the given resources and the
production feasibility frontier is attributable to the existence of the
unused resources associated with the 'slacks' in the domestic economic
organisation and these would be greater for the traditional sector than
for the modern sector. This 'vent-for-surplus' theory[4] has its clearest
application in the expansion of peasant exports from the underdeveloped
countries with an obvious hinterland of uncultivated land. But it is not
without some application to our model of the labour-abundant country
when it is remembered that the 'given' quantity of land depends not only
on physical endowment but also on the development of transport and
communications and economic organisation and that even a labour-
abundant country has both an extensive and an intensive margin of cultivation.

The combined effect of these three factors is likely to produce an
endogenous shift in the production feasibility frontier, depicted as a shift
from FF to FN_1 in figure 1. With the given international price ratio RR,
the country moves from B to its new equilibrium position C_1 on FN_1.
Once we have attained a neutral feasibility frontier such as FN_1, there is
little further scope for treating institutional changes as endogenous
factors in international trade. From now on, the only possible kind of
shift in the production feasibility frontier is the uniform outward shift
from FN_1 toward PP and this can be brought about mainly by an autonomous improvement in the domestic economic organisation. The
continuance of an open economy policy may exert a general educative
effect in improving the domestic economic organisation but since
institutional factors now affect the absolute advantage rather than the
comparative advantage of the country, there is no way of tracing the
specific indirect effects of international trade on the domestic economic
organisation. Meanwhile, of course, the initial data which we have
assumed constant, that is, the international price ratio, the best-known
techniques in the outside world and the country's factor endowments
would be changing owing to autonomous causes affecting the world
market conditions, technological innovations and to the autonomous
increase of population and capital accumulation. These changes would
open up a new differential gap between the production feasibility
frontier of the country and the new production possibility curve
embodying these changes in data. But since there has been some development in the economic organisation of the traditional sector, the

'institutional lag' or the time taken to adjust the production feasibility frontier to the production possibility frontier would probably become shorter than in the earlier stages of economic development with which we have been concerned in this paper.

The effect of international trade on the domestic economic organisation of a trading country is a relatively unexplored territory and we have only been able to cut a rough path through it. But it has been sufficient to bring out the important place which must be accorded to the development of the domestic economic organisation of an underdeveloped country in the theory of international trade and economic development. Once we give up the conventional assumption of perfect knowledge, the 'given' factor endowment and technology of a country (supposed to be known to the observing economist) are not known automatically and in a costless manner to the relevant producers and consumers. We cannot avoid the question how this relevant knowledge may be communicated in a more effective way by the development of the market and non-market institutions. In this setting, the basic notions such as the 'labour-abundant' country or its 'potential' comparative advantage remain somewhat ambiguous until we relate them to the development of the domestic economic organisation.

NOTES

[1] See R. I. McKinnon, *Money and Capital in Economic Development* (Washington, 1973) chap. 2.

[2] For example, the growth of labour-intensive exports of tea and silk from Japan during her initial phase of economic development owed much to the government's provision of technical and organisational services (cf. G. C. Allen and A. G. Donnithorne, *Western Enterprise in Far Eastern Economic Development*, London, 1954, p. 242). An even more striking example of the 'induced' technological and organisational innovation along the lines suggested by the Heckscher-Ohlin theory of factor proportions is to be found in the Japanese government's role in initiating and diffusing the labour-intensive and land-saving seed-and-fertiliser technology in agriculture in contrast to the labour saving innovations and mechanisation which characterised agricultural development in the United States (cf. Y. Hayami and V. W. Ruttan, *Agricultural Development: An International Perspective*, Part III, London, John Hopkins Press, 1971).

[3] For a well documented account of the role of foreign entrepreneurs in inducing the shifts in the production feasibility frontiers of the under-developed countries, see G. C. Allen and A. G. Donnithorne, *Western Enterprise and Far Eastern Economic Development*, Allen & Unwin (London, 1954) and also their *Western Enterprise in Indonesia and Malaya* (Allen & Unwin, London, 1957); also W. O. Jones, *Marketing Staple Food Crops in Tropical Africa* (Stanford Research Institute, Menlo Park, 1969) chap. 9.

[4] Cf. H. Myint, 'The "Classical" Theory of International Trade and the Underdeveloped Countries', *Economic Journal* (June, 1958).

Comment
Charles P. Kindleberger

The assignment given Professor Myint was limited to endogenous institutional variables. He has dutifully therefore eliminated from consideration exogenous institutional variables such as the multinational corporation, and endogenous non-institutional variables such as Nurkse's demonstration effect, (1953, pp. 63–67) although new wants are mentioned on p. 385.

Within these rather narrow limits, Myint has produced an elegant and cogent geometric analysis, using a physical production possibility curve, a neutral production feasibility curve which lies within the physical curve but restricted proportionately; a production feasibility curve based on a dual-sector economy, in which the traditional sector is more restricted than the modern sector because of less private integration in factor markets owing to high information costs, transports costs, etc. plus discrimination by government in the provision of public goods in favour of the modern sector; and finally a highly skewed dual-economy production feasibility curve, with increasing returns from learning by doing, etc. in the modern sector. The basis for discrimination by government in favour of modern industry and against the traditional sector is a somewhat irrational 'preference for industry' such as Cooper and Massell posited in their article on customs union in developing countries (1965, pp. 463 ff). Myint's endogenous institutional changes are seen in the correction of the discrimination of government and by private enterprisers against the traditional and in favour of the modern sector, so that the dual-economy production feasibility curve expands to the neutral production feasibility curve which expands with increasing perfection in factor markets and availability of information to the physical production possibility curve.

Distinguishing among various production possibilities curves has a distinguished history in international economic theory. The technique was used by Jaroslav Vanek (1959, pp. 198–208) to resolve the prolonged debate between Jacob Viner who believed in a real-cost theory and Gottfried Haberler who held to an opportunity-cost theory of trade. The real-cost production possibilities curve lies inside the opportunity-cost curve to the extent that there is disutility of effort by some factor or factors in each productive sector.

Myint's analysis, however, seems somewhat unduly restricted in its relevance for today's world by his small-country assumption that the terms of trade are fixed without regard to the developing country's trade. Much of the preference of developing countries for the modern sector, as noted by Cooper and Massell, proceeds from the implicit view that average and marginal comparative advantage differ from one another. In

Bhagwati's model of 'immiserising growth' (1958, pp. 201–5) in the traditional sector is avoided because while average comparative advantage dictates the export of its product, in which there are substantial gains from trade, marginal returns to expansion are negative: the loss in terms of trade outweighs the expansion of productivity. The issue has been treated not only by Bhagwati and others following him, but also in a thesis by Chacholiades (1964, pp. 106 ff) and a book by Burenstam Linder (1967). In Chacholiades' thesis the minimum subsistence wage below which workers refused to offer their labour lies above the wage which will clear the market for foreign-trade goods. Linder postulates an export maximum and a higher import minimum. Both analyses rest on assumptions of low elasticities and even kinked demand curves, which many economists in developed countries will find unpersuasive. But the possibility is real that countries cannot grow rich selling more tea, cocoa, jute, etc. even when it is produced with great efficiency though such possibilities may not properly be brought into a discussion of endogenous institutional factors. It is worth noting that growth in the import-competing commodity does not add to welfare until it has gone so far – in a two-country model – to reverse comparative advantage and allow the country to export the other product. As a consequence, borrowing to expand production in the import-competing commodity must proceed some distance, with new loans needed to pay interest on old loans, until the structure of comparative advantage is reversed. But this of course is the fault of two-country models. In the world of many commodities, there will almost certainly be some commodity or commodities, apart from the pregrowth export, in which incremental resources can be invested to add to income and welfare.

There is much in the Myint analysis to praise. Correcting for differentially high transaction costs in the modern and traditional sectors is clearly worthwhile. As part of the process, the attention called to the historic role of foreign entrepreneurs in traditional exports, e.g. Japanese tea and silk, is a useful corrective to the neglect of quality control in the trade practices of developing countries and I believe, the Socialist-bloc countries, until recently. Standardisation of commodity quality is an endogenous institutional change which extends the production possibility curve of a country. Prompt delivery dates are part of that quality control. These used to be carried forward by capitalistic merchants – whether foreign or indigenous – in organised markets, where the penalty for poor quality or for late delivery was private, and therefore assiduously avoided. In today's world where merchants are regarded as exploiters, and the public good of high standards, well met, is underproduced, this institutional gain must be provided, if at all, by laborious government effort.

As a final comment, let me suggest that the theory of international trade, in my judgement, must in the long run be extended in other directions to incorporate collective and public goods. On p. 381, Myint says as an *obiter dictum* that the theory of social choice with an effective voting system is clearly not applicable. But what kind of political behaviour should be incorporated in our models? Intuitively we believe that producers are better organised and more concentrated than consumers and therefore obtain tariffs, a collective good, which the disorganised consumers cannot afford to resist. The theory of collective goods suggests that organised groups can share out the transactions costs more effectively than disorganised ones. A recent thesis at Stanford University by Jonathan Pincus (1972) demonstrates this proposition for the U.S. Tariff of 1824 by showing that concentrated commodities got higher tariffs than widely dispersed ones. (It may be, however, that this theory fits the Tariff of 1824 better than any other tariff in U.S. history. It does not explain well the rise of free trade in Europe in the first three-quarters of the nineteenth century; see Kindleberger, 1975). If one opens the model up to include trade in intermediate goods, one can arrive at competition over tariffs between producers of imports, and those industries which use imports as inputs. This demonstrates further the weakness of the two-good model in which both goods are final product.

In the view of some analysts, government is the tool of the foreign entrepreneur, or of the foreign entrepreneur and his native collaborators. In some situations, however, it is clear that the government is antagonistic to these groups. As we explore the role of institutions in the dynamics of growth and foreign trade, I am convinced we shall need a more subtle theory of political decision-making than rational voting to convert what are now exogenous to endogenous institutional factors in the process. I suspect that the most promising avenue for development will prove to be the theory of collective goods.

REFERENCES

Bhagwati, J., 'Immiserizing Growth: A Geometrical Note', *Review of Economic Studies*, XXV, 68 (June, 1958).
Chacholiades, M., 'Balance of Payments Equilibrium with Imports as a Factor of Production', doctoral dissertation, M.I.T. (June, 1964).
Cooper, C. A. and Massell, B. F., 'Towards a General Theory of Customs Unions for Developing Countries', *Journal of Political Economy*, LXXIII, 5 (Oct., 1965).
Kindleberger, C. P., 'The Rise of Free Trade in Western Europe, 1820–1875', *Journal of Economic History*, XXXV, 1 (March, 1975).
Linder, S. B., *Trade and Trade Policy for Development*, (New York: Frederick A. Praeger, 1967).
Nurkse, R., *Problems of Capital Formation of Underdeveloped Countries*, (Oxford: Blackwell, 1953).
Pincus, J., 'A Positive Theory of Tariff Formation Applied to Nineteenth-century United States', doctoral dissertation (Stanford University, 1972 (to be published).

Vanek, J., 'An Afterthought on the "Real Cost-Opportunity Cost Dispute" and some Aspects of General Equilibrium under Conditions of Variable Factor Supplies', *Review of Economic Studies*, XXVI, 71 (June, 1959).

Summary of the Discussion

The discussion first considered the explanations and policy implications of the 'differential effects' of institutional limitations on the traditional and the modern sectors in less developed countries. It also dealt with the possibility of analysing these institutional factors within the framework of standard trade theory. This session was chaired by *Ronald W. Jones*.

Jagdish Bhagwati scrutinised the effect of institutional factors on the transformation curve. He noted that what Myint called the production possibility curve (*PP* in figure 1, p. 374) was not what is normally known as such, since it was defined using foreign rather than domestic knowledge of technology. He felt that the production possibility curve should relate to a country's own knowledge just as it related to its own resource endowments.

He was also puzzled by Myint's explanation of the differential impacts of institutional limitations on the modern and traditional sectors as reflected in the inward shift of the production feasibility curve. He felt that different limitations could have very different effects on the transformation curve. For example, in the case of interest rate differences between sectors, it was necessary to note that, the economy would operate on a restricted transformation curve in the usual way if such differentials reflected a factor price distortion. However, where the institutional differential was due to the different availability of public services in the two sectors, as noted by Myint, this was a very different matter indeed. There was no contraction of the production frontier, in the same sense as in the factor price differential case. Rather, one wanted now to distinguish between the short run and the long run when considering policy implications. Public sector investments could be reallocated in the long run between the two sectors eliminating the differential gap; while in the short run this differential, like the weather, could hardly be influenced. A similar problem was related to differential gaps caused by lack of knowledge. If foreign knowledge was not freely obtainable, Myint's analysis might give misleading answers since the differential gap could then only be reduced at a cost. Bhagwati concluded that the welfare consequences of these three institutional differentials should not be lumped together and analysed indiscriminately.

Several participants questioned the desirability of neutralising the higher costs faced by the traditional sector. *Bela Balassa* warned against uncritically adopting such policies since the alleged disadvantages of the traditional sector might not represent a distortion at all. The small-scale producer might pay more for a product simply because it costs more to

get it to him. Supplying the traditional sector with credit may involve
extra costs no less than supplying fertilisers. In order to determine the
need for government intervention, the difference between private and
social costs and benefits must be investigated in each particular case.
Balassa wondered if the paper considered sufficiently the economic costs
involved in small-scale retailing. He thought that extension services in the
agricultural sector may be an example of positive externalities justifying
government support. He also felt that McKinnon's argument for capital
market intervention was valid.[1]

Tibor Scitovsky observed that McKinnon's argument was implicit in
Myint's paper. Policies to provide credit to the small scale producer at the
same interest rate as to larger producers may be self-defeating. The profit-
maximising behaviour of financial intermediaries may force farmers to
have recourse to the black market at even higher interest rates. Government
policy to prevent an alleged discrimination of the farmer may therefore,
he claimed, actually lead to an even greater discrimination. Furthermore
he noted the distortions caused by government policies to benefit the
modern sector. Import substitution was an example of a policy which,
when successful, restricted a country's production possibilities.

Bo Södersten also suggested that high interest rates in 'informal
markets' reflected institutional limitations rather than market distortions.
High interest rates in the traditional sector had in some cases been shown
to reflect a very high time preference. However, government policies kept
interest rates artificially low in the modern sector, and the underdeveloped
state of savings institutions did not allow sufficient arbitrage between the
formal and the informal market to equalise interest rates. The development of savings institutions, he concluded, was therefore an important part
of the development process. *Charles Kindleberger* added that just as
interest rates may be high because of time preference, so wage rates for
shift work must be sufficiently high to offset a strong preference for
family life if factories were to run in three shifts.

Hollis Chenery suggested that standard trade theory was unable to
enlighten many important institutional problems. Myint's analysis,
although suggestive and impressive, contributed little to the formulation
of development policy, since it did not explicitly treat the non-trading
sector and since it exaggerated the ability of governments in LDCs to act
effectively. Countries do not aim at an efficient allocation of resources in
the trade sector, but strive to maximise some measure of consumption
subject to distributional considerations. The most efficient use of scarce
resources might be to do nothing to trade since it is only part of the
problem. Institutional reforms require administrative talent and he
emphasised that a government's organisational ability may be the
binding constraint on development. Since governments cannot remedy
all inefficiencies at once, the task was to identify which market impediments it was most profitable to remove. It was well known that capital,

labour, and natural resources were all underutilised in LDCs. Reforms on
the internal front, therefore, might be more important than earning
foreign exchange more efficiently. Thus, he felt that governments should
be viewed as striving to make more efficient use of the country's factors
of production in general, subject to the constraints imposed by trade and
by the availability of organisational ability.

Wassily Leontief likewise emphasised that the institutional limitations
treated by Myint applied to domestic as well as foreign transactions.
Furthermore he felt that Myint's analysis neglected to study how governments decide upon and implement policies. Social inefficiency can be
extremely profitable for certain interest groups and they will therefore
strive to maintain it. Like Kindleberger, Leontief suggested that it was
essential to view changes in institutions as the result of political struggles
between various interest groups. Policy advice, if offered at all, should
be how to change the power relations in a less developed economy.

Akin Mabogunje elaborated on this view and noted that systems of
land ownership and inheritance are institutional factors that may constrain development. Increased trade will not necessarily relax such
institutional constraints. It was necessary to differentiate between those
institutions that respond to increased trade and those that do not.

Bhagwati suggested an extension of Myint's analysis. He noted that
standard trade theory provided examples of how changes in policy-
imposed institutions could affect market institutions. Thus, free trade may
eliminate distortions emanating from domestic monopolies. Similarly
migration may eliminate distortions due to monopsonistic hiring in the
labour market. Bhagwati suggested that Myint's paper could easily be
extended to include such effects.

Åke Andersson noted that the communication network was an
institutional factor with differential effects in LDCs. Empirical studies
showed that it was very expensive to communicate within the underdeveloped world, especially for traders with a high opportunity cost for
time spent on the transportation system. Scale economies in the communication industry led to systems centred on the large cities of the
developed world. A telephone call, for instance, from one West African
country to another often went via European capitals. Such differential
capacity developments in the international communication network
needed to be considered in order to explain the specialised flows of commodities in international trade.

Hla Myint closed the session. He agreed with most of the criticisms made,
which he thought suggested that his critics had perhaps misunderstood
his position. He repeated that the whole point of his analysis was to show
that being on the inner feasibility curve was not a distortion, as some had
claimed, but a non-preventable cost. He had attempted to introduce the
institutional set-up as a new dimension in trade theory in addition to
technology and factor endowments. Confusing imperfections and non-

preventable costs, as some had done, could lead to the wrong diagnosis and to policy measures, which accentuated the problems. The introduction of usury laws, which had been mentioned several times in the discussion, was an example of this since higher rates of interest in the traditional sector generally reflect the unavoidably higher costs of lending money to many peasants. Governments should attempt to fill in the institutional shortcomings which his analysis revealed rather than intervene through the market. Cooperative arrangements to lower the costs of supplying these services presented one such possibility.

Once the nature of the institutional limitations was identified, his paper had concentrated on how the opening of trade might release forces which might improve the institutions. Recalling that the symposium dealt with positive rather than welfare analysis, Myint said that he had not specifically treated governments' general development policy nor the decision making process behind this policy. However, he had referred to the inadequate administrative ability of governments as an important example of incomplete institutional organisation. Drawing a parallel between the distribution of goods and the supply of public services, Myint noted that government administration was biased against the traditional sector. The middleman in the civil service was analogous to the middleman in the retail-wholesale network; the small chaps managing the village branches of public administration were treated very badly.

In conclusion Myint agreed with Kindleberger's observation (p. 388) that the task of the merchant in enforcing standards, controlling quality and fulfilling delivery dates was an important institutional factor in development. The problem in underdeveloped countries is that natural differences in the quality of agricultural products make standardisation difficult. The transition of the economic unit from the family producer via the Marshallian competitive firm to the multinational firm is accompanied by a development from heterogeneous to standardised and then to differentiated products. One task for underdeveloped countries was to introduce appropriate institutions to standardise products.

NOTE

[1] McKinnon, R. I., *Money and Capital in Economic Development*, The Brookings Institution (Washington, 1973).

12 Trade, Location of Economic Activity and the MNE: A Search for an Eclectic Approach

John H. Dunning

I.

The main task of this paper is to discuss ways in which production financed by foreign direct investment, that is, that undertaken by multi-national enterprises (MNEs), has affected our thinking about the international allocation of resources and the exchange of goods and services between countries. The analysis takes, as its starting point, the growing convergence between the theories of international trade and production, and argues the case for an integrated approach to international economic involvement, based both on the *location*-specific endowments of countries and the *ownership*-specific endowments of enterprises. In pursuing this approach, the paper sets out a systemic explanation of the foreign activities of enterprises, in terms of their ability to internalise markets to their advantage. It concludes with a brief examination of some of the effects which the MNE is allegedly having on the spatial allocation of resources, and on the patterns of trade between countries.

We begin by looking at the received doctrine on international economic involvement. Until around 1950, this mainly consisted of a well-developed formal theory of international trade and a complementary but less well-developed theory of capital movements. With the notable exceptions of John Williams (1929),[1] and Bertil Ohlin (1933), international economists of the interwar years were less concerned with explanations of the composition of goods and factors actually traded across boundaries (and implicitly at least, of the spatial distribution of economic activity) as with theorising on what would occur, if, in the real world, certain conditions were present. The Heckscher-Ohlin model for example, asserted that, provided certain conditions were met, countries would specialise in the production of goods which required relatively large inputs of resources with which they were comparatively well endowed, and would export these in exchange for others which required relatively large inputs of factors with which they were comparatively poorly endowed. The conditions included that countries had two homogeneous inputs, labour and capital, both of which were locationally immobile (that is, they were to be *used* where they were *located*); inputs were converted into outputs by the most efficient (and internationally identical) production functions; all enterprises were price-takers, operating under conditions of atomistic competition; there were no barriers to trade and no transaction costs; and international tastes were similar.

The Heckscher-Ohlin model has been criticised in the literature on various grounds, including the unreality or inapplicability of its assumptions. Here, we would underline some of the implications of three of these assumptions — factor immobility, the identity of production functions and atomistic competition. These are first, that all markets operate efficiently; second, there are no external economies of production or marketing; and third, information is costless and there are no barriers to trade or competition. In such a situation, international trade is the only possible form of international involvement; production by one country's enterprises for a foreign market must be undertaken within the exporting country; and all enterprises have equal access to location-specific endowments.

One of the deductions of the Heckscher-Ohlin theory is that trade will equalise factor prices. Replacing the assumption of factor immobility with that of the immobility of goods, it may be shown that movements of factors also respond to differential resource endowments. This was the conclusion of the early writings of Nurkse (1933), Ohlin (1933) and Iversen (1935) which explained international (portfolio) capital movements in terms of relative factor prices, or differential interest rates. For many years, trade and capital theory paralleled each other, it being accepted, that, in practice, trade in goods was at least a partial substitute for trade in factors. Eventually, the two were formally integrated into the factor price equalisation theorem by Samuelson (1948), and Mundell (1957).

In the late 1950s, there was a striking shift of direction in the interests of international economists brought on, *inter alia*, by the tremendous postwar changes in the form and pattern of trade and capital exports. Building on the empirical work of McDougall (1951) and Leontief (1953), and taking advantage of much improved statistical data, the 1960s saw the first real attempts to explain trade patterns as they were, rather than as they might be; contemporaneously, the emergence of international production as a major form of non-trade involvement was demanding an explanation.

Over the past 15 years, the positive theory of international economic involvement has 'taken off'. For most of the period, it comprised two quite separate strands. The first concerned explanations of trade flows. Here, contributions were mainly centred on introducing more realism into the Heckscher-Samuelson-Ohlin doctrine. Basically, there were two main approaches. The first was that of the neo-factor theories, which extended the two factor Heckscher-Samuelson-Ohlin model to embrace other location-specific endowments (notably natural resources) and differences in the *quality* of inputs, especially labour. The second group of theories were more path-breaking, as they cut at the heart of the Heckscher-Samuelson-Ohlin model by allowing for the possibility of differences in the production function of enterprises and of imperfect markets. These theories, which included the neotechnology and scale economy models, were different in kind to the neofactor theories, because they introduced explanatory variables which focused not on the specific resource endowments of *countries,* but on the exclusive possession of certain assets by *enterprises.* Sometimes, in addition to, but more often as a substitute for orthodox theories, these new hypotheses of trade flows were exposed to various degrees of testing. Yet as Hufbauer, in his masterly review in 1970 demonstrated, although the neofactor and the neotechnology theories performed well, they did scarcely better than the crude factor proportions theory. In his own words.'No one theory monopolises the explanation of manufacturing trade'.

The second strand of research in the 1960s centred on explaining the growth and composition of foreign direct investment, or of production financed by such investment. At first, causes were sought either from orthodox location theory (witness the plethora of microeconomic field studies and more macro-oriented econometric studies), or from neoclassical investment doctrine; but for various reasons, discussed elsewhere (Dunning 1973, Hufbauer 1973) neither approach proved very helpful. More rewarding were the attempts to identify the distinctive features of foreign *direct* investment in terms of *ownership* endowments of foreign firms. Though the germs of this idea were contained in the writings of Southard (1931) and Dunning (1958), it was left to Stephen Hymer in his seminal Ph.D. thesis (Hymer 1960) to explore it in depth. Out of this approach, later refined and extended by Caves (1971, 1974b), several hypotheses, focusing on particular kinds of ownership advantages of MNEs, were put forward, for example superior productive knowledge (Johnson 1970), better capabilities for product differentiation (Caves 1971), underutilisation of entrepreneurial and managerial capacity (McManus 1972, Wolf 1973) etc.; while a more behavioural perspective was taken by Vernon and his colleagues, notably Knickerbocker (1973), who chose to emphasise the role played by defensive oligopolistic strategy. These theories too have been subject to some testing[2]; again, it seems clear that no single hypothesis offers a sufficient explanation of non-trade involvement.

Though these new theories of trade and production originated quite independently of each other, by the early 1970s it was clear they were converging on, and even overlapping each other. Though expressed differently, the same variables were being increasingly used to explain both trade and non-trade involvement. Comparable to the technological gap theory of trade was the knowledge theory of direct investment; comparable to monopolistic competitive theories of trade, were theories of direct investment focused on product differentiation and multiplant economies. Yet, with the exception of Vernon's early integration of trade and investment as different stages of the product cycle (Vernon 1966), which took as its starting point the innovating advantages of *enterprises* in a particular country, and the later discovery of Horst (1972), that the same variable — *size* of firm — which best explained foreign investment, also explained investment plus trade, no attempt was made to integrate the two forms of involvement into a single theory — although the need for this was discerned by Baldwin (1970) and others. Nor, indeed, was there any explicit recognition that, because the decisions to trade or engage in foreign production are often alternative options to the same firm, any explanation of one must, of necessity, take account of the other.

The last three years have seen the first, albeit haltering, attempts to do just this. In a paper published in 1973, I suggested that only by considering trade and foreign production as alternative forms of international involvement in terms of *ownership* and *location* endowments could the economic implications of the U.K. joining the E.E.C. be properly evaluated. Seev Hirsch (1975) has formalised these concepts into a model, which specifies, very clearly, the conditions under which foreign markets will be, by alternative routes, serviced. Tom Parry has applied these same ideas to a study of the pharmaceutical industry (1975); his contribution is especially noteworthy as he has included licensing as a third form of economic involvement. Buckley and Dunning (1976) have examined comparative U.S. and U.K. trade and non-trade in these terms. In the belief that this is a helpful route towards an eclectic theory of international economic involvement, we now explore it in more detail.

II.

Exactly what is to be explained? Here an important point of taxonomy arises. A country's economic involvement outside its national boundaries may be perceived in two ways. First, it may mean the extent to which its own resources, i.e. those located within its boundaries, are used by economic agents (irrespective of their nationality) to produce goods or services for sale outside its boundaries; or the extent to which it imports either resources, or the products of resources located in other countries. This is the interpretation of orthodox international economics; *inter alia*, it implies arms-length trade in inputs and outputs. But secondly, a country's involvement may mean the extent to which its own economic agents[3] service foreign markets with goods and services, irrespective of where the resources needed to do this are located or used, and the extent to which its own economic agents are supplied goods by foreign-owned firms, irrespective of where the production is undertaken. Here, a country's economic space is perceived more in terms of the markets exploited by its institutions than of its geographical boundaries.

Like the distinction between gross national product (G.N.P.) and gross domestic product (G.D.P.),[4] which of the two interpretations is the more appropriate depends on the purpose for which it is being used; but for an evaluation of the contribution of a country's international economic involvement to the economic welfare of its citizens, the second has much to commend it, particularly where inward or outward investment account for a substantial proportion of its net capital formation.

Economic involvement by one country's enterprises in another may be for purposes of supplying both foreign and home markets. Production for a particular foreign market may be wholly or partly located in the home country, in the foreign market, in a third country or in a combination of the three. Similarly, production for the home market may be sourced from a domestic or a foreign location.

The capability of a home country's enterprises to supply either a foreign or domestic market from a foreign production base, depends on their possessing certain resource endowments not available to, or not utilised by another country's enterprises. We use resource endowments in the Fisherian sense (Johnson, 1970) to mean assets capable of generating a future income stream; they include not only tangible assets such as natural resources, manpower and capital, but intangible assets, such as knowledge, organisational and entrepreneural skills, and access to markets. Such endowments could be purely *location*-specific to the home country, in other words originating only from the resources of that country[5] but available to all firms, or they could be *ownership*-specific, that is internal to the enterprise of the home country, but capable of being used with other resources in the home country or elsewhere. In most cases, both location and ownership endowments affect competitiveness.[6]

For some kinds of trade, it is sufficient for the exporting country to have a location-endowment advantage over the importing country, that is, it is not *necessary* for the exporting firms to have ownership-endowment advantage over indigenous enterprises in the importing country. Much of the trade between industrialised and non-industrialised countries (which is of the Ricardian or H/O type) is of this kind. Other trade, such as that which mainly takes place between developed industrialised countries, is of high skill-intensive or sophisticated consumer goods products, and is based more on the endowment advantages of the exporting firms;[7] but, observe, this presupposes that it is better to use these advantages in combination with location-specific endowments in the exporting rather than in the importing (or in a third) country. Where, however, these latter endowments favour the importing (or a third) country, foreign production will replace trade. Foreign production then, implies that location-specific endowments favour a foreign country, but ownership-endowments favour the home country's firms; these latter being sufficient to overcome the costs of producing in a foreign environment (Hirsch, 1975) . (Again we assume that transfer costs can be considered as a negative endowment of countries other than the country of marketing.)

From this, it follows that any theory which purports to explain the determinants of any one form of international economic involvement is unlikely to explain the whole; nor, where that form is one of a number of possible alternatives, will it be adequately explained unless the forces explaining these alternatives are also taken into account. One should not be surprised, then, if trade theories of the neofactor brand, based on location-specific endowments will not normally be able to explain trade in goods based on ownership-specific endowments. But neither should one be disquieted if the neotechnology and monopolistic competitive theories of trade, based on ownership-specific endowments, are also inadequate where the *use* of such advantages is better exploited in conjunction with location-specific endowments of foreign countries.

It may be reasonably argued, however, that this latter criticism would be better directed against the way in which data on international transactions are collected and presented, and the way in which the exported ownership advantages are priced. First, trade statistics usually give details of the *gross output* of goods exported. But where exports contain a high import content, their total value may tell us little about the use made of indigenous endowments. This deficiency can only be overcome by recording exports on a domestic value-added basis. Second, trade statistics either ignore, or classify completely separately, intermediary goods, such as technology, management and organisation, which are exported in their own right. If these could be given a commodity classification, and their value added to the export of final products, then the ownership advantages of exporting enterprises would be better captured. Third, where trade takes place within the same enterprises, the recorded prices may bear little resemblance to arms-length prices, and so to the value of factor inputs used. If these problems could be overcome, a combination of the neofactor, neotechnology and monopolistic competitive theories of trade would probably explain trade patterns very well.

III.

So far we have not explicitly introduced the multinational enterprise (MNE) into our discussion. We define MNEs as companies which undertake productive activities outside the country in which they are incorporated. They are, by definition, also companies which are internationally involved. The extent to which they engage in foreign production will depend on their comparative ownership advantages *vis à vis* host country firms, and the comparative location endowments of home and foreign countries.

Unlike location-specific endowments, which are *external* to the enterprises which use them, ownership-specific endowments are *internal* to particular enterprises. They consist of tangible and intangible resources, including technology which, itself, dictates the efficiency of resource usage. Unlike location endowments, many ownership endowments take on the quality of public goods, that is their marginal usage cost is zero or minimal (hence, wherever a marginal revenue can be earned, but is not earned, they are underutilised); and, although their *origin* may be partly determined by the industry or country characteristics of enterprises, they can be used anywhere.

What, then, determines the ownership advantages which one country's enterprises possess over those of another? For our purposes, we distinguish between three kinds of advantage. The first comprises those which any firms may have over another producing in the same location. Here, Bain's classic work on the barriers to new competition (1956) provides the basic answer. Such benefits may lie in the access to markets or raw materials not available to competitors; or in size (which may both generate scale economies and inhibit effective competition); or in an exclusive possession of intangible assets, for example patents, trade marks, management skills, etc., which enable it to reach a higher level of technical or price efficiency and/or achieve more market power. These advantages, then, stem from *size, monopoly power,* and better *resource capability and usage.*

The second type of advantage is that which a branch plant of a national enterprise may have over a *de novo* enterprise (or over an existing exterprise breaking into a new product area), again producing in the same location. This arises because, while the branch plant may benefit from many of the endowments of the parent company, for example, access to cheaper inputs, knowledge of markets, centralised accounting procedures, administrative experience, R and D etc., at zero or low marginal cost, the *de novo* firm will normally have to bear their full cost. The greater the non-production overheads of the enterprise, the more pronounced this advantage is likely to be.

The third type of advantage is that which arises specifically from the multinationality of a company, and is an extension of the other two. Because such an enterprise operates in different economic environments, it is better placed to take advantage of different factor endowments and market situations. We shall return to this point later in the paper.

Most of these benefits, both individually and collectively, have been used by economists to explain the participation of affiliates of MNEs in the output of industries in host countries.[8] However, while recognising they are interrelated, there have been few explicit attempts either to explain the basis of the interrelationship or why the more marketable of the advantages are not sold directly to *other* firms. In consequence, not only has one of the fundamental attributes of MNEs been largely overlooked, but so also has the basis for much of the concern about the present international economic order. The substance of our thesis is not, in itself, new; it is more a reinterpretation and extension of an idea first formulated by

Coase in 1937, and, more recently, resurrected in the literature by Alchian and Demsetz (1972), Arrow (1969, 1975), Williamson (1971, 1975), McManus (1972), Baumann (1973), Gray (1973), Magee (1976), Murray (1974) and, perhaps most systematically of all, by Buckley and Casson (1976).

The thesis is that the international competitiveness of a country's products is attributable not only to the possession of superior resources of its enterprises but also to the desire and ability of these enterprises to internalise the advantages resulting from this possession; *and* that servicing a foreign market through foreign production confers unique benefits of this kind. Where, for example, enterprises choose to replace, or not to use, the mechanism of the market, but instead, allocate resources by their own control procedures, not only do they gain, but, depending on the reason for internalisation, others, (notably their customers and suppliers prior to *vertical* integration, and their competitors prior to *horizontal* integration), may lose. Internalisation is thus a powerful motive for takeovers or mergers, and a valuable tool in the strategy of oligopolists.

Now, it has long been recognised that such gains may follow from vertical integration, and to a lesser extent, from horizontal integration of a firm's activities; and much of current antitrust legislation is designed to prevent or minimise abuses arising as a result. But much less attention has been paid to the type of internalising practised by conglomerates, or that which reflects in the internal extension of a company's activities, or that associated with the internalisation of resources, products or markets over geographical space.

Consider, for example, the sectors in which the participation of MNEs, irrespective of their country of origin, is most pronounced in host countries. These are capital-intensive resource-based industries like aluminium, oil, copper, etc; R and D-intensive manufacturing industries; industries supplying branded consumer good products or those which require production processes which need large outputs to make them economic; capital or skill-intensive service industries, such as insurance, banking and large scale construction; and activities in which the spatial integration of inputs, products or markets is essential to efficiency, for example airlines, hotels etc. All of these not only require endowments in which MNEs have a comparative advantage, and which are difficult to acquire by *de novo* entrants; but more pertinent to our argument, they are all sectors in which there is a pronounced propensity of firms to internalise activities, particularly across national boundaries.

What then, are these incentives of firms to internalise activities? Basically, they are to avoid the disadvantages, or capitalise on the advantages of imperfections in external mechanisms of resource allocation.[9] These mechanisms are mostly of two kinds — the *price system* and *public authority fiat*. Where markets are perfectly competitive, the co-ordinating of interdependent activities cannot be improved upon; once imperfections arise or can be exploited through internalisation, this becomes a possibility.

Market imperfections may be both structural and cognitive. Uncertainty over future market conditions in the absence of competitive future markets, or about government policies, is another kind of imperfection. *Structural imperfections* arise where there are barriers to competition and economic rents are earned; where transaction costs are high; or where the economies of interdependent activities cannot be fully captured. *Cognitive imperfections* arise wherever information about the product or service being marketed is not readily available, or is costly to acquire. The cost of *uncertainty* may be gauged by the risk premium required to discount it, which may differ quite significantly between firms. From the buyer's viewpoint, market imperfections to avoid include uncertainty over the availability and price of essential supplies, and lack of control over their delivery timing and quality. From the *seller's* viewpoint, the propensity to internalise will be greatest where the market does not permit price discrimination; where the costs of enforcing property rights and controlling information flows are high; where the output produced is of more value to the seller than the buyer is willing to pay (again, possibly because of ignorance on the part of the buyer);[10] or, in the case of selling outlets, where the seller, to protect his reputation, wishes to ensure a certain quality of service, including after-sales maintenance. For both groups of firms, and for those considering horizontal integration, the possession of underutilised resources, particularly entrepreneurial and organisational capacity, which may be used at low marginal cost to produce products complementary to those currently being supplied, also fosters internalisation.

At the same time, to benefit from some of these advantages, an enterprise must be of sufficient size. This prompts firms to engage in product diversification or integration, which, in turn, increases their opportunities to profit from other internalising practices such as cross subsidisation of costs, predatory pricing, etc. One suspects that many of the advantages of conglomerate mergers are of this kind; and it cannot be a coincidence that, in recent years, takeovers and mergers have been concentrated in areas in which advantages of internalisation are most pronounced.

Public intervention in the allocation of resources may also encourage enterprises to internalise activities. Many policy instruments of governments, however justified in the pursuance of macroeconomic (and other) goals, may create distortions in the allocation of resources which enterprises may seek to exploit or protect themselves against. Some of these provoke reactions from all enterprises; others from only those which operate across national boundaries.

We confine our analysis to two kinds of government intervention especially relevant to the behaviour of MNEs. The first concerns the

production and marketing of public goods, which are not only characterised by their zero marginal cost, but by the fact that their value to the
owner may hinge on the extent to which others also possess it. Under
these circumstances, an orthodox perfect market is impossible, unless the
purchaser relies on the seller to withhold the sale of a good to other
buyers, or not to price it lower.

Some commodities and services produced by private enterprises also
have the characteristics of public goods. The major example is technology — an intermediary good which embraces all kinds of knowledge
embodied in both human and non-human capital (Johnson, 1970). The
significance of technology in the modern world economy needs no
elaboration: it is the main engine of development, a leading determinant
of both absolute and relative living standards, and a controlling factor in
the spatial allocation of resources. Its phenomenal growth since the
Second World War, especially in the field of information and communications technology, has undoubtedly facilitated the internationalisation of
firms, just as the railroad, telegraph and telephone helped the creation of
national enterprises a century ago.[11]

It is our contention that the need both to generate innovations and
ideas and to retain exclusive right to their use, has been one of the main
inducements for enterprises to internalise their activities in the last two
decades. Governments have encouraged this by extensively subsidising R
and D, continuing to endorse the patent system, and by recognising that,
in some industries, if the benefits of technological advances are to be
fully exploited, not only may it be necessary to restrict the number of
producers, but that enterprises should be free to internalise their
knowledge-producing with their knowledge-consuming activities. Even
without the intervention of governments, technology possesses many of
the attributes for internalising (or not externalising) markets. At the time
of its production, it is the sole possession of the innovator, who naturally
wishes to exploit it most profitably; it is costly and takes time to produce,
but there is no future market in it; it is often difficult for a potential
buyer to value, as its usefulness can only be determined after it has been
purchased. Yet often, for its efficient exploitation, it needs complementary
or back-up resources. These qualities apply particularly to the kind of
knowledge which *cannot* be patented, for example financial systems,
organisational skills, marketing expertise, management experience and so
on.

The second example of government intervention is particularly relevant
to the operations of MNEs. It both encourages such enterprises to
internalise existing activities, and to engage in new activities which offer
the possibility of internalising gains. It arises because of different economic
policies of national governments which often lead to distortions in the
international allocation of resources. Assume, for example, that an MNE
wishes to maximise its post-tax profits and that corporate tax rates differ

between countries. One way it can reduce its total tax burden is to capitalise on its intragroup transactions by manipulating its transfer prices, so as to record the highest profits in the lowest tax areas. Other things being equal, the more internal transactions the company engages in, the greater its opportunities for doing this; hence, in the case of MNEs, the added impetus to engage in a global strategy and to practise product or process specialisation within its organisation.

The MNE has other reasons for internalising its operations across boundaries. These include the desire to minimise the risk and/or costs of fluctuating exchange rates (Aliber, 1971); to cushion the adverse affects of government legislation or policy, for example in respect to dividend remittances; to be able to take advantage of differential interest rates and 'leads' and 'lags' in intragroup payments; and to adjust the distribution of its short-term assets between different currency areas. Some of these benefits of internalisation are now being eroded by government surveillance over transfer pricing and by the tendency for contractual arrangements between foreign and indigenous firms to replace equity investments of the former.

How far MNEs actually *do* manipulate intragroup prices to transfer income across national boundaries is still a matter for empirical research; so far the evidence collected is partial and impressionistic. Suffice to say there are many reasons why an MNE may wish to take advantage of such opportunities (Lall, 1973); and, that, however vigilant the tax authorities may be, in some areas, for example the pricing of intangible assets, the difficulty of (a) estimating the extent to which a transfer of goods or services has taken place, and (b) assigning a value to them, is a very real one.

We have illustrated, at some length, why firms and MNEs in particular, gain from internalising their activities, especially in respect of the production and marketing of technology. Another sector, in which MNEs are particularly active, is the capital-intensive resource-based industries. Here, all the traditional reasons for vertical integration hold good, in addition to those which result from multinationality *per se*; the classic example is the oil industry. They imply, for the most part, a vertical division of activity of firms, though the operations may be horizontal as well, where similar products are produced. Here too, the impetus to internalise transactions (as opposed to engaging in contractual arrangements) in the case of international vertical integration, is likely to be greater than in the case of domestic vertical integration.

It must not be forgotten, however, that there are costs as well as benefits to internalising economic activities; for an examination of these see Coase (1937), Buckley and Casson (1976). As markets become less imperfect the net gains of internalisation become less. The move towards externalising the marketing of many raw materials, partly stimulated by the actions of governments, testifies to this. In his study of U.K. direct investment overseas, Reddaway (1968) found that only 4 per cent of the output of U.K. plantation and mining affiliates, originally set up to supply the investing firms, were now directly imported by them.

We conclude, therefore, that the *ownership advantages* of firms stem from their exclusive possession and use of certain kinds of assets. Very often, enterprises acquire these rights by internalising those previously distributed by the market or public fiat; or by not externalising those which they originate themselves. This will only be profitable in imperfect market conditions, and where it is thought the co-ordinating and synergising properties of the firm to allocate resources are superior to those of markets or public fiat. It is possible to identify the source of such imperfections, both within countries and internationally, and to point to the types of activities which offer the greatest gains from internalisation. Of these, the production and marketing of intangible assets and of essential location-specific resources are the two most important. Both happen to be areas in which MNEs are particularly involved; the fact that the ownership advantages are exploited by foreign production is partly explained by *location*-specific endowments of the foreign country, and partly by certain ownership advantages which accrue only when a firm produces outside its national boundaries.[12]

IV.

What is the link between the above discussion and other explanations of international involvement? Simply this. The neotechnology theories of trade and the knowledge theories of direct investment both emphasise the possession of superior technology as an explanation of both trade and production, The monopolistic competitive theories concentrate on some aspect of 'arms-length' imperfect competition as the explanation for trade and investment.

It is our contention that the two approaches should be treated as complementary aspects of an eclectic theory of international involvement, which should embrace not only the product but also the factor and inter-mediary goods markets; and should acknowledge that the ownership advantages arise not only from the exclusive possession of certain assets, but from the ability of firms to internalise these assets to protect them-selves against the failure of markets (including the consequences of this failure for competitors' behaviour) and government fiat over the rest of their activities. Because it relates to the way in which the enterprise co-ordinates its activities, we call our approach a *systemic* theory of owner-ship advantages, applied to both trade and international production.[13]

In presenting the systemic theory, we accept we are in danger of being accused of eclectic taxonomy. We also acknowledge the interdependence between technology, imperfect competition and the internalisation process, and that it is not always easy to separate cause and effect.

But in the search for a composite measure of ownership advantage, a systemic approach has something to commend it. Empirically, there can be little doubt of the increase in the vertical and horizontal integration of firms, and of market and product diversification, which has enabled firms to benefit from the internalisation of their activities. This is demonstrated both by the increase in the concentration of enterprises in industrial economies in the postwar period, and by the growing importance of the pre- and post-production activities of firms. Other data suggest that about one-half of all exports of MNEs are intragroup in character.

But what is the positive value of the systemic theory? The theory suggests that, given the distribution of location-specific endowments, enterprises which have the greatest opportunities for, and derive the most from, internalising activities will be the most competitive in foreign markets. *Inter alia* these advantages will differ according to industry, country and enterprise characteristics. Hence, the ownership advantages of Japanese iron and steel firms over South Korean iron and steel firms will be very different from those of U.K. tobacco firms over Brazilian tobacco firms or U.S. computer firms over French computer firms. Enterprises will engage in the type of internalisation most suited to the factor combinations, market situations and government policies with which they are faced. For example, the systemic theory would suggest not only that research-intensive industries would tend to be more multinational than other industries; but that internalisation to secure foreign-based raw materials would be greater for enterprises from economies which have few indigenous materials than those which are self-sufficient; that the most efficient MNEs will exploit the most profitable foreign markets — compare, for example, the U.S. and U.K. choice of investment outlets (Stopford, 1976); that the participation of foreign affiliates is likely to be greatest in those sectors of host countries where there are substantial economies of *enterprise* size. Our theory is consistent with Horst's conclusion (1972) that most of the explanatory variables of foreign direct investment can be captured in the size of enterprise; indeed, one would normally expect size and the propensity to internalise to be very closely correlated, and MNEs to be better equipped to spread risks than national multiproduct firms.

What does the systemic theory predict that the other ownership theories do not? Taking the theories as a group, probably very little, except in so far as the independent variables fail to capture the advantages of internalisation. Indeed, we would argue that our theory is less an alternative theory of ownership advantages of enterprises, than one which pinpoints the essential and common characteristics of each of the traditional explanations. There is, however, one difference of substance. The systemic approach would argue that it is not the possession of technology *per se* which gives an enterprise selling goods embodying that technology to foreign markets (irrespective of where they are

produced) an edge over its competitors, but the advantage of internalising that technology, rather than selling it to a foreign producer for
the production of those goods. It is not the orthodox type of monopoly
advantages which give the enterprise an edge over its rivals — actual or
potential — but the advantages which accrue through internalisation, for
example transfer price manipulation, security of supplies and markets,
and control over use of intermediate goods. It is not surplus entrepreneurial
resources *per se* which lead to foreign direct investment, but the ability of
enterprises to combine these resources with others to take advantage of
the economies of production of joint products.

In other words, without the incentive to internalise the production
and/or sale of technology, foreign investment in technology-based
industries would give way to licensing agreements and/or to the outright
sale of knowledge on a contractual basis. Without the incentive to
internalise market imperfections, there would be much less reason to
engage in vertical or horizontal integration, and again, transactions would
take place between independent firms. This, we would argue, is the
distinctiveness of our approach.

V.

So far we have concentrated on the ownership endowments of its
enterprises as an explanation of a country's international competitiveness,
whatever the form of the involvement. We have argued that, although
the advantages are enterprise-specific, the fact that these may differ by
nationality of enterprise, suggests that such advantages, though endogenous
to the individual firms at that time, are not independent of their industrial
structure, or of the general economic and institutional environment of
which they are part. For example, U.S. government science and education
policy may be a key variable in explaining the technological lead of U.S.
firms in many industries; while, as Vernon (1974) has pointed out,
innovations respond to factor endowment and market needs, which also
influence the likely advantages of internalising those innovations. The
institutional arrangments by which innovations are rewarded are no less
relevant.

But these country or industry variables affecting ownership advantages
are not the same as the location-specific endowments to which we have
earlier referred. On our interpretation, these comprise three components —
the resources which can only be *used* by enterprises in the locations in
which they are sited, unavoidable or non-transferable costs such as taxes,
government constraints on dividend remission etc., and the costs of
shipping products from the country of production to the country of
marketing.

Each of these elements has received extensive attention in the literature of location theory, which usually assumes ownership endowments as the same between firms, and seeks to explain *where* they are exploited. Our concern here is a different one. Put in question form it is 'given the ownership endowments, is the location of production by MNEs likely to be different from that of non MNEs?' The systemic theory suggests that it is, and for three reasons. First, there may be particular internalising economies resulting from the friction of geographical space. Second, the location-specific endowments, which offer the greatest potential for internalisation are not distributed evenly between countries. Third, where there are differences in the market imperfections or Government policies of countries, then MNEs might be influenced in the extent to which they take advantage of these imperfections by internalising their operations.

In elaboration of these points, we would make four observations. First, various studies have underlined the advantages of both internalising R and D activities of enterprises and centralising them in or near the markets which stimulate such activities (Michalet, 1974; Vernon, 1974). In the case of U.S. based MNEs, this suggests that both *ownership* and *location* endowments work in favour of a home R and D base. In the case of MNEs from smaller home markets, this tendency may not be so pronounced. By contrast, because the advantages of internalisation are generally much less, it may be profitable to spatially disperse some kinds of manufacturing activities — especially where the production processes involved have become standardised.[14]

Second, a MNE which produces in different market environments, may well seek to co-ordinate its activities differently; the degree of uncertainty over local consumer tastes, future market conditions and government policy certainly varies between countries. For example, the less imperfect is the market for technology, the less likely is an enterprise to market technology-based products itself. Compare, for example, the role of foreign pharmaceutical companies in Italy, which does not recognise patent protection on drugs, with that of such companies in almost any other European country. By contrast, in some LDCs, MNEs may be reluctant to license local firms, because they feel that the complementary technology is insufficient to ensure the quality control they need.

Third, and perhaps most important, is the advantage which a diversified earnings base provides for an MNE to exploit differential imperfections in national or international markets and/or currency areas (Aliber, 1971), *inter alia*, through transfer-price manipulation; the use of leads and lags in intragroup transactions; the acquisition and monitoring of information; and the extension of benefits enjoyed by multiplant national firms at an international level. These are some of the (potential) advantages of internalisation afforded by international production, compared with international trade.

Fourth, there is the drive towards international production as part of oligopolistic behaviour (Knickerbocker, 1973). This is really a territorial extension of domestic strategy, and does not pose any new conceptual problems (but, see Vernon, 1974). Again, however, in so far as a company perceives its foreign interests to be part of a global strategy, rather than as an independent entity, the internalising advantages may be crucial to the locational decision of both leaders and followers.

VI.

To summarise: the international competitiveness of a particular country will depend on the ownership endowments of its enterprises and on its locational endowments, relative to those of other countries; and the transfer costs in moving goods and services from one country to another. The locational advantages will be the key influence of *where* production takes place, that is, the form of international involvement.

The origin of ownership endowments rests on internalising economies; these also may influence the location of enterprises. An eclectic or systemic theory of international competitiveness must thus embrace a theory of location and ownership endowments, the character of which we have discussed.

In the light of our analysis, what might one expect the impact of the MNE to be on location of production, the international diffusion or transfer of technology and trade patterns?

There are many different views about the affect of MNEs on the international distribution of resources. Partly, these reflect differences in the perspective one takes, for example that of a particular country or region, or that of all countries; or of the goals one is seeking to promote (such as increase in G.N.P., economic stability, economic independence, etc.). We shall confine ourselves to economic issues viewed in a global context. Here, there are two main viewpoints. The first is that MNEs promote a more efficient distribution of resources as, by internalising imperfect markets, they are able to overcome distortions in the economic system, such as barriers to the transfer of technology, tariff and non-tariff barriers, inappropriately valued exchange rates. Moreover, in a world of uncertainty and information imperfections, their more efficient scanning and monitoring processes, and their flexibility to respond better to market signals, is a useful conpetitive stimulus. In short, this view extols the MNE as an integrating force in the world economy, surmounting national barriers and improving the allocating of resources.

The second view asserts, that far from overcoming market imperfections, the MNEs are, themselves, a major distorting force in resource allocation; this is partly because they operate mostly in oligopolistic markets, and partly because of their ability to bypass market mechanisms and/or government regulations. As a result, it is argued, they engage in restrictive practices, raise barriers to entry, and, by their internalisation and centralisation of decision-taking, adversely affect the efficiency of resource allocation between countries. Far from promoting competition, the co-ordination of activities by entrepreneurs freezes existing production patterns, encourages agglomeration and makes it more difficult for countries to exploit their dynamic comparative advantages. Since MNEs *do* exert monopoly power, it is legitimate (on the lines of the optimum tariff argument) for home or host countries to impose restrictions on their activities.

The truth — in so far as it is possible to generalise — is obviously somewhere between these two extremes, with the balance steering one way or another according to (a) the efficiency of the resource allocative mechanism prior to the entrance of the MNEs and (b) the market conditions under which MNEs compete — which will vary, *inter alia*, according to industry and country.

But there are certain effects of MNEs, however they may be interpreted, which do seem to have been reasonably well established in the literature. We will touch on all three of these.

(1) In some instances, MNEs have been an integrating force and have taken advantages of existing factor endowments, thus promoting the more efficient use of resources. The best example, is where mobile resources of capital and technology are transferred from a capital and technology-rich country, and combined with immobile resources of labour and/or materials in labour and materials-rich countries, thereby helping these countries to exploit their dynamic comparative advantage. Other examples include what is currently happening in Europe as a result of the E.E.C., namely that the MNEs are rationalising their activities to take advantage of the economies of specialisation. This is a slow process, but no different, in principle, to the behaviour of multiregional (national) enterprises in the U.S., which may well be one of the explanations of the greater specialisation in the U.S. than within the E.E.C. as demonstrated by Hufbauer and Chilas (1973).

(2) There is some evidence of a spatial specialisation of the activities of MNEs and in particular, the centralisation of R and D activities in the home country. Something over 90 per cent of the R and D activities of Swedish and U.S. MNEs is undertaken in their home countries, and the proportion is probably not very different for most of the other leading investors. Hymer suggests that MNEs are encouraging the specialisation of activities, not for technological as much as organisational or strategic reasons, most of which enhance the incentive to internalise R and D in the home country. But, it does not necessarily follow that, without MNEs, the distribution of innovatory activities would have been any the less centralised. R and D among Japanese and European enterprises has certainly been stimulated by the competition from U.S. MNEs. The impact

on the U.K. pharmaceutical and semiconductor industries are classic
examples (Tilton, 1971 and Lake, 1975). In the LDCs, because of the lack
of indigenous competitors, the Hymer hypothesis has probably more
weight, though, even here, there are examples of MNEs setting up
specialised R and D facilities.

(3) In any analysis of the impact of MNEs on trade and location, it is
useful to distinguish between the different motives for foreign direct
investment. Kojima for example (1973) has distinguished between trade-
oriented and anti-trade-oriented activities of MNEs. He suggests that
current Swedish and Japanese investments are mainly made in areas in
which the home countries are losing a comparative advantage and host
countries are gaining it. These have been of two kinds; one to exploit
natural resources not available indigenously, and the other to switch
labour-intensive activities from high labour cost to low labour cost locations.
On the other hand, Kojima asserts that many foreign investments by U.S.
firms have been made to protect an oligopolistic position in world markets
and in response to trade barriers, and have transferred activities from
which they have a comparative advantage to where they have a disadvantage.
Such investments, he claims, are anti-trade oriented and run against the
principles of comparative advantage. Kojima cites here the extensive U.S.
foreign investments in the capital and technologically intensive industries.

The border between transferring a comparative advantage and creating
a new one is a narrow one, and the Kojima distinction between trade-
generating and trade-destroying investments is not altogether convincing.
Moreover, his approach tends to be a static one and is couched in terms
of first-best solutions. It also fails to consider vertical specialisation
within industrial sectors. Assuming technology (as in intermediate good)
can be sold for a competitive price between independent parties, one
might reasonably expect non-skilled labour-intensive operations of high
technology industries to be transplanted to those areas which possess
such labour in abundance; and countries with an abundance of materials
to produce such materials with technology developed by nations which
have a limited amount of materials. The Japanese and U.S. patterns may
be complementary to each other; their *ownership* advantages may reflect
country-specific characteristics. Evidence collected about the trading
patterns of U.S. MNEs (Lipsey and Weiss, 1973) supports this view. The
imports of U.S. MNEs tend to be more capital intensive than that of
other U.S. firms, mainly because of the ability of MNEs to export capital
and technology to undertake the labour-intensive production processes of
a capital-intensive product in low labour cost areas.

From a normative viewpoint, the point of greater interest is the extent
to which technology transfer through the co-ordination of the firm is
preferable to that of the market; and, on this subject, there has been only
limited research (Arrow 1969, Williamson 1975). Yet this, as we have
suggested, is a crucial issue, which both helps explain the growth of the

MNEs (relative to non-MNEs) and its effect on the spatial distribution of economic activity. Assuming perfectly competitive markets are not generally feasible (nor, from viewpoints other than economic efficiency necessarily desirable), under what circumstances is it preferable for the resource allocative process to be decided upon by markets or governments, however imperfect they may be, and under what circumstances by the co-ordinating activities of MNEs? For there is no *a priori* reason to suppose one form of resource allocation is preferable to the other. In remedying the imperfections and alleged distorting behaviour of MNEs, should not as much attention be given to removing some of the distortions of the environment in which they operate, so that they have less incentive to internalise their activities? To give a recent example, the replacement of fixed by flexible rates has decisively reduced the impetus for MNEs to engage in speculative or protective currency movements across boundaries. The candidate most in need of attention at the moment is technology. It is here where the present system of rewards and penalties leaves so much to be desired (Johnson, 1970) and it is here where both the incentive to internalise by MNEs *and* the potential for distorting behaviour on their part in exploiting the benefits of that internalisation arise.

In the last resort, however, we must acknowledge that it is not efficiency and certainly not efficiency viewed from a global standpoint, which is the standard by which the relative merits of internalisation of MNEs and imperfect markets of allocating resources is likely to be assessed. It is the effects of such patterns of resource allocation on the distribution of income between or within nations; on the relative economic power of countries or of different groups of asset owners; on the sovereignty of one country to manage its own affairs. It is these matters which are at the centre of the arena of public debate at the moment; and it is on such criteria as these that the actions of MNEs are judged.

Some countries facing the choice offered above, have clearly preferred to buy their resources in imperfect markets than through MNEs. Japan is the clearest example; while many LDCs are increasingly seeking to depackage the package of resources provided by MNEs in the belief that they can externalise the internal economies. Within the advanced countries, the non-market route is generally accepted. But, here too, there are murmurings of concern, articulated not only in such polemics as the *Global Reach* (Barnet and Muller, 1974) but in research studies done at the Brookings Institution (Bergsten, Horst and Moran, 1976) and by Peggy Musgrave (1975), on the effect of the (internalising) advantages of international production on the domestic economic power of U.S. corporations.

This particular form of the debate on the role of MNEs on trade and the transfer of technology and the location of production, is still in its infancy. It is an area hazardous and not altogether attractive for the academic economist; the issues are controversial; the concepts are elusive; the data are not easily subject to quantitative manipulation and appraisal, and the standard of debate is often low. But intellectually, it presents great challenge; it also offers much scope for the collaboration not only of economists of different specialities and persuasions, but between economists and researchers from other disciplines. For these reasons alone, it deserves to attract our ablest minds.

NOTES

[1] The following observation by Williams about industries which had expanded beyond their political frontiers is of especial interest to our discussion. 'They represent in some cases the projection by one country into others of its capital, technique, special knowledge along the lines of an industry and its market, as against the obvious alternative of home employment in other lines. They represent, in other cases, an international assembling of capital and management for world enterprises ramifying into many countries. They suggest very strikingly an organic interconnection of international trade, movement of productive factors, transport and market organisation.'

[2] See *inter alia* Horst (1972, 1974), Baumann (1974), Orr (1973), Wolf (1971), Caves (1974a), Buckley and Dunning (1976).

[3] Mainly enterprises: by a country's enterprises we mean those whose head offices are legally incorporated in the country.

[4] G.D.P. = incomes earned from domestic resources; G.D.P. = D.G.P. + income earned from assets abroad less income paid to foreigners on domestic assets.

[5] Proximity to the point of sale may be treated as a location-specific endowment for these purposes; distance (implying transport and other transfer cost) is thus considered as a negative endowment.

[6] Defined for our purposes as 'a country's share of foreign markets accounted for by its exports of goods (including intermediate goods and services), plus the output of its foreign affiliates; plus its share of domestic markets accounted for by domestic production and imports from its foreign affiliates.'

[7] For an elaboration of the complementarity between the neofactor theories of trade, see Hirsch (1975).

[8] See references in note 2.

[9] To avoid being subject to imperfections of markets when they are the weaker party to an exchange but to capitalise on imperfections where they are the stronger party.

[10] Such as particularly applies in the case of technically complex products and information.

[11] The transition from regional to national railroads in the nineteenth and early twentieth century was paralleled by the transition from national to multinational airlines after the Second World War.

[12] We have not the space to deal with the role of internalisation in prompting other forms of foreign direct investment; in some cases the co-ordinating advantages of the firm clearly transcends that of the market for technological reasons, such as airlines; in others it is more to do with con-

trolling information among interdependent activities, such as advertising, tourism; or as a form of oligopolistic strategy. In many cases, an investment based on technological innovation has managed to create its own barriers to entry through economies of size.

[13] Licensing and other forms of contractual arrangements of intermediate products.

[14] The pharmaceutical industry is perhaps the best illustration of this point.

REFERENCES

Alchian, A. and Demsetz, H., 'Production, Information Costs and Economic Organisation', *American Economic Review 62* (Dec., 1972).

Aliber, R., 'A Theory of Foreign Direct Investment, in C.P. Kindleberger (ed.) *The International Corporation* (Cambridge, Mass., M.I.T. Press, 1970).

Arrow, K. J., 'The Organisation of Economic Activity: Issues Pertinent to the Choice of Market and Non Market Considerations: in *The Analysis and Evaluation of Public Expenditures: the P.P.B. System*' Joint Economic Committee (Washington: U.S. Government Printing Office, 1969).

Arrow, K. J., 'Vertical Integration and Communication', *Bell Journal of Economics* (Spring, 1975) Vol. 5 No. 1.

Bain, J. S., *Barriers to New Competition*, (Cambridge: Mass.: Harvard University Press, 1956).

Baldwin, R. E., 'International Trade in Inputs and Outputs', *American Economic Review, 60* (May, 1970).

Barnet, R. J. and Muller, R. E., *The Global Reach* (New York: Simon and Schuster, 1974).

Baumann, H., *The Determinants of the Pattern of Foreign Direct Investment: Some Hypotheses Reconsidered*. Unpublished paper, 1974.

Bergsten, E. F., Horst, T. and Moran, T. E., *American Multinationals and American Interests*. (To be published by Brookings Institution, 1977.)

Buckley, P. J. and Dunning, J. H., 'The Industrial Structure of U.S. Direct Investment in the U.K.', *Journal of International Business* (Fall/Winter, 1976).

Buckley, P. J. and Casson, M., *The Future of the Multinational Enterprise*, (London: Macmillan, 1976).

Caves, R. E., 'Industrial Corporations: The Industrial Economics of Foreign Investment', *Economica 38* (Feb., 1971).

Caves, R. E., 'Causes of Direct Investment: Foreign Firms' Shares in Canadian and United Kingdom Manufacturing Industries', *Review of Economies and Statistics 56* (Aug., 1974a).

Caves, R. E., 'Industrial Organisation', in J. H. Dunning (ed.) *Economic Analysis and the Multinational Enterprise* (London, Allen and Unwin, 1974b).

Coase, R. H., 'The Nature of the Firm', *Economica 4* (Nov., 1937).

Dunning, J. H., *American Investment in British Manufacturing Industry* (London: Allen and Unwin, 1958).

Dunning, J. H., 'The Determinants of International Production', *Oxford Economic Papers 25*, (Nov., 1973a).

Dunning, J. H., *The Location of International Firms in an Enlarged E.E.C.: An Exploratory Paper*, Manchester Statistical Society (1973b).

Furubotn, E. G. and Pejovich, S., 'Property Rights and Economic Theory: A Survey of Recent Literature', *Journal of Economic Issues, 6* (Dec., 1972).

Gray, H. P., *The Economics of Business Investment Abroad* (London: Macmillan, 1973).

Hirsch, S., 'Capital and Technology Confronting the Neo-factor Proportions and Neo-technology Accounts of International Trade', *Welt Wirtschaftliches Archive 110* No. 4 (1974).

Hirsch, S., 'An International Trade and Investment Theory of the Firm', *Oxford Economic Papers 28* (July, 1976).

Horst, T., 'Firm and Industry Determinants of the Decision to Invest Abroad: An Empirical Study', *Review of Economics and Statistics 54* (Aug., 1972).

Horst, T., *American Exports and Foreign Direct Investments*. Harvard University of Economic Research Discussion Papers, 362 (May, 1974).

Hufbauer, G. C., 'The Impact of National Characteristics and Technology on the Commodity Composition of Trade in Manufactured Goods', in R. Vernon (ed.) *The Technology Factor in International Trade* (New York: Columbia University Press, 1970).

Hufbauer, G. C. and Chilas, J. G., 'Specialisation by Industrial Countries: Extent and Consequences' in H. Giersch (ed.) *The International Division of Labour* Problems and Perspectives (Tubingen: JCB Mohr (1974).

Hymer, S., *The International Operations of National Firms A Study of Direct Investment* (Unpublished Doctoral Thesis M.I.T., 1960).

Hymer, S., 'The Multinational Corporation and the Law of Uneven Development' in J. Bhagwati (ed.) *Economics and World Order* (New York: World Law Fund, 1970).

Iversen, C., *Aspects of International Capital Movements* (London and Copenhagen: Levin and Munksgaard, 1935).

Johnson, H., *Comparative Cost and Commercial Policy Theory for a Developing World Economy* (Stockholm: Almquist and Wiksell, 1968).

Johnson, H., 'The Efficiency and Welfare Implications of the International Corporation' in C. P. Kindleberger (ed.) *The International Corporation* (Cambridge, Mass.: M.I.T. Press, 1970).

Knickerbocker, P. T., *Oligopolistic Reaction and the Multinational Enterprise* (Cambridge, Mass.: Harvard University Press, 1973).

Kojima, K., 'A Macro-Economic Approach to Foreign Direct Investment', *Hitotsubashi Journal of Economics 14* (June, 1973).

Lake, A., *Multinational Firms and the U.K. Pharmaceutical Industry. A Study of Innovation and Imitation* Unpublished Paper (1975).

Lall, S., 'Transfer Pricing by Multinational Manufacturing Firms', *Oxford Bulletin of Economics and Statistics 35* (Aug., 1973).

Leontief, W., 'Domestic Production and Foreign Trade; the American Capital Position Re-examined', *Proceedings of the American Philosophical Society* Vol. 97 (1953).

Leontief, W., 'Factor Proportions and the Structure of American Trade; Further Theoretical and Empirical Analysis', *Review of Economics and Statistics 38* (1956).

Lipsey, R. E. and Weiss, M. Y., *Multinational Firms and the Factor Intensity of Trade.* National Bureau of Economic Research Working Paper No. 8 (1973).

MacDougall, G. D. A., 'British and American Exports. A Study Suggested by the Theory of Comparative Costs', *Economic Journal 61* pp. 697– 724 *62* 487–521 (1951 and 1952).

Magee, G. P., *Information and the Multinational Corporation: An Appropriability Theory of Direct Foreign Investment.* University of Texas, College of Business Administration Working Paper 77–11 (1976).

McManus, J. C., 'The Theory of the Multinational Firm', in G. Pacquet (ed.) *The Multinational Firm and the Nation State* (Toronto: Collier Macmillan, 1972).

Michalet, C., *Multinational Enterprises and the Transfer of Technology* Unpublished Paper for O.E.C.D. DAS/SPR/73. 64 (1973).

Muller, R., 'Global Corporations and National Stabilization Policy: The Need for Social Planning', *Journal of Economic Issues 9* (June, 1975).

Mundell, R. A., 'International Trade and Factor Mobility', *American Economic Review 47* (June, 1957) pp. 321–35.

Murray, R., 'Underdevelopment, International Firms and the International Division of Labour' in J. Tinbergen (ed.) *Towards a New World Economy* (Rotterdam: Rotterdam University Press, 1972).

Musgrave, P. B., *Direct Investment Abroad and the Multinationals: Effects on the U.S. Economy.* Prepared for the use of the Sub-Committee on Multinational Corporations of the Committee on Foreign Relations, U.S. Senate, Aug., Washington U.S. Government Printing Office (1975).

Nurkse, R., 'Causes and Effects of Capital Movements', (1933), reprinted in J. H. Dunning *International Investment* (Penguin Readings, 1972).

Ohlin, B., *Interregional and International Trade* (1933) (Cambridge, Mass.,: Harvard University Press; (rev. ed. 1967).

Orr, D., *Foreign Control and Foreign Penetration in Canadian Manufacturing Industries* Unpublished Paper (1973).

Parry, T. G., *The International Location of Production: Studies In the Trade and Non-Trade Servicing of International Markets by Multinational Manufacturing Enterprise* PhD. Thesis (University of London, 1975).

Reddaway, W. B., Potter, S. T. and Taylor, C. T., *The Effects of U.K. Direct Investment Overseas* (Cambridge (U.K.): Cambridge University Press, 1968).

Samuelson, P., 'International Trade and Equalisation of Factor Prices', *Economic Journal, 58* (June, 1948).

Southard, F. A., *American Industry in Europe* (Boston: Houghton Mifflin Company, 1931).

Stopford, J., 'Changing Perspectives on Investment of British Manufacturing Multinationals', *Journal of International Business Studies 7* (Fall/Winter, 1976).

Tilton, J. E., *International Diffusion of Technology: The Case of Semiconductors* (Washington D.C.: The Brookings Institution, 1971).

Vernon, R., 'International Investment and International Trade in the Product Cycle', *Quarterly Journal of Economics* 80 (1966) pp. 190–207.

Vernon, R., 'The Location of Economic Activity' in J. H. Dunning (ed.) *Economic Analysis and the Multinational Enterprise* (London: Allen and Unwin, 1974).

Weber, A., 'Location Theory and Trade Policy', *International Economic Papers 8* (1958).

Williams, J. H., 'The Theory of International Trade Reconsidered', *Economic Journal* 39 (June, 1929).

Williamson, O. E., 'The Vertical Integration of Production: Market Failure Considerations', *American Economic Review 61* (May, 1971).

Williamson, O. E., 'The Economics of Internal Organisation: Exit and Voice in Relation to Markets and Hierarchies', *American Economic Review: Papers and Proceedings* 66 (May, 1975).

Wolf, B., *Internationalization of U.S. Manufacturing Firms. A Type of Diversification* Unpublished Doctoral Dissertation (Yale University, 1971).

Comment
Nils Lundgren

I. THE GENERAL APPROACH

Professor Dunning's paper on the role of multinational enterprises in the international allocation of economic activity takes its starting point in some of the most promising advances in economic theory in recent years. His eclecticism leads him to apply elements from the theory of property rights, of information and transaction costs, of risks and uncertainty and of scale economies. These various elements are at present being used to develop the theory of the nature of the firm, a work initiated by Ronald Coase in his seminal article from 1937 and continued in particular by Alchian and Demsetz in the 1960s and 1970s.

This is an approach I fully agree with and have myself adopted in my studies of the multinational enterprise stimulated by the writings of Hymer, Kindleberger, Johnson and Caves. The early empirical work and much of the popular literature in the field was for a long time led astray by posing the wrong question to the wrong people. Questionnaires and interviews directed at managers of multinational firms sought an answer to the question of why the particular firms studied had invested abroad rather than at home. The answers to that question, of necessity, referred to various differences between home country and host country concerning wage levels, trade barriers, proximity to markets, supply of raw materials, taxation, etc. All these factors are well-known determinants of the international location of economic activity. They are simply expressions of comparative advantages appearing to individual firms as absolute advantages. As these studies implicitly are based on the assumption that no other firm could have made the investment, the real issue disappears. For obviously, the real issue is not why in this particular country, but why by this particular firm.

It is that question which leads us to the very basic problem of the nature of the firm. For there are good reasons to believe that domestic firms have some cost advantage over foreign firms in operating plants in a country. This leads us primarily to look for the more than compensating cost advantage enjoyed by foreign firms that successfully establish and operate subsidiaries in a country. We then decide that such firms must have some unique asset that generates an income flow which offsets the cost advantages of domestic firms. Such an assumption implies an analogy with the theory of national comparative advantage in international trade theory. Just as internationally immobile productive factors make pretrade cost structures different between countries and create a basis for international trade, firms seem to have productive factors that are immobile between firms and give rise to comparative advantages of firms in different product lines. These factors are what Professor Dunning calls *ownership-specific endowments.*

The nature of such firm specific assets can vary and Professor Dunning gives good examples in his analysis. In general, specialised knowledge about marketing, production, and product development or about co-ordination of such activities seems to be the heart of the matter. Combining two theories, the traditional one explaining the international location of economic activities and the firm-centred one explaining the allocation of activities between firms, we would seem to have the key to the pattern of multinational enterprise.

The story does not end there, however. We are still left with the problem of why firms with unique assets would establish subsidiaries abroad in countries with a comparative advantage in the relevant kind of economic activity. Why not sell the asset or the service from it to local firms which by assumption ought to be able to pay more for it than the foreign owner firm could hope to earn through a subsidiary? The most general answer to that is that the transaction costs in the market are too high. We have all been accustomed to treat such costs as market imperfections. In fact, no markets are perfect in the sense that information and transaction costs are zero. The economic problem of optimal allocation therefore covers the question of whether a market transaction is profitable given such costs and whether the alternative is no exchange at all or exchange in a different institutional setting. It was the message of Coase's 1937 article that the firm is such an institutional alternative to the market and, in fact, that the cost of market transactions was the basic explanation of why there are firms at all.

If we introduce this element, as Professor Dunning does, into the theory of multinational enterprise by assuming that the costs of transferring knowledge and co-ordinating economic activities from R and D and finance via production to marketing and after-sales service are lower inside firms than in market exchange between independent firms, we have a complete model predicting what we observe in the real world, i.e. multinational enterprises spreading over the globe. There is a long way to go in identifying the costs involved and measuring them, but I think we are on the right road.

II. A COUPLE OF OBJECTIONS

While I share Professor Dunning's general approach interpreted in the way briefly recapitulated above, I have a couple of objections against what I think he is saying about details and about some elements from other theories. It may be that I misunderstand his presentation, because it covers so much in only about 20 pages, however. The cost of an eclectic approach tends to be that one needs a lot of space to clear up the precise relations between the components because these have originally been shaped for other purposes.

(1) SCALE ECONOMIES

The presence of *scale economies* (falling unit costs) is maintained to be an important determinant of foreign investment. While I believe that to be true, I cannot see that Professor Dunning explains how. This is a pity because at the most elementary level scale economies obviously favour concentration of production to a few big plants and accordingly *ceteris paribus* lead to foreign trade rather than foreign investment. I assume that Professor Dunning has in mind scale economies at other points in the production process. If, as is likely, there are such economies in certain types of R and D and in finance, but *not* in production, traditional economic theory would predict that a few firms would specialise in R and D and finance in countries where scientists and bankers are abundant. These firms would sell their services to production firms established in countries where, for instance, engineers and skilled labour are abundant or where the markets are, etc. The missing link in this model that would lead to the establishment of multinational firms is obviously some transaction costs in the trade in such services between independent firms. It is not difficult to generate hypotheses. The uncertainty in small production firms as to the value of what is being offered for sale, for instance. As Arrow has pointed out, it is difficult to judge the value of knowledge without already possessing it. It is also a problem of defining property rights. The small production firms would be dependent on future decisions about R and D, etc., in firms abroad. They would like to have better information about that. Perhaps a man on the board of the R and D company? Or a demand that the R and D company shares the risk with the production company through a stake in its equity? The multinational enterprise is taking shape.

Another aspect of scale economies is the question of how firm-specific it is. Unless we supply the theory with some additional elements, any firm (or individual) could decide to set up a firm large enough to reap such economies. Furthermore, the relation to barriers to entry and market structure and thereby to market behaviour and market power is strategic. Oligopolistic firms may well want to invest abroad to keep out foreign competitors and they may want to follow each other with subsidiaries into new foreign markets. But why do they succeed, if indeed they do? The *desire* to have few competitors cannot be enough.

(2) EFFICIENCY OF MARKETS

It follows from the general approach which I share with Professor Dunning that the more efficient the spot and futures markets are for goods and services (including knowledge), the less scope there is for co-ordinating economic activities inside large firms rather than over markets with independent transactors. Patents are a kind of second-best system which creates a market for knowledge (both through the market for patents and through the market for licences). The patent system is accordingly an (imperfect) substitute for foreign investment. An efficient capital market is another substitute. We have all seen how often takeovers are explained by the need for capital to finance rapid expansion. The tendency towards financial empires in countries with primitive capital markets may be an illustration of the same phenomenon. The future may see breakthroughs for markets in knowledge, which would undermine the trend towards integrated multinational companies. Or it may see breakthroughs in the organisation of firms which will pull the other way. Government policy may furthermore encourage efficient markets or, perhaps more likely, discourage their emergence. I think this important aspect of the approach Professor Dunning has chosen deserves more attention than it gets in his paper. On page 407 I think he comes close to saying that the patents system has the opposite effect from what I claim here.

(3) PROTECTIONISM

Assume that a number of activities are most efficiently coordinated inside large firms and that these are all located in country A, which has an overall comparative advantage in that production line, and supplies country B with the final product through exports. Now let country B introduce a prohibitive tariff on this product. The result is likely to be that the suppliers in A set up subsidiaries in B and go on co-ordinating the whole set of activities. The government in B has, unconsciously, created a multinational firm!

I think this simple model illustrates one of the most important mechanisms behind the expansion of multinational firms. In Latin America it is easy to observe the mechanism because tariffs and similar visible trade barriers are used. In other countries protectionism is much more difficult to discern for the economist, though not for the traders. Typical examples are subsidies to local production, the threat of discrimination against imports in the future and discriminating public procurement. In fact, whenever the government is involved either directly in buying, as in the public sector and in government-owned firms or indirectly through active industrial policy, the tendency to favour or require local production is getting stronger. I do not think that IBM or

L.M. Ericsson would have established manufacturing subsidiaries abroad to the extent they have, if it had not been for their dependence on governments as customers and as subsidizers of local competitors.

The relation between protectionism and the formation of multinational firms obviously touches directly upon the subject of the conference and would therefore seem to merit some discussion.

(4) TRANSFER PRICING AND TAXATION

The opportunities to exploit international differences in tax rules by manipulating transfer pricing in trade between companies belonging to the same group have received much attention. Professor Dunning seems to give this phenomenon more weight than I think the research results motivate. There is no doubt that these opportunities are widely used in the sense that if we could identify all cases where the transfer price differs from the 'correct' arm's-length market price, we would find that they are many. However, recent research tends to play down the possibilities of large organisations to manipulate their information and control system in this way without losing efficiency and being let down by honest or dissatisfied employees. It would appear easier to have long-run stable divergencies between correct and actual transfer prices, however. I do not deny that at least less-developed countries could suffer important losses this way even today. What I do not believe is that these opportunities are an important determinant of the process towards more and bigger multinational firms. The whole national and industrial pattern seems to speak against such a hypothesis.

III. THE BASIC ISSUE

The basic issue in Professor Dunning's paper should be: How does the existence of multinational firms affect the global location of economic activity? This is a tall order and no one expects him to deliver all the goods in a conference paper at this stage of research in the field. The attempt at tentative conclusions on the last pages is very interesting and I do not object to it as far as it goes. I would like to add something to them, however.

First, I see a very important conceptual problem involved. If we, as social scientists, want to attribute causal effects to something in a system, that something should be exogenous. The emergence and growth of multinational firms is endogenous in the economic model Dunning and I agree on in basic outline. We explain the process by exogenous factors such as technical change, discoveries of natural resources, population growth, etc. To be able to study the effects of *multinational firms* on the location of economic activity, we have to specify a situation of comparison, where there are no such firms, but everything else is equal in some sense. As far as I can see the only way of solving that problem is to assume that foreign direct investment is prohibited, work out the basic properties of the world we would then have, and attribute the differences between that model world and the real world to the existence of multinational firms. Existing technology, natural resources, etc. would be assumed to be the same. In fact, technology is of course affected by the establishment of multinational firms, but this is perhaps a permissible first simplification.

Other problems arise in the same context. When we make statements about such effects, should we, and, in particular, do people, assume that direct investment has never been allowed anywhere, that prohibition is introduced today, that only their own country prohibits it (inward, outward, both?) or only that some restrictions on such investments are introduced? These conceptual problems may seem scholastic, but I refuse to be told about effects without seeing an explicit presentation of the situation with which we should compare. If the mind boggles, that is because one suddenly realises what we are trying to do. As economists we are used to analysing *marginal* changes and that is what I think we have to do. The question we should set out to answer is: if we introduce some restrictions (a tax on direct investment), what would happen to the location of economic activity? The changes then predicted, with the sign reversed, can legitimately be called effects of multinational firms.

I think that the kind of theory presented by Professor Dunning has something to say on this point. It has to do with the relative strength of the comparative advantages of nations, as compared to firms. With a credible guarantee of free trade (no protectionism of any kind) and a tax on foreign investment, I guess that IBM and L. M. Ericsson would tend to concentrate their production on the home country and some countries with cheap labour in a reasonably disciplined industrial environment. At the other extreme, the exploitation of bauxite would not move from Jamaica, because the national comparative advantage of that country is so extreme. In some cases ongoing economic activities would become unprofitable in the host country without becoming profitable in the home country, in which case they would be given up. Studying the relative strength of these basic factors would give us conclusions of the kind that I have developed further in my report to the Swedish government.

The following diagram may be a helpful illustration:

TABLE 1

National comparative advantage ＼	Firm-specific comparative advantage	
	extreme	inconsequential
extreme	I	II
inconsequential	III	IV

Typical case II industries are those exploiting raw materials. If copper-producing countries introduce prohibitive taxes on inward direct investment, copper mining will generally take place in the country, nevertheless. Typical case III industries may be electronics and engineering and presumably differentiated production in general. IBM or Philips would close down their production in Sweden, if a prohibitive tax was introduced, and move it to other countries such as Holland or West Germany. Case IV examples may be various base chemicals, flat glass, steel, and non-ferrous metals, where the product is standardised and could be produced by any of several firms as long as they are large enough to be able to co-ordinate successive stages of the production process within their own organisation. The production is almost footloose in the sense that any country situated not too far away from the market would do. The result is that there is no determinate solution in the model. In the real world this would correspond to high sensitivity to small differences in conditions. I would guess that this is why refineries, flat glass plants, and aluminium smelters so often become objects of tug-of-wars between multinational firms and between countries. There are simply no strong advantages favouring particular firms or countries. Case I is less easy to illustrate with examples, perhaps it is not an empirically important case.

In this systematisation cases III and IV are the most interesting from the point of view of the effects of multinational firms on the international location of economic activity. The hypothesis would be that the possibilities of establishing subsidiaries abroad leads to a more farreaching exploitation of national comparative advantages. On this account we should be able to treat the effects on location (and on welfare, efficiency and distribution) as analogous to the effects of freer trade. The analysis of case IV obviously requires a game-theoretical approach.

Summary of the Discussion

The discussion first considered how MNEs affected the international allocation of economic activities and how MNE analysis was related to trade and location theory. Explanations of why multinational productive activity occurred were compared. The need to distinguish between two questions was illustrated; first: where should different types of economic activities be located? second: should these activities, wherever located, be foreign or domestic owned? MNE firms were an alternative to the market in allocating resources, it was noted, and the discussion of the welfare implications of the emergence of MNEs emphasised that they could help as well as hinder the functioning of markets. Finally the question why certain countries had more multinationals than others was posed. This session was chaired by *Erik Dahmén*.

The discussion was opened by *Erik Dahmén*, who stressed the importance of the 'business level' approach as represented by Dunning's contribution. He believed that standard theories of resource allocation, trade and development paid insufficient attention to institutional changes, in particular those relating to communications developments, of which the emergence of MNEs was an important part.

John Dunning related the study of MNEs to the approaches of trade and location theory. Trade theory, he said, assumes resources to be trapped in different countries but mobile between firms, while the theory of MNEs assumes resources to be trapped in firms with different ownership advantages, but mobile between countries. Interfirm transfer of technology is prevented by market imperfections. Thus firms can be seen as an alternative to the market for allocating resources between countries. The study of MNEs was also related to location theory. While the basic question in location theory was where to locate a given productive activity, Dunning wished to explain whether a certain foreign market should be served by exports or by local production. This similarity in approach suggested that the study of MNEs could provide a link between trade and location theory.

Walter Isard, eager to realise the role of location theory, asked how the theory of MNEs could help to determine actual location decisions by firms. He suggested that the U.S. iron and steel industry was a prime candidate for multinational enterprise involvement as environmental regulations at home made air and water resources increasingly scarce, and wondered how MNE theory could help this industry to determine a suitable location for expansion.

Dunning replied that MNE theory could not answer Isard's question which did not concern the 'ownership advantages' of firms. Isard had asked whether production of a given firm will be located at home or abroad and not if production, whereever located, would be foreign or domestic owned. Dunning found the interesting question to be under what circumstances the company would be taken over by a foreign company, which is a multinational, or alternatively go overseas and itself become a multinational.

Harry Johnson added that since there is very little multinational investment in the iron and steel industry Dunning had been asked to answer a question for which his theory did not apply. *Assar Lindbeck* similarly remarked that Isard's case might be seen as an example of Lundgren's group IV (p. 425) containing industries for which no country had a particularly strong comparative advantage and no company a strong ownership advantage. As Wassily Leontief had noted in the discussion, there might be no unique solution for where a particular industry should be located. The steel industry could be located in many countries. If there were no strong ownership advantages it would tend to be locally owned. Factors such as environmental regulations and government subsidies would determine where the steel industry was actually located. Government-subsidised mills in Northern Sweden, Lindbeck suggested, might well export steel to the United States.

Lawrence Klein suggested that risk diversification was an important consideration for MNEs. Large companies spread their investments between countries in order to be less dependent on business cycles in a single country. IBM, he exemplified, would not be doing nearly as well if it invested its resources only in the American market and took a ride on the business cycle in the U.S.A. Instead, IBM spreads its investments between countries, rides the world cycle and staggers cyclical fluctuations.

Nils Lundgren was not convinced that the occurrence of risk was sufficient to explain the existence of MNEs. Financial markets provided an alternative way to spread risks. Shareholders could diversify their own portfolios instead of requiring the particular company they invest in to spread its risks by foreign investment. However, while portfolio diversification might be a satisfactory alternative for shareholders, he recognised that management and other employees might gain job security from investment abroad. Investment in other industries at home might not be feasible due to a lack of industry specific knowledge. In this sense risk spreading could contribute to explaining MNEs. Similar reasoning applied, Lundgren added, to Leontief's argument that firms in capital abundant countries tended to become multinational. Well-developed capital markets allowed firms to invest abroad in many ways other than direct investment – a point originally made by Charles Kindleberger and Stephen Hymer. Thus for capital abundance to be a sufficient explanation of the existence of MNEs, it was necessary to explain why multinationals should be more efficient than capital markets. Lundgren concluded that direct investment may involve something better than portfolio investment, namely exploiting firm specific knowledge.

Melvyn Krauss noted the particular uncertainty imparted by the risk for changes in government policies. A firm located in a single country risked being hurt by policies adopted by that country's government. He interpreted Lundgren's point to be that there was no market where firms could insure themselves against political risks.

Kindleberger suggested that a firm could become multinational as a result of a defensive investment strategy. It might fear a bilateral monopoly situation or fear being cut off from foreign supplies or outlets. BP constructs outlets in the U.S. for its North Sea oil even though there are enough outlets there and though U.S. firms with outlets are prospecting for oil. Fear that competitors will steal a march leads to investment abroad to defend market shares. Investments to defend foreign market shares, outlets or supplies could thus explain the emergence of multinationals in certain market forms. Such investments also suggested however that social inefficiency might accompany MNEs. He doubted that economists could identify those MNEs where there are real social advantages from resource allocation within firms compared with allocation by the market mechanism.

Jagdish Bhagwati suggested distinguishing between two kinds of multinational investments. Countries that follow import substitution-type policies typically attract direct investment of the tariff-jumping kind to supply the local markets. The national comparative advantage has then been created from the market side since the government eliminates the possibility of supplying its domestic market through imports. This type of investment, Bhagwati noted, is very different from the Heckscher-Ohlin type of national comparative advantage, which is based on an outward-looking trade policy. Therefore, firms that engage in outward-looking investments are probably free trade oriented, and constitute a pressure group for free trade, whereas those that service domestic markets, made profitable because of quantitative restrictions and tariffs, are basically protectionists.

Dieter Biehl also remarked that government policy led to MNEs serving foreign markets by local production rather than by exports. He mentioned that Volkswagen preferred to produce in the United States to avoid accusations by the U.S. government of dumping.

Government tax policy could also help explain the emergence of the MNE. The so-called favourable foreigner's effect in the framework of the corporation tax in Germany meant that due to the split rate system operating (51 per cent for retained and 15 per cent for distributed profits) total tax payments of a subsidiary of a foreign-based multinational may be up to 20 per cent lower compared with the tax payment of a comparable national German company. Even more taxes could be avoided if the foreign parent company instead of supplying its subsidiary with equity capital grants loans to its subsidiary, since interest paid on loans is deductible from gross profits before tax.

Klein and Lindbeck debated the importance of the changing dollar value of the yen in determining Japanese investment in the U.S. during the 1960s and 1970s.

In the early 1960s, *Klein* said, President Kennedy urged Japanese industrialists to invest in America. They answered that American businessmen were so shrewd they would have exhausted all profit opportunities. Now they have changed their minds and the typical Japanese multinational wants to break into the American market.

Lindbeck objected that the reason for foreign firms to invest in the U.S. was not that American firms have become less shrewd, but rather that the dollar had been overvalued during the 1950s and early 1960s, with low profit margins in the U.S. relative to Europe. The devaluations of the dollar have resulted in an undervalued dollar. Profit margins in the U.S. have increased relative to other countries, and foreign businessmen, including the Japanese, are clever enough to go in.

Bela Balassa added that changes in real wages had acted in the same direction as exchange rate changes, making it more profitable to invest in the United States than it was ten years ago.

Lundgren observed that both commercial policy and exchange rate changes tend to move production from one country to another but do not themselves explain why that production is owned by a multinational. If exchange rate changes move production that in accordance with MNE theory is in the hands of a multinational firm, a direct investment results; this is a case of a visible hand leading to the same results as the invisible hand. Standard theory applies even though we have multinationals, he emphasised.

Max Corden added that only if the visible hand of the MNEs internal planning process allocated resources differently, were new ingredients needed amongst standard trade theory considerations to determine the location of economic activity between countries. He suggested that the standard factors from trade and location theory influenced the location of activity, but that additional considerations might affect the location of ownership of MNEs. There must be some reasons why some countries — for instance Switzerland and Holland — generated more MNEs relative to their size than others. This question, also posed by Leontief, was well worth studying, he felt. Once we had a theory of the location of activity and a theory of the location of ownership, Corden concluded, it was necessary to relate the two and ascertain whether a bias towards multinationals in a country also affected its allocation of activity. Would allocation of foreign production activity in the rest of the world be different if owned by country *A* rather than country *B*?

Fritz Machlup asked if the concepts used in MNE theory were operational in the sense that the social scientist could determine when the firm was more efficient than the market in allocating resources. *Lundgren* replied that these concepts in fact were operational since firms were continuously making calculations to determine whether external or internal transactions were more profitable.

Dunning closed the discussion. He thought that he could fit Kindleberger's type of defensive investment into his general scheme by saying that it was motivated largely by a desire to stop other oligopolists from benefiting from internalisation advantages.

In reply to Bhagwati he argued that some import-substituting investments are part of the natural course of the product cycle, while export-oriented investments may be generated by government policies such as export rebates. Therefore, one could not argue that import-substituting multinationals generally operate within a protectionist or imperfect market framework while exporting multinationals do not.

Elaborating on Corden's and Kindleberger's comments Dunning emphasised the need to distinguish between international production which helps to integrate and perfect markets, and that which does the opposite. Whether the visible hand working through the multinational firms improves the market outcome or not, depends on which type of market its internal organisation is replacing. If the markets are highly imperfect, then the multinational may well be operating as a perfecting and integrating force, which increases world welfare. On the other hand one could point to situations where the imperfections created by the multinational are greater than those of the markets which they are seeking to replace, because we know that multinationals tend to operate within oligopolistic market environments. In consequence it is possible that the allocation of resources resulting from bypassing normal market mechanisms gives a less desirable result. Furthermore, the location of ownership directly affected the location of economic activity. For instance he believed that there would not be much manufacturing industry in Taiwan, Singapore or South Korea, without foreign-owned, in particular U.S.-owned, companies. There is consequently an interrelationship between the two distinct concepts of ownership and activity location.

Answering Isard, Dunning said he could envisage change of ownership due to the introduction of new techniques within the iron and steel industry, at least when one is concerned with iron ore exploration in different parts of the U.S. It is conceivable that the change of ownership by bringing in new types of techniques could affect the extent to which iron ore is exploited by one area rather than another according to the production techniques in question. Agreeing with Assar Lindbeck, he said that the fact that there are strong environmental controls in the U.S. might mean that some iron and steel companies might find it more profitable to integrate backwards vertically in other countries, which is what is happening for rather different reasons in the Japanese case.

Dunning also noted the importance of economies of scale. One of the chief reasons for the emergence of international companies, engaging in trade as well as in production, was to take advantage of these economies not only in production, but also and perhaps more so in research and development. He distinguished between plant economies of scale, which tend to concentrate production in particular areas, and firm economies of scale, particularly those associated with R and D, which might cause the concentration of the location of R and D activities, but which could lead to a dispersion of activities of production throughout the world.

Finally Dunning emphasised that international trade in intermediary products deserved further study. He mentioned as particularly interesting trade in technology and in research-intensive products. There were peculiar examples as Taiwan, exporting research-intensive products while the United States provided the technology to produce these products. He had the impression, however, that trade theorists still tended to look at trade between developed and developing countries in the form of industrial goods versus primary goods and sometimes on a horizontal basis when trade was between industrialised countries. He suggested analysis by trade theorists of vertical integration or diversification of activities particularly, but not necessarily, within MNEs. Unfortunately, Dunning noted, one cannot apply traditional trade analysis to these empirical problems because of the data limitations since the export of technology is not shown in the commodity trade classifications but registered as royalties and fees, and these are not classified in the same way as commodities.

13 International Circumstances Affecting the Development and Trade of Developing Countries

Akin L. Mabogunje

This paper is divided into five parts. The first section sets out the facts of current international trade and development and summarises the basic elements of current international trade theory. The second and third parts provide a critique of this theory in terms of the circumstances of developing countries today. Borrowing from the methodology of contextual criticism of Gunnar Myrdal, a distinction is made between criticisms which relate to issues inherent or *immanent* in the acceptance of the theory as a reflection of reality (these are dealt with in Section II) and criticisms which go beyond the domain of or are *transcendental* to the considerations and presuppositions of the theory (these are examined in section III). Leading on from these, a fourth part adumbrates a new economic order in which developing countries can fashion development paths which are more consistent with their resources and circumstances and which provide them with a more realistic basis for participating in international trade.

I. INTERNATIONAL TRADE: DEVELOPMENT AND THEORY

The Second Development Decade opened with the real output of developing countries growing at a rate of 5·3 per cent and well below the 6 per cent target laid down in the International Development Strategy. During the first two years of the Decade, countries accounting for more than half the total population of the developing world showed a rate of growth of per capita output of less than 1·5 per cent and many of them actually recorded negative rates.[1] The few developing countries which achieved growth rates of per capita output of 5·5 per cent or more accounted for only 15·5 per cent of total LDC population. They consisted mainly of petroleum-exporting countries and those countries with a fast-growing manufacturing export sector.

The poor performance of developing countries is closely associated with the continued decline in their share of world exports. Whilst in 1950 their exports accounted for nearly a third of the world total, by 1972 their share had dropped to less than 20 per cent and might have been worse if the petroleum-exporting countries had not maintained their relative position over the period. By contrast, the developed market-economy countries with which virtually all developing countries traded increased their share of world exports from 60 to over 72 per cent and during the 1960s their combined output grew at an annual rate of 8 per cent (current prices).

The phenomenon whereby out of two international trading groups one continues to prosper from the gains from trade whilst the other suffers only adverse consequences due not to a fall in the actual volume of commodities exchanged but largely to price movements, poses serious problems for our understanding of the basis of current international trade theory. In order therefore to appreciate the nature of the international circumstances which militate against the development and trade performance of developing countries, we shall summarise the salient features of this theory.

The basic questions to which the theory of international trade sets out to provide answers are: under what conditions would two nations engage in the exchange of commodities? What factors would determine the prices at which they trade their commodities and the quantity of commodities they exchange? What type of gains or advantages accrue to each nation in the transaction? The questions have engaged the attention of eminent economists over the years and their analyses and theoretical constructs have often been intellectually stimulating and mathematically elegant.

Given certain well-known assumptions, the Heckscher-Ohlin-Samuelson model states that two countries will engage in trade due to different relative factor endowments and each will export the commodity that uses relatively intensively its relatively abundant factor. Trade will result in complete equalisation of factor prices so that the immobility of factors between countries does not prevent the maximisation of world output and hence the realisation of international economic efficiency.

This model has been criticised on a number of grounds. The most notable are its assumption of perfect competition and its disregard for technological progress. The model has also been criticised for its comparative static character which diverts attention from the fact that international trade, as presently operative between developed and developing countries, has tended to breed inequality and to widen the gap between the two groups of countries.

II. TRADE THEORY AND THE CIRCUMSTANCES OF DEVELOPING COUNTRIES

This theory provides developing countries with very little guidance as to how to behave in the face of a continued worsening of conditions for their major commodities in world markets. Part of the problem is, perhaps, that to a considerable extent many developing countries do not satisfy the criterion of 'nationhood' in the terms required by the theory. The concept of a nation, although not considered central to international trade theory, turns out to be one of its most important, if implicit, assumptions. The major attribute of nationhood is the sovereignty or power to exercise independent actions within defined territorial limits. This power extends beyond political control of citizens and embraces, in particular, the ability to intervene effectively in the more vital field of economic relations, national and international. It is the ability to exercise this power that in the final analysis ensures that the terms of trade between two countries reflect an acceptable division of the gains from trade.

(1) FORMER COLONIAL STATUS

Perhaps the most important international circumstance affecting the trade and development of developing countries is therefore their erstwhile colonial status which, even today, affects their capacity to act fully as 'nations'. For the purpose of this paper, it will be more instructive to use the developing countries of Africa to illustrate the consequences of this historical diminution of sovereign rights. Particularly in West Africa, the origin of the present problem can best be understood by going back to the period between 1830 and 1880 which preceded the colonial conquest. This was a period when European influences began to be greatly incubated in Africa but on terms and conditions determined by the Africans.[2]

One of the important consequences of the loss of control due to cononial status was the fragmentation of the continent into trading spheres for individual European nations. A continent whose population as of 1972 was less than 375 million was split into 56 'national' entities with an average national population of 6·7 million and a median population of only 3·7 million.

The small size of the majority of African countries has constituted a major obstacle not only to their freedom of action in the field of international trade but also to their ability effectively to undertake their own development. The history of colonial exploitation in most of these countries depicts the following five stages of development whereby each country was transformed from a primitive 'reserve' outside the world market into a truly underdeveloped economy, dominated by and integrated into the world market:

(a) The stage of exploratory trading economy usually based on identifying the range of raw materials available in the area and deciding on which ones to stimulate and concentrate exploitative effort. This is the stage when many colonial trading companies are established and make easy monopoly profits without either risks or great investment;

(b) The stage of infrastructural investment mainly in transport (ports, railways and roads) and in limited social overheads especially related to urban development and involving the installation of water supply, electrification, sanitary equipment as well as schools, hospitals and housing;

(c) The stage of accelerated development came at the end of the Second World War and was marked by greater investment in both social overhead capital and productive activities. The aim was to rebuild Europe's losses in the war through planning the development of the colonies and ostensibly investing in the welfare of their people;

(d) The stage of rapid growth in the bureaucratic machinery of colonial exploitation soon followed and quickly encouraged a pattern of public expenditure with a high propensity to import. The economy soon gets to a stage where imports start to outstrip exports and the country, in consequence, depends on 'aid', technical assistance and capital inflows from the metropolitan countries;

(e) The stage of stagnation when the 'dualistic' structure of the economy is most marked and is characterised by an increased dependence on the metropolitan country, a most glaring difference in the distribution of growth between the various sectors of the economy and per capita product, and most important, by the stagnation or even decline of the agricultural sector which still provides employment for the vast majority of the population.

Samir Amin (1973, p. 298) has monitored this pattern in French-speaking West Africa. Referring to it as 'outward-directed' growth or growth based on external demand and external financing, he showed how, on the eve of the Second World War, most of the French West African countries had hardly gone beyond the exploratory trading stage. Real colonial exploitation by then had touched little more than Senegal, with the other territories remaining still an unexploited 'reserve'. Indeed, in the period between 1920 and 1940, the external trade of Senegal alone accounted for nearly 60 per cent of the total for French West Africa. This total itself had doubled in real volume during the period, giving a growth rate of 3·5 per cent per annum, a rate two to three times lower than the postwar rate. Public expenditure during this period grew at a rate of around 2 per cent per annum whilst the role of external finance was negligible, averaging less than 2 per cent of total public spending.

The period of accelerated development opens with the plans of the *Fonds d'Investissement pour le Développement Économique et Social des Colonies* (F.I.D.E.S.). The flood of investment made possible under this programme went not only to further improve infrastructure but particularly to bring about rapid extension in areas of export production.

Indeed, during the period 1948 to 1960, economic growth in French
West Africa paralleled the growth in external financial contribution. Thus,
whilst the real annual growth rate of export earnings was 4·7 per cent,
that for all income from abroad was 6·8 per cent.

The reason for this large volume of external financing was that well
before 1960, the accelerated rate of colonial exploitation had produced
a crisis in the public finances of the various territories. Economic growth
had lagged behind current public expenditure and there was need to
meet a growing proportion of that expenditure out of the budget of the
metropolitan country. Even before their independence, the economy of
these colonies was already stagnating and unable to provide the
necessary resources for administering the country.

The position did not improve appreciably with independence. If anything, the gap between the rate of growth in current government
expenditure, which was increasing, and the rate of growth of the economy,
which was slowing down, continued to widen. Effort to increase taxation, as
was widely practised in the decade immediately following independence,
merely postponed the day of reckoning. The situation reflected the
paralysis of national saving capacity which, despite the growth in gross
domestic product, remained unable to bring about an automatic and
spontaneous transition from growth stimulated from abroad to
internally generated and self-financing growth. During 1960–70 local
savings accounted for no more than 1 per cent of the region's gross
domestic product. Nothing illustrates better the completely dependent
nature of the economy of the region and its total lack of internal dynamism.

(2) MONETARY DEPENDENCE

The situation is further accentuated by continued monetary dependence
in each of these countries. For most of them political independence had
not led to the establishment of national central banks. Their monetary
transactions continue to be handled by the Central Bank of the West
African States (B.C.E.A.O.). This bank, a legacy from colonial times,
provides a common currency for seven of the former nine states (excluding
Mali and Guinea) of French West Africa. In 1962 the B.C.E.A.O. was
reconstituted and the seven countries concluded with France a co-
operation agreement by which France guaranteed the convertibility into
French francs of the €.F.A. francs issued by B.C.E.A.O. The member
countries undertook to keep their external reserves in an operations
account opened by the B.C.E.A.O. at the French Treasury, with which a
special relationship was also established. This relationship included the
maintenance of a fixed exchange rate between the C.F.A. and the French
franc, unlimited access to French francs, and freedom of transfer between

France and these countries. This relationship limits the control these countries have over their own currencies. In a period of great instability in the exchange rate of the franc, most of these countries have suffered with France and their capacity to import outside of the franc zone has been considerably impaired.

The position is not much better in many other African countries which have their own Central Banks since virtually in all cases their reserves continued to be held in the major international currencies. The only advantages that such countries have had is the freedom to switch their reserves from one international currency to another and to decide whether or not to devalue their currencies with that of the metropolitan country. Considerable attention has been paid to the consequences of this aspect of economic dependence in recent years and the pressure of developing countries to have a more stable international currency in the form of Special Drawing Rights is only an initial stage in the move to reduce the level of dependency. But as long as the currency situation in developing countries retains its present features these countries will suffer adversely in their participation in international trade.

(3) THE ROLE OF MULTINATIONAL CORPORATIONS

Another important circumstance affecting the development and trade of developing countries is the overwhelming role of multinational corporations in mediating the pattern, scope and content of their international economic relations.[3] The multinational corporations not only strengthened the process of colonial exploitation of developing countries but also deepened the pattern of their dependency especially where these countries adopted a strategy of industrialisation based on import substitution.

The strengthening of the process of colonial exploitation is notable in the concentration of most of the investment of these corporations on petroleum and other extractive mining activities.[4] Exploitation of such minerals as copper, tin, bauxite, nickel and iron ore have been undertaken not only to meet current needs of the developed countries but also to stockpile against future needs and the possibility of changing policies in the developing countries concerned.

But perhaps the most farreaching impact of multinational corporations on the development and trade of developing countries has been through industrialisation based on the principle of import substitution. This principle requires the replacement of the importation of consumer goods by the importation of the technology, the capital, skilled manpower and often the semiprocessed raw material needed for 'assembling' these goods in the developing countries. According to Hirschman, the principle of import substitution is based on the notion of doing 'last things first'.

Advanced technology is imported into the developing countries to enable
them to go through the motions of manufacturing their own consumer
goods. It can thus be argued that this function of 'technology transfer',
so efficiently undertaken by multinational corporations, has the effect of
subverting authentic technological development in these countries.
Irrespective of whatever growth is achieved in gross domestic product,
the importation of highly sophisticated production methods destroys the
basis of local technology and renders the population in developing countries
technologically unable to meet the challenges of their own environment. To
this extent, therefore, the role of multinational corporations in the industrialisation process in developing countries may serve to delay their technological progress and impede the long-term chances of their development.

Whilst not all developing countries, particularly the smaller ones, can
hope to achieve any remarkable technological progress if allowed a
different path of development, it remains true that most of the technology
imported into virtually all Third World countries has been very inappropriate in the sense of usually being capital-intensive while the real need is
for labour-intensive technology. The effect of this has been to compound
the employment problems of these countries and to stultify their development through unrequited expectations from massive investment in
education, health and other social infrastructure. The political instability
which often accompanies such mismatch between social investment and
economic opportunities confounds the long-term prospects of overall
development in these countries.

If only on these scores, the impact of multinational corporations on
the development and trade of the less-developed countries deserves serious
reappraisal. In terms of their actual operations also, the role of these
corporations has not always been compatible with the best interest of
developing countries. Various studies have been undertaken by the
Secretariat of the United Nations Conference on Trade and Development
(U.N.C.T.A.D.) which reveal that on at least three grounds the activities
of the multinational corporations have been prejudicial to development
and trade of developing countries.

(a) First, these corporations often impose export restrictions on their
subsidiaries and affiliates in the developing countries. Such restrictions can
take the form of market sharing whereby the subsidiaries are permitted to
export to certain countries and precluded from doing so to others; or it
may involve the retention by the parent company of the primary
responsibility for the multinationals' export activity and an insistence that
its prior approval must be obtained for any exports by its subsidiaries.
Sometimes, the restriction takes the form of permission to export to or
only through special firms. All of this can work against the trade and
development of a developing country especially where the subsidiary of a
multinational corporation occupies a prominent position in the domestic

market and is barred from exporting to other markets and especially to
nearby markets which may otherwise have been allocated to the parent
or to another affiliate company.

(b) Second, multinational corporations often tie the import of raw
material and intermediate goods required to be used for domestic
production closely to sources of supply within the corporation structure.
Such tied purchasing arrangements have often frustrated the principle of
import substitution since it prevents the growth of backward linkage
relation involving the development of local sources of raw material.[5]
Moreover, this tying of inputs to specified sources enables multinational
corporations to exploit the technique of transfer pricing to the disadvantage of developing countries. Prices which the corporation charges
for inputs supplied by its subsidiaries or affiliates are to a large extent
determined arbitrarily in the absence of world market prices. In general,
therefore, transfer pricing is used as a means of minimising the tax
liability of the corporation as a whole through limiting or increasing
profits made by its subsidiaries for tax purposes or to reduce the impact
of customs duties or accumulate surplus funds in 'safe' currency areas.

(c) Finally, multinational corporations engage in tremendous surplus
creaming through easy movement of funds out of developing countries.
Apart from the use of arbitrary transfer pricing, they utilise a variety of
other methods to repatriate high profits out of these countries. One of
these methods is deferred payment by affiliates to a subsidiary in a
developing country for goods that have been purchased from the latter.
On the other hand, a subsidiary in a developing country may be
instructed to make immediate payment for all purchases made from affiliates, instead of being permitted the normal 30- or 90-day payment
period.

It might, of course, be argued that any developing country can well
protect itself against the machinations of multinational corporations.
Such an argument would have missed the real essence of the problem
posed by these corporations. Apart from the fact that most of these
practices are carried out on an informal basis, without written or
juridical records, so much secrecy in fact surrounds them that even
developed countries, when they are on the receiving end of these
operations, have not always succeeded in getting at the information
necessary for taking appropriate action. Moreover, in terms of resources,
most developing countries are weak relative to the multinational
corporations and find themselves in a pathetically helpless position to
stand up to them. However, developing countries, following the example
of the Andean group of countries, may eventually face up to the problem
of multinational corporations. The Andean countries through harmonisation of policies and concertion of effort are beginning to curb some of the
more notorious of the restrictive practices of multinational corporations
including those involving the use of imported technology.

(4) TRADE POLICIES OF DEVELOPED COUNTRIES

These constitute another major international circumstance affecting the development and trade of developing countries. Industrial countries use quantitative import restrictions, variable import levies, tariffs expressed in *ad valorem* or specific terms or a mixture of both to restrict the imports of agricultural commodities from developing countries. For some of these countries, these commodities provide a very high percentage of their total foreign exchange earnings.[6] In consequence, any restriction of access to the markets of developed countries quite naturally exerts a downward pressure both on the volume and the prices of their agricultural exports.

(5) STRUCTURAL CHANGES

Besides such direct action, indirect consequences of the structural changes accompanying the continued economic growth of developed countries have had adverse effects on the trade and development of developing countries. One of these, arising from rapid scientific and technological progress in the petrochemical industries, is the continuing fast expansion in the output of new types of synthetic material and their growing substitutability for natural products usually exported by developing countries. Lower demand for the specific agricultural raw material weakens the bargaining power of the developing countries for a more equitable price.

Of equally negative significance for development and trade of developing countries is the changing composition of the industrial output of developed countries. In recent years, greater importance has come to be attached to chemical and engineering industries whilst those industries which depend largely on agricultural raw material, notably textiles, clothing, timber and vegetable oils, have become less significant. Moreover, highly sophisticated technology now ensures that production processes use less and less volume of these raw materials per unit of manufactured output. This development also affects the international trade of the less-developed countries in certain mineral ores such as tin.

In short, international trade as currently carried on is clearly a classic case of 'unequal exchange' in which the developed countries have all the advantages on their side whilst the developing countries are generally in a relatively weak bargaining position to protect their interests. The fact that they have been able to force the issue in the market for a critical product like petroleum through harmonisation of policies in the Organization of Petroleum Exporting Countries (O.P.E.C.) is the exception that proves the rule. Even here, the exposed nature of the economies of these countries has meant that the inflationary consequences of the so-called 'oil crisis' have been passed on to them and there is already growing doubts as to who has gained from this 'heroic' effort. Certainly, the transfer of inflation due to this crisis has served only to exacerbate the prevailing poverty crisis in many developing countries.

Confronted by these stark realities of foreign economic relations, international trade theory offers the less-developed countries very little guidance for behaviour. The role of multinational corporations which straddle the activities of exchange between the trading partners whilst acting for the interest of only one of them confounds all the assumptions that international trade can be seen by developing countries as a most important factor in their development.

III. TRADE THEORY AND AVAILABLE GLOBAL RESOURCES

There is, however, an aspect of this problem which transcends both the theory and the present trading reality and poses a more fundamental question as to the future pattern of international trade. This transcendental dimension derives from considering the present pattern of international trade within the global context of available natural resources and viable development options open to developing countries. An important aspect of international trade theory concerns the gains from trade between the two parties. This aspect emphasises the opportunities which international trade provides for both parties for consuming more of certain goods. Indeed, the theory assumes that the parties concerned have identical consumption tastes 'in the strict sense of identical homothetic utility functions'.

On this issue, Johnson (1968) in fact tried to project a more positive role for the monopolistic competitive advantages enjoyed by multinational corporations in the markets of developing countries. According to him, the consumer in a developing economy cannot maximise his satisfaction unless he involves himself in a perpetual learning process concerning the new goods and services being placed at his dosposal. This process entails the acquisition of knowledge about the new technologies of consumption based on new capital-intensive technological discoveries. Since such a consumer has limited time to devote to this learning process, it is economical for the producer to undertake the adaptation of commodity consumption to rising incomes so as to minimise the associated education process for the consumer. Moreover, the producer, in this case the multinational corporations, has both the resources and the economic incentive to do so. From this point of view, monopolistic competition in developing countries can be seen more 'as a rational and dynamic mechanism of social adjustment of consumption patterns to economic development rather than as a socially undesirable imperfection of market structure, which ought to be reduced or eliminated by social policy in the interests of promoting the consumer from "exploitation".'

If the effect of the operation of multinational corporations and of current international trade patterns were to be considered wholly in these benevolent terms, the question then is: how far can it succeed in bringing about the development of developing countries, a development which involves the acquisition of tastes, styles and standards of living similar to or comparable with those currently enjoyed by the developed countries? This is today the most fundamental question that every developing country has to answer as it confronts the growing apparent intractability of the complex of development problems which it has to resolve and the limited set of options open to it. In this regard, it is important to bear in mind what can best be regarded as the new 'development ethics' that is pervading the activities and aspirations of governments in most of these countries and is supported and reinforced by the international community. These ethics oblige every government to strive to improve the socio-economic conditions of all strata of its population and to mobilise them to participate actively in their own development. In other words, the development of these countries is increasingly being seen as involving the acquisition of certain tastes, style and standard of living not simply by a wealthy minority but by the large majority of the populace. How far will this be possible if those tastes style and standard of living are to be of the type currently enjoyed in Western capitalist countries with which they largely engage in international trade?

The present standard of living in the developed countries of Western Europe, North America and Japan can be said to be based on an industrialisation programme that depends on, among other things, a considerable consumption of steel and energy.[7] In spite, however, of a 20-fold difference in total consumption, the overall growth rate for each group of countries is nearly the same. This means that, accepting the current pattern of international trade and development, the gap between the developed and developing countries would have become an unbridgeable chasm by the year 2000. The effect of a greater rate of population growth in the developing countries will be to make the gap in *average* individual consumption even larger. According to Oyawoye (1975), assuming that the developed countries can be persuaded to reduce their growth rate of steel consumption from 6 per cent to 2 per cent annually and the developing countries can step up their growth rate from 6 per cent to 10 per cent, this will only marginally reduce the gap by making the consumption of developing countries by the year 2000 rise to half of what developed countries consumed in 1975.

Such a seemingly favourable but most unlikely event would then have brought total world consumption of steel to 1300 million tonnes in the year 2000 as against the 2150 million tonnes which the rich countries alone would have consumed in that year if the present rate of 6 per cent growth were maintained.

The same situation is revealed when one considers energy consumption.

According to Marois, 5000 million tonnes of coal equivalent is consumed each year by the developed countries compared to about 200 million tonnes in the developing countries. This corresponds to per capita consumption of 6 tonnes and 0·3 tonnes, respectively. The rate of increase for both developed and developing countries is approximately 5·5 per cent per annum in spite of the 25-fold difference between them.

Many of the minerals needed for the present level of consumption in developed countries are produced in those countries. This is not to minimise the vital contribution of developing countries to the mineral markets but to emphasise that some of the myths about their rich mineral wealth do not stand up to close examination. Moreover, given the non-renewable nature of these particular resources and the rate at which foreign enterprises are exploiting and evacuating them out of developing countries to stockpile elsewhere, their availability for a pattern of development similar to that of the present developed countries would pose many serious problems.

The logical conclusion to which we are drawn is that developing countries have only two development options open to them. One is to continue along the existing development path based on the notion of achieving a pattern and style of consumption similar to that of the developed countries. The other is to accept the non-viability of this course of action and to settle down to fashioning a new developmental goal more consistent with their local resource endowment and socio-cultural disposition. Either of these choices has farreaching implications for international trade. The first choice involves an acceptance of their current dependency status and a need to adjust to the dominating role of multinational corporations whilst, maybe, searching for ways and means of minimising some of the deleterious effect of their present methods of operation. Such a choice also accepts an outward-directed orientation for the economy and would seek to achieve 'development' through trying to attract more and more foreign enterprises and aid.

The second choice focuses on the economy itself and on the vital importance of transforming those basic structural elements which at present impair its capacity to respond effectively to new societal goals. Taste and consumption patterns are strongly conditioned and influenced both by the strength of the productive sectors of the economy and the value preferences of a society. The ability of developing countries to bring about such fundamental structural transformation to their economy and society, however, depends essentially on how far they can exercise their sovereign rights of who and what to allow into their countries or keep out of them. Under such a situation, international trade will continue to play a vital role in development but its priorities in each developing country will be determined by the needs of that country rather than directed and manipulated by powerful agencies operating outside the country and with interests not always convergent with those of the country.

IV. CONCLUSION: A NEW DEVELOPMENT ORDER

This outline of the options open to developing countries commands attention only to the extent that it can be shown to represent real hard choices from which an escape is not possible. Of course, it is possible to argue that a third option exists somewhere between the two described above but the trend towards stagnation in the developing countries emphasises that such a third choice is a chimera. Even those countries which are enjoying the vicarious boom arising from high oil prices still have to face the problem of how to restructure their economy to increase its capacity for self-sustained development. And that problem entails what to do with foreign enterprises which dominate their economy and determine how it is linked with the present pattern of international trade.

A conceivable escape has sometimes been suggested as possible through the regional groupings or economic unions of developing countries. Such a union, it is claimed, by ensuring a larger market increases the bargaining power of developing countries *vis-à-vis* the multinational corporations, expands their opportunity surface for discovering new resources and for undertaking larger and more viable enterprises, and makes their impact on world trade more easily felt. These are advantages whose significance cannot be overestimated. Indeed, in various parts of the Third World developing countries are already striving to create the necessary institutions to achieve such regional economic organisation and their efforts in this regard need to be greatly supported by the international community. But even when they have succeeded in forming and operating the new economic-political entity, they will soon come face to face with the overriding issue of how far their development strategy can be based on existing patterns of international trade and its implications for the style and standard of living of their people and their overall economic well-being.

A recent preoccupation of the international community is the discussion of what is called 'the new economic order'. This preoccupation has arisen in the wake of attempts by petroleum-producing developing countries to intervene in the world market for their commodity. The resultant adjustment forced on the developed countries which have controlled this market up to then has been termed a 'crisis'. Yet, for developing countries, this so-called oil crisis is only a scratch on the all-pervading poverty crisis under which they have been suffering for so long. Attempts to understand the basis of this poverty crisis is starting to reveal not only the part played by international trade as currently structured by the instrumentality of multinational corporations but also by the presuppositions surrounding this trade with respect to the development goals possible of attainment by developing countries.

This presupposition is entailed in the fact that international trade, as presently organised, represents the final global extension of an economic order based on the operation of a self-regulating market which emerged in Europe in the wake of the industrial revolution late in the eighteenth century. This economic order requires that not only goods and services but also the factors of production, including labour, be treated as commodities for which there are prices which the market determines and seeks to regulate in response to the blind forces of supply and demand. But labour is not a discrete commodity. It is an attribute of human beings who cannot be shoved about, used indiscriminately, or even left unused, without affecting also the human individual who happens to be the bearer of this peculiar commodity.

When in the early years of the emergence of this economic order in Europe, the system was allowed to operate unfettered, its impact on the masses of the people who must offer their labour in the 'market' was to reduce them to the very depths of abject and humiliating poverty.[8]

For the second half of the nineteenth century and even till today, societies in the developed countries continue to be protected by their governments against the full exposure to the operation of the self-regulating markets both in its national and international manifestations. The colonial and imperial adventure of European countries in the nineteenth century, however, extended this system to the developing countries. Neocolonial relations and the operations of multinational corporations have succeeded in strengthening and sustaining it even after the developing countries have gained some semblance of independent political power. If the lot of people in these countries is, therefore, to be improved, if the gruelling poverty in which most of the people currently wallow is to be relieved, then as happened in Europe in the nineteenth century, governments in those countries must devise ways and means of protecting their people against full exposure to the self-regulating international trade market especially in the highly oligopolistic form represented by the operations of multinational corporations.

A new economic order to be meaningful must therefore make it possible for developing countries to come to grips with the problems of the structural transformation of their economy and their society. Such concern with structural reforms may involve a certain degree of temporary withdrawal from or decline in the intensity of participation in international trade. The nature of the international circumstances which have affected and continue to affect the trade and development of developing countries has been so pernicious that nothing short of major structural transformation in a degree of solitude can ensure that these countries create within their borders those institutions, attitudes, and life patterns which can guarantee not only their full development but their long-term effective participation in international economic relations as real and truly independent national entities.

NOTES

[1] United Nations, *Review of International Trade and Development, 1973,* (New York, 1973), Sales No. E.74. II.D. 14, p. 15.

[2] In describing the situation at this time, Brunschwig (1963, p. 212) for instance, noted:

> Black Africa was shaken and changed, just as Europe had been by the coming of the inventions and discoveries which brought it out of the Middle Ages. . . . The evolution took place at the pace of the Black, who was free to accept or refuse the novelties: the African did not feel dominated or constrained. In general he dealt on equal terms with the foreigners and did not feel himself being carried away in spite of himself on to a path which was alien to him. This evolution could have continued. It was interrupted in the last quarter of the nineteenth century. The European conquest did not give a different direction to the path on which the African had now started. The break did not come from a change of direction, but from a brutal thrust which took away from the Africans control over their progress.

[3] Of the total book value of direct foreign investment of these corporations estimated as over $150 billion in 1971, about a third was invested in developing countries. Of this amount, the United States accounted for over 55 per cent, followed by Britain with about 20 per cent and France about 7 per cent.

[4] In 1969–70, these two activities represented 86 per cent of total multinational investment in Western Asia, 74 per cent in Africa, 55 per cent in Southern and Eastern Asia and 22 per cent in Latin America.

[5] The refusal of a consortium of multinational corporations to develop the ample bauxite resources of Ghana as a complement to their investment in the Volta Hydroelectricity Scheme is a good case in point.

[6] As of 1970, food and animal feeds accounted by value for some 26 per cent of the total export from developing countries (or 44 per cent if fuel exports were excluded). This ranged from over 39 per cent for the Americas, 29 per cent for Africa to just about 6 per cent for West Asia.

[7] As at present, these countries together consume nearly 500 million tonnes of steel per year, corresponding to nearly 600 kg per person. At the other extreme, the developing countries consume 25 million tonnes of steel each year, corresponding to about 20 kg per person per year (see Marois 1974, p. 151).

[8] As Polanyi (1944, p. 73) observed about this system as it took root in England in the early half of the nineteenth century:

> the system in disposing of a man's labour power, would incidentally dispose of the physical, psychological and moral entity 'man' attached to that tag. Robbed of the protective covering of cultural institutions, human beings would perish from the effects of social exposure; they would die as victims of acute social dislocation through vice, perversion, crime and starvation. Nature would be reduced to its elements, neigh-

bourhoods and landscapes defiled, rivers polluted, military safety jeopardised, the power to produce food and raw materials destroyed. Finally, the market administration of purchasing power would periodically liquidate business enterprises, for shortages and surfeits of money would prove as disastrous as floods and droughts in primitive society. Undoubtedly, labour, land and money markets are essential to a market economy. But no society could stand the effects of such a system of crude fictions even for the shortest stretch of time unless its human and natural substance as well as its business organisation was protected against the ravages of this satanic mill.

REFERENCES

Amin, S., *Neo-Colonialism in West Africa* (London: Penguin Books. 1973).

Brunschwig, H., *L'Avènement de l'Afrique Noire* (Paris, 1963).

Johnson, H. G., 'The Theory of International Trade', paper presented at the International Congress on the Future of International Economic Relations, Montreal, Canada (Sept., 2–7, 1968).

Marois, M., *Towards a Plan of Actions for Mankind. Problems and Perspective* (Amsterdam, 1974).

Oyawoye, M. O., 'Development and Management of Mineral Resources in Africa', Presidential Address, Geological Society of Africa (Khartoum, 1975).

Polanyi, K., *The Great Transformation* (New York, 1944).

United Nations, *Review of International Trade and Development, 1973*, (New York, 1973) Sales No. E.74 II.D. 14.

Comment
Michael Michaely

I.

Professor Akin L. Mabogunje's paper on this topic,[1] which I am assigned
to discuss, presents a farreaching thesis on the role of international trade
of less-developed countries. In the author's words (p. 443)

> The logical conclusion to which we are drawn is that developing
> countries have only two development options open to them. One is to
> continue along existing development paths based on the notion of
> achieving a pattern and style of consumption similar to that of
> developed countries. The other is to accept the non-viability of this
> course of action and to settle down to fashioning a new developmental
> goal more consistent with their local resource endowment and socio-
> cultural disposition.

The author thus clearly argues, here as elsewhere in the paper, for a
policy of closing off the LDCs, at least partly, from the effects transmitted
from the outside world through international trade. This plea is based on
two separate sets of arguments — though the distinction is not always made
clear in the paper.

First, as would appear from the lines just quoted as well as from the
ensuing discussion, international trade relations may be considered harmful
because they lead to modifications of the fabric of society. This argument
cannot be discussed in terms of conventional welfare criteria, to which we
are so used, in which welfare of individuals is considered in isolation, and
welfare is not additive among members of society. The argument on hand
not only implies additivity, but assumes some collective welfare which
transcends the individual, and which conceivably may be impaired (by
some standards of the judge) even were each and every member of the
society to feel that his own welfare has been raised. Gains from trade are
inferred by conventional welfare theory, from the fact that members of
society avail themselves of new options opened by trade. With the change
in welfare criteria, such inference would no longer be justified.

The other set of arguments makes the claim that — if I interpret the
author correctly — international trade might have been beneficial to the
less-developed world; but it is not so in fact, the way it is actually conducted. The world is viewed as consisting of two groups, the developed
countries and the less-developed countries, each working perhaps (so the
paper implies) as a collective. The developed part of the world exploits,
through international trade relations, the less-developed part. This
exploitation takes two inter-related forms:

(a) The developed countries make the LDCs produce and export to the DCs goods whose production and export is not beneficial to the LDCs, and in which the latter would not specialise were it not for the coercive power of the DCs. In this way, international trade has led to the reduction of welfare of LDCs, in comparison with the autarky position in this part of the world before colonisation and the opening of trade relations.

(b) The superior bargaining power of the DCs has led to unfair terms of trade. Thus, 'international trade as currently carried on is clearly a classic case of "unequal exchange" in which the developed countries have all the advantages on their side whilst the developing countries are generally in a relatively weak bargaining position to protect their interests'. (p. 440). Hence, international trade 'has tended to breed inequality and to widen the gap between the two groups of countries' (p. 433). The inferior bargaining power of the LDCs is presumably due to political status: 'perhaps the most important international circumstance affecting the trade and development of developing countries is the fact of their erstwhile colonial status, a fact which, even today, affects their capacity to act fully as "nations". (p. 434).

In the following, I do not propose to discuss the issue of the effect of trade relations on welfare through the changes it introduces into the social structure: this may be argued only by making subjective value judgements, to which all of us are equally entitled and by which no argument is resolved. I shall submit, on the other hand, a few comments on the issue of colonial status, and on the structure and terms of trade between the developed and less-developed parts of the world.

II.

The terms of trade may be said to be detrimental to the party concerned in two different ways — and Professor Mabogunje argues the existence of both.

One is a movement of the terms of trade through time against the party: 'Of two international trading groups one continues to prosper from the gains from trade whilst the other suffers only adverse consequences due not to a fall in the actual volume of commodities exchanged but largely to price movements . . . . ' (p. 433).

Pessimism over the course of change of the terms of trade of primary products, the major export category of the LDCs, versus manufactured goods — their main imports — was for a while widespread. It was certainly the prevailing view among policy-makers in the LDCs soon after the Second World War, and was a main source of motivation for the import-substituting policies of many LDCs, as well as for development theories such as those of Nurkse or Prebisch. Such pessimism is much less popular today, on very good grounds. Prices of primary goods are vulnerable, subject to large short-term fluctuations, and the examination in isolation of specific short periods of several years may create the impression of a general worsening of the terms of trade of primary goods. But the investigation of longer periods — be they of the last ten years, of the whole post-war period, of the twentieth century, or even beyond — fail to reveal any consistent trend of the terms of trade against primary goods. Nor would it seem, on balance, that *a priori* considerations should lead us to expect such deterioration in the future, even if predictions of the total exhaustion of many primary sources within two generations were to be taken with a grain of salt. I should thus submit that deterioration over time of the terms of trade of LDCs may be excluded from the consideration of international circumstances affecting the LDCs as a group. Of course, specific countries may on occasions be adversely affected.

The other claim about the terms of trade of LDCs is concerned not with their movement over time, but with their absolute level. In one sense or another, this level is argued to be unfair, leading to the exclusive reaping of the gains from international trade by the group of developed countries, with no gain — or a slight one, at best — to the LDCs. At its extreme, this argument goes as far as to claim that trade — as it has been conducted — has actually led to the LDCs being worse off than without trade. In its less extreme version, the argument states that although trade might be better than autarchy, the amount of trade is too large: the tradeable sector is overdeveloped, at the expense of the non-tradeable sector; likewise, the specialisation pattern within the tradeable sector is different from what it would have been in a free world market; and, finally, that trade is conducted under terms of trade less favourable to the less-developed country than those that would prevail with a genuinely free, competitive international trade. Part of the argument may be summarised by means of figure 1 (being confined to two goods, such diagrammatic analysis cannot deal with the *structure* of trade).

In a model of two goods, X and M, PQ is the transformation (production-possibility) curve of the two goods in a given, politically dependent less-developed economy. A is the autarchy position in the economy, indicating the amounts of X and M which are both produced and consumed without trade. With a completely free world trade, at relative prices indicated by the slope of ww, this economy would specialise in X, producing the combination B and trading X for M at the world price — the consumption point being somewhere on ww to the left of B. Trade would definitely lead, under such circumstances, to the increase of the country's welfare. Assume now, however, that an outside power prevents trade at free world prices, constraining the country to trade under the less favourable terms indicated by the slope of cc. The country would still specialise in the production of X, although less than under free trade. Production would be at point C, and consumption somewhere to its left on cc. The country is clearly

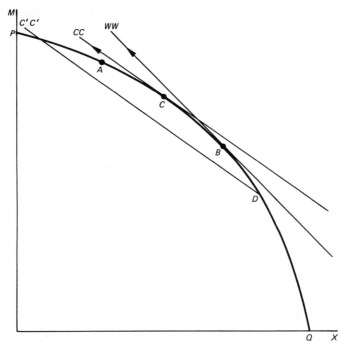

Figure 1

worse off than with free international trade; but it is still better off with
trade, as it is conducted, than under autarchy.

Assume now further, however, that the outside power not only dictates
less favourable terms of trade, but also leads to the expansion of production of X beyond its size in a free domestic market. This may be done by a
variety of means, ranging from the employment of indentured labour to the
use of tax or subsidy schemes. Production may then be at a point such as
D, with trade along $c'c'$ and consumption somewhere on this line to the
left of D. The country may easily be in such case worse off than under
autarchy. Moreover, one could conceive of a case where by such means of
intervention the economy could be led to specialisation in the *wrong*
good – a case in which trade (cum domestic intervention) clearly leads
to the reduction of the economy's welfare.

Whether one or another of the possibilities indicated by such simplified
analysis has in fact been the lot of various LDCs is a matter to be discussed
by the use of empirical, historical evidence. Failing such evidence, one may
only indicate presumptions. It seems reasonable to assume that the political
domination of an LDC by an outside power has most often led to the
country's trade being conducted under the conditions symbolised by the
line cc – that is, under terms of trade less favourable than those that

The International Allocation of Economic Activity

would prevail in a completely free world trade. It may also be presumed
that means of internal intervention have frequently led to an overexpansion
of the export sector of a dependent LDC. Whether this has gone often, or
at all, far enough to make the country worse off than without international
trade, must be an open question.

III.

In the preceding discussion, a major element was the political domination
of an LDC by an outside power. This dependent status is a necessary, but
not sufficient condition (unless the colonial power is a small economy)
for the conduct of trade under less favourable terms for the LDC than
those that would prevail in a free world. Another necessary circumstance is
that in the colonial power, the right to trade with the dependent LDC
should be restricted to certain firms, which would thus enjoy a monopolistic or monopsonistic position. That such restrictions were indeed quite
widespread, during the colonial era, is only too well known.

A question of prime importance, in discussing current and recent
developments, is to what extent do historical patterns of trade remain in
force beyond the termination of political dependence. Since most LDCs
have actually assumed a status of independence during the last generation,
the significance of the answer to this question is quite obvious.

A pioneering research on this topic has recently been conducted by
Professor Ephraim Kleiman, at the Institute of International Economic
Studies in Stockholm.[2] Kleiman finds, first, that trade of the dependent
countries — both exports and imports — does tend to be confined very
heavily to the respective metropolitan powers. This is more true for the
French than for the U.K. dependencies, and applies even more to the
dependencies of the smaller colonial powers (Belgium, Italy, or Portugal).
Taking the trade with all LDCs as the standard of measurement (the
'normal'), the U.K. trade with its dependencies appears (in the early
1960s) to be three times the 'normal'; the French respective trade —
eight times the normal; and the Portuguese trade — as high as 70 times.
Or, to make another illustration, exports to the U.K. amounted to 42 per
cent, and exports to France to less than 2 per cent, of the total exports
of the U.K.'s dependencies; whereas these shares amounted to 2 per cent
and 53 per cent, respectively, in the exports of French dependencies.

Kleiman employs various measures to estimate the effect of termination
of political dependency on the share of the metropolitan power in the
erstwhile dependency's trade. One is a cross-section comparison of groups
of countries classified by their age as independent countries — including
the group of still-dependent countries. Another is a time-series study of
individual countries from the verge of acquiring independence and onward.
The various measures are quite consistent in giving an indication that the

share of the former colonial power declines to about one-third within a generation following independence. This would, in turn, imply that most, but not all, of the special trade relationships of the metropolitan countries with its dependency tend to disappear within one generation.

Another interesting finding in Kleiman's study is that trade has tended during the 1960s to grow less in former dependencies which have acquired independence than in LDCs as a whole. That is, on net terms, trade of former dependencies has tended not just to shift from one trade partner to another but also to decline (relatively to trade of others). Whether this confirms that prior to independence the tradeable sector had indeed been overgrown, or whether this autarchic development is due to other circumstances or policy targets, cannot quite be answered by these findings.

Along similar lines to those of Kleiman's study, I have examined the possible impact of the political status on the rate of growth.[3] The time-series comparison for ten countries which have gained their independence at some time in the postwar period, and for which the required data are available, is presented in table 1.

TABLE 1 AVERAGE ANNUAL INCREASE OF PER CAPITA G.N.P., 1950–74 (IN PER CENT; IN PARENTHESES – NUMBER OF YEARS)

Country	Before Independence	After Independence
Algeria	1·5 (12)	4·9 (12)
Ghana	1·2 (7)	1·1 (17)
Kenya	1·0 (13)	3·1 (11)
Malawi	2·2 (15)	4·1 (8)
Malta	4·0 (20)	5·0 (4)
Nigeria	2·2 (10)	4·7 (14)
Tanzania	3·1 (11)	2·9 (13)
Uganda	0·5 (12)	1·5 (12)
Upper Volta	0·6 (10)	0 (14)
Zaire	0·8 (10)	3·2 (14)
Mean of ten countries	1·7	3·1

In the large majority of the ten countries – as well as for the group as a whole – the rate of growth appears to have been significantly higher after gaining independence than before it; this is true for seven countries, whereas the reverse relationship holds in only one (Upper Volta), while in the remaining two (Tanzania and Ghana) the rate of growth is practically the same in the two sub-periods.

A similar impression is gained from a cross-section analysis for the period 1951–62, presented in table 2 (after 1963 the number of

TABLE 2 AVERAGE ANNUAL INCREASE OF PER CAPITA G.N.P.,
DEPENDENT AND INDEPENDENT COUNTRIES 1951—62
(IN PER CENT; IN PARENTHESES — NUMBER OF COUNTRIES)

Year	Dependent countries	Independent countries
1951	5·6 (10)	2·8 (23)
1952	3·8 (10)	3·0 (23)
1953	−0·7 (10)	2·2 (23)
1954	3·2 (10)	2·3 (23)
1955	2·8 (9)	3·0 (23)
1956	2·8 (10)	0·7 (22)
1957	2·0 (10)	2·5 (22)
1958	−1·8 (9)	0·7 (23)
1959	1·7 (9)	2·2 (24)
1960	1·2 (9)	2·8 (24)
1961	−4·5 (6)	1·9 (27)
1962	−4·8 (5)	3·4 (28)
Mean of twelve years	0·9	2·0

dependent countries drops drastically to a single country from 1967 onward and is certainly too small for a meaningful comparison). Again, it appears that in most years the rate of growth was higher among independent than among dependent countries; this is true also for the average of the period 1951—62 as a whole.

Although these findings cannot be considered a full-proof evidence, they seem to suggest that the gaining of independence leads to an increase in a country's rate of growth. The search for possible explanations of this effect is beyond the scope of this brief paper. It may only be pointed out that while, as a rule, independent countries receive less (in relation to G.N.P.) foreign capital inflow than dependent territories, their relative import surpluses have been generally higher. This may indicate that at least one of the sources providing for a faster growth following independence is the use (sometimes to depletion) of existing accumulations of foreign-exchange reserves.

IV.

Leaving aside the issue of the fairness and equity in the existing pattern of trade and terms of trade, and the historical costs and benefits of inter-national trade to the less-developed world, it may be asked how effective would be a future improvement of the terms of trade of LDCs. Such an improvement seems to be a major component of the 'new international economic order' envisaged by the 'Third World'. Would a *feasible* change in the terms of trade be a significant factor in determining the pace of development of LDCs? We may try to answer it by resort to an arithmetic exercise, in which the magnitudes for 1970 (the most recent year for which aggregated data are readily available) will be taken as the starting position.[4]

These data are as follows, in rough terms (excluding oil from primary goods and the O.P.E.C. countries from LDCs): (i) Exports of primary goods from LDCs to DCs amount to $33 billions (at current, 1970 prices); (ii) exports of primary goods from DCs to LDCs amount to $9 billions; and (iii) the G.N.P. of LDCs is approximately $400 billions.

Now make the following, quite extreme, assumptions: (a) LDCs, by establishing effective cartels, increase permanently the price level of their primary-goods exports threefold; (b) this increase has no effect at all on the quantity of imports of these goods by DCs; and (c) likewise, this increase has no effect at all on the prices of exports from DCs to LDCs.

With these data and these assumptions, the increase in prices of exports of primary goods by LDCs will raise their annual export receipts by 66 billion dollars, or some 16 per cent of their G.N.P. The assumptions used are, however, highly implausible. Even maintaining the assumption that effective cartels are established — with all its implications about capacity to ration, to limit entry to the market, etc. — the other assumptions must be qualified. For assumption (b) to hold, the price increase should have no impact on demand for the primary goods by DCs, via either income or substitution effects; and no impact on local supply of these goods by DCs. Assumption (c) would require, *inter alia*, that even primary goods whose prices are increased in exports of LDCs would keep unchanged price tags when the goods are exported by DCs; and that the price of value added in exports of manufactures from DCs to LDCs would not only fail to rise, but would actually fall to offset the increase in the price of imported inputs. If assumptions (b) and (c) are replaced by more realistic and plausible assumptions, it would appear that a 5 to 7 per cent increase in their income level is the maximum that LDCs as a group may expect from a permanent threefold increase in the prices of primary-good exports. Several individual countries would, of course, enjoy a much more substantial improvement. My casual impression is that these would be, by and large, the high-income LDCs, whereas the poorest nations would fare worst.

The *once and for all* increase of 5 to 7 per cent in the income level of LDCs, derived in this exercise, should be put in the proper perspective. It is roughly equivalent to, say, the excess of the *annual* rate of increase of G.N.P. in a country like Korea — which has relied heavily on trade in its development course — over the average rate of increase of G.N.P. in LDCs. In such a comparison, the improvement due to changes in the international terms of trade almost fades into insignificance. This is, of course, a very simpleminded exercise. It overlooks issues such as the shadow price of foreign exchange, the possible effect of the terms of trade on domestic income distribution, or the impact on savings. Yet, it may suggest that as a factor in encouraging or inhibiting a rise in the standard of living of LDCs, possible changes in the international circumstances are far less important than domestic circumstances and the policies pursued by the less-developed countries themselves.

NOTES

[1] The topic for this session was International Circumstances Affecting the Development and Trade of Less-Developed Countries — Including the Effects of Decolonisation.

[2] Ephraim Kleiman, 'Trade and the Decline of Colonialism', Institute for International Economic Studies, Seminar Paper No. 49 (July, 1975). An abbreviated version has appeared under the same title, in the *Economic Journal*, 86 (September, 1976) pp. 459–490.
by Thomas Birnberg and Stephen Resnick, 'A Model of the Trade and Government Sectors in Colonial Economies', *American Economic Review*, LXIII (September, 1973), pp. 572–587.

[3] A most valuable assistance in this investigation has been provided by Mr. Matti Gutraich.

[4] This draws on a memorandum I have circulated at the World Bank in September 1975.

14 Transitional Growth and World Industrialisation*

Hollis B. Chenery

In the past 25 years, world population has nearly doubled and world output has tripled. This rapid growth has been accompanied by an accelerated shift of economic activity, and particularly of industry, from the old industrial centres to newly developed countries and to countries in the process of development. The reallocation of economic activity can be thought of both as reflecting the internal dynamics of national growth, as well as the international spread of technology and changing comparative advantage. An integrated treatment of the international allocation of production and trade must deal with both of these aspects.

The principal reallocation of economic activity in the postwar period has been a shift of manufacturing from the old industrial centres to a group of countries that have been catching up to the industrial leaders. I will identify the latter group as the *transitional countries*. They have either achieved the income levels and industrial structure of the original group in the past quarter-century or are in a position to do so by the year 2000. From the vantage point of 1976, there are eleven 'newly developed' market economies with a total population of some 250 million, and seven centrally planned economies that have nearly completed a similar transformation. Another 30 countries are well advanced in this transition.

This paper examines the uneven spread of industry among countries from two points of view; first, as a central feature of the internal transformation required by a developing economy, and then as part of the process by which a rapidly growing country has to readjust the structure of its trade in response to its changing comparative advantage and external market conditions. The analysis in three parts:

*I am indebted to Moises Syrquin, Don Keesing, Larry Westphal and Vinod Prakash for advice. Statistical calculations were performed by Hazel Elkington. This study grows out of a series of comparative analyses of development patterns, as well as several case studies of industrialisation. Principal results are given in Chenery (1960, 1964, 1969), Chenery, Shishido and Watanabe (1962), Chenery and Taylor (1968) and Chenery and Syrquin (1975).

(a) The nature of transitional growth and of the countries that are completing the transition;

(b) Alternative strategies of industrialisation and their impact on individual industrial sectors;

(c) The changes in factor proportions and comparative advantage associated with different development patterns and their effect on trade in manufactures.

I. TRANSITIONAL GROWTH

Kuznets (1966) summarises in the term 'modern economic growth' the set of processes by which the first group of industrial societies has developed.[1] Although the growth processes of the next wave of developing countries are similar in many respects to those of the first group, there are also important differences. These stem mainly from the existence of the advanced countries as sources of technology, capital and manufactured imports, as well as markets for exports. Although they do not necessarily change the goals of the society — which are derived in large part from the experience of the leading countries — these differences in the international environment broaden the range of opportunities of the follower countries, particularly as to the extent and form of international specialisation that they choose.

(1) NATURE OF THE TRANSITION

The transition from the economic structure of a poor country to that of an advanced society involves changes in the composition of demand, production, trade, and employment, all of which are highly correlated with the level of per capita income. In extending Kuznets' analytical framework to permit a more systematic study of transitional countries, Chenery and Syrquin (1975) compared the cross-sectional patterns to time series for the period 1950–70. We have also attempted to identify the principal factors that cause the growth of individual countries to deviate from the average patterns and have explored some of these relations by simulating the effects of different trade patterns.

In the present context, I am primarily concerned with those aspects of transitional growth that affect the rate and pattern of industrialisation and hence determine its uneven spread among developing countries. The proximate causes of these intercountry differences may be identified as:

(a) variation in overall rates of growth;

(b) variations in initial factor proportions and in their rates of change;

(c) differences in the response of demand to growing income;
(d) resulting differences in trade patterns and capital inflows.

Our results reinforce Kuznets' finding that the developed countries have quite similar economic structures, despite earlier variation in the timing of industrialisation and growth of G.N.P. There is also considerable uniformity among countries at the lowest income levels. The convergence at high income levels supports the concept of a 'transition' and leads to the description of many aspects of structural change by a logistic or other function having lower and upper asymptotes. Most of the transition from the lower to the upper asymptote takes place between the income levels of $150 and $1500 (in 1973 dollars).[2]

Of the factors affecting industrialisation, the most uniform are the decline in the share of food in consumption (and the corresponding rise in non-food components) and the rise in the share of investment in G.D.P. The most variable factors are natural resource endowments and the development strategies adopted by countries in relation to their opportunities for trade and capital inflows. Subsequent analysis will bring out the effects of these factors on the timing and pattern of industrialisation.

The transition can be usefully divided into an earlier and a later phase by measuring the halfway point in each development process. For example, on average, the share of industry (manufacturing plus construction) in G.D.P. increases from an average of 12·5 per cent for underdeveloped countries to 38 per cent for developed ones. This process is half completed at an income level of about $450, which is close to the average for all processes. On the other hand, the rise in the share of manufactured exports in G.D.P. (from 1·1 per cent to 13 per cent) takes place much later in the transition and is half completed only at an income level of $1000. In the following discussion the countries that have completed more than half of the normal changes in the structure of production and trade will be classed as 'transitional' and those that have not reached this point as 'less developed'.[3]

Apart from the initial differences in factor endowments, the major factors that we have identified as having a systematic effect on development patterns — particularly on patterns of trade and industrialisation — are country size and the capital inflow. Large countries are characterised by relatively smaller shares of both trade and capital inflows in G.D.P., and for this reason their production patterns are determined to a much larger extent by the pattern of internal demand. The opposite can be said of smaller countries, in which trade is a substantial fraction of G.D.P., domestic markets are small, and the production structure can be much more specialised.

The combination of size, resources and trade patterns has led us to identify three principal development patterns associated with the following groups of countries:[4]

(a) Large countries, which are characterised by relatively low ratios of trade to G.N.P. and usually low capital inflows ('large' is defined as a population of 15 million in 1960);

(b) Small countries relatively specialised in primary exports, described as 'primary oriented' (SP);

(c) Small countries relatively specialised in the export of manufactured goods and services ('manufacturing oriented' or SM).

These patterns provide the starting point for the analysis of the timing and pattern of world industrialisation in the remainder of this paper.

(2) TRANSFORMING THE PRODUCTIVE STRUCTURE

The transformation of the production structure from primary production to industry lies at the heart of transitional growth. Given the fairly uniform changes in internal demand that take place with rising levels of income, the main sources of variation in this transformation lie in the opportunities for international trade. Since trade in services is relatively unimportant, the transformation can be described as a shift in the source of supply of tradeable commodities from primary products to manufactured goods.

The three patterns identified above are associated with different initial factor endowments and different changes in comparative advantage over time. Countries with larger populations usually have more diversified natural resources as well as a larger domestic market at each level of per capita income. They also have higher internal transport costs and tend to substitute internal for external trade in bulky commodities. Large countries therefore have a relatively low share of exports in G.D.P., on the order of 10 to 15 per cent. Large domestic markets also lead to the earlier development of industries having economies of scale and hence to an early rise in the share of manufacturing in G.D.P.

Smaller countries have more specialised economies and their exports typically range from 20 to 30 per cent or more of G.D.P.[5] Countries lacking a favourable resource base for primary exports must develop a specialisation in manufacturing (or service) exports at a relatively early stage, while the resource-rich, primary-oriented countries can continue to exchange primary exports for manufactured imports up to relatively high levels of income. However, apart from the exceptional small oil producers, all of the countries that have achieved per capita income levels of $2000 or more have also industrialised to the point where industrial output exceeds primary production.

The average effects of these factors on the transformation of the productive structure are brought out in cross-country regressions for the main branches of industry. These results — which are analysed in greater detail in the following section — provide a basis for comparing the timing of the transformation of production among countries representative of each development pattern.

Although the share of traded goods in G.N.P. declines somewhat as income rises, the main variation in the transformation is in the shift from primary production to industry. In figure 1 the normal change in composition of tradeable output is shown for each of the three patterns, along with the actual transformation experienced by several transitional countries over the period 1950–73.[6] The full list of transitional countries is given in tables 1 and 2.

The average patterns show a considerable variation in the timing of the shift from primary production to industry. The share of manufacturing output reaches that of primary output at about $500 in the large country and SM patterns, but only at $1200 in the SP pattern. The variations among individual countries are even greater, with Malaysia and Venezuela lagging considerably behind the SP norm because of their exceptionally favourable primary exports and Brazil and Israel leading the normal timing of the L and SM patterns. For most rapidly growing countries, however, the growth vectors tend to parallel the normal direction of change.

These examples illustrate the variation in growth patterns that is observed in transitional countries as a result of differences in their resource endowments and development policies. Despite this variation, it is clear that over the whole range of the transition the effect of rising income on the growth of industry is much more important than the difference in trade patterns. A rapidly growing country specialising in primary production can easily have a greater increase in industrial output per capita than a more slowly growing country specialising in industry – compare Malaysia and India, or Venezuela and Argentina. I will, therefore, examine the differences in growth rates among the transitional countries before proceeding to analyse the spread of industry as a consequence of transitional growth.

(3) THE TRANSITIONAL COUNTRIES

As defined above, the transitional countries are those that are in the process of catching up to the income levels and economic structures achieved by the old industrial countries before 1950. Three groups of transitional countries are listed in tables 1, 2, 3 and 4: (a) the newly developed market economies; (b) the newly developed centrally planned economies; and (c) market economies in the later stage of the transition.[7] Some of the marginal choices are arbitrary, but none of them affects the overall picture that emerges.

The newly developed countries all had levels of per capita G.N.P. (at market prices) of over $1400 in 1973; they ranged from $400 to $1300

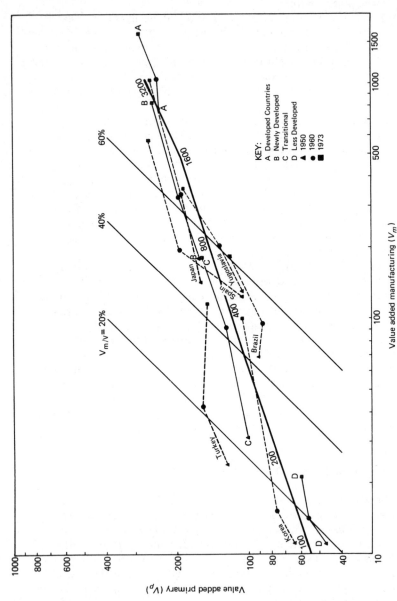

Figure 1a: Transformation of production: large countries (L)
US$ 1973 per capita

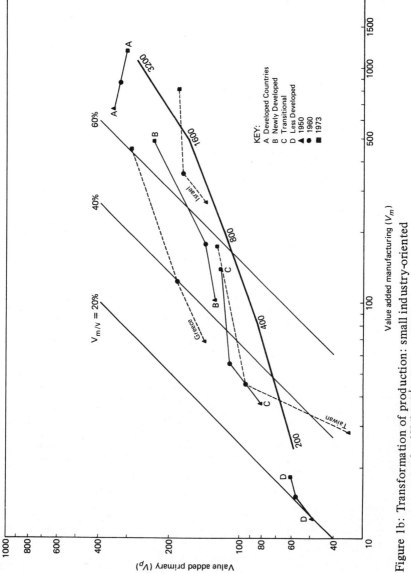

Figure 1b: Transformation of production: small industry-oriented countries (SM) US$ 1973 per capita.

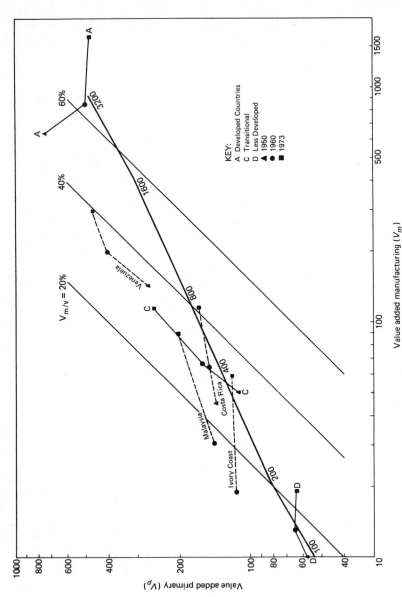

Figure 1c: Transformation of production: small primary-oriented
countries (SP). US$ 1973 per capita.

TABLE 1 BASIC DATA FOR NEWLY DEVELOPED COUNTRIES*

| | 1950 | | | | | 1973 | | | | | Annual average growth rates G.D.P. per capita | |
	G.D.P. mp., US$ 1973 (bill.)	Pop. (mill.)	G.D.P. per capita $	Manuf. prodn. $ (mill.)	Prim. prodn. $ (mill.)	G.D.P. m.p. US$ 1973 (bill.)	Pop. (mill.)	G.D.P. per capita $	Manuf. prodn. $ (mill.)	Prim. prodn. $ (mill.)	1950–60	1960–73
Large countries												
Japan	46.4	82.9	560	11795	13095	392.0	108.4	3618	111956	28028	7.6	9.1
Italy	38.6	46.8	824	7866	7943	134.2	54.9	2446	37883	13706	5.4	4.4
Spain	13.1	27.9	470	3415	2940	59.9	34.7	1725	19823	9193	5.2	6.3
Argentina	17.5	17.1	1027	4814	2656	40.2	24.3	1656	15383	5546	1.4	2.6
Total	115.6	174.6	662	27890	26634	626.4	222.3	2818	185045	56473	5.9	7.0
Small industry-oriented countries												
Israel	1.7	1.3	1335	334	176	10.1	3.2	3145	2628	580	1.4	5.7
Puerto Rico	1.5	2.2	672	243	344	7.0	2.9	2413	1623	217	5.3	6.0
Ireland	1.6	3.0	529	398	464	6.3	3.0	2063	2323	1143	4.8	7.1
Greece	3.4	7.6	445	511	1068	16.3	9.0	1812	4041	2586	4.8	7.4
Singapore	0.7	1.0	704	84	27	4.1	2.2	1893	931	97	0.4	7.6
Hong Kong	0.8	1.9	408	93	26	5.8	4.2	1394	2335	160	3.6	6.9
Portugal	3.2	8.4	386	918	1102	11.4	9.0	1270	4536	1531	3.4	6.9
Total	12.8	25.4	507	2581	3207	61.0	33.5	1822	18417	6314	4.0	7.0
All newly developed	128.4	200.0	642	30471	29841	687.3	255.8	2688	203462	62787	2.9	9.2

Source: World Bank. G.D.P. is gross domestic product at market prices.
*Totals may not add due to rounding.

TABLE 2: BASIC DATA FOR TRANSITIONAL COUNTRIES*

	1950					1973					Annual average growth rates G.D.P. per capita	
	G.D.P. m.p. US$ 1973 (bill.)	Pop. (mill.)	G.D.P. per capita $	Manuf. prodn. $ (mill.)	Prim. prodn. $ (mill.)	G.D.P. m.p. US$ 1973 (bill.)	Pop. (mill.)	G.D.P. per capita $	Manuf. prodn. $ (mill.)	Prim. prodn. $ (mill.)	1950–60	1960–73
Large countries												
South Africa	8·7	12·9	676	1431	2719	26·3	24·3	1083	6131	5204	1·7	2·4
Yugoslavia	6·0	16·3	370	2131	1726	20·3	21·0	970	7507	3986	4·3	4·3
Mexico	12·5	26·3	475	3037	2876	50·7	56·0	905	12874	5838	2·4	3·2
Brazil	17·4	52·0	335	3586	4708	77·7	101·1	769	18605	12077	3·0	4·2
Iran	5·2	16·3	319	533	1577	31·0	32·1	964	4609	12787	3·0	6·4
Turkey	5·5	21·0	261	499	2559	21·5	38·2	563	4404	5640	3·4	3·4
Colombia	3·2	11·3	281	520	1292	10·1	22·5	449	1966	3134	1·5	2·5
South Korea	2·4	18·9	128	202	1210	13·1	32·9	398	3296	3489	2·6	7·0
Total	60·9	175·0	348	11940	18668	250·7	328·1	764	59392	52155	2·8	4·1
Small industry-oriented countries												
Lebanon	1·0	1·7	604	135	197	2·7	3·0	906	394	257	0·2	3·1
Panama	0·4	0·8	442	37	96	1·5	1·6	950	250	246	1·9	4·6
Taiwan	1·3	7·6	168	211	260	10·0	15·4	648	2679	1909	4·9	7·0
Peru	2·9	8·2	356	377	967	9·2	14·5	631	1960	2060	2·6	2·5
Tunisia	0·7	3·3	223	58	192	2·6	5·5	468	275	598	3·0	3·5
El Salvador	0·4	1·9	227	57	173	1·3	3·8	352	251	318	1·9	1·9
Total	6·7	23·5	286	875	1885	27·2	43·8	623	5809	5388	2·6	4·1

Small primary-oriented countries

Venezuela	4·4	5·0	884	709	1329	18·0	11·3	1591	3332	5259	3·3	2·1
Saudi Arabia	1·9	5·1	370	157	996	15·2	7·7	1967	1006	10800	3·2	11·0
Jamaica	0·5	1·4	325	52	143	2·0	2·0	1000	285	381	6·9	3·6
Uruguay	2·6	2·2	1170	589	301	2·9	3·0	960	641	502	-1·5	-0·4
Iraq	0·6	5·1	124	39	140	3·8	10·4	362	392	1855	6·7	3·3
Chile	1·5	6·1	256	246	274	7·3	10·2	713	1909	1386	4·1	4·9
Costa Rica	0·3	0·9	367	48	120	1·4	1·9	730	215	311	3·5	2·7
Malaysia	2·0	6·1	331	177	807	6·7	11·3	593	1028	2296	0·8	4·0
Algeria	2·6	8·2	317	338	902	8·3	14·7	567	1125	1887	4·3	1·2
Nicaragua	0·3	1·0	285	34	104	1·1	2·0	561	251	277	2·1	3·7
Dominican Republic	0·6	2·1	301	110	177	2·6	4·4	577	425	662	2·2	3·4
Guatemala	0·9	2·8	314	105	292	2·7	5·2	512	419	750	0·7	3·3
Zambia	0·7	2·4	310	24	85	2·1	4·6	442	275	764	2·7	0·7
Rhodesia	0·7	2·7	281	108	223	2·4	5·9	400	592	505	1·5	1·6
Paraguay	0·4	1·4	299	70	177	1·0	2·4	417	166	318	0·5	2·2
Syria	0·8	3·2	237	136	188	2·8	6·9	396	530	475	-0·3	4·2
Ivory Coast	0·6	2·5	235	44	297	2·5	5·9	420	346	706	1·0	3·7
Ecuador	0·8	3·2	242	116	309	2·7	6·8	394	497	895	1·9	2·4
Total	22·3	61·5	363	3101	6862	85·1	116·6	730	13434	30029	2·5	3·5
All transitional	89·9	260·0	346	15915	27415	363·1	488·4	743	78635	87572	3·1	3·9

*Totals may not add due to rounding.

in 1950. They include seven centrally planned and eleven market
economies. The dividing line between this group and the remaining transitional countries is based primarily on the extent to which they have
transformed their productive structures as well as on the income level
reached. (Venezuela and Saudi Arabia are thus considered transitional,
even though their per capita incomes are over $1600.) On this test, the
newly developed include only large countries and small, industry-oriented,
countries, although several of them (Ireland, Argentina) were primary-
oriented at an earlier period. The remaining transitional countries have per
capita incomes above $400 or the equivalent volume of manufacturing.

Tables 3 and 4 give data for the five country groups broken down by
patterns of resource allocation. On this basis, the breakdown of world
population in 1973 was as follows: old developed (13 per cent), newly
developed market (7 per cent), newly developed centrally planned (9 per
cent), transitional market economies (13 per cent), transitional centrally
planned (23 per cent),[8] and other developing countries (35 per cent).

The effect of transitional growth on relative income levels is shown
in figure 2. The accelerated growth of both the centrally planned and
other newly developed countries has permitted them to double, or even
triple, their income levels in the past 25 years. Both groups have grown at
rates above 4 per cent per capita, and most of the market economies have
accelerated since 1960.

The total G.N.P. of the transitional countries has grown about as
rapidly over this period, but their per capita growth was reduced to 3·9
per cent by higher population growth (2·8 per cent *vs.* 1·1 per cent for
the newly developed). In contrast, the G.N.P. of the poorer developing
countries has risen at only 4·1 per cent — about the same rate as the old
developed countries — and high population growth has reduced their per
capita growth to less than 2 per cent.

II. INDUSTRIALISATION

To understand the uneven growth of industry, it is necessary to separate
the effects of differences in country growth — which were summarised in
the preceding section — from changes in internal demand and international
specialisation. This will be done by considering first the spread of industry
to the transitional countries, where differential growth rates are the
dominant factor, and then analysing the differences in the patterns of
industrialisation that are associated with differences in scale and factor
proportions.

(1) THE UNEVEN SPREAD OF INDUSTRY

The growth of manufacturing in each of the five major country groups is

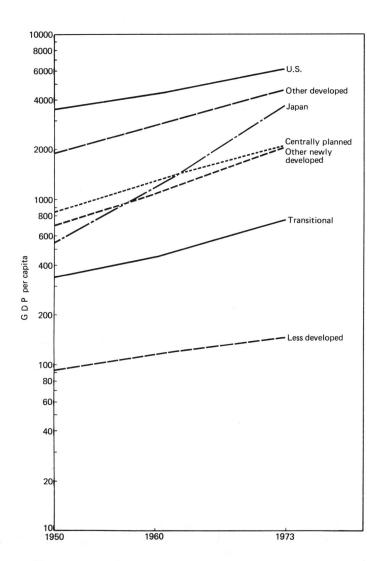

Figure 2: Rise in per capita income: country groups US$ 1973.

TABLE 3: OUTPUT*

Countries	1950					1973				
	G.D.P. m.p. US$ 1973 (bill.)	Pop. (mill.)	G.D.P. per capita $	Manuf. prodn. $ (bill.)	Prim. prodn. $ (bill.)	G.D.P. m.p. US$ 1973 (bill.)	Pop. (mill.)	G.D.P. per capita $	Manuf. prodn. $ (bill.)	Prim. prodn. $ (bill.)
A. Old developed										
1. U.S.	545·1	152	3580	153·7	40·3	1293·8	210	6149	362·3	58·2
2. Other	416·5	215	1937	122·0	54·6	1191·4	267	4458	400·4	84·3
Total	961·6	367	2619	275·7	94·9	2485·2	478	5203	762·7	142·5
B. Newly developed										
1. Japan	46·4	83	560	11·8	13·1	392·0	108	3618	112·0	28·0
2. Other large	69·2	92	754	16·1	13·5	234·4	114	2057	73·1	28·4
3. Small manuf.	12·8	25	507	2·6	3·2	61·0	34	1822	18·4	6·3
Total	128·4	200	642	30·5	29·8	687·3	256	2688	203·5	62·8
C. Transitional										
1. Large	60·9	175	348	11·9	18·7	250·7	328	764	59·4	52·2
2. Small manuf.	6·7	24	286	0·9	1·9	27·2	44	623	5·8	5·4
3. Small prim.	22·3	62	363	3·1	6·9	85·1	117	730	13·4	30·0
Total	89·9	260	346	15·9	27·4	363·1	488	743	78·6	87·6
D. Less developed										
1. Large	58·6	653	90	7·0	30·4	154·4	1089	142	22·9	65·4
2. Small manuf.	3·5	28	125	0·3	1·3	8·7	51	171	1·3	2·9
3. Saml prim.	11·5	91	126	0·9	5·3	27·3	164	166	3·2	10·5
Total	73·6	772	95	8·2	37·1	190·3	1303	146	27·3	78·8
Total market economies	1253·6	1599	784	330·3	189·2	3726·0	2525	1475	1072·2	371·7
E. Centrally planned										
1. USSR	149·8	180	832	31·3	55·6	506·5	250	2028	199·8	116·8
2. Other	80·6	89	910	21·9	24·0	220·4	105	2103	89·2	40·8
Total	230·4	269	858	53·2	79·7	726·9	355	2050	289·0	157·6

Source: World Bank. Data for centrally planned countries from U.S. Congress, Joint Economic Committee, 1973, 1975.

*Totals may not add due to rounding.

TABLE 4: ANNUAL AVERAGE GROWTH RATES AND OUTPUT SHARES: MANUFACTURING*

Countries	Growth rates 1950–60				Growth rates 1960–73				Manufacturing % G.D.P.		
	G.D.P.	Per capita G.D.P.	Manuf. prodn.	Prim. prodn.	G.D.P.	Per capita G.D.P.	Manuf. prodn.	Prim. prodn.	1950	1960	1973
A. Old Developed											
1. U.S.	3·3	1·5	3·0	1·6	4·3	3·1	4·4	1·7	28·2	27·4	28·0
2. Other	4·7	3·7	6·1	1·3	4·6	3·7	4·7	2·4	29·3	33·4	33·6
Total	3·9	2·6	4·5	1·4	4·4	3·4	4·6	2·1	28·7	30·2	30·7
B. Newly developed											
1. Japan	9·0	7·6	10·5	3·2	10·3	9·1	10·1	3·5	25·4	29·2	28·6
2. Other large	5·6	4·6	6·1	4·1	5·4	4·3	7·3	2·6	23·3	24·6	31·2
3. Small manuf.	5·6	4·0	7·3	2·4	8·1	7·0	10·2	3·4	20·1	23·7	30·2
Total	6·9	5·7	8·1	3·6	8·1	7·0	9·0	3·1	23·7	26·7	29·6
C. Transitional											
1. Large	5·6	2·8	6·4	4·3	6·9	4·1	8·4	4·8	19·6	19·9	23·7
2. Small manuf.	5·4	2·6	6·7	5·4	7·0	4·1	10·1	4·1	13·0	14·8	21·3
3. Small prim.	5·5	2·5	5·4	6·6	6·4	3·5	7·5	6·6	13·9	13·9	15·8
Total	5·6	2·7	5·7	5·0	6·8	3·9	8·3	5·3	17·7	18·1	21·7
D. Less developed											
1. Large	4·1	2·0	4·6	4·0	4·4	2·0	5·8	2·9	12·0	12·5	14·8
2. Small manuf.	4·8	2·3	5·2	4·4	3·5	0·7	7·0	2·7	9·3	9·5	14·8
3. Small prim.	4·0	1·3	5·8	3·7	3·7	1·1	5·7	2·5	7·7	9·1	11·7
Total	4·2	2·0	4·8	4·0	4·3	1·8	5·8	2·9	11·2	11·9	14·4
Total market economies	4·4	2·4	5·0	2·9	5·2	2·8	5·5	3·1	26·4	27·7	28·8
E. Centrally planned											
1. USSR	6·1	4·3	10·1	3·7	4·9	3·7	7·1	2·9	20·9	30·2	39·4
2. Other	5·1	4·2	7·4	3·2	4·0	3·3	5·4	1·7	27·2	33·8	40·5
Total	5·8	4·2	9·1	3·6	4·6	3·6	6·6	2·6	23·1	31·3	39·8

*Growth rates for G.D.P. and for individual sectors of G.D.P. are calculated initially on the basis of constant prices in domestic currency in order to avoid the distorting effect of disparate changes in prices and exchange rates.

shown in figure 3. While the general pattern is similar to that of figure 2, the 'catching up' phenomenon of the three transitional groups is even more pronounced. Tables 3 and 4 show that the net shift in the distribution of world manufacturing is quite substantial. There has been a decline in the share of the old developed countries from 72 per cent to 56 per

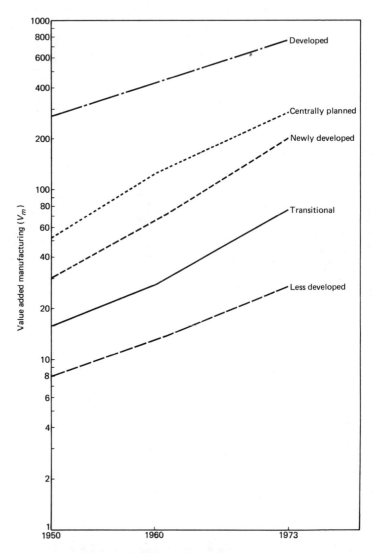

Figure 3: Growth of manufacturing: country groups.
US$ 1973 (billion).

cent and an increase of more than 50 per cent in the shares of each of the three transitional groups. I will limit further analysis of this shift to the market economies, since the centrally planned economies constitute a more closed system in which market forces operate only to a limited extent.[9]

This international spread of manufacturing can be attributed to three sets of factors: (a) differences in the growth of G.N.P. among countries; (b) variation in the income elasticity of demand with the level of income; (c) changes in international specialisation. From the data presented in tables 3 and 4 it is possible to separate the effects of differences in aggregate growth from the other factors, leaving further analysis to the national and sectoral level.

To separate the effects of income growth from other influences on manufacturing output, I will use the following formula:

$$\Delta V_m = V_m{}^T - V_m{}^o = m^o(Y^T - Y^o) + \Delta m Y^T$$

where V_m = value added in manufacturing, Y = G.N.P., and $m = V_m/Y$. The first term, $m^o(Y^T - Y^o)$, can be considered as a growth effect, while the second term, $\Delta m Y^T$, includes all the factors causing a change in the share of industry in G.N.P. – the 'industrialisation effect' (an alternative formulation is given in Solow's Comment, p. 494). Application of this decomposition to the data in tables 3 and 4 gives the following results for the period 1950–73:

		Δm	$\Delta m Y^T$	ΔV_m	$\dfrac{\Delta m Y^T}{\Delta V_m}$
A1	United States	$-\cdot2\%$	$- 3$	208	$- 1\%$
A2	Other Developed	$4\cdot3\%$	51	278	18%
B	Newly Developed	$5\cdot9\%$	41	173	23%
C	Transitional	$4\cdot0\%$	15	63	23%
D	Less Developed	$3\cdot2\%$	6	19	32%
	Total		110	741	

This breakdown shows that even in the newly developed and transitional groups, where the rise in the share of industry is large, it accounts for only 23 per cent of the total increase in manufacturing.[10]

This analysis confirms that at least three-quarters of the net shift of industry to the newly developed and transitional countries can be attributed to their higher growth rates. Table 4 shows that the rate of growth of manufacturing is more closely related to the overall growth of the economy than it is to the pattern of specialisation. However, in individual sectors of industry, changes in international specialisation will be shown to play a much more important role.

(2) SOURCES OF INDUSTRIALISATION

While the largest increase in industrial activity is concentrated in countries in the later stages of the transition, the timing of industrialisation is greatly affected by market size and the availability of primary resources. When industrial growth is decomposed by sector, the leads or lags can be shown to be greatest in the intermediate products and capital goods that are most affected by economies of scale.

To progress further in understanding these factors, it is necessary to examine their interaction. Since only a few countries have completed the transition, I will combine the results of a model that simulates industrialisation by country with evidence from cross-country regressions.

The following interindustry model was designed initially to explain the pattern of industrialisation in Japan and then reformulated to simulate the effects of alternative development policies.[11] It distinguishes between the effects of changing domestic demand and changing net trade in each sector and also measures the effects of technological change.[12] In the case of Japan, the model was estimated for 1914, 1935, 1955 and 1965, covering a six-fold increase in per capita income.

The basic relations in the historical version of the model are summarised in the following equations:

$$X_i + M_i = C_i + I_i + E_i + \Sigma a_{ij} X_j \ (i = 1 \ldots n) \tag{1}$$

$$Y = \Sigma V_i = \Sigma v_i x_i \tag{2}$$

$$\Sigma E_i + F = \Sigma M_i \tag{3}$$

$$X_i = \Sigma r_{ij}(D_j + T_j) \ (i = 1 \ldots n) \tag{4}$$

Where:

Y = G.D.P.
F = capital inflow
X_i = production in sector i
C_i = public and private consumption
I_i = investment use
E_i = exports
M_i = imports
$T_i = E_i - M_i$

$D_i = C_i + I_i$

V_i = value added in sector i

a_{ij} = input of commodity i per unit of output of commodity j

v_i = ratio of value added to production in sector i

Equation (1) is the basic equation for an open Leontief system in which supply from domestic production plus exports must be equal to final demand — internal and external — plus intermediate use in other sectors of the economy. Equation (2) is the national accounts identity defining G.D.P. from the production side. Equation (3) states the balance of payments constraint for an economy with a net inflow of capital.

Equation (4) is the standard solution for a Leontief model in which the exogenous elements are consolidated into two factors: internal demand (consumption plus investment) and net trade (exports minus imports). In analysing changes over time, the input coefficients are assumed to change and the elements of the Leontief inverse are therefore dated.

To apply this model to the historical analysis of structural change, the growth of each element can be separated into two parts: expansion proportional to G.D.P. plus a deviation from proportional growth. For the growth in output of sector i from period 1 to period 2, this deviation is defined as:

$$\delta X_i^{12} = X_i^2 - \lambda X_i^1 \tag{5}$$

Where $\lambda = Y_2/Y_1$. Deviations in the other elements of equation (1) can be written in the same form. When they are substituted into equation (4), the expression for the deviation of output from proportional growth becomes:

$$\delta X_i^{12} = \sum_j r_{ij}^2 \left(\delta D_j^{12} + \delta T_j^{12} + \lambda S_j^{12} \right) \tag{6}$$

The deviation from proportional growth in each sector is therefore expressed as a function of the change in composition of demand, the change in net trade, and the effects of changes in input coefficients.[13] The last element is usually described in the Leontief system as 'technological change' although it also includes substitution in response to changes in relative prices.

If there is no change in technology or in the ratio of net trade in each sector to G.D.P., equation (6) provides an algebraic statement of Nurkse's concept of balanced growth which allows for intermediate use as well as changes in the composition of final demand. When these elements are estimated from historical data, equation (6) therefore provides a measure of the 'balanced growth' element for each sector.

The application of this analytical framework to Japan is based on an input-output system of 23 sectors, of which 14 are branches of manufacturing.[14] The calculation described in equation (6) was applied to each sector and repeated for different time periods. My comments are limited to explaining the rise in the share of manufacturing output in two periods shown in table 5: the early transition (1914–35) and the later transition (1935–65). This division minimises the disruptive effects of the Second World War. In 1935 Japan had an income level of about $350 (1973 prices), typical of the midpoint of the transition, and by 1965 it had reached $1260. Over this 50 year period G.N.P. expanded eleven-fold and industrial production 28 times. The share of industry in G.N.P. increased from 18 per cent to 47 per cent in constant (1960) prices.

Table 5 shows that the non-proportional growth of demand accounted for 58 per cent of the total rise of the share of industry in G.D.P. (defined to exclude food processing). This 'balanced growth' effect was somewhat more important in the earlier stage (65 per cent) and somewhat

TABLE 5
SOURCES OF INDUSTRIALISATION IN JAPAN – 1914–1965*

	1914–35	1935–65	1914–65
		Index of Growth	
1. G.N.P.	2·10	5·25	11·01
2. Population	1·32	1·42	1·87
3. G.N.P. p.c.	1·62	3·70	5·90
4. Exports	3·95	1·92	7·60
5. Industrial production	2·92	9·63	28·15
		Share of Industry in G.N.P.	
6. Food processing	9·7%	6·5%	4·4%
7. Non-food	8·5%	19·0%	42·2%
	(1914)	(1935)	(1965)
		*Sources of Industrial Growth**	
8. Demand effects	65%	42%	58%
9. Trade effects:	26%	4%	15%
(a) Exports	(30)	(−6)	(12)
(b) Imports	(5)	(10)	(4)
10. Technological change	9%	54%	26%

Sources: Chenery and Watanabe (1975) and Chenery, Shishido and Watanabe (1962).
**Computed from equation (6). Industry omits food processing.

less important in the later stage (42 per cent). The expansion of manufactured exports was the next most important cause in the early stage (30 per cent), in which the effect of import substitution was negligible. These effects were reversed in the later stage, in which the economy adjusted to the wartime loss of exports largely by import substitution.

Perhaps the most interesting feature of this analysis is the measure that it provides of technological change.[15] For the whole period of the transition, the increase in intermediate demand resulting from changes in input—output coefficients — which include price effects as well as changing technology — account for 26 per cent of the rise in the share of manufacturing. In the later stages of the transition they are much greater than the effects of changes in specialisation.

The overall pattern of Japanese industrialisation can best be understood as an adaptation to Japan's limited natural resource base. Over the 50 years of the transition, there was virtually no increase in primary exports. The substitution of manufacturing for primary production took place indirectly through international trade and more directly through technological change and substitution.[16] Both import substitution and export expansion started in the simpler, labour-intensive sectors of manufacturing, primarily textiles, and then spread to other sectors, primarily basic metals and metal products. Although the expansion of manufactured exports (instead of primary products) in the early stage of the transition has been followed by only a few developing countries, the later stages of import substitution and export expansion are similar to the general pattern of trade adjustment described in section III.

(3) EFFECTS OF SPECIALISATION

Although no studies of industrialisation comparable to that for Japan have been completed, there are several other ways to generalise these results. Cross-country regressions show the variation of sector production with income levels, country size and export patterns, and indicate the sectors which are most affected by market size and resource endowments. An alternative approach is to estimate the variation of the exogenous demand elements in equation (4) directly as a function of income and population and then to simulate the growth of sectoral output with income.[17]

The Chenery-Taylor regressions were estimated for twelve sectors of manufacturing for large and small countries separately, with the levels of primary and manufacturing exports included as explanatory variables.[18] Most sectors showed a large and significant effect of variation in primary exports, indicating that there is some substitution of manufacturing for primary exports in almost all sectors, either through exports or import substitution. As expected, these estimates of the effects of specialisation are much larger for small countries than for large ones.

The regression results provide a convenient way to identify the main sectors in which countries specialising in primary exports lag in shifting to manufacturing as well as those affected by economies of scale. To bring out these lags, table 6 gives a summary of the difference between the three development patterns over the transition. The sectors are listed in approximately the order of their normal development and grouped into 'early', 'middle' and 'late'.

The main differences are between the values for the small, primary-oriented (SP) countries on the one hand and the other two groups. They are concentrated in the industries usually classed as 'heavy' — chemicals and petroleum, paper, basic metals, and metal products. To bring out this relationship more sharply, the growth of heavy industry with the level of income in each of the three patterns is shown in figure 4. These results

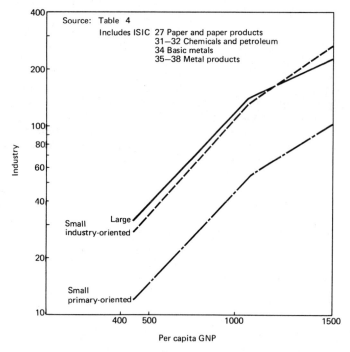

Figure 4: Growth of heavy industry. US$ 1973 per capita

suggest that the SP countries in effect substitute primary exports for about half of the amount of basic industry produced in the other two patterns throughout most of the transition.

The effects of market size are less apparent in this comparison, since

TABLE 6: VARIATION IN SHARES OF VALUE ADDED WITH PER CAPITA G.D.P.*

G.D.P. per capita $	Large countries			Small industry-oriented countries			Small primary-oriented countries		
	300 %	700 %	1000 %	300 %	700 %	1000 %	300 %	700 %	1000 %
Early industries									
20–22 Food, bev., tob.	3·68	3·84	3·96	4·86	4·76	4·78	4·38	4·68	4·83
29 Leather prods.	0·21	0·21	0·19	0·35	0·28	0·26	0·14	0·19	0·20
23 Textiles	2·80	3·00	2·76	2·43	2·38	2·38	1·04	1·09	1·12
Middle industries									
33 Non-met. mineral prods.	1·31	1·69	1·60	0·95	1·44	1·74	0·66	0·89	1·03
30 Rubber prods.	0·58	0·76	0·73	0·39	0·40	0·41	0·12	0·15	0·20
25–26 Wood prods.	1·18	1·79	1·95	2·43	2·17	2·10	0·54	0·91	1·26
31–32 Chemical and pet. coal prods.	2·37	3·50	3·78	1·80	2·65	3·19	0·73	1·18	1·50
Late industries									
24 Clothing and footwear	1·40	2·35	2·57	2·62	2·25	2·12	1·07	1·46	1·70
28 Printing and publishing	1·03	1·67	1·78	0·61	1·13	1·49	0·46	0·70	0·92
34 Basic metals	1·64	2·88	3·04	0·69	1·36	1·87	0·02	0·09	0·17
27 Paper and paper prods.	0·52	0·95	1·13	0·67	1·45	2·05	0·09	0·22	0·32
35–38 Metal prods.	2·98	5·62	6·68	2·78	6·61	9·61	1·79	3·44	4·58
	(19·70)	(28·24)	(30·17)	(20·58)	(26·88)	(32·0)	(11·04)	(15·00)	(17·83)

Source: H. B. Chenery and L. Taylor, 'Development Patterns: Among Countries and Over Time', (1968), pp. 406, 407.

they are partly concealed by aggregation. As might be expected, scale effects are more pronounced at low income levels and in sectors such as basic metals and chemicals that are known to have substantial economies of scale (see Haldi and Whitcomb, 1967). A more sensitive indicator is provided by the level of exports from these sectors, which is discussed in the next section.

III. CHANGING COMPARATIVE ADVANTAGE

Comparative advantage changes much more rapidly in transitional countries than in either the developed or less developed groups. Not only do the transitional countries grow more rapidly than the income groups above and below them but they devote an increasing share of their resources to the formation of both physical and human capital. As a result the stock of reproducible physical capital (excluding residential building) may double in ten years and the stock of human capital in fifteen years, thus tending to close the gap with the developed countries. On the other hand, exportable natural resources, which provide the principal basis for comparative advantage in the less developed countries, become relatively scarcer during the later stages of the transition. Sooner or later there has to be a shift away from primary exports toward manufactures.[19]

Since data on factor proportions are not yet available on a comprehensive basis, I will limit my discussion to the indirect evidence for some of the countries following each of the major development patterns. These observations suggest that, in addition to changes in factor proportions, increases in the size of the domestic market with rising income play a large role in determining comparative advantage in transitional countries. Although the changing trade patterns of the smaller countries can be interpreted in terms of the Heckscher—Ohlin analysis of comparative advantage, the export and import patterns of larger countries are better understood as a reflection of the internal pattern of development.

(1) SCALE AND FACTOR PROPORTIONS

When natural resources are treated as a separate factor of production, along with physical capital and skilled labour, the Heckscher—Ohlin model provides a good explanation of the main features of trade between the less developed and the developed countries. Most poor countries are at a disadvantage in producing manufactured goods, not only because of limited capital and skills but also because of the smaller size of their domestic markets. The traditional colonial exchange of primary products and handicrafts for manufactures and processed raw materials can indeed be taken as the prototype for the factor-proportions explanation of trade and of its benefits to each party.

All of these factors change in transitional countries as income levels rise. However, the relative availability of natural resources continues to dominate the trade pattern up to high levels of income. Since the changes in factor proportions and their implications for trade vary according to the development pattern, I will take each pattern separately.

Industry-oriented Countries

Industry-oriented countries are defined as those which, at each level of income, have a relatively high proportion of manufactured goods in their total exports.[20] In most cases of successful development following this pattern — Japan, Israel, Singapore, Hong Kong, Taiwan, Korea — the relation of this trading pattern to the limited natural resources of the country is obvious. In the early stages of development, exports have been based on relatively cheap labour (both skilled and unskilled) and have then become increasingly skill intensive. Success in exporting particular commodities has often led to associated research and technical training, so that the initial comparative advantage has been reinforced.

Although a number of other countries have attempted to follow this pattern of development, many have failed because of an inability to establish efficient export industries that would sustain continued growth. Among the successful cases, the availability of external capital for the first decade or so in countries such as Taiwan, Israel, Korea and Puerto Rico has sustained rapid import growth until the export base could be established.

The small, industry-oriented pattern of trade is, perhaps, the 'purest' case of Heckscher-Ohlin specialisation, particularly in its early stages. As these economies have developed. learning by doing and technological adaptation have increasingly replaced the measurable differences in factor costs as the basis for export expansion and make it difficult to describe the trade pattern as resulting primarily from factor endowments.[21]

Primary-oriented Countries

Most small primary-exporting countries maintain this export pattern until near the end of the transition. Manufactured exports normally reach a share of 20 per cent of total exports only at income levels above $1000 per capita. The delayed development of manufacturing also has a substantial effect on the type of manufactured goods that are exported. However, as comparative advantage based on natural resources declines, a shift to manufactured exports becomes necessary. If this happens at income levels between $500 and $1000, the country will have relatively high wages and will not find its comparative advantage in the labour-intensive industries that are the first to develop in the SM pattern. In the more extreme cases, such as Venezuela or Iran, the country may shift directly into capital-intensive exports of manufactures based on its raw materials and abundant capital.

This need to shift from primary exports to manufactures at some point in the future may not be adequately signalled by market forces, particularly in the case of mineral exporters whose exports will be limited by future supplies. Since the exchange rate responds to the present rather than the future demand and supply of foreign exchange, it may be necessary for the government to provide incentives to develop industries that will be needed to supply exports ten or fifteen years hence but which would not have a comparative advantage in relation to present primary exports. Few governments have had sufficient foresight to bring about this reorientation of trade without a balance of payments crisis and protracted slowdown in growth, as in Uruguay, Chile, Colombia, Sri Lanka, and many other cases.[22]

Large Countries

At very low income levels the comparative advantage of larger countries is mainly determined by their natural resources, as in the case of the smaller countries. However, some industries are established for the domestic market in large countries at much lower levels of per capita income, as was shown in table 6. Once basic metals, chemicals, machinery and equipment, and other 'scale economy' industries are in operation, they provide a basis for exports that does not exist in smaller countries whose factor endowments are otherwise similar.[23] The manufactured exports of the larger transitional countries are therefore a mixture of the labour-intensive commodities that are typical of the SM countries and 'scale economy' products.

Because of the combination of changing scale and factor proportions, the export patterns of large countries are harder to relate to factor-proportions or other simple models of trade. Although economies of scale are relatively less important in richer countries, they cannot be ignored in analysing the trade patterns of transitional countries.

Finally, since exports are only 10 to 15 per cent of G.N.P. in large countries, the added cost of not conforming to comparative advantage in their trade patterns is considerably less than for smaller countries. In fact, the loss in growth that is caused by periodic import shortages in countries that have given insufficient attention to exports is often considerably greater than the loss that would be occasioned by an inefficient choice of export commodities. In comparing the performance of some of the more successful large developing countries in recent years (Yugoslavia, Brazil, Korea) with some of the less successful ones (Argentina, Philippines, India), it is the policy of export promotion by the former group and its absence in the latter that stands out as the crucial difference, rather than the better choice of export sectors.

(2) EFFECTS ON MANUFACTURED EXPORTS

The general characteristics of the three patterns of trade and development outlined above can only be verified through more detailed statistical analysis than has yet been done.[24] Some of the available data for the period since 1960 are summarised in tables 7 and 8, which illustrate the following points.

At the aggregate level, manufactured exports have been growing some 50 per cent faster than manufacturing production in almost all groups of countries, the main exceptions being the richest (the United States) and the poorest. A growing share of manufactured output is therefore being exported from all of the transitional groups. While the share of the transitional countries rose only from 2 per cent to 3 per cent of the manufactured exports of the market economies between 1960 and 1971, the newly developed group increased its share from 13 per cent to 21 per cent. The transitional countries are in a position to make an increase of similar magnitude in the next twenty years.

Table 8 relates the export volumes and the factor proportions embodied in manufactured exports to the income levels and development patterns of the exporters. Since it is based on data at the SITC two-digit level, a factor index is derived from the relative shares of two labour-intensive, low-skill industries (textiles and clothing) and two generally higher skill and more capital-intensive sectors (chemicals and machinery).[25] These four groups account for about 60 per cent of world trade in manufactures.

There are two main conclusions from this stage of the analysis:

(a) *Volume of industry exports.* The SM countries are very specialised at all income levels except the lowest, in which industrial specialisation is only beginning. In the first three groups, manufactured exports are 40 to 50 per cent of manufacturing value added (equivalent to perhaps 20 per cent of total output) in SM countries. In the large countries the share exported is less than half as great, while in the SP countries only 5 per cent of manufactured goods are exported.[26]

(b) *Factor proportions.* The factor-proportions index shows the expected rise with income level in all three trade patterns.[27] However, at the same income level, the SM countries generally have the lowest skill intensity and the SP countries the highest. This is consistent with the arguments advanced above.

(3) GROWTH AND SPECIALISATION

In conclusion, I will return to the main questions raised at the beginning of this essay: (a) What has been the nature of the uneven spread of

TABLE 7: MANUFACTURED EXPORTS (UNCTAD 'A') US$ 1973 (1960 PRICES)*

Countries	1960 ratio to value added in manufacturing	Manufactured exports			Annual average growth rates	
		1960 $ Bill	1965 $ Bill	1971 $ Bill	1960–65	1965–71
A. Old developed						
1. U.S.	0·100	20·62	26·37	36·17	5·0	5·4
2. Other large	0·249	40·76	56·09	92·35	6·6	8·7
3. Total large	0·166	61·38	82·46	128·52	6·1	7·7
4. Small manuf.	0·403	18·50	29·03	44·19	9·4	7·3
5. Small prim.	0·028	0·30	0·89	1·48	24·3	8·9
Total	0·188	80·17	112·38	174·20	7·0	7·6
B. Newly developed						
1. Japan	0·162	5·16	11·45	25·69	17·3	14·4
2. Other large	0·167	4·89	9·34	16·95	13·8	10·4
3. Total large	0·164	10·05	20·79	42·64	15·7	12·7
4. Small manuf.	0·400	2·03	3·22	5·99	9·7	10·9
Total	0·182	12·08	24·01	48·63	14·7	12·5
C. Transitional						
1. Large	0·048	1·00	2·07	4·42	15·7	13·5
2. Small manuf.	0·147	0·25	0·71	1·50	23·2	13·3
3. Small prim.	0·123	0·65	0·79	1·09	4·0	5·5
Total	0·068	1·90	3·57	7·01	13·4	11·9
D. Less developed						
1. Large	0·114	1·25	1·80	2·24	7·6	3·7
2. Small manuf.	0·100	0·05	0·06	0·12	3·7	12·3
3. Small prim.	0·127	0·19	0·25	0·36	5·6	6·3
Total	0·114	1·49	2·10	2·72	7·1	4·4
Total market economies	0·179	95·64	142·07	232·55	8·2	8·6

Source: Vinod Prakash, 'Statistical Indicators of Industrial Development: A Critique of the Basic Data'. IBRD, Development Economics Staff Working Paper No. 189 (September, 1974).

*Totals may not add due to rounding.

TABLE 8: SELECTED EXPORT CHARACTERISTICS

		Trade pattern		
Country group	*Large*	*SM*	*SP*	*Total*
A. *Developed*				
1. E_m/V_m (%)	18·6	52·4	7·1	22·1
2. E_m/E (%)	74·1	70·7	16·6	71·3
3. Chemicals and machinery ($ bill.)	84·31	23·32	0·75	108·38
4. Textiles and clothing ($ bill.)	7·41	4·85	0·06	12·32
5. Factor index $\frac{(3)}{(3+4)}$	0·92	0·83	0·93	0·90
B. *Newly developed*				
1. E_m/V_m (%)	24·4	36·1		25·5
2. E_m/E (%)	85·4	62·9		81·7
3. Chemicals and machinery ($ bill)	24·45	1·68		26·13
4. Textiles and clothing ($ bill.)	5·38	2·37		7·75
5. Factor index $\frac{(3)}{(3+4)}$	0·82	0·42		0·77
C. *Transitional*				
1. E_m/V_m (%)	9·2	47·9	4·9	11·3
2. E_m/E (%)	30·7	57·9	4·1	23·1
3. Chemicals and machinery ($ bill.)	1·88	0·83	0·23	2·93
4. Textiles and clothing ($ bill.)	1·35	0·94	0·11	2·39
5. Factor index $\frac{(3)}{(3+4)}$	0·58	0·47	0·68	0·55
D. *Less developed*				
1. E_m/V_m (%)	9·3	7·0	4·8	8·7
2. E_m/E (%)	20·6	15·3	5·6	17·4
3. Chemicals and machinery ($ bill.)	0·24	0·04	0·05	0·32
4. Textiles and clothing ($ bill.)	1·19	0·01	0·05	1·26
5. Factor index $\frac{(3)}{(3+4)}$	0·17	0·77	0·46	0·20

TABLE 8: SELECTED EXPORT CHARACTERISTICS (Contd.)

		Trade pattern		
Country group	Large	SM	SP	Total
Total				
1. E_m/V_m (%)	18·9	48·9	6·0	21·6
2. E_m/E (%)	71·1	68·5	8·0	65·8
3. Chemicals and machinery ($ bill.)	110·87	25·87	1·03	137·76
4. Clothing and textiles ($ bill.)	15·33	8·16	0·22	23·72
5. Factor index $\dfrac{(3)}{(3+4)}$	0·88	0·76	0·82	0·85

Source: U.N. Trade Statistics.

industry? (b) What has been the relative importance of differences in growth rates and of changes in international specialisation to this result?

Whether we look at total manufacturing or at the trade in manufactured goods, it is clear that the accelerated growth of the transitional countries has been the main agent of change in the world distribution of industrial activity. This conclusion is accentuated by the fact that large countries comprise three-quarters of the population of all three groups — newly developed, centrally planned and transitional — and their growth patterns have been determined as much by the changing internal pattern of demand as by changes in international specialisation.

These aggregate figures understate the importance of changes in specialisation for the more dynamic industrial sectors. The relatively large internal markets of some of the transitional countries have made possible the development of industries characterised by economies of scale at income levels as low as $400 per capita or even less. Some of these countries (Yugoslavia, Brazil, Spain, Mexico, Korea, India) have started to emerge as significant exporters of 'scale commodities' in the past decade, and they may well develop a more pronounced comparative advantage in them in the future. Apart from scale effects, the emerging patterns of both primary and manufactured exports from the transitional countries seem to accord quite well with their changing factor proportions, once the growing scarcity of their primary resources is recognised.

In the analysis of trade relations, the transitional countries should be recognised as a separate group with factor proportions intermediate between the old developed countries on the one hand and the less developed ones on the other. The newly developed countries have already lost their comparative advantage in many branches of textiles, clothing, electronics and other labour-intensive activities to countries with lower wages, and further differentiation of this sort is to be expected. To reflect this phenomenon, trade theorists will have to deal with several factors and several countries, relying more heavily on empirical observation for their simplifying assumptions. As the theory of transitional growth becomes better articulated and embodied in dis-aggregated models,[28] it offers opportunities for a better integration with the theories of international trade and location.

NOTES

[1] The fifteen countries that were fully developed before the Second World War are the United States, Canada, Sweden, Switzerland, Australia, New Zealand, United Kingdom, Denmark, Norway, Belgium, France, Germany, Netherlands, Austria and Finland. (Here, as elsewhere, I omit countries of under one million population such as Iceland and Luxembourg.) The basis for selection is given in Chenery and Syrquin (1975, p. 10). For 1950, my list of developed countries is the same as that given by Kuznets (1966, table 7.1), with the omission of Italy and Japan.

[2] All data used in this paper are taken from the Economic and Social Data Bank of the World Bank. Measurement of the transition on this basis for ten development processes is given in Chenery and Syrquin (1975, p. 21). The basic sample consists of 101 non-communist countries for the period 1950–70. The original G.N.P. estimates were in 1964 dollars at factor cost, as then calculated by the World Bank. A conversion factor of 1.61 is used to convert to G.D.P. in 1973 market prices (see World Bank *Atlas*, 1975).

[3] These criteria are elaborated in Chenery and Syrquin (1975, p. 20).

[4] This classification was originally proposed by Chenery and Taylor (1968). It was modified by Chenery and Syrquin (1975) to take account of differences in development policies.

[5] The results of multiple regression analysis (Chenery and Syrquin, p. 41) show the share of exports falling from 26 per cent of G.D.P. at a population of 5 million to 11 per cent at 100 million, with little effect on per capita income.

[6] These diagrams omit construction from industry and, hence, differ from those in Chenery and Syrquin (1975).

[7] The more advanced centrally planned economies – U.S.S.R., German Democratic Republic, Czechoslovakia, Poland, Hungary, Romania and Bulgaria – are treated as 'newly developed' in tables 3 and 4. The centrally planned transitional economies – Albania, Cuba, North Korea, China – are omitted for lack of comparable data.

[8] China is included in this group although it would not qualify on its present income level.

[9] This decision is also dictated by the lack of comparable statistical information. For the centrally planned economies, I have utilised estimates

by the Joint Economic Committee of the U.S. Congress (1973, 1975) which show lower growth rates than the official sources used by the United Nations.

[10] When this calculation is done in current prices, the largest effect on the international distribution of industry is in the United States, where a combination of rising prices of services and low income elasticity of demand has reduced the share of manufacturing by 4·5 per cent of G.N.P. A similar drop in the share of manufactures in current prices is also apparent in other rich countries since 1960.

[11] The original model was presented in Chenery, Shishido and Watanabe (1962). Policy simulations are given in Chenery (1969) and Chenery and Raduchel (1971).

[12] The antecedents for this analysis are found in Nurkse's theory of 'balanced growth' and the extensive discussion that it generated. The best statement of the original thesis is found in Nurkse's Wicksell lectures (1959). Scitovsky (1959) and Streeten (1959) showed that economies of scale would lead to an alternation of investment among sectors, a phenomenon that was examined in a general equilibrium framework by Chenery and Westphal (1969).

[13] The derivation of this expression and the definition of S_j are given in Chenery, Shishido and Watanabe (1962).

[14] The original analysis for 1914–55 has been re-estimated for the years 1914–65 in Chenery and Watanabe (1975).

[15] Since input-output tables do not exist for the prewar period, technological change is inferred from equation (6) for each sector as a whole. The estimate for the prewar period is quite approximate.

[16] A detailed analysis of the nature of technological change and its effect on reducing the demand for primary outputs is given in Chenery, Shishido and Watanabe (1962).

[17] Preliminary results of the simulation analysis are given in Chenery (1969).

[18] The study of Chenery and Taylor (1968) was based on some 40 countries for the period 1953 to 1965. This analysis is now being extended by the World Bank through 1973 for a larger sample of countries.

[19] A few small petroleum exporters provide the main exception to this generalisation.

[20] From a theoretical standpoint, a definition based on factor proportions would be preferable. However, the available data show a fairly high correlation between a classification based on natural resource endowments per capita and that used here (Chenery, 1964).

[21] See the comparison of alternative trade hypotheses by Hufbauer (1970).

[22] In theory, future prices of foreign exchange derived from planning models could provide the basis for investment decisions that could avoid this problem. In practice, governments respond initially by protection and import substitution, which makes the subsequent shift to manufactured exports more difficult.

[23] Estimates of scale economies by S.I.T.C. category are given in Hufbauer (1970).

[24] Hufbauer's 1970 study of trade in manufactures, which includes ten transitional and fourteen developed countries, is the most useful test of alternative hypotheses that has been made. His sample excludes the primary-oriented countries.

[25] Analysis now under way at the three-digit level will yield a more precise index.

[26] Table 8 is based on a restricted definition of manufactured exports, which includes food processing with primary exports.

[27] The inclusion of Hong Kong, which has a high proportion of textile and clothing exports, lowers the average of the newly developed group.

[28] Interindustry planning models for transitional countries — such as Bruno's study of Israel (1966) and Westphal's analysis of Korea (1971) — provide a promising basis for extending the concept of dynamic comparative advantage in a form that can take account of most of the elements discussed here.

REFERENCES

Bruno, M., 'Optimal Patterns of Trade and Development', in H. B. Chenery (ed.) *Studies in Development Planning* (Cambridge: Harvard University Press, 1971).

Chenery, H. B., 'Patterns of Industrial Growth', *American Economic Review, 1—4*, 50 (Sept., 1960), pp. 624—654.

Chenery, H. B., 'Land: The Effects of Resources on Economic Growth', in K. Berrill (ed.) *Economic Development with Special Reference to East Asia* (New York: St. Martin's, 1964).

Chenery, H. B., 'The Process of Industrialization'. Harvard University Center for International Affairs, Economic Development Report No. 146 (Dec., 1969).

Chenery, H. B. and Raduchel, W. J., 'Substitution in Planning Models', in Chenery (ed.) *Studies in Development Planning* (Cambridge: Harvard University Press, 1971).

Chenery, H. B., Shishido, S. and Watanabe, T., 'The Patterns of Japanese Growth, 1914—1954', *Econometrica*, 30 (Jan., 1962), pp. 98—139.

Chenery, H. B. and Syrquin, M., *Patterns of Development 1950—1970* (London: Oxford University Press, 1975).

Chenery, H. B. and Taylor, L., 'Development Patterns: Among Countries and Over Time', *Review of Economics and Statistics*, 50 (Nov., 1968), pp. 391—416.

Chenery, H. B. and Watanabe, T., 'The Role of Industrialization in Japanese Development, 1914—1965' (1976) unpublished.

Chenery, H. B. and Westphal, L. E., 'Economics of Scale and Investment Over Time' in J. Margolis (ed.) *Public Economics* (New York: St. Martin's, 1969).

Haldi, J. and Whitcomb, D., 'Economies of Scale in Industrial Plants', *Journal of Political Economy* 75 (Aug., 1967), pp. 373—385.

Hufbauer, G. C., 'The Impact of National Characteristics and Technology on the Commodity Composition of Trade in Manufactured Goods', in

Vernon, R. (ed.) *The Technology Factor in International Trade* (New York: Columbia University Press, 1970).

Kuznets, S., *Modern Economic Growth* (New Haven: Yale University Press, 1966).

Nurkse, R., *Patterns of Trade and Development*, The Wicksell Lectures, (Stockholm: Almquist and Wiksell, 1959).

Scitovsky, T., 'Growth — Balanced or Unbalanced?', in M. Abramovitz *et al.* (eds.) *The Allocation of Economic Resources* (Stanford: Stanford University Press, 1959).

Streeten, P., 'Unbalanced Growth', *Oxford Economic Papers*, 11 (June, 1959), pp. 167–191.

U.S. Congress, Joint Economic Committee: Reorientation and Commercial Relations of the Economies of Eastern Europe; A Compendium of Papers (USGPO, 16 Aug., 1975), pp. 256–257. *Soviet Economic Prospects for the Seventies; A Compendium of Papers* (USGPO, 27 June, 1973), pg. ix.

Westphal, L. E., 'An Intertemporal Planning Model Featuring Economies of Scale', in Chenery, H. B. (ed.) *Studies in Development Planning* (Cambridge: Harvard University Press, 1971).

Comment
Robert M. Solow

This excellent and substantial paper rests on a broad hypothesis that will
be familiar to everyone who knows Chenery's work. The hypothesis is that
modern economic development is an identifiable process of growth and
change whose main features are the same in all countries, past and near
future. This does not mean that the same events, in the same magnitudes,
must happen in the same sequence everywhere. Chenery does not claim
that economic development is as pre-programmed as the life-cycle of the
salmon. There is room for local variation because of different local conditions; I will list some of those in a moment. But it does mean that newly
developing countries can learn from the historical experience of old
developed countries (except for one very important circumstance: the
new countries must inevitably develop and industrialise, as the old ones
did not, in a world that already contains many large developed countries).
This has some relevance to the questions raised by Professor Mabogunje.

I suppose that the main reason for trying to establish these 'laws of
development' (assuming that they exist) is to learn from them what sort
of policies 'work' — because they 'go with the flow' — and what sort do
not — because they go against the inner necessities of modern development.
In just the same way, you would want to understand the life-cycle of the
Atlantic salmon, whether your purpose was to catch them, or to help them
survive, or both. But except for casual remarks, this is a positive paper, not
a normative paper.

I mentioned that there is room in Chenery's view of development for
local variation in the pattern and pace of industrialisation, depending on
local conditions. These local conditions play the part of 'exogenous
variables' in this theory of the process of development. It is worth listing
what the main ones are.

The most important exogenous variable is probably the local endowment of natural resources, including arable land. The oil countries provide
only the most extreme and recent example, but it obviously matters a lot
for the possible patterns of development whether a country does or does
not have rich supplies of exportable natural resources, including potential
agricultural crops of food and fibre. (I will come back to the oil countries
in a moment.)

A second important exogenous variable in Chenery's scheme of things
is the absolute size of a country's population (and land area). A large
population generates a large internal market, which may permit the
exploitation of economies of scale without the necessity to penetrate
export markets. Even without economies of scale, there is something to
be said for a large internal market in a world of imperfect international

markets, changing obstacles to trade, transportation costs, uncertainty and risk-aversion. In any case, it appears from Chenery's data that large countries exhibit systematic differences from small countries in the typical pattern of industrial growth. Countries that are large in land area are also more likely to have diverse natural-resource bases.

A third important exogenous variable is the availability of an inflow of external capital. One might think that capital movements ought to be endogenous in a theory of economic development, and to a certain extent they undoubtedly are. But one only needs to mention the important cases of Taiwan, South Korea and Israel to realise that the flow of international capital is not simply a matter of the economic calculus.

Finally, one ought to mention internal policy choices as a sort of exogenous variable helping to determine the course of economic development, at least in the sense that one would not expect a descriptive theory in its early stages to be able to explain those choices.

I take it to be the Chenery view that if you select or invent an unnamed country, and tell me only its resource endowment, its size, its realistic hopes for aid and other capital inflows, and the sort of development policy it pursues (plus a few other things), I should be able to tell you the rest of its story as it passes up the ladder from the poverty level of $100–200 of G.D.P. per capita, into the transitional stage, through the newly developing stage, into the *arriviste* situation, with a per capita G.D.P. of $3000 or more, when it can begin to think about having nuclear bombs and missiles of its own.

With that background, the basic empirical proposition of the paper is that the main identifiable feature of modern economic development is a shift from primary production (including agriculture) to manufacturing. Manufacturing output tends to catch up with primary output at a G.D.P. of about $500 per captia (in 1973 prices); except that small countries with a rich resource base naturally reach this stage later, with a G.D.P. of some $1200 per capita. It has to be said that the data seem to support this generalisation handsomely. I think figures 1(a), (b) and (c) are rather impressive.

Up to this point, I have only one criticism to make. There is an awful lot of G.D.P. that is neither manufacturing nor primary production: mainly construction, transportation, public utilities, and services. I gather that in earlier work, Chenery has lumped construction with manufacturing as 'industry'. For most purposes, presumably, generating electricity, running railroads, operating telephone networks, and even managing banks and insurance companies are thoroughly modern economic activities, and ought to be included with 'industry'. A problem arises with services, some of which belong in the modern sector and some of which do not. It would be interesting to know if similarly strong patterns of development emerge from a more exhaustive classification of economic activity. Maybe the data just won't permit that to be worked out.

Suppose we accept the descriptive truth of Chenery's Law (which, by the way, has antecedents going back to Colin Clark and Simon Kuznets at least, not to mention Hegel). Why does it hold? Why should the path of economic development lead from primary production, through manufacturing, to tertiary industry? At one extreme, this sequence might be a logical necessity, in the sense that one could hardly imagine anything else; it might follow from fundamental economic reasoning. At the other extreme, it might merely be a matter of the newly developing countries imitating the old developed countries, with no more significance than Coca Cola or rock music. (If the data were available, who knows what cross-country regressions on those commodities would show?)

Actually I think — and probably Chenery would agree — the truth is between those extremes, and the standard pattern of economic development is something like a historical likelihood or near-necessity. The modern world could have evolved somewhat differently, but since it did not, it would be extraordinarily difficult to change the standard pattern now. In particular, I would guess that the standard pattern draws its force from two sources: first, the pattern of income elasticities of demand for broad classes of commodities, which is partly social-imitative in origin, but undoubtedly partly biological as well; and second, the nature of modern technology, especially the fact that some particular industries require more skilled labour than others, and/or require more capital than others, and/or have stronger economies of scale than others. It is easy to show in a diagram how appropriately shifting transformation curves, superimposed on an appropriately biased indifference map, can lead exactly to the pattern found by Chenery in the data.

This line of thought suggests two further detailed comments. First, the centrally planned economies already show some deviations from the standard pattern; and it is possible, of course, though not certain, that China will eventually deviate even further. Table 4 shows that by 1973, the centrally planned economies already had a larger fraction of G.D.P. in manufacturing than the developed market economies (40 per cent as against 30 per cent), and the fraction was still apparently rising in those countries, though it had already levelled off in the old developed economies and in Japan. This is a case where the rest of G.D.P. is important: manufacturing and primary production together account for a larger fraction of G.D.P. in the centrally planned economies than in the old developed or newly developed market economies. Presumably it is consumer services, including housing and transportation, that are being squeezed. The pattern of income-elasticities of demand is more malleable, and more ignorable, than the nature of modern technology. (Witness the fate of China's backyard steel furnaces. There is information for Professor Mabogunje here, too.) The track of China through the Chenery diagrams will be interesting to see.

Second, I am inclined to think that the oil-exporting countries of the Middle East are simply anomalies from the Chenery point of view, and perhaps should be excluded from his routine cross-country analyses. Here I am speaking with great ignorance; but my tourist-magazine picture of the terrain suggests that there cannot possibly be any comparative-advantage sense in going through the standard pattern in those places. Is it possible that it would really be more sensible for Saudi Arabia and Kuwait to invest abroad and live off the proceeds than for them to establish a conventional manufacturing economy in an inhospitable climate and peculiar location? I can easily understand the nationalistic and socio-psychological reasons that would work against some unorthodox solution. After all, it has been suggested that if North America had happened to be settled from the west rather than the east, New England — the part of the U.S. that I live in — would still be uninhabited. I am merely suggesting that the Chenery patterns may not extend to such unusual combinations of resource endowment, terrain, and climate. (Professor Chisholm suggested to me that a ship-repair industry would make some locational sense, and I agree. But that is not a manufacturing society.)

I want to turn next to a second substantive conclusion of the analysis in this paper. It has to do with the change in the geographical distribution of manufacturing activity in the world between 1950 and 1973. The paper argues that the change has indeed been substantial: the share of the old developed countries fell from 72 per cent to 56 per cent, so that the share of the transitional countries rose by half. Moreover, a decomposition of the shift into effects due to differential rates of growth among groups of countries and effects due to differing rates of industrialisation 'confirms that three-quarters of the net shift of industry to the newly developed and transitional countries can be attributed to these higher growth rates'. In other words, the industrialisation effect within the newer countries is not so important as the fact that their overall growth is faster, so that they would acquire a larger share of the world's manufacturing even if the ratio of manufacturing to G.D.P. did not change at all.

I have two comments to make on this part of the analysis. First, it seems to me that the geographical redistribution of world manufacturing production is a little less impressive than the raw data suggest. It is true that the share of the old developed countries fell from 72 per cent to 56 per cent; but their share of the world's population also fell between 1950 and 1973, from 20 per cent to 16·5 per cent. The shift is there, all right, but some of it reflects the shift in the distribution of the world's population, and may indeed be caused by it.

On the other hand, I think there is a sense in which Chenery's calculation may understate the importance of differential growth as against industrialisation. The decomposition technique used in the paper is subject to the oldest index-number problem, one that arises in every attempt at an additive decomposition of a multiplicative relation (manufacturing output = share of manufacturing in G.D.P. x G.D.P.). In order to make everything come out neatly with no positive or negative loose ends,

Chenery weights the change in G.D.P. with the *initial* share of manu-facturing, and the change in the manufacturing share with the *terminal* G.D.P. That is: $m_T Y_t - m_O Y_O = m_O(Y_T - Y_O) + (m_T - m_O) Y_T$. This decomposition yields the figures given on page 473. Of course it would make just as much sense to interchange the timing of the weights and write the decomposition $m_T Y_T - m_O Y_O = m_T(Y_T - Y_O) + (m_T - m_O)Y_O$. In that version, the relative importance of the industrialisa-tion effect in the newly developed, transitional, and less developed groups falls from 23 per cent, 23 per cent and 32 per cent respectively to some-thing like 5 per cent, 5 per cent and 12 per cent. Probably the average of these figures and those reported by Chenery is the best bet; it corresponds to weights halfway between the initial and terminal ones. Fortunately, this amendment strengthens Chenery's conclusion (as it must, because the newer countries have been increasing their manufacturing share faster than their output share). Clearly differential growth is by far the stronger force.

Finally, the paper has some interesting things to say about the importance of international trade in permitting small developing countries to specialise and thus to exploit ordinary returns to scale in production and marketing, as well as various intertemporal gains from specialisation. Export patterns also apparently have their regularities. Chenery remarks that the eventual 'need to shift from primary exports to manufactures at some point in the future is not adequately signalled by market forces, particularly in the case of mineral exporters whose exports will be limited by future supplies'. I am curious about that point, although I think it may very well be true. There is, after all, no simple externality involved in the coming exhaustion of cheap supplies of natural resources, nor in the future higher profitability of manufactured exports. Presumably no one ought to see this coming better than the operators of the mineral deposits themselves. If it were a matter of information, then correct information would be all the incentive necessary. I wonder if the key to this is not that old chestnut, the difference between private and social rates of dis-count. Primary exporters and others in transitional countries are probably very risk-averse, and they surely live with plenty of risk. Maybe they see the future as clearly as anyone, but discount it more heavily than we, as outsiders and relatively secure outsiders, think they should. That would be consistent with Chenery's observation that few governments seem to be able to muster the required foresight until they are forced into a re-orientation of trade by a balance-of-payments crisis. Governments, especially insecure governments, have been known to discount the future more heavily than wise people like professional economists think is socially appropriate. I am interested in this possibility because it may suggest the appropriate corrective incentives — though I should call attention to the fact that if the operative inefficiency is the use in private (and public) decisions of an excessively high discount rate, that will affect many more things than just the choice of export industries.

Comment
Jagdish N. Bhagwati

I wish to make two comments on Hollis Chenery's most interesting paper. The first comment is meant to be constructive in regard to the debate at this symposium on the utility of the 'small' models of trade theory, in particular of the 2 x 2 x 2 model (which several of those here who have failed to keep up with the many recent theoretical developments still erroneously consider to be all that there is to trade theory). It should be useful therefore to show how small models can yield big insights (just as big models often yield small insights) by demonstrating how some of Hollis Chenery's regressions can be 'explained' by the classroom results of trade theory in its simplest, 2 x 2 x 2 version.

This can be done simply by taking his regressions on the increasing share of manufacturing in national income as per capita income grows: regressions which, in one form or another, have been run with success earlier in Chenery (1960), in Chenery and Taylor (1968) and indeed elsewhere. What needs to be explained then is a shift in the productive structure as per capita income grows.

Now, instead of thinking cross-sectionally, consider conveniently what happens to the production structure as per capita income grows for an open economy. Two cases must be distinguished, one where consumption bias will influence the production structure and the other where it will not and therefore production bias must be invoked to explain the observed shift in production structure.[1]

The first case arises when we assume that the growing, open economy is large in the Samuelson sense, that it can influence its terms of trade. Then, it is clear that if the income elasticity of demand for manufactures exceeds unity, this will *ceteris paribus* increase the excess demand for manufactures after per capita income expands and thus lead to an increased (relative) price of manufactures and hence to a production shift in favour of manufactures.[2] The 'consumption bias' in favour of manufactures will then lead to a production shift towards manufactures. and indeed this may well be an important explanation of Chenery's results, especially as the tending of manufacturing share in national income to rise slackens off at high per capita incomes where services may be characterised by higher income elasticities of demand than manufactures.

But take the alternative case of a small country instead. In this case, the consumption bias will *not* affect the production structure. But then the trade theorist can immediately think of theorems on *production bias* that can possibly give us the results that Chenery's regressions embody. Essentially, these theorems define sufficiency conditions for expansion in income to yield biased shift in production at constant commodity prices: thus, in figure 1, growth shifts the production possibility curve from AB to $A'B'$ and, at given commodity price-ratio PC, the production structure shifts in favour of manufactures (from P to P').

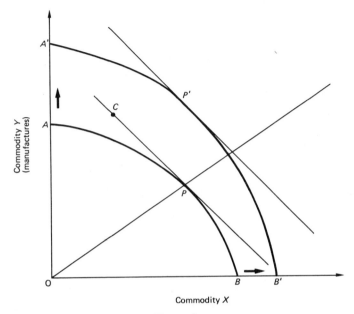

Figure 1

Since per capita income may increase due to capital accumulation, the Rybczynski theorem is relevant: an increase in the relative endowment of capital will bias the production structure in favour of the capital-intensive commodity. Now, if manufactures are capital-intensive (as they seem to be), the growth of per capita income will clearly be attended by production bias in favour of manufactures (as illustrated in figure 1). This would, *ceteris paribus*, lead then to the observed shift in production structure.

The other source of growth in per capita income is technical change. Here too, we know from trade theory that relatively faster Hicks-neutral technical change in manufactures will produce a production bias in favour of them. Again, it is not unreasonable to think that the evidence, both casual and econometric, points to manufactures being more technically progressive.

However, as Findlay and Grubert (1959) have noted in a classic paper, if the technical change is capital-using (as is empirically the case for manufactures), the production bias may be reversed (as the effect of the bias in technical change is as if overall capital supply was diminished, thus making the Rybczynski effect go in the opposite direction to that implied by the technical change *per se*). Hence, the production bias in manufactures would follow from their greater technical progressivity only insofar as (heuristically) the neutral change effect dominates the biased change effect: as might well be the case.

While therefore trade theory can illuminate Chenery's econometrics and is thus in harmony with developmental analysis, my second comment suggests conflict with Chenery's notion that his several regressions represent, as it were, each a sequence which countries 'will follow' as their incomes grow. This is for the simple reason that a country's trade pattern and volume and its production pattern are, to a trade theorist, the result of *interaction* between the country's own endowments and demands and the rest-of-the-world's endowments and demands. Thus, if a country goes from, say, $500 per capita income to $750 per capita income, Chenery's regressions, if used for prediction, would imply that one could read off the changes in the country's trade and production *without reference* to what had happened to other countries in the rest of the world, *whereas* a trade theorist would consider this to be an incomplete and therefore possibly erroneous procedure.

NOTES

[1] By production (consumption) 'bias', we mean a non-proportional shift in production (consumption) pattern when, consequent upon growth, *commodity prices are held constant.*

[2] Needless to say, one can envisage a number of 'pathologies' that could reverse the sign on any of the steps in the preceding argument.

REFERENCES

Chenery., H., 'Patterns of Industrial Growth', *American Economic Review*, Vol. 50 (1960), pp. 624−54.

Chenery, H. and Taylor, L., 'Development Patterns: Among Countries and Over Time', *Review of Economics and Statistics*, Vol. 50 (1968).

Findlay, R. and Grubert, H., 'Factor Intensities, Technological Progress and the Terms of Trade', *Oxford Economic Papers* (1959), pp. 111−21.

Summary of the Discussion

The first part of the discussion concerned positive and normative aspects of trade, growth and development. Akin Mabogunje developed his views on these relationships and the ensuing discussion attempted to clarify the contributions to development resulting from policies of openness and of autarchy. The policies toward multinational enterprises received special attention. The second part concerned how the statistical regularities observed by Hollis Chenery could be used and interpreted. The relationship between Chenery's approach and trade theory as well as the role of economic policy in his model received particular attention. How did trade and exchange rate policy influence the path and timing of development? This session was chaired by *Erik Lundberg*.

Michael Michaely summarised the reasoning which he believed lay behind some people's aversion to trade in LDCs. The steps in this reasoning were as follows

(a) The LDCs deserve a larger share of world income,

(b) because in the past they were exploited by other parts of the world,

(c) through international trade;

(d) in order to improve their relative position, the LDCs should therefore restrict international trade.

While he accepted the first statement, Michaely could only partly accept the second. Exploitation was not a necessary condition for the LDCs to 'deserve' an increased share of world income. This could be motivated entirely by considerations of equity. While agreeing that some trade was necessary for exploitation to have occurred at all, he rejected the conclusion that international trade was bad and that LDCs would have been better off without it. In fact, empirical studies showed clearly that expansion of exports is a major instrument of growth. There is a clear positive correlation between the share of exports in G.D.P. and the rate of growth.

Bela Balassa had the impression that the paper presented trade and foreign investment as a zero-sum game. In general, he viewed transactions between developed and developing countries as mutually beneficial. Nevertheless, he recognised that especially the latter could be subject to exploitation by foreign private firms. He referred to his ongoing study of Ghana, Senegal, the Ivory Coast, and Mali, which had documented a number of cases of exploitation by multinational corporations due to unequal bargaining power. He cited the example of an Italian assembly plant in Mali which had promised to contribute to Mali's industrialisation but in fact so much overpriced components that Mali incurred a net loss of foreign exchange. Similarly, a French multinational firm was found by the study to have overpriced wheat in the Ivory Coast by 25 per cent for ten years. These and similar cases of exploitation arose because governments lacking administrative capacity and ability allowed multinationals to exploit a bilateral monopoly situation. Governments must have the ability to 'shop around' if they were to change this. He suggested that there was a difference between export-oriented policies and import-substitution policies. The latter could provide the multinational firm with an opportunity to exploit the country by charging a high price to the domestic consumer, while with the former the multinationals had to accept world market prices. By contrast, the policy of export orientation in the Ivory Coast had led to a substantial expansion of small-scale peasant agriculture.

Kjeld Philip observed that most LDCs in fact regulated the activities of multinational firms. These had to fulfil a number of conditions in order to obtain the necessary government permissions. Thus, governments can in principle determine the conditions for establishment and conduct of multi-nationals. However, competition between countries may result in multi-nationals being let in on easier terms and in greater numbers than if the LDC's coordinated their policy.

Akin Mabogunje replied that he was not one of those people in the LDCs who considered international trade bad. He had wished to stress the need to re-examine the way economists tended to link trade to develop-ment. Trade may well be an engine of growth, he said, but it may not necessarily solve a country's development problems. Growth, especially the particular pattern imposed by the demands of the developed countries, does not automatically induce the necessary structural changes. Everyone realised, he observed, that mining towns turned into ghost towns if such basic changes were not introduced before the mine was exhausted. There-fore, Mabogunje warned against an emerging multinational institution — droves of itinerant economists, who on their stops around the world advised the LDCs that more trade would solve all their development problems.

As a frequent adviser, *Balassa* wished to comment on Mabogunje's attitude to trade and development patterns as expressed in his paper. He noted that the choice between Western and indigenous consumption patterns was a normative, not a positive, issue. As an economic adviser he was content to accept the development patterns which followed logically from most governments' welfare functions. The question, how-ever, was under what circumstances this could be done and what measures were available to achieve it. The changes suggested for a 'new life-style' overruled, as Michaely had pointed out in his Comment, practically every-one's preferences. This might be possible in very primitive economies but countries already embarked on 'capitalist development' like Brazil, South

Korea, Kenya, and the Ivory Coast could not return to an autarchical pattern. In addition to being primitive, a country must have a dictatorial government and receive considerable foreign aid to be able to pursue such a policy. Balassa felt that Tanzania had been able to follow a similar course for those reasons, but these conditions were not fulfilled in many other countries. So, he suggested, one should not oversimplify the choice between trade-oriented and autarchic development strategies.

Tibor Scitovsky, coming to the defence of the maligned advisers, noted that accepting the aim of greater self-sufficiency does not preclude a certain amount of international contact and reliance on foreign loans and imports. Even economists who desired greater self-sufficiency were among those advocating more trade. A given degree of self-sufficiency can be achieved more cheaply and perhaps earlier by making greater use of comparative advantage on the way to that aim.

While sympathising with Mabogunje's dissatisfaction with the lack of development in the presence of growth, *Fritz Machlup* felt that his complaint about the advice they received was unfair. Machlup doubted that countries which had taken 100 to 200 years to develop, could advise other countries how to develop in 25 years. Some may think they have the formula, but he remained unconvinced.

Philip noted that there is a time-lag between growth and development. Incomes from additional exports such as oil in Nigeria could be squandered on higher salaries to civil servants or invested in expansion of the infrastructure. However, investment in education, roads, telecommunications, etc., provides development not today but 20 years from now. Thus growth is perhaps a necessary first step for development.

Mabogunje closed this part of the discussion. He repeated that he was not against trade, which may indeed by an engine of certain types of growth. He was dissatisfied that trade had not led to development, judging from West African experience. Simply increasing the volume of production would not change the basic structural characteristics of preindustrial economies. In Ghana and Senegal trade had not changed the basic fabric of society and he feared that, similarly, the discovery and subsequent exploitation of oil deposits in Nigeria would not lead to a pattern of sustainable development. He suggested that trade could distort the use of productive factors and in particular of the allocation of research resources. In Nigeria, for instance, agricultural research for 70 years had been directed toward the cultivation of cocoa rather than of yams. The earnings from cocoa exports which were intended for importing capital goods were instead used to import food to feed the population. At the same time there were vast areas of uncultivated land. Replying to Machlup and Scitovsky, he suggested that development could not wait 100 years and that self-sufficiency to be worth the name had to be achieved within a period of 40 years.

The discussion then turned to Hollis Chenery's paper. *Michaely* believed that the paper's main point was related to the previous discussion concerning growth and development. He interpreted the frustration experienced by someone who claimed to be growing but not developing to mean that something was lacking for his size of income. The task was to establish what. (By way of analogy, illustrative for those who knew him, Michaely recalled the exclamation of a London haberdasher upon failing to find a suit to fit him: 'The trouble, Sir, is that for your size you are too short'.) Chenery's contribution, he suggested, lay in indicating the right economic dimensions and their proportions, given a country's income. Thus, 'frustrated' countries which felt they were growing but not developing could find out what was wrong for their size of income by consulting Chenery's charts.

Michaely recommended that Chenery's analysis be extended to analyse more closely why countries deviate from the 'normal' development path, if it was good to deviate, and if so in what direction. Furthermore, one should study how Chenery's various categories — natural resources, size, capital inflows, and development policy — influence growth. A casual look at the world indicated that it was not advantageous to be well endowed with natural resources. The fastest growing countries were those without natural resources. Was this perhaps a misleading observation?

A related point concerned the role of economic policy. In particular, Michaely suggested explicit recognition of the role of exchange rate policy (in its widest sense — including the operation of tariffs, subsidies, etc.). The exchange rate, Michaely recalled, was a basic element in Ohlin's model: the model is not closed, and the pattern of trade not determined, until the exchange rate is introduced. The exchange rate is undoubtedly also the major instrument through which the pattern of trade might be changed from what it would be when left to be determined by the economy's exogenous circumstances. If Nigeria or Norway, for instance, do not wish to let the availability of oil determine their pattern of specialisation the most obvious instrument to use would be exchange policy. Therefore, Michaely suggested that the rate of exchange — not as an instrument of balance-of-payments adjustment but as an instrument which participates in determining the pattern of specialisation — is an element which should be included in the Chenery analysis.

Ronald Findlay asked if Chenery's Law could predict the timing as well as the course of development given the basic data. He recalled that Rostow's Law could predict when a country would reach a particular stage of economic growth and asked if Chenery would also be willing to time the transition from one income level to another. Was perhaps the speed of transition related to the natural resource endowments, as suggested by Michaely, to the choice of economic system etc?

Gary Hufbauer asked what role Chenery left to the normal armoury of policies in his highly determinate world. He suggested for instance that the exchange rate and commercial policy chosen by a country might not affect the path it followed, only the speed at which it travelled that path. If so, there was still a lot of room in Chenery's world for policy and for such institutions as the Bank and the Fund.

Following this line, *Balassa* emphasised the role of commercial policy in determining an economic structure beneficial for development. He noted that Chenery had attributed three-quarters of the 'net shift of industry to the newly developed and transitional countries to . . . higher growth rates'. But he had not gone on to answer the question why this group of countries in fact grew faster than others. Part of the answer could be found in Chenery's paper since it showed that in each of the groups constituting transitional and newly developed countries, export policy was a major factor in explaining different growth performances. Thus export-oriented countries did better than others in the group of large developing countries (Brazil, South Korea, Yugoslavia versus the Argentine, the Philippines, India) as well as in the group of small countries (Hong Kong, Taiwan versus Chile, Sri Lanka, Uruguay). Furthermore this was true for socialist as well as for non-socialist countries. As he had shown elsewhere, the inward-looking policies of the Argentine, Chile, Hungary and Czechoslovakia had resulted in similar experiences which contrasted sharply to that of outward-looking policies of Norway and Denmark.[1] Japan would seem to be an exception to the observed relationship of trade policy and growth performance. Chenery's table 5 shows that in the period 1935–65 Japan combined a policy of import substitution with high growth rates. Balassa, however, considered Japan to be a special case. First, it was a very large country and therefore could afford much more import substitution than other transitional and newly developed countries. Second, the period 1935–65 was dominated by the depression and by war preparations. Balassa suggested that subdividing the period would give different results. In 1960–65 Japanese exports of manufactures grew annually at 17·3 per cent and in 1965–69 at 14·4 per cent which much exceeded the growth of G.N.P. Therefore, during this period exports made a positive contribution to Japanese growth.

In this connection Balassa commented on a suggestion in Solow's Comment that governments in the small, resource-rich countries might lack sufficient foresight to reorient trade away from primary-product exports. He did not agree with Solow that market failure was the cause of this, ascribing it instead to bad policies. These countries were unable to exploit economies of scale within the confines of small domestic industries. They adopted import substitution in industries where this was very costly, and having established small-scale firms it became difficult to shift to exporting manufactured goods competitively.

Dieter Biehl applied Chenery's Law to the regional case. He referred to results in two German studies which presented data for countries as well as for the regions in the E.C.[2] Disregarding problems of comparing time-series and cross-section data, he felt that the material

suggested that the decline in the share of industry and the increase in the
share of the service sector was much more pronounced when regional
data was used.

Findlay objected to Chenery's use of the term 'balanced growth' to
describe a statistical decomposition. The concepts balanced and unbalanced
growth referred to different development strategies; Nurkse had
advocated developing on a broad front while Hirschman and others
preferred to push faster on a narrow front. This bore no relation to
Chenery's use of the term and his choice of words might confuse the
reader.

Jagdish Bhagwati suggested how Chenery's results could be arrived at
by using the simple models of trade theory. He developed his observations
at greater length in a Comment presented after the symposium and
reproduced on pp. 496—498. Also Balassa and Findlay related Chenery's
approach to trade theory. *Balassa* objected to Chenery's statement that
trade theorists did not consider the effects of differences in growth rates.
There was, he noted, a rich literature from Hicks to Johnson on the
effects on trade of changes in technology and in factor endowments. Consequently he felt there was no conflict between trade theory and the
Chenery model; in fact the latter was quite consistent with models containing three countries and three factors.

Findlay also felt that the conflict between the Chenery model and
trade theory was more apparent than real. Chenery, he observed, seemed
to think that while he was concerned with production and consumption,
trade theorists were concerned with exports and imports. However, Findlay
knew of no trade theory which ignored production and consumption and
reminded that trade is obtained as the difference between consumption
and production of a good. Findlay seized this opportunity to welcome
Chenery to the company of trade theorists and hoped that he would cease
making hostile remarks about 2 x 2 x 2 models.

Chenery closed the discussion. He suggested that the next step was to
introduce additional explanatory variables which would reduce the
magnitude of observed deviations from his regression lines. Even though
he had obtained high coefficients of determination, his main variables —
income, population, capital inflow and natural resources — left a lot to be
explained. While his analysis provided a standard of comparison, it should
not be interpreted as explaining the development of individual countries,
even though they adher to the norm, since it minimised the role of
economic policy.

Like Solow and Michaely, he felt that discovering laws of development
would enable countries to formulate policies that were consistent with the
basic relationships revealed by past experiences. This kind of policy-making
could clearly be improved, he felt, and questioned the value of, for
example, the U.N.I.D.O. target to have 25 per cent of world industrial
production located in the LDCs by the year 2000, since such a develop-

ment was not in line with past experience. Furthermore, he suggested that 20 years ago countries trying to industrialise had failed to appreciate the constraints of historical necessity and overexpanded industry at the expense of other sectors.

Thus he viewed his analysis as an appropriate background against which to study such issues of economic policy. In particular, he felt it was suggestive for a country's choice of trade policy. The three types of countries in his analysis faced different problems, implying different roles for trade policy. He stressed the differences faced by large and by small countries. For instance, large countries might find it less important to earn foreign exchange efficiently than small countries, but still find it very important to earn some foreign exchange. He felt that many countries had misread this message.

Similarly he observed that exchange rate policy was of varying importance for various countries. The exchange rate is a critical instrument for small countries to establish an outwardly oriented manufacturing industry. On the other hand, it plays quite a different role for the primary exporter and again is less crucial for large countries than for smaller, more specialised economies.

In reply to Findlay, Chenery maintained the usefulness of associating his accounting framework with the concept of balanced growth. He agreed with Nurkse that internal factors had more to do with overall resource allocation than did external factors. However, he felt that Nurkse's theory of balanced growth tends to neglect the contribution that trade could make to development.

Chenery emphasised the role of trade in developing countries. Trade provided, he felt, the best way to introduce the flexibility needed to avoid serious bottlenecks and misallocation of resources in these countries. LDCs were characterised, he claimed, by underutilised resources. Even the slowest growing poor countries had excess capacity in their capital stocks. India, for instance, would grow faster given its existing resource stock if it could import goods, such as spare parts, which it could not produce itself. This ability to adjust to imbalances was one of the main factors explaining differences in growth rates, he believed. Trade provided a possibility to solve such bottlenecks and whether it was a least cost adjustment or not was secondary to being able to adjust at all. Communist countries saw trade as an advantageous way to obtain necessary inputs even at prices 50 per cent above the shadow price of foreign exchange since imports released resources for other uses. Thus, while there is great diversity in the way countries handled trade problems, they must solve them in order to develop successfully.

In reply to Bhagwati, Chenery attempted to relate his approach to the simple models of trade theory. He suggested that once he had empirical measures of countries' endowments of the factor categories, as suggested by Bertil Ohlin, it would be possible to categorise half a dozen typical situations of factor proportions. Such realistic combinations of three or four factors could provide a basis for empirical studies of the relations between trade and development.

NOTES

[1] Balassa, B., 'Growth Strategies in Semi-Industrial Countries', *Quarterly Journal of Economics* (February, 1970).
[2] Fels, G., Schatz, K. -W., and Walter, F., 'Der Zusammenhang zwischen Produktionsstruktur und Entwicklungsniveau', *Weltwirtschaftliches Archiv*, Bd. 106 (1971) Heft 2, pp. 240–278; Biehl, D., Hussmann, E. and Schnyder, S., 'Zur regionalen Einkommensverteilung in der Europäischen Wirtschaftsgemeinschaft', *Die Weltwirtschaft*, Heft 1 (1972), pp. 64–78.

15 A Multiregional Input-Output Model of the World Economy

Wassily Leontief

I. INTRODUCTORY REMARKS

From the time Ricardo proposed to explain international exchange of goods and services in terms of their comparative (or opportunity) costs, pure theory of international trade was dominated by the general equilibrium approach. Professor Ohlin deepened the foundation of its original classical formulation by showing that differences in comparative costs can in their turn be explained by regional differences in the relative supply of labour, capital and natural resources. Because of the obvious practical difficulties of empirical implementation of any general equilibrium theory, most of the concrete quantitative explanations of actually observed interregional flows of goods and services have, nevertheless, been conducted in terms of the Marshallian partial equilibrium approach.

This paper presents a brief summary description of a multiregional input-output model of the world economy intended to provide concrete factual explanation of interregional flows of goods and services in general equilibrium terms. Instead of being viewed in isolation, interregional transactions are being treated in that system as subsets of much larger sets of variables comprising the regional levels of output, consumption and investment of all different goods and services as well as the exploitation and allocation of estimated regional reserves of specific natural resources. Environmental repercussions of economic activities are accounted for through introduction into the system of distinct sets of variables representing the generation and abatement of a selected group of polluting substances.[1]

II. THE INPUT-OUTPUT STRUCTURE OF PRODUCTION AND CONSUMPTION

The input-output method used in this study provides the means for describing the complex and highly differentiated structure of the world economy in great detail. Each of the fifteen regions into which all the developed and less developed countries are grouped for the purposes of this analysis is visualised as a set of 48 producing and consuming sectors connected with each other and with the economies of other regions by steady flows of goods and services. Extractive industries absorb, in addition to inputs received from other sectors, renewable or non-renewable primary (that is, natural) resources. Households absorb consumers' goods and supply labour; the public sector is represented by government activities of several different kinds. Pollutants are treated as byproducts of regular production or consumption processes, and their elimination (abatement) as a special type of 'productive' activity. Besides the flows of current inputs, each sector also employs 'stocks' of buildings, machinery, inventories of raw and semifabricated materials (usually referred to, respectively, as fixed and working capital) and — in the case of the household sector — residential housing, sewage systems, etc.

The 'cooking recipe' (technological mix) used in a particular industry at any given place and time determines the amounts of all the inputs, including labour, required to produce a given amount of its output. In the case of households, it is the 'consumption recipe', which depends on the income level and the combination of biological needs, social conditions and cultural standards, that determines the contents of a typical household shopping basket.

A set of regional input and consumption coefficients describes the combination of goods and services required by each one of the productive sectors of a particular economy per unit of its output and, in the case of private or public households, per unit of their aggregate expenditures and income.

For the purposes of numerical computation, the schematic image of the world economy described above is reduced, primarily but not exclusively, to a system of linear input-output equations. This analytical tool has been designed with the view of being able to absorb, with as little distortion as possible, large variegated sets of quantitative data. Array upon array of technical 'mixes' describing the present or the projected future input requirements of all the different branches of mining, agriculture, manufacturing and various service industries, as well as the contents of typical shopping baskets of private and public households in each of the fifteen different groups of countries, had to be fitted into the structural framework of an analytical description of the world economy and committed to the electronic memory of a large computer. So were alternative estimates of the total stocks of different mineral and other natural resources. The technical coefficients permitting estimation of the amounts of various pollutants generated in many of the production and consumption processes were ascertained, too, as well as the input requirements of processes designed to suppress or at least to reduce the flows of these undesirable byproducts of the regular economic activities.

Separate estimates of the key urban environmental amenities (such as water supply, and liquid and solid waste collection) and housing had to be made. They, too, were included in the analytical design and entered into the computer.

III. INTERNATIONAL TRADE, PRICES AND FINANCIAL TRANS-ACTIONS

The economies of individual regions are linked with each other through flows of internationally, or rather interregionally, traded goods.

While the inputs and outputs of goods and services classified as 'domestic' must be balanced within each region, the consumption of internationally traded goods has to be balanced only for the world as a whole. Export surpluses and import surpluses of each commodity or commodity group must add up to zero on the international scale. The worldwide input-output system must contain a set of equations stating this in algebraic terms.

In principle, the composition of each region's exports and imports should be examinable and, consequently, also predictable in terms of comparative production costs and the structures of demand. However, the lack of sufficiently detailed factual information precludes, at this stage of analysis, the possibility of explaining interregional commodity flows in such fundamental terms.

The quantity of a particular type of good, say, steel, exported from a given region, say, North America, is treated as a fixed share of aggregate world exports (which, of course, are equal to aggregate world imports) of that good. The quantity of steel imported into the North American region is, on the other hand, regarded as representing a given share of the total amount of steel consumed in that region. Thus, the domestic outputs and the global input – or rather its separate regional components – are the variables that enter into the determination of the internal input-output balances of the trading regions.

With sets of appropriate 'trade coefficients' incorporated in our system of equations, any projected change in regional inputs and outputs of internationally traded goods will thus be accompanied by appropriate shifts in each region's pattern of exports and imports.

More-over, the quantities of internationally traded goods flowing into and out of every region are related to – and determined simultaneously with – their flows between the different sectors of each region.

In terms of this approach, all the exports of a particular good can be viewed as if they were delivered to a single international trading pool and all the imports as if they were drawn from that pool. The worldwide trading balance (to be distinguished from the monetary payments balance, considered below) requires that the sum total of all regional exports of each good delivered to its pool equal the sum total of all regional imports drawn from that pool.

The fact that this formulation does not involve any analysis of bilateral (that is, region to region) trade flows, should be viewed, at this stage, as its strength rather than its weakness. Detailed analysis and explanation of the network of interregional shipments — involving the consideration of such factors as differential transportation costs — can and should be separated from the analysis of long-run patterns of what might be called the interregional division of labour.

The introduction of prices and income variables leads, as explained below, to the important question of the total value of the exported and imported goods and the problem of capital flows and of other types of international transfers.

The same sets of technical coefficients that govern the physical relationships between the inputs and the outputs within the structural framework of a particular economy also determine the relationship between prices of various goods and services, on the one hand, and the 'value added', that is, the wages, rents, profits earned and taxes paid by the industries that produce them, on the other hand.

Given the price received by an industry for a unit of its output and the prices paid by it for the inputs purchased from other industries, one obviously can determine how much of its receipts will remain (after all, these purchases have been made) to be paid out as 'value added' or, if worse comes to worse, how much subsidy (negative value added) that industry will have to receive to keep going.

Given the 'value added' to be paid out by each industry (per unit of its output), one can reverse the question and ask what prices would have to be charged for the products of different industries so as to enable each of them to balance its revenue with its total outlays — the latter defined to include payments for purchased supplies as well as the value added.

This latter approach is used to compute, by solving the appropriate set of price/value-added equations, the corresponding prices of their products from the given — or rather the projected — values added paid out by producing sectors of advanced industrialised areas (exemplified by the North American region). Such computations naturally, must also take into account the expected changes in the technical input coefficients. Prospective changes in the prices of various raw materials derived in this way will, necessarily, reflect the rise in the capital and other input requirements of primary extracting industries expected to be brought about by the depletion of the more accessible resources and consequent shift to inferior reserves of natural resources.

Having determined the prices of internationally traded goods on the basis of conditions expected to prevail in the highly developed regions, we can then insert these prices in the equations describing the price/value-added relationships reflecting the technology and resource endowments assumed to exist at that time in other, less developed regions. With prices considered as given, the solution of these equations yields the values added, that is, the net income comprising wages, profits and rents that can be expected to be earned by the various industries in the less developed countries.

Extractive industries exploiting rich natural deposits in some of the less developed areas can be expected to yield in the future, as they already do, much higher values added (rents and profits) than their counterparts operating under much less favourable natural conditions in the developed industrialised countries. The opposite will probably be true in the case of some of the manufactured goods. Squeezed between world prices reflecting the advanced technology and labour skills of the developed regions and high domestic costs, industries producing such goods for export in the less developed countries can be expected to yield only very low or even negative 'values added'. In the latter case, they could exist only if supported by direct or indirect subsidies.[2]

This, incidentally, is a situation that could not have been envisaged if the principle of cost minimisation had been formally applied on a world-wide scale. The simultaneous operation of high-cost and low-cost facilities under conditions in which the latter could actually satisfy the entire demand obviously violates that principle. It is equally obvious, however, for many different reasons, that such situations not only prevail now, but will continue to exist in the future.

The *trade balance* of a country or region in the model depends on the quantities of goods imported and exported and on the prices at which they have been purchased or sold. Unlike outputs which are treated as physical quantities only, export and import totals, as well as trade balances, are computed in current prices.

In addition to the items entered in the balances of trade, the balance of payments includes such financial transactions as capital transfers (securities and loans), international interest and other income payments and official aid.

These variables are incorporated in the system of input-output equations that also contain all the structural data used in deriving the alternative projections of possible future states of the world economy presented in 'The Future of the World Economy'.

For the purpose of developmental projections, the balance of trade of a particular region can be treated as one of the given variables and its Gross National Income as one of the unknown variables, or vice versa. After having set, for example, numerical gross product targets for less developed areas, one can determine what import surplus the attainment of these targets would entail under given structural conditions. Or, on the contrary, having fixed the allowable import surplus of a region, one can compute the attainable level of Gross National Product. In other formulations of the problem, both the payments deficit or surplus and the level of consumption of the less developed countries are treated as variables dependent, for instance, on given prices of the raw materials that they sell and the manufactured goods that they buy on international markets.

IV. FLEXIBILITY AND INTERDEPENDENCE WITHIN THE EXISTING STRUCTURAL CONSTRAINTS

The model as a whole contains more variables than equations. The structural relationships described in it can thus be satisfied by many (strictly speaking, infinitely many) different combinations of the unknown magnitudes that enter into it. By fixing the magnitudes of some of the variables from the outside one by one, we can reduce the total number of unknowns so as to make that number equal to the number of equations and thus arrive at a unique solution. By varying the magnitudes of one or several of the externally fixed variables, it is thus possible to obtain a series of alternative projections showing in each case how the dependent variables would have to shift to preserve the internal balance of the system within its given structural framework.

Because of the general interdependence among all parts of the system, the level of each type of economic activity in each corner of the world, so long as it has not been fixed by assumption, is bound to respond in one way or another to every primary change introduced in any other part of it. Many of the remote indirect repercussions turn out to be so small that they could be neglected, while others are much larger than one would intuitively expect them to be.

For purposes of scientific explanation or projection one would be inclined to observe, or to fix by assumption, the magnitudes of what might be called causal factors and use the analytical system to ascertain their necessary effect. For purposes of practical action, however, the relationship between causes and effects can also be approached from the other end. In explaining, for example, the means of narrowing the gap between the levels of per capita consumption in the less developed and the more advanced regions, the inquiry might move not from causes to effects, but from desired effects to the causes capable of bringing them about. Instead of fixing (among others) the magnitude of variables that represent the level of capital transfer from developed to the less developed areas or, say, the stringency of antipollution standards imposed on industries operating in the latter groups of countries, and then computing the corresponding income levels, we can start out by postulating the target income levels for all regions and then proceed — by solving the appropriate system of equations — to find out what combinations of larger capital transfer would permit the attainment of these predetermined goals.

In examining the state of the world economy as projected by the model, we do not necessarily need to know which of the variables were fixed in advance, that is, before the computation started, and which were treated as unknowns to be derived. The total picture would remain the same if the roles were, so to say, reversed, that is if some of the numbers obtained through the original solution were considered as given, while some of those originally fixed were treated as unknowns.

A description of a particular hypothetical state of the world economy can be interpreted as providing answers to all kinds of questions. In fixing developmental goals such as have been defined in the context of the Second United Nations Developmental Decade, variables which describe the future state of the economic system are usually designated as target variables. These typically are the levels of per capita G.D.P., private and public per capita consumption and their respective rates of growth. The number of variables that in one context or another can be viewed as representing causal factors, such as domestic savings, external balance, labour force participation, prices of raw materials and so on is, on the contrary, quite large. Hence, after inserting in the system the prescribed or desired magnitudes of target variables, one will often find that the number of the remaining unknowns exceeds the number of equations. This means that many different combinations of causal instrumental factors could bring about, within the given set of technical and structural limitations, the attainment of the same prescribed goals.

At this point one might ask, why not maximise? Why not find out what combination of causal or policy-controlled variables would, for example, maximise the level of consumption or the welfare index defined in some specific terms? The response to this question is fundamentally the same that was given above to the question about the optimal international division of labour. Any attempt at general overall maximisation would inevitably drive a system beyond the valid limits of the simplified analytical formulation erected on a still relatively weak and fragmentary data base and certainly beyond the range of what can actually be expected to happen.

It is more a question of analytical convenience than of fundamental difference when one speaks, on the one hand, of given magnitudes or unknown variables (for example, regional income levels, international trade flows, capital transfers) and, on the other hand, of numerical coefficients describing the structural characteristics of the system (for example, technical input coefficients of various industries, estimated reserves of raw materials, etc.). What is treated today as a given structural characteristic of the economic system, tomorrow might be explained in terms of some more fundamental factors and relationships, the existence of which empirical inquiry has as yet not been able to ascertain or to measure with sufficient precision.

The system is described in terms of sets of linear equations and the computer programme developed to solve them enables not only the

authors of the report, but also the prospective users to ask and to answer —
with minimal computational efforts — such questions as how an unknown
(for instance, the investment level of a particular less developed area)
would react not only to shifts in the values of some externally fixed
variables (such as the level of foreign aid received), but also to a structural
change (such as, for instance, a reduction in the magnitude of a technical
coefficient describing the amount of electrical power used per unit of
output by the chemical industry).

The input-output model of the world economy on which this Report
is based is capable of answering a great variety of questions. Since that
system is complex and large, the formulation of specific questions and
the interpretation of answers that come out of the computer in the form
of figures is a task that has to be approached with great care and
circumspection.

V. FORMULATION OF THE MODEL

The schematic overview of its structure presented below should suffice
for a general understanding and a correct interpretation of the principal
conclusions.

The 2625 equations contained in the model consist of 15 interconnected regional sets, one for each of the fifteen regional blocks. Each
regional set consists of 175 equations that describe — in terms of 269
variables — the interrelationships between the production and consumption of various goods and services — and, in particular, of specific natural
resources — within a particular region; 229 of these variables are region-
specific, while 40 represent the export-import pools of internationally
traded goods and the balance or imbalance, as the case may be, of that
region's international financial transactions.

(1) REGIONAL BREAKDOWN

The fifteen regions, with the abbreviated designations used for each region
in all the tables, as well as the total population and average per capita
G.D.P. figures for the year 1970, are listed in table 1.

Basically, the geographical groupings aim at a reasonable degree of
homogeneity in the economic variables that characterise nations combined
in a single regional unit. A primary criterion employed in this classification
scheme was the level of economic development as measured by per capita
income levels and the share of manufacturing activity in total G.D.P.
Further aggregation was based on the identification of certain variables
that are of particular importance to the study. Thus, the major oil-
exporting countries were grouped together and, for African nations, a

TABLE 1
CLASSIFICATION OF REGIONS*

Name	Designation	Identifying number	Population 1970 (millions)	G.N.P./cap 1970 (1970 US$)
Developed:	:DC			
North America	NAH	1	229·1	4625
Western Europe, high income	WEH	4	282·0	2574
U.S.S.R.	SUH	6	242·8	1791
Eastern Europe	EEM	7	105·1	1564
Western Europe, medium income**	WEM	5	108·1	698
Japan	JAP	9	104·3	1916
Oceania	OCH	15	15·4	2799
Africa, medium income**	SAF	14	21·5	786
Developing Group I: (Developing with major mineral resource endowment)	:LDC-I			
Latin America, low income	LAL	3	90·0	443
Mid-East/Africa, oil producers	MDE	11	126·5	286
Africa, tropical	TAF	13	141·4	168
Developing Group II: (Other developing)	:LDC-II			
Latin America, medium income	LAM	2	191·4	594
Asia, low medium-income	ASL	10	1023·2	120
Africa, arid	AAF	12	131·2	205
Asia, centrally planned	ASC	8	808·4	167

*Complete listing of countries included in each region is presented in Annex I of 'The Future of the World Economy'. The classification is influenced by the level of development the regions are likely to reach by the year 2000.
**These two regions, Western Europe medium income and Africa medium income, are classified in Developing Group II in the printout of scenario A which appears in Annex VI of 'The Future of the World Economy'.

TABLE 2

```
UN40M    WORLD MODEL REGION BLOCK                      (175X269)

NUMBERING SYSTEM SHOWN: REAL


          GNP   1      BAL   6     LABOR11    NFISH31    RSS  39     RSM  60     IEQP 97   ·SEQP  2    HRSS  7
            CONS  2      IMPRT 7     NUTRN12    HFISH32    MRSLK48    XT   62     IPLT 98    SPLT  3    ECUMR16
            OSAVE 3      EXPRT 8     EMA  14    EFISH33    AGR  57    XNT  81     INVCH99    SINVY 4    SCUMR
            INV   4      POP   9     EMTOT22    AGS  34    RSR  58    ABATE87    IIRR  0    SFAS  5    HEC
              GOV   5      URBAN10    XFISHZ0    GMSUB38    AGM  59    ABSLK92    ILAND 1    SLAND 6
```

	GNP	BAL	LABOR	NFISH	RSS	RSM	IEQP	SEQP	HRSS
1 GNP	M + + + :	- +	P :	:	:	:	P	: +	:
2 SAVE	% - P :		:	:	:	:	:	P	:
3 INV	- :		:	:	:	:	: + +	P P	:
4 GOV	% - :		:	:	:	:	:	:	:
5 BAL	: -	:	: P P	:	:	:	:	M :
6 IMPRT	: -	:	: P	:	:	:	:	:
7 EXPRT	:	:	: P	:	:	:	:	:
8 LABOR	L L :	L L :	- L :	L : L	L L L :	L L L L	:	L L :	:
9 NUTRN	M :	M :		M :	:	:	:	:	:
11 EMA	E :	E E :	-	E : E	E E E :	E E E M	:	:	:
19 EMNA	:	:	+ -	:	:	:	E :	:	:
27 ABDET	:	:	:	:	:	:	M - :	:	:
32 AGS	C C :	C U :	M : M M M · M :	· : ·	· · · : · · ·	: S S S S S :	:		
36 RSS	C C :	C U :	· :	· : ·	· · · : · · ·	: S S S S S :	:		
45 AGR	C C :	C U :	· :	· : ·	· · · : · · ·	: S S S S S :	:		
46 RSR	C C :	C U :	· :	· : ·	· · · : · · ·	: S S S S S :	:		
47 AGM	C C :	C U :	· :	· : ·	· · · : · · ·	: S S S S S :	:		
48 RSM	C C :	C U :	· :	· : ·	· · · : · · ·	: S S S S S :	:		
50 XT	C C :	C U :	· :	· : ·	· · · : · · ·	: S S S S S :	:		
69 XNT	C C :	C U :	· :	· : ·	· · · : · · ·	: S S S S S :	:		
75 IEQP	:	:	:	:	:	: -	: G	:	G
76 IPLT	:	:	:	:	:	:	G G	:	
77 INVCH	:	:	:	:	:	: -	G	:	
78 ECUMR	:	:	:	: G	:	:	:	:	G - +
87 SEQP	:	K	K :	K : K	K K K : K K K K	:	K K : -	:	
88 SPLT	K :	K K :	K :	K : K	K K K : K K K K	:	K K : -	:	
89 SINVY	:	:	:	K : K	K K K : K K	:	:	· :	
90 SFAS	: G	:	:	:	:	:	:	- · :	
91 SLAND	:	:	:	K :	K :	:	:	- :	
92 MAGS	:	:	:	A :	:	:	:	:	
96 MAGR	:	:	:	: A	:	:	:	:	
97 MRSS	:	:	:	A · :	:	:	:	:	
6 MRSR	:	:	:	: A	:	:	:	:	
7 MAGM	:	:	: D	:	:	:	:	:	
8 MRSM	:	:	:	:	:	:	:	:	
10 MXT	:	:	:	:	:	: A	:	:	
29 MSER	M :	:	:	:	:	:	:	:	
30 MTR	M :	M M :	:	:	:	:	:	:	
31 MAID	M :	:	:	:	:	:	}	:	
32 EAGS	:	:	:	:	:	:	:	:	
36 EAGR	:	:	:	:	:	:	:	:	
37 ERSS	:	:	:	:	:	:	:	:	
46 ERSR	:	:	:	:	:	:	:	:	
47 EAGM	:	:	: D	:	:	:	:	:	
48 ERSM	:	:	:	:	:	:	:	:	
50 EXT	:	:	:	:	:	:	:	:	
69 ESER	:	:	:	:	:	:	:	:	
70 ETR	:	:	:	:	:	:	:	:	
71 EAID	:	:	:	:	:	:	:	:	
72 ECAP	M :	:	:	:	:	:	:	:	
73 MCAP	:	:	:	:	:	:	:	:	
74 DUMMY	:	:	:	:	:	:	:	:	

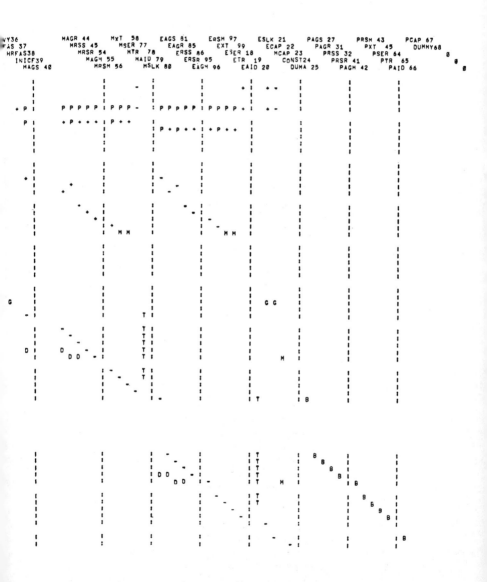

distinction was made between those receiving less than 250 mm (10 ins.) of rainfall annually, and those receiving more. As might be expected, the criteria outlined were not applied without exceptions. In general, the regional groupings respect continental boundaries so as to facilitate the comparison of the projected results with the economic data produced by various international agencies. An exception to this rule was made for the oil-producing countries of the Middle East and Africa which were grouped into one region. In a few other instances, geopolitical considerations overrode the economic basis for aggregation.

Table 2 presents in a schematic form a block of equations pertaining to a single region. The letter or symbol placed in each cell of the table represents the coefficients of variables (named at the heads of the relevant columns) that enter into the linear equations (or a linear approximation of a non-linear equation) described by each row. Thus, for example, the symbol, @, at the intersection of row (50) and column (81) stands for the set of technical coefficients that represents inputs of traded goods (*XT*) per unit of output of non-traded goods (*XNT*). Note, however, that this very large table is itself still in summary form: the variable *XT* actually represents the class of 19 traded goods; the variable *XNT* represents the class of six non-traded goods; and the symbol @ represents the coefficients of a 19 x 6 portion of the regional input-output table. A key to the symbols for the various coefficients in table 2 appears in table 3.

TABLE 3

Key to coefficient symbols in table 2

A	Import to output ratios
B	World export pool shares
C	Consumption coefficients
D	Margin trade to physical units
E	Emissions coefficients
G	Growth rate type parameters
K	Capital coefficients
L	Labour coefficients
M	Miscellaneous parameters
P	Prices
S	Structure of investment demand
T	Marginal trade composition
U	Urban amenities input structure
X	Exogenous data for calibration 1970
%	Ratio applicable to context
@	I—A input-output coefficient

The equations, or groups of similar equations, represented by a particular row in table 2 can be conveniently identified by the name of the 'leading' variable that the equation explains or defines in terms of some other variables.

Some of the variables are measured in appropriate physical units, the others in value ($) units. Dollar figures describing the values of outputs, inputs, exports, imports or stocks of particular goods in base year (1970) prices can be interpreted as measurements of their physical amounts.[3]

An equation or a group of similar equations can be reconstituted from each row by multiplying each coefficient entered along the row (not forgetting to take into account the sign) with the variable identified by the symbol located above it in the top row of the table, and then setting the sum or the terms so formed to equal zero.[4]

For example, the equation corresponding to the first row of coefficients reads:

$$-M_1 * GDP + CONS + INVS + GOV + EXPRT - IMPRT + P_1 * URBAN + P_2 * ABATE + INVCH = 0$$

where $M_1 = 1 + M_2$

M_2 = per cent of G.N.P. spent on pollution abatement in 1970
P_1 = per capita cost of urban service
P_2 = abatement costs per unit of pollution abated

(2) MACROECONOMIC BALANCE

Equations (1) to (9) in table 2 describe balances for the macroeconomic variables. They show how the principal elements of the regional accounts — regional G.D.P., gross investment, employment, etc. — are related to the levels of other activities in the system and to each other. The multiplication of G.D.P. with M_1 in the first term of equation (1) compensates (as can be verified by appropriate substitutions) for the cost of abatement, $P_2 * ABATE$, that is already included in the conventional measure of the Gross Domestic Product for the base year 1970. Since regional accounts for future years are also expressed in 1970 prices, only an increase in the proportion of pollution abated (M_2) will be registered as an increase in G.D.P. To take account of abatement over xpenditures in G.D.P., any increment in the rate of abatement over that actually realised in 1970 (such as M_2) is multiplied by the 1970 'prices' (the unit cost) of abatement and summed into the Gross Domestic Product. Inventory change is treated analogously to investment, but in compliance with standard conventions it is recorded as a distinct element of G.D.P.

Personal consumption of specific goods is treated as a function of income per capita. The coefficients in columns (2) and (9) are terms in the linear approximations of the consumption functions for the region. The coefficients, *C*, of column (2) measure the amounts of specific agricultural products (*AGS*), metal and energy resources (*RSS*), and industrial products (*XT* and *XNT*) consumed per dollar of additional total expenditure. The coefficients in column (9) represent the population term in the linearised consumption functions. They show, for any given level of consumption expenditure, how the amounts of the various specific products will increase or decrease with an increase in population (with the total consumption expenditure held constant). Housing is treated as household investment. The capital coefficients, *K*, in columns (2) and (9) represent the consumption expenditure and income terms that determine the stock of housing required at any given spending and population level. Expenditures on collection of household liquid and solid wastes and water supply are specified as 'urban amenities'. Their level in any given region depends on the size of the urban, rather than the overall population.

The second equation determines DSAVE, that is, the positive or negative excess of desired private saving over the actual volume of investment. It is essentially a slack variable (see endnote 4 on pp. 529–30). While government saving is set equal to government investment, the desired (or potential) supply of private savings is determined as a given per cent of G.D.P. plus net inflows of foreign capital and foreign aid.

For a single region, unless explicitly set equal to zero, a positive or negative DSAVE can exist. By the internal logic of the system, it has to be matched by a shortfall or an excess of the actual, as compared to the normal (corresponding to the normal saving ratio) level of consumption, a positive or negative (as the case may be) element in aid and capital flows, or some combination of the two.[5]

Each year's investment is the sum of four components: equipment, plant, land development, and irrigation investment. Rows (75), (76) and (87) to (91) of table 2 show further details of the treatment of investment in this system. In any given year, the stocks of plant and equipment capital required to support current production are determined by capital coefficients (*K*). Investment required over a ten-year period (say, between 1970–80) must cover depreciation as well as the difference between current requirements and the stock of capital at the beginning of the decade. Equation (91) keeps track of the requirements of arable land, but the levels of investment in land development and irrigation are set exogenously in the present system. Columns (97) to (101) show the industrial composition of the four different types of domestic investment, that is, the proportional allocation of a dollar's worth of equipment investment among the sectors producing machinery, electrical machinery, etc., and the industrial composition of inventory change.

Row (8) contains labour coefficients, representing employment per unit of output in the various industrial, household and government sectors. Only in the developed countries are labour coefficients specified for agriculture. Thus, total regional employment includes the entire employed labour force in the developed regions, but excludes the agricultural labour force in the lower income regions.

(3) INPUT-OUTPUT BALANCES

Rows (11) to (69) of table 2 describe the input-output balances of the system. Rows (50) to (68) show the total requirements of nineteen internationally traded manufactures per unit of output of the corresponding domestic producing sectors. The purchasers of these inputs include household consumers, government, investment, as well as other industrial sectors. Separate rows identify specific products measured in physical units, in other words specific agricultural products (AGS) and specific resource products (RSS). Residual agriculture (AGR, or all agricultural production except animal and milk products, cereals, high protein crops, and root crops), residual resource (RSR, or all minerals other than the six metals and three energy resources specifically enumerated), and food and resource processing margins are also shown separately, but they are measured in 1970 value units.

(4) POLLUTION AND ABATEMENT EQUATIONS

Equations (13) to (31) are the pollution balances of the system. Rows (11) to (15) are the equations for setting the levels of abatement activities. Rows (16) to (23) contain the emissions coefficients which measure the quantities (metric tonnes of biological oxygen demand, suspended solids, particulate matter, etc.) emitted per unit of output of each economic activity. Emissions coefficients are specified for urban households as well as for all agricultural and industrial processes. Net total emissions (EMA) measure the volume of each pollutant that is emitted minus the amount treated by the abatement sectors ($ABATE$). Abatement activities do in their turn generate pollution; hence, they can eliminate only a fraction of the pollution that they treat. Thus, particulate abatement eliminates more than 99 per cent of the emissions treated, while primary water treatment eliminates only 80 per cent of the suspended solids and none of the nitrogen pollution in the water it treats. The coefficients in rows (24) to (31) measure residual pollution after treatment by the abatement processes. This pollution ($EMNA$) is not abatable in the sense that it is the proportion of treated emissions remaining after treatment. The variable $EMTOT$ is the sum, for each pollutant, of untreated emissions and residual emissions after the abatement processes have been applied. Thus, $EMTOT$ measures the total volume of emissions remaining to render whatever damage or discomfort can be attributed to pollution.

While worldwide environmental consciousness is growing rapidly, proven abatement technologies are acknowledged to be available for only a very limited list of pollutants. For the rest (since no abatement is technically feasible at present), the level of gross emissions by producers and households is necessarily equal to the level of net emissions. The levels of emissions of these pollutants can be estimated by the multiplication of the emissions coefficients for non-abatables by the levels of industrial and household pollution determined through the solution of the model. Developmental projections presented in the Report contain such estimates for one non-abatable pollutant (pesticides) only.

(5) INVESTMENT BALANCES

Required stocks of plant and equipment (*SPLT, SEQP*) are computed by multiplying sectoral production levels by their respective capital co-efficients (rows 84 and 99). In 1970, investment in plant and equipment (equations 75 and 76) is determined by multiplying the required stocks by the sum of the growth rate and the estimated rates of replacement of the stocks in question. In later years, replacement investment is still considered a fixed percentage of the capital stock in place, while investment for expansion is computed as the difference between required capital (*SPLT, SEQP*) and that in place ten years earlier (*HPLT, HEQP*), referred to in some tables as 'historical stocks'.

Since the differences between the output levels of two different years, and consequently the corresponding capital stock, are in many cases treated as unknowns to be determined through the solution of the system of (non-linear) equations, the computations described above may involve the use of iteration, that is, a method of stepwise successive approxima-tions.

Equations (78) to (86) cumulate the consumption of mineral resources over successive decades. Information on cumulative resource extraction provides a basis for projecting the future costs of extraction: as the more accessible reserves of a particular mineral in a given region become exhausted, the next layer involving higher extraction costs begins to be exploited.

(6) INTERNATIONAL TRANSACTION EQUATIONS

The remaining equations in the table determine the imports and exports of the various types of goods and services discussed above. This system does not identify the region of origin of any region's imports, nor the destination of any region's exports (see p. 510 above). Instead, every exporter sells to a 'pool' of traded goods, from which importing regions draw their imports. Equations (92) to (131) deal with imports. In general, imports are specified as a given ratio of imports to domestic output. The import/output ratios, A, are derived from a set of import coefficients,[6] each one of which represents the proportion of total domestic consumption of a particular good that is satisfied by imports in a particular region. Imports of services, primarily foreign travel, are tied directly to G.D.P., and imports of transportation to total imports. Thus, every region draws an amount from the world pool of specific products in accordance with its domestic consumption and its import coefficients.

Each region is assigned a given share of the total export pool for each commodity. Equations (132) to (172) state that a region's exports of each kind of output are a given proportion, B, of the total world pool. World pools are represented by the pool variables, $PAGS, PAGR, PRSS$, etc.

In comparing a table describing the composition of exports of a region with one listing the imports of that region we find that the region is in most instances an importer and exporter of the same goods. This reflects the process of classification which groups together different kinds of goods. Moreover, when the exports and the imports of countries combined into a single region are aggregated, the flow of goods traded between any two often are not netted out but rather are listed both as exports and imports of this region. Hence, coefficients and export shares generally depict gross rather than net trade. An exception is made for specific metal and energy resources, which are treated on a net basis. Their margins, however are carried on a gross basis. Thus, a region can be both an importer and an exporter of metal-refining services, but it can only appear as either a net importer or a net exporter of metal content. Resource refining margins traded by any region are assumed to be equal to their 1970 volumes plus a specified proportion of imports or exports of specific resource products in excess of the base year. Agricultural margin trade is computed by multiplying the trade in each of the specific agricultural products by a region-specific processing margin percentage.

Interregional financial transfers are separated into capital flows, which change a region's international indebtedness and thus also generate interest payments and aid payments which are treated as pure grants.

The balance of payments, $BAL,$ is the sum total of deficits or surpluses — as the case may be — of the following three external accounts: the difference between the value of exports and imports of the region, $EXPRT - IMPRT$; the difference between the capital inflows and the capital outflows, $ECAP - MCAP$, of the regions; the difference between the foreign aid obtained and supplied by the region, $EAID - MAID$: and the net foreign income payments (mainly interest payments) received or made by the region. In other words, the balance of payments, BAL, by definition, is the net flow of foreign short-term credit. It represents a gap (positive or negative) between the long-term financial intakes and outlays of a given region.

The cumulative level of indebtedness which constitutes the base for the determination of annual interest payments is computed so as to include not only cumulative ordinary capital flows, but also cumulative annual positive or negative balances of payments defined above.

VI. IMPLEMENTATION

The task of assembling data for the world system involved two major endeavours: the estimation of structural coefficients for each region in the base year, 1970, and the projection of changes in these base year co-efficients for the years 1980, 1990 and 2000. Both of these efforts posed serious problems and it would be presumptuous to claim any degree of statistical authority even for the base year data.[7] Estimates of future coefficients are, for obvious reasons, even more uncertain. It is our belief that the estimates, while rough, are generally plausible, and that they provide a solid base for future improvements.

Many international, regional and national institutions, including statistical, research, and other types of institutions contributed specialised information for this effort. Their cooperation was important, yet much remains to be done. The full potential of this initial study will be realised only if it stimulates various institutions to undertake efforts to improve the data at all levels of the system.

The analytical structure requires systematic estimation of a comprehensive set of input-output accounts, including current and capital account transactions, exports and imports, and the balance of payments for each of the 15 regions of the world. In addition to the conventional production accounts in value units, balances in physical units were constructed for four types of agricultural products (livestock, cereals, high-protein crops, root crops), fish, six metals (iron, copper, aluminium, nickel, zinc, lead), three fossil fuels (coal, petroleum, natural gas), eight pollutants (particulate air pollution, suspended solids, biological oxygen demand, phosphorus, nitrogen, dissolved solids, solid wastes, pesticides), and fertilisers.

Detailed data on trade flows were obtained from United Nations sources. These were aligned and aggregated in accordance with the regional and product specifications of the world system to provide estimates of import coefficients and export shares for all traded commodities, including the specific agricultural products. The trade coefficients for the metal and energy resources were not readily attainable from the United Nations statistics; they were reconstructed from other sources, as were the aid and capital flows for the base year. The United Nations statistics furnished base-year values for most of the macrovariables of the system: G.D.P., population, urban population, government expenditures, and labour force. FAO sources furnished data on the production and con-

sumption of specific agricultural products and on some of the major
agricultural inputs.

Regional input-output tables and the input structures for agriculture,
mining and pollution abatement were not so readily available. While
input-output tables are published for more than 70 countries, there are
no comprehensive regional accounts. Individual country tables are constructed with differing classifications and accounting conventions, and
expressed in terms of their own price units. Years of painstaking analysis
and data refinement would be necessary before we could combine
individual country tables to construct meaningful regional tables.
Furthermore, for several of the developing regions there were only one or
two country tables available, and for China and some of the African
regions there were none. The same sort of problems made it impossible to
observe directly the composition of consumption and investment
expenditures in each region. In the absence of adequate region-specific
data it was necessary to estimate many, but by no means all, of the
structural coefficients of the system as functions of per capita gross
national product on the basis of cross-country regressions. The basic
strategy consisted of reconciling and adjusting the prices of a small group
of input-output tables and consumption vectors and determining how
individual coefficients or groups of coefficients vary with income levels
in the sample of comparable tables.

The diagram (table 4) summarises the methods used to estimate the
base-year data and to project the model's coefficients into the future.
Each of the blocks in the diagram represents a set of coefficients in the
world model. The 'texture' of each block — whether it is dotted, cross-
hatched, etc. — denotes the kind of methodology used to estimate the
base-year coefficients. The numbers (1, 2, 3 and 4) refer to the methods
used to project the coefficients for the base year into the future.

The great majority of the parameters were estimated on the basis of
cross-national regressions of specific coefficients or weighted sums of coefficients on national per capita income (taken to represent an index of the
overall level of the economic and technical development of the country in
question). While information from the input-output tables and other
economic statistics of fifteen or more countries were consulted in cross-
sectional analysis, the actual regressions were often computed on the basis
of only eight countries, namely those for which the Kravis study provided
some basis for an international price standardisation.[8] Coefficients that
were estimated from cross-national regressions were entered into the system
as reference tables for each of eleven 'benchmark' levels of per capita income.

This procedure was used for estimating those coefficients indicated
on the diagram by unmarked (plain) cells, including those for energy and
capital inputs into agriculture, investment, consumption structures, an
urban amenities vector, and the industry input-output tables. Thus, for
example, the input—output coefficients for a given region are assumed to

TABLE 4 COEFFICIENT ESTIMATION AND PROJECTION FOR A SINGLE REGION BLOCK

	Agriculture	Metals	Energy	Input-output	Investment	Inventory	Pollution	Consumption	Urban	Government	Fish	Exports
Agriculture	2	0	0	4	0	4	0	1,2	0		0	4
Metals	0	0	0	2	0	4	0	0	0	0	0	2
Energy	1,2	3	3	2,4	0	4	4	1	2	1	1	2
Industry and services (fertiliser) 2	4 / 4	3	3	1,2	4	4	4	1	2	1	4	1
Capital	1,2	3	3	1	0	0	4	1	2	1	1	0
Pollution	2	0	0	2	0	0	4	0	1,2	0	0	0
Labour	1,2	3	3	1,2	0	0	4	1	2	1	1	0
Imports	2	2	2	1	0	0	0	0	0	0	1	0

Coefficient projection methodology

1 Income dependent
2 Specially projected
3 Changing with resource depletion
4 Held constant

Region-specific

Column scaled

Benchmarked

Other

0 No entry

Row scaled

depend only on its income level rather than on other region-specific characteristics. Such an assumption does not, of course, take into account potentially great differences in the sectoral input proportions among regions with similar income levels but with different consumption habits or technologies.

Input-output tables do not normally include the detail on mining and resource processing margins requisite for the present system; therefore, the coefficients for mining and resource consumption had to be estimated from special studies. To estimate each region's input structure for mining, we began with the input coefficients for mining from the detailed, 485-sector United States input-output table and modified each column to take into account interregional differences in the average costs of extracting each specific resource. In the case of most of the metals, interregional differences in mining costs were not known directly. In these cases we assumed that cost differences were proportional to interregional differences in the average grades of the particular ore mined. The regional labour costs for mining were estimated by the same methods as the other labour coefficients in the system.

The specific resource-consumption per unit of output of each industrial sector was first estimated from unpublished, detailed time series information from the United States, obtained from the U.S. Bureau of Mines. The detailed energy-consumption coefficients for the United States were available from special studies by the University of Illinois, Centre for Advanced Computation. Since the intensity of consumption of the specific resources varies significantly from region to region, it was essential to modify the first round of estimates of the coefficients, based on United States data, to bring them into conformity with the regional consumption control totals. The estimates of the total regional consumption of each specific resource were obtained from the statistics of regional production, imports and exports. Each row of the resource-consumption coefficients was then scaled so as to bring the regional consumption of each resource into agreement with the base-year resource-consumption statistics.[9] In the diagram, the coefficients which were scaled by region-specific row multipliers are designated by horizontal stripes; those scaled by the column multipliers are indicated by vertical stripes.

The labour coefficients were first estimated on the basis of cross-country regressions. The discrepancies between the regional employment control totals and employment estimates computed from the preliminary labour coefficient estimates resulted in large part from the special characteristics of agriculture in each region. Since the agricultural work-force assumes unknown, but potentially significant, proportions of hidden unemployment in developing countries, we did not attempt to estimate the labour coefficients in agriculture for regions with per capita income below $1000 per annum. The agricultural labour coefficients for the developed countries were scaled so as to reproduce available statistics

of the agricultural labour force in the base year. When this was done, the
labour requirements computed on the basis of the full set of labour coefficients for each region agreed quite closely with the independent
statistics of the total regional employment.

The consumption structures for the base year are based on cross-
country regressions on income per capita for ten countries, using the price-
adjusted consumption data of the Kravis study.[10] The household capital
coefficients, representing investment in housing, were estimated from
information on the regional rent differentials furnished by Lakshmanan.[11]
The consumption of selected agricultural products was estimated from
the region-specific consumption functions published by F.A.O. Food
consumption is specified in physical units, with the appropriate food-
processing margins and other agriculture expressed in value terms. Urban
amenities per urban resident are specified in a vector representing the
services of water supply, sewage disposal, and solid waste collection. These
services are characteristic of urban life but not generally of rural life throughout the world. These coefficients were estimated in special studies by
Lakshmanan. Household emissions of water pollution and solid waste
loads are tied to the urban amenities column because the abatement of
these pollutants is not normally required in a rural setting. Finally, the
benchmark vectors of government expenditure proportions are based on
cross-country regressions of expenditures of per capita national income
in three broad categories — education, defence, and 'other'.

Returning again to the diagram of Table 4, dotted areas identify sectors
where neither the region-specific nor the scaled or benchmark treatments
seemed appropriate. No information exists, for example, on the costs of
pollution abatement for medium or low income countries; hence, it was
necessary to assume that abatement involves the same (the U.S.) technology
throughout the world. Similarly, the pollution emission coefficients were
based primarily on U.S. data. Presticides, where emissions are region-
specific, and solid waste emissions, which are benchmarked, are
exceptions. Others were weighted on the basis of differences in the
detailed process mix in the different geographical regions, but otherwise
similar matrices were used for all regions.

VII. CONCLUDING REMARKS

The description of the multiregional input-output model of the world
economy presented above is not detailed enough to provide a basis for
systematic assessment of its specific strengths and weaknesses. In the
context of this Symposium it might contribute to bringing into full
relief three areas of contrast between alternative ways of posing and
answering the problems of the interregional division of labour and international trade.

(a) The contrast between the general equilibrium and the partial equilibrium approach.

(b) The contrast between aggregative analysis and a disaggregated approach aimed at describing and explaining the phenomenon in greater and in more concrete detail.

(c) The contrast between general theoretical formulation which provides a convenient basis for pure deductive reasoning, and theoretical modelling aimed at concrete empirical implementation.

The world model described above has already been tested in the preparation of several alternative projections of the development of the world economy from 1970 through 1980, and 1990 to the year 2000.[12] It can and will presently be used as an analytical tool for a systematic study of the structural characteristics of the existing interregional distribution of economic activities and international flows of goods and services that correspond to it.

NOTES

[1] This paper is based on the Preliminary Report on *The Future of the World Economy* prepared for the United Nations Department of Economic and Social Affairs by a team led by Anne P. Carter, Wassily Leontief, and Peter Petri (New York, 1976). The Report was published in book form by Oxford University Press in April, 1977.

[2] It has been impossible to carry out a full analysis of the price and rent implications of the world system within the time limitations of the present report. Such an analysis is, however, planned.

[3] The unit used in such measurement being defined as the amount of that good that could be purchased for $1 at its 1970 price.

[4] Certain variables are identified as 'slacks'. Their meaning and their use require explanation. Formally, a 'slack' is an extra additive variable introduced into an equation. There are several different reasons for using this device. If a slack is treated as one of the unknowns (the magnitude of which can be determined simultaneously with the magnitude of all the other variables), the final result will be the same as would have been obtained if the equation in question were simply eliminated from the system; except that the magnitude of the slacks as it came out in the numerical solution will indicate by how much the relationship into which it was inserted would have to change in order to be compatible with the rest of the system.

A general computer programme for manipulating a large system that contains equations which are kept in force for some solutions and have to be suppressed for some others can thus be greatly simplified by the use of slacks. If the value of slack entered into an equation (and with it into the computer programme) is set at zero, that equation is kept in force. To switch it out one simply has to treat the slack as one of the unknown variables.

Treated as an exogenously determined variable, a slack can also be employed conveniently to introduce a change in the shape of the equation (and consequently of the relationship described by it) in which it enters, for instance, an upward or a downward shift in a curve.

[5] The 'balance of payments' is a slack variable as described in endnote 2, page 529.

[6] By import coefficients we mean: (imports/total regional use). For computational convenience, the model actually uses import ratios (imports/regional output), even though the concept of the import coefficient is more satisfactory for analytical purposes. The two concepts are related by a simple algebraic formula as long as regional outputs are non-zero.

[7] In many respects the 1970 solution was made to be consistent with actual 1970 data; in other respects it was found more meaningful to construct and use 'normal 1970' data, that is, data that exclude peculiarities due to 1970 alone. For example, most balance of payments statistics are based on 1969–71 averages due to the great variability of some of these measures. Also, investment and inventory change are based on 1961–70 growth rates rather than on actual 1970 observations. This facilitates comparisons between 1970 and the later projections.

[8] Irving B. Kravis, *et al.*, *A System of International Comparisons of Gross Product and Purchasing Power* (The Johns Hopkins University Press, Baltimore, 1975).

[9] In scaling, a set (a column or row) of coefficients is stepped up or down in the same ratio. The ratio is chosen so as to bring the sum of the scaled coefficients to a given marginal row or column total.

[10] Kravis, *et al.*, *op. cit.* (endnote 8).

[11] T. R. Lakshmanan, *et al.*, 'Urbanization and Environmental Quality: A Preliminary Note', (Mimeo) (April 1, 1975).

[12] These are presented in the U.N. Report referred to above.

Comment*
Lawrence R. Klein

I. THE FUTURE OF THE WORLD ECONOMY

This is a stupendous model — a truly beautiful piece of work — that makes a unique contribution to the conference, namely, portrays a realistic model of general equilibrium in the global sense. It is not only global in that it is a world model, but also by extending the boundaries of strict economic analysis to such important subjects as food, resources, pollution, and demography, mostly but not entirely in a full feedback mode. It is right in step with this symposium through its detailed emphasis on trade and payments.

This model does not, by a wide margin, cover everything of relevance but it covers much more than many other economists have tried, and at a detailed level of sector disaggregation.

Many of the comments that have been going back and forth at this Symposium about simple (small) models and more complicated or realistic (larger) models are carrying on the discussion at an entirely different order of magnitude. This is a large system, rich in detail, that few have tried to comprehend, operate or build. It puts our discourse on a new plane that I find especially appealing. Simple systems are all right for making a teaching point, but not for making realistic decisions. I am sure that the regional scientists among our group will join me in supporting this large-scale general equilibrium approach — with lots of numbers.

There is an understated sentence near the beginning of Section I. 'The future can rarely be predicted with precision . . . '. How well we know this, but the authors have wisely chosen to use scenario analysis; in other words to lay out alternative assumptions and work out the dynamic trend paths for each to the year 2000, reported at decade intervals beginning in 1970.

This is enough in praise of the work at hand. I did not come to this hemisphere just to say nice things about this volume. There is so much in it, that surely there is much to criticise as well as to praise. I offer my suggestions, however, intended in an constructive way, although I know

*At the symposium Wassily Leontief reported on his work for the United Nations Department of Economic and Social Affairs, which had just appeared in a preliminary version as A. P. Carter, W. Leontief, and P. Petri, *The Future of the World Economy*, United Nations (New York, 1976). His contribution to the present volume gives a summary description of the multiregional input-output model used in the United Nations study. Professor Klein's Comment refers to the U.N. publication.

that a great many of them are going to be rejected out of hand, on the basis of prior discussions on related topics.

(1) GENERAL CRITIQUE

The equations of economic behaviour and technology embedded in this system are, in my way of thinking, too simple. There are too many proportionality relations, not enough dynamic relations with lag distributions (having many of the same steady state properties, though) and not enough detail on institutional relations dealing with taxes, transfers, subsidies, and the monetary system.

Naturally, much of the system's technology is contained in the co-efficients of different regional input-output tables, and these must be allowed to change over time. I find the mechanism of change in the I–O coefficients to be somewhat unsystematic. It is my view that the system of I–O coefficients must be related to the pricing system, through the medium of input-demand relationships. This is not done, and I feel that there is a problem in catching substitutions that are induced through price changes. In recent years, we have seen extremely large changes at the level of input prices, especially concerning traded goods, and there are probably more to come. The system should be designed so as to capture the effects of these changes as they occur later in this century.

Prices are in the system and play a significant role. This is to be noted and applauded, but I should note that the treatment of prices is more informative from the supply than from the demand side, and the joint interaction of supply/demand. Prices are determined from the solution of the I–O dual problem, (supply side) and the value-added proportion which includes many demand side influences. The whole set of calculations, however, are in normalised prices. They reflect relative price shifts but try to finesse the problems of inflation or deflation. To some extent, this may seem to be justified in a long-run trend model, but have not the last 25 years been strongly influenced by inflationary price movements to an extent that would lead us to be conscious and wary of absolute price movements in the next 25 years?

I raise this question because the model, while enormously rich in many technical details, lacks an explicit monetary sector and covers up many basic economic distinctions between nominal and real calculations. The tax-subsidy-transfer system in most (but not all) parts of the world is fundamentally specified in nominal rather than real terms, and the capital flow sections of the payments balances — very important for many of the scenarios — should also be in nominal terms, not to mention the complications of a numeraire currency. The problem is that the world accounting wealth constraint must be in nominal terms and must be imposed for long-range scenarios in order to guard against the build-up of accounting imbalances. Such flows as investment income (national, regional, or international) and capital movements, apart from direct investments, have no unique real or physical counterpart. It distorts the structure of the system to model these, as is done in this report, in real rather than nominal valuations. Complicated as the model is, it must unfortunately be made a shade more complicated in order to function as a complete system.

Another general issue is the completeness of the system. The various scenarios search and cover the two-dimensional plane of real production (income) growth and population growth. I think that these ought to be endogenously generated within the system. The general equilibrium model surely ought to be able to project a solution for real growth; moreover, aggregate growth should be in a feedback relation with the component sectors that make up total growth. I feel that there is a certain emptiness in a model that does not provide a projection of the most central variables without their having been assumed in the first place. Similarly, population projections affect the economy and are affected by the economy. The world's best demographic scholars have frequently been led badly astray by economic impacts on birth, family formation, and other population measures. Is the problem adequately handled by assuming a wide range of population projections from high to low? I would prefer to see the demographic variables integrated into the economic solution in full feedback form.

The model and its scenarios, apart from their 1970 base, look forward. There is certainly nothing bad about this as long as they also take a retrospective glance. In a system as deep and complicated as the present one, the reader and user need a feeling of credibility. It is not a 'black-box' system but it is certainly a 'strong box' that requires knowledge of an intricate combination lock. Short of becoming locksmiths, we might feel much better about the contents if there were a strong dose of retrospective testing. How well does the model fit the facts of the past two or three decades? Is there a readily ascertainable scenario that approximately reproduces quantitative history? How well is mid-decade of the 1970s described by the model? In the next section, I shall comment in some places on 1980 values because we may know a fair amount about some of these already in 1976.

Associated with the procedure of validation testing that I find wanting, is the concept of error analysis. Both on the basis of *a priori* statistical reasoning and on historical performance, there are error magnitudes that should accompany the various scenarios. I am quite sure that the appropriate error bands are fairly large — not so large as to negate the great value of the findings — but large enough to request that we be provided with a detailed analysis of their magnitude and nature.

Finally, the system is occasionally linearised, and for the most part, it is a linear model. Given the recent advances in computer technology, I find this kind of approximation to be unnecessary. To the extent that nonlinear effects can build up in a few decades of simulation, it would seem preferable to retain them in the specification and even add some relevant non-linearities to the overall model, using some more powerful methods of computer simulation in order to work out the scenario details.

(2) SPECIFIC CRITIQUE

Methodological issues are the main things to be discussed in connection with this report, but the various scenario values both from the side of results and assumptions are informative, occupying a large portion of the total manuscript. I do not want to 'nit-pick' unimportant matters to the neglect of the main results, but I do want to see what guidance for model appraisal can be ascertained from the various figures or particular concepts used. These specific points are raised partly in response to the above cited lack of validation testing.

  I shall take up points of issues essentially in order of appearance. (Page references in the following text are to the preliminary version of *The Future of the World Economy* by A. P. Carter, W. Leontief and P. Petri, New York, 1966.)

  (a) Real growth of the developed countries has been historically at 4·5 per cent, but one of the points of analysis should be to determine if such a rate can be maintained in the future as a consequence of energy and other resource limitations; therefore an assumed rate of growth seems to dodge one of the most important issues to be determined by the analysis. My own predilection is for a lower rate in the long run but not, as indicated later, simply because higher growth breeds lower growth along a mechanical curve extrapolation (pp. 9 and 13).

  (b) It is suggested that an investment ratio of 35 to 40 per cent may be required to support a sustained growth rate of 9 to 10 per cent. Do not the Japanese results of the decade of the 1960s contradict this assertion? By the figures given here for 1970, the Japanese investment ratio reached only 20 per cent. There are a number of good explanations for the Japanese performance, but mainly they are not captured by the present model structure (p. 32).

  (c) It is an interesting and, indeed, fascinating finding of this study to see that world trade growth is projected above the rate of world G.D.P. growth but is not the annual rate of 6 per cent trade growth on the low side in view of historical performance and recent trends, especially the opening of larger growth potential in trade with the centrally planned economies (p. 371)?

  (d) Some of the scenario results indicate reversals of trend movements and this may be plausible, but it is often hard to see why it occurs, particularly at distant specific intervals. Why should the balance of payments of developing market regions show a deficit in 1980, a surplus in 1990, and a deficit again in 2000? Are there some Kuznets' long swings inherent in the structure of the system? A somewhat more bothersome result in individual lines of the complete simulation tables shows not only smooth reversal curves, but also some very sudden, jerky movements. Given the simplified set of proportionality relationships in what is basically a linear model, it is not clear that there is a basis for projection of specific large movements that change character of parts of a solution in a hazy or murky distant future. In a model like this, we should probably stick to smooth scenarios in the absence of very specific information (pp. 41 and 93).

(e) Export shares of the world total for a particular good are fixed. This, I believe, could be considerably improved, even allowing for some flexibility in altering fixed shares, by relating the flows to relative prices – or else how could one have explained the past two decades of Japanese export growth at an accelerated rate? There are undoubtedly many new developments on the horizon like Japan's of the 1950s and 1960s and the model ought to have a perceptive way of spotting them (pp. 60 and 64).

(f) '. . . the balance of trade of a particular region can be treated either as one of the given variables and its Gross National Income as one of the unknown variables, or vice versa'. Again referring back to an earlier comment about the endogenisation of G.N.P., I would prefer to treat neither as given and both as variables generated by the model. In present studies of public policy formation through the medium of econometric models, there is much attention devoted to optimising loss functions containing targets and instruments over a future horizon. Excellent algorithms with computer programmes have been provided to work out 'optimal' simulation paths. It is not that the 'optimal' paths are demonstrably superior to those of this paper, but they have a certain objectivity and systematic regularity that has much to recommend. Although these programmes have been mainly applied to national models, they could be applied to the present world model (pp. 65 and 66).

(g) The keeping of agricultural yields at their 1970 levels seems to be unduly pessimistic. Prediction of harvests has been admittedly difficult, or even disastrous, of late, but this is such an important area of activity for the present model, it would seem that something better could be done, especially by taking agricultural investment and the use of more sophisticated intermediate inputs into account (p. 89).

(h) Scenario A assumes that DC employment levels are equal to labour force levels. Is this plausible, feasible or worth considering? It is only one of many scenarios, but I find it to be highly unrealistic (p. 109).

(j) The three alternative assumptions for scenario generation UN/B, UN/A–1, UN/A–2 give the respective world G.D.P. results for the year 2000; $13,250 billion, $11,999 billion, and $12,651 billion. Aren't these various results quite close together? It appears that they differ by much less among themselves than I would expect forecast errors to be. There needs to be a richer array of scenario alternatives that give wider ranges of world possibilities by the year 2000 (p. 111).

(k) The International Development Strategy calls for a growth rate in excess of 6 per cent for LDC during the second half of the present decade. Last year was a poor, inauspicious start. It may be possible to exceed 6 per cent with some help from O.P.E.C. countries, but it may be an overly optimistic target (p. 119).

(l) Scenario X. The Japanese rate seems low at 4·9 per cent, the Western Europe (medium) rate seems high at 7 per cent and the East European rate seems low at 4·9 per cent. The Middle East at 9 per cent is quite optimistic. The Middle East rate of 11·9 per cent for 1971—80 seems to be an outside estimate in view of the recession effects and cutbacks of 1974—75 (pp. 127 and 128).

(m) Personal consumption ratios of between 50 and 70 per cent are quite low, and will be hard to achieve — doubly so if special measures are taken to facilitate a more equal distribution of income. It is generally thought that Japan's takeoff into high growth was greatly assisted by an unequal income distribution that promoted high savings rates (pp. 130 and 133).

(n) The idea that primary industries, especially agriculture will expand at a slower rate than G.N.P. is interesting but might lead to problems as this differential persists over time (p. 133).

(p) There is a strong emphasis in the report on higher growth in heavy industry than in light industry. Is this feasible and is it desirable? I have doubts but would disagree with the conclusions that higher growth in heavy sectors is pronounced and that it is essential. The O.P.E.C. countries that aspire to growth and diversification are looking a great deal towards light industry. Japan got a major start from light sectors and has transferred these activities now to Taiwan, Hong Kong, and South Korea. These latter areas may be able to take off from light rather than heavy activities (p. 137 and 138).

(q) 'The imports of a given commodity in a given region are assumed to be proportional to the gross domestic output of the commodity'. Soviet grain imports do not follow this rule. The same is true of other countries whose imports are often an inverse function of domestic output in order to make up the shortfall (p. 143).

(r) Assumptions of scenario H are implausible, namely that the Middle East, Latin America and the U.S.S.R. would be the sole petroleum exporters after 1980. North Sea, Nigeria, Indonesia, China, Mexico, Canada, and others will surely be active in export markets for petroleum (p. 168).

(s) Should the price of petroleum be tied to cost of production of oil from shale by the year 2000? This seems to be a rather poor working hypothesis (p. 183).

(t) The coal price figures for 1980, 1990, 2000 are quite low. Contrary to the report's assertion, I would say that its present movement is now very much in the train of oil and natural gas prices (pp. 253 and 254).

(u) Some of the relative price movements look very implausible to me — copper in 2000 (high), coal low throughout, electricity low now and throughout. These are only a sampling of problematic cases (pp. 290 and 291).

Scenario X. Some bothersome results are:

The choppy nature of nickel net exports, and the path and choppy nature of coal net exports (p. 328).
Comparative G.D.P. performance of U.S.S.R. low relative to that of Western Europe (medium) (p. 329), and
the payments surplus build-up in U.S.S.R. and Eastern Europe (p. 329).
The import surplus of Middle East by 1990 and continuing (p. 334).
The G.D.P. rise of South Africa from 1980 (p. 339).

These are only some prominent examples.

16 Concluding Remarks

W. Max Corden and Ronald E. Findlay

We shall devote the first part of our concluding remarks to some reflections about trade theory provoked by the conference papers, and even more by the discussion, then we shall attempt some comparison of international trade theory and location theory — one aim being to see what trade theory can learn from location theory — and finally we shall comment on the papers and discussion dealing with development economics.[1]

But first let us say that it is impossible to summarise the conference. The papers and discussion certainly can — and will have to — stand on their own. Nor would it be appropriate for us to give grades — whether on insight, techniques, clarity of exposition and simplicity of language, or knowledge of the history of thought — much as we might enjoy doing so. The topic has been 'the international allocation of economic activity', conceived here as a study in positive rather than normative economics (though occasionally papers and discussants departed from the limitation to positive economics). All conceivable aspects of the topic seem to have been explored or touched upon. The main limitation has been that all but two of the papers have dealt with generalisations and with theory, and the discussion has been only about models and generalisations, any empirical content being very casual indeed (with the exception of Branson's extensive comments). Other than in Isard's paper, there have been no substantial case studies. The two empirical papers have had rather little connection with the main theme of the conference.

We have found the conference very stimulating, suggesting numerous directions for further theoretical and empirical research. The present volume that has come out of it may well be influential in redirecting theoretical developments, and in particular, in encouraging trade and location theorists to familiarise themselves with each others' works and to improve their models as a result.

With these introductory remarks to our conclusion, let us then turn to the first of our main topics.

I. INQUEST ON TRADE THEORY

One of the themes of the papers at this conference and, even more, of the discussions, has been, what might be called, an 'inquest on trade theory', namely reflections on the value of the established formal theory in explaining the international allocation of economic activity. We have had among us not only many of the leading makers and refiners of the modern theory — above all Haberler and Ohlin — but also some critics, as well as representatives of what has appeared as the alternative 'paradigm' of location theory. This has been stimulating. It raises in particular the question in our minds whether one can summarise the main inadequacies in standard trade theory, as they emerge from remarks at this conference, the aim being to provide signposts for further development. In order to do this it seems necessary first to provide a quick survey of the main elements of the modern theory.

The core of modern trade theory as it is usually taught is, what might be called, the narrow factor-proportions model. This is the house that Samuelson built and many others refined. It contains the essential Heckscher-Ohlin model, that countries tend to export those goods that are intensive in the factors in which countries are well-endowed. The core theory has two goods, two factors and two countries (above all, two factors), and assumes that production functions in different countries are identical. This core theory yields the result that free trade would lead to factor price equalisation (given the assumption of commodity price equalisation through trade and no factor reversals), and a number of other, now familiar, results.

It is obvious that the core theory — as indeed all versions of trade theory — is heuristic, and contributors to it do not believe that the world actually consists of two factors, two commodities, and so on. It also needs to be stressed that this narrow Samuelson theory is not what can reasonably be described as trade theory, but only as its formal core as usually taught. It is certainly not the house that Ohlin built.

Thus, the second stage is to conceive of a wider core theory, which might be called the broader factor proportions theory. Above all, one allows here for more than two factors. Some of the factors can be specific to particular industries, this being simply a limiting case of factor intensity. It is this broader factor proportions theory which Ohlin pioneered and expounded in the great book *Interregional and International Trade* that we have all been rereading for this conference.

The broader theory argues that the pattern of trade depends to a great extent on the interaction of relative factor intensities of goods and services with relative factor endowments of particular countries. The work of Leontief brought out the inadequacy of the narrow two-factor theory in explaining the pattern of U.S. trade, but the subsequent empirical work by Hufbauer, Baldwin, Vanek and others, seems to have given strong support to the broader theory, in which one distinguishes skilled from unskilled labour as factors, or alternatively human capital from raw labour, and also allows for natural resources. Branson's valuable survey at this conference is relevant here. Thus, at the minimum, one needs a four-factor model (natural resources, physical capital, unskilled labour and skilled labour), and possibly one has to allow for more factors, notably some natural resources specific to particular products. Some formal theoretical work has been done on this broader multifactor theory, though the neat results of the narrow theory can hardly be maintained. It should be noted here, incidentally, that the two-goods assumption has been necessary only for simple expositions of the narrow theory, but not for its principal results.

The third stage is to allow for different technologies or production functions between countries. In a sense this is a break with the fundamental Heckscher—Ohlin approach, which might prefer to explain apparently different production functions in terms of different factor endowments. But there is certainly no difficulty in incorporating different production functions in the formal theory, and it has been done often enough.

Different production functions can result rather narrowly from differences in technical knowledge — from a failure for available knowledge to be transmitted fully among countries (but does that not mean that there is really a difference in human capital?) — or they can be explained in institutional or historical terms. At this stage of the analysis a large number of considerations which trade theory is sometimes accused of ignoring (notably differences in social attitudes to various kinds of productive activity and organisation) can certainly be incorporated, and in practice this has probably not been done enough, other than at the most formal level.

The fourth stage is to allow for economies of scale. The role of economies of scale — or, more broadly, economies of agglomeration — has been stressed at this conference by the location theorists, so we have been very conscious of them. It is true that the core theory, whether in its narrow or broader version, ignores economies of scale, and it is a fault of many standard expositions that they are underplayed. But it certainly cannot be said that trade theorists have ignored economies of scale. Ohlin devoted the important chapter III of his book to the subject, Meade dealt with them in *Trade and Welfare* and in *A Geometry of International Trade*, and there is indeed an extensive literature. Economies of scale underlie two recent approaches to the explanation of trade in manufactures, namely the Linder theory, which argues that countries tend to export goods for which there is a relatively high domestic demand, and the Grubel-Lloyd explanation of intraindustry trade.

The fifth stage is to allow for endogenously varying factor supplies. This is a particularly important development. The core theory, as usually expounded, certainly assumes factor supplies in different countries to be fixed. That is, above all, a characteristic of the standard geometric expositions. It seems almost the essence of trade theory that it takes as given the factor endowments of different countries, and then explores the effects of differences in such endowments for the international allocation of economic activity and for trade.

Yet it would be quite wrong to suggest that the major writings on trade theory have not allowed for variable factor supplies. Here, above all, one must refer to *Interregional and International Trade.* This book has an extensive discussion of the effects that trade has on factor supplies or services, referring to domestically originating factor services. In addition, it need hardly be mentioned, it showed how international factor movements are essentially alternatives to trade in their effects on factor prices. The variability of factor supplies was, indeed, a crucial ingredient in this book. In a famous article Mundell explored the relationship between international factor movements and international trade in terms of the narrow core model, coming out with somewhat extreme results which really brought out the extreme nature of the core model. There was also a very thorough analysis of international factor movements in Meade's *Trade and Welfare.* Papers in international monetary economics that allow for international capital mobility must run into their hundreds, but we also have now a number of rigorous analyses of the effects of capital mobility on trade in real-theory models.

The sixth stage is to allow for growth (notably by capital accumulation) and time, and to make the theory dynamic. This has also been done. To begin with, we have fully worked out models, essentially comparative static, which explore the effects on the terms, volume and pattern of trade of given increases in factor endowments and changes in production functions. These are simple extensions of the narrow-core model. In addition we have models which explore the effects of trade on growth, making growth endogenous. In the more elaborate models, trade affects capital accumulation, which in turn affects trade, the path of changing factor endowments and production patterns being traced out. The trouble about these latter models is that they are elaborate and, generally, very mathematical, so that their results have not yet been widely understood or used, and they have not provided any basis for empirical works.

The seventh and last stage is to allow for commercial policy, taxes and subsidies, in affecting the pattern of trade and allocation of resources. It need hardly be said in this audience that this has been one of the main concerns of trade theory. In fact, it has been its first concern, the motive force for the original development of the theory as well as much subsequent development. Here it need only be noted that in the last ten years the multicommodity theory of tariff structure and effective protection has greatly refined this area, going well beyond the models and conclusions of the core theory, and emphasising the positive economic issue of how a complicated structure of tariffs, subsidies, taxes, quotas and so on, may affect the allocation of resources within a country.

The question now arises where the gaps are in the theory, and hence where further development is needed. As mentioned earlier, in making these rather brief remarks we are influenced by the considerations stressed at this conference, especially those highlighted in location theory, and we hope that some guidance for future research directions may be suggested. We have in mind that trade theory may benefit by incorporating within it elements of location theory, just as location theory might benefit by learning from trade theory.[2]

We deal here with five topics in turn, being inevitably brief. When we say that there are gaps in the theory, or that more needs to be done, we do not mean to assert that nothing has been written along the lines suggested. We are simply suggesting more emphasis in these directions. This does not seem the place for a conscientious survey of trade theory drawing attention to all the papers and books, some pioneering, that have dealt with some of these matters. So we wish to be excused in advance.

(1) ECONOMIES OF SCALE

The theory of international trade with economies of scale, and also economies of agglomeration (involving external economies of scale), is clearly underdeveloped. We need some clear and useful multigood models, rigorously specified, and yielding perhaps testable propositions, with scale economies as a central feature.

(2) TRANSPORT COSTS

The location theorists have directed our attention to transport costs, again interpreted more broadly as distance costs, and including costs of transmitting information geographically. Of course we have not ignored transport costs in trade theory. We have seen them as simple barriers to trade, at the limit creating the category of non-traded goods. But trade theory has not allowed systematically for transport costs differing between goods affecting the allocation of resources.

Here would seem to be an obvious application of the multicommodity general equilibrium theory of tariff structure and effective protection, tariffs being replaced by a structure of transport costs for this purpose. This theory, for example, would tell us that the relationship between transport costs on inputs relative to transport costs on final goods (and, more generally, transport costs at various stages of a multistage production process) are relevant for resource allocation. What trade theory can contribute to location theory — rather than just rediscovering the results of location theory — is the general equilibrium implications which have been fully worked out for the effects of tariff structures.

(3) FACTOR MOBILITY

We have models in which trade and international factor movements are alternatives. We also have models in which trade brings about some changes in factor supplies without changing the basic factor endowment characteristics of countries. But the direction in which we need to go is to develop comprehensible models in which there is both trade and extensive international factor mobility, with some factors highly mobile, others less so, and others immobile. One would then get much closer to location theory, which is concerned with the geographical allocation of economic activity, resources moving not just between industries in a given area, but also moving between areas. One could imagine, for example, a model where natural resources and unskilled labour are immobile between countries, skilled labour is partially mobile and capital is highly mobile. Because of some immobility of knowledge and of social institutions, production functions might differ between countries, the mobile factors tending to move in the direction of the favourable production functions (and climate). We come back to all this at more length later in our fuller discussion of location theory.

(4) MULTINATIONALS

International factor mobility — both of capital and of managerial labour — is encouraged by multinationals, as is the international transmission of knowledge. Hence if we are to allow for the great importance of multinationals in international trade we must certainly extend our models in the factor and knowledge mobility direction. But there is more to multinationals than this, as pointed out in Dunning's paper at this conference, and in his and other papers elsewhere.

First, one needs to allow for non-market links between countries, for the market being bypassed in some international trade flows. Secondly, one needs to get beyond the competitive model (though this has been done to a limited extent in tariff theory), and allow for international oligopoly. Thirdly — and this is the particularly interesting point that emerges from Dunning's paper — one needs to explore rigorously the relationship between the location of economic activity and the location of ownership. For this purpose one will need to develop a systematic theory of ownership location: why are some countries much more the originators of multinationals (and their citizens, presumably, the owners) than others, discounting for economic size of various countries? Is this related to the location of economic activity, some activities being more 'multinational-prone'? And does the location of ownership in turn influence the location of the activity?

(5) DYNAMIC OR HISTORICAL MODELS

Finally, in the programme and in the discussion of this conference there has been a useful emphasis on the role of history in determining the international location of economic activity. In comparative static models one can take history into account in rather a formal way by allowing production functions to differ between countries and at various points in time. But this is hardly dynamic or very productive of insights. One needs models with lags, where the past governs the present, and where putty-capital (physical and human) turns into clay-capital once installed, though the clay may subsequently depreciate (slowly melt away?). We do have a few such models, but this approach needs to be put more at the centre of our exposition.

II. TRADE THEORY AND LOCATION THEORY

Less than ten years separate the publication dates of Ricardo's *Principles* and von Thünen's *Isolated State*, the two great works from which modern trade theory and modern location theory trace their respective descents. However, it would seem that trade theory established itself as a unified and comprehensive body of analysis much earlier than location theory, as a result of the systematic development of Ricardian doctrine by J. S. Mill, Marshall, Edgeworth and many others, whereas von Thünen's work, as Isard has pointed out, was relatively neglected during the nineteenth and early twentieth centuries. Consequently when Alfred Weber, the next major figure in location theory, began writing in the first decades of this century, he had to contend with a very influential body of doctrine on international trade and commercial policy that for the most part ignored the spatial dimension of economic activity. Location theorists from Weber to Isard have not ceased to complain about this state of affairs, whereas on the other side only Bertil Ohlin appears to have been willing to attempt a genuine integration of trade and location theory.

In his 1911 article on 'Location Theory and Trade Policy'[3] Weber accuses classical trade theory of 'putting the cart before the horse' in its doctrine of the international division of labour. According to Weber the proper way to analyse this problem is to begin by assuming a uniform distribution of population and resources over geographical space, with the existence of transport costs tending to produce a uniform pattern of production. Specialisation and concentration of production arise only because of some tendency for labour and/or natural resources to be relatively more abundant in some region, which causes a deviation from the 'norm' of uniformity. While the difference of emphasis is interesting, there is clearly no real difference between Weber's approach and that of the classical trade theorists; indeed it would seem to make more sense to start from the undoubted existence of differences in the endowment of labour, capital and natural resources between regions rather than with some abstract postulate of uniformity.

Weber also offered some fascinating speculations about the future course of world industrialisation. It is particularly instructive to see how his geographical determinism led him astray. He took it as axiomatic that iron and steel production must be concentrated close to large coal deposits, because of the overwhelming influence of transport costs. As economist Bela Balassa and geographer Michael Chisholm have both pointed out at this conference, the tremendous reduction in transport costs that we have seen in this century has meant that the iron and steel industry is now much more 'footloose' than Weber could have imagined. The entire phenomenon of Japanese heavy industry, for example, is inexplicable in his terms, since it is based entirely on raw materials imported over relatively long distances.

The most recent expression of the need to introduce space and transport cost into trade theory has been by Isard and Peck (1954).[4] They present empirical evidence on the importance of distance in interregional and international trade and also show how the pattern of specialisation in a Graham-type linear model of production and trade is influenced by transport costs. It is unlikely that any trade theorist has ever believed that transport costs were irrelevant or unimportant in accounting for the pattern and volume of trade. The usual neglect of transport costs in trade theory seems rather to be due to the fact that practitioners in this field have felt that they have had more to contribute to other determinants of the pattern of trade, such as the influence of demand or factor proportions, leaving distance and transport to the attention of the location theorists. Such intellectual division of labour is after all not uncommon; even though it may sometimes lead to unfortunate results.

Isard, in his writings and at this conference, has stressed repeatedly that trade theory and location theory become indistinguishable when merged into a full-blown general equilibrium system. In a formal sense he is undoubtedly right. However, it may also be true that this unity is only achievable at such a high level of generality that it is not of much use to anybody and that, as a practical matter, it is best for trade and location theorists to go their separate ways, a point of view expressed at this conference by Harry Johnson and Ronald Jones.

Before considering whether this view is justified, a few words should be said about whether location theory itself has a general equilibrium framework or not. Location and transportation problems frequently take the pattern of costs as given exogenously and then seek the optimal location of a plant or choice of transport routes. This tends to have a partial equilibrium flavour to trade theorists, who like to think of costs as determined endogenously by tastes, technology and factor endowments. Haberler's penetrating survey of trade theory, for example, has made this criticism of location theory, and it has been expressed at this conference also. However, there are several contributions to location theory and regional economics that have appeared in the last twenty years which are undoubtedly within an explicit general equilibrium framework, such as the work of Isard, Lefeber, Moses and Andersson for example. The emphasis in these models has been on transportation activities, however, and they are not very interesting on the factor supply or consumer preference side which is where the trade models are strongest.

The tradition in trade theory from Ricardo to Samuelson has been to consider a world in which assorted bundles of factor supplies are 'trapped', as Ronald Jones picturesquely expressed it, in different locations. Together with an exogenously given technology these factor supplies determine production possibilities surfaces for each 'country' and these, in conjunction with tastes, determine the pattern of production, consumption and trade. The immobility assumption has bothered several people, particularly J. H. Williams, since it is palpably and increasingly contradicted by the facts. Heckscher and Ohlin have both had many interesting things to say about international factor mobility, and Jones himself has been in the forefront of recent modelbuilding in this area. The theme of increasing international factor mobility rose again and again at the conference and it is clear that this is going to be one of the dominant concerns in international economics for the next few years at least.

Formal models in trade theory have tended to make alternative extreme assumptions about factor mobility, either perfect immobility, in which case factors are content with whatever price they receive in their native habitat, or perfect mobility in which case factors move instantaneously in response to any international price differential. Kemp, Jones and Chipman, for example, in their well-known papers, assume that labour is perfectly immobile while capital is perfectly mobile. Mixed cases, in which both factors are responsive in some degree to price differentials but still have some local preference, are clearly more realistic but not so easy to handle analytically. The factor mobility question is obviously related to that of transport costs and location discussed earlier, and it may therefore be worthwhile to sketch out a possible general equilibrium framework to cover all these issues.

Suppose the world to be an archipelago of different islands, endowed with varying types and amounts of natural resources and with some initial distribution of population and capital. Technology for producing commodities and transporting goods and people from island to island is also given, as are the tastes of the individuals regarding work and leisure and the consumption of different goods as well as the locational preferences regarding work and consumption of each individual. With suitable restrictions on the technology, tastes and initial endowments it would seem that a set of prices could be found at which each individual is maximising his utility and at which demand is equal to supply for all goods and factors. The location of factors and production, as well as the pattern of international trade, would all be determined simultaneously. Some factors might move and others might stay put, depending upon the entire system of relative prices in the general equilibrium.

Notice that we cannot construct a production possibilities surface *a priori* for any of the islands, since its factor endowment is endogenous. Furthermore, factor price equalisation would not hold since identical inputs from a production standpoint might have different locational preferences. But such phenomena as temporary migration, tourism and other realistic details could easily be fitted in. There is therefore no ground for saying that trade theory, or location theory for that matter, is 'unrealistic' and unable to accommodate these features of the modern world.

Such an extensive general equilibrium system, however, would be dangerously close to a map on the scale of one to one. The challenge to trade theory or trade *cum* location theory is to find some suitably simplified model or set of models that is capable of yielding specific, empirically refutable implications about the international allocation of economic activity in a world in which political boundaries are no longer barriers to the movement of factors in the absence of controls.

III. TRADE THEORY AND ECONOMIC DEVELOPMENT

Finally, the relevance of trade theory for the problems of the developing countries and the study of development patterns was another lively issue at the conference. One aspect of the discussion was the relationship between trade theory and the ideas underlying Professor Chenery's well-known econometric studies of the association between various structural features of development and the levels of per capita income and total population.

It would appear that the uniformities that Chenery finds in his cross-section can be fitted rather neatly into a simple model of trade and growth. A sufficient set of assumptions would be similar tastes and technology, just as in the standard Heckscher—Ohlin model, together with Engel's Law on the demand side and the hypothesis that the manufacturing sector is more capital-intensive than the primary producing sector. Then the higher the endowment of capital relative to labour the higher will be per capita income and the higher the share of manufacturing and the lower the share of primary production. Specific natural resources can easily be included in the primary sector's production function, and increasing returns to scale in the manufacturing sector, to increase the flexibility of the model and to improve its predictive power. We are therefore somewhat baffled as to why Professor Chenery should feel that the approach of trade theory to these problems is either contradictory to or irrelevant to his own con-

ceptual framework which derives from the early development theory of
Rosenstein-Rodan, Lewis and Nurkse.

An increasingly widespread point of view, eloquently expressed at the
conference by Professor Mabogunje, is that participation in the existing
system of world trade is harmful to the long-run growth prospects of the
developing countries. It is alleged that far from being an 'engine of growth'
as in D. H. Robertson's famous phrase, or even a 'handmaiden of growth'
as Irving Kravis more moderately puts it, the current pattern of international specialisation condemns the less developed countries to poverty
and stagnation, with all the advantages accruing to the more developed of
the 'unequal partners'. An inward-looking or autonomous development
strategy, based on some form of 'balanced growth' is advanced as a
preferable alternative.

The more rational proponents of this strategy, however, wish it to be
followed over a wider area than the individual nation, to take advantage of
specialisation and economies of scale, but they wish the partners to be
other nations at a similar level of development so that the possibility of
domination and 'exploitation' of a weaker partner by a stronger does not
arise. This approach to world trade is reminiscent of the English football
league with its four divisions of teams who only play against other teams
in their own division.

It is probably true that international trade, by itself, cannot raise the
rate of growth unless it stimulates capital accumulation or unless the terms
of trade continuously improve over time. There is no substitute for raising
productivity through the accumulation of physical and human capital and
technological progress, in an environment in which there are strong
incentives for entrepreneurs, private or public, and workers and farmers to
perform to the best of their ability. The many instances which can be cited
of particular economies which went through a long cycle of involvement in
international trade on the basis of the export of one or two primary commodities, and had little to show for it afterwards, do not prove that trade
is not beneficial to development. Japan with its raw silk, and above all our
host country for this conference, with its lumber and iron ore, show con-
clusively that the export of primary products need not be the 'blind alley'
that it is often alleged to be.

Engaging in international trade is certainly not a sufficient condition,
and perhaps, for a very large country with a highly diversified resource
base, not even a necessary condition, for economic development. Even a
fraction of the gains from trade, however, if channelled in the right
direction over a sustained period, can be of crucial significance in shifting
the margin from relative stagnation to steady growth. Most of the often-
cited cases where trade did not lead to development are also cases where
there was wasteful government expenditure, irresponsible monetary
policy, and extensive and unpredictable controls at the microeconomic
level. Why is it not these factors, instead of participation in international

trade, that are held responsible for the failure to achieve anything substantial in the way of economic development?

The 'unequal partners' approach to international economic relations ignores the possibility of mutual gain from international trade, that was demonstrated long ago by Ricardo. In international trade, unlike football, both teams can win. It is, however, undoubtedly true that different patterns of specialisation have different long-run consequences for economic development which should be brought into the analysis. Primary product specialisation can frequently lead to a distribution of income and wealth that is highly unequal and oriented towards luxury consumption. It may fail to generate the dynamism that is often associated with industrialisation, involving learning by doing and the economies of large-scale production. However, a society that is determined to achieve economic progress always has the option of using taxation and other measures to channel resources into the desired direction. As Cuba discovered rather painfully, sugar is politically neutral, and can be made to serve the cause of the socialist revolution just as well as that of a reactionary and corrupt clique.

We suspect that what both Professors Chenery and Mabogunje were reacting to, in their different ways, was the old-fashioned static view of comparative costs, which gave the impression that countries were somehow assigned immutable roles in the international division of labour. The last twenty years or so has seen a flood of research in which capital accumulation and technological progress are firmly integrated into the traditional body of doctrine and also linked with the 'dual economy' models and other approaches of recent writers on economic development. This has been a natural extension of the factor proportions approach to the international allocation of economic activity, pioneered by Eli Heckscher and Bertil Ohlin.

NOTES

[1] These remarks were prepared at the conference, though written up later. Max Corden prepared and delivered section I and Ronald Findlay sections II and III, though the general arguments right through the paper represent the views of both authors and are the fruits of their common discussion.

[2] At this point in our verbal presentation we ought to have made the following point, which seemed self-evident to us at the time. Our failure to do so led to misunderstanding from some members of our audience.

Our criterion for deciding in which direction trade theory ought to be extended is empirical relevance. Trade theory is heuristic, so that it cannot be expected to provide a precise detailed picture of the real world, but its usefulness depends on important features of the world about us being incorporated in it. We believe that the considerations which we proceed to discuss here are empirically relevant, but in the time available we could hardly substantiate this with data. In any case, the importance of economies of scale, multinationals, etc., seemed rather obvious. We also think it appropriate that the theory be logically coherent and fully worked out, but our criterion for incorporating a particular variable or characteristic is not its contribution to the elegance of the theory or its amenability to geometry or mathematics. See the discussion following this paper.

[3] 'Die Standortlehre und die Handelspolitik', *Archiv für Sozialwissenschaft und Sozialpolitik*, 32 (2), pp. 647–77. English translation, International Economic Papers No. 8 (1958).

[4] Isard, W. and Peck, M. J., 'Location Theory and International and Interregional Trade', *Quarterly Journal of Economics*, vol. 68 (February, 1954).

Summary of the Discussion

Max Corden and Ronald Findlay had accepted the task of reflecting on, if not summarising, the papers and discussions of the symposium. Their concluding remarks, which started as an inquest performed on standard trade theory, related the contributions and observations previously made by the participants to that discipline, the aim being to identify serious inadequacies and to trace important paths of further theoretical development. This session was chaired by *Robert M. Solow.*

The Chairman recalled that an inquest was something performed on corpses, but listening to Corden and Findlay he had had the feeling that in this case the corpse was conducting the inquest. Looking forward to a lively trial in which testimonies from representatives of other approaches would also be presented, he declared the discussion open.

Walter Isard remarked that one could in a symmetrical way conduct an inquest on location theory. However, like Dieter Biehl, he felt that the aim of the symposium was to consider the international allocation of economic activity from the viewpoint of both trade and location theory. There existed, he thought, a general theory — an 'allocation theory' — including these theories as special cases. Such a synthesis he felt was very much in line with Bertil Ohlin's work. By making different types of simplifying assumptions in the general theory, these special cases focused on different aspects. Location theory emphasised scale economies and transportation costs, usually ignoring the existence of different nations, while trade theory focused on, for example, the effects of national policies such as tariffs and exchange rate changes ignoring the elements mentioned by Corden. Neither theory, he thought, treated dynamic problems. Isard believed that the theories were far apart only when extreme cases were compared and that there could be more synthesis than commonly recognised, in particular by the pure trade theorists who were unaware of developments in location theory. He viewed the contributions to the symposium by Chenery and Leontief as applications of this general theory which he urged be further developed to become realistic and operational.

Michael Chisholm suggested that an important step in approaching such a general model would be for trade theory to treat distance costs and factor mobility. This could be done in models with a limited number of factors and countries by subsuming the problems of overcoming distance plus the characteristics of the commodities and factors moved in terms of propensities to move over space. Such simple models incorporating the appropriate spatial elasticities in a trading system might help to bridge the gap between location and trade theory.

Charles Kindleberger, elaborating on the effects of distance costs, noted that goods and factors do not move smoothly over space but instead follow information networks. He suggested that the concept of nodes used in location theory had something to contribute to international economics. Trade theory did not use this concept much, but in finance it was contained in scale economies and perhaps also in dynamic putty-clay views of history. In fact places were arranged hierarchically, particularly in finance, and it was important to specify the pattern of agglomerations. Entrepôts, centres, relays, emporia, etc., fulfil in space something close to a monetary function. Once we extend the analysis from two to three countries, we must consider that they do not trade equally with each other but use one as a relay or as a numéraire in a special sense. Telephone calls from French to British West Africa go through Paris and London. Money payments from Latin America to Africa go through New York and London and that is normal. This geographical information network approach is useful and he felt it could have been stressed more by the location theorists.

Erik Lundberg recognised that this had been a conference of theorists about methodology and model building. Corden and Findlay, he noted, had suggested a number of variables and relations that should be incorporated into trade theory to perfect it. But he lacked a discussion of the relative importance of different problems. With the exception of the empirical contributions by Chenery and Leontief, such considerations appeared all too often only as casual illustrations. Theorists, he suggested, should first determine what problems are important to analyse and then construct the simplest possible models for analysing satisfactorily the chosen problem. Too little had been said about the 'demand' for improvements in methodology and in model building. Letting trade theory be developed from the 'supply side' by trade theorists tended only to result in further improvements of already sophisticated models.

Melvyn Krauss agreed with the general principle that trade theorists should develop simple models to help understand the real world. He felt, however, that over the past twenty years the two-sector model had become a relevant tool of analysis and was not just a game that trade theorists played.

Assar Lindbeck suggested that it would have been useful if Corden and Findlay had stated more precisely what questions they were trying to answer. The mechanisms considered and the assumptions of a model should be chosen with a view to the problems it was designed to analyse, he noted, and not only because these mechanisms and assumptions were mentioned in the conference.

Wassily Leontief claimed that trade theory was fundamentally non-operational as were the suggestions to combine location theory and trade theory. As long as we construct non-operational systems in which each concept is defined in terms of the others with some verbal reference to some vaguely conceived and unmeasured facts, he said dismally, we shall sit in a charmed circle admiring an Emperor without clothes. Neither

simple nor complicated models would help. Bertil Ohlin's original
contribution had seemed to indicate a 'path toward observation and
explanation', he felt, but trade theorists were moving away from it and
towards more complication by introducing still more general considerations. What we need, Leontief said, was not a general theory but the ability
to explain specific situations. If an outsider, ignorant of our traditions and
courtesies, heard these suggestions for complicating our models, he would
leave to seek explanations elsewhere. In order to progress, he concluded,
we must realise that trade theory had not advanced much since Ohlin's
work.

Hollis Chenery noted that theory tended to feed on theory and become
non-operational and irrelevant as long as it lacked a methodology for
integrating the results of empirical inquiry into theory. Corden's outline,
he felt, ignored the step of testing theories and of incorporating empirical
results into them. And, he claimed, more than casual empirism was
required to identify the phenomena that needed to be reconciled with
existing models. The procedure by which this is usually done is that there
appears an article followed by other articles and then by a survey; and, he
suggested, once a hypothesis is included in a survey, it is incorporated into
the body of accepted trade theory and finds its way into the textbooks.
He missed reference to works which like Hufbauer's and Stern's
attempted to sift alternative hypotheses and to find variables which were
measurable or for which there were proxies. These problems of empirical
testing were a necessary part of theorising, he said, and the interaction
between empiricists and theorists was necessary to perfect theories that
could explain real world phenomena.

Chenery saw two alternatives. One approach, represented by Leontief's
and Klein's models, was to construct bigger models and utilise computer
techniques to solve for and simulate results. However, the more complicated a model, the more difficult it was to winnow out its general
principles from different simulations. The second alternative was to construct and test simple models, using the results to refine different parts of
the overall system (for example, specific forms of consumption and
production functions). The use of these empirical formulations leads to
models that are less general in form but whose relevance to actual
economic behaviour can be tested.

Since trade theorists advise people who cannot prove their predictions
wrong, progress has not been comparable to that in other fields. By contrast,
business cycle theory, for instance, had been completely transformed
because it had had to confront empirical evidence over the last twenty
years. Business cycle theorists had used econometric methods, simulated
results and tested the effects of alternative policies. As a result it had also
become a more policy-oriented field, He noted that there was no similar
pressure of events disproving trade theorists' claims to be able to determine
comparative advantage or to predict a country's trade pattern. Trade

theorists, he concluded, would have to apply more econometrics and other criteria than elegance and 'cleanness' in order to address the subject matter of the symposium: the international allocation of economic activity.

Jagdish Bhagwati rejected the charge of non-operationality levelled by Leontief and Chenery against trade theorists. Both the Ricardian and the Heckscher-Ohlin trade models were operational and had been subjected to empirical tests. Nor did he feel that the interaction between theorists and empiricists had been neglected to the extent suggested by Chenery. There is certainly a need for econometrics at some stage, but there were, he noted, no facts without theories to begin with.

Lindbeck illustrated that simple models were useful even for empirically inclined people by adding that, without the simple two-by-two model, the Leontief paradox and the analytical and empirical development it generated would never have appeared.

Bertil Ohlin observed that it was of course important to have operative and measurable variables and models. It was also desirable to keep in mind the kind of policy problems which economists wished to solve later on — with the aid of the preparation which their positive theory provided. He felt that it would be shortsighted to draw narrow limits for such a theory. A positive analysis which in its selection of subjects paid attention to the probability of later application to policy problems might be very valuable. Besides, there was something that could be called a general understanding of an economic development. One never knew when it might be useful for an analysis of policy problems to have a deep understanding of what is happening when a development changes its course. It can also help the economic historians. Natural scientists are often told by the public that they should not pursue their research if they cannot guarantee its usefulness. He found this a rather 'unscientific' attitude.

Corden and Findlay closed the discussion. *Corden* noted that while they had selected two issues central to the development of trade theory, the central issue of the discussion had been a fundamental attack on the whole method used by trade theorists. However, he felt that the attack was ill-founded and that their position had been misinterpreted.

He had attempted to discuss what the most suitable techniques were for positive analysis of the international allocation of economic activity. The role of trade theory was to provide a tool kit suitable for thinking about these problems and a methodology suitable for making generalisations. Different problems require different tools and it was necessary to know how to choose the tools that were appropriate for each particular case. To explain why Australia exports wool and Japan electronics requires one set of tools, while setting up a world model for the United Nations requires another. It was important to present students in textbooks with a useful set of tools. His presentation was based on the assumption that trade theory could be improved and he and Findlay had made some suggestions for improvement as a result of the proceedings of the symposium.

Trade theory should not be viewed as an alternative to empirical approaches but as a basis for such applications. Contrary to some of the previous speakers he felt that in fact the interaction between empirical work and trade theory had been very close, as represented for instance by the work of Gary Hufbauer.

Nor did Corden admit that trade theory could be criticised as being unrealistic or practically irrelevant. Trade theory had always dealt with practical matters and with important policy questions, he noted. In fact, modern development in the field more or less started with a tariff on imports of wheat into Great Britain — the Corn Laws. Even the origin of the Stolper-Samuelson theorem goes back to a policy study, he noted.[1] He suggested that some of his own work was more relevant to actual policy than even the U.N. input-output model.

Corden finished by asking if there were anything in trade theory not in location theory. If not, trade theory was just a special case of location theory. He suggested that trade theory did have something lacking in location theory. While location theory had differences in locational costs it did not explain them, whereas trade theory thanks to the Heckscher-Ohlin model could explain cost differences between countries in terms of factor intensities and factor endowments. The 'trapping' of factor supplies therefore was the distinguishing feature of trade theory, not the absence of economies of scale. Once location theory could explain locational cost differences in a general equilibrium way, Corden concluded, it would have everything trade theory had, and something else as well.

Robert Solow added that this did not mean that if location theory were more general than trade theory, so much the worse for trade theorists. Quite the contrary! The special case was always the interesting case provided it was true. Generality was by and large the thing to be avoided since it went with emptiness. The world knew two kinds of theorists: when presented with a true theorem one kind would instantly try to generalise it, the other kind would instantly look for a good strong special case. Being the second kind of theorist, Solow preferred not to yield to generality for its own sake.

Findlay concluded that the purpose of their attempt to depict a general equilibrium system of a spatial economy had been to show that the logic of trade theory and that of location theory could in a general sense be integrated. He was reacting against those who believed that trade theory in an essential way was limited to 2 x 2 x 2 models with fixed and immobile factors, while their own theory was more general. But he pointed out that this integration of trade and location theory was on a purely conceptual or formal level and that the general model was rather useless. Like Solow, he did not feel that this level of generality was much to strive for if one wanted operational models and preferred instead to develop simple models which presented interesting special cases.

Trade theory could be made operational in two different ways: (a) by building input-output and link models, or (b) by a suitable choice of simple models. There was no disagreement between Leontief and Lundberg and himself on this point. He did however feel that trade theory was basically operational. Although there were practical difficulties in measuring many of its concepts, he could not agree that concepts like factor proportions, production functions, and technological diffusion were non-operational.

The Chairman, admiring the skill with which intelligent people could argue that the kind of work they like to do is the kind of work everybody ought to do, declared the last discussion of the symposium closed.

NOTE

[1] A critical link in this chain is M. C. Samuelson, 'The Australian Case for Protection Re-examined', *Quarterly Journal of Economics*, 54: 148 (November, 1939), which was a contribution to the lively debate inspired by J. B. Brigden, *et al.*, *The Australian Tariff — An Economic Inquiry* (Melbourne, 1929).

Previous Nobel Symposia

Symposia 1–17 and 20–22 were published by Almqvist and Wiksell, Stockholm and John Wiley and Sons, New York; Symposia 23–25 by the Nobel Foundation Stockholm and Academic Press, New York; Symposium 26 by the Norwegian Nobel Institute, Universitetsforlaget, Oslo; Symposium 27 by the Nobel Foundation, Stockholm and Almqvist and Wiksell International, Stockholm; Symposium 28 by Academic Press, New York; Symposium 29 by the Nobel Foundation, Stockholm and Trycksaksservice AB, Stockholm; Symposia 30 and 31 by Plenum Press, New York; Symposium 32 by the Nobel Foundation, Stockholm; and Symposia 33 and 34 by Plenum Press, New York. The present volume is Symposium 35.

Index